LL

ENVIRONMENTAL LAW

THE LAW AND POLICY RELATING TO THE PROTECTION OF THE ENVIRONMENT

paper

D0294109

BALL & BELL ON
ENVIRONMENTAL LAW

THE LAW AND POLICY RELATING TO THE PROTECTION OF THE ENVIRONMENT

Fourth Edition

Stuart Bell LLB Hons, Barrister

BLACKSTONE PRESS LIMITED

First published in Great Britain 1991 by Blackstone Press Limited, Aldine Place, London W12 8AA. Telephone: 0181–740 2277

© S. Ball and S. Bell, 1991
© S. Bell, 1997

First edition 1991
Second edition 1994
Reprinted 1994
Third edition 1995
Fourth edition 1997

ISBN: 1 85431 686 9

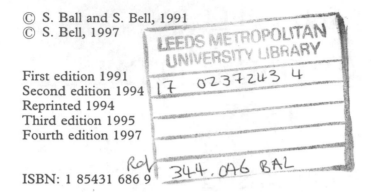

British Library Cataloguing in Publication Data
A CIP catalogue record for this book is available from the British Library

Typeset by Style Photosetting Ltd, Mayfield, East Sussex
Printed by Ashford Colour Press, Gosport, Hants

This book is printed on recycled paper

Contents

The scope of this book — Some themes of the book — The shape of the book — The history of environmental law — The modern age of environmental law — The future of environmental policy — The future of environmental law — The costs of compliance — The costs of non-compliance — Policy and environmental law

Some major features of environmental legislation — Informal sources of law and practice — European Communities (EC) law — International law — Judicial review — Remedies — Procedure — Standing — Restrictions on judicial review — The Ombudsman

Department of the Environment, Transport and the Regions (DoE) — Other parts of Central Government — Parliamentary Select Committees — Royal Commission on Environmental Pollution (RCEP) — Other advisory bodies — The Environment Agency — Sewerage undertakers — Countryside bodies — Local authorities — Decision-making in local authorities

The development of a general environmental secrecy policy — Mechanisms
of secrecy — Commercial confidentiality — 'Green nutters' — Administration costs — The Royal Commission's approach — The effect of secrecy
upon risk perception — Environmental rights — The recommendations of
the Royal Commission — Water pollution — Other registers in the water
industry — Waste management — Registers in relation to contaminated land
— Integrated pollution control — The Chemical Releases Inventory — Air
pollution — Access to information held by local government — The Environmental Information Regulations 1992 — The public's utilisation of
registers

The characteristics of the common law as a mechanism of environmental
protection — Is the common law as a protection mechanism dead? — Civil
liability in statutes — Other private law remedies — The law of tort and
environmental protection — The law of nuisance — Defences to a claim for
nuisance — Private rights under the common law and the grant of planning
permission — An assessment of nuisance as a tool for environmental
protection — Public nuisance — Trespass — Negligence — The rule in
Rylands v *Fletcher* — Defences — The usefulness of the rule in *Rylands* v
Fletcher — The protection of riparian rights — Civil law remedies —
Statutory nuisance — The control of statutory nuisances — The categories
of statutory nuisance — What is required to satisfy the local authority? —
Who is the 'person responsible'? — The abatement notice — Defences —
The right of appeal against an abatement notice — Individual actions by any
person — Sentencing powers for contravention of an abatement notice —
The use of injunctions and proceedings in the High Court

The main features of town and country planning — Town and country
planning as a tool of environmental policy — Town and country planning and
some themes of this book — The planning legislation — What is town and
country planning? — Planning policy — Deregulation — Local planning
authorities — Forward planning: development plans — The history and
future of development plans — Local plans — Unitary development plans —
Development plans and development control — Non-statutory plans and
guidance — Development control: definition of development — Material
change of use — Use Classes Order — Existing uses — The General
Development Orders — Is planning permission required? — Applying
for planning permission — Decisions by the local planning authority —

Alternative and special procedures — Special areas — The Secretary of State's powers — Summary of rights of third parties — The local planning authority's discretion — The presumption in favour of the development plan — Other material considerations — Conditions — Legal tests for the validity of conditions — Conditions and policy — Planning conditions and pollution control — Planning obligations — Planning appeals — Procedure on appeals — Challenging the decision of the Secretary of State — Enforcement of planning law — Enforcement notices — Stop notices — Injunctions — Other enforcement powers — Enforcement where there is no breach of planning law — Planning and hazardous substances

10 Environmental assessment   277

What is environmental assessment? — Environmental Assessment Directive — Environmental Assessment Directive and direct effect — Is the project subject to environmental assessment? — Environmental assessment and permitted development — Pre-application procedures for establishing the need for environmental assessment — Pre-application directions from the Secretary of State — Challenges to the decisions of the Secretary of State or local planning authority — Other procedures for determining the need for environmental assessment — The environmental statement — Undertaking the process of environmental assessment — Environmental assessment in simplified planning zones and enterprise zones — Environmental assessment in practice — The case for reform? — The next phase?: Strategic environmental assessment

11 Integrated pollution control   299

Pollution of the atmosphere — Pollution on land — Control of water pollution — The administrative jungle and the mechanisms of protection — Consequences of the fragmented approach — Time for a change — Best practicable environmental option — The EC's role in change — *Vorsorgeprinzip:* anticipation through foresight — HMIP: a unified body — The Environment Agency and IPC — The introduction of integrated pollution control — Organisation and administration of the system of integrated pollution control — Role of the Secretary of State — The requirement for authorisation — Determination of the need for an authorisation — Prescribed processes — Meaning of process — Release of prescribed substances — Exceptions — Overlapping controls — Planning permission — Contaminated land — Applications for authorisation — Fees — Public participation and other consultation procedures — Call-in procedure — Commercial confidentiality and national security — The determination of an application — BATNEEC — Integrated pollution control notes — Implementation of the IPC system — Transfer of authorisations — Enforcement powers — Offences and remedies — Corporate liability — Crown immunity — Appeals — Integrated pollution prevention and control

15   Disposal of waste to sewers   483

Trade effluent discharges — Applying for a trade effluent consent — How are consents set? — Trade effluent charges — Public participation — 'Red List' substances — Enforcement — Discharges from sewage works — Domestic sewage discharges

16   The conservation of nature   490

History — Types of legal protection — The nature conservation agencies — The protection of individual animals and plants — Habitat protection— Sites of special scientific interest (SSSIs) — Duties on owners and occupiers — Specific nature conservation duties — Nature conservation orders — National nature reserves (NNRs) — Local nature reserves — Marine nature reserves (MNRs) — Limestone pavements — Management agreements — Planning permission — Loss and damage to SSSIs — The international perspective — EC Wild Birds Directive 79/409 — EC Habitats Directive 92/43 — The 1994 Regulations — European marine sites — European sites and other regulatory systems — The Ramsar Convention — Summary of protection of internationally important sites

17   The protection of the countryside   521

Town and country planning — Extra protections — The Countryside Commission — Landscape protection and management agreements — Agriculture and landscape

18   The protection of trees and woodlands   532

Trees and planning permission — Tree preservation orders (TPOs) — Conservation areas — Compensation — Felling licences — Proposals for change — Hedgerows

Bibliography   540

Index   553

Preface

It is perhaps inevitable that in the two years since the publication of the third edition of this book there have been further changes in environmental law, although the pace of domestic legislative change appears to have slowed down in comparison to the heady days of the early 1990s. In an area which is becoming increasingly complex, both in terms of policy challenges and the types of legal mechanism which are used in an attempt to address these challenges, the sheer amount of information is a little daunting. The following analysis seeks to identify some of the more important issues which have emerged over the last two years and those areas which are likely to continue to be developed in the short period before the Millennium.

At an international level we have had the Rio II Conference in New York early in the summer of 1997. It was rather depressing to note the lack of progress made on the admittedly vague commitments made at the first conference in 1992, but this was compounded by the fact that when pushed to make further commitments, national interests were preferred to establishing definite targets. On the positive side, the UK did appear to be taking the lead on some of the more important issues, and if only parts of the rhetoric expressed by some of the major nations were turned into reality, progress is not out of the question.

Within the European Union we have seen the introduction of a new Directive on Integrated Pollution Prevention and Control and significant amendments made to the Directive on Environmental Assessment. On the horizon we have major initiatives on the use of economic instruments, a White Paper on a Community-wide scheme on liability for environmental harm, and a new framework Directive on water resources. This last proposal reflects the move away from the traditional use of 'daughter' Directives towards a more integrated approach. Overall, there is likely to be continued emphasis on the quality of the implementation of existing and future European legislation rather than on the wholesale introduction of wide-ranging new initiatives. The European Court of Justice has continued to be active over the last two years, dealing with various issues including *Tombesi* (on the difficult question of the definition of waste), *Arcaro* (on the direct effect of the Cadmium Directive and consequently other 'daughter'

Directives) and the *Dutch Dykes* case (on the enforcement of the environmental assessment Directive in national courts).

On the domestic front we are still seeing the 'bedding down' of the
institutional and legal changes brought about by the Environment Act 1995
and in particular the creation of the Environment Agency on 1 April 1996.
Thus we have seen the development of central policy aims for the EA
including guidance from the Secretary of State, advice on meeting the goal of
sustainable development and the tricky issue of cost benefit analysis in
decision making. New legislation has been passed in relation to special waste
(which after many years of waiting finally implements the Directive on
Hazardous Waste) and the recycling and recovery of packaging waste (again
implementing European legislation).

The full implementation of the main environmental law statutes has led to
disputes involving the interpretation of many of the legislative terms. These
have included *R* v *Secretary of State and Compton, ex parte West Wiltshire* (on
Part I of the EPA 1990), *Shanks and McEwan (Teesside) Ltd* v *Environment
Agency* (on the definition of 'knowingly' in relation to waste management
offences), and *R* v *Carrick DC, ex parte Shelley* (on the duty under the EPA
1990 to inspect and deal with statutory nuisances). There have also been
continued attempts to address and consolidate the law on standing for
environmental pressure groups. After what appeared to be clarification of the
position in the *ex parte Greenpeace* and *Pergau Dam* actions, we were once
again left in a state of confusion with the decision in *ex parte Garnett* (which
attempted to restrict the class of those claiming *locus standi*). Happily, Sedley
J appears to have restored some sort of judicial balance with the decision in
ex parte Dixon which liberalises the law on standing to such an extent that
only 'troublemakers' or 'busybodies' will now be excluded. In any event, the
juiciary may well be overtaken by the legislators if proposals to introduce an
Environmental Court go ahead. In the common law, we have seen further
ambivalence displayed by the House of Lords towards the development of the
law of nuisance as a tool for environmental protection in *Hunter* v *Canary
Wharf* (where the right to sue in nuisance was inextricably linked to the
ownership of land). As a postscript to this round-up of cases we have also
seen the generally poor manner in which the courts have dealt with the
interpretation of European law, including a range of decisions dealing with
environmental assessment culminating in the decision of Hidden J in *R* v
North Yorkshire CC, ex parte Brown (where it was held that the Directive did
not have direct effect — notwithstanding the opposing view of the Advocate-
General in the *Dutch Dykes* case which was being heard in parallel and which
was quoted to the English court); the long saga of *Lappel Bank* with the
House of Lords referral to the ECJ in *R* v *Secretary of State for the Environment
ex parte RSPB* in which the ECJ surprised no-one (other than the House of
Lords seemingly) in relying on existing European case law and holding that
economic criteria did not justify the failure to designate a Special Protection
Area under the Wild Birds Directive. Unfortunately, this judgment came too
late for Lappel Bank which had been turned into a large storage area for cars
in the intervening period. In contrast, there has now been one referral to the

ECJ from the High Court. In *R* v *Secretary of State for the Environment and MAFF, ex parte Standley*, the ECJ has been passed to interpret aspects of the Nitrates Directive.

As previous editions of this book have stressed, the role of policy in the environmental field is as important as that of law, and although new legislation and case law is the traditional life blood of legal textbooks, potentially the most significant change in the short period since the last edition of this work occurred in May 1997 when the Labour Government was elected. One of the major difficulties with a change of Government is that, to a far greater degree than changes in law, the potential effects are completely unpredictable. There has been a slight feeling of an interregnum in the first few months of the new administration (in relation to environmental policy at least — admittedly somewhat of an exception in the spectrum of policy making). It is difficult to discern any major policy shifts although this could have more to do with the need to evaluate the legislative and institutional upheavals of the last years of the Conservative administration rather than any lack of desire to introduce new measures.

In writing a book of this sort, where some consideration is given to the policy aspects of the administration of environmental protection, there is always some difficulty when there is a signficant change in the policy makers. The identity of the 'British' approach to environmental regulation which is discussed in this book is heavily characterised by ideologies which were an integral part of the Conservative administration. This identity is too deeply ingrained in the tools and mechanisms of environmental protection for radical alterations to be made in the short term. Thus, issues such as deregulation and the use of the market as a regulatory tool continue to be covered, notwithstanding the fact that some of these identified characteristics would not fall easily within the general political aims of the new administation.

During the last election campaign you would have been hard pressed to find any major ongoing debate on environmental issues between the main political parties. It would be wrong, however, to assume that the issues were therefore unimportant in political terms. All three main parties produced their 'greenest' manifestos yet and there is increasing acknowledgment that environmental policy will continue to be integrated into the mainstream — a point recognised with the birth of the new 'Super Ministry' of the Department of Transport, Environment and the Regions.

Although it is important to consider the possible nature of environmental law and policy under a Labour Government, it is also perhaps a good time to reflect upon some of the remarkable changes which have occurred over the last 18 years of Conservative administration. We have seen the increasing formalisation of environmental standards (even though the practical aspects of implementing these standards are often ignored), the modernisation of pollution control techniques with the introduction of new systems of Integrated Pollution Control, waste management and water resource protection, formal environmental assessment for major projects, and last but not least the gradual unification of pollution control functions in the Environment Agency. Of course, most (but not all) of these changes were introduced via the EC but this shouldn't hide the fact that the modernisation of environmental regulation has taken place over a relatively short period of time and under an administration which was not necessarily noted for the strength of its policies on environmental protection.

On the other side of the coin, some things haven't altered very much at all. Although the nature of the regulatory system may have changed drastically, the enforcing authorities are still mainly characterised by low resource levels and poor morale. Moreover, there has been little significant shift in the enforcement of environmental law during the last 18 years. For a brief period the National Rivers Authority increased prosecution rates for water pollution offences but more recently the figures have stabilised. On the Environment Agency's most recent figures, there were over 20,000 substantiated water pollution incidents in 1996. Of these only 225 were prosecuted. Of course, not all of the incidents would have warranted prosecution but questionmarks remain over the remaining 99% of the polluters.

So will the Labour Government take a different approach? The lack of electoral debate on environmental issues indicates that there is a degree of underlying consensus on the broad issues of environmental regulation. Of course, there are political differences between the parties but the overall approach from the Labour Government should be similar in many aspects to the progress made by the Conservatives, particularly over the last five years. One of the main obstacles to predicting the direction of future policy is that there is not a great deal of definitive material on environmental policy which has been issued by the Labour Party. The manifesto served up a mixture of vague commitments with the usual platitudes about ensuring higher levels of environmental protection and wanting to pursue rigorous levels of enforcement. The main policy document called *In trust for tomorrow* was issued in 1994 as a report of the Labour Party Policy Commission on the environment. In addition to concrete commitments on a range of issues it also contained radical proposals on such things as an Environmental Ombudsman, compensation for environmental damage and stronger habitat protection. The status of this document is now somewhat uncertain and there have been a number of instances where the Government has made decisions which contradict some of the policy statements made (most notably in relation to opencast coal mining).

With the caveat that there is uncertainty surrounding the general policy direction of the Labour Government left in the vacuum of the possible abandonment of *In trust for tomorrow*, what then can we expect to see over the next five years?

(a)   It will come as no surprise that the most significant shift in policy (which would probably have occurred whoever came to power) will be away from direct regulation to the use of economic instruments. In addition to the attraction of raising revenue from sources which are politically 'soft', it should ensure that the costs of pollution are internalised. It would be no surprise if there was direct taxation on polluting industries over the next two or three budgets. The Treasury has identified two main targets, the mining of aggregates and those who discharge polluting substances into water.

(b)   There is a strong sense that the new administration will attempt to integrate environmental policy into other Departments. Although there were halfhearted attempts to do this under the Conservative administration it was generally recognised as being unsuccessful. John Prescott has far more general political clout than his Conservative predecessors and the effect has already been seen with the proposals to create an Environmental Audit Committee and the announcement of a White Paper on integrating transport. The main consequence of this integration will be that there is less emphasis on the pollution control aspects of environmental regulation and more on general issues such as transport, economic instruments, the use of regional strategies to address environmental problems and meeting the goal of sustainable development.

(c)   One of the few concrete proposals put forward by the Labour Party whilst in opposition would see the creation of an Environmental Court to deal with both criminal and civil environmental cases. The policy document *In trust for tomorrow* proposes that the Court will allow environmental groups to bring claims without any need to show that they had a particular interest in the claim itself and where such a claim was brought in the public interest, the unsuccessful plaintiffs would not have to pay the defendant's costs.

(d)   An increasing emphasis will be placed upon strategic decision making at a regional level. In pollution control there is an element of this with the creation of regional divisions of the Environment Agency with Advisory Committees dealing with local strategy to address local issues. Although many decisions may be devolved to the regions it is difficult to see a wholesale decentralisation as there are too many ways in which Central Government or other national bodies (such as the EA) dictate the policy which guides individual decision making. Perhaps, more importantly, the final say in many decisions still lies with the Secretary of State, either by way of appeal or statutory direction.

(e)   The final prediction (which is put forward more in hope than in certainty) is that there will be a long overdue revision of the law of nature conservation and habitats protection.

When we move away from the broad policy themes towards the more difficult issue of individual decisions we can seen that the change of administration is unlikely to make much of a difference. We have seen Labour policy U-turns in relation to the approvals for the Birmingham Northern Relief Road and the Cardiff Bay Barrage. These should not necessarily be viewed as a foretaste of things to come. Instead they reflect the polycentricity (i.e., multi-faceted nature) of environmental decision making.

There are many other issues which the incoming Government will have to tackle as a legacy of the last administration or as a result of new European initiatives. These 'poisoned chalices' include legislation to deal with contaminated land (already much delayed and controversial), recycling and recovering packaging (which is set for review less than a year after the legislation was passed), the widening of the Integrated Pollution Control regime and environmental assessment. Whilst broad policy statements are interesting and stimulating, the real test comes when the specifics need to be translated into often unattractive legislative packages. The devil, as they say, is always in the detail.

Inevitably, perhaps, the increasing sophistication of environmental regulation has led to certain 'growing pains' and presented us with deeper issues which need to be addressed. The introduction of a basic system of environmental regulation means that more fundamental challenges await — challenges which address the nature of responsibility for environmental problems which is shared between policy makers, legislators, industry and consumers. This shift away from traditional models of pollution control towards policies dealing with sustainability is gathering pace. The role of the individual in environmental protection is likely to be addressed with increasing regularity, starting with the stark choices which face us on transport policy and housing. Environmental law can help to shape the framework within which those decisions are made, but it does not make the issues any simpler.

Writing a book is never an easy task and this edition has been particularly difficult. As some readers will be aware, Simon Ball, my original co-author, died in late 1996 at the age of 39. Simon believed that environmental law has developed into a separate academic discipline which is more than a simple aggregation of a series of statutory provisions. He played an integral part in that development by not only delving into the deeper, more theoretical aspects of environmental law and policy but also by attempting to distil some of the principles for those who come to study it for the first time. When we wrote the first edition of this book we did so with the aim of providing a rudimentary commentary on the framework of environmental law and policy which would not only give an overview of the substantive provisions but also attempt to place them in some sort of practical and policy context. I quite happily confess that Simon always had a much broader vision of the subject than I, but he was always eager to share it freely amongst his peers and students so that he could continue to develop and revise his ideas. Perhaps more importantly, environmental law was not merely an academic exercise for Simon — he really did believe in the adage 'Think globally, act locally'. I know that he is sorely missed by many people. This edition is dedicated to him.

In an area which is as complicated as environmental law it is customary (and necessary) that I finish with the usual acceptance of responsibility for any errors. There are sections of the book which were written jointly with Simon and therefore still contain references to our combined view of matters. I have retained these for the sake of accuracy although any errors are still mine alone. I have endeavoured to state the law as at 1 September 1997.

Stuart Bell
September 1997

Abbreviations

AONB	area of outstanding natural beauty
APC	air pollution control
AQMA	air quality management area
AQS	air quality standards
BATNEEC	best available techniques not entailing excessive cost
BOD	biochemical oxygen demand
BPEO	best practicable environmental option
BPM	best practicable means
COPA 1974	Control of Pollution Act 1974
COSHH	Control of Substances Hazardous to Health
CRI	Chemical Releases Inventory
DoE	Department of the Environment
EA	Environment Agency
EC	European Community
EPA 1990	Environmental Protection Act 1990
ESA	environmentally sensitive area
HMIP	Her Majesty's Inspectorate of Pollution
HSA	hazardous substances authority
HSC	hazardous substances consent
HSE	Health and Safety Executive
IEA	Institute of Environmental Assessment
IPC	integrated pollution control
IPPC	integrated pollution prevention and control
LAAPC	local authority air pollution control
MAFF	Ministry of Agriculture, Fisheries and Food
MHLG	Ministry of Housing and Local Government
MNR	marine nature reserve
NCC	Nature Conservancy Council
NNR	national nature reserve
NRA	National Rivers Authority
RCEP	Royal Commission on Environmental Pollution
SEPA	Scottish Environment Protection Agency
SSSI	site of special scientific interest

TPO	tree preservation order
WDA	waste disposal authority
WRA	waste regulation authority

Table of Cases

Table of Statutes

Table of Statutory Instruments

PART I   GENERAL PRINCIPLES OF ENVIRONMENTAL LAW

ONE

What is environmental law?

In the 1980s some commentators doubted whether the issue of 'the environment' would last. They have been proved wrong, since it is clearly one of the big issues, perhaps the biggest issue, of the 1990s.

It is a big issue in political terms, since protection of the environment is high on most people's priorities for the 1990s. As a result political parties and governments are falling over each other in their eagerness to appear green, even if as yet their actions rarely match their rhetoric. It is big in terms of the size of the problems faced and the solutions required; global warming, the destruction of the ozone layer, acid rain, deforestation, overpopulation and toxic waste are all global issues which require an appropriately global response. It is big in terms of the range of problems and issues — air pollution, water pollution, noise pollution, waste disposal, radioactivity, pesticides, countryside protection, conservation of wildlife — the list is virtually endless. In the words of the White Paper on the Environment, *This Common Inheritance* (Cm 1200, 1990) the issues range 'from the street corner to the stratosphere'. Finally, it is big in terms of the knowledge and skills required to understand a particular issue. Law is only one element in what is a major cross-disciplinary topic. Lawyers need some understanding of the scientific, political and economic processes involved in environmental degradation. Equally, all those whose activities and interests relate to the environment need to acquire an understanding of the structure and content of environmental law, since it has a large and increasing role to play in environmental protection.

The scope of this book

Faced with all these elements of 'bigness', authors of books on environmental law have to make many choices, otherwise each book would become unmanageably large. Inevitably what is included in this book reflects the personal interests and prejudices of the authors. The shape and structure of this book — what is included, what is omitted, what is covered in detail, what is covered in outline, how it is put together — must therefore be explained.

The book is entitled 'Environmental Law' and an explanation of these two words will clarify some preliminary points about its content.

Environmental

This is a difficult word to define. Its normal meaning relates to 'surroundings', but obviously that is a concept that is relative to whatever object it is which is surrounded. Used in that sense environmental law could include virtually anything; indeed, as Einstein once remarked, 'The environment is everything that isn't me'. However, 'the environment' has now taken on a rather more specific meaning, though still a very vague and general one, and may be treated as covering the physical surroundings that are common to all of us, including air, space, waters, land, plants and wildlife.

A definition of this nature is used in the Environmental Protection Act 1990 (EPA 1990), s. 1, which defines the environment as consisting of 'all, or any, of the following media, namely, the air, water and land'. Rather than offering a hostage to fortune by attempting to lay down some impossibly precise definition, we propose to adopt this one for the general description of the book's content. A more precise description can be given simply by stating what is and what is not covered by the book. We intend to concentrate on those laws and practices which relate primarily to the protection of the whole or part of the general surroundings, as opposed to those where the true objective is the protection of public health, or individual people such as workers or consumers.

Obviously, it is not possible to consign some areas of law with certainty to one category or another and, as a result, the exact dividing line between what is and what is not included is rather artificial. But a line has to be drawn somewhere. Accordingly, we cover the law and practice on the protection of air, water and land against pollution, and the protection of the ecosystem, together with those ancillary issues which help to explain these areas, such as public participation, access to information, remedies and procedures.

Such things as consumer protection laws, product liability laws, health and safety legislation and animal protection laws are not covered, although they can often be relevant to solving environmental problems. There are also a number of areas of what is undeniably environmental law which are omitted on grounds of space. The growing package of legislation on the protection of the cultural heritage is omitted. Little will be said about radioactivity, where the law is very complex indeed and where there is a large overlap between the environmental and human protection parts of the law. The provisions in the EPA 1990 on the introduction of genetically modified organisms into the environment and on litter are also omitted.

Law

This book is not intended to be merely a description of the various rules and regulations, although obviously that is a part of any useful book on the law. Such a description would give little clue to what happens in practice. Whether, and how, the law is enforced is just as important as what the law is. Indeed, given the discretionary nature of many of the powers and duties imposed on environmental decision-makers, it is unreal to draw a hard and fast distinction between what the law is and how it is used. This book will therefore seek to emphasise policy as much as law, and practice as much as principle.

There are some other general limitations on the subject matter of the book in addition to the ones mentioned above. It is not about all those laws which 'relate to' the environment, since that too could cover virtually anything. We intend to concentrate on those laws and practices which have as their object or effect the *protection* of the environment. Those things which merely have an indirect impact on the state of the environment, such as tax levels, grants and incentives, are thus excluded from full coverage, although their relevance is referred to in passing and they may frequently be of crucial importance to the policy-maker.

In addition, for reasons of space, we intend to concentrate on domestic laws and practices. We will not attempt to deal with truly international problems in any detail, a choice which is justified by the publication of the excellent and comprehensive *International Law and the Environment* (Birnie and Boyle, 1993). Even so, the importance of international agreements in influencing and moulding our domestic law should be recognised.

The crucial relevance of European Communities (EC) law must be emphasised. We adopt the attitude that EC law *is* domestic law in the sense that it cannot be ignored even though it does not always give rise to enforceable obligations and remedies. Therefore EC controls, both current and proposed, will be integrated into each part of the book where relevant. In addition, there is a separate chapter on the basic constitutional rules of the EC and on the history, philosophy and current direction of its environmental policy. It is hard to overestimate the central importance of EC law and policy to British environmental law. This importance is often masked by the fact that in the environmental field EC law tends to require some form of implementation in this country before it is formally recognised. Once implemented, the EC derivation of the rule is then frequently forgotten because the domestic law is cited as the applicable law.

Some themes of the book

This description of the scope of the book highlights a number of important themes. One is that there is a great deal of interaction between rules which have as their main objective the protection of the environment and those which aim to protect people. Just as in nature conservation it has become accepted in the last 30 years that there is no use in protecting individual animals or species unless you also protect their habitats, in all matters we now accept that protection of human beings involves protection of their environment. The converse is also true in that many rules originally aimed at protection of people end up protecting the environment. For example, standards in relation to radioactivity are often set with the protection of humans in mind, but have an important impact on environmental levels of radiation. Similarly, the presence or absence of laws on cruelty to animals has a significant impact on nature conservation even though that is not their primary motive.

A related theme is that the rules are simply the tools of the trade of law-makers, environmental protection agencies and environmentalists. A rule which has as its objective one goal is frequently of enormous use in an entirely different way. For example, the law of nuisance owes its existence and shape to the objective of protecting property rights, but it still has an important, though often unpredictable, part to play in regulating environmental standards in the interests of the community. This is one of the major themes of this book: that there is often more than one way of tackling a problem and that the environmental lawyer must be seen as a problem-solver who chooses the most appropriate tool for the particular problem encountered. Often this will involve using a combination of different tools. As an example, many rules of property law may be used to further environmental ends: the Royal Society for the Protection of Birds follows a policy of buying land for nature reserve purposes on the principle that the exercise of ownership rights will often provide a better method of protection than many statutory designations or protections. This is not to say that the whole of property law must be somehow annexed as a part of environmental law, but that environmental lawyers should make use of any piece of law which has a relevance to the problem in hand.

A further issue relates to the nature of law. It is often stated that law is not constructive; that it does not build houses or plant trees. We regard this as an inaccurate notion. There is no doubt that many laws do lay down straightforward negative rules restricting specified forms of behaviour. But many laws lay down rights as well as wrongs. Much of environmental law consists of setting out a framework for behaviour — who should make decisions, how they should make them, what procedures must be followed. Such law is clearly not just negative.

In *Countryside Conflicts* (Lowe et al., 1986), the authors state that, 'planning control is no more than an essentially negative power; a device for stopping objectionable proposals'. This pessimistic view, which is undoubtedly widespread (especially amongst non-lawyers), seems to miss the point that planning law, like much of environmental law, is also about positive concepts, as expressed in the word 'planning' and illustrated by the production of development plans as an integral part of the process. In relation to pollution control, a similar point can be made by noting that the regulatory agencies spend a far greater proportion of their time providing positive advice on how to reach the standards they set than on enforcing those standards through legal threats and remedies.

This distinction between negative and positive tools links to a division in the subject matter of environmental law. It is common to equate environmental protection with pollution control. However, whilst pollution control undoubtedly represents a major part of environmental law, there are many other issues, such as the retention of biological diversity and the preservation of landscape, which also make up the subject. These issues often require slightly different legal mechanisms.

Finally, and perhaps most importantly, the law provides remedies. To many people, whether they are environmentalists or industrialists or lawyers giving advice, this is the most central aspect of law, since they want to know what they can do about a situation. One of the interesting developments of recent years has been the search for adequate remedies for environmental problems. Legal tools have been accepted as legitimate devices for helping to solve environmental problems. Law plays an often underrated but enormously important role, alongside scientific, technological, social and economic solutions, in helping to combat environmental degradation. In this role, many novel legal concepts have been developed.

The shape of the book

A major aim of this book is to illustrate the proposition that there is developing such a thing as environmental law. Most lawyers are brought up on the idea that there are a number of core, or basic, subjects which are essentially about techniques and in which a set of central organising principles can be distilled from the law. Criminal law, constitutional law, public law, contract law, torts, equity and property law would be good examples. The traditional view would then be that, alongside those basic subjects, are as many areas of law as there are areas of life, in each of which the techniques of the basic subjects are used; for example, the law relating to family relationships, the law relating to housing. But over a period of time, there is no doubt that these topic-related areas build up their own principles and reasoning processes. A good example of this process would be the development of the principles of public law over the last 40 years.

We would argue that environmental law is starting to acquire its own conceptual apparatus, in the sense that there is being built up a set of principles and concepts which can be said to exist across the range of the subjects covered. This is very much at an early stage, but the process of establishing environmental law as a separate discipline has begun. This makes it important to explain some general concepts, such as the 'polluter pays' principle, near the beginning of the book (see p. 124). It also explains the division of the book into two parts, one on the general themes of environmental law and the other on specific environmental issues. As suggested above, an environmental lawyer ideally needs to understand both parts in order to possess the tools required to carry out the task of solving particular problems properly.

Part I of the book looks at those general issues which cut across all issues of environmental protection, but which are in practice an essential part of any understanding of the law. The discussion in this part should also provide a form of vocabulary to help with an understanding of the context of the specific laws and practices which are dealt with in Part II.

Part I thus covers the nature of the regulatory systems adopted for environmental protection, the sources of the law, the institutions and agencies involved in environmental protection, the process of setting environmental standards and the different types of standard that may be adopted, the role of the EC, secrecy and freedom of access to information, the role of the common law and the important question of how environmental laws are actually enforced.

In *Part II* the specific laws relating to particular environmental issues are treated on a chapter by chapter basis. However, there is a significant problem of organisation here. Should the law be divided up according to the medium in which the environmental threat manifests itself (i.e., air, water, land etc.)? Should it be divided according to the identity of the polluter (e.g., cars, factories, power stations etc.)? Should it be divided according to the nature of the pollutant (e.g., radiation, lead, pesticides, CFCs etc.)? Or should it even be divided according to the nature of the target which is being protected (e.g., people, animals, ecosystems, the atmosphere)?

There is no single answer. The laws are not designed on any one of these four axes, but on all four at once. The best that can be done is to select groupings of laws that more or less hang together in a way that makes sense to someone faced with a problem. It must then be remembered that in reality all these things interrelate, so that a problem on the disposal of waste to land cannot be considered without some consideration of the law on incineration, or discharges to water, or recycling. Integrated pollution control and the adoption of the related concept of best practicable environmental option in the EPA 1990 are explicit recognitions of this interrelation.

Certain issues also play a role which it is impossible to explain in terms of any one of the four axes set out above. The law on town and country planning is an example. It clearly has a central role in protecting against threats to amenity and is in other ways an important part of the law on environmental protection. For example, hazardous or undesirable developments can be prevented or subjected to conditions, making the need for planning permission an essential part of most systems of pollution control. But it also has a role in organising economic development which is outside environmental law in its strict sense.

As a result the chapter divisions in Part II may be seen as artificial in a number of ways. We try to cover the protection of the major environmental media — air, land and water — from pollution, at the same time as considering the various means of disposing of waste — sewage disposal, incineration, landfill, discharge to rivers, discharge to the sea, reuse and recycling.

Environmental protection law is undoubtedly undergoing a period of unprecedentedly rapid change (see below). It is therefore intended to give special prominence to those areas where there have been recent changes and to refer to potential future developments wherever possible. In a subject area such as this, where activities have to be planned reasonably far in advance, it is always best to know what is likely to happen in the future as well as what is actually the law at the time. In this sense environmental law is forward-looking law.

The history of environmental law

An understanding of the current state of environmental law requires some understanding of its history. Not surprisingly for such a densely populated country, environmental controls have a long history, going back to medieval statutes on small-scale pollution and the development of private law principles to deal with threats to communal assets such as water. Of course, until recently, few would have thought of these laws as part of something called 'environmental law', since their main focus was on the protection of private and common property.

Britain's position as the cradle of the Industrial Revolution led to the very early development of public controls specifically related to environmental protection. The most significant provisions were developed in response to public health problems in the mid-nineteenth century, culminating in the landmark Public Health Act 1875.

Britain can boast what is normally considered the world's first national public pollution control agency, the Alkali Inspectorate, which was established by the Alkali Act 1863 to control atmospheric emissions primarily from the caustic soda industry. Water pollution controls followed in the Rivers Pollution Prevention Act 1876, although these proved to be virtually unenforceable in practice. Britain also introduced some of the earliest provisions on town planning. The first legislation to cover this subject was the Housing, Town Planning etc. Act 1909, which again derived from public health pressures and which vested controls in local authorities, at this stage on a non-obligatory basis. Obligatory town and country planning controls were introduced on a nationwide scale in 1947 — again early in world terms.

In addition to these public controls, the law of nuisance was developed (especially in the nineteenth century) as a means of providing private redress for environmental harm, although on a very selective basis. Britain also had some of the earliest voluntary bodies concerned with environmental protection.

National, centralised control of problems (such as through the Alkali Inspectorate) was very much the exception in this period of development, and most public health and environmental protection was carried out at a local level by a vast array of local boards and, at a later stage, local authorities. Some uniformity was effected by the Public Health Act 1875, which produced model by-laws for such things as the design and layout of housing, but most of the early provisions reflect a tendency (which is still apparent) to regulate only the most dangerous or sensitive matters at a central level.

In these formative years, law-making tended to be ad hoc in the extreme. This is self-evident with case law, which by its very nature must react to the facts of cases brought. But legislative changes were also reactive, with Parliament tending to legislate for problems on an individual basis, in isolation from other areas and without any thought for wider development or consolidation of the law. For example, one effect of the early Alkali Acts and the controls over atmospheric emissions is reputed to have been an immediate worsening of water quality as industries chose liquid discharge as a replacement method for the disposal of their wastes. The same reactive tendency can be seen more recently. A good modern example is the enactment of the Deposit of Poisonous Wastes Act 1972, which passed through Parliament in only a few days in response to a much-publicised discovery of the fly-tipping of poisonous waste near a school playground.

As a result, environmental law has traditionally been split amongst a number of statutes, many of them covering much other material with little to do with environmental protection. Grandiose titles have often concealed the fact that an Act only covers part of the law on a particular area. For example, the Wildlife and Countryside Act 1981 did not really have much to offer for the protection of the wider countryside outside sites protected for nature conservation and landscape purposes, and even the Control of Pollution Act 1974, which was the first of the modern breed of large statutes concerned exclusively with pollution control, had very little to say about air pollution.

One reason for this fragmentation was often lack of Parliamentary time provided by the Government of the day, fuelled by the perceived lack of importance of environmental issues. This is undoubtedly changing rapidly as the political importance of environmental protection has grown immensely in recent years. But many environmental measures in the past have resulted from single issue campaigns, or from private members' bills. For example, one of the reasons why the protection of birds has always been at a greater level than the protection of animals and plants is the passage of the Protection of Birds Act 1954 as a Private Member's Bill sponsored by the Royal Society for the Protection of Birds. A further example to show that this still happens is the Control of Pollution (Amendment) Act 1989, a Private Member's Bill to require the registration of carriers of controlled waste, passed in response to fly-tipping in London.

One effect of this long, and unplanned, history is that modern Britain has inherited a far less coherent system of pollution control than many other countries. The same historical factors also explain the relatively large number of agencies dealing with environmental matters, although recent changes in institutional responsibility have significantly improved matters in this respect.

A further effect is the survival of anachronisms. The name 'Alkali Inspectorate' lasted until the 1980s (when it became part of Her Majesty's Inspectorate of Pollution) and, although there have been changes in the EPA 1990, we still have laws on statutory nuisances which retain the essential shape they were given in the Public Health Act 1875. Anachronisms may also be seen in the limitations on access to environmental information and public participation in environmental decision-making (see Chapter 7) and in the still widespread immunity of the Crown in relation to environmental regulation (although this is being removed gradually).

Of course, as well as a long history of pollution control, Britain has a long history of pollution. This has left a legacy of problems that require urgent action, such as abandoned waste tips, derelict land, discharges of toxic wastes and untreated sewage into estuaries and the sea, and a host of other matters. There are other problems, stemming from the fact that many matters were not perceived as problems in the past, or that lower standards were accepted then. For example, perpetual planning permissions for peat extraction or gravel extraction were commonly granted in the 1940s and 1950s. Many of these are in areas now accepted as sensitive and worthy of protection, but under the current law the permission may only be removed by the payment of compensation for the loss of development rights.

Britain's ageing industrial base also creates difficulties when new, improved controls and standards are introduced. Fairness requires that existing producers are given some time to adapt to new standards, yet there is at the same time a problem of unfairness if controls are introduced so as to produce an inequality between new and existing producers.

The modern age of environmental law

Environmental law has changed rapidly in the last few years, and further change can be expected in the future to reflect the vastly increased prominence of environmental issues. Although it is not possible to specify a precise date or event, the modern age of environmental law can tentatively be said to have begun some time in the early 1970s.

There has been an obvious shift in the emphasis of the law since then to reflect newer environmental concerns. Many problems were simply not perceived as such in the 1960s, or were subordinated to other more pressing matters, such as the raising of living standards or the provision of full employment. The emphasis at that stage was on health and safety matters, a point well illustrated by the placing of the Alkali and Clean Air Inspectorate within the Health and Safety Executive when it was established in 1974. Land use was also emphasised; indeed, it could be argued that the very fact that Britain had (and still has) what is probably the world's most advanced system of land use planning led to the concentration of controls at that stage rather than to encouraging the development of adequate continuing pollution controls.

By comparison, the focus of modern legislation is on the control of pollution, and growing concern is being expressed about global and transfrontier problems, the control of hazardous substances and processes, the minimisation and management of waste, and the conservation of natural resources and protection of ecosystems. In short, current concerns tend to reflect the need to control the almost inevitable by-products of the modern, technological, industrial age.

In terms of legislation, the law is becoming more concentrated in a smaller number of Acts. The *EPA 1990* contains the main bulk of provisions on air pollution from stationary sources, waste management and disposal, the integrated control of the most potentially polluting processes, litter, the environmental impact of genetically modified organisms, noise and statutory control of environmental nuisances. The *Water Resources Act 1991* contains the law on water pollution and water resources, whilst the *Water Industry Act 1991* covers matters relating to water supply and sewerage. The *Wildlife and Countryside Act 1981* includes much of the relevant law on nature conservation in Parts I and II. The *Environment Act 1995* introduced new legal provisions in relation to liability for contaminated land. It also created the Environment Agency, which took over functions related to integrated pollution control, waste regulation, water pollution and water resources, and radioactive substances, although without any major changes in the substance of the law. The *Town and Country Planning Act 1990* includes in consolidated form most of the relevant statutory law on town and country planning and tree protection, though the related Planning (Listed Buildings and Conservation Areas) Act 1990 and Planning (Hazardous Substances) Act 1990 now include separate treatment of listed buildings and hazardous substances consents. There is also the Planning and Compensation Act 1991, which made some significant amendments to the 1990 Acts.

None of these Acts is a full code in relation to the relevant subject matter. There are numerous individual issues which are dealt with by separate pieces of legislation, such as on mobile sources of pollution, or on pesticides. There are other issues where the controls are still spread amongst a large number of Acts, such as in relation to landscape protection. It is also necessary to point out that much of the detailed law in any area is actually provided in statutory instruments and a wide range of other documents made under the relevant Acts. The process of producing a coherent body of environmental law, begun in the Control of Pollution Act 1974 (which put most of the law on water pollution and waste disposal in one place, but which is now virtually fully replaced by later legislation in England and Wales), has certainly moved forward some distance.

One of the important features of this process is that the development and direction of the statutory controls is more planned than before. The main Acts referred to above are all Government-sponsored Acts, illustrating an increasing tendency to plan and interlink legislation properly, although there is still a habit of including unrelated matters in legislation just in case no other opportunity arises in a packed Parliamentary timetable. For example, the EPA 1990 includes miscellaneous provisions on the control of dogs, the dismantling of the Nature Conservancy Council and the prohibition of straw and stubble burning. The publication of the wide-ranging White Paper on the environment, *This Common Inheritance* (Cm 1200, 1990), underlined this commitment to a planned development of environmental policy. The important aspect of the White Paper was not the new policies it included (these were very limited and many of the proposals had a distinctly recycled feel to them), but its mere existence as a declaration of the importance of the environment and of having a definite set of policies towards its protection.

There is also an increasing institutional coherence. The National Rivers Authority was established in 1989 as a national body regulating water pollution and a number of other activities affecting water quality. Her Majesty's Inspectorate of Pollution was established in 1987 to bring together a number of sectoral Inspectorates and was given integrated powers over the most hazardous industrial processes in the EPA 1990, an Act which also created greater coherence in relation to the control of air pollution by local authorities and the management of waste and waste disposal. Once again it is clear that controls over stationary sources of pollution are more coherent than those over mobile or non-point sources. The year 1996 saw the creation of a unified Environment Agency for England and Wales with responsibility for integrated pollution control, the regulation of waste, the control of radioactivity and the regulation of water pollution.

A different aspect of developments in relation to institutional responsibilities has been the policy of splitting production from regulation. This may be termed the need to differentiate the poachers from the gamekeepers. In recent years this was achieved by the creation of the National Rivers Authority. Prior to that the regulation of water pollution was the responsibility of the regional water authorities, who were also responsible for causing pollution from sewage works which they operated. A more recent example is the enforced separation of waste regulation functions from waste disposal functions in the EPA 1990 (see Chapter 13), a process that has been taken further in the Environment Act 1995.

A final change, which may be seen from the examples referred to, is that environmental protection is becoming increasingly centralised, although this must be seen against the perspective that, as stated above, the system inherited from earlier years was particularly decentralised. There are many reasons for this — the increasing technological and scientific demands on pollution controllers, Central Government antipathy towards local government, increased emphasis on uniform and integrated planning of solutions to problems, and the impact of EC membership. This issue is considered further in Chapter 5.

A most important factor in all of these changes has been the influence of the European Communities (EC). The EC has a well-developed environmental policy and has passed numerous pieces of environmental law. At a general level, membership of the EC has led to the consideration and adoption of new methods of control and to the need to confront environmental issues in an organised way at Central Government level. More specifically, EC legislation and pressure has led to many actual and proposed changes in the law (often after British resistance), for example, on sulphur dioxide emissions, the dumping of sewage sludge in the sea and reductions in emissions from vehicles. Other changes have been more indirect; for example, the Wildlife and Countryside Act 1981 was necessary to comply with EC Directive 79/409 on Wild Birds, and the opportunity was taken to modify other areas of the law at the same time. Without the EC obligation there must be some doubt whether any legislation would have been brought forward at that time and even greater doubt as to whether it would have been persevered with in the light of the widespread opposition to the Government's original proposals, which were significantly altered as the Bill passed through Parliament.

The future of environmental policy

In the light of EC membership, and the pressure now brought to bear by the whole international community on environmental issues, it is difficult to disentangle British policies from global and regional ones. It is also difficult to predict the future accurately in this area because environmental policy is currently a highly political area. For example, it is difficult to imagine many issues that could raise a greater number of separate, highly-charged, political issues than the proposals for some form of 'carbon tax'. Nevertheless, a number of key directions for future policy present themselves:

(a) The emphasis is shifting away from the more traditional reactive methods of solving environmental problems towards the prevention of harm.

This is illustrated by the progressive adoption of laws that set standards for products or the processes by which they are made, rather than for discharges or emissions. The introduction of integrated pollution control, a process-based control, is an important step in this direction.

(b)   The importance of the market in controlling environmental problems will continue to be stressed. Originally, this stemmed from the philosophical basis of the Conservative Government whilst it was in power. Subsequently, it has been related to the preference for market mechanisms (often referred to as 'economic instruments'), which may help to prevent pollution occurring by sending signals to consumers about the true environmental costs of their activities. Examples can be seen in the proliferation of schemes for charging for environmentally harmful activities, in the increasingly frequent reference to the 'polluter pays' principle and direct measures such as the introduction of the landfill tax. The current Government has made it clear that over the next few years there will be more reforms of the taxation system to increase incentives which will reduce environmental damage. The two most likely candidates for change are taxes on the quarrying of aggregates and water pollution (by way of an increase in charges). In addition, the EC is looking at a variety of economic instruments including full cost recovery pricing for water pollution (i.e., charging for the full environmental costs for the use of water, see further p. 447) and direct taxation of materials (e.g., the controversial carbon tax).

(c)   The EC also stresses the role that mechanisms other than administrative regulation have to play in the protection of the environment. The key concept in its fifth Action Programme on the Environment, covering the period 1993 to 2000 and entitled *Towards Sustainability,* is that of 'shared responsibility'. This means that responsibility for environmental problems is shared between govemment, producers and consumers. By suggesting that producers and consumers should be empowered to make decisions that have an impact on environmental performance, it heralds the development of a wider range of legal and policy responses to environmental problems.

(d)   A further matter that links all of the above together is the provision of information about the environment. It is obvious that increased interest in environmental issues has led to a political need for greater access to information. But there is a further reason why freedom of information is a central issue. This is that market mechanisms do not work, and concepts such as shared responsibility mean nothing, unless there is access to accurate information. As a result, wide-ranging provisions on access to information have been enacted at both EC and domestic levels — see Directive 90/313 and the Environmental Information Regulations 1992 (SI 1992 No. 3240).

(e)   An important issue is the internationalisation of many problems. A number of high-profile issues, such as global warming, depletion of the ozone layer, the protection of the rainforest, and attempts to save the whales, have galvanised interest in environmental issues, and there is no doubt that the future agenda will increasingly be set on the international stage.

Of course, the clearest expression of this process was the United Nations Conference on Environment and Development (UNCED), held in Rio de

Janeiro in June 1992. Although this was rightly criticised for failing to produce anything of enormous immediate significance, it did produce agreement on a number of things. These included a framework convention on climate change, a convention on biological diversity, a declaration on the sustainable development of forests, and Agenda 21, which is effectively a very wide-ranging environmental action plan for the next century. The implications of these commitments are currently being fed through into domestic policies, so Rio is probably most accurately seen as the beginning of a process rather than the end of one. This process of internationalisation of environmental policy received a setback at the Rio II summit held in New York in June 1997. Although the political rhetoric about the need for global cooperation was much to the fore again, the evidence from many countries suggested that many of the specific targets which were agreed at Rio would not be met. Furthermore, there was relatively little consensus on the setting of future targets.

(f)   A central strand of policy at Rio was the emphasis on the conservation of natural resources. The key concept was that of 'sustainable development', an idea that was originally developed by the World Commission on Environment and Development (the Brundtland Commission) in its report, *Our Common Future*, in 1987. *Our Common Future* defined sustainable development in general terms as 'development that meets the needs of today whilst not affecting the ability of future generations to meet their own needs', thus suggesting that global resources (including environmental resources) should be measured, with the objective of ensuring that they are not depleted over time. Clearly, this idea requires some further development itself, in particular in relation to how one goes about measuring intangible global assets and whether it is permissible to substitute one type of asset for another. One thing that is clear is that sustainable development still represents a commitment to growth. In *This Common Inheritance* the Government stresses the view that continued growth is a necessary (although not a sufficient) condition for maintaining the quality of life, and this view is reiterated in *Sustainable Development: The UK Strategy* (Cm 2426, 1994), the Government's strategy document on the matter. The idea of sustainable development should therefore be distinguished from the concept of sustainability, which merely reflects the state of something being sustainable in the long term.

(g)   At a national level, a change in Government raises inevitable questions about the way in which domestic environmental policy might develop over the next few years. Whereas certain initiatives such as the increasing use of economic instruments are accepted across the political parties (with differences over detail rather than principle), there are a number of policy shifts on the horizon. These could include: the integration of environmental policies with other areas of policy; the decentralisation of power from central government to the regions, particularly in relation to strategic environmental planning; and an increased emphasis on issues which are central to open access to environmental justice, including greater access to information.

Perhaps most significantly, the full implications of sustainability will need to be addressed and difficult choices made. These are most obvious in relation to steps that are being taken to reduce waste (of materials and energy) by tackling the problem at source. The policy is now that waste reduction is to be preferred to recycling, and recycling to disposal. The minimisation of waste is clearly going to be an important feature of future production measures, not least because of the spiralling cost of waste disposal. Other areas which are destined to be controversial are transport policy and housebuilding. The nature of the controversy reflects the fact that the most important message of sustainability appears to be getting across. This is that there is not some remote category of people called 'polluters' and everything will be all right if they can be controlled, but that environmental protection is a matter for everyone and involves everyone making informed choices about their own lifestyles.

The future of environmental law

An introductory chapter may seem a strange place to consider the future of the law, since any such discussion must inevitably involve an understanding of the present position. However, it is useful to sketch out some general ideas about the direction in which environmental law might be going at this stage so as to set the rest of the book in context.

The starting point is to repeat the proposition that environmental law has not been developed as a self-contained discipline, but has simply borrowed concepts from other areas of law. One result is undoubtedly a degree of incoherence, but another is that the objective of the protection of the environment is not always best served by the legal mechanisms available, because these other areas were not developed with the particular problems of environmental protection in mind. For example, the private law concentrates on the protection of private interests and has difficulties when it comes to protecting common or public interests in the unowned environment. No damages are payable for harm to the environment as such, and only those with personal or property rights may bring an action (thus excluding animals, trees, rivers etc). No value is placed on the environment itself and environmental protection is simply an incidental by-product of the protection of other interests. As Lord Scarman pointed out in 1974 in *English Law — The New Dimension*:

> For 'environment' a traditional lawyer reads 'property': English law reduces environmental problems to questions of property . . .. The judicial development of the law, vigorous and imaginative though it has been, has been found wanting.

Public law does recognise the public interest, but difficulties arise out of a lack of acceptance of the idea that the environment has some independent status or value, as distinct from rights conferred on individuals and communities. Even the criminal law struggles with environmental 'crimes', since it has often been pointed out in the courts that many of the offences created are not criminal in the 'true' sense (see the acceptance by the House of Lords in

Alphacell Ltd v *Woodward* [1972] AC 824 that water pollution offences are in the category of 'acts which in the public interest are prohibited under a penalty'). Finally, the structure of the judicial system (with its emphasis on adversarial and backward-looking two-party litigation and with its procedural rules which are not user-friendly to those wishing to bring environmental cases and which fail to give the public interest a separate voice) is not particularly well-suited to consideration of environmental disputes, because typically they have multiple causes, give rise to complex scientific arguments, involve a complex interplay between public, private and criminal law, and require the balancing of difficult political or policy questions.

With these current defects in mind, the following thoughts can be put forward about the future development of environmental law.

(a)   In terms of civil law, there may well be a development of some sort of redress for purely environmental harm. For example, current EC proposals on civil liability envisage damages being payable for impairment of the environment (see, for example, the EC Commission Green Paper, *Remedying Environmental Damage*, 1993).

(b)   At a wider level, the work of environmental philosophers may be adopted so as to establish a legal concept which accords the environment some status in its own right (one hesitates to use the unclear phrase 'environmental rights', which might be better used to describe procedural rights possessed by individuals, such as rights to information, rights to be consulted, rights to have reasons provided for a decision and rights to make a complaint). This could be achieved by the recognition that, in line with the discussion about sustainability above, the planet is effectively held in trust for future generations. It could thus lead to the development of some sort of public trust doctrine. However, the development of such a concept is fraught with problems, since there is an all too obvious potential conflict between the precautionary and restrictive measures that are often required for sensible action on the environment and the traditional legal emphases on personal freedom and protection of property. This conflict can only really be resolved by the development of some sort of 'environmental constitution' that sits alongside other constitutional protections.

(c)   With regard to the criminal law, one reason that is often given for the failure to enforce against environmental laws is that a criminal remedy is inappropriate. Consideration may, therefore, be given to the 'decriminalisation' of whole areas of environmental law, so that a distinction could be drawn between, on the one hand, infringements that are properly characterised as administrative in nature and, on the other, truly criminal breaches, such as blatant cases of environmental vandalism. One advantage of this may be to encourage stiffer penalties for those in the second category. In similar vein, consideration should be given to the idea that fines imposed for environmental offences (of either type) should be paid into special funds for the enhancement or protection of the environment. This is not currently possible owing to the Treasury's insistence that all fines go into central funds — an attitude which does not fit easily with the 'polluter pays' principle.

(Indeed, many of the market mechanisms favoured by Government simply do not work — in the sense of providing an appropriate incentive to act in a particular manner — without an element of earmarking of funds.)

(d) There is, perhaps, a growing realisation that the different areas of law — public law, private law, criminal law — merely provide, in the environmental context, a set of different tools to achieve a specified objective, in this case the protection of the environment. For example, in relation to contaminated land it is clear that someone has to 'pay' for the contamination, either by cleaning it up, or by living with the consequences. There are essentially four possible options: the polluter could be made liable; the current owner or occupier could be liable; the State could pay (i.e., through some public clean-up mechanism) — this really means that the the public pays through some form of taxation; or, finally, the loss could lie where it falls, meaning that the environment and the local community effectively 'pay'. For a policy-maker the issue is how to come up with a solution that is effective, efficient and fair, whilst the tools that are available include, but are not limited to, legal mechanisms. The interesting thing about the solution provided in the Environment Act 1995 is that it combines the various tools in quite a sophisticated fashion and produces a situation where the public interest is protected by a combination of mechanisms that borrow from public, private and criminal law (see Chapter 13).

(e) The above example raises the question of whether the development of the law is a matter for the courts or for Parliament. In *Cambridge Water Co. v Eastern Counties Leather plc* [1994] 2 AC 264, Lord Goff stated in respect of environmental protection:

> . . . given that so much well-informed and carefully structured legislation is now being put in place for this purpose, there is less need for the courts to develop a common law principle to achieve the same end, and indeed it may well be undesirable that they should do so.

This can be interpreted as a reflection of the fact that Parliament is able to create a coherent and structured system, rather than one developed on an ad hoc, case-by-case basis; but it also reflects the point that Parliament has a greater democratic legitimacy than the courts when it comes to allocating responsibility for environmental harm. In the same passage Lord Goff also stated:

> As a general rule, it is more appropriate for strict liability in respect of operations of high risk to be imposed by Parliament, than by the courts.

This raises a different point about the *nature* of the liability that should be imposed. At present there is a clear division between those, such as the Government and most industrial organisations, who see the imposition of strict liability as unfair and punitive and therefore wish to retain a fault-based system as far as possible, and those, including the EC Commission in its Green Paper, *Remedying Environmental Damage*, who see strict liability as the most efficient and effective method of allocating responsibility for environmental harm. This issue is likely to remain a controversial one for many years.

(f) Notwithstanding the above points, there is an increasing likelihood that a separate court or tribunal dealing with environmental cases will be established. This follows considerable debate which has taken place over the last few years (see the articles referred to in the bibliography). Some tentative steps have already been taken with the amalgamation of the system of administrative appeals within the Planning Inspectorate. It is quite easy to establish a prima facie case that the current legal system does not work too well when confronted with environmental disputes, and that a new structure and set of procedures could work better. It must be borne in mind, however, that in many ways it is the substance of the law that is the problem, not the procedures, although the two are related.

(g) What, then, is the current approach of the British courts? Whilst acknowledging the dangers of generalisation, it is possible to detect different approaches to different types of cases. In the civil or common law cases, the courts appear to be keen to restrict the extension of liability for environmental harm unless there are clearly identifiable parameters within which future decisions can be made. In *Hunter* v *Canary Wharf Ltd* [1997] 2 WLR 684 and *Cambridge Water Co.* v *Eastern Counties Leather plc* [1994] 2 AC 264 the House of Lords refused to extend common law principles to accommodate the concept of environmental damage or damage to those who did not have any property interests. In *Merlin* v *British Nuclear Fuels plc* [1990] 2 QB 557, the High Court decided that the entry of radiation into a house did not amount to 'injury to any person or damage to any property' within the meaning of the Nuclear Installations Act 1965, s. 47. This case has now to be viewed in the light of the decision in *Blue Circle Industries Ltd* v *Ministry of Defence* [1997] Env LR D7 (in which actual physical damage brought about from radiation was actionable).

(h) Administrative challenges to environmental decisions have also been dealt with in a very narrow fashion by the courts. There have been a series of challenges to administrative decisions ranging from the acceptance of derogation from standards set under the Drinking Water Directive to failure to designate a special protection area under the Birds Directive. Whilst the courts have not rejected every challenge, it is uncommon for environmental decisions to be overturned. Although this often reflects the essentially discretionary nature of the decision-making process in many environmental matters, it also suggests that, in the main, the courts have been very cautious when it comes to developing new ideas on environmental protection.

(i) A final example of the judicial reluctance to develop the law on environmental protection can be found in relation to cases which have an aspect of European law to them. Time and time again the courts have appeared to be unwilling to develop the principles of European environmental law or to refer the most complicated matters to the European Court of Justice under the Article 177 procedure. In *R* v *Secretary of State for Trade and Industry, ex parte Duddridge* [1995] Env LR 151, the Divisional Court (subsequently upheld in the Court of Appeal [1996] Env LR 325) refused in very clear terms even to consider the application of the precautionary principle set out in Article 130R(2) of the EC Treaty as part of English law. There are other decisions where it is interesting to contrast the ECJ's view with the conclusions of the domestic courts (see, for example, *Aanemersbedrijf P.K. Kraaijeveld BV* v *Gedeputeerde Staten van Zuid-Holland* (case C-72/95) [1996] ECR I-5403 on the direct effect of the Environmental Assessment Directive and the UK cases (p. 282) or the decisions in the *Lappel Bank* case, p. 513). It is quite clear from these cases that, on the whole, the courts in the UK struggle with the application of European environmental law.

(j)   In relation to criminal cases, however, the courts have increasingly adopted a purposive approach to construing statutes. For example, in the case of water pollution offences, the interpretation that successive courts have been willing to place on the word 'cause' has been very wide (see p. 453). This can also be seen in relation to waste management offences (e.g., *Shanks and McEwan (Teeside) Ltd* v *Environment Agency* [1997] Env LR D8). This purposive approach appears to stem from the judicial desire to provide law that is effective in terms of environmental protection. One of the exceptions to this purposive approach is in the case of nature conservation matters. In *Southern Water Authority* v *Nature Conservancy Council* [1992] 1 WLR 775, the House of Lords adopted a very literal interpretation of the Wildlife and Countryside Act 1981 in finding against the NCC (see p. 503).

(k)   There is another area where the courts have proved active. In recent years, there has been an increased willingness to develop judicial review mechanisms to provide for openness in decision-making and accountability to the public for decisions made in its name. For example, the courts are now accepting a wider role for environmental and other public interest groups in litigation. In *R* v *Inspectorate of Pollution, ex parte Greenpeace Ltd (No. 2)* [1994] 4 All ER 329, Otton J decided that Greenpeace had *locus standi* to challenge the decision to allow the thermal oxide reprocessing plant at Sellafield to start operating. He pointed in particular to the campaigning group's genuine interest in the issues raised and to its expertise and resources, and even referred to it as 'eminently respectable and responsible'. In *R* v *Secretary of State for Foreign and Commonwealth Affairs, ex parte World Development Movement Ltd* [1995] 1 WLR 386 (the *Pergau Dam* case) a similarly wide approach was also adopted, leading to the suggestion that the very restrictive ruling in *R* v *Secretary of State for the Environment, ex parte Rose Theatre Trust Ltd* [1990] QB 504 is unlikely to be followed in future. This liberalisation of the judicial attitude towards standing was confirmed with the decision in *R* v *Somerset County Council, ex parte Dixon* [1997] NPC 61, where Sedley J decided that the only real restriction on the right to bring a challenge should be to exclude applicants in any case where they are merely a 'busybody' or 'troublemaker', who has no real interest in the outcome of the challenge. This widening of *locus standi* will be encouraged by the recommendations of the Law Commission in *Administrative Law: Judicial Review and Statutory Appeals* (Law Com. No. 226, 1994) that *locus standi* should be found where the application is in the 'public interest', that unincorporated associations should be enabled to make applications in their own name, and that costs should be awarded from central funds where there is a public interest challenge.

(l) Despite the negative points that have emerged in the previous discussion, there will certainly be a continuing increase in environmental litigation. The increased formality of many areas of environmental policy increases the possibility of a successful public law challenge; practising lawyers are increasingly aware of the possibilities thrown up by legal action; environmental interest groups have learnt the usefulness of the legal process in making political points as well as in winning cases; and EC law throws up a whole new area of litigation arising out of the doctrines of direct effects and indirect effects and the decision in the *Francovich* case (see Chapter 4).

(m) Finally, whatever happens in relation to these major issues, there will continue to be some fine-tuning of the mechanisms that already exist. One of the defects of the law has been its piecemeal development, and it is clear that measures that have proved successful in one area are likely to be adopted in others.

The costs of compliance

Whatever the exact direction that the law takes, one thing is clear about the future; the cost of compliance with the law is going to rise sharply, both for polluters and for society in general. This is mainly because regulatory standards are getting stricter and are being enforced more rigorously. But there are other factors, such as a heightened perception of the true environmental cost of many activities and the greatly increased pressure that is being brought to bear by the public, environmental groups and green consumers and investors.

The cost of sewage disposal illustrates the point. Disposal to the sewers has traditionally been thought of as a fairly cheap and efficient way of disposing of wastes. But the introduction of integrated pollution control means that increased controls will be applied to discharges of prescribed substances to the sewers. The costs of sewage treatment are also increasing because of changes relating to the disposal of their own wastes by sewage works. For example, the standards set for discharges to controlled waters are being tightened as the Environment Agency reviews existing consents, and this will carry a new urgency in the light of the need to meet the requirements of EC Directive 91/271 on Urban Waste Water Treatment. The cost of disposal of sewage sludge will also rise. Not only is the cheap option of dumping sewage sludge in the sea being phased out, after strong international pressure, but the cost of disposal on land is likely to rise significantly. Incineration is another possibility for disposal of sludge, but that too is coming under increasingly tight regulation. The privatised nature of the sewerage undertakers emphasises the need to take these factors into account. At the moment these sewerage undertakers are reviewing existing trade effluent consents for discharges to the sewers, and it is clear that in the next few years conditions restricting the discharge of certain substances will increasingly be imposed and that charges for discharges to sewers will rise.

The costs of non-compliance

Apart from the direct cost to business of complying with stricter regulatory controls, the potential liabilities for non-compliance are also increasing. These liabilities fall into five general categories:

(a) *Criminal liabilities.* The number of criminal offences for non-compliance with environmental legislation is immense, and in recent years the regulatory agencies have shown an increased willingness to resort to prosecution. Private prosecution is also a possibility. Fines will be the normal penalty, though in a number of cases sentences of imprisonment have been imposed (there is normally a potential personal liability for directors and senior managers). Maximum fine levels have risen in recent years, as have actual levels of fines imposed.

(b) *Administrative sanctions.* In most regulatory systems there is a range of options available to the regulator, including variation, suspension or revocation of a licence. Since these steps may lead to the closure of a plant, they are obviously of great importance.

(c) *Clean-up costs.* In most environmental legislation there is a power to clean up after a pollution incident and recover the cost from the polluter or (in some cases) the occupier.

(d) *Civil liability.* There is growing interest in the 'toxic torts', although many of the actions have in fact been around for a long time. Many environmental actions rest upon strict liability. Although liability may often be difficult to establish, the size of claims may be very high indeed.

(e) *Adverse publicity.* In practice the publicity attracted as a result of infringements of the law may be as costly as any direct costs.

In the light of all these risks, not to mention the increased costs of waste disposal and of complying with stricter standards, some of the most significant recent developments in the environmental field relate to management issues. For example, a British Standard on Environmental Management Systems (BS 7750), relating to the adoption of an appropriate management system, was introduced in 1994. The EC has agreed a Regulation on Eco-Management and Auditing (Regulation 1836/93), which goes further in some respects by requiring a public statement of environmental performance, external verification procedures, and a commitment to continuing improvements in environmental performance. Both these schemes are voluntary in the sense that there is no compulsion to join them. However, it appears that the pressures from supply chains and from the public may well be such that in practice many firms will be forced to introduce some form of environmental auditing of their business (see further p. 124).

Policy and environmental law

A final introductory thought, but a most important one, is that environmental law is a political discipline. It is political in the narrow sense that major differences can be discerned between political parties as to the correct policy to apply. These differences do not normally relate to the ends to be achieved, but to the methods to be adopted in doing so, and the costs to be incurred. A clear example is the controversy provoked by the passage of the Wildlife and Countryside Act 1981 over whether voluntary or compulsory controls should be adopted in relation to the protection of important natural sites (see Chapter 16). A further example relates to the whole history of town and country planning in the 1980s, when the very dramatic changes to planning policy led to disagreement and dispute. These are clear examples of the application of 'Thatcherism' to the environment, as a Government with a deep suspicion of planning and regulation sought to grapple with a system based on coherent planning for the future. However, there are others which relate to such things as privatisation and deregulation. The Deregulation and Contracting Out Act 1994 shows that little has really changed since the 1980s and also emphasises the point that the whole context of environmental law may well change if a different administration is elected.

Environmental law is also political in the wide sense that it involves the making of policy decisions about the best way to achieve certain objectives. This is emphasised in this book by looking at law as being about techniques or tools for solving problems. It is not just lawyers and environmentalists who have a choice of tools they may use to achieve a particular objective. Legislators and policy-makers also have a range of tools available to them. The law is one tool alongside such things as fiscal policy, education, research, and voluntary solutions. There are different types of legal mechanism that may be used, such as the setting of environmental quality objectives, or of strict limits on emissions, or controls attached to processes or products. These various possibilities are discussed in detail in Chapter 5, but it ought to be recognised that, in order to combat complex problems of pollution and environmental harm, a combination of methods is often required.

It is impossible to say that Britain always adopts one method rather than another, but it is clear that the tendency has been to adopt flexible mechanisms of control, where what is permitted is judged by reference to its effect on the receiving environment. As a result, the British approach to pollution control tends to be fairly pragmatic, and involves a great deal of discretion. This discretion is normally exercised by specialist regulatory agencies, although local authorities also have very significant environmental protection functions. An important point is that this discretion is exercised on grounds that are not restricted to environmental factors. There is a traditionally close connection in British environmental regulation between social, political and economic factors and decisions on environmental protection.

This emphasis on taking into account a wide range of factors before making a decision links to a fundamental point about the way that 'pollution' and 'environmental harm' are defined. Once again, it is difficult to formulate precise definitions, but a general guide would be to say that they cover situations where there is an excess of something over what is desirable. There is no doubt that they are relative concepts; one person's waste is another's raw materials. As a result, Nicholas Ridley's famous comment that 'Housing is not a form of environmental pollution' can be seen as inaccurate in some cases.

The level of pollution is also relative. For example, because of the self-cleansing properties of the environment, it may well be said to be less polluting to discharge into a large fast-flowing river than into a small sluggish one, and higher levels of pollution from industrial sources may be tolerated in one area than in another because of the corresponding advantages of the economic prosperity that the industries bring. It is nonsensical to talk of getting rid of pollution. It only makes sense to consider how to reduce it and the levels which are acceptable.

Everything therefore depends on what is considered acceptable. This involves economic, political, social and cultural criteria as well as scientific and environmental ones. It is therefore important to understand that, in implementing environmental protection policies, regulatory agencies are effectively carrying out a political balancing process. As Hawkins puts it in *Environment and Enforcement* (1984), 'The power to define and enforce consents is ultimately a power to put people out of business, to deter the introduction of new business or to drive away a going concern'.

TWO

Sources of environmental law

Most of the formal sources of environmental law are statutory. Compared with subjects such as contract or tort there is very little judge-made law, and most of what there is consists of interpretations of statutory provisions. Obviously there are areas of the common law which can be used to promote environmental protection, such as the law of nuisance, or the rules on restrictive covenants, but the environmental advantages they bring tend to be incidental to the main purpose of the law concerned. For a discussion of the common law's contribution to environmental protection see Chapter 8.

Some major features of environmental legislation

Environmental statutes tend to exhibit a number of features:

(a) they are often framework Acts, requiring delegated legislation to be made to make them effective;
(b) their commencement is often delayed or staged;
(c) they include unclear definitions;
(d) they confer wide discretions.

Delegated legislation
Much of the detail of environmental statutes is left to be worked out in various forms of delegated legislation, such as regulations, rules, orders and schemes. This is particularly true of some of the main pieces of legislation in environmental law — the EPA 1990, the Water Resources Act 1991 and the Water Industry Act 1991, the Environment Act 1995 and the Town and Country Planning Act 1990. In each case a person who read the Act on its own would get a very limited view of the law. For example, the general requirement that an authorisation must be obtained from the Environment Agency before 'prescribed processes' are carried on is laid down in the EPA 1990, s. 6, but the list of processes is prescribed in Regulations, as are the

detailed procedures for acquiring an authorisation. In the Town and Country Planning Act 1990, the central definition of what requires planning permission owes just as much to statutory instruments — the General Permitted Development Order and the Use Classes Order — as to the general definition laid down in s. 55 (see Chapter 9).

Delegated legislation may take a number of forms. In most cases, it is made by the Secretary of State or some other member of the Government (such as the Minister of Agriculture). But this is not necessarily the case, and it does not always involve the use of statutory instruments laid before Parliament. For example, the Environment Agency has the power to issue charging schemes under s. 41 of the Environment Act 1995, although approval of the scheme is required from the Secretary of State and the Treasury, and either House of Parliament can annul any statutory instrument by resolution.

Very wide powers are often granted in relation to matters that are delegated. In some cases, such as the General Permitted Development Order, and the Use Classes Order and the producer responsibility provisions in the Environment Act 1995, ss. 93–95, this virtually amounts to giving the Secretary of State a power to rewrite the Act. There are obvious problems of accountability with such an approach, since far less Parliamentary scrutiny is given to delegated legislation than to Acts of Parliament. There is also the prospect that the powers may not be used. For example, under the Control of Pollution Act 1974, powers were given to the Secretary of State to make regulations on precautions to be taken over the control of potentially polluting matter, and on water protection zones (s. 31(4) and s. 31(5) respectively), yet none were ever made.

In addition to the normal range of secondary legislation, there is what could be called 'tertiary' legislation, made up of different forms of rules, guidance and advice. There is no set legislative pattern to this type of 'rule', although it appears to be becoming more popular with Government as environmental regulation becomes more complex. There are many different types of such legislation and they have a tremendous impact upon the way in which environmental law operates in practice (see further p. 28).

Commencement

Legislation often requires implementation by statutory instrument before it comes into force. The Control of Pollution Act was enacted in 1974, yet Part II relating to water pollution was not brought into force until 1986, and then only in a piecemeal and gradual manner. Some parts of the Act were never brought into force (e.g., s. 46(1)–(3) on the powers of water authorities to vary consents after an act of pollution). Apart from the suspicion that such delays are used for political purposes, this gradualist approach obscures what the law is and brings it into disrepute by creating uncertainty for the public, regulatory bodies and industry alike.

The EPA 1990 included a provision for most of it to be brought into force by commencement order. This led to the provisions on waste management licensing not being brought into force until May 1994. As far as integrated pollution control is concerned, the provisions of the Act have been brought into force, but were not applicable to individual processes until the commencement date published in Regulations had passed (see p. 329). It seems contrary to the rule of law that the decision on whether, and how far, to implement enacted legislation should be left entirely to the discretion of the Secretary of State. However, that is the position and the same approach has been adopted for the Environment Act 1995, virtually all of which requires a commencement order before it comes into force.

Definitions

Definitions are often left unclear in the legislation. Normally this is to preserve flexibility in the application of the law. For example, until the enactment of the EPA 1990, the central concept in the law on air pollution was that of 'best practicable means' (BPM). This phrase was never statutorily defined. Instead, it was explained in relation to different processes in BPM Notes published by Her Majesty's Inspectorate of Pollution (HMIP) and its predecessors. Even these were not comprehensive, since an important feature of BPM was that it allowed flexibility to cater for local and individual circumstances. Interestingly, the BPM Notes were often drawn up in consultation with interested parties, including representatives of the industry concerned.

The same approach is adopted for the definition of the key phrase in Part I of the EPA 1990 — 'best available techniques not entailing excessive cost' (BATNEEC). Integrated pollution control (IPC) and local authority air pollution control (APC) Guidance Notes explaining the content of BATNEEC have been published for each prescribed process, although with less reliance on the industries concerned.

A similar process can be seen in the Town and Country Planning Act 1990, where fundamental concepts such as development and material change of use have deliberately been left as open as possible in the legislation. In this case, they have been further defined by the courts in numerous cases, but the original flexibility has been retained by the courts' insistence that the application of the law to the facts of any individual case is a matter for the relevant decision-maker (the so-called 'fact and degree' test). If anything, this approach is becoming more common. In the Environment Act 1995, Part II, a new system providing for remediation of contaminated land is established, yet the fundamental question of whether land is 'contaminated' will owe as much to guidance issued by the Secretary of State which local authorities must follow, as it does to the partial definition set out in the Act. What should be determined as a matter of law is thus relegated to a matter of administrative discretion. An even more remarkable example is provided by the Deregulation and Contracting Out Act 1994, which includes a general power for any Minister to amend or repeal existing legislation by means of a statutory instrument if it appears that the measure imposes a burden on any trade, business or profession, and that the amendment or repeal will reduce that burden. These examples illustrate a clear shift in power away from Parliament and the courts to the executive Government.

Discretions

Wide discretions are frequently given in the legislation. This is a particularly clear feature of British environmental law (see p. 111). There are many examples, ranging from the discretion given to the Secretary of State on the form of delegated legislation, through discretion as to whether an area should be designated for special protection, discretion on the setting of standards (e.g., in the permitted level of a pollutant discharged or emitted), to discretion over the enforcement of the law. In all areas of environmental law it is hard to get away from discretionary decision-making.

However, two important trends must be pointed out at this stage — the increased structuring of the discretions and the increased role of Central Government. In the past, it has been normal for environmental legislation to grant public agencies and bodies a large amount of discretion, often in the form of a subjective power which is then regulated by the courts. Over the last few years, the agencies have themselves structured the exercise of their discretions through such things as internal agency guidelines and strategies, and have thus made the whole system more formalised (a good example is the adoption by the EA of a formal policy on prosecution and other enforcement action). This gives the courts a greater potential role in environmental decisions. However, the effect is arguably limited by the other trend which, as pointed out above, is that ever greater powers are being given to Central Government to dictate the sorts of considerations that must be taken into account in any exercise of a discretion. This process is seen very clearly in the Environment Act 1995. As a specific example, s. 39 imposes a requirement that the Environment Agency take into account the likely costs and benefits before making decisions; but, more generally, the whole way in which the Environment Agency will operate will be decided by guidance and directions issued by Central Government.

These features of environmental legislation help to explain some of the essential characteristics of the 'British approach' to environmental protection, such as flexibility and pragmatism (see p. 107). The width of the discretions given also militates against uniformity in either the definition or the application of the law.

Informal sources of law and practice

One particular result of giving wide discretion to decision-makers is that the concept of environmental 'law' expands to include a wide range of matters. For example, the IPC and APC Guidance Notes mentioned above are crucial to any understanding of what is actually required of industry in relation to pollution, even though they have no formal legal effect other than as matters to be taken into account by the appropriate enforcing body. Similarly, in areas of the law that depend on the discretionary balancing of policy factors, an understanding of the sources of policy is central. In many cases, prevailing policies effectively make or change the law. One of the most famous of policies in town planning — the Green Belt — has no statutory foundation at all (apart from around London). It stems entirely from a Central

Government restraint policy dating back to the 1950s, which has been applied on a local basis in many areas. In theory, the whole idea of Green Belt could be amended, or even scrapped, tomorrow merely by a change in Government policy.

The story of town planning in the 1980s illustrates this point graphically, since what amounted virtually to a revolution in town planning law took place with very few changes to the legislation and delegated legislation. The main vehicle of change was Central Government Circular guidance on policy, which could be imposed on local authorities through the appeal system. It is arguable that a student of current planning law would learn more about what will happen in practice by reading Government policy documents than by reading the legislation.

The range of what must be considered as law is also widened by some of the features of environmental law. It is law in action rather than law for lawyers. It involves the solving of practical problems, so everything which is likely to have an impact on the solution of a problem should be understood, including policy and evidence of practice. It is also a forward-looking law; because of the need to plan for the future, it is desirable to know what the law is going to be as well as what it is.

Thus, the sources of environmental law are far wider than Acts of Parliament, delegated legislation and cases. Much of what constitutes law in its wider sense is in Circulars and policy documents issued by Central Government or the regulatory agencies. (It should be noted that there are normally different Circulars issued by the Department of the Environment and the Welsh Office, but these normally say the same things. In this book references to Circular numbers are to those issued by the Department of the Environment — see further above.)

It may also be argued that 'law' should include the actual practice of agencies with responsibilities in the environmental field; an argument which is at its strongest when dealing with enforcement. This makes it desirable that as much as possible about the practice and policy actually relied upon by decision-makers is published officially, an aim which (sadly for writers of environmental law books) is not yet met in practice.

European Communities (EC) law

It would not be proper to conclude a discussion of the sources of the law without a reference to EC law, which is of enormous importance in the environmental field. Membership of the EC has clearly involved a distinct loss of sovereignty for Member States, and in this country this is given constitutional force by the European Communities Act 1972. Section 2(1) provides that EC legislation is recognised as law in Britain, although by no means all EC environmental legislation is directly effective in the sense that it can be relied upon by individuals before it is implemented by domestic measures (see p. 66).

By virtue of the European Communities Act 1972, s. 2(2), EC legislation can be transposed into domestic law by delegated legislation even if there is no parent statute authorising it. For example, Directive 85/337 on Environmental Impact Assessment was implemented in British law through the passage of regulations by reference to that subsection. This power has a technical limitation, since no provisions extra to the EC legislation may be added without a new piece of enabling legislation. For example, this explains why the domestic regulations on environmental assessment originally went no further than required by the Directive (some would argue that they did not actually go as far as that), but that limitation was removed by a new statutory power to make regulations on environmental assessment under the Planning and Compensation Act 1991, s. 15.

EC law is explained in greater detail in Chapter 4, but an important point to establish here is that, as with the position in domestic law, EC environmental law consists of far more than legal rules. It is as necessary to understand the policies, principles and future direction of EC law as it is to understand its current legal content.

International law

International law governs relations between states. Unlike EC law, it has no direct effect on domestic law or on individuals. However, it will often have an indirect effect, for example by publicising a particular issue, by laying down generally accepted standards, or by imposing political pressure on states to change their laws or practices. Thus the North Sea Conferences have had an important impact on British domestic policies in relation to the dumping of sewage sludge in the North Sea, which will now cease. Many pieces of legislation include powers for the Government to introduce changes into domestic law in order to comply with international obligations. For example, the EPA 1990, s. 156 enables the Secretary of State to make regulations to modify other parts of the Act in order to comply with EC or international obligations.

For the most part, international environmental law consists of Conventions agreed by signatory states, such as the Ramsar Convention on Wetlands of International Importance (see p. 519), or the Vienna Convention for the Protection of the Ozone Layer. These may provide general guidance on activities or they may lay down precise standards and requirements (for example, the Montreal Protocol to the Vienna Convention does this). The important point is that such law is not ultimately binding, except in a political sense, because of the lack of sanctions available for non-compliance. However, it is often implemented by domestic or EC legislation, a process which has happened to the Montreal Protocol. It is anticipated, by analogy with the development of international law in other spheres, that it will develop some generally agreed principles to cover such things as trans-boundary pollution, that will apply even without the need for a treaty.

Judicial review

Environmental enforcement authorities are public bodies exercising public powers. Mostly, these powers are exercised under statute and consequential delegated legislation. However, in exercising these powers, it may be that such bodies do not follow statutory procedures, that they arrive at decisions unfairly, or that they attempt to make decisions which they have no power to make. The High Court oversees the exercise of these powers by administrative bodies by means of judicial review. The main ground for judicial review is that an administrative body has made a decision which was outside the statutory powers given to it (i.e., *ultra vires*). This may happen in one of three ways.

(a) No power to make the decision itself
If the Environment Agency decided to issue a trade effluent discharge consent for a discharge made to a sewer, a matter which is controlled by the privatised water services company, then the decision would be subject to judicial review because it could not be made within the statutory powers under the Water Resources Act 1991.

(b) The improper exercise of discretion
This principle was first expounded by Lord Greene MR in the case of *Associated Provincial Picture Houses Limited* v *Wednesbury Corporation* [1948] 1 KB 223:

> . . . a person entrusted with a discretion must, so to speak, direct himself properly in law. He must call his own attention to the matters which he is bound to consider. He must exclude from his consideration matters which are irrelevant to what he has to consider. If he does not obey those rules, he may truly be said, and often is said, to be acting 'unreasonably'. Similarly there may be something so absurd that no sensible person could ever dream that it lay within the powers of the authority. Warrington LJ in *Short* v *Poole Corporation* gave the example of the red-haired teacher, dismissed because she had red hair. That is unreasonable in one sense. In another it is taking into account extraneous matters. It is so unreasonable that it might almost be described as being done in bad faith; and, in fact, all these things run into one another.

Therefore, the improper exercise of discretion can be crudely subdivided into a number of different categories: taking into account irrelevant considerations, failing to take into account relevant considerations, and acting so irrationally that the decision could only have been made in bad faith. Examples include taking into account the political party that an applicant supported when deciding an application for a waste disposal licence, and failing to consider the special attention to be paid to the provisions of the development plan when considering a planning application.

(c) Procedural unfairness
Although, in theory, the review of decisions made with procedural impropriety falls within the unreasonableness ground above, it is distinct enough to form its own head of review. There are two elements making up procedural

fairness. These are that every person has a right to a fair hearing and that there should be no bias in a decision-making process. The right to a fair hearing includes the right to meet any case put against an applicant and the right to present cogent and coherent evidence in support of a case. The prohibition against bias covers such situations as local authority planning committee members participating in decisions to grant planning applications on land which they own. In such circumstances it is impossible for the decision-maker to reach a fair decision.

When a decision is made in any of the above circumstances, an aggrieved person has the right to apply to the High Court for judicial review. Such a right should not be confused with any statutory right of appeal, which may give rise to a reconsideration of the merits of a case, rather than consideration of questions of law. Indeed, theoretically, a court exercising its power of judicial review is not entitled to substitute its own decision for that of the administrative body. This general right to challenge administrative decisions is supplemented in certain cases by specific statutory rights to challenge decisions. For example, s. 288 of the Town and Country Planning Act 1990 makes provisions for High Court challenges to decisions of the Secretary of State on points of law. Although there are procedural distinctions between the two types of challenge (in particular there are often much stricter time limits), the substantive issues remain broadly the same. It is important to note, however, that the statutory challenge is often an exclusive power which prevents any further challenge under general judicial review proceedings.

Remedies

The High Court has several remedies available to it to overturn a decision made unlawfully.

(a) Certiorari
An order of certiorari is used to quash an administrative decision made unlawfully. Thus, where a noise abatement order has not been made correctly because of procedural defects, the order itself would be declared null and void.

(b) Prohibition
Where there is a threat that a statutory power will be unlawfully exercised then a prohibition forbids a statutory body from exercising its power in the threatened way.

(c) Mandamus
An order for mandamus forces a statutory body to carry out its statutory duty. For example, where the Environment Agency is under a statutory duty to supervise sites governed by a waste management licence under the EPA 1990, such an order would force them to carry out this supervision properly. This is perhaps the remedy which is most obviously concerned with the control of

environmental bodies. Many authorities are under a duty to carry out activities which have a consequential effect on environmental protection. A failure to carry out these duties may be due to the 'unreasonableness' of the body making the decision. Thus, the rights of people aggrieved by such a lack of activity are considerably enhanced.

(d) Declaration

The reform of judicial review procedures in 1977 added the remedies of declaration and injunction to the other remedies. When a declaration is sought the court seeks to give a statement as to the legal relations between the parties, but that is all it does and the declaration cannot be enforced. A declaration seeks no more than to state the legal position and does not seek to change the respective legal positions of the parties. Thus, a declaration is suitable for a situation where there are uncertainties over whether or not a certain set of facts falls within a category of law.

(e) Injunctions

Although an injunction is available as a remedy under the judicial review procedure, it is the least used remedy, since it is not available against the Crown. As much of environmental protection is carried out by Crown bodies, such a remedy is limited.

Procedure

The procedure for judicial review is contained within the Rules of the Supreme Court, Order 53. An application has to be made within three months from the date when the grounds of the application first arose, unless the court considers that there is good reason for extending the period (Ord. 53, r. 4). This time limit does not apply where there is any other statutory provision which has the effect of limiting the time within which an application for judicial review may be made (Ord. 53, r. 4(3)). In addition, the court may refuse to hear an application if there has been undue delay in bringing it, even if it is brought within the three months period (see, for example, *R v Swale Borough Council, ex parte Royal Society for the Protection of Birds* [1991] 1 PLR 6).

However, in order to bring a claim for judicial review, the applicant must show a 'sufficient interest' in the decision or power to which the application relates (Supreme Court Act 1981, s. 31(3)). There has been some suggestion that this interest has to be greater where the application is for the remedies of prohibition or certiorari, but it is generally accepted that the only test is to show a sufficient interest for remedies. The phrase 'sufficient interest' is of tremendous importance in matters of environmental protection. As will be shown in Chapter 8, the protection of private law rights is contained within the common law and thus anyone seeking to protect their own private interests in land may resort to the common law rather than going through the even more expensive procedure of judicial review. But it is clear that somebody with a private interest in land affected by an administrative decision would have 'sufficient interest' or *locus standi*. It is more difficult to show that a person has the necessary standing by virtue of an interest in the environment as a whole, as it is not generally accepted that there are 'environmental rights' available to the public at large.

Standing

The basis of the law on standing is contained in *Inland Revenue Commissioners v National Federation of Self Employed and Small Businesses Ltd* [1982] AC 617, where Lord Wilberforce said that the decision as to who had a 'sufficient interest' under the Supreme Court Act 1981, s. 31 had to be considered with the known merits of a case:

> It will be necessary to consider the powers or the duties of those against whom the relief is asked, the position of the applicant in relation to those powers or duties, and to the breach of those duties said to have been committed. In other words, the question of sufficient interest cannot, in such cases, be considered in the abstract, or as an isolated point: it must be taken together with the legal and factual context.

In the planning system many actions have been brought by interest groups, where sufficient interest can be demonstrated by objecting to proposals or giving evidence at a local inquiry (see *Save Britain's Heritage* v *Number 1 Poultry Ltd* [1991] 1 WLR 153 or *R* v *Hammersmith London Borough Council, ex parte People Before Profit* (1982) 80 LGR 322). In purely environmental matters, however, it is suggested that such an interest would be more difficult to show. In *R* v *Secretary of State for the Environment, ex parte Rose Theatre Trust Co.* [1990] 1 QB 504, Schiemann J considered an application made by the Theatre Trust Company in relation to the Secretary of State's refusal to schedule the site of the Rose Theatre in Southwark (which was being developed) as an ancient monument under the Ancient Monuments and Archaeological Areas Act 1979. In deciding whether or not the company had any standing to bring an action in judicial review, he decided that, although it was not necessary for an applicant to demonstrate a financial or legal interest in the matter complained of, the statute giving rise to the power or duty had to be examined and the question asked as to whether or not the construction of that statute gave the applicant a right to have a duty performed. As the power confirmed by the Act in that case was specifically to be exercised by the Secretary of State in the public interest, on the construction of the Act the judge decided that no individual citizen or company had the right to challenge the decision in any event.

This decision is perhaps not as wide-ranging as it would seem. In many environmental regulations the purpose of the legislation is to protect certain groups or certain areas. For instance, under the Clean Air Act, it is clear that protection is to extend to a local authority's area and therefore a resident within that area would be entitled to expect that the statutory obligations would be carried out properly under that Act. Similarly, the waste disposal regime contained within Part II of the EPA 1990 seeks to control the disposal of waste so that it does not cause harm to the environment or to human health. This may be given a broad construction by the courts and it would, it is suggested, give wide rights of standing to all those who were intended to be protected.

Guidance on this matter was given more recently in another decision of Schiemann J, *R v Poole Borough Council, ex parte Beebee* [1991] JPL 643. In this case he considered whether various environmental groups had sufficient standing to challenge a decision by Poole BC to grant itself planning permission for housing on a site of special scientific interest. The British Herpetological Society was held to have standing because of its long association with the site (indeed, one of the conditions of the planning permission was that the Society would be allowed to mount a rescue of reptiles and amphibians from the site). The World Wide Fund for Nature, which was involved mainly to fund the action, was stated not to have standing. It was made clear, however, that the Nature Conservancy Council would also have standing in such a case because of its official responsibilities for nature conservation.

In any case, the authority of the *Rose Theatre* case has been challenged in two recent decisions, and it is, perhaps, unlikely to be followed in the future. In *R v Inspectorate of Pollution, ex parte Greenpeace Ltd (No. 2)* [1994] 4 All ER 329, Greenpeace challenged the decision to allow the thermal oxide reprocessing plant at Sellafield (THORP) to commence operations. Pointing to Greenpeace's genuine interest in the issues raised and to its expertise and resources, Otton J decided that the group had sufficient interest, although he did note that it also had many members in the region who may be affected. In *R v Secretary of State for Foreign and Commonwealth Affairs, ex parte World Development Movement Ltd* [1995] 1 WLR 386 (the *Pergau Dam* case), the court, if anything, went even further in allowing a pure public interest claim to proceed, since there were clearly no local residents involved. In particular, it was emphasised that if the applicants were not granted *locus standi* then a clear illegality would not be subject to challenge.

Even this decision did not stop attempts, some of them successful, to argue that any persons challenging a decision required a special private interest in the subject matter of the challenge (e.g., see *R v N. Somerset DC, ex parte Garnett* (unreported)). In *R v Somerset County Council, ex parte Dixon* [1997] NPC 61, however, the decision in *Pergau Dam* was reaffirmed and the law on standing continued to be liberalised. In that case, the answer to the question of who had sufficient interest in the subject matter of the challenge was wide enough to include anyone who was not a busybody or a troublemaker. Public law challenges were concerned with the abuse of power, not the protection of private rights and therefore the classes of those who sought to draw attention to those abuses must include anyone who had a genuine interest in the subject matter of the challenge irrespective of any private law interest.

This liberalisation of the law on standing reflects the recommendations of the Law Commission. In *Administrative Law: Judicial Review and Statutory Appeals* (Law Com. No. 226, 1994) it recommended that *locus standi* should be found where the application is in the 'public interest', unincorporated associations should be enabled to make applications in their own name, and costs should be awarded from central funds where there is a public interest challenge.

It should be noted that there is one exception to all of this. The Attorney-General, as guardian of the public interest, always has *locus standi*. An applicant without 'sufficient interest' could therefore ask the Attorney-General to bring an action on their behalf. This is called a 'relator' action. The shadow applicant pays the costs but manages to side-step the rules on standing. However, the Attorney-General has an unchallengeable discretion whether to bring an action in this manner.

Restrictions on judicial review

There are a number of restrictions on the use of judicial review as a method of controlling the activities of enforcement bodies. First, as stated previously, the matter is not a hearing of the merits of a case. Thus, when a decision is quashed or a duty is enforced, it does not necessarily mean that the final decision of the administrative body will be to the liking of the person seeking judicial review. A good example of this is in the case of the judicial review of planning decisions. If an Inspector, on appeal, makes a decision which is contrary to the Inquiries Procedure Rules (for instance by not taking into account written representations from objectors), the resulting decision may be challenged. The Inspector's decision in those circumstances could be overturned by the High Court, but the final decision would be referred back to a fresh Inspector, who could very well arrive at the same decision as the first Inspector, even though taking into account the representations made.

Furthermore, where individuals with 'sufficient interest' apply for judicial review of a decision they have to be able to show that they have suffered prejudice. Therefore, although the court is not entitled to make a judgment on the merits of the individual case, it may well be that the substance of the point raised by the interested party shows an unlawful act, but, on the facts of the individual case, the applicant did not suffer any prejudice from the decision itself. Thus, where an interested party was not entitled to put its views across at a planning inquiry, there may well be a breach of the right to a fair hearing. However, where it could be shown that other people had put over a similar case, a judicial review remedy may be refused.

Where there are other remedies available, the court has a discretion to refuse an application for judicial review. Therefore, in the situation where an applicant is seeking an injunction and also has private rights which could give rise to a similar remedy under the common law, a court can refuse to exercise its discretion in relation to the public law remedy.

Overall, the role of judicial review in controlling administrative actions has grown in importance over the past 20 years. The introduction of new concepts to govern the full breadth of administrative action gives rise to an important avenue of redress to the private individual.

The Ombudsman

There may be instances where, although there is no abuse of the statutory power which would render a decision reviewable, there is some maladministration which could give rise to a public complaint. In such cases a complaint can be made to the Ombudsman in control of those activities. In the case of Central Government activities (e.g., the Department of the Environment) the investigating Ombudsman is the Parliamentary Commissioner for Administration, whereas in the case of complaints against a local authority, the matter is dealt with by the Commissioner for Local Administration. The governing factor in such complaints is whether or not the authority concerned have acted within appropriate standards of administrative conduct, rather than whether or not they have acted lawfully.

Complaints to the Ombudsman normally go through either a local councillor or an MP (depending upon the level of authority concerned), although they need not do so in all cases. The nature of the Ombudsman remedy is both singular and advisory. Therefore, an aggrieved party who has other rights of action, whether under the common law or by means of judicial review, must pursue that particular avenue, as long as it is realistic to do so. Secondly, an Ombudsman has no statutory power to impose an award of damages, or to alter the legal position (e.g., by quashing a decision). Normally, the Ombudsman will make a recommendation for compensation which, although having no statutory backing, is accepted by the statutory body concerned in over 95% of cases. The role of the Ombudsman should not be underestimated. The incidence of complaints to the Ombudsman has risen in recent years because it is a quick, cheap, and often effective mechanism for channelling complaints about public authorities. It is a mechanism which the public are happy to utilise because of its informal nature and simple procedure. It is perhaps worthwhile to point out that the stages of a complaint are relatively straightforward and provide an adequate opportunity for the proper presentation of grievances. It is also important that the Ombudsman has significant investigatory powers: these will have an impact on the practices of the public bodies over which jurisdiction is exercised.

THREE
Environmental protection agencies

For many years the number of different agencies involved in environmental protection reflected the fragmented nature of policy and law enforcement in this area. Some rationalisation was brought about with the establishment of the National Rivers Authority (NRA) and Her Majesty's Inspectorate of Pollution (HMIP). Until the establishment of the Environment Agency (EA) by the Environment Act 1995, however, the spread of responsibilities remained wide.

The introduction of the EA has seen an amalgamation of three of four main regulatory agencies — the NRA, the WRAs and HMIP (local authorities being the fourth). It should also be borne in mind that the increase of guidance on both technical and policy matters has meant that the role of local authorities may change. There are, however, a range of other bodies with powers and responsibilities for environmental protection. Some of these bodies exercise purely policy-making functions, whilst others are out specific regulatory agencies.

One of the notable changes brought about by the EA has been the implicit recentralisation (in one sense) of many regulatory powers. In particular, the Environment Act 1995 has seen the move towards centralised strategies in relation to air quality and waste. In addition, local authorities are under a duty to have regard to guidance from the DoE and the EA when operating the provisions in relation to contaminated land. Whereas most powers will be exercised by local offices with regard to local conditions, the overall emphasis is on central guidance to improve the consistency and quality of decision-making.

A side-effect of this recentralisation is the consequential loss of accountability. A distinction needs to be drawn between those bodies which are elected and those which are not. The EA has no direct accountability and, in the light of the wide discretionary powers which it exercises and the policy which it is responsible for, this is a central issue.

Department of the Environment, Transport and the Regions (DoE)

Central control of the majority of environmental matters falls to the 'super ministry' created by the Labour Government in May 1997. As the name suggests, the Department is also responsible for transport policy and the decentralisation of decision-making and policy to the regions (in England — Scotland, Wales and Northern Ireland are dealt with separately).

Control is mainly manifested at the level of policy, but since environmental law is essentially about the taking of discretionary, political decisions, this means that the DoE has an enormous impact, even if this is not always apparent from a bare statement of the law. However, three important qualifications must be made about the role of the DoE.

First, it is not the only part of central government which sets policy in relation to environmental matters. Indeed it is arguable whether there is such a thing as a national environmental policy, as opposed to individual policies on individual issues. Other Government departments, such as the Ministry of Agriculture, Fisheries and Food (MAFF), the Department of Trade and Industry and the Treasury, exercise enormous influence in their own fields. The Welsh, Scottish and Northern Ireland Offices also exercise responsibility within their own geographical areas (a responsibility which will increase under the proposals for a Scottish Parliament and Welsh Assembly). It is also true to say that, under the Conservative Government, the DoE was not a particularly strong Department within central government, even in relation to environmental matters. There is more than a suspicion that this position will continue under the Labour administration, particularly when the position of Environment Minister (under the Secretary of State) is not presently a Cabinet post in stark contrast to that of the Transport Minister.

Secondly, it has few operational powers relating to environmental protection. Those that it does have are often delegated to others. For example, although planning appeals are made to the Secretary of State, in the vast majority of cases they are decided by members of the Planning Inspectorate, which has been an executive agency of the DoE and the Welsh Office since April 1992. Indeed, since that time the Inspectorate has become responsible for a wide range of appeals in relation to environmental matters, including appeals concerning waste management licences, discharge consents and local authority air pollution control authorisations.

Thirdly, it is not concerned simply with environmental protection. It has a very wide portfolio, which includes responsibility for local government (including the vexed question of local government finance), housing, transport infrastructure and the water industry. It is fairly clear that some of these areas not only take priority over environmental protection but are often in direct conflict with environmental aims.

Some of these points require amplification. The Secretary of State has very wide legislative and quasi-legislative powers which stem from the framework nature of the main environmental protection legislation, and also from the need to update legislation in the light of EC requirements. Very wide discretionary powers are also granted: for example, the decision whether to declare an area an urban development area is virtually an unfettered discretion given to the Secretary of State.

There are also very wide powers in relation to appeals against decisions made by the regulatory bodies. This is most obvious in the planning area, but an appeal to the Secretary of State is a common feature of many of the regulatory systems covered in this book. This reflects the political (i.e., policy-based) nature of much of this area of law. For example, it is significant that the Planning Inspectorate has always been kept within the DoE, rather than being moved to the Lord Chancellor's Department. This reflects the fact that the important feature of its decisions is that they are based on policy rather than on any notion of judicial fairness, despite the increasing formality of planning procedures.

The DoE may impose its policies in a number of ways. One is by changing the law (a feature of the British system of Government is that the Government is rarely defeated in Parliament). Another is through exercising powers granted under the legislation. This may include the making of directions, the power to approve actions of regulatory bodies, the power to make appointments to the various regulatory bodies, or the power to hear appeals. Interference has been at its clearest in town planning, where there is the greatest opportunity to disagree over matters of policy. Although the DoE has reserved the main legislative powers in the Environment Act 1995, the transfer of a variety of powers to the EA has been viewed suspiciously by some observers. A third method is by the manipulation of available resources. The DoE and the Treasury have complete responsibility for the budgets of a number of the regulatory agencies (e.g., the Countryside Commission and the Nature Conservancy Councils). They also control local government finances very tightly. One avenue for future development here is the way that regulatory agencies are being encouraged to acquire some financial independence by charging for parts of their work. This theme has been developed strongly in the Environment Act 1995, with a range of revenue-raising measures (see p. 52).

Given the importance of independent regulatory agencies in environmental law, it is also significant that the DoE is the channel through which Parliamentary accountability of a number of these agencies, such as the Countryside Commission, is provided.

Other parts of Central Government

Important roles are played by other government departments in particular sectors. For example, control of agricultural matters is largely the responsibility of MAFF, whilst many policy decisions of central importance to global warming and acid rain are made by the Department of Trade and Industry. The Department of Culture, Media and Sport, created (under the name National Heritage) in April 1992, has responsibilities in relation to ancient monuments and the listing of historic buildings.

An important aspect of decisions is how far they take into account environmental considerations. A number of pieces of legislation now include general requirements to take the environment into account. For example, there is a very vague, but potentially useful, duty imposed on all public bodies in the Countryside Act 1968, s. 11. This states, 'In the exercise of their functions relating to land under any enactment every Minister, government department and public body shall have regard to the desirability of conserving the natural beauty and amenity of the countryside'.

There have been a number of attempts to see this sort of duty imposed on a wider basis throughout all Government departments. In 1990, the White Paper, *This Common Inheritance* (Cm. 1200, 1990), contained proposals for 'greening' each Government department by nominating a Minister to be responsible for considering the environmental implications of its policies and programmes. There was also a strong link with a second proposal that there should be an appraisal of the policies of each department in the light of their environmental implications.

The implementation of these duties was, at best, patchy, with little public information available on the manner in which the proposals were working in practice. When the Labour Government came to power, these deficiencies were to be addressed by the creation of a centrally appointed environmental audit committee, which would carry out this appraisal as an independent body.

Parliamentary Select Committees

Parliamentary Select Committees may be said to perform the functions of scrutinising the day-to-day activities of Government. They also, in the environmental field, help to inform public debate outside Parliament. In the House of Lords, the European Communities Sub-Committee has been especially important in analysing the potential impact of proposed EC legislation. In the House of Commons, the Select Committees are organised so as to mirror government departments. There is thus a House of Commons Select Committee on the Environment. This body has had a large impact on the direction of environmental policy, and can be said to be very influential in this area. Sir Hugh Rossi was the Chairman between 1983 and 1992, and in that time the Committee concentrated on environmental (as opposed to local government or housing) issues, conducting inquiries into such matters as Acid Rain (1984), the Operation and Effectiveness of Part II of the Wildlife and Countryside Act 1981 (1985), Pollution of Rivers and Estuaries (1987), Air Pollution (1988), Toxic Waste (1989), Pollution of Beaches (1990), the Draft EC Directive on Landfill (1991), and the Government's Proposals for an Environmental Agency (1992).

There is little doubt that the reports of these inquiries, all of which have been unanimous on a cross-party basis, have an influence on Government. As an example, the Report on Contaminated Land (January 1990) recommended the creation of public registers of contaminated land, a recommendation that was introduced into the EPA 1990, although the Government rescinded the commitment to introduce these registers. Nevertheless, the introduction of the new contaminated land provisions in the Environment Act 1995 owes a lot to the early recommendations of the Select Committee.

Royal Commission on Environmental Pollution (RCEP)

This is a rather rare beast, a standing Royal Commission with its own Secretariat. It has been in existence since 1970 and has produced 19 Reports on a variety of matters. These Reports have enormous authority in relation to the subject matter discussed and exert a significant influence on the direction of future policy, although by no means all the recommendations of the Royal Commission are implemented. The Royal Commission has been a particularly strong supporter of the widening of access to environmental information, and can also claim to have popularised the concept of 'Best Practicable Environmental Option'. Important Reports have been the Fifth Report, *Air Pollution Control: An Integrated Approach* (Cmnd 6371, 1976), the Tenth Report, *Tackling Pollution — Experiences and Prospects* (Cmnd 9149, 1984), the Eleventh Report, *Managing Waste: The Duty of Care* (Cmnd 9675, 1985) and the Twelfth Report, *Best Practicable Environmental Option* (Cm. 310, 1988). The most recent Reports are the Seventeenth Report, *Incineration of Waste* (Cm. 2181, 1993), which supports the development of incineration linked to energy recovery, the Eighteenth Report, *Transport and the Environment* (Cm. 2674, 1994) and the Nineteenth Report, *Sustainable Use of Soil* (Cm. 3165, 1996), which advocates the protection of soil quality.

Other advisory bodies

In addition to the RCEP, the Government has established a number of non-statutory advisory bodies with various roles. In particular, three bodies established as a result of the publication of the UK's Strategy on Sustainable Development assist with the consideration and implementation of environmental policy and the strategy for sustainable development. The UK Round Table on Sustainable Development consists of 30 members from a selection of bodies, including non-governmental organisations, business, local government and the Church. Unfortunately, it received a set-back when the first of its recommendations — to insert a duty on OFGAS to have regard to sustainability in the Gas Bill — was rejected. It has set aside five main issues for discussion, including sustainable transport, energy policy and environmental auditing.

Secondly, there is a five person panel of advisors known as the Government's Panel on Sustainable Development. This Panel reports directly to the Prime Minister and advises upon issues arising from the strategy. Some critics of the Round Table group (who have suggested that it is a cosmetic exercise) think that the panel will have much more influence over policy. It has a number of topics on its agenda, including the use of economic instruments in environmental policy and environmental education and training.

Finally, the Government launched its 'Going for Green' initiative, which is intended to involve voluntary groups within the community to promote sustainable development.

The Environment Agency

The history of the Environment Agency (EA) is long and tortuous. In 1989 the House of Commons Select Committee on the Environment, in its Report on Toxic Waste, recommended that an Environmental Protection

Commission should be established with responsibility for the whole range of pollution control matters. This recommendation was rejected by the Government, a stance that was reiterated in the White Paper, *This Common Inheritance* (Cm 1200, 1990). One reason given was that there had been many changes in relation to environmental protection in recent years, and that such a major change might have to wait until things had settled down. The White Paper did suggest, however, that consideration would be given to the establishment of an umbrella body overseeing the work of HMIP and the NRA. It also proposed that HMIP should become a separate executive agency within the Government (i.e., a 'Next Steps' agency) 'as soon as possible', although it would still remain part of the DoE. This mechanism was popular with the Conservative Government as a means of providing regulatory agencies with a degree of independence, whilst at the same time injecting some basic management principles and subjecting the agencies to some of the rigours of the marketplace.

However, in an important reversal of policy, in July 1991 it was announced that it was the Government's intention to create a unified environmental protection agency, a move that had already gained the support of all other political parties. Details of what was intended gradually emerged. There were two main points of argument which led to a significant period of delay. One was whether the waste regulation duties of the local authorities should be included within the agency's ambit — to do so would create a uniformity of practice that was lacking, but would obviously reduce local accountability. The other was whether the NRA should be brought within the agency *en bloc,* or whether only its pollution control functions properly belonged there. The Minister of Agriculture argued strongly for the NRA's non-pollution control functions to be devolved to the Ministry of Agriculture, Fisheries and Food, but that was strongly opposed by environmentalists and the NRA itself, who argued that the need to retain integrated catchment management was at the heart of everything that the NRA did.

After some discussion and consultation the Government accepted that the EA would take over all the powers and functions of HMIP and the NRA, together with the waste regulation duties of the local authorities.

The Environment Agency: an overview
The name of the Agency is misleading. It does not have control over all environmental regulation. Despite Government statements made during the discussion which led to the creation of the EA, the Drinking Water Inspectorate is not included (although there is an outstanding Labour Party commitment to reverse this); nor are any direct functions relating to nature conservation (although there are a number of general duties relating to sites which are of nature conservation interest). These omissions (when coupled with the areas of environmental regulation which remain with local authorities) meant that at the time of its creation, the EA was effectively a pollution control authority with a large number of water-related functions such as land drainage and flood defence (with the interesting side effect that the number of staff in these areas outnumber those in pollution control).

The functions of the EA largely reflect the pre-existing functions of the NRA, HMIP and the waste regulation authorities. A detailed description of each of these areas of responsibility can be found in Part II of this book. They include:

(a) *Water-related functions.* The EA has responsibility for a wide range of matters relating to water and water resources (see further Chapter 14), including:

(i)   control of pollution of water resources under Part III of the Water Resources Act 1991 (e.g., the setting of water quality objectives, the use of powers to prevent pollution and the enforcement of pollution control);
(ii)   management of water resources (e.g., abstraction licensing, drought orders and powers to secure adequate supplies from the water companies);
(iii)   supervision and administration of flood defences;
(iv)   fisheries regulation;
(v)   navigation, harbour and conservancy duties.

(b) *Waste-management-related functions.* The EA has responsibility for a range of waste management functions (see further Chapter 13), including:

(i)   licensing waste management facilities (including supervision of waste management activities and taking action against breaches);
(ii)   the registration of activities which are exempt from the waste management licensing system;
(iii)   the registration and regulation of waste carriers and brokers;
(iv)   the administration of the surrender of waste management site licences;
(v)   the enforcement of the duty of care under the EPA 1990, s. 34.

(c) *Industrial processes.* The EA has responsibility for the control of all emissions from industrial processes under Part I of the EPA 1990 which are prescribed for central control (see further Chapter 11).

(d) *New functions.* In addition to the functions which have been transferred from the pre-existing agencies, the Environment Act 1995 created a range of new functions for the Agency, including:

(i)   the role of enforcing authority in relation to 'special sites' under the provisions in Part IIA of the EPA 1990 concerning the regulation of historically contaminated land (see p. 413);
(ii)   the administration and regulation of the producer responsibility initiative under ss. 93 and 94 of the Environment Act 1995 (see p. 369);
(iii)   the issuing of guidance in relation to various matters including IPC processes and contaminated land;
(iv)   the carrying out of research and the provision of information on the environment (including the setting up of public pollution control registers);

(v)   statutory consultees in relation to the National Air Quality Strategy and the National Waste Strategy.

Scotland

Slightly different administrative and regulatory arrangements apply in Scotland. Prior to the implementation of the Environment Act 1995 there were a variety of regulatory bodies responsible for environmental protection. The river purification authorities were responsible for the control of water pollution, and integrated pollution control was regulated by Her Majesty's Industrial Pollution Inspectorate (HMIPI). The local authorities (the district and island councils) acted as waste regulation authorities (although there was no separation of regulatory and operational functions as in England and Wales) and as enforcing authorities for air pollution control under Part I of the EPA 1990.

The Environment Act 1995 introduced a unified agency for Scotland known as the Scottish Environment Protection Agency (SEPA). The range of powers, functions, aims and duties applicable to SEPA broadly reflect the position of the EA. There is, however, a narrower regulatory focus on fundamental pollution control matters without the wider issues of water resource management which were transferred from the NRA to the EA. This focus is reflected in the title of the agency (with the significant omission of the word 'protection' from the Anglo-Welsh agency) and the fact that there are some minor variations in the legislative provisions which could become more significant with the passage of time (e.g., SEPA does not have a 'principal aim' as specified under s. 4 of the 1995 Act for the EA (see below)).

There are two major differences in the scope of the powers of the two agencies. First, SEPA has control over all prescribed processes under Part I of the EPA 1990, whereas in England and Wales control remains divided between the EA and the local authorities. Secondly, as mentioned above, SEPA has none of the non-pollution-related water management functions. The majority of these remain with the new unitary local authorities created by the Local Government etc. (Scotland) Act 1994. The position of the water and sewerage undertakers is also different in Scotland. Unlike England and Wales, which has privatised water companies, Scotland has three public non-departmental water authorities created under the provisions which led to the local government reorganisation referred to above.

Although the statutory provisions governing SEPA and the EA are broadly the same there are minor variations. For the purpose of this book, reference is made to the situation in England and Wales. The corresponding position in Scotland is covered in other texts such as *Green's Guide to Environmental Law in Scotland*, ed. Reid (W. Green and Son, 1992).

Structure of the agency

The EA is an independent corporate body (Environment Act 1995, s. 1(1)) and does not have Crown immunity, although partial immunity can be granted where the agency exercises its functions under an agreement to carry out a Ministerial function (s. 38). In order to assist with the carrying out of its functions, the agency is under a duty to establish an Environment Protection Advisory Committee (EPAC), made up of people with a 'significant interest' in the agency's functions. An EPAC is established for each agency region. Once established, the agency is under a duty to consult the committee and consider any representations made by it.

The regional structure of the agency was the subject of much debate as a result of the very different administrative boundaries used by the NRA, HMIP and the WRAs. Whereas the NRA and HMIP were split into regional sections (eight and three, respectively) the WRAs were split on the basis of local authority areas. In the end, the EA was organised on a regional basis, but the water management boundaries remain based on the NRA's river catchment areas, whilst the pollution control functions are organised largely on the basis of county authority boundaries (in the case of water management areas the district boundaries are sometimes used where they provide a convenient 'match').

General powers and duties

The EA is subject to a complicated framework of duties, aims and objectives. Some of these have been transferred from the NRA, but most are either new in substance or scope. Some of these objectives were subjected to a good deal of Parliamentary scrutiny during the passage of the Environment Bill (which led to the introduction of the 'principal aim' of meeting the objective of sustainable development under s. 4), but there is still a lack of clarity in many of these statutory aims and objectives.

These aims and duties are designed to underpin the policy decisions of the agency, but do not fetter that discretion unduly. The duties are expressed in a variety of ways (see below), with the agency being required to 'have regard to' some duties whereas others have to be 'taken into account'. When it comes to individual decision-making, the agency has a wide discretion and the weight which attaches to each duty will be variable. Therefore, it would be difficult to challenge legally any decision made by the agency on the basis that it had failed to carry out the duty unless the agency had acted unreasonably in the *Wednesbury* sense.

It is important to bear in mind that the aim, objectives and duties are not framed in a statutory vacuum. In addition to the general matters set out in the Environment Act 1995 there is an increasing range of specific statutory objectives which are set out in relation to individual functions of the agency. Many of these have been imposed as a result of the need to meet EC legislation which favours the use of such specific targets. For example, the agency must seek to achieve water or air quality objectives when exercising its functions in determining authorisations and consents and in doing so it must place those objectives above the general aims and duties.

Principal aim and objectives of the agency

Section 4 of the Environment Act 1995 defines the principal aim for the EA: in discharging its functions the EA is required so to protect or enhance the environment, taken as a whole, as to attain the objective of achieving sustainable development. Although this may be the first time that such an overarching duty has been imposed upon an environmental agency, the extent to which this section creates a legally enforceable obligation upon the EA is a little uncertain. A number of factors, set out in s. 4, are designed to influence the implementation of the duty in practice.

First, the agency must take into account the likely costs of achieving the principal aim. This was inserted into s. 4 to ensure that environmental considerations are not paramount when pursuing the aim of sustainable development, and the cost of the pursuit of the principal aim is to be taken into account. This reflects the policy distinction between the aims of sustainability and sustainable development (see p. 15).

Secondly, the principal aim is to be pursued in relation to the conservation and enhancement of the environment 'taken as a whole'. This was introduced to ensure that the decision-making process was not overburdened by detailed consideration of impacts on individual environmental media. Instead the Government suggested that there should be an integrated analysis of all impacts, and decision-making should take into account these overall factors. Another interpretation of this provision could be used to justify attaching less weight to any one individual factor on the basis that the factors 'when taken as a whole' lead to a particular conclusion.

Thirdly, the principal aim has to be viewed in relation to all of the other objectives which apply to the EA (surprisingly there are no other statutory 'aims' — which rather begs the question over the use of the word 'principal'). The 'principal' aim will only take precedence over other statutory objectives where there is a direct conflict between the two. Thus it would appear that in a situation where the agency is making a decision to act and it cannot meet both objectives, the principal aim would take precedence. Confusingly, however, the aim is stated to be 'subject to' other provisions of the Act, which would include the other objectives. This confusion over the hierachy of the principal aim and the other statutory objectives underlines the difficulty of introducing a principal aim which does not actually create any legally enforceable rights. It rather defeats the purpose of a 'principal aim' when it is subject to the myriad of other statutory objectives and functions.

Finally, the agency must have regard to guidance issued by the Secretary of State when discharging its functions (s. 4(3)). Guidance on the principal aim was issued in November 1996. The guidance is contained two short, relatively bland, sections which do little more than express very general objectives and strategic aims. The emphasis on the EA's contribution to sustainable development centres on the need to take a holistic approach to the protection and enhancement of the environment; to take a long term perspective of the implications and effects of carrying out its functions; to enhance and protect biodiversity; to discharge, where possible, its regulatory functions in partnership with regulated organisations; to develop a close and responsive relationship with the public; and to provide high-quality information and advice on the state of the environment.

The role of guidance is central to meeting the principal aim. One of the inherent dangers of using such guidance to flesh out such a statutory provision is that it is capable of change without recourse to legislation. This could have a significant impact upon the manner in which the EA carries out its functions without the scrutiny which is afforded to legislative proposals. There are two safeguards to prevent the abuse of this process. First there is a duty on the Secretary of State to consult before issuing such guidance and secondly a draft has to be put before both Houses of Parliament with rights of veto available if either House resolves to do so (s. 4(5)–(7)).

On any analysis (legal, philosophical or even semantic), the complexities of the principal aim obscure the nature of the legal obligation which is created. Whilst the creation of a policy framework is long overdue, the real issue which remains to be clarified is the way in which this principal aim will be taken into account in relation to individual decision-making and the setting of strategic aims. There is a real danger that the width of the discretion given to the agency when merely having regard to the guidance will mean that the principal aim is little more than a statement of intent which will not be subject to judicial scrutiny. Notwithstanding the uncertainty over the nature of the legal obligation created by the aims and duties, they are still of importance in internal decision-making within the agency and as political levers for environmentally sensitive decisions.

Other aims, objectives and functions

In addition to the principal aim of the EA, a range of other duties and objectives is set out in ss. 5–9 of the Environment Act 1995. These relate to the following areas:

(a) *Pollution control functions.* Under s. 5 of the Act, the EA is under a duty to exercise its functions for the purpose of preventing or minimising, or remedying or mitigating the effects of, pollution of the environment. This section distinguishes between the agency's pollution control functions and the other non-pollution powers and functions (e.g., flood defence and fisheries). This distinction is carried over in s. 7 which provides that the agency, when formulating or considering any proposals, is to *have regard to* the desirability of conserving and enhancing natural beauty and the conservation of flora, fauna and geological or physiographical features. In relation to non-pollution powers and functions this duty is raised so that the agency is required to *further* the conservation etc. This distinction reflects the fact that the EA cannot be said to be furthering environmental conservation when it is issuing consents, authorisations or licences for activities which by definition will be polluting.

(b) *General environmental duties relating to water.* Section 6 of the Act provides for general environmental duties in relation to the water industry. The duties generally reflect some provisions of the Water Resources Act 1991, s. 16 (since repealed), and the Water Industry Act 1991, s. 3 (in relation to the water companies' environmental duties). Other the duties under the Water Resources Act 1991, s. 16 are transferred to the Environment Act 1995, s. 7 (see below). Under s. 6 the duties relate specifically to promoting the conservation or enhancement of the natural beauty and amenity of waters (including land associated with such waters) and the conservation of flora and fauna which are dependent on the aquatic environment. These duties are not particularly onerous, requiring action only when the agency considers that it is desirable to do so. The desirability of carrying out this duty will be affected by the duties under s. 7 and the principal aim under s. 4.

Subsections (4)–(6) of s. 7 cover access to water, or lands associated with such water, for recreational purposes.

(c)   *General environmental duties.* The EA's general environmental duties are found in s. 7 of the Act. These duties also apply to the relevant Secretaries of State. The duties are divided into two. Subsections (1)–(3) cover environmental duties whereas subsections (4)–(6) cover the duties in relation to public recreational access to water. Once again these are adapted from the duties found within the Water Resources Act 1991, which applied previously to the NRA. The duties apply to the EA when considering or formulating 'proposals'. Although there is no definition of 'proposals' within the Act, the term would include all strategic policy-making (such as the strategies on air quality and waste) and would arguably cover individual decision-making on licence applications.

These general duties are divided into duties which apply to pollution control functions of the EA (see above); duties which apply to the non-pollution powers and functions; and duties which apply to both.

In relation to non-pollution control functions the EA is under a duty to further the conservation and enhancement of natural beauty and the conservation of flora, fauna and geological and physiographical features of special interest. In addition the EA must have regard to a range of matters including the desirability of protecting heritage sites or public access to areas of natural beauty, the effect of proposals on the beauty of any area and the effect on the economic and social well being of rural communities.

(d)   *Environmental duties with respect to sites of special interest.* There are specific duties in relation to notification and consultation in the case of any land of a special conservation interest which may be affected by any works carried out by the EA or by any authorisation which it is considering (see further below).

The Secretary of State has the power to issue codes of practice under s. 9 of the Environment Act 1995 to assist the EA in carrying out any of the duties referred to above. This provision replaces the Water Resources Act 1991, s. 18, but as the NRA's duties have been transferred to the EA, the only code passed under that Act, the Water and Sewerage (Conservation, Access and Recreation) (Code of Practice) Order 1989 (SI 1989 No. 1152) still applies to the EA. The code of practice under this Order was issued jointly by the Secretaries of State and MAFF after consultation with a range of interested bodies. Contravention does not give rise to any criminal offence or civil right of action, but will be taken into account by relevant bodies in deciding whether to use any powers available to them.

The cost-benefit duty
Probably the most controversial duty imposed upon the EA is the duty to take into account the costs and benefits of exercising its powers. Section 39 of the Environment Act 1995 provides:

[The EA] —

(a)   in considering whether or not to exercise any power . . . or
(b)   in deciding the manner in which to exercise any such power,
shall, unless and to the extent that it is unreasonable for it to do so in view
of the nature or purpose of the power or in the circumstances of the
particular case, take into account the likely costs and benefits of the
exercise or non-exercise of the power or its exercise in the manner in
question.

'Costs' are defined as environmental as well as personal costs (s. 56(1)) and
although 'benefits' are surprisingly (given the mutual relationship between
the phrases) not defined, the term would arguably include environmental
benefits in addition to any personal benefits.

There are two important restrictions on the application of the duty. First, it
does not apply if it would be unreasonable in the circumstances of a particular
case. The clearest example of this would be where emergency action was
required by the EA. Secondly, the duty does not affect the exercise of other
mandatory obligations such as complying with environmental quality objectives. In such circumstances, the decision-making discretion of the EA is
constrained within the pursuit of the specific objective and the costs and the
benefits become less relevant. The general cost-benefit duty does, however,
apply where the EA can select from a range of potential options when seeking
to achieve these objectives and the costs and benefits of each of those options
can be considered when selecting which is the most appropriate.

The main controversy over this section was centred around the extent to
which it could be used to challenge a decision of the agency on the basis that
the benefits of a proposed action or strategy could not be shown to outweigh
the costs. Thus, the exercise of any regulatory power by the agency, including
powers to investigate, prosecute or require preventative or remedial measures,
could be challenged where the duty was not carried out. The danger of
challenge could, in turn, lead to excessive bureaucracy as each decision would
be subjected to detailed scrutiny by the agency and those affected by the
decision alike.

These dangers do not reflect the essentially discretionary nature of the
decision-making power of the agency. Taking account of costs and benefits
does not necessarily mean that the agency has to demonstrate that the costs
outweigh the benefits (or vice versa) or even that, once it has carried out such
an appraisal, it must act in accordance with the conclusions. A requirement
to take account of costs and benefits arguably does no more than raise an
evidential presumption that they will be considered. In classic administrative
fashion it does not prescribe the weight which should be attached to such
costs or benefits and therefore any decision based on such an analysis will be
difficult to challenge.

The Secretary of State has issued non-statutory guidance on the cost-
benefit duty as part of the explanatory document which accompanies the
statutory guidance on the principal aim of the EA. The guidance emphasises

the importance of carrying out environmental appraisals before exercising decision-making powers. In addition, the guidance points out the difficulties in quantifying environmental costs, benefits, and places, and sets out a number of factors which may be relevant in reaching a decision. Arguably the most important section of the guidance stresses the fact that in many situations, the application of the duty will require the exercise of judgment by the EA — a judgment which is likely to be unchallengeable in the courts.

In addition to this general duty under s. 39, the agency has to consider the costs associated with other duties. Thus there is a duty to consider 'any likely costs' when seeking to achieve its principal aim under s. 4 (see above) and the agency must set out the costs and benefits for exercising its options under the pollution control functions in s. 5.

Unification of administrative and regulatory powers

In addition to the general aims and objectives, the Environment Act 1995 unified a variety of the powers which were previously found in disparate legislation. The aim is to provide consistency and uniformity in a range of areas, including inspection, entry, enforcement and fees and charges.

Inspection, entry and enforcement powers

The EA has a range of inspection and enforcement powers. These powers are exercised for the purpose of:

(a)   determining whether any environmental legislation is being complied with;

(b)   exercising or performing any of the Agency's pollution control functions;

(c)   determining whether or how a pollution control function should be exercised.

Section 108 of the Act provides that an officer appointed by the Agency can, when there is no emergency:

(a)   enter premises at any reasonable time,

(b)   be accompanied on to premises by a police constable should the officer apprehend that they will be obstructed in their duty;

(c)   make any investigation as necessary including: measurements, taking samples, photographs and questioning individuals (answers given to such questions will not be admissible in any prosecution brought against *that person*);

(d)   carry out experimental borings and install and maintain monitoring equipment (with at least seven days notice):

Where occupants are likely to refuse entry, the officer can seek a warrant prior to entry onto premises. Documents which are subject to legal professional privilege are exempt from the above requirements. In cases of emergency entry can be gained at any time, with force if necessary. In such circumstances no prior notification is required when setting up monitoring equipment or carrying out experimental borings. Under s. 110 it is an offence to intentionally obstruct an authorised officer in the exercise of his or her duties.

In addition, there are specific powers to requisition information in writing in relation to individual functions (e.g., EPA 1990, s. 71, in relation to waste management offences). The answers to such requisitions are not subject to the rule against self-incrimination (referred to in s. 108), as the person served with such a requisition has the ability to consider any responses in the light of legal advice (see *R* v *Hertfordshire County Council, ex parte Green Environmental Industries* [1997] Env LR 114). Powers of entry in relation to the non-pollution control water functions are to be found in the Water Resources Act 1991, s. 169.

Schedule 22 to the Environment Act 1995 has amended the provisions relating to enforcement powers for individual functions (e.g., waste management and pollution of controlled waters) so that there is no significant imbalance in the powers which are available to the agency for each of these functions. For example, ss. 90A, 90B, 49A and 49B of the Water Resources Act 1991 (as inserted by the Environment Act 1995) give the agency the power to serve an enforcement notice where there has been, or is likely to be, a breach of a condition of a discharge consent. This is a new power which widens the range of enforcement options in relation to water pollution.

Fees and charging schemes

It is intended that the EA should seek to operate on a cost recovery basis (i.e., the amount of money it receives in charges and fees should cover its administrative expenses). Sections 41 and 42 of the Environment Act 1995 provide the power to introduce charging schemes for all forms of environmental licensing. The agency can exercise this power itself, unlike some of the previous powers to raise fees and charges which were exercisable by the Secretary of State (e.g., waste regulation and IPC under the EPA 1990). To ensure that the schemes are subject to proper scrutiny, each must be published in draft and approved by the Secretary of State and the Treasury before it can come into operation. Furthermore, the scheme must be made by statutory instrument and can be annulled by either House of Parliament.

There are no restrictions on the amount which can be charged nor on any differentials in charging to reflect the administrative burden of each individual application. At present, all charges are levied on a fixed basis with variations for certain classes of licence. This does not, however necessarily reflect the amount of administrative effort involved in the processing of each individual application. There have been some suggestions that charging schemes should be developed which would accurately reflect the amount of work required.

There are separate annual charging schemes for IPC and the waste management licensing system. The scheme in relation to discharge consents has effect for a five-year period with annual revisions of the fee levels.

In addition to this specific power, the agency has general powers to charge for any services provided in connection with environmental licences under s. 37(7) and (8) (there are further incidental powers under s. 43). This would cover any advice or assistance provided to applicants when preparing applications. The use of this power would enable the agency to introduce charging rates which more accurately reflect the administrative burden without necessarily complicating the existing charging schemes.

Directions from the Secretary of State

The Secretary of State has a wide range of powers to issue directions to the agency. These directions can be of a specific or general nature. In relation to individual functions they include:

(a)   directions requiring the inclusion of specific conditions in IPC or waste management licences (see EPA 1990, ss. 7(3) and 35(7);

(b)   directions requiring the agency to take specific enforcement action in relation to IPC and waste management licences (EPA 1990, ss. 12–14, 37, 38 and 42);

(c)   directions requiring the agency (amongst other things) to carry out surveys of waste arisings in relation to the national waste strategy (s. 44A);

(d)   directions made in the interests of national security or mitigating the effects of a civil emergency (Water Resources Act 1991, s. 207).

The Environment Act 1995, s. 40, gives the Secretary of State a further general power to issue any directions of a specific or general character.

Overlap with other agencies

Although the EA has responsibility for the majority of powers in relation to pollution control, there are still a number of other bodies with direct responsibility for environmental protection. In particular, local authorities play an important role in regulating contaminated land, statutory nuisances, noise, air quality and planning. In addition, the water service companies' control over discharges to sewers remains unaffected by the Environment Act 1995 (although there is a power for the EA to apply its general environmental duty to any proposals relating either to the functions or land-holdings of the water companies (s. 7(3)).

There are, however, some overlaps between the EA and nature conservation bodies. English Nature, the Countryside Commission for Wales, the National Parks Authorities and the Broads Authority are under a duty to inform the EA of the identity of any land which may be affected by the Agency which is of special nature conservation interest because of its flora, fauna or geological or physiographical features (s. 8). Where the EA has been notified of the identity of such land, it is under a duty to consult with the relevant body before carrying out or authorising works which would destroy, damage or significantly prejudice those features notified. This applies to all authorisations which are regulated by the EA. Although nature conservation bodies have always been consultees on applications for regulatory consents previously, this duty to consult is considerably wider and would include not only actions carried out by the EA itself but enforcement actions which would require remedial measures to be undertaken by third parties.

Sewerage undertakers

In relation to discharges to sewers, the licensing body is the privatised sewerage undertaker, which grants what are called trade effluent consents. This is an unusual example of a private body undertaking an environmental regulation function, although it is arguable that a sewerage undertaker is in reality doing little different from a private waste disposal contractor in providing a method of waste disposal through privately owned facilities. Appeals against trade effluent consent decisions go to the Director General of Water Services (OFWAT), who is appointed under the Water Industry Act 1991 and whose main functions relate to the regulatory control of the newly privatised water industry. The sewerage undertakers have been largely unaffected by the introduction of the EA. For a further explanation of the water industry see Chapter 14.

Countryside bodies

Within the countryside, the absence of a controlling 'Department of Rural Affairs', such as many other countries possess, is crucial. In the past the dominant force has tended to be MAFF, simply by virtue of the weight of resources available to it. This has traditionally been a very insular Ministry, although under the Agriculture Act 1986, s. 17, the Agriculture Ministers are now required to seek to achieve a balance between the interests of agriculture, the economic and social needs of rural areas, and conservation and recreation.

There are, however, other independent agencies within the Government responsible for specific matters. In England there is a Nature Conservancy Council for England (known as English Nature) and a Countryside Commission, which have responsibilities for nature conservation and for recreation, landscape and amenity respectively. This division of responsibility reflects a split in functions decided upon as long ago as 1949 and some reasons behind this are explained in Chapter 16. The Nature Conservancy Council was organised on a Great Britain basis until 1 April 1991 when, for largely political reasons, it was split into three separate national bodies by the EPA 1990. (In this book, for ease of reference, these are referred to generically as the Nature Conservancy Councils.) In Wales, the nature conservation functions were amalgamated with the amenity functions in a new Countryside Council for Wales. In Scotland, a similar body called Scottish Natural Heritage has been established under the Natural Heritage (Scotland) Act 1991, which also combines the two functions. There is no intention at present to combine English Nature and the Countryside Commission for England.

Local authorities

There has been a great deal of restructuring in local authorities over recent years. In 1986, the abolition of the metropolitan county councils led to the creation of two separate structures for local government in England and Wales (with slight variations in the case of London). As a result of further local government reorganisation under the Local Government Act 1992, there are now three main types of local authority:

(a) *Single-tier London boroughs and metropolitan districts.* In metropolitan areas, there is a one-tier system, the metropolitan district councils. These obviously have responsibility for all matters, although some functions (police, fire and transport) are run by joint boards of the councils.

(b) *Non-metropolitan areas.* In non-metropolitan areas, there is a two-tier system of county and district councils. In constitutional terms these two tiers are equal, but they have differing responsibilities. County councils have responsibility for the police, fire services, personal social services, transport, highways, education, libraries, strategic planning and development control in certain prescribed 'county matters' including waste disposal and minerals development. District councils have responsibility for housing, general development control, recreation, environmental and public health.

This split causes problems for the public which often finds it difficult to identify which tier is responsible for any particular matter. The problem is particularly acute in the environmental sphere because of the overlapping powers of the two tiers (e.g., in town planning). This confusion was cited as one of the factors which led to the reorganisation of local government and the introduction of unitary authorities.

(c) *Unitary authorities.* This third class of local authority was created after a review of local government considered a large number of proposals to introduce more single-tier authorities to replicate the powers of the metropolitan district councils.

At present, there are 35 metropolitan district councils, 33 London borough councils (including the City of London), 36 county councils, 264 district councils and 25 unitary authorities. All undertake a wide variety of tasks in relation to environmental protection. There are five main areas to consider:

(a) Town and country planning
The local authority is normally the local planning authority. This means that it is responsible for the making of development plans and for the control of development. The powers also incorporate responsibility for related matters, such as tree preservation orders, listed building protection, conservation areas, hazardous substances consents, the control of derelict land, and the protection of the countryside. As explained above, planning functions are split between county and district councils, with county councils being responsible for strategic planning and for national parks, minerals and waste disposal matters, whilst district councils have responsibility for other development control decisions. The scope for conflict between the two tiers was lessened slightly by the reduction in the range of county functions in the Local Government, Planning and Land Act 1980.

(b) Public health matters
Local authorities have always had responsibility for a very wide range of matters under the Public Health Acts. In particular, this involves duties in

relation to the control of statutory nuisances, the law on which was remodelled in the EPA 1990, Part III (see Chapter 8). Local authorities also have powers as principal litter authorities in relation to the duties and offences laid out in the EPA 1990, Part IV.

(c) The control of noise
Local authorities have primary responsibility for the control of noise from premises. In the past these provisions have been separate from those relating to statutory nuisance, but in the EPA 1990 the two sets of powers are treated together (see Chapter 8).

(d) Air pollution
Local authorities have long had responsibility for the control of smoke, dust, grit and fumes under the Clean Air Acts and related legislation. In the EPA 1990, Part I, they are given more complete powers to control air pollution from plants which are not the responsibility of the EA under integrated pollution control.

(e) Contaminated land
Perhaps the biggest change for local authorities brought about by the Environment Act 1995 is the shift away from waste management (which was absorbed, minus the waste collection authorities by the EA) to the regulation of contaminated land. In a role which echoes the position of local authorities in respect of statutory nuisances, there is a duty to inspect local authority areas for the presence of contaminated land and to take action against the person responsible for the contamination or the owner/occupier of the land in question. Unfortunately, little has been said about the resources available to some of the smaller authorities to actually carry out such a change of role. A more detailed explanation of the roles is given in Chapter 13.

In addition to these areas, it is clear that local and regional policies on such things as transport provision, recreation and strategic planning specifically and all of an authority's functions generally all have a part to play in the protection of the environment and the pursuit of sustainability.

Decision-making in local authorities

Local authorities are elected bodies. In theory it is the elected councillors who make the ultimate decisions, usually through the appropriate committee. However, in practice, most actual decisions are taken by officers, with the committee rubber stamping them. The councillors are always free to disagree with the recommendation of an officer, but, in so doing, they must be careful to act only on grounds permitted in the relevant legislation, otherwise their decision will be capable of being challenged as *ultra vires*. The constitutional monopoly of the elected councillors has also been removed. The Local Government Act 1972, s. 101, provides that the local authority may delegate any of its powers (apart from a few that must be exercised by a resolution of the whole council, such as the adoption of a local plan) to committees, or to specified officers.

This structure makes councils accountable to the electorate. But it also means that the range of considerations taken into account by local authorities is necessarily wider than those which relate simply to environmental protection. Local authorities, because of their elected status, have a democratic right to balance the advantages of conflicting courses of action which is arguably lacking in many other bodies, even if it does occasionally mean that strange decisions are reached.

In addition, all local authorities are subject to rules on the ability of the public to attend meetings and to receive information about the council's activities. Originally, the Public Bodies (Admission to Meetings) Act 1960 gave members of the public a right of admission to meetings of local authorities. This was extended in the Local Government Act 1972, s. 100, to cover all committee meetings. That provision was itself greatly expanded in the Local Government (Access to Information) Act 1985, which added new ss. 100A — 100K to the 1972 Act. In essence, a member of the public has a right not only to attend meetings of the council and its committees and sub-committees, but also to have access to agendas, minutes, and background reports. This enables information to be obtained on such things as the grounds for a decision, or whether the councillors have diverged from the recommendation of an officer. This written information must be available at all reasonable hours at the offices of the council, and members of the public may make copies of it. Under the statutory provisions, the information must be made available to the public at least three clear days before a committee meeting and this is generally the practice of local authorities. There is, however, some authority to suggest that where the information is particularly complex it must be made available as soon as possible (see *R* v *Rochdale Metropolitan Borough Council, ex parte Brown* [1997] Env LR 100).

There are limitations. There is a list of exempt information, and the council may resolve to exclude the public if publicity would be prejudicial to the public interest. This may cover meetings such as those to consider whether to recommend that enforcement action is taken on a particular issue, since it may be rendered useless if prior warning is obtained. However, in practice, many local authorities not only allow access to meetings, but permit objectors to address the meeting.

Unlike the questions of secrecy and access to environmental information covered in Chapter 7, the purpose of these powers is to show openness in decision-making and to give an impression of public accountability in what is accepted to be a political system. These powers should therefore be compared with the restrictions on access to meetings of most of the other regulatory bodies discussed.

Mention of local authorities would not be complete without a reference to their current finances. It is quite clear that with restrictions on spending they are unable to carry out properly many of the tasks entrusted to them in the environmental area, thus calling into question the effective enforcement of parts of environmental law.

FOUR

The European Community and the environment

Notwithstanding its economic basis, the EC is a major and increasing source of British environmental protection law. It also has a central and profound influence on the direction of environmental policy, both at a Community level and within each Member State. As a result, every subject covered by this book is affected, either directly or indirectly, by the activities of the EC.

There are four main ways in which the EC plays a role in shaping British environmental law and policy:

(a)   Some pieces of EC legislation lay down rules and standards that are directly enforceable in Member States without any need for further implementation. In these cases EC law is British law.

(b)   Other pieces of EC legislation are addressed to Member States and require changes in British law or administrative practice. This is normally the situation in relation to environmental legislation, because of the predominant use of Directives, which are not necessarily directly effective within Member States (see p. 65). British law is therefore not the same as EC law until the EC law has been implemented. In such cases the precise role of the EC in initiating the change is often forgotten, since the domestic legislation resulting from the EC requirements will constitute the law which is applied in practice. An important point to note is that EC law and British law often differ in such circumstances, because EC law frequently consists of aims and goals and procedural frameworks rather than precise legal rules, and allows for some discretion in the Member States as to how and when to implement it.

(c)   The third role is somewhat wider and rests upon the constitutional position that Britain now occupies as a Member State of the EC. The EC not only passes environmental laws, it has an environmental policy. This policy and the general economic and environmental principles which underpin it exert an important influence on British policy-making and on British attitudes towards environmental law and its enforcement. The direction in which environmental protection will go therefore depends as much on wider

European attitudes as it does on ingrained British ideas, although of course British ideas will in turn help to mould the general EC view and to affect the attitudes of the other Member States.

(d)   Finally, the economic policies of the EC have a profound effect on the direction of both EC and domestic environmental law. Environmental protection cannot be isolated from economic policy and the substantial completion of the single internal market by the end of 1992 has had significant spin-off effects on the environment. Indeed, many 'green' commentators would argue that the economic policies of the EC, based as they are on economic growth and on economies of scale in industrial and agricultural production, are themselves antithetical to the achievement of the aims of a clean environment and conservation of natural resources.

The specific pieces of EC law and policy that have an influence on British law will be integrated into the relevant chapters of the rest of the book. This chapter will concentrate on more general matters, such as the place of environmental policy within the EC, the history and principles of that policy, the institutions of the EC and their law-making and enforcement powers, and the way in which the policies and laws are implemented in Britain. However, it must be stressed that all the nuances of EC law cannot be covered in one chapter; accordingly, this chapter will concentrate on those issues which are of relevance to environmental protection and will not seek to provide an exhaustive account of general EC law principles.

The nature of the EC

The EC is more than just a free trade agreement between 15 fairly similar Western European states. It has institutions and law-making powers of its own, making it a form of supranational state in which the Member States have limited their sovereign rights, albeit within limited fields (although for political reasons the extent of this is often denied).

The activities over which the EC has powers are set out in the Treaties which establish the EC, which are effectively the EC's constitution. In the past there have been three Treaties and three linked Communities, the European Economic Community (EEC), the European Coal and Steel Community (ECSC) and the European Atomic Energy Community (Euratom). It has been the EEC, established by the Treaty of Rome, which has been the central Community and to which environmental policy relates. The Treaty of Rome was amended by the Single European Act 1986, which first introduced references to the environment, and all the Treaties were further amended by the Treaty on European Union, signed on 7 February 1992 at Maastricht. Rather confusingly, this Treaty, which came into force on 1 November 1993, altered the name of the EEC Treaty to the EC Treaty. In this book all references to Treaty Articles are to the EC Treaty, as amended. The formal title of the EC has also altered to the European Union (EU), but in this book we will retain the more familiar initials 'EC'. Most recently, less significant amendments to the Treaty were agreed at the Amsterdam Summit in summer 1997.

The institutions of the EC

The four main EC institutions are the Commission, the Council, the Parliament, and the European Court of Justice. Each has powers and duties specified in the Treaty and an obligation to further the aims of the EC. There is also an advisory Economic and Social Committee and the European Environment Agency.

The European Commission

The Commission is the executive of the EC. It consists of 20 independent members appointed by the Member States (two each from the five larger states — Germany, France, Britain, Italy and Spain — and one each from the others), serviced by a large number of officials. It has responsibility for implementing EC policies and initiates and draws up proposals for legislation for the Council to approve. It also has a major responsibility for policing and enforcing EC law, in which role it has extensive investigatory powers.

It is the Commission which draws up the environment action programmes and drafts proposed EC legislation. By means of information agreements with the Member States, the Commission is informed of proposals for domestic legislation and these often give rise to a Commission proposal for a common policy across the EC. However, the ambivalent nature of the Commission must be appreciated. On the one hand it is often the driving force behind new environmental policies: on the other it is responsible for enforcing the economic aims of the EC (see its position in the *Danish Bottles* case — p. 81).

Internally the Commission is divided into a number of Directorates. Directorate General XI (DG XI) deals with Environment and Nuclear Safety. As a result of the formal adoption of the principle that environmental policies should form a component of the EC's other policies, DG XI has had its hand strengthened slightly in relation to its dealings with other Directorates, such as those with responsibility for transport and energy policy, which have traditionally tended to have greater influence.

The Council of Ministers

The Council is a political body made up of one representative of each Member State. The identity of this representative alters according to the nature of the business. Thus, transport ministers normally agree transport measures, environment ministers normally agree environmental measures and so on. As a body it has a duty to ensure the attainment of the Treaty objectives, but clearly national interests play a central role in the Council's decisions.

As a result the Council's voting procedures are crucial. There are some differences in the procedures to be adopted for different matters. Some pieces of legislation have to be passed unanimously by the Council, acting on a proposal from the Commission, and after consultation with Parliament and the Economic and Social Committee. Others can be passed by a qualified majority of the Council, a system of weighted voting in which Member States can be outvoted (see p. 78).

The European Parliament

The European Parliament is mainly a consultative and advisory body, although it does have some supervisory powers over the Commission and the budget. The advent of direct elections in 1979 revitalised the European Parliament and it has been a significant mouthpiece of concern over environmental issues ever since. For example, it set in motion a ban on imports of sealskin products. It also has an important role in ensuring a certain amount of openness in EC decision-making, particularly through its Committee on the Environment, Public Health and Consumer Protection which scrutinises legislative proposals. The deliberations of the Council and the Commission are secret, and debates on proposals for legislation in Parliament are the only truly open part of the EC's decision-making process.

Consultation with Parliament has always been a mandatory requirement, in the absence of which a piece of EC legislation will be void. The Single European Act 1986 increased Parliament's powers over legislation in a significant way by introducing the 'cooperation procedure', which empowers it to reject or propose amendments to legislation subject to qualified majority voting. The procedures are complex, but in essence the Council will adopt a 'common position' based on the Commission's proposals. If Parliament rejects this 'common position', the Council may only adopt the measure if it does so unanimously. If Parliament proposes amendments, the Commission must reconsider the matter. It may choose to insert Parliament's amendments and, if it does so, the Council has a choice: it can either agree the amended proposal by a qualified majority, or it can agree some other formula unanimously, or it can allow the proposal to lapse. This procedure was used in relation to Directive 89/458 on Emissions from Small Cars, when Parliament inserted a stricter test than that wanted by the majority of the Council or originally proposed by the Commission. The Commission agreed with the stricter test and amended the proposal, thus effectively forcing the Council to agree also, or face not having a Directive at all (see Haigh and Baldock, *Environmental Policy and 1992*, 1989).

The cooperation procedure is now set out in Article 189C, which was added by the Maastricht Treaty. However, as a further complication, it also introduced a new 'co-decision procedure' in Article 189B, which involves the resolution of disputes through a Conciliation Committee, made up of representatives of the Council and the Parliament, and which provides an enhanced role for the Parliament. Of greater practical importance to environmental law is the fact that the Maastricht Treaty also extends the scope of qualified majority voting so that it will cover most pieces of proposed environmental legislation (see p. 79). As a result, though in future there will be three different procedures through which environmental legislation can be passed (under Articles 189C, 189B, and where unanimity is still required), in most cases Parliament will have a significant involvement, thus going some limited way towards tackling the problems of secrecy and lack of democratic accountability inherent in EC legislative procedures.

The European Court of Justice

The European Court of Justice consists of judges appointed by common agreement of the Member States. It is assisted by Advocates-General, one of whom makes reasoned submissions to the Court in each case. It has supreme authority on matters of EC law. This means that it has ultimate power to interpret the meaning of the Treaties and of any legislation made by the other institutions. The Court can thus, if asked, review the legitimacy of the actions of the other institutions, provide answers on matters of EC law to Member States' courts and declare whether Member States are implementing EC law properly.

Article 177 plays a major role here. Under Article 177, any court or tribunal in a Member State can refer any matter of EC law to the European Court of Justice for its interpretation of the law. This procedure aims to ensure uniformity between Member States in their application of the law. It also provides a method of obtaining an authoritative ruling. Since the Court is the ultimate arbiter of any law having an EC input, Article 177 references should be made where there is any doubt as to the meaning of EC law, or the compatibility of domestic law with it. However, one drawback is that national courts effectively have a discretion whether to make a reference or not.

In carrying out its functions the European Court of Justice has been exceptionally activist and creative. It has developed several novel principles, including the doctrines of the supremacy of EC law and of direct effects, and has been responsible for extending the scope of the powers of all the institutions (including itself). It has done this by adopting a purposive approach to interpretation in which it looks as much at the spirit as at the letter of the law. On matters of EC law, therefore, the Court's view is central to any discussion of the law. For example, in *Vessoso* (cases C-208 & 207/88 [1990] ECR I-1461, it ruled that the definition of waste in the framework Directive on Waste 75/442 included waste which was to be recycled, since it was waste as far as the disposer was concerned irrespective of the intentions of the recipient.

The Court gives one agreed judgment. These are often very brief and formal and for the full reasoning the opinion of the Advocate-General must be read, although sometimes the Court and the Advocate-General do not agree. The European Court of Justice should not be confused with the European Court of Human Rights, which exists to police the European Convention on Human Rights.

The European Environment Agency

The European Environment Agency is a new body provided for in Regulation 1210/90. However, the Regulation only came into force when it was agreed in October 1993 that the headquarters of the Agency would be in

Copenhagen. The Agency has been established with the limited role of gathering information and data on the state of the environment in the EC. A report on the state of the environment must be published every three years. It also has functions relating to the dissemination of that information and the harmonisation of methods of measurement of data throughout the EC. This will include such things as the development of adequate forecasting and cost-benefit techniques. In order to help with these tasks, the European Environment Information and Observation Network will be established, under which Member States must inform the Agency of their main national environmental information networks, which the Agency will then integrate into an EC Network. In recognition of the international nature of environmental pollution, the Agency is open to non-EC members.

The Agency has not been given any enforcement or policing powers in relation to environmental legislation, despite a determined attempt by the European Parliament to introduce such powers by proposing amendments to the Regulation. However, there is a provision in the Regulation that requires the Council to reconsider the scope of the Agency's powers within two years of the Regulation coming into force, in particular specifying a possible role in the monitoring of the implementation of EC environmental legislation. In time, therefore, the Agency may well evolve into a European Environment Inspectorate.

As a separate, complementary, development, in 1992 various national agencies (including the then HMIP) established an informal network of environmental enforcement agencies known as the 'Chester Network' after its first meeting place. The original purpose of the Network was to facilitate the exchange of information and experience on common problems relating to standard setting and enforcement. In parallel to the setting up of the Network, the Fifth Environmental Action Programme recognised the unsatisfied need for a proper follow-up of the application of Community environmental legislation by announcing the setting up of an implementation network comprising representatives of relevant national authorities and of the Commission in the field of practical implementation of Community measures. The Chester Network was then modified to create the informal EU Network for the Implementation and Enforcement of Environmental Law (IMPEL). IMPEL has a wide mandate to consider the implementation of environmental legislation, including mainly questions of how to ensure better enforcement by national, regional and local bodies.

Sources of EC law

EC law is contained in the Treaties, legislation passed by the institutions, international treaties to which the EC is a party, and the judgments and principles of the European Court of Justice.

To understand the relevance of these sources, an explanation of the concepts of the supremacy of EC law and direct effects is required. The doctrine of the supremacy of EC law is that, where there is a conflict between EC law and national law, EC law prevails, even if the national law is later in time; national courts should thus apply EC law rather than national law which does not comply with EC law. This is, however, intimately linked with the idea of direct effects. A law has direct effects if it gives rise to rights and obligations which can be enforced by individuals and companies before national courts. If an EC law is directly effective in this sense, the doctrine of supremacy means that the non-conforming national law can simply be ignored.

Not all EC law is directly effective in this sense. For any provision to be directly effective it must be sufficiently clear and precise to form a cause of action. It must also be unconditional and must not require further definition at the discretion of the Member State. There are also limitations on direct effects related to the source of the EC law. Treaty Articles and Regulations are capable of having direct effects, as long as they fulfil the above tests. For Directives, the Treaty suggested that they would not be capable of having direct effects. However, the European Court of Justice has indulged in some significant judicial legislation and has decided that Directives may have direct effects if the action is against the State or an emanation of the State, but not if against another private body. Since most environmental legislation is in the form of Directives, this is of great importance. In the field of environmental law, the doctrine of direct effects has not developed as rapidly as in other areas. Indeed, there is some doubt about the applicability of the doctrine to the traditional forms of environmental Directives following the decision in *Arcaro* (case C-168/95) [1996] ECR I-4705 (see p. 69).

Even if not directly effective, EC law may have some effect in domestic courts. The European Court of Justice held in *Von Colson* v *Land Nordrhein-Westfalen* (case 14/83) [1984] ECR 1891 that domestic legislation must be interpreted so as to comply with EC law if the domestic law was passed to implement it. Since then, the European Court of Justice has decided in *Marleasing SA* v *La Comercial Internacional de Alimentación SA* (case C-106/89) [1990] ECR I-4135 that national courts should interpret national legal provisions in accordance with EC law, irrespective of whether they pre-date or post-date it. However, it appears that national courts may decline to adopt this approach in circumstances where to do so would breach the legitimate expectations of parties to the action.

Treaty provisions

The provisions of the EC Treaties lay down the powers of the EC institutions and the procedures for decision-making as well as laying down certain substantive legal requirements. They are of enormous importance in actions before the Court relating to the legality of EC actions. In addition, some Treaty provisions are directly effective (e.g., Article 119 on equal pay), but this is not the case for the Articles concerned with the environment.

Regulations

Regulations are legislative acts of general application. They are normally directly effective, as long as they are sufficiently precise. However, there are few Regulations in the environmental sphere, except those relating to the process of giving effect to international treaties, agricultural policy and administrative matters, such as the European Environment Agency and the eco-auditing and eco-labelling schemes.

Directives

Directives are addressed to Member States and are binding as to the result to be achieved. They are well-suited to environmental measures, since they leave the choice of how to implement them to the Member States, which will each have different methods for setting environmental laws. Most EC environmental legislation is in the form of Directives.

Normally implementation is required within a specified time period (often two years). This will be done by the Member State changing its domestic law and it will be in breach if it has not *fully and correctly* implemented the Directive within the time limit. In Britain, once the Directive is implemented the domestic rule will constitute the relevant law.

A distinction must be drawn here between formal and actual compliance. Changing the law to comply with EC law constitutes formal compliance. However, this is no guarantee that the law is complied with in practice since, for example, a regulatory agency may exercise its discretion not to enforce the law. Increasingly the Commission is looking for evidence of both formal and actual compliance, although its lack of resources for monitoring develop-ments in all the Member States hampers this. The creation of the European Environment Agency may well help here in the future.

A Directive cannot be relied upon in the courts of a Member State unless it is directly effective. Originally it was assumed that Directives could not be directly effective, since discretion was given to the Member States on the method of their implementation. But, the European Court of Justice has held that Directives which are sufficiently precise as to the ends to be achieved are directly effective once the time limit has expired. However, even then, Directives have direct effect *only* against a Member State or an emanation of the State (this is known as vertical direct effect), not against another private body or person (horizontal direct effect). The reason for this distinction is that the State itself cannot plead a failure to implement the Directive properly as a defence — a form of estoppel principle (see the European Court of Justice decision in *Marshall* v *Southampton and South West Hampshire Area Health Authority (Teaching)* (case 152/84) [1986] QB 401). The continuing existence of the distinction was re-asserted in *Dori* v *Recreb Srl* (case C-91/92) [1994] ECR I-3325.

An 'emanation of the State' has been defined widely by the European Court of Justice in *Foster* v *British Gas plc* (case C-188/89) [1991] 1 QB 405, where it was stated that:

a body, whatever its legal form, which has been made responsible pursuant to a measure adopted by the State, for providing a public service under the control of the State, and has for that purpose special powers beyond those which resulted from the normal rules applicable in relations between individuals, is included among the bodies against which the provisions of a Directive capable of having direct effect might be relied upon.

One limitation is that it is up to the national courts to apply this test. However, in *Griffin* v *South West Water Services Ltd* [1995] IRLR 15, it was decided, in the context of employment law, that a privatised water company is an emanation of the State. The judge made it clear that it is the functions that the body carries out, rather than its precise legal ownership and structure, which determine the point. It is thus likely that all the privatised utilities will be treated as emanations of the State, at least as far as their 'public' functions are concerned.

The effect of these cases is that some environmental Directives will be directly effective in some circumstances. If that is the case, an incompatible domestic law can be ignored and the Directive applied instead by the national court. A number of environmental Directives have now been held to be directly effective in British courts (see p. 93). Other remedies for failure to implement a Directive are also discussed below.

Decisions, Recommendations and Opinions
Decisions are binding on the individual or group to whom they are addressed, and may also be directly effective. They are again rare in environmental law, being limited mainly to matters of monitoring and information gathering, but precautionary steps in relation to CFCs were taken in the 1980s by means of Decisions. The institutions may also issue Recommendations and Opinions. These are not binding and only have a persuasive effect.

Court decisions
The decisions of the European Court of Justice give rise to law and this has been a particularly fertile area. The Court has borrowed and developed general principles of law from the jurisprudence of the Member States, such as the principles of natural justice, proportionality, certainty, equality and the protection of legitimate expectations. The concept of proportionality is a particularly important one in environmental law and was applied in the *Danish Bottles* case (*Commission* v *Denmark* (case 302/86) [1988] ECR 4607 (see p. 81)).

Validity of EC legislation

The validity of Regulations, Directives and Decisions can be challenged within two months under Article 173. This Article sets out grounds which are slightly wider than the English *ultra vires* rules. As a judicial review action it also requires the applicant to have *locus standi*. Member States, the Commission, the Council and Parliament have it, whilst an individual has to show direct and individual concern. Such a requirement virtually restricts individuals to challenging Decisions addressed to them.

Compliance by Member States with EC law

Under Article 5, Member States are required to 'take all appropriate measures, whether general or particular, to ensure fulfilment of the obligations arising out of this Treaty or resulting from action taken by institutions of the Community'. A further requirement is to 'abstain from any measure which could jeopardise the attainment of the objectives of the Treaty'. Abiding by EC law therefore entails a positive and a negative obligation: implementation of relevant Directives, and not doing anything contrary to EC law. Since environmental law consists mainly of Directives, compliance will be discussed in terms of them.

In order to comply with a Directive, a Member State must implement it fully and within the time limit. Any incompatible law must be repealed. It is irrelevant whether other States have also failed to comply.

It thus appears that there are a number of ways in which there may be non-compliance with a Directive:

(a) failure to implement at all within the time allowed (the case law is clear that there is no real excuse for this, since the Member State will have agreed the time limit in the first place);

(b) failure to implement all the requirements of the Directive;

(c) implementation by adopting an incorrect interpretation of the Directive, the European Court of Justice being the ultimate arbiter of this point;

(d) attempting to implement by mere changes in administrative practice; *Commission* v *Belgium* (case 102/79) [1980] ECR 1473 makes it clear that a change in the law is required, because administrative measures may be altered at any time by the administration;

(e) inadequate implementation in practice.

This last type of non-compliance arises where a Member State has passed all the legislation required to implement a Directive, but there is no compliance in fact. For example, it could arise where a Member State fails to enforce the provisions of a law, or where standards laid down in a Directive are not adhered to in practice. In *Commission* v *United Kingdom* (case C-337/89) [1992] ECR I-6103, the European Court of Justice effectively equated non-compliance in fact with non-compliance in law. It decided that, by failing to comply with the maximum admissible concentration of nitrate in drinking water in some supply zones, the British Government was in breach of Directive 80/778 on Drinking Water. This raises some important points, because in a decentralised country the national Government is not necessarily the body that was actually responsible for the breach and, indeed, may not, in some cases, be in a very strong position to rectify matters. Nevertheless, it appears that the national Government will be held responsible as a matter of EC law.

Each Member State will normally be required to send a 'compliance letter' to the Commission explaining the measures that have been taken to ensure compliance with a Directive. These provisions are often stated in each individual Directive, but have not always been adhered to rigorously in the past. Accordingly, a Directive relating to the harmonisation of provisions on reports on the implementation of environmental Directives was passed in 1991. This will no doubt increase the Commission's ability to identify non-compliance, as will the creation of the European Environment Agency, though at present it is quite clear that complaints from environmental groups and individuals in Member States are the most significant sources of information on non-implementation.

Remedies for non-compliance

If a Member State does not implement a Directive properly, or maintains in force a law which is contrary to EC law, there are only a limited number of options. The main responsibility for ensuring compliance rests with the Commission, which has a discretion to start infringement proceedings. Its current policy is to start these automatically in cases where any failure to comply is alleged.

These infringement proceedings have various stages. The Commission will write to the State informally, asking it to explain its position. If a satisfactory answer is not received, a formal letter will be sent, and the State's observations will be formally required. If the Commission is still not satisfied that the matter can be settled, it will issue a Reasoned Opinion, explaining what it thinks are the main features of the non-compliance. Most cases are resolved at these preliminary stages, and there are obvious parallels with the graded procedures adopted in practice by most regulatory agencies when dealing with breaches of domestic environmental law.

Under Article 169, the Commission then has a discretion to bring the Member State before the European Court of Justice. Another Member State may join in Article 169 proceedings as a third party to argue for one side or the other (for example, Britain did this to support the Commission in the *Danish Bottles* case). If the Commission does not bring infringement proceedings, another Member State may bring them under Article 170, although this is very rare. An individual has no *locus standi* to bring infringement proceedings, or to compel the Commission to do so, but is limited to drawing an alleged non-compliance to the attention of the Commission.

The European Court of Justice is the ultimate arbiter of whether there has been compliance in law, and will give a decision on whether the State is in breach of EC law, but in the past it had few powers to enforce its ruling. Nevertheless, States normally have complied as a matter of political necessity. Otherwise the Commission or another Member State can reinstitute the infringement proceedings (again this is rare). The Maastricht Treaty has changed matters considerably. Under a new Article 171, the Commission may issue a Reasoned Opinion if it considers that a Member State has not complied with a judgment of the Court. If the Member State then continues to fail to comply, the Commission can bring the case back before the Court, which may impose a penalty. It is proposed that the level of financial penalty will depend upon the seriousness and duration of the violation. The seriousness of the violation will be evaluated on a case-by-case basis, taking into account such factors as the clarity of the rule which has been breached and the seriousness of the environmental damage or harm to human health involved. The duration of the violation runs from the date of the first court hearing and it is relevant to consider the cooperation of the Member State in seeking to resolve the matter after the hearing.

In addition to these two variable factors, there is a degree of weighting which is applied taking into account the Member State's influence over the law which has been violated (i.e., the number of votes it has on the Council of Ministers and its gross domestic product). If all of these factors resulted in the maximum daily penalty it could lead to significant fines (well in excess of 500,000 ECUs in some cases), which could be a serious deterrent. The Commission has also discussed the possibility of withholding EC funds provided for environmental matters in the event of non-compliance.

In addition to these formal infringement procedures, the Court of Justice has used the concept of the supremacy of Community law to develop various strands of case law which relate to the question of compliance with EC law. Two of these — the doctrine of direct effects and the interpretation principle established by *von Colson* and *Marleasing* (known as 'indirect effects') — have already been mentioned above. But it is worth summarising them again because, when these judicial developments are all taken together, they ensure that a lot of pressure can be exerted on Member States to implement Directives properly and in full.

(a)   The doctrine of direct effects is of great importance, since directly effective EC laws can be relied upon in the courts of Member States without the need for implementation: any incompatible national law can simply be ignored. If a national court is unwilling to accept that a Directive is directly effective, the applicant may ask it to refer the question to the European Court of Justice under the Article 177 procedure. The main drawback of the direct effects doctrine is that for Directives it only applies vertically against emanations of the State. Not only does this restrict its application in the environmental sphere, because many potential claims will be horizontal ones against private companies for failing to meet specified standards, it also creates problems of fairness, since public and private bodies are treated differently. This limitation of the doctrine was very clearly illustrated in the decision of the ECJ in *Arcaro* (case C-168/95) [1996] ECR I-4705 in which the Cadmium Directive 85/513, a daughter Directive of the Dangerous Substances Directive 76/464 was held not to be directly effective against the representative of a precious metals plant as he was not 'an emanation of the State'. Perhaps more significantly the Advocate General thought that the Directive was not unconditional or sufficiently precise to be capable of being recognised as having direct effect. He noted that the national authorities which granted the authorisation to discharge cadmium were permitted to impose more stringent limits than those imposed by the Directive. In the circumstances this amounted to a considerable discretion which rendered the Directive imprecise and incapable of having direct effect. It had previously been thought that whereas framework Directives did not lay down sufficiently precise standards, Directives which imposed discharge limits would be sufficiently precise. The court expressly did not consider this part of the Advocate General's opinion and we are left with a degree of uncertainty.

In the light of Article 130T of the Treaty, which allows Member States to introduce or maintain tighter standards in respect of any environmental legislation, it could be argued that if the Advocate General's opinion were to be followed in other cases, *no* environmental Directive could have direct effect — an unattractive proposition to say the least. Even if this constitutional basis for rejecting the direct effect doctrine was found to be incorrect, many environmental Directives follow the pattern of the Dangerous Substances Directive and the daughter Cadmium Directive, and the doctrine of direct effect in the case of environmental Directives would be very limited indeed.

The seeming decline of the doctrine of direct effect is also reflected in the decision of the ECJ in *Comitato di Coordinamento per la Difesa della Cava* v *Regione Lombardia* (case C-236/92) [1994] ECR I-483, in which the court found that Article 4 of the Framework Directive on Waste (75/442) did not have direct effect. Although the direct effect doctrine is far from dead it may be more fruitful for an individual to bring a claim based on the expanded *Francovich* principles (see further Holder: 'A dead end for direct effect? Prospects for enforcement of European Community environmental law by individuals' (1996) 8 JEL 322).

(b)   The indirect effects doctrine established in *von Colson* and *Marleasing* (that national laws should be interpreted so as to comply with EC law) avoids one of the limitations of direct effects by allowing horizontal actions. But it can be criticised for imposing unfair burdens on private bodies, since they will often have relied on the provisions of British law in carrying out their activities, only to find that their expectations are not met when the law is interpreted in a wider manner. It remains to be seen how far this doctrine will have an impact in British law, since it ultimately depends on the willingness of British judges to adopt the EC interpretation and on the existence of some national law that can plausibly be 'interpreted' in the appropriate manner.

(c)   The third development stems from the decision of the European Court of Justice in *Francovich* v *Italy* (cases C6 and 9//90) [1991] ECR I-5357. The case concerned the rights of employees in the event of their employer's insolvency, but it laid down the important general principle that a Member State could in some circumstances be liable to an individual for harm caused by a failure to implement a Directive. In effect, the decision created a new tort. The Court laid down three requirements:

(i)   that the result pursued by the Directive involved the conferring of rights for the benefit of individuals;

(ii)   the content of those rights could be determined by reference to the Directive; and

(iii) there was a causal link between the failure to implement the Directive and the harm suffered by the individual.

Requirement (i) creates a possible difficulty in relation to some environmental laws. Whilst it is clear that Directives such as the Drinking Water Directive (80/778), or the Directive on Freedom of Access to Information on the Environment (90/313), give rights to individuals, in many cases the Directive is primarily directed towards protection of the environment. However, it is suggested that most Directives laying down standards can be interpreted as conferring implied rights on individuals. This conclusion is supported by decisions of the European Court of Justice, such as in *Commission* v *Germany* (case C-131/88) [1991] ECR I-825. Requirement (ii) lays down a clarity requirement that must be determined on a case by case basis. Requirement (iii) emphasises that there must be some harm caused to the plaintiff — the action cannot be used to make a general point about non-implementation. However, the causation issue is also tricky, since in most situations the harm will be caused by an operational failure rather than by the Government's non-implementation.

The *Francovich* principle has been significantly widened with the decision of the European Court of Justice in *Brasserie du Pêcheur SA* v *Germany* (cases C-46 and 48/93) [1996] QB 404. The court held that the obligation to compensate parties for breaches of European law applies to any breach and is not limited to claims which stem from the failure to implement. *Francovich* itself concerned the straightforward situation where there was a decision of the ECJ under Article 169 establishing Italy's failure to comply with a relevant Directive (thus demonstrating that failure to pass any implementing legislation was clearly covered).

In *Brasserie du Pêcheur* the court distinguished Directives which give a wide discretion on manner of implementation from those where the obligation is more certain. In situations where there is little discretion, a failure to transpose a Directive would mean that a Member State would incur liability in line with the *Francovich* principles. In cases where there is a wide discretion on implementation there would be a right to receive compensation where three conditions were met:

(i)   the rule of law must be intended to confer rights on the individuals;

(ii)   the breach must be sufficiently serious; and

(iii)   there must be a direct causal link between the breach of the obligation resting on the State and the damage sustained by the injured parties.

It is the second criterion which distinguishes these conditions from the *Francovich* principles. A breach would be serious, for example, if a Member State persisted with the breach in the face of an ECJ ruling or other settled case law which made it clear that the conduct in question constituted an infringement. There is, however, the interesting case (in terms of environmental Directives) of non-implementation in practice (e.g., through non-enforcement of the law). It would not necessarily be easy to argue that non-enforcement was serious in the context of the *Brasserie du Pêcheur* decision, however, if this is covered it would add yet another dimension to the development of the *Francovich* principle. In any event, in the light of the criticisms of the enforcement record of Member States (see p. 88) it would seem that the issue is a 'serious' one in a political if not a legal sense.

(d)   The fourth development that is of significance arises out of *R* v *Secretary of State for Transport, ex parte Factortame Ltd* (case C-213/89) [1991]

1 AC 603, in which it was decided that a national court must set aside national procedural laws that represent an obstacle to the implementation of EC law. Since an important limitation of the doctrines explained above is that there needs to be a cause of action in national law in order to raise the EC issue, this raises some interesting possibilities. In many typical environmental cases the applicant will either fail to establish *locus standi* for a judicial review action, or will be unable to bring an action in tort because it has no interest that the law recognises (for example, the plaintiff may be an amenity group, or may have suffered only economic loss). The judgment in *Factortame*, relying on Article 5 of the Treaty, suggests it is strongly arguable that such restrictive national laws should be dispensed with where a matter of EC law is concerned.

These various developments give rise to a range of propositions. For example, if a consumer were to become ill as a result of drinking water from the public supply that did not comply with the standards laid down in the Drinking Water Directive (80/778), it would seem that there is a claim either directly in tort, relying on the direct effect of the Directive, or under the *Francovich* doctrine, even if the water did comply with national standards. A more far-reaching example might be where an environmental group wished to challenge the non-implementation of a Directive (or even a failure to enforce it, since the two are arguably the same thing in practice). In addition to making a complaint to the Commission, it could seek a declaration claiming that directly effective standards were not being enforced, and argue on the basis of *Factortame* that the rules on *locus standi* should not be used to deny it access to the courts. It might even carry out a clean-up operation and claim its expenses under *Francovich*, even though such a claim would be bound to fail if only national laws were used. Many of these very interesting propositions are likely to be tested in the courts over the next few years.

The common market

The fundamental basis of the EC has always been economic. The primary aims were originally set out in Articles 2 and 3 of the Treaty of Rome, which established the EEC in 1957. These are the creation of a 'common market' (i.e., a fully integrated single internal market within the boundaries of the Member States) in 'goods, persons, services and capital', together with the progressive harmonisation of the economic policies of the Member States. In order to achieve these primary aims, internal barriers to trade and competition need to be dismantled, so that there are no internal frontiers to hamper the free movement of goods, persons, services and capital, and no discrimination between people or firms on the grounds of nationality. This policy of free competition may be referred to as the provision of a level playing-field for producers across the EC. Common tariff barriers against the outside world are also to be erected and common policies developed in relation to certain key sectors of the economy, such as agriculture, transport, coal and steel, and energy.

This fundamental economic basis remains. In 1985, the Member States agreed to push for the completion of a fully integrated internal market by the end of 1992, and this requirement was incorporated into the Treaty as Article 8A by the Single European Act 1986. There is little doubt that this led to fresh impetus towards economic integration, although there is equally little doubt that full integration will have to wait for some time after 1992 in some sectors (e.g., fiscal policy).

It is clear that there is a fundamental conflict between some of these aims and the protection of the environment. This problem has been tackled by the creation of an environmental policy.

The EC's environmental policy

There was no mention of the environment in the original Treaty of Rome. To some extent this was because the primary aims of the EEC were, as explained above, economic, but it was mainly because the potential environmental impact of the expansionist, growth-related economic policies adopted at the time was not perceived. By the early 1970s, however, the need for some form of policy on the protection of the environment was accepted. There were two reasons for this. One was the acceptance of the interrelationship between economic growth and environmental degradation. The other was that the environment was then emerging as a significant political issue. Environmental protection thus fits into the activities of the EC in two overlapping ways: first as an adjunct to economic policy, and secondly as a positive end in itself.

In October 1972, declaring that 'economic expansion is not an end in itself', the Heads of State of the Member States accordingly requested the Commission to draw up an EC environmental policy. It responded by formulating the first Action Programme on the Environment. (This has been followed by four further Action Programmes in 1977, 1982, 1987 and 1992. This was the effective beginning of what is now a very wide-ranging environmental strategy. (Even so, it was not actually the beginning of EC involvement in environmental matters — as long ago as 1967, Directive 67/548 provided specifically for the classification, packaging and labelling of dangerous substances.) Well over 200 items of environmental legislation have now been agreed as part of this policy, ranging across the whole spectrum of matters covered by this book.

The constitutional basis of the EC's environmental policy

The constitutional basis for an environmental policy must be considered in two distinct phases: before and after the Single European Act 1986. The history of the development of the EC's environmental policy will be considered first, because it is a good illustration of the way that the institutions have in practice widened the scope of what the EC deals with by a generous reading of the Treaty.

Before 1986 the legal justification for the policy was not entirely clear. In practice, two Articles of the Treaty, Articles 100 and 235 (the former relating to the harmonisation of national laws in order to further the establishment of the common market, the latter relating to the EC's general and residual powers), were used as justification. Directives relating to pollution control and common standards tended to be justified on the basis of Article 100, whilst those where the content was almost purely environmental, such as Directive 79/409 on Wild Birds, were justified on the basis of Article 235. It was quite common for both Articles to be cited, just in case of a challenge.

In cases that did come to the European Court of Justice, the environmental policy was supported, which is not surprising since it had been formulated with the agreement of all the Member States. In *Commission* v *Italy* (case 91/79) [1980] ECR 1099, the Court held quite clearly that environmental matters may fall within Article 100. It stated:

> Provisions which are made necessary by considerations relating to the environment and health may be a burden on the undertakings to which they apply, and if there is no harmonisation of national provisions on the matter, competition may be appreciably distorted.

Then, in *Procureur de la République* v *Association de Défense des Brûleurs d'Huiles Usagées* (case 240/83) [1985] ECR 531, on the legitimacy of Directive 75/439 on Waste Oils, the European Court of Justice stated that environmental protection was 'one of the Community's essential objectives', and as such it justified some restrictions on the operation of the common market. In a sense this amounted to a rewriting of the Treaty by the European Court of Justice as a matter of political reality.

In 1986, the Single European Act went some way towards reflecting the reality of the situation by amending the Treaty to add a whole new title relating to the protection of the environment. (It also added some express social aims, such as protection of the health and safety of workers, consumer protection, and research and technological development, to reflect a similar expansion of activity in those fields.) By adding new Articles 130R, 130S and 130T, the Act introduced explicit law-making powers in relation to environmental matters. In addition, it effectively amended Article 100 by adding a new Article 100A, which has been of great importance for the development of environmental policy, even though it is primarily aimed at speeding up the completion of the single internal market. These changes not only regularised the existing *de facto* position, they also established some clearer constitutional rules than there had been in the past on the extent of the law-making powers and on how decisions were to be made.

The Maastricht Treaty continued the process of integrating environmental matters into the heart of the EC's activities by making further amendments to the Articles mentioned above. It also recognised for the first time that the development of 'a policy in the sphere of the environment' is one of the EC's main activities (see Article 3), and replaced Article 2, which sets out the objectives of the EC, with a new version that includes the tasks of promoting throughout the Community 'a harmonious and balanced development of economic activities' and 'sustainable and non-inflationary growth respecting the environment'. Article 2 thus acknowledges that there is a balance to be struck between economic and environmental factors. Of course, there remains a very live political debate about how far this widening of the aims of the EC has moved it away from a strictly economic union towards political union. Environmental policy is perhaps a good indicator of this process, since the more that explicit environmental objectives are adopted, the more it looks as if the EC is moving towards full political union.

Further amendments to the Treaty were agreed at an Intergovernmental Conference held in Amsterdam in June 1997. Although the amendments are not as significant as the changes brought about after Maastricht, they continue the development of European environmental policy. The changes include:

(a) The setting of a new main goal of attaining sustainable development within the Treaty. The Community must 'promote balanced and sustainable development of economic activities'. This goal is reinforced by a new Article 3 which provides that 'environmental protection requirements must be integrated into the definition and implementation of Community policies and activities . . . in particular with a view to promoting sustainable development'. This is the first time that there has been any challenge to the pure economic basis for the Community since its creation. The process of integrating environmental considerations into the whole sphere of European legislation and policy will certainly create interesting precedents for domestic policy.

(b) Greater freedom of access to environmental information. A new provision grants free access to information from documents of the Council, the Commission and Parliament with exceptions only on grounds of public and private interest. The precise details of the implementation of this new provision are to be left to the individual institutions within two years of the Treaty coming into force.

(c) An amendment to Article 130S. This is intended to resolve disputes between Parliament and the Council by introducing a method of holding negotiations at the end of the decision-making process in cases where the parties cannot agree on any particular legislative proposal.

(d) Proposals to amend the qualified voting procedure to include the four areas which are subject to unanimous decision-making after the Maastricht amendments (economic instruments, land use planning, water resources and energy). It is understood that this proposal has little chance of being implemented.

Articles 100 and 100A

Article 100 enables Directives to be made that seek to harmonise laws and administrative practices of Member States which directly affect the establishment or functioning of the common market. The normal methods of achieving this are to lay down uniform, common standards or to outlaw specified discriminatory practices.

The relationship with the environment here is that a unified internal market depends upon trade and competition not being distorted by Member States applying different rules and standards. The EC therefore tries to harmonise laws in all the Member States so that a producer in one country does not have an unfair advantage over one in another. A law permitting producers in one country to pollute more than an equivalent producer in another country is seen as anti-competitive, since it amounts to a form of disguised subsidy. In this sense environmental policy is little more than incidental to the central economic policy.

By inserting Article 100A, the Single European Act introduced qualified majority voting for many proposals of this nature. However, as a safeguard, it also required as an objective that, if action is taken under Article 100A concerning health, safety, environmental or consumer protection, a high level of protection should be taken for those standards (Article 100A(3)). In addition, it added a power for Member States to derogate from the common standards in certain limited ways (Article 100A(4) — see p. 81).

The Maastricht Treaty made little change to these Articles, except that Directives proposed under Article 100A will in future be subject to the 'co-decision procedure' established in Article 189B, rather than the 'co-operation procedure' of Article 189C, thus extending the role of the European Parliament for Directives agreed under Article 100A.

Articles 130R, 130S and 130T

These Articles provide a specific justification for environmental protection laws, even where there is no direct link to the economic aims of the EC. Article 130S provides the mechanics by setting out the voting procedures in the Council (see below). In contrast with Articles 100 and 100A, either Directives or Regulations are possible, although few environmental Regulations have been made. A further contrast is that, whilst Articles 100 and 100A require the uniform application of standards, under these Articles that is not always required, since the motivating force behind them is the improvement of environmental standards rather than the creation of the common market. Accordingly, Article 130T specifically provides for the possibility that stricter measures than those agreed under Article 130S may be employed by Member States, as long as they are compatible with the rest of the Treaty (for fuller discussion of the need for uniformity, see p. 80).

Article 130R(1) lists as *objectives* of the EC's environmental activities the preservation, protection and improvement of the quality of the environment, the protection of human health, and the prudent and rational utilisation of resources. Article 130R(2) sets out four central *principles* of EC environmental policy, which should be taken into account when framing policy and legislation:

(a) preventative action should be preferred to remedial measures;
(b) environmental damage should be rectified at source;
(c) the 'polluter pays' principle; and
(d) environmental policies should form a component of the EC's other policies.

These principles are discussed further on p. 83.

Under Article 130R(3), the EC institutions are required to *take account of* available scientific and technical data, environmental conditions in the various regions of the EC, and the balanced development of those regions when preparing any proposals. In addition, some form of cost-benefit analysis should be performed before environmental measures are agreed — another example of the close interrelationship between environmental and economic matters.

The international dimension is covered by Article 130R(5). Many pollution, conservation and environmental matters, such as acid rain, the protection of migratory species, or pollution of the North Sea, are international in scope. A supranational body such as the EC is well-placed to tackle them by having a common internal environmental policy with uniform standards. It may also act by putting forward a common platform in dealings with the rest of the world. Article 130R(5) specifically permits the negotiation and conclusion of international agreements, a power which justifies the EC's independent involvement in international treaties and dealings with Eastern Europe.

There is one rather unclear limitation on these powers. Article 130R(4) stated that the EC should take environmental measures which can be better attained at an EC level than at a domestic level. This has always been known as the principle of subsidiarity, and it suggested that the true purpose of EC environmental legislation should be the establishment of common policies and standards rather than any interference in local issues. But there was some disagreement over its exact meaning. Some argued that it was a competency clause, which prevented the EC from interfering in matters which are better attained at a national level. But it specifically did not say that the EC may *only* take decisions which can more effectively be taken at Community level, and an alternative (and preferable) view is that it was only a guideline (see Krämer, *EEC Treaty and Environmental Protection*, 2nd ed., 1995, p. 59).

The Maastricht Treaty appears to resolve this argument. It deleted Article 130R(4) and inserted a general principle of subsidiarity in Article 3B, which applies to all EC activities. This states:

In areas which do not fall within its exclusive competence, the Community shall take action, in accordance with the principle of subsidiarity, only if and in so far as the objectives of the proposed action cannot be sufficiently achieved by the Member States and can therefore, by reason of the scale or effects of the proposed action, be better achieved by the Community. Any action by the Community shall not go beyond what is necessary to achieve the objectives of this Treaty.

This is clearly a competency clause, but it remains to be seen how far it will restrict the development of EC environmental policy, since as a matter of law (as opposed to policy) it would seem that nearly all current EC environmental law could be justified under this test (see p. 89 for a discussion of what has happened on this point).

The Maastricht Treaty made a number of other amendments, including renumbering some of the existing provisions. The amended version of Article 130R(2) states that EC action on the environment must aim at a high level of protection, thus bringing it into line with Article 100A. More significantly, the Treaty also added to the list of basic principles in Article 130R(2) 'the precautionary principle'. This principle is normally taken to mean that measures should be taken even before a causal link has been established between pollution and environmental harm. As such, it adopts a far more cautious and proactive approach to possible environmental harm than a principle based on prevention of harm and it could therefore have very far-reaching effects on the scope of EC environmental law in the future.

A new Article 130S(5) provides that if a measure agreed under Article 130S involves disproportionate costs for a particular Member State, the Council may allow for temporary derogations and/or for financial support to meet those costs out of the special Cohesion Fund. This provision was inserted to buy off complaints from a number of the less-developed Member States that the burden of EC environmental policy fell unfairly on them since it hindered their industrial and economic development. They perceive this to be unfair because the other Member States have arguably reached their current level of development only by taking advantage of the absence in the past of the standards now imposed by modern environmental laws.

Article 235

Article 235 is a catch-all power which permits the institutions of the EC to take appropriate measures to attain any of the objectives of the EC that cannot be achieved through other powers. It has frequently been cited in the past as a justification for environmental actions, especially those relating to international action, although there is no longer any great need to do so in the light of Articles 130R and 130S.

Qualified majority voting

The system of qualified majority voting in the Council in theory allows environmental policy to be pushed forward at a faster rate than where unanimity is required. One obvious reason is that the possibility of a national veto is reduced. For example, the objections of the Danish Government (which wanted stricter standards than those proposed) to Directive 88/76 on Emissions from Large Cars resulted in it being outvoted in the Council. More recently, the British Government was outvoted on the EC list of hazardous wastes adopted pursuant to Directive 91/689 on Hazardous Waste. However, another reason is that the system encourages the Member States to reach a compromise position within the Council. The combined effect may enable some proposed Directives to avoid the fate of, for example, Directives 88/609 on Emissions from Large Combustion Plants (which deals with the causes of acid rain) and 85/337 on Environmental Impact Assessment, both of which were delayed for many years by the opposition of one or two Member States. However, this does not mean that Directives will always be agreed swiftly, even with qualified majority voting, because there are also complex political considerations to take into account, although less-developed Member States may now be bought off by concessions based on Article 130S(5). The increasing involvement of the European Parliament is also relevant to whether a compromise position can be reached.

Prior to the Single European Act 1986, unanimity was required for all environmental legislation, whether agreed under Article 100 or Article 235. This was changed by the Act, so that, in order to move more quickly to the single internal market, a qualified majority would suffice for Directives agreed under Article 100A. Unanimity was still required under Article 130S, although a little-used exception was introduced in the second subparagraph to cover situations where a unanimous Council had agreed in advance that a qualified majority would apply.

This was changed again by the Maastricht Treaty, which amended Article 130S so that most environmental legislation agreed under it is subject to qualified majority voting. The only types of environmental legislation where unanimity is still required are those primarily of a fiscal nature (for example, the proposed carbon tax), measures relating to town and country planning or land use (unless they are concerned with waste management), measures concerning the management of water resources, and measures affecting national policies on energy supply (for example, a proposal restricting the use of coal on environmental grounds).

Which Article?

The difference in the voting procedure in the Council has been one reason why, since the Single European Act, the Article that is used in adopting a Directive is important. Another reason relates to the involvement of the European Parliament. The Single European Act introduced the 'co-operation procedure' for Directives adopted under Article 100A, thus giving the Parliament a greater input (as to which, see p. 61) than it had for Directives agreed under Article 130S. Once again, the Maastricht Treaty changed things by applying the new 'co-decision procedure' set out in Article 189B, which gives Parliament even greater influence, to Directives agreed under Article 100A. For Directives agreed under Article 130S (apart from the exceptional cases where unanimity is still required), the 'co-operation procedure' as set out in Article 189C applies.

The question of which Article is appropriate in any given case has been tested on a number of occasions in the European Court of Justice. In *Commission* v *Council* (case C-300/89) [1991] ECR I-2867, the Court annulled Directive 89/428 on the Titanium Dioxide Industry on the grounds that the wrong Article (and thus the wrong voting procedures) had been used. The Commission, in proposing the Directive, had argued that it could be adopted under Article 100A, because it related to the harmonisation of rules relating to an industrial process. The Council, however, unanimously agreed that it should be adopted under Article 130S, since the content of the Directive related to environmental protection. The Court of Justice decided that the Commission's argument was essentially correct. It stated that where environmental measures also contributed to the establishment of the internal market they fell within Article 100A, thus suggesting that most environmental Directives could be based on Article 100A. It also noted that, where there was a choice between alternative Articles, Article 100A should be chosen because it allowed greater input from Parliament through the co-operation procedure. This decision opened the way at the time for the wider use of qualified majority voting on environmental matters.

However, in a later case, *Commission* v *Council* (case C-155/91) [1993] ECR I-939, which concerned the correct legal basis of Directive 91/156 amending the framework Directive on Waste 75/442, the Court of Justice altered its view and adopted instead a test based on the centre of gravity of the Directive. In this case it decided that the principal objective of the Directive, which was the protection of the environment, was the crucial factor, and not any ancillary effect on the functioning of the internal market. Directive 91/156 could thus be distinguished from Directive 89/428. This centre of gravity approach has now been further supported in *Parliament* v *Council* (case C-187/93) [1994] ECR I-2857, where the Court of Justice refused an application by the Parliament for the annulment of Regulation 259/93 on transfrontier shipments of hazardous waste because, even though it had obvious effects on free movement of goods, the Regulation fell within the framework of the Community's environmental policy. The conclusion is probably that most environmental Directives should now be based on Article 130S, although it remains possible to adopt harmonisation Directives having some environmental elements under Article 100A.

Is uniformity required?

There is a difference between Articles 130S and 100A over whether Member States may diverge from the standards laid down. Article 130T allows Member States to apply more stringent environmental measures than those agreed under Article 130S, as long as they do not distort trade between Member States. But, for Directives agreed under Article 100A, uniformity is required throughout the EC: the standards that are set must be common, otherwise the objective of a common market is not achieved. Article 130T cannot be used to justify a derogation from a Directive agreed under Article 100A. For example, in *R* v *London Boroughs Transport Committee, ex parte Freight Transport Association Ltd* [1990] 3 CMLR 495, the Court of Appeal held that the Committee's requirement that silencers be fitted to air brakes in certain London streets was illegal because it contravened Directive 70/157 on the approximation of exhaust systems (which was held to be directly effective). The Directive had been agreed under Article 100A and therefore stricter standards were an infringement of the common market. This decision was overturned by the House of Lords on appeal, though without challenging the point in issue here (see [1991] 1 WLR 828).

There is one exception under Article 100A(4). National provisions may be stricter than the Directive if the Directive was adopted by a qualified majority, the national provision is justified by the need to protect the environment or the working environment, and the Commission verifies this. This exception was intended to cover the situation where a Directive was agreed under Article 100A despite the opposition of a Member State. It was central to the political balance agreed in the Single European Act because it provided a palliative to qualified majority voting. Article 100A(4) has been invoked successfully by the German Government in relation to what effectively amounts to a ban on the use of pentachlorophenol in Germany, although not before the original decision by the Commission to accept the ban was annulled by the European Court of Justice (see *France* v *Commission* (case C-41/93) [1994] ECR I-1829). The Court did not address the scope of Article 100A(4) directly, but it did state that the exception should be interpreted restrictively because it derogates from the single internal market and therefore suggests that it applies only where a Member State has an *existing* piece of legislation that is more stringent than the Directive at the time the Directive is adopted.

However, this interpretation is somewhat at odds with Directive 94/62 on Packaging and Packaging Waste. As well as imposing requirements on the composition and recoverability of packaging, this controversial Directive imposes a duty on Member States to establish national systems to provide for the collection and recovery of packaging (many Member States already have such schemes). It then provides for recovery and recycling targets, in relation to which it is interesting to note that, whilst the Directive was adopted as a harmonisation Directive under Article 100A, Member States were allowed to set higher targets if they wished. In addition, three Member States (Portugal, Greece and Ireland) were allowed to meet lower targets. It is clear that these differences were agreed because of the political difficulties that arose in the negotiation of the Directive, but it is hard to see how this fits in with the normal requirement of uniformity under Article 100A (see London and Llamas, 'EC Packaging Directive' (1995) 145 NLJ 221).

The *Danish Bottles* case

The interests of environmental protection may also be used as a defence in other ways. For example, Article 36 permits national laws which are effectively restrictions on imports (under Article 30), if there is a genuine need to protect, amongst other things, the environment, public health or national treasures.

The very important decision of the European Court of Justice in the *Danish Bottles* case (*Commission* v *Denmark* (case 302/86) [1988] ECR 4607) amplifies this point into a more general rule. The Court concluded that the protection of the environment is one of the EC's so-called 'mandatory requirements'. As such it can justify an interference with the operation of the common market, as long as the method adopted is proportionate to the aim which is being protected. However, it will not justify derogation from a Directive agreed under Article 100A.

The case arose from a Commission challenge to Danish laws which required beer and soft drink containers to be returnable, arguing they were a form of disguised discrimination against foreign manufacturers and hence an impediment to free trade under Article 30. The European Court of Justice held in clear terms that it was permissible to use environmental protection as an excuse for such discrimination. It went on to hold that such a derogation from the free market must be proportionate to the end to be achieved. Since a returnability requirement was clearly more environment-friendly than a recycling one, this requirement was acceptable. But a further licensing requirement, whereby only a limited number of container shapes was permitted, was disproportionate and thus illegal in EC law.

This decision has an obvious impact on the ability of Member States to pass environmental legislation that is stricter than in other Member States and which thus interferes with the common market. But it also has an impact on the attitude of the Commission, since in order to re-establish the single internal market, it will seek to lay down common standards by proposing EC legislation. There is an incentive to move towards common standards based on the stricter environmental protection legislation of the non-conforming State, using Article 100A(3) as a justification.

Some extension of the *Danish Bottles* principle can be seen in the *Wallonian Waste* case, *Commission* v *Belgium* (case C-2/90) [1992] ECR I-4431. This case concerned what was effectively a ban on waste imports imposed by the Walloon Regional Executive. The European Court of Justice decided that waste constituted goods for the purposes of the Treaty and thus there was a clear infringement of the provisions on free movement of goods. However, it went on to decide that the ban was justified on environmental grounds. In so doing, it held that wastes are goods of a special character. Accordingly, the general principle set out in Article 130R(2), that pollution should be rectified at source, was called into play to suggest that wastes should be disposed of as close to their place of origin as possible. This enabled the Court to avoid the otherwise inevitable conclusion that the ban was discriminatory and is an important example of how these general principles can be used so as to have an impact on the development of the law. A further interesting feature of the case was the rather bizarre (but logical) result that the ban was legal as far as it applied to ordinary wastes, but not as far as hazardous wastes were concerned, because Directive 84/631 laid down an exhaustive system for the transfrontier shipment of hazardous waste. Therefore, in accordance with the argument accepted by the Court of Appeal in the *London Boroughs Transport Committee* case (see above), the ban on hazardous waste was illegal because it contravened the provisions of the Directive.

Some attempt to formalise these decisions has been made by the Maastricht Treaty, which added a new paragraph to Article 130R(2). This allows Directives seeking to harmonise EC laws to include a safeguard clause permitting a Member State to take *provisional* measures for environmental reasons. This does not appear to alter anything decided by *Danish Bottles,* but the Article does add a further requirement that such measures are subject to inspection by the Commission.

The scope of EC environmental policy

The Action Programmes on the Environment have laid down certain basic principles of EC environmental policy. The most important are set out in Article 130R(2). They are that:

(a)   preventative action is to be preferred to remedial measures;
(b)   environmental damage should be rectified at source;
(c)   the polluter should pay for the costs of the measures taken to protect the environment (the 'polluter pays' principle, see p. 124); and
(d)   environmental policies should form a component of the EC's other policies.

These are not directly enforceable obligations, but they will be taken into account in drawing up environmental and other EC legislation. They also influence domestic pronouncements and policies and, as illustrated above, can be used in the development of EC environmental law. The Maastricht Treaty added an important new principle, the precautionary principle.

The Action Programmes also plan future action in relation to the environment. The first two Action Programmes were reactive in nature and concentrated on pollution control and on remedial measures. This fitted in with the economic justification of environmental policy under Article 100, but was also designed to tackle the most obvious and pressing problems first. The third and fourth Action Programmes emphasised preventative measures at the same time as continuing the work on pollution control. For example, a number of Directives were agreed on product standards and on the design of industrial plant and processes. They also stressed the need to integrate environmental protection into other EC policies. Whilst there are not too many clear examples where this has happened as yet (the designation of environmentally sensitive areas for agricultural grant purposes is one of the few direct examples), the importance of this principle for the shape of future policy should not be underestimated. However, perhaps the most significant feature of the third and fourth Action Programmes was that attention was increasingly paid to structural, or 'horizontal', measures that laid down procedures or ancillary administrative matters. For example, legislation was passed on the assessment of the environmental impact of major projects (85/337), eco-labelling (Regulation 880/92), freedom of access to environmental information held by public bodies (90/313), and eco-management and audit (Regulation 1836/93).

There is no doubt that the amendments made by the Single European Act aided this shift in emphasis by encouraging more wide-ranging measures. For example, because of Danish objections to the use of Article 235, it was accepted after the passage of the Wild Birds Directive 79/409 that no further legislation would be passed on wildlife unless it related to trade. Such a limitation is now clearly removed, as the passage of the Habitats Directive 92/43 illustrated. As a further example, Directive 90/313 on Freedom of Access to Information on the Environment was made under Article 130S and there is little doubt that it would have been difficult to justify such a measure under Articles 100 or 100A.

The fifth Action Programme, entitled *Towards Sustainability*, was agreed at the end of 1992. It will cover the period 1993 to 2000. As its title suggests, it stresses the sustainable management of natural resources and provides a more wide-ranging environmental policy than before. It further switches the emphasis away from grouping environmental controls by reference to environmental media, such as air, water or land, to looking horizontally at all the environmental implications of various sectors of the economy. In particular, as part of the principle of integrating environmental policies within the EC's other policies, it concentrates on the following sectors: industry, transport, agriculture, energy and tourism.

A central concept in the scheme of the fifth Action Programme is that of 'shared responsibility'. This is the idea that responsibility for solving environmental problems is shared between government, industry and consumers. This heralds a movement away from using legislation and regulation to solve problems towards a greater use of financial and other market mechanisms. It also suggests a more inventive use of legal instruments, including civil liability and voluntary mechanisms, and the provision of more information on the state of the environment.

The range of environmental Directives

It is not possible in the space available to list all EC Directives that relate to the environment. What follows is a selective list intended to illustrate the major areas of EC involvement. Greater detail on individual Directives is given in the relevant chapters of Part II of this book and in Haigh, *Manual of Environmental Policy: the EC and Britain* (Longman, looseleaf), which explains each Directive in turn. Where the number of a Directive is given below, it normally refers to the original piece of legislation, which may subsequently have been amended. In some cases, such as in relation to the use and production of CFCs or emissions from vehicles, no number is given simply because the amount of legislation is very great.

EC Directives have been made in relation to the following:

(a) setting quality standards for water (e.g., Surface Waters for Drinking 75/440; Drinking Water 80/778; Bathing Waters 76/160; Water Standards for Freshwater Fish 78/659; Shellfish Waters 79/923; Nitrates 91/676);

(b) setting emission standards for discharges to water (e.g., Dangerous Substances in Water 76/464; Groundwater 80/68);

(c) setting quality standards for air (e.g., Smoke and Sulphur Dioxide 80/779; Nitrogen Dioxide 85/203; Lead in Air 82/884);

(d) setting emission standards for emissions to the atmosphere (e.g., various Directives on Emissions from Vehicles such as 70/220, 88/76, 89/548 and 91/441; Emissions from Industrial Plants 84/360; Emissions from Large Combustion Plants 88/609; New and Existing Municipal Waste Incinerators 89/369 and 89/429; Hazardous Waste Incinerators 94/67);

(e)   setting noise standards (e.g., Noise in the Workplace 86/188; various Directives on Noise from Vehicles; Noise from Construction Plant 84/532);

(f)   controlling emissions of dangerous pollutants (e.g., Dangerous Substances in Water 76/464; Toxic Waste 78/319 as amended by 91/689; Mercury 84/ 156; Lindane 84/491; Cadmium 83/513; Disposal of PCBs 76/403 and various Directives on CFCs, Lead and Pesticides);

(g)   controlling the disposal of waste (e.g., Framework Directive on Waste 75/442 as amended by 91/156; Toxic Waste 78/319 as amended by 91/689; Sewage Sludge 86/278; Urban Waste Water Treatment 91/271);

(h)   controlling the storage and use of hazardous materials (e.g., Major Accident Hazards 82/501 (the 'Seveso' Directive); Asbestos 87/217);

(i)   controlling dangerous activities (e.g., Transfrontier Shipment of Toxic Waste Regulation 259/93);

(j)   setting product standards (e.g., Lead in Petrol 88/195; the various Directives on Noise and Emissions from Vehicles; Classification, Packaging and Labelling of Dangerous Substances 79/831);

(k)   setting standards for the operation of certain industries (e.g., Emissions from Industrial Plants 84/360; Titanium Dioxide Industry 78/176 and 89/ 428; Emissions from Large Combustion Plants 88/609);

(l)   procedures for the planning of development (e.g., Environmental Impact Assessment 85/337);

(m)   protection of wildlife (e.g., Wild Birds 79/409; Habitats 92/43; Trade in Endangered Species Regulation 3626/82);

(n)   protection of the countryside (e.g., the Agri-Environment Regulation 2078/92);

(o)   the use and release of genetically modified organisms (e.g., 90/219 and 90/220, as amended by 94/15);

(p)   recycling and waste reduction (e.g., Packaging and Packaging Waste 94/62).

There are also important Directives and Regulations on an ever-widening range of ancillary matters. Regulation 1210/90 establishes the European Environment Agency. In addition, it replaces the current programme on the collation of information on the environment (CORINE) with new regimes of environmental monitoring and dissemination of information. Directive 90/ 313 on Freedom of Access to Information on the Environment is another essential part of the process of providing accurate information, which is so important if responsibility for environmental improvement is to be shared between regulators, industry and the public. Regulation 880/92 on Eco-Labelling and Regulation 1836/93 on Eco-Management and Audit further emphasise the role that voluntary initiatives by business will play in future policy. Lastly, there is the Financial Instrument for the Environment (LIFE), contained within Regulation 1973/92, which provided financial support for environmental matters, especially on the promotion of sustainable development and nature conservation, up to a total of 400 million ECUs by the end of 1994.

The types of mechanism used

It is very difficult to draw any firm conclusions from such a wide range of Directives. As one would expect, they utilise a wide range of techniques, selecting different tools for different jobs. Some of these issues are covered in Chapter 5, where, in particular, the differences between Britain and the other Member States over the types of standard to be adopted in relation to Directive 76/464 on Dangerous Substances in Water are discussed.

Two mechanisms that require some consideration at this stage are limit values and framework Directives. Limit values relate to a process whereby standards are set that require a certain minimum or maximum threshold level to be reached, but allow Member States to impose more stringent standards if circumstances require. They are thus of great use for creating general uniformity throughout the EC whilst retaining some flexibility on the ground.

Framework Directives lay down a general framework or structure of controls and come in two general types. The first type is illustrated by Directive 76/464 on Dangerous Substances in Water, which sets out a framework of controls and principles that could be applied in the future by further Directives. These Directives (sometimes called 'daughter Directives') are used to set limit values for particular dangerous substances. The second type is illustrated by Directives 75/442 and 91/156 on Waste, which set out general requirements and procedures, but leave it to Member States to set specific standards. This second type is becoming very common, in part as a recognition of the doctrine of subsidiarity, but also because of the EC's increasing emphasis on structural and procedural measures. For example, the Directive on integrated pollution prevention and control is of this general type. This has one important impact on the enforcement of EC environmental law — framework Directives are far less likely to be directly effective than the more specific 'regulation-style' Directives that were often used to set EC standards in the past. For example, in *Comitato di Coordinamento per la Difesa della Cava* v *Regione Lombardia* (case C-236/92) [1994] ECR I-483, the European Court of Justice decided that Article 4 of Directive 75/442 (as amended by Directive 91/156), which requires Member States to take the necessary measures to ensure that waste is disposed of without harming human health or the environment, was not sufficiently precise to be directly effective because of its essentially programmatic nature. In the light of the decision in *Arcaro* (case C-168/95) [1996] ECR I-4705 it might be considered that the distinction between framework Directives and the more specific Directives is more blurred than originally thought, at least in terms of the inapplicability of the direct effects doctrine.

The future of EC environmental policy

There are a number of trends in relation to the future of the EC's environmental policy which may be picked out.

(a)   Future policies are increasingly likely to be preventative in nature. The focus of attention in environmental and safety matters is shifting from straight regulation of activities to precautionary measures, such as the fixing of product standards (e.g., on lead content in petrol), or plant design standards (e.g., Directive 84/360 on Emissions from Industrial Plants), or the avoidance of problems through waste reduction and recycling (e.g., Directive 94/62 on Packaging and Packaging Waste). In particular, the existence of the single internal market demands that emphasis is placed on products and processes so that free competition does not lead to a lessening of standards and to environmental degradation.

(b) Cross-media approaches to pollution control are likely to be encouraged, along the lines of integrated pollution control in this country. Most of the existing Directives have tended to concentrate on one particular sector, whether an industry, a substance or an environmental medium. The IPPC Directive is a major step towards a more integrated approach (see p. 336).

(c) The integration of environmental matters into other policies, as required by Article 130R(2), is likely to increase, especially since this is essential for pursuing effective preventative measures. In this respect, Green Papers have been issued on such things as the urban environment and the impact of transport on the environment.

(d) One of the impacts of the single internal market is likely to be a concentration of economic activity in the geographical centre of Europe. The potential effects of this on more marginal areas have already been recognised through the EC's Regional Policy and the environmental effects will require tackling. One way of doing this will be through the Cohesion Fund and the support available under the LIFE programme.

(e) Ancillary measures, such as freedom of information, the encouragement of public participation in decision-making, and the creation of environmental rights are likely to be stressed, following the lead of Directive 90/313 on Freedom of Access to Information on the Environment and Directive 85/337 on Environmental Impact Assessment, which encouraged openness in the planning of environmentally significant developments. This is crucial to the success of many of the EC's programmes, since consumers can only take responsibility for environmental affairs if they are given sufficient and accurate information on the environment and the environmental performance of polluters.

(f) This previous point links to the need for an increased democratisation of the EC's decision-making processes. At present, efforts in this regard are effectively channelled into the granting of greater powers to the European Parliament.

(g) Action on international problems, such as global warming, acid rain, ozone depletion and oil pollution, will continue to be taken, since the EC is well placed to tackle these problems. This book has not dealt in detail with these issues, but the role of the EC has been significant in coordinating a European-wide response and this will continue. In particular, the EC has stressed in *Towards Sustainability* the role that it can play in combating climate change. It may well be that the main contribution that the EC will make in this area is the development of some form of 'carbon tax', although this is a matter which is currently fraught with political difficulties.

(h)   As on the domestic scene, economic and fiscal instruments can be expected to be developed. The Environment Council accepted the idea in principle at its meeting in October 1990. This commitment to financial instruments is reiterated in *Towards Sustainability*. Included within the category is the use of civil liability, and it is significant that the EC published a Green Paper on environmental liability in 1993 entitled *Remedying Environmental Damage* (COM(93)47 final). This expressed a preference for the use of strict civil liability, coupled with a clean-up fund where liability could not be established. There is no doubt that this will prove to be very controversial, as was the Commission's draft Directive on strict civil liability for damage caused by waste when it was published (see p. 430), but it can be anticipated that the civil law will play an increased role in EC law in the future. Although the development of a common liability scheme is considered to be a priority within the Commission the chequered history of the Green Paper demonstrates the controversy that the proposals have created. It is likely that the ideas will be developed with the production of a White Paper following on from a Communication produced by the Commission (see further p. 127).

The Commission has also paved the way for the greater use of other economic instruments by way of environmental taxes. A Commission Communication on Environmental Taxes and Charges in the Single Market (COM (97) 9 final) supports the use of environmental tax measures as an appropriate way of internalising the costs of pollution with the caveat that any new measures should not act in a manner which would distort the internal market. The experience of using environmental taxes will be monitored carefully throughout the Community.

(i)   The Commission has also stated an intention to concentrate on the enforcement of existing legislation. In a Communication to the Council and European Parliament on Implementing Community Environmental Law, the Commission reported that at October 1996, in relation to environmental matters, there were over 600 outstanding infringement cases against Member States with over 85 awaiting determination by the ECJ, with further cases being registered with the Commission at the rate of over 250 a year (over 20 per cent of all infringement cases). This is probably the tip of the iceberg as only the most serious cases will be reported to the Commission and these will not involve the thorny question of under-enforcement (i.e., although there has been formal compliance in terms of the transposing legislation there has been no implementation in practice).

The suggestions for improvement put forward in the Communication included:

(i)   The development of standards for inspection tasks by authorities in the Member States which would ensure that annual reports were compiled. These reports would enable the Commission to arrive at an informed view of the successful transposition and implementation of European legislation.

(ii)   The creation of an official grievance procedure in each Member State, possibly by means of a 'European Ombudsman'. This would ensure that complaints were handled swiftly at a local rather than Community level.

(iii) Increasing the opportunity for environmental cases to be dealt with by national courts through broader access to justice on Community environmental issues. This might involve relaxation of the rules on *locus standi* to include recognised environmental non-governmental organisations (which would fall in line with the decision of Otton J in *R* v *Inspector of Pollution, ex parte Greenpeace Ltd (No. 2)* [1994] 4 All ER 329, see p. 34).

The role of the European Environment Agency and associated organisations, such as IMPEL, is likely to develop as coordination and cooperation between Member States improves. This in turn could give rise to even more infringement proceedings if the Agency's monitoring powers mature.

(j) A final theme relates to the concept of sustainability. It is clear that the EC will emphasise the minimisation of waste and the recycling of waste that is produced. One example of this is a proposed framework Directive on energy efficiency (the SAVE programme), which has already given rise to Directive 92/75 on Energy Labelling for Domestic Appliances. But perhaps the most important steps here relate to packaging, where Directive 94/62 on Packaging and Packaging Waste sets recovery and recycling targets and seeks to reduce the excessive amount of packaging that is used.

In summary, the main agenda for the EC until the turn of the century has been set by the fifth Action Programme, *Towards Sustainability*. This reflects the shift in emphasis in all Member States towards considering the use of financial and other instruments as a means of ensuring environmental improvement, rather than always using methods connected with regulation by a public body. The Regulations on Eco-Labelling and Eco-Management and Audit are important examples of such methods, since they create voluntary schemes which industry can choose whether to join or not. But that is not to say that mandatory regulatory schemes will no longer be used, as most recent Directives on IPPC and environmental assessment illustrate.

Subsidiarity

One doubt attached to the future direction of environmental policy relates to the concept of subsidiarity (i.e., the requirement added by Article 3B of the Maastricht Treaty that the EC should only make laws that are best made at that level, leaving Member States to take measures that are better taken at a national level). This could be used to slow down progress on EC measures, or even to repeal existing legislation. The concept was discussed at the Edinburgh Summit in December 1992, which reached such conclusions as that the Community should only legislate to the extent that is necessary, that framework Directives should be preferred to detailed ones and that voluntary codes should be considered where appropriate. In the event, the hit-list of Directives that were candidates for amendment or repeal did not include any environmental measures. However, the threat posed by subsidiarity was shown by the British Government's action in bringing forward a list of Directives it wished to see amended and a further list of proposals it wished to see discontinued. The first category included the various Directives on air quality standards, drinking water, bathing waters and hazardous waste, whilst the second included the proposed Directives on landfill, packaging waste and ecological quality of water, as well as the proposal to extend the Directive on environmental impact assessment to plans, policies and general programmes in addition to specific applications for development. It appears that this threat has been resisted by the EC institutions and that the most that will happen is that some Directives, especially those on water quality, will be re-assessed in the light of current scientific knowledge and that future Directives are more likely to take the form of framework Directives, leaving precise standards to the Member States.

EC environmental law and Britain

There is little doubt that the EC's environmental policy and the various Directives and Regulations adopted in pursuance of it have had an important influence on British environmental law. They have led directly to new legislation, new standards being adopted, significant changes in Government policy, and also a general reassessment of the whole British approach to pollution control. It is not practical to provide an exhaustive list, but the following examples should give a flavour of the impact of EC environmental law. Further examples are covered at relevant places elsewhere in the book.

(a)   New domestic legislation has been passed in relation to: environmental assessment (see the various regulations explained in detail in Chapter 10); drinking water quality (see the Water Supply (Water Quality) Regulations 1989 (SI 1989 No. 1147)); the protection of important natural habitats (see the Conservation (Natural Habitats etc.) Regulations 1994 (SI 1994 No. 2716)); the definition of waste (see the Waste Management Licensing Regulations 1994 (SI 1994 No. 1056), sch. 4); the recovery and recycling of packaging waste (see the Producer Responsibility Obligations (Packaging, Waste) Regulations 1997 (SI 1997 No. 648); and access to environmental information (see the Environmental Information Regulations 1992 (SI 1992 No. 3240)).

(b)   New standards have been adopted for such things as air quality (see the Air Quality Standards Regulations 1989 (SI 1989 No. 317)), emissions from cars (e.g., in relation to lead and carbon dioxide) and bathing waters (in order to reflect the standards laid down in Directive 76/160). In addition, consents for discharges to controlled waters incorporate standards laid down in EC Directives, as do the water quality objectives which underpin many decisions on the control of water pollution.

(c)   The impact on policy can be seen clearly in the case of the privatisation of the water industry. The Government originally intended to privatise the whole industry, including the regulatory aspects, but was forced to create a public regulatory agency (in the form of the National Rivers Authority) when it became clear that a private regulator would not fulfil the requirement for a 'competent authority' to have responsibility for overseeing the Directives on water pollution. A different example is that Directives 91/271 on Urban Waste Water Treatment and 76/160 on Bathing Waters have led to important changes in capital spending programmes in the water industry. It is also arguable that the partial shift in British policy from basing controls on the impact on the receiving environment to using concepts based on best available techniques has been strongly influenced by the EC. Finally, the existence of EC standards has been of great importance for environmental groups, who have something with which to compare British practice when publicising alleged deficiencies in environmental performance.

As noted earlier, the influence has not all been in one direction, although it is clear that in the past Britain has often been in a minority over particular measures (for example, the problems encountered in the drafting of Directive 76/464 on Dangerous Substances in Water are discussed in Chapter 5). As far as the future is concerned, it is significant that the ability to veto measures is now restricted by the qualified majority voting procedures used for most EC environmental legislation and that the EC has recently been extended by the accession of three new Member States, each of which could be said to have fairly strong environmental credentials. A further issue is that the role of the UK Parliament in agreeing EC legislation is minimal, apart from the House of Lords Select Committee on the European Communities, which issues reports on proposed legislation frequently (for example, its comments on the EC Commission Green Paper, *Remedying Environmental Damage*, are a very constructive contribution to the debate on strict liability for environmental harm).

As with all Member States, not all Directives have been implemented fully, although the British record is actually better than most. There has been a particular problem in Britain with implementing on time. Britain has now formally been found to be in breach of EC Directives on two occasions. In *Commission* v *United Kingdom* (case C-56/90) [1993] ECR I-4109, the European Court of Justice held that Britain was in breach of Directive 76/160 on Bathing Waters in relation to standards at Blackpool and Southport beaches. In *Commission* v *United Kingdom* (case C-337/89) [1992] ECR I-6103, the European Court of Justice decided that there had been a failure to implement Directive 80/778 on Drinking Water by (i) failing to ensure that water used for food production purposes was covered by the implementing regulations (a failure now rectified), and (ii) failing to comply with the maximum admissible concentration of nitrate in some supply zones. This second part of the decision is very important, because the Court decided that the duty to comply with maximum admissible concentrations is an absolute one, thus effectively treating non-compliance in practice in the same way as formal non-compliance and opening the way for future infringement proceedings based on a failure to enforce EC standards properly in practice. In Britain this is of importance because of the way that much of the practical implementation of the law is delegated to independent agencies and quangos.

In this context, the Court of Appeal decision in *R* v *Secretary of State for the Environment, ex parte Friends of the Earth* [1995] Env LR 11 is instructive. The case arose out of the European Court of Justice decision on Directive 80/778 on Drinking Water referred to above. The Court of Justice had decided that the duty to comply with the standards laid down in the Directive is absolute, rather than simply to take all practicable steps to comply, as had been argued by the British Government. When it later transpired that certain water companies were supplying water that was in breach of the pesticide standards set out in the Directive, the Secretary of State had accepted undertakings from them about their plans to remedy the situation, rather than making an enforcement order. This was challenged by Friends of the Earth, but the Court of Appeal accepted that, whilst the *primary* duty imposed by the Directive on the Government was absolute, this then gave rise to a *secondary* duty to comply with the judgment. It appears that this secondary duty is not absolute in the same way, but is capable of being qualified by practical considerations.

The Commission has initiated infringement proceedings against the UK Government for the continued failure to implement the Drinking Water Directive. Once again, there is an alleged failure to comply with the parameters for pesticides. In addition, the system of water company undertakings under the Water Industry Act 1991 is alleged to be unlawful as it does not allow for the direct enforcement of the Directive standards by affected individuals (an interesting contrast to the judgment of the Court of Appeal). Further infringement proceedings are possible over Directive 76/464 on Dangerous Substances in Water (although it appears that all the Member States are in the same position over failures to introduce pollution reduction programmes for 'black list' substances) and Directive 85/337 on Environmental Impact Assessment, where infringement proceedings were started over the failure to carry out an environmental assessment of the East London River Crossing (the route of which was to have cut through Oxleas Wood site of special scientific interest), although this project was subsequently abandoned by the Department of Transport.

It is also possible that actions will be commenced in relation to the actual implementation of a number of Directives in practice, including Directives 90/313 on Freedom of Access to Information on the Environment and 92/43 on Habitats. This is related to the way in which Directives are now being implemented. In response to worries about the formal transposition of Directives into British legislation, the tendency nowadays is for implementing regulations to repeat the wording of the relevant Directive and to make little attempt to 'translate' what are often unclear terms into the sort of precise language that is normal in British legislation. The regulations implementing both of the above Directives illustrate this point perfectly. The result is that the meaning of the regulations remains unclear and that fuller enlightenment must await either administrative guidance (which gives undesirably wide powers to the administration and is, in any case, not conclusive), or a decision by the courts (normally this would involve a judicial review action, with all the difficulties and expense that entails). For example, it is unclear exactly which bodies and what categories of information are covered by the Environmental Information Regulations 1992, but conclusive answers to these points will only be given should an aggrieved party bring a challenge against a body which it believes has failed to comply with the Regulations. Such a round-about method of discovering the scope of the law is most undesirable.

This raises the issue of the attitude that the British courts have adopted towards EC environmental law. At a general level they have come to terms with the supremacy of EC law, although this has come about indirectly through the European Communities Act 1972, s. 2, which provides the constitutional basis for the application of EC law in Britain. One result is that they have been willing to construe domestic legislation to comply with EC law if it was passed in order to implement it. The clearest example is provided by *Litster* v *Forth Dry Dock & Engineering Co. Ltd* [1990] 1 AC 546, where the House of Lords adopted a purposive interpretation of the Transfer of Undertakings Regulations in accordance with the relevant Directive. However, it is not yet clear whether the British courts will be willing to follow the *Marleasing* case and apply the doctrine of indirect effect where no intention to implement EC law can be discerned (see the House of Lords' decision in *Duke* v *GEC Reliance Ltd* [1988] AC 618). In addition, the *Francovich* principle has not yet been tested in the British courts.

As far as the doctrine of direct effects is concerned, the position is equivocal. In *R* v *London Boroughs Transport Committee, ex parte Freight Transport Association Ltd* [1990] 3 CMLR 495, the Court of Appeal held that a requirement in Directive 70/157 on Noise from Vehicles was directly effective; in *Twyford Parish Council* v *Secretary of State for Transport* (1990) 4 JEL 273, it was held that the requirement to carry out an environmental assessment was directly effective in relation to projects covered by Annex I of Directive 85/337; and in *R* v *Secretary of State for the Environment, ex parte Friends of the Earth* [1995] Env LR 11, the Court of Appeal accepted implicitly that the standards laid down in Directive 80/778 on Drinking Water were directly effective (as, indeed, was clear from the European Court of Justice decision in *Commission* v *United Kingdom* (case C-337/89 [1992] ECR I-6103). On the other hand, in the *Petition of the Kincardine and Deeside District Council* (1991) 4 JEL 289, the Scottish Court of Session decided that the requirement to carry out an environmental assessment was not directly effective in relation to projects covered by Annex II of Directive 85/337 because of the discretion given to Member States, and in *Wychavon DC* v *Secretary of State for the Environment* [1994] JEL 351, Tucker J appeared to hold that *none* of the provisions of Directive 85/337 has direct effects. This decision has been followed in a number of subsequent cases without any real analysis of the other competing decisions, in particular, in *R* v *North Yorkshire County Council, ex parte Brown* [1997] Env LR 391, where Hidden J held that the Directive did not have direct effect. This decision was swiftly followed by the judgment of the ECJ in *Aannemersbedrijf P.K. Kraaijeveld BV* v *Gedeputeerde Staten van Zuid-Holland* (case C-72/95) [1996] ECR I-5403, where the court held that national courts were responsible for filling in any gaps in national legislation where projects which were covered under the Directive were omitted nationally but without reaching any precise con-clusion on whether the Directive had direct effect. With the continuing confusion it is not surprising that the applicants in *Brown* were granted leave to appeal to the Court of Appeal so that the issues could be clarified. In addition, in the *Twyford* case, the judge refused relief to the applicants on the ground that they had not suffered substantial prejudice, whilst in both the *Twyford* and *Wychavon* cases, the judges stated that they would have exercised their discretion not to grant relief to the applicants, even if they had agreed with their legal arguments. It is hard to reconcile the reasoning in these cases with accepted principles of EC law.

It is also significant that the courts have shown a marked reluctance to refer matters to the European Court of Justice under Article 177. A clear example is the Court of Appeal's decision in the *Lappel Bank* case where, although the judges were split on the interpretation of Directive 79/409 on Wild Birds, they declined to make a reference, although the House of Lords later rectified the position by making a reference (see p. 513 for a fuller explanation of this case). It may also be asked why no reference was made in the *Twyford*, *Kincardine*, *Wychavon* and *Brown* cases, where the EC law issue was demonstrably unclear from the fact that different decisions were reached on it although Hidden J appeared to have little difficulty in reconciling the opposing views in *ex parte Brown*. The High Court has, however, also made its first reference on the implementation of the Nitrates Directive 91/676 (see *R v Secretary of State for the Environment, ex parte Standley* 268 ENDS Report 47).

It can be argued that, compared with the willingness that the European Court of Justice displays to adopt robust interpretations of the law, the performance of the British courts is far from impressive. For example, whilst the Court of Justice has been willing on a number of occasions to interpret the somewhat vague provisions of environmental Directives as laying down clear objective criteria (see, for example, *Commission v United Kingdom* (case C-56/90 [1993] ECR I-4109, where it stated that the criteria for designation as a traditional bathing water were objectively clear from Directive 76/160, and *Commission v Spain* (case C-355/90) [1993] ECR I-4221, where it held that the requirements for classification as a special protection area for birds were objectively clear from Directive 79/409), the British courts have always managed to find some hurdle to explain why the applicant should not succeed.

As a final example, in *R v Secretary of State for Trade and Industry, ex parte Duddridge* [1995] Env LR 151, the Divisional Court refused to apply the precautionary principle as part of English law. This principle is now enshrined within Article 130R(2) of the EC Treaty, as amended at Maastricht, but the court decided that it only laid down a general principle upon which EC policy on the environment should be based and did not impose any immediate obligations on Member States. Whilst this is not entirely surprising, the fact that the court also described the proposition that the principle should be adopted as part of British law as a matter of commonsense as 'startling' does, perhaps, illustrate that British judges may struggle when it comes to developing new principles to cope with the peculiarities of environmental litigation.

FIVE

The regulation of environmental protection

Despite the current vogue for suggesting economic or fiscal mechanisms for combating environmental problems, the system of regulation by public bodies remains the prime tool for environmental protection in this country. This commitment to regulation was reiterated in the White Paper *This Common Inheritance* (Cm 1200, 1990), which stated that 'administrative controls will for the foreseeable future remain at the heart of Britain's system of environmental control — just as they are in many other countries in the world', even at the same time as the possibility of using economic mechanisms is suggested as a future, additional, tool. More equivocally in *This Common Inheritance — The Second Year Report* (1992), the Conservative Government stated that there should in future be a presumption in favour of using economic instruments as opposed to direct regulation. The move away from common models of direct regulation appears to be gathering momentum. In the light of a statement of intent issued by the Treasury after the first Labour budget, it is likely that there will be continued emphasis on the use of economic instruments over the traditional forms of regulation. Whatever the political rhetoric, however, the use of taxation and subsidies will always be secondary to regulation in its widest sense.

What does regulation mean in this context? At one level all the word means is the use of rules to control activities. These could be criminal law rules, or civil law rules, or private non-legal rules operated by a body such as a trade association, or maybe even the 'rules' of the free market. In this book, however, the word regulation is used to mean administrative or bureaucratic regulation (i.e., the application of rules and procedures by public bodies so as to achieve a measure of control over activities carried on by individuals and firms).

Other means of controlling activities, such as the criminal law, the civil law and the use of the market, will be considered later, but since these are often subsidiary to administrative regulation, this will be explained first.

Administrative regulation

Administrative regulation is far more than just the setting of rules on what can and cannot be done. It denotes a coherent *system* of control in which the regulating body sets a framework for activities on an ongoing basis, with a view to conditioning and policing behaviour as well as laying down straight rules.

The advantages of such a system include the ability to provide uniformity, rationality and fairness between those who are regulated. Some form of public accountability is also produced by having a public body responsible for regulation. In particular, one advantage over the criminal law is that a coherent link can be made with other policies, so as to balance all relevant factors. This is often seen as an important part of the British approach to regulation: that it involves an explicit balancing of environmental factors with such things as economic and social considerations.

British regulatory systems can be said to exhibit a pragmatic and flexible approach. The same mechanism is not used for each situation. In some cases the reason is simply that it is recognised that a control mechanism that works for one problem is unlikely to work for a different one. This is a good illustration of the use of law as a tool or a technique to help to solve particular problems. In other cases, there are historical reasons, since one of the features of having a long history of environmental control is that the administrative structures have built up piecemeal and in response to problems as they arise. For example, many controls have in the past been given to local authorities purely because they happened to be dealing with similar matters already, or because there was no other relevant body around at the time.

The processes of regulatory decision-making

Before looking at the main features of regulation in this country, it is necessary to summarise the main processes or stages in regulatory decision-making. These are:

    (a)   the establishment of general policies;
    (b)   the setting of standards or specific policies in relation to the environmental issue concerned;
    (c)   the application of these standards and policies to individual situations;
    (d)   the enforcement of standards and permissions;
    (e)   the provision of information about the environment and the regulatory process.

(a)   The establishment of general policies

The process of establishing general policies is not really part of the regulatory system, but a necessary precondition for any system of environmental control. Having said that, one of the most obvious features of the British political system is the absence of formal national policies in many areas. Even where there are local or sectoral plans, there is often no national plan, or, if there is, it is made up of somewhat imprecise and flexible policies laid down in a variety of documents. A good illustration of the flexible nature of policy-making in Britain is provided by the town and country planning system, where the 'national plan' is to be found scattered amongst numerous Circulars, Planning Policy Guidance Notes, Ministerial decisions, White Papers and other assorted policy statements.

Given the essentially political nature of much of environmental law, the general tenor of the policies tends to be decided by Central Government. The presumption in favour of development in town planning is one example, but general decisions on energy and transport policy, such as the favouring of road transport over rail, or the retention of a nuclear power programme, are others. Certain political philosophies may also be imposed by Central Government; good examples are the principle of voluntariness in relation to controlling agricultural activities, or the policy of privatisation. However, because of the decentralised nature of much of pollution control, some general policies are effectively decided by bodies other than the elected Central Government. Other policies stem from general assumptions about the nature of the regulatory system itself — which we later refer to as the 'British approach' to environmental regulation (see p. 107).

A final factor is that the shape of many policies is now decided, or at least affected, by the EC. Arguably some of the most significant impacts on the environment in the next few years will follow from the establishment of the single European market and the countervailing powers adopted by the EC in terms of such things as regional and social policy.

(b)   The setting of standards or specific policies in relation to the environmental issue concerned
Any system of control must have some objectives that are set for it, otherwise it runs the risk of ceasing to be rational, uniform or fair. These may be fairly explicit objectives, such as air quality standards with specific maximum concentrations for a range of pollutants, or they may be far more vague, such as a water quality objective to the effect that a river should be capable of supporting fish.

In the past reliance has usually been placed on rather vague standards, such as the test of nuisance at common law, or the idea that best practicable means should be used to reduce gaseous emissions to the atmosphere. In addition, standards were often set in an informal manner, as used to happen with non-statutory water quality objectives. More specific and more formal standards are becoming far more common, a good example being the publication of Process Guidance Notes for processes covered by Part I of the EPA 1990. In the development control system, policies of this type are set out in development plans and in Planning Policy Guidance Notes. There is often overlap between this stage and stage (a) above.

(c)   The application of these standards and policies to individual situations
This is often seen as the central part of the regulatory process. There are numerous examples where a permission, authorisation, consent or licence is

required from a public body. (Different pieces of legislation use different words but they all mean essentially the same thing.) Whether one is granted, and the nature of any conditions attached, will normally be a discretionary decision, but one that is made by reference to the general standards established at stage (b). The application of standards may also be seen in such processes as court actions for nuisance and the specific application of whether best practicable means or best available techniques are being used.

(d) The enforcement of standards and permissions

In practice, one of the most important areas of environmental law is whether the legal instruments that are available are used, since there is often considerable discretion given to the regulatory body. 'Enforcement' covers a far wider range of matters than the single question whether to prosecute for breaches of the law. In any regulatory system, there is normally a whole range of administrative and other remedies available in addition to prosecution. The question of which remedy to use is also tied up with how the regulator should proceed. There is a wealth of evidence to show that informal methods of enforcement are often preferred, and that regulators normally adopt a 'compliance strategy' towards enforcement, rather than a 'sanctioning strategy' (i.e., one based on confrontation, see Chapter 6). Questions of inspection and monitoring also arise as part of the enforcement process.

(e) The provision of information about the environment and the regulatory process.

A theme which runs through the regulatory process concerns the openness of the system. This includes such questions as the production of official information on the state of the environment, the availability of public registers, and the publication of information about how the regulatory system itself works. Britain's traditionally secretive administrative processes are slowly becoming more open. This is most obvious in relation to stage (c), but is also apparent in the extension of public registers, enabling more information to be available for enforcement purposes. It may also be seen in the increased willingness of the Government to issue consultation papers before changes in the law and practice are adopted.

Anticipatory and continuing controls

Regulatory mechanisms may be divided into two general types, anticipatory controls and continuing controls.

Anticipatory controls

These are measures in which controls are imposed on an activity at its commencement in order to forestall potential environmental problems. Usually the objective is to prevent the activity unless certain requirements or conditions are met. The category includes a wide range of licensing-type controls, where permission of some sort is required before an activity may be started or carried on. These are normally complemented by a combination of criminal and administrative sanctions if the activity starts without permission, or if the permission is contravened.

The range of possible anticipatory controls is quite wide. It includes:

(a) An outright ban (e.g., the intended ban on the use of CFCs in products, or the prospective ban on the dumping of sewage sludge at sea). Of course, there is no *necessity* for a public regulatory body to be involved here, but someone will need to police the ban.

(b) A prohibition on an activity unless a particular body is notified in advance (e.g., the requirement under the Wildlife and Countryside Act 1981, s. 28 that owners and occupiers of a site of special scientific interest notify the relevant Nature Conservancy Council of any intention to carry out a potentially damaging operation, thus forewarning the Council of a possible need to take further protective steps).

(c) A prohibition on an activity unless it is registered, registration being something that cannot normally be refused by the registering body (e.g., there is a requirement that carriers of controlled waste register with the Environment Agency).

(d) A prohibition on an activity until a licence, permission, authorisation or consent is obtained, where the granting of the permission is at the discretion of the regulating body.

In relation to this last type, there are two distinct categories of permission or consent. Some are one-off permissions which, once granted, create what are in effect permanent rights because it is difficult to vary or revoke them. A good example is the granting of planning permission, where revocation entails the payment of compensation. Others provide for variation or revocation in the light of future circumstances. Most pollution control consents fall into this category, examples being the requirement to obtain an authorisation from the Environment Agency for carrying on a prescribed process, or a consent for a discharge to controlled waters.

Continuing controls
These are measures where the carrying out of an activity is controlled on a continuing basis. Typically they relate to the way an activity is carried on, so another way of referring to them would be as *operational* controls. An obvious example is the ongoing duty to comply with the terms of a consent, licence, authorisation, or permission granted by a pollution control authority, which will normally be combined with a range of other regulatory controls relating to monitoring and enforcement. The distinction between anticipatory controls and continuing controls is thus that one relates to *whether* an activity should be carried on in the first place, whilst the other relates to *how* it is carried on once it has started.

Of course, anticipatory and continuing controls are mutually supportive and most regulatory systems combine the two types of mechanism. Anticipatory controls still require some monitoring to ensure that the prohibited activity is not being carried on. Conversely, most continuing controls rest on the need for some initial permission before an activity may be started; indeed, the threat of withdrawal of the initial permission may well constitute the strongest inducement to comply with continuing regulatory requirements. For example, planning permission is required before a new activity is started, but that permission will often include conditions that require some adherence to defined standards over a period of time, such as permitted working hours or noise limits. Similarly, consents, authorisations and licences obtained from pollution control authorities normally combine the initial need for a consent with an ability to vary the requirements as the situation changes. This mutually supportive position is reinforced by the fact that many activities are subject to the requirements of more than one regulatory system.

Planning and prevention

The town and country planning system is the major system of anticipatory control in environmental law. To a large extent this stems from the very nature of planning control. It involves the preparation of plans, which may then guide future behaviour. The controls are necessarily imposed at the outset, whilst most pollution control mechanisms basically assume a continuing activity. Planning also mainly concerns land use, siting and locational issues that logically pre-date the operational controls.

A further reason results from practice. In these other systems, it is rare for the initial consent to be refused or revoked (although this power does remain as a threat for those who contravene the continuing controls). For example, it appears that no instance was ever recorded of a certificate of registration being refused under the Alkali Acts, either at the outset or on renewal (see Wood, *Planning Pollution Prevention,* 1989). In other areas of pollution control, the record may be slightly different, but there are still few examples of a consent from a pollution control authority actually being refused where there is already a planning permission.

One result is that the main burden of deciding whether a particular plant should go ahead normally falls upon the local planning authority. By way of example, a new factory will require planning permission as well as consents for emissions from the EA, and maybe the sewerage undertaker and local authority (in its capacity as regulator of air pollution) as well. It will be the local planning authority that decides whether to have the factory in that particular place. The pollution control authorities tend to see their task as setting limits on what is acceptable in terms of pollution from the site proposed rather than as stopping the development going ahead at all. Traditionally, these authorities have had little scope for saying, 'this development would be better somewhere else', though that is a matter they could raise when consulted by the local planning authority over the development proposal. (For an analysis of the relationship between the systems of planning and pollution control, see *Gateshead Metropolitan Borough Council* v *Secretary of State for the Environment* [1995] JPL 432.)

This is perhaps inevitable given the differences in nature between local planning authorities and other regulatory bodies. A local planning authority has a specific remit under the Town and Country Planning Act 1990, s. 70 to consider *all* material factors relating to a development, whilst other bodies often have a more limited range of relevant factors to consider in making their decision. It is also an elected body, where ultimate power resides with elected members, and therefore has greater legitimacy in terms of making a balanced policy decision to refuse a development.

Standards in environmental law

Most environmental controls rely on some form of measurable standard. This standard may be used as a guideline (i.e., an objective) or it may be used as a means of defining what an individual or firm may do. Indeed, one of the distinctive features of environmental regulation is that the regulatory body often has responsibility for defining the standard as well as enforcing its application.

There are a number of different types of standard, but a crude division can be made into those which are set by reference to the *target* which is being protected and those which are set by reference to the *source* of the pollution. Source-related standards may be further divided into emission standards, process standards and product standards. There are other factors that have a significant impact on the nature of a standard, such as whether it is centrally or locally set, uniform or flexible, precise or imprecise.

The following summary is not intended to be an exhaustive list of the various types of standard (from the list of variables above obviously the number of potential types is very great), but is an attempt to introduce a basic vocabulary of terms. It also aims to illustrate some of the more common methods used, together with some thoughts on their relative strengths and weaknesses. In a sense, these are the tools available to the legislator in deciding how a regulatory system is to work.

(a) Environmental quality standards (target standards)
Some standards concentrate on the effect on a particular target. In many cases, the protected target may be human beings and the standard is accordingly set by reference to the effect on them (e.g., the effect of radiation on workers). However, since this is a book about environmental protection, it will concentrate on situations where the protected target is the environment, or part of it. The phrases 'target standards' and 'environmental quality standards' will therefore be treated as interchangeable.

The effect on the target may be measured in different ways. It may relate to a biological effect, thus channelling all information directly into a consideration of the actual impact of a pollutant (e.g., a standard requiring that a discharge to water is not harmful to fish or aquatic animals). Alternatively, it may relate to the exposure of the target, from which certain biological or other effects may be presumed. In the environmental field, however, it will more usually relate simply to some measurable quality of the receiving environment, such as the level of a particular pollutant.

An environmental quality standard can therefore be defined as a standard where conformity is measured by reference to the effect of a pollutant on the receiving environment. It is unusual for the selected target to be the whole environment. More commonly a particular medium will be chosen as the reference point, such as air or water. In order to retain flexibility, there will frequently also be a geographical limitation: the standard may thus be set by reference to a particular river or area, or may be even more specific, such as where air quality or noise levels are fixed within factories or any other enclosed area.

Examples of environmental quality standards include:

(a)   setting air quality standards for the maximum or minimum concentration of any specified substance in air (e.g., the Air Quality Standards Regulations 1989 (SI 1989 No. 317) set mandatory standards for sulphur dioxide, nitrogen dioxide, lead and smoke);

(b)   setting water quality standards for the concentration of specified pollutants in 'controlled waters' (see p. 463, where the establishment of statutory water quality objectives is discussed);

(c)   the nuisance test at common law, under which property owners are entitled to the enjoyment of their property without unreasonable interference from neighbours.

It will be clear that these standards may be set by reference to any number of parameters. For example, a water quality standard could be set specifically for the maximum concentration of zinc, or a whole range of parameters may be used, as is the case for drinking water. It will also be clear that the standard can be precise or imprecise — the nuisance standard is a good example of an imprecise standard.

(b)   Emission standards

An emission standard can be defined as a standard where conformity is measured by reference to what is emitted rather than the effect on the receiving environment. Emission standards thus tend to concentrate on wastes produced. For example, the content of a discharge from a pipe or chimney could be controlled by reference to an emission standard.

Examples of emission standards include:

(a)   the maximum content of a particular substance in a liquid discharge from a pipe to a sewer or 'controlled waters';

(b)   the noise level measured as it emanates from a building;

(c)   the maximum content of a particular substance in an emission from chimney or exhaust pipe.

(c)   Process standards

A standard may be imposed on a process either by stipulating precisely the process which must be carried on, or by setting performance requirements that the process must reach. In the second case there would be a choice as to how to reach these requirements. These standards may relate to the whole of the process or, alternatively, to a part of it, such as the way that a product is made or the way effluent is treated. They may include requirements about the technology that is used, the raw materials, or operational factors such as whether the process is being carried out properly.

Examples of process standards include:

(a)   a requirement that a particular pre-treatment plant for effluent be used;
(b)   a stipulation on the height of a factory chimney;
(c)   a stipulation about the use of a particular grade or quality of fuel;
(d)   a requirement that the 'best available techniques not entailing excessive cost (BATNEEC) are used (see p. 325), though the general requirement is often translated into a set of emission standards in practice;
(e)   conditions attached to the operation of a landfill site or incinerator.

It is clear that current practice is to emphasise the use of process standards, and this is illustrated by their use in Part I of the EPA 1990. They are a good means of preventing harm to the environment arising in the first place.

(d)   Product standards

Product standards may be defined as where the characteristics of an item that is being produced are controlled. This may be done with the aim of protecting against damage the product may cause whilst it is being used, or when it is disposed of, or even during its manufacture. Examples include:

(a)   a requirement that all new cars are capable of running on unleaded petrol;
(b)   a requirement that cars are fitted with catalytic converters;
(c)   it may even be thought that requirements on the labelling of goods are a type of product standard.

Interrelationship of standards

Of course, these four types of standard are not exclusive of each other. An emission standard will often be set so as to achieve an environmental quality standard. Product standards for a car will include many matters relating to the emissions from it, such as lead, carbon dioxide or noise. In addition, the cumulative effect of these emissions will have an impact on the attainment or otherwise of any environmental quality standard.

Taking one particular, toxic pollutant, lead, environmental concentrations may be controlled in a number of ways:

(a)   Environmental quality standards may be set, stating that levels of lead should not rise above a certain level in the air, in water, or in the soil.
(b)   Emissions of lead may be controlled, so that any emission, whether into air or water or on to land, should not include more than a specified concentration of lead, to be set in some form of permission or consent.
(c)   Processes may be regulated to reduce the use of lead, or to reduce by good design possible emissions and escapes of lead into the environment.

(d)   Products likely to include lead may be regulated, either to ban its use (e.g., lead fishing weights) or to limit the use of lead (e.g., setting maximum amounts of lead in leaded petrol).

Other characteristics of standards

As stated earlier, a number of other matters are also important in relation to the nature of a standard. The standard may be a precise one, such as one set by reference to a scientifically provable maximum or minimum — often a numerical value. Alternatively, it may be an imprecise one, such as a requirement that 'best practicable means' (BPM) or BATNEEC are used, or one applying the common law test of nuisance.

The standard may be a uniform one across the country (or the EC), or it may vary from area to area. Indeed, it may be set on an individual basis. Certain matters demand uniform standards. For example, uniformity is normally desirable for emissions from mobile sources such as cars, otherwise problems are caused at boundaries. For similar reasons, most product standards are set on a uniform basis. It is strongly argued by some that uniformity creates equality, a particularly important consideration in the context of the EC and the single internal market. Limit values, as used by the EC in a number of Directives, create a special form of uniformity. They require that a certain standard is reached, but allow Member States to impose more stringent standards if circumstances require.

The standard may be set centrally or locally. This distinction tends to reflect the same division as that between uniform and individualised standards, since centrally set standards will usually be uniform whilst locally set ones will vary with the discretion given to the decision-maker. In this context, it must be remembered that traditionally, few standards in Britain have been set by legislation. Often this exercise was left to local bodies, although this is changing as EC standards permeate domestic environmental law.

Strengths and weaknesses of different types of standard

Obviously it is not possible to cover all types of standard, but it is possible to see the relative strengths and weaknesses of the more commonly used examples.

Environmental quality standards, by concentrating on what it is that requires protection, are able to deal with inputs to the environment from all sources and via all potential pathways, whilst the other mechanisms, used on their own, tend to permit cumulation of any particular pollutant. For the same reason, environmental quality standards can also cater for potentially harmful combinations of substances on the environment. They can thus enable a policy-maker to identify areas where work is needed, and channel resources effectively. They can also be tailored for particular circumstances, for example by being more stringent in sensitive areas than in others.

However, there are a number of limitations to environmental quality standards. They require constant monitoring of the environment, which may prove to be impractical or expensive. Enforcement poses difficulties, since failure to reach a standard may alert us to the existence of a problem, but does not necessarily tell us the cause or how to remedy it. For example, in order to clean up a river which is chronically contaminated with organic wastes, a regulator would first have to identify the causes of the pollution and then find some method of restricting inputs that was fair and enforceable. A further problem of environmental quality standards is that they may give no incentive to polluters to improve their performance in areas where the standard is already being met.

The very nature of environmental quality standards is that they tend to be set as *objectives* rather than as legal requirements, except in those situations where there is a limited number of sources and targets, such as enclosed work environments. This use as objectives makes them useful at the strategic and planning stages of the regulatory process (see pp. 96–7). For example, development plans often set environmental quality standards, even if they are frequently very imprecise, such as a policy that developments liable to cause a nuisance should not be permitted in a defined area.

By contrast, the strength of emission standards is that they are relatively easy to control and monitor by sampling at the point of emission. Enforcement is also easier because of the simplicity of the causation requirements where there is a point of discharge. In addition, an emission standard may be tightened progressively to encourage a discharger to improve the process, whilst still retaining choice as to how this is done.

A main drawback of emission standards relates to the difficulty of controlling diffuse (or non-point) emissions, such as fertiliser or pesticide run-off, by these means. There is also the difficulty (shared with process standards and product standards) of organising a system that can cope with an accumulation of similar emissions in one area, such as car exhausts in Los Angeles or similar industrial concerns in one water catchment area. This second difficulty is not an insoluble problem, however. It may be tackled by setting very strict local emission standards, by linking them explicitly to an environmental quality standard, or by applying the 'bubble' approach (i.e., by aggregating together all emissions in a particular area and permitting a total amount of emissions for that area).

Process standards are obviously limited to where there is a process to control and thus tend to apply mainly to the manufacturing industry. Their main strength is that they may be set so as to prevent a problem arising in the first place. They may also help to pool resources for research at a central level. There is a potential disincentive for producers to find more effective ways of reducing pollution, unless the standards are made progressively stricter, or are periodically altered, or are set at levels that force the producer to develop the technology so as to reach the standard (so-called 'technology forcing' rules).

Product standards are similarly limited to where there is a product and have similar strengths and weaknesses as process standards. As stated above, both categories also have difficulty in catering for the cumulative effect of pollutants on their own.

Locally set and centrally set standards: Britain versus the EC

It has often been noted that Britain and the rest of the EC do not seem to see eye to eye on pollution control. This is sometimes translated into a conflict between a British preference for locally set and variable (i.e., non-uniform) emission standards, set by reference to local environmental quality, and an EC preference for centrally set uniform emission standards. Haigh (in *EEC Environmental Policy and Britain*) points out that any conflict on these grounds has been much exaggerated (see below).

Nevertheless, these two types of standard provide an excellent opportunity for a case study on their relative strengths and weaknesses.

Locally set and variable emission standards set by reference to local environmental quality

Each of the features of this combination of ideas merits some mention. Referring everything to environmental quality can be said to target controls where they are needed — at the protection of the environment. In this way, the impact of non-point emissions and background levels of pollution may be taken into account, as well as discharges from pipes and chimneys. The fact that neither the emission standards nor the environmental quality standards are uniform provides flexibility. This enables more sensitive areas to be protected more strictly, or polluters who are seen as more useful to the community to be treated more leniently. In all cases, a great deal of discretion is granted to decision-makers. It is also argued that, since standards can be varied to take account of local circumstances, the mechanism is economically efficient. For example, greater pollutant loads could be permitted in remote, unpopulated areas or where the self-cleansing properties of the local environment are greater.

Centrally set uniform emission standards

These have obvious advantages. Uniform standards are easily imposed, easily implemented and easily monitored. They are fair between polluters since all are treated the same, and they avoid difficult problems about allocating the right to pollute amongst different polluters. As a result they may be relatively cheap for the regulator to operate, because they involve less administrative discretion than variable standards. They also fit in well with the economic principles of the EC's common market.

On the other hand, they can be said not to allow local conditions to be taken into account, because there is no flexibility (although this can be provided at the enforcement stage). They are meant to be unable to deal with the situation where there is a number of polluters in one area, since there is no jurisdiction to reduce the emission standard to fit local conditions. They are also sometimes said to lead to the possibility of a uniformly polluted country if there is one relevant discharge in every area. These last two criticisms are rather too general, since good use of preventative controls would help in both cases.

Why Britain and the EC differ

It is not difficult to think of reasons why Britain may differ from other Member States within the EC. As an island, Britain has no frontiers. Thus, the argument about fairness has never had the impact that it has in France and Germany, which share the Rhine as a border, and where the inequality of one factory being allowed to discharge more than another on the other bank is obvious. Other factors stem from the 'British approach' to pollution control, such as that Britain has a tradition of discretionary, local decision-making and a system based on pragmatism, in which the effects on the environment are balanced with social, economic and political factors.

But the main argument for the British position probably stems from self-interest. With its rainy climate, fast-running streams, ample coastline and relative remoteness, Britain can claim a comparative advantage when it comes to pollution. Put very crudely, the same discharge is supposed to cause less pollution in Britain than in other countries, because of its lesser effect on the environment. When it comes to setting standards, some people in Britain do not see why stringent uniform standards should apply across the EC if they have no justification in terms of environmental protection in the British context, even if they provide that protection elsewhere.

As stated earlier, the differences have been exaggerated. Even discounting the influence of EC legislation, there are many examples of uniform emission standards applying in Britain, although this is sometimes hidden by being the product of administrative practice rather than legislative action. This is especially the case in relation to dangerous substances, where no amount of discretionary balancing with other factors will make them safe. Also the differences set out above relate mainly to water pollution, which is, arguably, the area where Britain has the greatest comparative advantage. Even in relation to water pollution, the differences have mainly surfaced over one particular Directive — the framework Directive 76/464 on Dangerous Substances in Water. It was in relation to this Directive that Britain's position led to alternative regimes being adopted for the control of dangerous substances (see p. 439). But, as Haigh points out, it seems that what the other EC Member States saw as cause for concern was not the use of environmental quality objectives to define the context for the setting of variable discharge consents, but the fact that these quality standards were, at the time, informal, unpublished, and set by regional authorities. It is not hard to imagine that other Member States thought they were being told that the British approach to controlling dangerous substances was that 'it all depends on the circumstances'.

As a final point, it should be noted that in any case Directive 76/464 did *not* lay down uniform emission standards. It laid down limit values, and many of the arguments against uniform emission standards do not apply to these, because there is the flexibility to have a stricter standard if desirable.

The 'British approach' to regulation

Since administrative regulation can take many forms, it is important to establish the distinctive features of the British style or approach. In other words, what types of rules and standards are employed? How are they set and by whom? How are they enforced and by whom? What role does the public play in these processes?

In *National Styles of Regulation* (1986), Vogel identifies a number of characteristics of the British style. The book claims to be 'an examination of British environmental policy as seen through the eyes of a student of American politics', and consists of a comparison of approaches to environmental regulation in Britain and the USA. Vogel writes that Britain's regulatory style is characterised by flexibility and informality, and summarises the system as involving:

> An absence of statutory standards, minimal use of prosecution, a flexible enforcement strategy, considerable administrative discretion, decentralised implementation, close co-operation between regulators and the regulated, and restrictions on the ability of non-industry constituents to participate in the regulatory process.

At the risk of producing an unmanageable list, to these points could be added others, such as delegation of decision-making to autonomous quasi-governmental and non-governmental bodies, extensive use of industrial self-regulation, a limited availability of legislative and judicial scrutiny of regulators, a gradualist approach to change, reliance on scientific knowledge for decision-making and habitual reference to economic factors before decisions are made.

Vogel compares this approach with that of the USA, which he characterises as rule-oriented, normally employing rigid and uniform standards, and making little use of industrial self-regulation. In addition, less use is made there of administrative discretion, prosecution is much more common, there is great executive and judicial scrutiny of regulators and technology-forcing rules are favoured. All of these features lead to conflict between regulator and regulated and to an adversary mentality.

Of course many of these differences are not unique to environmental regulation in the two countries, but are a matter of general political culture. They probably stem from different attitudes towards regulation engendered by different population densities and degrees of cultural homogeneity. In Britain the need for a balancing process is all too clear, whilst in the USA the 'frontier mentality' is understandably more prevalent.

At this point a warning should be given. Since the 1960s the situation in the USA has changed dramatically, and what Vogel describes in the 1980s is quite different from what happened before. Similarly, the British approach is currently changing quite rapidly. The informal and flexible basis remains, but the approach has undoubtedly got more open, more centralised, more legalistic and more contentious, especially in the last 10 years or so. The changes in legislation have been substantial, but there have also been more disguised internal changes of practice by regulators. As a result, Vogel's analysis is beginning to look outdated.

One crucial factor in this change is the attitude of the EC. The British approach has tended to conflict with that adopted by other Member States and has had to be modified to fit in with that. At the same time, the increased profile of environmental issues, particularly international ones requiring common responses, has led to some changes of style out of political necessity. A further factor which influenced the change away from the traditional British approach was the political preferences of the Conservative administration which governed during a period of radical change in the regulation of environmental protection. The major policy features of the administration included the rejection of long-term planning in favour of market forces, deregulation of unnecessary bureaucratic controls, privatisation of public services, imposition of strict spending controls on public bodies, the general weakening of local authority power, and the use of voluntary controls allowing choice wherever possible. All of these have all left significant legacies for the incoming Labour administration. At the time of writing it is too early to assess the potential effects of the change in government but it is likely that many of the previous policy aims will be adapted rather than radically altered. The only obvious changes in policy which can be identified at this early stage are the integration of environmental policy into other areas and the emphasis on local decision-making via the establishment of regional bodies.

The following sections will explore some of the manifestations and implications of the British approach, and will seek to illustrate just how it is changing and in what direction. However, it must be stressed that this is only a general approach. No-one would suggest that all these symptoms are displayed by each of the various regulatory processes in the country, merely that these are recognisable general features.

The implications of the British approach also vary at the different stages identified earlier, with the result that, for example, general policy-making remains mainly a central function, rather than being particularly decentralised (although many of these general policies are now in practice agreed at international or EC level). Nevertheless, the general features of the regulatory system can be illustrated by considering a number of key issues.

Decentralisation

Decision-making is decentralised in three ways: by being given to a wide range of bodies, by significant use of delegation, and by geographical decentralisation.

There are a range of bodies exercising environmental responsibilities (see Chapter 3). Although the creation of the Environment Agency unified a variety of pollution control functions, Britain still has a large number of autonomous or semi-autonomous environmental agencies, such as the Nature Conservancy Councils, the Health and Safety Executive, the Nuclear Installations Inspectorate, and the Countryside Commission. Local authorities also have wide-ranging environmental protection powers in relation to such things as air pollution, contaminated land, noise control, town and country planning and environmental health. Traditionally, there has also been decentralisation within central government. For many years the nominal responsibility for environmental policy has rested with the Department of the

Environment. This has obscured the fact that many decisions and policies which have important environmental effects have been made by other Departments including the Department of Trade and Industry (e.g., on power stations and transmission lines), the Department of Transport (e.g., on emissions from vehicles and the routes of new roads) and the Ministry of Agriculture, Fisheries and Food (e.g., on agricultural support schemes). The diversity is compounded by the tendency to have separate bodies in Wales and Scotland. Under the newly created Department of the Environment, Transport and the Regions (referred to in this book as the Department of the Environment for the sake of brevity), there has been some acknowledgement that there is a need to re-integrate certain aspects of environmental policy and the introduction of the Environmental Audit Committee should ensure that the environmental implications of all decision-making are at least considered, although previous attempts to set up a similar body under the Conservative administration did not meet with much success. Although these moves suggest a greater use of centralised policy-making powers, these must be balanced against the re-emphasis of regional policy-making and the plans for devolution for Scotland and, to a lesser extent, Wales.

Even within the Department of the Environment, matters are often delegated. For example, appeals against refusals of planning permission are normally dealt with by the Planning Inspectorate Executive Agency, although this remains formally part of the Department of the Environment.

Over the years this decentralisation of power has tended to result in a rather incoherent environmental policy, with very little uniformity across the country. Even such a central function as the monitoring of the environment has tended to be done in an uncoordinated way. There have been a number of changes in recent years which have altered matters. For example, the regulation of water pollution was organised on a regional basis until 1989, when the NRA was established as a national body covering England and Wales. HMIP was created in 1987 to draw together a number of inspectorates at that time operating separately within the Department of the Environment and the Health and Safety Executive. Both these institutional changes clearly fostered uniformity in decision-making. The Environment Act 1995 created the Environment Agency for England and Wales and the Scottish Environment Protection Agency for Scotland, thus continuing the process of producing a more coherent and uniform institutional structure.

Decisions are also commonly made locally. Local authorities have the wide powers referred to above, whilst many of the inspectorates and other agencies operate on a regional basis, granting some discretion to local decision-makers. There is a philosophy underpinning this, of course. The British approach is geared pragmatically towards the protection of the receiving environment, so it is sensible that decisions are taken by people or bodies with a knowledge of local conditions, whether environmental, social or economic.

An important change has been the centralisation of policy decisions in recent years. This has been most marked in relation to matters where there is conflict between central and local government. For example, in the town and country planning system, increased intervention in local decisions by

Central Government was the major issue of the 1980s. It was manifested mainly through hard-hitting and directory Circulars, which were applied on appeal so as to alter the policy context of most planning decisions, though there were also changes to the law and in institutional structure designed to reduce local control, through such creations as urban development corporations. However, centralisation is also a reality in relation to pollution control. For example, local authorities have lost a significant amount of discretion in relation to air pollution as a result of the implementation of Part I of the EPA 1990, whereas the EA has taken over the waste regulation functions previously carried out by local authorities. Even in an area where local authorities have been given new powers, such as in the regulation of historic contamination under Part IIA of the EPA 1990, they are obliged to act in accordance with central guidance or are subject to technical advice from the EA.

Centralisation may also be seen at work in the control of public spending. The regional water authorities were severely limited for many years in their ability to make capital expenditure decisions, and the same is true for local authorities. For bodies such as the Countryside Commission which rely almost entirely on Government grant, the position is even clearer.

Finally there is a very significant element of centralisation involved in the relationship between Britain and the EC. Not only is EC decision-making essentially secret, but there is little input to it by local or regional bodies in Britain. However, the crucial point is that EC law is binding on Member States. The requirement to conform with it, coupled with the policy goal of uniformity throughout the EC, means that power is taken away from local and non-governmental bodies and given to central bodies. This is clearly true in relation to the first two stages of the regulatory processes identified earlier (the policy-making and objective-setting stages), and it is becoming increasingly true for the third stage (the operational stage of setting individual consents) as well.

Discretion

The amount of discretion is great at all the stages of regulatory decision-making. Parliament rarely sets firm policies and standards in legislation, allowing for these to be defined in delegated legislation or through administrative guidance. For example, in the town and country planning system the nature of central guidance is nowhere dictated in the legislation, but is set out in Government Circulars and Planning Policy Guidance Notes, which may be altered at any time.

At the standard-setting and consent-setting levels the discretion is usually given to the relevant regulatory body. As examples, local planning authorities have the ability to grant or refuse planning permission as they think fit (subject mainly to the Secretary of State's control over policy on appeal), the Environment Agency has discretion over the setting of standards for discharges to water and in the definition of 'best available techniques not entailing excessive cost' (BATNEEC).

A similar wide discretion can be seen at the enforcement stage. There are few statutes which lay down duties to enforce the legislation, or which set out statutory factors to take into account, and usually the decision whether to take action is taken by the regulatory body on the basis of practical and political factors which are not mentioned in the legislation. Since many of the most important remedies are administrative remedies which are unavailable to individuals, this discretion is of enormous practical importance. Enforcement is discussed in greater detail in Chapter 6.

Judicial interference is frequently limited by the width of discretions given in legislation. This is best illustrated in the town and country planning legislation, where there is a clear policy of judicial non-intervention in decisions about the weight to be attached to material considerations. An example of this policy was shown in *London Residuary Body* v *Lambeth London Borough Council* [1990] 1 WLR 744, where the Secretary of State's decision to grant planning permission for office development in London County Hall was held to be unchallengeable by the House of Lords. This was so even though he had accorded overriding weight to the presumption in favour of development where there was nothing else in favour of the development and some grounds against. A different example is the decision in *R* v *Secretary of State for the Environment, ex parte Rose Theatre Trust Co.* [1990] 1 QB 504, where a decision by the Secretary of State not to make the site and remains of the Rose Theatre a scheduled ancient monument was held to be unchallengeable because of the width of the discretion given in the legislation. There are few cases on the extent of the discretion given to pollution control authorities, but it can be expected that the courts would adopt a similar non-interventionist stance there.

As a result of all these factors, and also the general British preference for variable rather than uniform standards, the British system of environmental control has become characterised by flexibility and lack of uniformity.

Gradualism and reliance on scientific evidence

The place of these ideas as two of the key tenets of British pollution control is emphasised in Department of the Environment Pollution Paper No. 11, *Environmental Standards — The UK Practice*. This very readable document was published in 1975 and is now somewhat out-of-date, but it has great significance in terms of explaining the British approach to pollution control, since it is effectively a justification of that approach in the face of alternatives being put forward within the EC.

The philosophy of gradualism is that pollution controls should be strengthened gradually as economic circumstances, the goodwill of producers and scientific abilities allow. This links very strongly with the related idea that decisions should be taken on the basis of a reliable scientific base, although it should be recognised that science does not necessarily produce facts in the environmental sphere, but estimates of risks or probabilities. There is accordingly always a political factor involved in whether to accept a risk or not (see below).

One major effect of these two ideas has been that environmental controls have tended to be reactive rather than anticipatory. They have rarely been concerned with laying down a framework in advance, leading to the fragmentation of the system and to its lack of uniformity. A more specific effect is that time is normally given for changes to be made in order to give industry time to adjust capital programmes and work methods. In relation to the requirement that best practicable means be used, it was normal practice to allow any process to continue for its operational life (often 10 years) before declaring it in contravention of the requirement, even though it may have been superseded before then. A similar discretion is provided for in relation to BATNEEC under the EPA 1990, but the time allowed for changes is typically much shorter.

The extended time scale for implementing the 1990 Act (full implementation did not take place until 1996), apart from being a comment on the complexity of the new requirements, is a further example of the gradualist approach. Interestingly, the timetable for the introduction of Part I of the Act was laid down after an undertaking was given in Parliament to do so, and thus avoid a re-run of the non-implementation of the Control of Pollution Act 1974. At the EC level, this approach is also reflected in the time scale allowed for implementation of Directives, which is normally at least two years, and often five years. A final example is that the British have frequently rejected the use of 'technology-forcing' rules. These represent the setting of a rule which is stricter than currently achievable, though with a time scale for its achievement. The theory is that producers will thus be forced to adapt their current technology to meet the requirements. This concept is much used in the USA, but in Britain the potential cost to industry is more frequently used to argue for a gradual change.

The importance of context

In establishing environmental controls, importance is nearly always attached to economic and other factors. As Pollution Paper No. 11 puts it:

> The tendency in setting standards in the UK is less to seek an absolute scientific base than to use scientific principles and all relevant and reliable evidence, then to try and progressively reduce emissions in a way that is consistent with economic and technological feasibility and with what at any one time is thought to be an acceptable ultimate objective.

It is difficult to separate the reasons for this policy from its effects. One reason is undoubtedly the historical influence that the town and country planning system, with its explicit requirement to balance all material considerations, has had on the development of the law, but a major reason must relate to the definition of pollution and the objectives of environmental controls.

Pollution has been defined as a relative concept, in the sense that there is no absolute rule about what amounts to pollution. The same applies to other forms of environmental change, such as urban or agricultural development. It is not possible to eradicate pollution, merely to reduce it. It follows that, at some stage, a choice has to be made about what is, and what is not, permissible. This is ultimately a political question, and involves a balancing of various factors. However, there are two possible objectives of pollution control. One is to aim to reduce pollution to 'acceptable' levels. An alternative is to aim to reduce pollution as far as possible. In Britain the first approach is implicitly adopted in relation to most substances. This explains the inevitability of a political balancing process, and also the preference for variable environmental quality standards. The second approach tends to lead to a reduction in discretion and to greater reliance on uniform standards, because if one producer can reduce to a particular level others should be able to do so as well.

The contextual approach accepts, therefore, that there is always going to be a trade-off between environmental protection and other factors, such as cost. This is fundamental to most British environmental controls. For example, it is reflected in the phrase 'best available techniques not entailing excessive cost' (BATNEEC) which is the cornerstone of Part I of the EPA 1990. The best available techniques part of the formula suggests that every step should be taken to protect the environment, but the not entailing excessive cost part qualifies it by reference to economic factors. One of the most interesting features of the interpretation of the 1990 Act is proving to be the way that the balance is being struck in practice between the two parts.

This philosophy of balancing environmental protection with material welfare is apparent in most areas of the law. It explains the wide discretions given to decision-makers, the emphasis on decisions being taken by reference to local factors, and the practice of defining some concepts after consultation with the industry involved. The emphasis on balance also explains such fundamental features of British law as the preference for flexible environmental standards rather than uniform ones, and the flexible and cooperative enforcement strategies that are employed by regulatory agencies.

Are things changing?

As the previous section suggests, a number of things appear to be changing in relation to the traditional British approach to regulation. In particular, there is an increasing tendency for standards to be set centrally (which often goes hand in hand with more uniform standards), and a related tendency for them to be set out more explicitly in legislative instruments or formal policy documents. This has been referred to as 'the new formalism' by Macrory (see 'Environmental Law: Shifting Discretions and the New Formalism' in *Frontiers of Environmental Law,* ed. Lomas, 1991).

A number of examples could be used to illustrate the point. Perhaps the clearest relates to the way that EC standards are imposed through Directives, thus effectively replacing local discretion with central prescription, but there are also examples from domestic legislation. In relation to water pollution, a major change over the next few years will be the setting of statutory water quality objectives by the Secretary of State for stretches of controlled waters. The Environment Agency is under a duty (under the Water Resources Act 1991, s. 84) to exercise its powers so as to ensure, as far as it is practicable to do so, that the statutory water quality objective is achieved at all times. This covers, amongst other things, its powers in relation to setting discharge consents and clearly entails the whole process becoming more open and predictable (see p. 463). A similar process can be seen at work in the town planning requirement (in the Town and Country Planning Act 1990, s. 54A) that decisions are to be made in accordance with the provisions of the development plan, unless material considerations indicate otherwise (see p. 251). A third example can be taken from Part I of the EPA 1990. The very full, clear and precise advice provided in Process Guidance Notes as to the meaning of BATNEEC in relation to each process has in practice reduced the discretion of individual inspectors quite significantly. As a result, the in-built conflict between the two parts of the BATNEEC definition that is referred to above seems to be being decided very much in favour of BAT, particularly as far as local authority air pollution control is concerned. This is because individual inspectors, who have to cope with a very wide range of different processes, are likely to impose the standards in the relevant Process Guidance Notes in full unless the operator can come up with a good reason why they should not.

As well as centralising decisions and reducing discretions, this new formalism also increases the potential role of the courts. It has already been noted how the courts have played a lesser role in the development of environmental policy in this country than in, for example, Germany or the USA. This is probably because of the wider discretions provided in the legislation, which are often unchallengeable. However, the development of more explicit standards, coupled with clear operational duties imposed on the regulatory agencies, means that a greater number of decisions may potentially be challenged through judicial review. A good example is the duty imposed on the Environment Agency under the Water Resources Act 1991, s. 84, referred to above: it is quite possible that this could be used in the future to compel the agency to adopt a certain course of action. The likelihood of the courts playing an increasing role in the development of environmental law is further increased by recent developments in relation to judicial review and EC law. For example, the concept of the supremacy of EC law has been used to develop various doctrines with the aim of ensuring not only that legislation is passed to implement EC Directives, but also that the laws that are passed are implemented and enforced in practice.

Of course, much of this discussion is only of real relevance to regulatory systems. If, as may be the case in the future, market mechanisms are preferred to regulation, they may represent a force moving in the opposite direction. One of the potential results of deregulation and a shift towards the use of market mechanisms is a decentralisation of decisions from Government to consumers and industry.

There is another general change that can be identified, which is that there is a discernible shift away from reliance on flexible standards based on the impact on the receiving environment towards standards based on the use of the best available techniques. This is seen at its clearest in relation to Part I of the EPA 1990, where the conditions attached to authorisations are set by reference to BATNEEC, but it is also an inevitable by-product of a more centralised and formal system. It also follows from the increased involvement of lenders, insurers and other stakeholders in decisions on environmental management, since they are likely to insist on the use of the best available techniques as a protection against liability or loss of their stake.

Deregulation

This term appears to carry three separate, but overlapping, meanings. One refers to the so-called 'war on red tape', which the last Conservative Government pursued over their final years of government: in other words, that excessively bureaucratic procedures and practices should be removed or simplified. A second meaning relates to the general disinclination to use regulatory mechanisms unless they are necessary, which often translates into favouring voluntary and market-style mechanisms. A third meaning can be discerned in terms of a policy not to interfere with the operations of business. It is clear that the last Government pursued deregulatory policies in each of these senses for many years: the pursuit of these policies culminated in the announcement, in 1993, of a 'deregulation initiative', which formalised the process and resulted in the active search for examples of perceived over-regulation by government departments.

The Deregulation and Contracting Out Act 1994 was the main manifesta-tion of this process and still remains on the statute book notwithstanding the change of Government. It includes a general power for any Minister to amend or repeal existing legislation by means of a statutory instrument if they are of the opinion that the measure imposes a burden on any trade, business or profession, and that the amendment or repeal will reduce that burden. There are some limited consultation and procedural requirements that temper this very wide power, but it is clear that it could be used in the future to attack a number of environmental protections. In addition, s. 5 of the 1994 Act empowers Ministers to 'improve' various enforcement procedures (a term which includes such things as revocation and variation of a licence, as well as criminal prosecution) by statutory instrument. For example, the Minister may, in relation to any specific enforcement regime, require that a business be notified in advance of any intention to take enforcement action and afforded an opportunity to make representations and be entitled to a written statement explaining why remedial action is being taken. The Act also provides some very vaguely worded provisions allowing Ministers to provide for appeals against enforcement action. Whilst it is arguable that these provisions, if used, would create greater accountability in terms of enforce-ment decisions taken by regulatory agencies, it is difficult to see how these two new powers remove 'red tape' in the first sense used above, since they appear to impose extra requirements. The real justification behind them appears to be in accordance with the third meaning of deregulation used above.

Some of the effects of the Act can be seen in the EA's Code of Practice on Enforcement (see further p. 147). Although other environmental targets have been identified, the real impact of the deregulation initiative on environmental law remains to be seen. In particular there is a great deal of uncertainty over the future of the initiative given the seeming antipathy of the present administration to the idea of deregulation.

Meanwhile, it did result in some limited changes in the Environment Act 1995. Schedule 10 to the Water Resources Act 1991 was altered so as to reduce the amount of public involvement in the setting of discharge consents. The schedule also extended the period within which consents may not be varied from two years to four. However, somewhat ironically, the other matter in the 1995 Act which could be said to be deregulatory in the first sense used above actually had the effect of increasing environmental protection, since s. 111 repealed the requirement for a tripartite sample in certain legal proceedings, thus making it easier for the EA to bring prosecutions.

Market mechanisms or the use of economic tools

These rather general phrases are meant to encompass all approaches which seek to use prices or economic incentives and deterrents to achieve environmental objectives. This could be done, for example, by encouraging pricing systems that signal the true environmental costs of products to consumers, thereby making environment-friendly items cheaper than those that pollute or waste natural resources. In a sense, therefore, these economic tools or instruments are the exact opposite of using the free market, since they normally involve an interference or intervention in the free market for the purpose of environmental protection. However, they do involve the use of the market in the sense that they are normally designed to allow consumers and industry to make choices about their actions. By way of contrast, many people would argue that most, though certainly not all, regulatory systems tend to operate so as to remove choice.

There is thus a potential confusion in referring simply to 'using the market' for environmental protection ends, since that runs together the policy of allowing an unrestricted free market to allocate resources on the assumption that that is somehow more efficient, and the separate policy of intervention in the market for protective purposes. As Nicholas Ridley, a devoted free marketeer, wrote in an explanation of the Conservative Government's environment policy whilst Secretary of State for the Environment: 'It is an essential part of the free market philosophy that regulation by Government is necessary to secure the public interest in environmental protection' (*Politics Against Pollution: The Conservative Record and Principles*, Centre for Policy Studies, 1989).

Annex A to the White Paper *This Common Inheritance* (Cm 1200, 1990) discusses a range of different ways in which economic instruments may be used to further environmental protection. These build on five general categories identified by the Organisation for Economic Cooperation and Development, namely, charges, subsidies, deposit or refund schemes, the creation of a market in pollution credits and enforcement incentives. It is accepted in the White Paper that charges and subsidies have constituted the main uses of economic instruments so far. It also becomes clear that some of the mechanisms are self-standing whilst others, such as most charging schemes, require a regulatory framework and proper policing, so they must be seen as additional to, rather than separate from, regulatory systems.

In addition to direct economic instruments there are some recent examples of legislative schemes which have the indirect effect of creating a market which has environmental benefits. Indeed, although they do not involve any direct taxation, many of those affected by the legislation view the effects in that way. For example, the legislation dealing with the obligation imposed on producers of packaging to meet certain recovery and recycling targets will effectively create a market in packaging recovery notes (PRNs) by compelling producers to demonstrate compliance with the statutory targets through the purchase of PRNs from authorised reprocessors (see further p. 369). This, in turn, should act as a direct financial incentive to reduce the amount of packaging in circulation. The creation of the market is, of course, an indirect effect of the legislative provisions, but it is nevertheless an intended effect. Similar points could be made about the legislative scheme dealing with contaminated land — the use of a legislative scheme to drive the market and to act as an incentive to promote the cost-effective remediation of contaminated land has appeal as it provides the certainty of regulation in addition to the political acceptability of the use of the market.

A selection of economic tools or instruments is considered below.

(a) Charges for the administrative cost of operating the regulatory system

This now goes under the title of 'cost recovery charging' and has been adopted in relation to a number of regulatory activities. The idea is to recover the regulatory costs that are incurred in granting applications or consents, or in such things as inspecting, monitoring or policing those consents. The current policy is not to charge for the general costs of operating the whole regulatory system, but to limit the charge to the amount which can be referable to each consent or discharge. In the interests of administrative simplicity, the charges are normally arranged in bands, rather than being worked out individually.

For example, in relation to water pollution, a scheme of charging for applications for consent was introduced in October 1990. This was intended to recoup the costs of administering the application procedures for discharge consents. More significantly, annual charges to recover the cost to the NRA (and subsequently the EA) of policing any discharges to controlled waters were introduced on 1 July 1991 (see the *Scheme of Charges in Respect of Applications and Consents for Discharges to Controlled Waters*). These are set so as to recoup the costs associated with inspecting and monitoring discharges, not the full cost of monitoring water quality, which will still be paid for by the taxpayer (see p. 52).

Similar schemes were introduced from 1 April 1991 for applications and authorisations for operating a process subject to integrated pollution control (*HMIP Integrated Pollution Control Fees and Charges Scheme (England and*

Wales)) and for local authority air pollution control *(Local Enforcing Authorities Air Pollution Fees and Charges Scheme (England and Wales))*. In the Integrated Pollution Control Scheme, the various processes subject to integrated pollution control have been divided into components and a flat rate is payable for each component. This is an attempt to cover the approximate cost to the EA of granting and monitoring an authorisation. A further scheme has been introduced for waste management licences.

Cost recovery charging systems may be progressive and thus have a beneficial environmental effect. For example, the charging schemes referred to involve higher charges for discharges which cost more to monitor, and these are often those which cause more pollution.

Fees for planning applications were introduced in the early 1980s. At present there are standard fees set according to the size and nature of the proposed development and they do not reflect the full cost to the local planning authority of processing the application, much less the cost of policing the system of planning controls. However, it is proposed to increase these fees over the next few years so that more of the full cost of the system is recovered.

There always has been a rather different system of charging for discharges to sewers. This involves a rate for domestic consumers which is linked to property value, and a variable rate for trade dischargers linked to the volume and strength of the discharge as measured by Chemical Oxygen Demand. This produces a relatively unsophisticated method of charging for the cost of sewage treatment according to the demands made upon the system by the discharge. An incidental effect of concentrating on volume is, however, to reduce the level of water used and the level of waste, and thus to encourage both conservation of resources and recycling.

(b)   Charges reflecting the full environmental cost of an activity
The system of charging for sewage discharges shows the potential for use of charging systems which aim to charge for the full environmental cost of an activity. Such systems may be seen as the true environmental or pollution taxes referred to by Pearce, Markandya and Barbier in *Blueprint for a Green Economy,* 1989. The most controversial example is the so-called 'carbon tax'. The objective behind this idea is to raise the price of fossil fuels to reflect their true (and hitherto uncosted) environmental effect, thus curtailing their use and reducing the greenhouse effect. There are distinct problems with such an idea. One is obtaining sufficient information about the discharge or process to make the taxes work properly. This would seem to demand a strong regulatory structure to police the system, although self-monitoring methods may have a large part to play in this respect. Another is the problem of obtaining accurate information about environmental effects on which to base the tax levels.

There is no doubt that this is an idea which is going to be greatly used in the future, and the Government has, on a number of occasions, promised to consider it for discharges to 'controlled waters'. However, despite the recommendation of the Royal Commission on Environmental Pollution in its

Sixteenth Report, *Freshwater Quality* (Cm 1966, 1992), that a system of charges reflecting impact on the environment should replace the present system of cost-recovery charges in order to act as an incentive to clean up environmentally harmful discharges, little has yet happened. It is significant that powers to introduce such environmental charges were not included in the Environment Act 1995. The proposed framework Directive on Water Resources has raised the prospect of a system of cost-recovery charges again, and we can expect a continued debate on the issue over the next few years (see further p. 445).

(c)   Charges to finance environmental or pollution control measures
A number of examples may be given here. The EA may, under the Water Resources Act 1991, s. 161, pass costs incurred in preventing or remedying water pollution back to the person who caused it. The EA may also recover costs incurred in cleaning up unlawful deposits of waste from the occupier or the person who made the deposit (EPA 1990, s. 59). In relation to statutory nuisances, there are similar clean-up and cost-recovery powers available to local authorities in EPA 1990, s. 81.

Fines levied in court for offences may also be seen as a form of environmental charge. Indeed, given the nature of environmental offences and the limited moral blame often attached to them, many people treat fines as administrative penalties rather than as true criminal sanctions. The typically low level of fines means that their economic effect is limited, though levels are rising steadily, for example, the maximum fine for many environmental offences was raised to £20,000 on summary conviction by the EPA 1990. In the Crown Court, Shell (UK) was fined £1m for polluting the River Mersey, in addition to which it paid a reported £6m in clean-up and other costs. However, at present there is no way of ensuring that fines are actually used for the benefit of the environment or that part of it which is damaged. One interesting development in this respect is the decision in *Herbert* v *Lambeth London Borough Council* (1991) 90 LGR 310, that a compensation order may be made under the Powers of Criminal Courts Act 1973, s. 35, where damage has been caused by a statutory nuisance, although there is a statutory limit of £5,000 on the sum which may be awarded.

Civil law remedies may also be seen as achieving the same objectives. Many statutes now include civil liability for damage to people or their property, and the creation of a remedy of breach of statutory duty may act as a potent method of reallocating costs. The drawback at present is that few civil actions recognise fully the costs involved in environmental damage. The law has never developed any concept of 'environmental rights', with the result that the only possible civil law claimants are people with private rights. Put more simply, animals, birds and plants do not have civil law rights. The debate on the introduction of liability for environmental damage is likely to intensify with the European Commission pressing for a unified liability scheme amongst Member States. The history of these proposals can be traced back to the draft Directive on Civil Liability for Damage Caused by Waste (COM 91 219 (final)) which has since disappeared without trace. This introduced the concept of 'impairment of the environment' and provided that any plaintiff should be entitled to recover for costs incurred in preventing or remedying harm to the environment (in addition to damages for injury to persons or property), as well as obtaining injunctive remedies. This approach was very broadly followed in 1993 by the Lugano Convention on Civil Liability for Damage Arising from Activities Presenting a Danger to the Environment. There are current proposals to develop a liability scheme, the detail of which will be contained in a White Paper, to be published before the end of 1998. In introducing a Community-wide liability scheme the Commission could recommend that the EC accede to the Convention or it could propose a new Directive which would establish the regime in Member States. The inclusion of damage to the unowned environment will probably be an integral part of any new proposal. Whatever approach is taken, it may signal a new development of environmental 'rights'.

(d)   Charges levied on polluting materials or processes

Instead of a charge being levied on the results of pollution, it could be levied on a process or a product. The best example is the landfill tax that was announced by the Chancellor of the Exchequer in November 1994 and which was introduced in October 1996. The idea is that a tax is payable on all waste that is disposed of to landfill. It is expected that the amount of the tax will be passed back by the operators of the landfill site to the originators of the waste, thus increasing the cost of landfill and acting as an incentive to reduce the amount of waste produced. The potency of the incentive relates to the level of the tax. Originally, it was proposed by the Government that the tax should be based on the value of the waste, but it was pointed out by many commentators that this might lead to cost-sensitive producers of waste sending it to cheaper sites, which are likely to be precisely those sites where environmental standards are lowest, and lead to undesirable transportation of wastes in an attempt to find a cheaper site. It was subsequently announced that the tax would be based on the weight of the waste, with inert wastes (such as demolition wastes) subject to a lower rate to reflect their lesser environmental impact. Landfill operators are able to obtain rebates from the tax by setting up environmental trusts which promote sustainable waste management practices (see further p. 367).

The tax is somewhat of a breakthrough since, although it has been appreciated for some time that taxes could be used to combat pollution and contamination problems, little has been achieved. However, the Treasury has always vigorously opposed any attempt to earmark taxes and charges for specific spending purposes (a process known as 'hypothecation') and, without that, a subsidiary aim of environmental taxes, which is that they should be linked directly to environmental spending, will not be achieved. For example, the proceeds from the landfill tax could be used to fund the clean-up of 'orphaned' closed landfill sites (i.e., those where the original operator cannot be found or does not have the resources to afford the clean-up), although the environmental trust funds may also be used in the same way. Nevertheless, the introduction of a landfill tax may well herald a faster development of environmental taxes in the future.

An alternative is that a charge may be reduced for relatively environment-friendly activities. The most obvious example is the reduced tax payable on unleaded petrol compared with leaded petrol. This has led to a significant rise in the use of unleaded petrol over the last few years. A further example is the EPA 1990, s. 52, which introduced the concept of waste recycling credits for authorities or others who retain waste for the purpose of recycling it.

(e) Subsidies and grants

These are commonly used for environmental ends, although their use within the EC is restricted by the rules on illegal state aids. For example, subsidies are available for the construction of facilities for the improvement of the treatment of agricultural water and silage effluent — both particularly potent, and increasingly common, causes of pollution. Care has to be taken that the subsidies achieve the result intended. Some subsidies on forestry and agriculture, for example, have been accused of having detrimental environmental effects because of their inability to select between beneficial and non-beneficial projects.

Compensation payments for environmentally sensitive activities may also be seen in this category. The prevailing policy in relation to countryside protection has tended to be one of voluntariness, whereby farmers and landowners are compensated for agreeing to forgo certain advantages in the interests of the environment. Sometimes this is through the payment of direct compensation and sometimes through the negotiation of management agreements. For example, management agreements may be agreed in relation to the protection of national nature reserves or sites of special scientific interest, and similar methods are being used in other designated areas such as environmentally sensitive areas and nitrate sensitive areas.

(f) The creation of a market in pollution credits

A further instrument is the use of tradeable quotas, or emissions trading. These are methods of creating a market in the right to pollute. For example, a total for emissions of a specified substance may be set for a particular area. Firms may then bid for the right to take up a part of that total. Prospective or new polluters would have to buy the rights of existing holders if there was no spare capacity. By restricting the available emissions, prices would be driven up, providing an incentive to reduce emissions or to develop alternatives.

The idea is most developed in the USA, but the groundwork for its use in Britain is laid in the EPA 1990, s. 3(5), which allows the Secretary of State to establish total emissions of any substance either nationally or for a limited area, and to allocate quotas, with power progressively to reduce the total allowed. This idea is designed for use in relation to the commitment to cut carbon dioxide emissions by specified dates (currently the EC commitment is to stabilise emissions at 1990 levels by 2000), as agreed internationally as a method of combating global warming. Once again, a regulatory structure would be needed to police the system.

(g) Deposit and refund schemes

Although deposit and refund schemes are clearly severe interferences with a free market, it is also clear that they may have an enormous impact on the amount of waste produced. Traditionally, the Conservative administration favoured voluntary mechanisms here, rather than ones imposed by law. By way of example, the British Government intervened in the *Danish Bottles* case (*Commission* v *Denmark* (case 302/86) [1988] ECR 4607) in the European Court of Justice, supporting the EC Commission's argument that a Danish law requiring drinks containers to be returnable was contrary to the free market principles of the EC. The Court of Justice upheld most of the Danish scheme despite its clear anti-competitive effect, on the grounds that the aim of environmental protection justified some interference with the operation of the single internal market within the EC. It will be interesting to see how the Labour Government develops the use of such schemes.

Future uses of economic instruments

The above summary is not intended to be an exhaustive list of those mechanisms which might be tried, or even of those which are already in use, but to give an idea of the type of instrument that may be available. As stated before, there is little doubt that market-related instruments will increasingly be used in the future. Indeed, they could currently be said to be 'flavour of the month' as far as environmental regulation is concerned.

One reason for this is that market mechanisms have a degree of political acceptability which crosses current party political ideological boundaries. There is a strong link with the principle of choice, the idea that people should be given a choice of how to act, as long as their actions do not breach some generally accepted limits. This idea is seen most strongly in the realm of town and country planning where the importance attached to market forces is made explicit in much of Central Government policy advice. The principle is also seen in relation to such things as the adoption of voluntary methods of protection in the countryside (see Chapter 17) and the preference for pollution control systems which set objectives whilst leaving producers to work out for themselves how to achieve them. There is also a strong link with the related policy of deregulation pursued throughout the 1980s and 1990s and explained in White Papers such as *Lifting the Burden* (Cmnd 9571, 1985) and *Building Businesses, Not Barriers* (Cmnd 9794, 1986). Amongst other things, this policy amounts to a rejection of imposed restrictions in favour of agreed ones and a removal of unnecessary state powers.

Within the EC, the Commission has also suggested a shift in EC environmental policy towards the greater use of economic instruments rather than the administrative regulation approach. Appropriately enough, this suggestion was originally linked to the EC-wide system of environment-friendly labelling for goods, recognising that in order for any of these market-based methods to work there needs to be accurate information available to consumers and regulators. It is significant that EC action has been concentrated in this area in the 1990s. For example, 1990 saw the agreement of Directive

90/313 on Freedom of Access to Information on the Environment and Regulation 1210/90 on the establishment of the European Environment Agency, which will initially have a role in acquiring and disseminating information about the state of the environment in the EC.

The polluter pays principle

The EC can claim another important contribution to the development of economic instruments; its environmental policy has always included the adoption of the 'polluter pays' principle, although it was probably the Organisation for Economic Cooperation and Development (OECD) which first popularised the idea in the early 1970s (see OECD, *The Polluter Pays Principle*, 1975). The principle basically means that the producer of goods or other items should be responsible for the costs of preventing or dealing with any pollution which the process causes. This includes environmental costs as well as direct costs to people or property. It also covers costs incurred in avoiding pollution, and not just those related to remedying any damage. There is a very strong link between the principle and the idea that prevention is better than cure. It will also be clear from the foregoing discussion that these costs should include the full environmental costs, not just those which are immediately tangible.

The relevance of this principle to the discussion of economic instruments is obvious, since a producer will have to pass on any costs in the price of goods to the ultimate consumer. However, this is only a principle, it has no legal force and there is no agreed definition that has anything approaching the precision of a statute. On the contrary, there has frequently been dispute over its exact scope, especially over the limits on payments for damage caused. It is essentially a guide to desirable courses of action, but it is fairly clear that it has rarely been fully satisfied in either EC or British environmental legislation.

As a result the principle has sometimes seemed to be all things to all people, and has even been used to justify views with which it has little connection, for example the suggestion that producers may pollute as long as they pay for it. That is a complete misunderstanding of the principle's true meaning, and the potential abuse of such an imprecise phrase should be appreciated.

Eco-auditing and environmental management systems

Within the context of economic instruments, it is appropriate to consider briefly the development of environmental management systems and environmental auditing, a rare area where Britain can claim to lead the world in the development of an environmental concept. Many firms are now tackling the increased pressures and potential liabilities imposed by environmental law by adopting some form of environmental management system. Indeed, it is likely that compliance with a recognised system will soon become a requirement of the purchasing policies of some major purchasers, or be required by a firm's lenders or insurers. Some form of environmental reporting in company accounts is also likely to be required in the future.

There are three main systems currently being put forward, though there are other industry-based systems as well:

(a) The British Standards Institute has developed a British Standard 7750 on Environmental Management Systems, which was launched in 1994 following a pilot programme. BS 7750 is a voluntary system in the sense that a firm can choose whether to adopt it or not. It is based on a quality management approach similar to BS 5750 on Quality Management, with the result that no specific levels of environmental performance are stipulated, the setting of the firm's environmental objectives being a matter for the firm itself. However, the firm must have a publicly available environmental policy, which must include at a minimum a commitment to meeting legal standards and a commitment to improved environmental performance. Having established an environmental policy, the firm should carry out an initial review of its position, including the compilation of a register of relevant legislation and policy requirements and a separate register of environmental effects. It should then set environmental objectives and targets, establish a management programme so that these targets can be met, and set up the appropriate operational controls and records systems. Finally, the company should audit its activities to check conformity with the programme, and review the policy and objectives in the light of that audit.

(b) EC Regulation 1836/93 on Eco-Management and Audit came into force in April 1995, having been agreed in 1993. Since a Regulation is directly applicable in Member States, it becomes part of British law automatically without the need for implementing legislation and will thus lay down a uniform EC-wide system.

The objectives of the EC Eco-Management and Audit Scheme (EMAS) are similar to those behind BS 7750, in that they are to promote improvements in industry's environmental performance by the establishment and implementation of environmental management systems by companies, and the systematic, objective and periodic evaluation of the environmental performance of these systems. One area where the EC Regulation goes further than BS 7750 is in requiring the provision of information on a firm's environmental performance to the public. For example, an environmental statement, which must include such things as a summary of the relevant figures on pollutant emissions, waste generation, raw material usage and energy and water consumption, must be published every year. This statement has to be validated by an independent, accredited verifier, who will also verify the company's policy, objectives and audit programme for conformity with the Regulation.

(c) The International Organisation for Standardisation (ISO) has issued an Environmental Management Standard known as ISO 14000. The standard deals with similar matters to BS 7750 and the EMAS scheme. Associated with the basic standard are a number of other related ISO standards (14000 series) providing guidance on various environmental issues, including auditing, qualification criteria, environmental labelling and life-cycle assessment.

BS 7750, EMAS and ISO 14001 represent a significant step forward in improving and formalising environmental management systems. They are not without criticism as the standard of the accreditation bodies can differ. Generally it is accepted that (in the case of BS 7750) accreditation provides significant advantages in terms of customer requirements, corporate image and liability minimisation.

So what is the difference between the three standards? They have similarities in terms of the constituent components. Each requires:

- An understanding of the environmental impacts created by the business.
- An environmental policy stating the intention and principles of the organisation in relation to its overall environmental performance.
- Broad and detailed environmental goals with specific performance targets.
- An environmental management programme which is designed to meet those goals.
- Appropriate control procedures for activities.
- A system for internal auditing of the EMS.

The similarities between BS 7750 and EMAS are striking. The only major difference is that under EMAS there are additional requirements for the preparation of a publicly available environmental statement based on a preparatory environmental review. The compatibility between EMAS and BS 7750 means that if a site has been certified to BS 7750, the basic management system will also satisfy the corresponding requirements of EMAS. Thus for companies attempting to gain accreditation under BS 7750 there is no need to incur further costs in having these aspects separately verified for the purposes of registration under EMAS.

The introduction of ISO 14001 is also expected to slot into any existing accreditation under BS 7750. It is likely that ISO DIS 14001 certificates will be added to BS 7750 certificates issued, subject to the certification body checking that the organisation with the certified EMS has properly considered a further 14 points in the light of ISO 14000 requirements. These include:

- A commitment to 'prevention of pollution'.
- A commitment to comply with legislation and other requirements.
- A management review is undertaken by top management.
- Training must include awareness of the environmental benefits of improved personnel performance and roles and responsibilities in emergencies.
- Continual improvement is not qualified (as it is under BS 7750).

Of course in some cases no change will be necessary as BS 7750 certification might have included these aspects.

Accreditation under the new standards should have great significance where a business is involved in European and world markets. It is quite clear that EMAS and ISO 14001 will have a significant impact in those markets over the next 10 years.

One further factor which is relevant to this discussion is the attractiveness of registration in terms of developing a targeted approach to enforcement. Industry groups and the Departments of the Environment and Trade and Industry under the Conservative Government suggested that sites which are certified to these environmental management standards should be subjected to less regulatory scrutiny and pay lower fees and charges as a result of the reduced supervision time required.

Mention should also be made of eco-labelling. There is an EC Regulation on the subject (880/92), which was implemented in Britain through the establishment of an Eco-labelling Board in November 1992. The essence of the scheme is that criteria are developed to enable the environmental impact of a product to be analysed by taking into account the whole of its life cycle. Criteria are currently being developed for a limited range of products, with the intention that a proportion of the products within the range can be awarded an eco-label. Despite delays caused by methodological problems, the first eco-labels for washing machines and a small range of other products have now been agreed.

The civil law as a tool for environmental protection

The detailed role of the civil law is considered in Chapter 8. However, as pointed out in the section on charges (see p. 120), the civil law can be seen as a form of market mechanism, so it is worth making a few general comments about civil liability in this chapter. There is little doubt that the last few years have seen a great increase in interest in the use that can be made of civil law mechanisms — by policy-makers as well as by lawyers. Recognising that civil liability appears to fit in well with the basic principles of EC environmental policy, such as the polluter pays principle, the EC issued a Green Paper on civil liability in 1993 entitled *Remedying Environmental Damage* (COM(93)47 final). It is likely that this Green Paper will be revised before the end of 1998 when it is expected that the Commission will submit a White Paper on the introduction of a Community-wide liability scheme. The Green Paper comes down generally in favour of the development of regimes based on strict liability, where causation rather than fault would be the dominant factor behind a finding of liability. Where no liability could be shown, or where the person liable has gone bankrupt or is untraceable, some form of fund paid for by relevant industries or activities would be established to compensate plaintiffs. One unresolved issue relates to whether all activities should be subject to strict liability, or whether it should be limited (as it has generally been in Britain) to specific, more hazardous activities. The proposed EC Directive on Civil Liability for Damage Caused by Waste envisages a wide-ranging liability for all waste (although little movement is expected on the introduction of these proposals), whilst the Council of Europe

Lugano Convention on Civil Liability for Damage Resulting from Activities Dangerous to the Environment, 1993, as its name suggests, proposes strict liability for only a limited range of activities.

The imposition of civil liability has other effects as well as simply sorting out the question of liability for specific incidents. It acts as an incentive to act in a particular way, because of the high possible risks. In so doing, it fulfils the precautionary principle and fits in well with the current EC emphasis on shared responsibility, since producers will act so as to reduce and manage risks themselves. It thus acts as a stimulus to integrate risk management principles into all levels of business decision-making, as there is little doubt that the threat of civil action is a potent one, especially in an age when insurance against such risks is hard to obtain.

The criminal law as a tool for environmental protection

The criminal law can be used either to provide direct criminal sanctions for environmental harm, or in a subsidiary and complementary role within a regulatory system. It tends to be of greater use in the second way. This is because the main purpose of the criminal law is to punish clearly identified wrongs. Yet, in relation to many environmental matters, it is often impossible to identify wrong without reference to other factors. For example, it is clearly desirable to have industry and many other activities which may cause pollution. The question is not a simple one of whether to have them, but a more difficult one of how much pollution is acceptable (see also the definition of pollution on p. 23). That requires a balancing of the various factors involved against what is reasonable — a discretionary, political process, for which the regulatory system is well-suited. The criminal law is rather inadequate for such a balancing process, and thus tends to be used mainly to deal either with clear acts of environmental vandalism, or to support the regulatory system once it has decided what is and what is not acceptable.

There are a number of examples of offences which stem directly from environmental harm. Under the EPA 1990, s. 87, it is an offence to drop or deposit litter in a public or other specified place. In the Water Resources Act 1991, s. 85, there is a general offence of causing or knowingly permitting any poisonous, noxious or polluting matter to enter controlled waters. It is not always necessary to show actual harm to the environment, (e.g., see, in the case of water pollution, *R* v *Dovermoss Ltd* [1995] Env LR 258): in some cases an activity may be prohibited because harm can be assumed to follow or because the risk of harm is too great to take. For example, under the Clean Air Act 1993 it is an offence to emit dark smoke from premises.

However, even in these cases, enforcement is often left to a public body. One reason for this is practical, given the difficulty in some situations of identifying and proving environmental harm. Another reason is that the right of prosecution has often been restricted in English law. This is becoming less common, but a good example is the restriction in relation to water pollution. Under the Rivers (Prevention of Pollution) Acts 1951 and 1961, which established a system of consents for discharges to water for the first time and also a general pollution offence in similar terms to the Water Resources Act 1991, s. 85, it was provided that a prosecution could only be brought by a water authority, or with the consent of the Attorney-General. This restriction was removed by the Control of Pollution Act 1974, with the result that there is now a right of private prosecution for all the basic water pollution offences.

A third reason for enforcement being left to public bodies is the lack of available public information relating to pollution. Under the Rivers (Prevention of Pollution) Acts, there was no public register of consents, samples taken of water quality, or samples taken of discharges; indeed it was an offence for water authority officers to disclose such information gained in the course of their duties. Under the Control of Pollution Act 1974, a system of public registers was first established, which is starting to remove the secrecy of earlier years. Similar limitations on private prosecution and access to information have been present in most areas of environmental law over the years.

The most frequent use of the criminal law is therefore in a subsidiary capacity to administrative controls (i.e., to the regulatory system). Many criminal offences consist not of committing a direct act of pollution, but instead of ignoring the dictates of the regulatory body. Under the Water Resources Act 1991, s. 85, it is a criminal offence to discharge trade or sewage effluent without, or in breach of, a consent from the EA. In relation to town and country planning, the offence consists not of breaching planning control but of ignoring an enforcement notice. This makes the criminal offence truly subsidiary to the regulatory process, since only the local planning authority may issue an enforcement notice, thus taking the possibility of enforcement away from the public. The scope of these offences has been widened with the unification of enforcement powers within the Environment Agency

All of these matters have an effect in decriminalising the law. The offence is not directly linked to the environmental harm, but to an administrative process. Enforcement is normally by an administrative body and often for breach of an administrative requirement. The message that is given is that these things are truly related to administrative processes rather than the criminal law. In addition, the low sentences that are imposed (sometimes because only low sentences are available), the marked reluctance to prosecute, the limited amount of moral censure that has traditionally been attached to environmental offences, the lowly status of many who are selected for prosecution and the escape of many major industrial polluters from prosecution (all factors which are discussed elsewhere in this book) tend to emphasise the decriminalisation of the laws. Once again, however, there is no doubt that things are changing very rapidly as a result of changes in the perception of the general public. One development in the future may well be the making of an overt distinction between 'administrative' offences against the regulatory system and true environmental offences, with higher personal penalties being available in the latter category.

SIX

The enforcement of environmental law

The British approach to enforcement

Essentially, enforcement is carried out by regulatory bodies. Although there are supplementary powers available to those with private rights under the common law, there are inherent disadvantages in relying upon extra-statutory powers to control the protection of the environment (see Chapter 8). Moreover, the right to bring private prosecutions is unavailable for the majority of administrative breaches (see p. 129).

The identity of the enforcement model exercised by those regulatory bodies is strongly underscored by the themes which dominate Part I of this book. For instance, flexibility in both the setting of standards and the methodology of pollution abatement, use of non-statutory 'guidance' to control emission standards, large degrees of open texture within statutory definitions to enable enforcement bodies to utilise discretionary powers and the reliance upon self-policing based upon the mutual self-interest of industrialists and enforcement officers are characteristic of the British approach to enforcement. One important point, however, needs to be made at the outset of this chapter: most of what follows is a discussion of the enforcement attitudes towards breaches of pollution control legislation. There is very little discussion of the wider issues of enforcement in the field of environmental protection generally. There are a number of reasons for this. First, the bulk of the theoretical research on the enforcement of environmental rules has taken place in the field of pollution control. Secondly, other areas rely much more heavily on other controls such as the use of voluntary mechanisms. In the case of nature conservation, for instance, the range of enforcement mechanisms is narrow and the system is largely maintained through the use of management agreements, which provide civil sanctions for breach (for further discussion of the enforcement strategies in relation to nature conservation see Withrington and Jones 'The enforcement of conservation legislation: protecting sites of special scientific interest in Howarth and Rodgers (eds), *Agriculture, Conservation and Land Use* (University of Wales Press, 1995). Thirdly, the

general principles discussed can be applied in other areas with slight modifications. For example, enforcement in the planning system is strongly influenced by the models which are discussed below, but with the important
distinction that there is an underpinning, explicit, policy background by
which all enforcement action is to be judged, in the form of the local
development plan and any other relevant considerations such as national
policies. Finally the description of the enforcement model in relation to
pollution control does tend to throw the issues surrounding the enforcement
of environmental law into sharpest relief and whilst it does not illustrate all
of the problems it provides an initial building block upon which other models
can be imposed.

It is possible to identify two different models which are utilised in the
enforcement process: first, the cooperative (or conciliatory) model and,
secondly, the confrontational approach. The cooperative approach is characterised by the development of a continuing relationship between enforcer and
polluter. Thus, mutual respect and trust develop which can be utilised to
ensure that there is compliance with a system of law, or, in the case of
environmental protection, of quality standards. The confrontational approach
involves the penalising of activities. At its extreme, such an approach can
result in the punishment of every breach.

The nature of enforcement mechanisms in environmental protection

Regulatory enforcement is concerned with the use of tools or mechanisms to
achieve an objective. It is not *only* concerned with punishment but also with
bringing about compliance.

At one end of the enforcement spectrum, powers of prosecution enable
regulatory bodies to punish one-off incidents, but the use of the criminal
sanction is only one in a variety of mechanisms used to control activities.
Formal enforcement tools which are more administrative in nature are also
available. For instance, the EPA 1990 contains provisions which allow for
authorisations to be varied or revoked and for activities to be prohibited or
to be subject to enforcement procedures without any reference to the criminal
courts. When the Environment Agency was created, the range and scope of
these administrative enforcement mechanisms were increased with the unification of enforcement powers for all environmental media. Thus the EA now
has the power to take action against breaches of a discharge consent by way
of enforcement notice (see the Water Resources Act 1991, s. 90B, inserted
by the Environment Act 1995, sch. 22). This seemingly minor change in the
law could have a marked practical effect on the manner in which the law is
enforced by increasing the enforcement options available to the EA without
the need for criminal sanctions — once again illustrating that the selection of
legal mechanisms is an integral part of any regulatory system.

Furthermore, there are 'informal' tools. The word 'informal' here does not
necessarily indicate that such controls are not serious. There are stages in all
enforcement procedures which can be identified as being the 'last warning'
or penultimate step before 'formal' action. These are not formal sanctions in

the true sense. For example, the service of an abatement notice or a notice for the requisition of ownership details under the Town and Country Planning Act 1990 are 'formal' steps which can lead to prosecution although there is no element of punishment explicit in such action when taken in isolation.

Further down the severity scale of regulatory enforcement lie such informal mechanisms as threats or an increased number of visits from an enforcement officer. Such tools will be used at an initial stage in an enforcement procedure, but do not constitute sanctions.

Lastly, there are informal problem-solving mechanisms. The idea that the regulatory bodies can be viewed as consultants or educators underpins the cooperative approach so prevalent in Britain.

Throughout any discussion of the legal context of the practical enforcement of pollution control, it must be borne in mind that those bodies who regulate activities often do so with an 'active' discretion; that is to say a discretion which actually defines the limits of what is permissible in any case. Such an approach is clearly evidenced by the use of non-statutory guidance notes to set emission standards. Moreover, there is further discretion over and above this 'active' discretion; when enforcement bodies decide whether or not to seek a sanction for the breach of these standards.

The legal context

The vast majority of pollution offences are defined as offences of strict liability. That is to say there does not need to be proof of any negligence or fault on behalf of the defendant/offender for liability to attach. Indeed, most pollution offences tend to be accidental in the sense that there is no premeditation on behalf of the person responsible. However, with offences of strict liability, theoretically every breach should amount to an offence as there is no element of fault, the absence of which can be offered as a defence. Nevertheless, when the figures are examined, the incidence of prosecution for environmental pollution offences is remarkably low. By way of example the South-West and Southern Water Authorities brought no prosecutions for water pollution offences in 1988 and 1989. Other authorities were also relatively reluctant to prosecute. This should be viewed against a background where figures show that in certain areas as few as 35% of discharges of trade effluents are made at levels which are in compliance with their consents. Thus, there is an apparent dichotomy between the theory of strict liability and the exercise of the discretion as to enforcement. How has this situation arisen?

The pollution control system in Britain has all the characteristics of an administrative and bureaucratic regulatory system. Within the wider definition of regulatory systems it falls into the same class as many other analogous systems, including the system of the criminal law.

However, one of the major differences between the regulatory system of pollution control and the criminal regulatory system is that the central aim of the pollution system is to *prevent* harm to the environment and/or human health rather than to detect and then punish those who cause harm. Often, under environmental legislation, enforcement agencies utilise regulations to control continuing activity rather than to penalise single offences. The basis of this mechanism of control is the fostering of an ongoing relationship between the enforcers and those who pollute. By encouraging the use of a system which controls activities rather than punishes, this relationship is cultivated.

This relationship can only exist because of the wide amount of discretion used in interpreting regulations; this allows 'technically' guilty offenders in breach of regulations to avoid liability. The methods that the enforcement authorities use are largely peculiar to the pollution control system. The enforcement agencies will normally carry out specific statutory enforcement activities only when there is a belief (on behalf of the individual officer of the agency concerned) that the continuing relationship between the enforcers and the polluters is being ignored. The breakdown is characterised by an increasing unpleasantness and a move away from a cooperative approach for as long as an unauthorised activity is carried on.

There have been three main studies carried out which have examined the activities of enforcement bodies in England. The first and second, *Environment and Enforcement* (Hawkins) and *Policing Pollution* (Richardson, Ogus and Burrows) investigated the enforcement mechanisms utilised under the old-style water authorities. The third, *The Reasonable Arm of the Law* (Hutter) looked at the role of local authority environmental health officers. By questioning officers at length about their attitudes to enforcement in relation to both 'offenders' and the offence itself, all three studies provide an in-depth study of the themes of environmental enforcement. Further studies carried out in Scotland gave similar findings (see Watchman, Barker and Rowan-Robinson 'River pollution: a case for a pragmatic approach to enforcement' [1988] JPL 764).

The evidence presented in these three studies demonstrates that the enforcement agencies often walk a tight-rope between a cooperative approach and the effective enforcement of environmental legislation. *Policing Pollution* indicated that out in the 'real world' of environmental enforcement the final sanction of prosecution for the breach of a regulation was very rarely used. In the study it was shown that officers believed that prosecutions tended to upset offenders to such an extent that any cooperation or continuing relationship built up between the two parties was quickly and effectively demolished. Moreover, officers tended to utilise a quasi-enforcement system based upon 'informal' mechanisms of enforcement as perceived by individual officers rather than as provided for in regulations.

It was shown that prosecution was used only in approximately 10 cases out of every 3,000 breaches of the trade effluent discharge consent system. These statistics raised an obvious question — why was there such a reluctance to prosecute on behalf of the enforcement authorities?

The attitude towards the offence

One of the main reasons for encouraging a cooperative, continuing relationship rather than a confrontational approach is the moral ambivalence surrounding regulatory offences. For a long time pollution offences were regarded as morally neutral. Research suggested that although the enforcement agencies were enforcing the same standards for all polluters they were not necessarily concerned with the standards themselves. Instead they tended to look at the intent behind the act of pollution.

The discretion used in enforcing the strict regulations were identified as being within a 'doughnut-ring' of decision-making. Enforcement officers used this discretion to attach moral blame to a particular incident by altering the level of a particular sanction involved with the moral opprobrium which they felt towards the activity. This was one explanation of the extremely low prosecution rate, as the enforcing authorities were reluctant to use the ultimate sanction of prosecution unless the level of moral blame was at the top end of the scale, which could be equated with gross criminal negligence or actual intent on behalf of the offender. Most accidents were and are not viewed as being morally offensive as 'they could have happened to anyone'. Secondly, the enforcement agencies tended to have grave doubts about the level of criminal penalties involved for breach of the regulatory system. The fines were notoriously low and therefore were not always seen as an effective sanction when compared to the profits which were often generated from the polluting activities. Additionally, the low level of punishment tended to reinforce the view that it was not only the enforcers who had morally ambivalent views of the offence, but the judiciary as well.

Moreover, the typical attitude to 'white collar crimes' suggested that offences committed as a result of industrial activity were less heinous than normal offences. It was often said that pollution was a natural consequence of industrial activity which also created jobs. For the balance to be weighted in favour of protecting against harm to the environment therefore, the need to protect had to outweigh significantly the utility of the process in creating jobs.

Traditionally, those who have polluted have been of a high status in society and those affected by pollution of low status. Pollution was more commonplace in working-class areas of high industrial activity. Indeed, many of those living in the area were working in the factory which was polluting the area. It was often seen as a way of life rather than a matter for complaint.

Commentators have also identified the existence of the so-called capture theory in the relationship between the polluters and enforcement agencies. The capture theory testifies to the belief that large corporations (as the traditional polluters) have a large degree of control over the enforcers by using the traditional power-relationship model. Thus, the smaller enforcement agencies are traditionally in awe of the larger powerful corporations who not only are worth many millions of pounds but also have tremendous influence.

Attitudes towards the offender

The attitude towards the offender was not necessarily based upon the actual cause of the pollution incident but what the enforcement agencies believed to be the cause of the pollution incident. Research has shown that where there were problems with trade effluent discharges, offenders were far more likely to be prosecuted if they made their relationship with the enforcement agency more difficult. The reverse was also true: if the offender had a good relationship with the enforcement agency then it was less likely that a prosecution would ensue. This brought an element of 'just deserts' into the enforcement process; moral blame was more likely to attach to an offender where previous warnings had been given of a particular danger. The work of the enforcement agencies was technically and scientifically based rather than based on the sanctions available under the law. They had perceived that their relationship with the offender was designed to help to achieve a particular solution rather than enforcing the regulations by the letter of the law. Cooperation with the polluters to achieve a better quality environment rather than confrontation was always seen to be their objective.

Enforcement agencies tended to view offenders in three different groups:

(a)   Business firms seen as amoral calculators. The view of the enforcement agencies was that certain businesses are motivated entirely by profit and would disobey the law when they calculated that it was in their interest to do so. The enforcement agencies tended to view this type of operation with considerable disdain and were far more likely to want to prosecute every breach.

(b)   Firms seen as political citizens. The operators of these businesses were perceived as going about their business properly and any breach of the regulation was likely to be on the basis that the operators felt that the regulation was unreasonable and was requiring them to carry out actions which were unnecessary in a purely commercial sense.

(c)   Firms seen as organisationally incompetent. These firms could be characterised as ignorant and beset by organisational difficulties rather than possessing any particular moral attitude. In practice, non-compliance by them was perceived by the enforcement agencies as bad housekeeping derived from a lack of understanding or a lack of responsibility on behalf of the individuals in charge of industrial processes. Enforcement agencies were unwilling to identify such firms as amoral calculators because of their perception of the individuals within them.

In the last type of case, the enforcement agencies utilised a cooperative approach which gave them the role of educator/consultant rather than policeman. Another underlying reason or justification for this cooperative approach was shown perversely in the enforcement agencies' attitude to those who they viewed as being amoral calculators. It has been said that where an amoral calculator was identified it was quite clear that they would enforce the regulations strongly and severe punishment would result. However, it was argued that the understaffing of the enforcement agencies meant that prosecutions in all cases of breach would be impossible and therefore it was imperative that the cooperative approach be taken. It was felt that industry could 'pull out the plug' if a confrontational approach were taken. Indeed, one officer was quoted as saying 'if we lose cooperation we lose control'. Thus, the need for cooperation was mutual.

The use of sanctions other than prosecution

As the regulatory system of pollution control was and is concerned with the continuing prevention of harm, the availability of sanctions other than prosecution could be considered to be an influential factor in deciding whether or not to prosecute.

Many contraventions are of a chronic nature rather than an acute, one-off accident. In such circumstances, the use of non-criminal sanctions may be more appropriate. Variation and enforcement notices etc. permit a continuation of the cooperational approach as they allow for a remedy without any explicit punishment. As such, they offer an opportunity for a greater flexibility for negotiation and cooperation. However, where there is a one-off pollution incident the use of such sanctions is limited.

Even where non-criminal sanctions are used there is still scope to punish the uncooperative offender as most of the non-criminal sanctions have as their ultimate step the prosecution for breach.

The process of enforcement

Having examined some of the attitudes that the enforcement agencies have towards both the offender and the offence, how do they translate these attitudes into the process of enforcement?

In *Policing Pollution,* Richardson suggested that there was often a pattern of enforcement which was adopted by the old-style water authorities to underpin the cooperational approach. A six-fold process was identified:

(a) presenting the problem;
(b) problem solving;
(c) presence;
(d) threats;
(e) taking a legal sample;
(f) prosecution.

(a) Presenting the problem

The first stage in the process of enforcement was identified as the setting up of a reasonable image of the enforcers. The idea being that they wished to present themselves as reasonable people making reasonable demands.

This was achieved by appearing authoritative and stating the problems that a company faced. This approach was strongly linked to the view of the firm as a political citizen. By appearing authoritative but reasonable it was hoped that a solid base could be established on which to build a relationship of mutual trust.

(b) Problem solving

After a problem had been presented, the next phase of this quasi-enforcement system involved an investigation to find a reasonable solution. Sometimes, in complicated cases, the attempt to find a solution using the cooperational method obscured the fact that standards were being breached. There was often a perception amongst enforcement bodies that where a problem was complex then it was only to be expected that there would be a failure to attain the required standard.

(c) Presence

Policing Pollution suggested that not all traders responded to these first two steps in the enforcement process. If there was little effort made to cooperate, enforcement officers would become more assertive. This attitude was founded upon a belief that the longer an offender failed to comply, the more likely it was that the business could be identified as an amoral calculator. Consequently, it was less important to follow a strategy of cooperation because a greater degree of moral blame could attach to the offender. In an attempt to increase the severity of the pressure upon an offender, the next 'step' in this process was an increase in presence. Any offender persisting in non-compliance was visited regularly and constant check-ups were made. This was hoped to have the effect that 'big brother was watching' and firms would recognise the futility of continuing to confront the enforcement agencies.

(d) Threats

Although a heightened degree of presence carried with it an implied threat, continuing non-compliance often resulted in explicit threats. Even here, there were grades of threatening behaviour. For example, at one end of the spectrum there were verbal warnings, whereas at the other formal letters on headed notepaper signed by the Chief Inspector/Head of Committee/Chief Executive etc. Throughout this process, officers could also assure themselves of the reasonableness of their actions, which reinforced their view that they were still attempting to seek compliance rather than punishment.

(e) Taking a legal sample

The penultimate step before prosecution was the taking of a formal legal sample. Such samples form the essential evidence on which a prosecution can be founded. Indeed, in the case of the Water Resources Act 1991, such a sample has to be taken to be admissible. This was seen to be a very serious step and one which was not taken lightly. As a serious step, officers were wary of utilising such powers regularly. As a 'last chance' mechanism, the value of such a procedure would be lost if samples were taken regularly without any consequential prosecution in the case of continuing non-compliance. Although the nature of the formal sample procedures has been abolished under the Environment Act 1995, the formal step of 'taking a sample' still continues.

(f) The prosecution

Within the system of enforcement for water pollution the final step was, and is, prosecution. *Policing Pollution* and *The Reasonable Arm of the Law* indicated that there were no particular objective factors which determined the incidence of prosecution. Thus, it made little difference that one area was heavily populated and another more rural, or one industrialised and another residential. Even within regions figures varied.

Although these steps of enforcement characterised the water authorities' operations prior to privatisation under the Water Act 1989, other enforcement agencies have also been identified as using a similar framework. Indeed, in *The Reasonable Arm of the Law,* Hutter puts it thus:

'Enforcing the law' to an environmental health officer means securing compliance with the law through persuasion and advice, rather than the apprehension and subsequent punishment of offenders. The law is regarded as a means to an end rather than an end in itself and officers consider themselves to be delivering a service both to the local community — by promoting and maintaining a required standard of public health — and, in some respects, to the regulated — by advising them on how best to attain these standards, rather than being members of an 'industrial police force'.

This methodology of compliance rather than sanction is unusual in that, in a heavily regulated system, those outside the enforcement agencies would assume that the regulations are being enforced properly. What effects does this have?

Lack of public confidence in the enforcement system

The public are often the main source of primary information regarding pollution incidents. Enforcement agencies are often understaffed and overworked. Not all pollution occurs between 9.00 am and 5.00 pm and certainly not when an officer happens to be on site. Many prosecutions are instigated by vigilant members of the public.

Often third parties are viewed with mistrust by both enforcers and polluters. Complaints from the public can put a cooperational relationship in jeopardy. The enforcers are faced with a dilemma, should they proceed against an activity to the detriment of the trust built up or should they continue to seek the cooperation of an offender but risk the wrath of a disappointed third party?

An argument has been put forward by Hawkins that the enforcement bodies often choose a third way. In *Environment and Enforcement* he suggests that selective enforcement *enhances* the public's view of the enforcers. By choosing 'high profile' cases the agencies could attempt to draw attention to their own effectiveness:

A policy of fuller enforcement expressed in a swelling prosecution rate cannot be employed as an indicator of efficiency, for in an environment of ambivalence this risks being treated as evidence of agency harassment. It is rather in the careful and sparing selection of cases for prosecution that the agency is best able to protect its own interest by showing that 'something is being done'.

However, the Tenth Report of the Royal Commission of Environmental Pollution quoted a poll commissioned by the EC which found that 93% of interviewees agreed with the proposition that stronger measures should be taken to protect the environment against pollution. This led later on in the Report to the comment that 'The success of our regulatory authorities needs to be judged on their performance rather than their methods'. This reiterated their finding in the Sixth Report in 1976 that the public lacked confidence in the Industrial Air Pollution Inspectorate because there was a view that the interests of the Inspectorate were too closely linked with those of industry. The point being made stressed the public's misunderstanding of the conciliatory approach. In traditional regulatory systems, there may be a degree of discretion, but this would normally stem from a desire to police effectively by means of not overloading the system. It is difficult for the public to understand that using a conciliatory approach is, by its very nature, helping to secure compliance.

The close links between industry and their enforcers can be directly attributed to this non-confrontational approach. In an era of increasing environmental awareness the public need to *see* that the law is being used effectively. It is difficult to explain to a member of the public that the cooperational strategy will secure environmental quality improvements where a company is clearly breaking the law. Actual proof of the breach of a regulation would normally result in enforcement and thus the public perceive that the enforcement of statutory regulations in the environmental field is not a worthwhile process.

Differing levels of enforcement

One of the findings of the different research projects carried out in the 1980s was that there were various levels of enforcement in different geographical locations. For instance, in *Policing Pollution,* it was shown that in a three-year period 48 prosecutions were brought by a 'northern water authority' for the contravention of trade effluent consents. In a 'southern water authority' not a single prosecution was brought over the same period. Indeed, officers within that authority only had 'a very hazy impression of the prescribed route that the decision [about whether to proceed with the prosecution] would take'. Secondly, the figures for the northern water authority for prosecution stemmed mainly (some 90%) from one division of that authority.

This lack of uniformity could be a consequence of the 'doughnut-ring' model of decision-making. Many different factors need to be taken into account when considering whether or not to bring enforcement action, and clearly within one authority more factors would preclude a prosecution than promote it. Put another way, the many different factors, including the personalities of the officers themselves, alter the width of the 'doughnut-ring' when deciding whether or not to prosecute. The wider the discretion, the more uncertain a system becomes.

The counterbalance to discretion is certainty, and, depending upon the width of the discretion used, there will be varying degrees of certainty as to whether or not a particular regulation will be enforced. Uncertainty detracts from the power of the regulatory framework. Some officers were disturbed by this lack of uniformity. They favoured a more explicit policy applicable at least throughout the whole authority, if not nationwide. They were evidently anxious to ensure procedural reasonableness and the application of predetermined rules to guide the exercise of their discretion.

The concern expressed stems from the need for a degree of certainty to ensure that both enforcers and industry know where they stand in relation to any breach. Certainty brings fairness of a different sort from that in a system where there is a wide discretion. If all those controlled by the regulatory system know the parameters within which they can work, and that such parameters are applied equitably throughout the system, then clearly there are greater degrees of moral and legal authority. When the enforcement agencies express concern over the uniformity of regulatory enforcement, it is quite clear that the system itself cannot be operating with total efficiency.

Administrative difficulties

Aside from the attitudes that enforcement agencies have towards the offence and the offender, other external factors have had a marked effect upon the efficient enforcement of environmental regulations. These can properly be related to all the usual problems facing administrative and bureaucratic systems.

As was seen in Chapter 3, the traditional model for environmental regulation in Britain has been to set up large administrative bodies charged with both organisational and regulatory responsibilities. Thus, agencies have been both poacher and gamekeeper. This of course can lead to fundamental difficulties because of the contradictory nature of these two functions. The two main examples of this dual role were in the control of water pollution under the regional water authorities and the control of the disposal of waste to land through the county-wide waste disposal authorities. Both these authorities carried out activities which were the subject of control which had to be policed by themselves. The water authorities operated sewage treatment plants, and the waste disposal authorities were site operators disposing of waste within their own area. Additionally, these two bodies possessed the regulatory powers for the supervision of private sector activities. The failure to separate the two contradictory roles created great problems. Often the gravest breach of regulations came from the operational arm of the regulatory authorities. For instance, pollution from the water authorities' sewage treatment plants was perhaps the most significant factor in the deterioration of water quality. In the waste disposal sector, the Commons Environment Committee stated:

> . . . many local authorities appear to have concentrated on their operational activities to the detriment of their regulatory duties . . . [some waste

disposal authorities] regard keeping consignment notes in a box in the corner as adequately discharging their record-keeping responsibilities.

This dual role led to two difficulties in enforcement. First, the private sector argued that it was inequitable for the enforcement agencies to prosecute when their own operations were also in breach. Secondly, it led to a desire to use the conciliatory approach because many officers within the enforcement agency empathised with those in the private sector as to the problems faced in pollution avoidance. Their officers had experienced difficulties within their own agency and thus were far more likely to be sympathetic in enforcing the law generally.

Staffing and funding levels

To maintain a proper level of enforcement, adequate resources have to be made available both in terms of personnel and funding. Environmental enforcement bodies have, in the past, had to cope with cuts in funding and understaffing. The funding limits imposed on local government are well documented. Progressive cuts in funding and low morale have led to a smaller complement of staff attempting to deal with a large number of complaints and quite often a lack of expertise in some technical areas. Whilst the position in other regulatory bodies is not so severe there are still significant shortfalls in funding and staff.

These problems have a knock on effect in terms of monitoring and inspection rates. Figures for monitoring visits have always been below the essential level: approximately 60% of the necessary inspections were carried out by HMIP even with a full complement of staff. The birth of the Environment Agency has done nothing to reverse this trend and there will continue to be a need to target resources at the most obvious cases.

Changes in attitudes to enforcement

Most of the research referred to so far in this chapter dates back to empirical studies in the mid 1970s to the early 1980s. Perceptions of environmental difficulties have changed dramatically since that time. New environmental quality objectives imposed by the EC have meant that the enforcement agencies are being placed under increasing pressure to take a proactive approach to enforcement and to use prosecution as the short term weapon to bring industry into line in the long term. For instance, the EPA 1990, s. 7, provides for such objectives to be taken into account when authorising processes subject to integrated pollution control and air pollution control. Similarly the Water Resources Act 1991 makes water quality objectives a statutory consideration. The evidence of this fundamental change in the control of pollution in Britain can also be seen with the introduction of the Air Quality Standards Regulations 1989 (SI 1989 No. 317). This move towards fixed standards and away from individualised flexible enforcement requires the redefinition of the enforcement of environmental protection.

The redefinition of the regulatory role

With the creation of the National Rivers Authority under the Water Act 1989 and the formation of the new system of regulation in the waste disposal industry under the EPA 1990, there was a move away from the dual-function approach of the 1970s and 1980s. The NRA and the waste regulation authorities had almost total regulatory control without the problems of operational complications to blunt their effectiveness. This, in turn, allowed the NRA to become the self-styled 'Water Guardian' and to concentrate on the policing side of its role in order to achieve compliance by confrontation. This was evidenced by an increase in the incidence of prosecution since its creation. Figures show that the number of prosecutions for water pollution rose at least 25% each year in the initial years of its life.

The incidence of prosecution was only one piece of evidence of a changing attitude to enforcement. In the first of a series of water quality papers, the NRA outlined its approach to enforcement. In addition to the conciliatory model, there was a desire to prosecute where a discharger had shown little care in attempting to comply with consent obligations. Informal, internal guidelines offered guidance as to when prosecution would be pursued. These guidelines, which were used on a national basis, attempted to class incidents by reference to objective standards such as numbers of fish killed or repetitious breaches. Theoretically this demonstrated a consistency of decision-making and avoided previous concerns about the unreasonable exercise of discretion. Although at first glance this may not have been far away from the previous attempts at moral judgment in exercising enforcement discretion, it did, however, demonstrate that the NRA was far more likely to consider accidents as requiring enforcement action even where moral opprobrium was low. Furthermore, the NRA brought a large number of prosecutions against the privatised water services companies. According to prosecution figures, four of the 10 most prosecuted companies were (and are still) from the water industry. This has had an indirect effect upon those who discharge into sewers controlled by the companies. Where levels of prosecutions against the private water companies rise, they in turn have to enforce trade discharge standards, thus increasing the enforcement pressure considerably.

The creation of the waste regulation authorities meant an end to the difficulties which faced officers under the previous local-authority-controlled waste disposal authority, who were required to police sites operated by their own authority. The arm's-length waste disposal companies have always been subject to the same degree of control as private operations, although in practice the regulatory relationship may be affected by the fact that the regulator and the regulated may have often worked together for many years.

The creation of the Environment Agency should, of course, continue the redefinition of the regulatory role as the links with local authorities are finally severed and there is an increasing integration of the enforcement functions in relation to varying pollution control responsibilities. Arguably, there have always been different approaches to enforcement taken by the various pollution control authorities and the regulatory role has differed. For example, the NRA had a more aggressive reputation than HMIP, which sought the role of educator rather than policeman. All of these different approaches have had to be absorbed within the agency and it may take some time to assimilate these different cultures. It will be interesting to see whether a new enforcement model will emerge or if there will be a straightforward adaptation of one of the existing models. The Code of Practice on Enforcement is intended to underpin the integration of enforcement and bring some transparency into the enforcement practice (see further p. 147).

The redefinition of the enforcement agencies' relationship with industry

The traditional image of the enforcement agencies collaborating with industry over a table in a room at the factory with a cup of tea while 'problem-solving' is fast disappearing. Most enforcement agencies were renowned in the past for their ability to be sympathetic in suggesting ways to abate pollution. Indeed most guidance notes controlling the processes within an industry were drafted with close assistance from those who operated the processes themselves.

HMIP took a different stance when drawing up the guidance notes to govern integrated pollution control and air pollution control. The Inspectorate specifically rejected the Chemical Industry Association's claims that it should be involved throughout the process of drawing up the guidelines. The dismay expressed by the association emphasised the about-turn in this traditional relationship. It was suggested by some within the association that, in the absence of representations from industry, the system would be unworkable as a large number of appeals against unreasonable authorisations would overload the Inspectorate.

HMIP stressed the advisory capacity of all consultees. The then Director, Frank Feates, pointed out that he would be happy to take into account the views of the Chemical Industry Association but that these views would not be the overriding consideration. Other bodies would also be entitled to make representations.

Furthermore, the Inspectorate made it clear that it saw its role as having four main strands:

(a) a preventative approach;
(b) a positive but structured relationship with operators;
(c) the provision of information and guidance to industry on an arm's length basis; and
(d) a systematic targeting of resources towards the highest priorities.

These strands included a possible suggestion that those producers supplying high quality pollution technology will be the proper people to advise HMIP as to what constitutes the 'best available techniques'. This move indicated that the Inspectorate and now the Agency will take into account a much wider sample of opinions when deciding the framework which it governs. Thus, the 'active' discretion in standard-setting and methods of abatement has an objective basis.

There are other more far-reaching changes, however, which go beyond formal enforcement to more proactive issues, such as the setting of consent levels. In its first water quality paper, *Discharge Consent and Compliance Policy: A Blueprint for the Future*, the NRA made a number of recommendations stressing the importance of tighter numeric consents with percentile limits for 'environmentally significant discharges'.

This confrontational style has also spread into the way in which prosecutions are presented. When the facts of a pollution incident are put before the court, an assessment is made of the damage caused by the pollution in ecological as well as scientific terms. Photographs are often used to display vividly to a court what is meant by the dry, and often incomprehensible, scientific evidence. Attempts are made to explain to the court in lay terms both the short- and the long-term effects of the pollution caused. These sometimes emotive prosecutions are bound to have a confrontational effect and will undoubtedly undermine any continuing relationship to some extent.

Unfortunately, the size and complexity of the task facing the enforcement agencies has undermined the attempt to move away from the cooperative approach. The number and poor quality of IPC applications, for instance, has led to disproportionate amounts of time being spent upon administering the system of authorisations. In local authorities an acknowledged shortfall in the number of APC applications has largely been overlooked, whilst monitoring and enforcement visits have fallen.

The redefinition of the importance of environmental protection

The changes in emphasis in the regulatory system are not solely ones of detail and are more than superficial. Underlying the changes is a fundamental shift in the way that environmental problems are perceived, not only by the public but also by the enforcement agencies themselves. The concept of the environment having rights of its own is increasing in importance, and generally the desire to protect the environment has begun to undermine previous assumptions made as to the benefits of industrial activities which cause pollution. As environmental issues have become more important in the public eye, the desire to ensure that environmental standards are maintained has increased generally. These changes have brought about a retreat from the cooperational approach to a new, more ambivalent standard. That is not to say that the enforcing agencies are ambivalent as to the difficulties faced by industrialists. However, they are now balancing the cooperational and the confrontational approaches in order to achieve environmental quality improvements.

When public interest in the environment increases, the moral opprobrium attaching to pollution increases. Incidents such as the Camelford disaster, where aluminium sulphate was put into the drinking water supply, have supported the view that the public is now ready to perceive incidents of environmental pollution as being more than mere administrative difficulties. The distinction between this particular branch of white collar crime and other more recognisably 'criminal' activities is becoming blurred.

This change in emphasis has had a consequential effect upon areas of environmental regulation. First, there has been an increase in the fines and penalties for pollution offences. Historically, it was unusual for a prosecution for environmental pollution to be heard anywhere other than the magistrates' court. The level of fines imposed by the magistrates tended to reflect the public opinion of white collar crime being a morally neutral offence. Although many environmental pollution offences are triable either in the magistrates' court or the Crown Court, the option to try the matter in the Crown Court, with the opportunity to seek an unlimited fine and even imprisonment, was not often taken.

It is now becoming more usual for matters to be committed to the Crown Court. Perhaps the most celebrated Crown Court prosecution, of Shell (UK) in February 1990 for an oil spillage into the River Mersey, reflects the latent powers of the Crown Court which have not been very much in evidence. In that case the total of the fine and compensation costs amounted to several million pounds, which cancelled out much of the annual profit derived from the process which caused the pollution. In that particular situation, it was clear that the Crown Court judge not only viewed the offence with the seriousness that it required but also took into account (perhaps subconsciously) the need to make the polluter pay. Moreover, the judge specifically pointed out that the level of fine was 'lenient' taking into account all the mitigating factors.

The notoriously low levels of fine, which have traditionally undermined the use of prosecutions, have been increased to take into account the need for the magistrates to have wider powers to reflect the seriousness of offences which do not merit being heard in the Crown Court. As a consequence, most of the offences of environmental pollution under the EPA 1990 have had the maximum fine level in the magistrates' court increased from £2,000 to £20,000. This is also mirrored in the increased penalties in the Planning and Compensation Act 1991. Furthermore, there are explicit references in some Acts to the financial benefit which has accrued or is likely to accrue to an offender (for example, see the Planning (Listed Building and Conservation Areas) Act 1990 and *R* v *Chambers* [1989] JPL 229). Finally, the demand for increased fines to take into account the potential profits from pollution was made explicit by the Government in the White Paper, *Crime, Justice and Protecting the Public,* which said:

> Companies which see commercial advantage in creating pollution or neglecting safety precautions cannot be punished effectively by fines at the level given to most offenders.

It then goes on to say that higher levels of fines should be imposed to take into account both the means and the resources of the offenders.

Although there are still difficulties in ensuring that there are sufficient funds and sufficient manpower to meet the increasing work in detection, these difficulties are being addressed. Furthermore, charging schemes to cover the cost of administering applications for authorisations under the IPC and APC systems and under the Water Resources Act 1991 ensure that the levels of funding for the administrative side of the regulatory function can be properly balanced to take into account the complexity of the work required.

The development of enforcement policy

In 1990, the Conservative Government expressed its aim of enforcing standards rigorously and it comes as no surprise that the Labour Party has given a similar commitment in its main policy document, *In Trust for Tomorrow*. It is clear that the enforcement of environmental regulations is considered to be important, at least rhetorically. Before 1990, however, the state of environmental law did not lend itself to flexible enforcement and there were many loopholes and gaps in the law. The overhaul of the Control of Pollution Act 1974 with the introduction of the EPA 1990 and the Water Resources Act 1991 was intended to herald a new era for environmental law. The creation of the Environment Agency under the Environment Act 1995 takes this a stage further. It will, of course, be some time before we gain a clear picture of the effects that these institutional changes may bring, but in a period of rapid change it is instructive to reflect on the progress which has been made in the first half of the 1990s before turning to consider the possible future of enforcement policy in the era of the Environment Agency.

During its lifetime, the NRA used a specific enforcement policy with prosecution as an active component. The use of prosecution was, however, aimed at punishing accidental breaches as opposed to chronic or persistent foreseeable breaches, which tended to be dealt with via the conciliatory model outlined above. Compliance levels continued to be relatively low, with industrial operators achieving 65% compliance with their consents in 1993–4. One of the factors in the lack of prosecutions for these chronic breaches was that the selection of enforcement mechanisms was restricted, as the NRA did not possess any of the traditional administrative powers (e.g., enforcement notices).

In addition relatively little use was made of the preventative or remedial powers provided in the Water Resources Act 1991, s. 161. The primary reason for this was that there was inherent uncertainty surrounding the expenditure of money which could not necessarily be recovered from the party responsible for the pollution.

Unlike the NRA, HMIP did have a wide range of enforcement options and used them fully in pursuing a less confrontational enforcement strategy. Whereas prosecution rates were remarkably low (with an average of 14 prosecutions per year) enforcement notices were used in increasing numbers. Many of these were served in the initial phase of the implementation of Part I of the EPA 1990 required the updating of old equipment or the installation of additional equipment to deal with the upgrading of existing processes.

The continued use of these administrative sanctions helped to foster the conciliatory approach between HMIP and industry. The use of enforcement notices after a pollution incident or to deal with chronic breaches gives the 'offender' some time to deal with the cause of the problems without the ignominy of a prosecution. The service of the notice is seen as part of the enforcement process without excluding the possibility of prosecution either for breach of the enforcement notice or for any continuing breaches.

The Environment Agency

The creation of the Environment Agency has yet to have a significant impact upon the old enforcement practices of the separate regulatory bodies which were integrated into the new Agency. The institutional and cultural barriers to integration will take some time to break down sufficiently to ensure that a coherent enforcement strategy is adopted throughout all of the divisions of the EA. There have been two main steps which have been taken to ease this integration: the introduction of a Code of Enforcement; and the assimilation of the enforcement powers which are available to deal with the different aspects of pollution control. Arguably, the former has more to do with the deregulatory initiatives of the last Government then a desire to improve the consistency of environmental enforcement.

Enforcement Code

Although environmental enforcement agencies have long had unofficial enforcement policies, the EA has published a formal Enforcement Code. The Code comprises a general statement of its enforcement policy, a guide to enforcement for its officers, a guide to the rights of businesses when enforcement action is proposed against them and the EA's prosecution policy. The most significant change brought about by the new Code (which has no statutory authority) is that businesses have been given a new non-statutory right to object to enforcement measures proposed by the EA.

This 'right' is open to businesses (or presumably individuals) which have been notified that enforcement action is to be taken against them, and entitles them to a letter explaining the reasons for the enforcement action and giving them the opportunity to make representations to the EA official concerned. They will have 10 working days after being told that an enforcement notice is to be served on them to lodge such objections. This right to object will not extend to cases where officers believe that immediate action is necessary. They will, however, have to provide a written statement explaining their reasons for taking immediate action as soon as practicable.

The Code sets out four principles of the EA's enforcement practices. These are to apply the law 'proportionately', consistently and transparently, and to target action at activities giving rise to the most serious environmental damage or where the hazards are least well controlled. The EA will expect 'relevant good practice' to be followed and, where this has not been established, will expect businesses themselves to assess the risks of their activities and satisfy it that any necessary actions will comply with the law.

The prosecution policy is not very detailed and is restricted to the principles the EA will apply. Prosecution will be 'considered' in circumstances where:

(a)   it would draw attention to the need to comply with the law;

(b)   a conviction would act as an example to others;

(c)   a breach of the law gives rise to a potential for considerable environmental harm;

(d)   the gravity of an offence, taken with the general record and approach of the offender, warrants it.

Where enforcement action is anticipated the Environment Agency's policy gives a business the following rights:

(a)   the right to a letter, on request, explaining what needs to be done and why — when warranted, officers express an opinion that something should be done — without taking formal action;

(b)   the right to a 'minded to' notice and an entitlement to have its point of view heard by the agency before formal action is taken;

(c)   when immediate action is taken, the right to a written statement explaining why this is necessary (i.e., why immediate rather than another course of action, and the consequences of failing to take action); and

(d)   the right to be told exactly what rights of appeal it has when formal action is taken.

These rights reflect the principles set out in the Deregulation and Contracting Out Act 1994 (see further p. 116). Although the code provides a transparent approach to enforcement it is unlikely that it will have any marked effect on existing practices. Indeed, it is arguable that the code simply formalises the enforcement strategy which had been identified over 10 years previously. The creation of a formal conciliation scheme merely reinforces the traditional approach by legitimising the attempts to reach a settled agreement.

Assimilation of enforcement powers

As discussed in Chapter 3, the Environment Act 1995 amended existing legislation to ensure that the Environment Agency has the full range of administrative mechanisms available to deal with all of the pollution control functions. The main changes were made to the powers under the Water Resources Act 1991 dealing with water pollution. The insertion of s. 90B into the Act makes provision for the service of enforcement notices. Whilst this gives the agency another enforcement tool to use in dealing with non-accidental causes of pollution, it may also be used as a 'softer' option in place of prosecution. In addition there are now extra powers available to prevent pollution. The works notice procedure under the Water Resources Act 1991, s. 161A, means that the previous uncertainty over cost recovery has been eased.

These legislative changes give the EA a greater flexibility in dealing with different sources of pollution, but an increase in the number and type of enforcement powers will not necessarily mean that there will be any significant shift in attitudes to enforcement, notwithstanding the potential increase in enforcement action. It is important to point out that the use of these administrative sanctions may have a larger impact on an 'offender' than any criminal sanctions which a court might impose. The costs involved in carrying out improvements which are imposed by an enforcement notice have no direct relationship to the nature of any breach and are therefore much more difficult to predict. The courts do have powers to remedy the effects of any pollution caused in relation to certain offences (see, e.g., EPA 1990, s. 27, in relation to Part I offences), but the powers are not utilised regularly.

The future

Although there have been significant institutional and legislative changes since the introduction of the EPA 1990 and the Water Resources Act 1991 there has not been any notable shift in the incidence of enforcement actions. This raises the question whether the explanations set out earlier in this chapter still apply. One thing is certain — the factors governing any decision to enforce are still complex and differ on a case-to-case basis. It is possible, however, to identify a slight shift away from the traditional views of the offender and the offence, which bears out the redefinition of many of the critical factors as set out above. The creation of a unified national agency with centralised policies will encourage a much more uniform application of enforcement powers (but some mild regional differences can still be identified).

Although decisions to prosecute are still made on a discretionary basis there is much more public scrutiny of individual incidents and it would be unlikely for the moral blameworthiness of an offender to be a material factor in determining whether to take enforcement action. Environmental harm is now often the most relevant factor in the determination and serious incidents rarely escape some form of sanction.

The true picture is that although there has been some movement away from the traditional conciliatory approach, cooperation between industry and the regulators has not broken down. Indeed, the EA has taken an active role in advising industry on improving its performance (with subsequent financial savings for the companies involved see 242 ENDS Report 6). In reality the general consensus between the two sides of the enforcement system is never likely to break down fully, as detection and enforcement of every breach would be impracticable and undesirable. It is likely that increasing emphasis will be placed upon the use of self-monitoring in order to detect breaches (see further Howarth, 'Self-monitoring, self-policing, self-incrimination and pollution law (1997) 60 MLR 200). In addition performance indicators (such as certification for BS 7750, EMAS or ISO 14000) may be recognised as a benchmark for a 'lighter touch' approach to enforcement which recognises the higher levels of compliance such certificated companies have to achieve. Using such mechanisms to decrease the scope of the inspection and monitoring duties would enable the agency to concentrate on the most blameworthy offenders.

The converse argument is that neither of these approaches necessarily guarantees that companies will comply and there have been examples of certificated companies being prosecuted for environmental offences. There are more fundamental objections to the reliance upon self monitoring, which centre around the rule against self incrimination and the transfer of a crucial regulatory function to the regulated.

Enforcement and deregulation

Perhaps the biggest general influence over the enforcement policies of all enforcement agencies (especially local government) is Central Government's commitment to removing what is viewed as unnecessary and interfering regulation. Since the introduction of the new statutory regime under the EPA 1990 and the Water Resources Act 1991, industry has argued that the legislation is too complex and compliance involves excessive amounts of both expenditure and other resources. This complaint has found a sympathetic response with the introduction of the framework of the Deregulation and Contracting Out Act 1994 (see p. 116 for an explanation of the provisions of the Act). Although the full impact of the Act upon environmental legislation has yet to be determined, the potential implications of the provisions were demonstrated with the publication of the proposals of the seven Business Deregulation Task Forces (organised into industry sectors) which were appointed by the Conservative Government to examine opportunities for reform.

The Task Forces chose to emphasise the gap between the intention of Central Government when making law and policy and the manner in which that intention was implemented by enforcement authorities on the ground. The proposals from the Task Forces ranged from planning (including the extension of permitted development rights and a requirement for local planning authorities to accept the recommendations of a Development Plan Inspector) and waste management to IPC, LAAPC and water pollution. Some of the recommendations were accepted and implemented in subsequent legislation. The clear danger of the 'Task Force' approach is that it tackles the perceived problems of over-regulation from only one perspective. Although some environmental legislation is complex, there are often legitimate reasons for having such requirements. Whilst removing such hurdles means that business can operate without interference, it should only be necessary where the environmental impact of the change can be accurately predicted to be insignificant.

Although the 1994 Act has not implemented any of the other recommendations of the Task Force, the new power is available to enable any future proposals to be enacted. It is not possible to predict accurately the future role of the Act but the passage of the Environment Act 1995 through Parliament may give some indication of the Government's attitude to the administrative approach to enforcement. For example, the contaminated land provisions were weakened considerably during the Bill's passage and a number of preconditions to the serving of a remediation notice were imposed (see p. 410). Other examples include the cost benefit duty under s. 39 and other similar provisions (see p. 49). Ironically, the deregulation initiative which started out as a 'war on red tape' has now developed (particularly in relation to enforcement) into a situation where the enforcement agencies have to carry out numerous theoretical and practical exercises before commencing any enforcement action.

Public participation in the enforcement process

Having examined closely the way in which regulatory bodies enforce the law, it must be pointed out that there are residual powers providing for direct action to be taken by members of the public. It is likely that the next phase of environmental enforcement will be supplemented by a greater degree of public participation in the enforcement process. Generally, there is a constitutional right to bring private prosecutions for statutory offences. However, in environmental matters, this right has often been specifically limited by the statute concerned (e.g., in air pollution legislation). The Control of Pollution Act 1974 did not have any prohibition on prosecutions for offences of water pollution and anglers' associations and others took action themselves against water authorities. This trend has continued under the EPA 1990. Unfortunately, such powers are often overlooked. Indeed, as the Environmental Protection Bill passed through Parliament, the Labour Party proposed an amendment in order to include a clear reference to the public right to prosecute. This was rejected as unnecessary. As the public become aware of their rights, any action on the part of the regulatory bodies may become superfluous.

In order for non-statutory enforcement bodies or individuals to take enforcement action, members of the general public need to have proper access to environmental data. To bring a prosecution, information is required so as to identify properly the breaches of any regulation. Of course, a major weakness in the environmental regulatory system in Britain is the difficulty of achieving access to environmental information.

SEVEN

Access to environmental information

As we have seen in Chapter 3, the system of the enforcement of pollution control is exercised in the main by statutory enforcement agencies. These enforcement agencies do not necessarily, however, engender public confidence. As restrictions on the right to take action by private prosecution are removed, the general public is able to enforce the law where, for instance, an enforcement agency fails to prosecute for a regulatory breach. These powers of prosecution have significant powers connected which can require further remedial action. For example, under the EPA 1990, s. 26, where a prosecution is successful a court can order action to be taken within a certain time-limit to ensure that any breach complained of is remedied. These powers potentially allow the general public to have a degree of control over the enforcement of pollution control.

Why then do the public not take more action? There are a variety of reasons which include high cost, apathy, ignorance of the powers available and a fear of the legal system. However, even if these difficulties could be overcome, access to the information which could form the basis of an enforcement action has traditionally been limited.

Most environmental offences involve the carrying out of unauthorised activities. These may arise from the breach of a condition in an authorisation or they may be entirely unauthorised actions. To assess levels of compliance, the public require access not only to information concerning the details of an authorisation but also to monitoring data which can provide an assessment of the success of the controls.

The enforcement agencies, of course, have specific and wide-ranging powers to enable them to obtain information. These powers are not available to the general public, but the information obtained by the appropriate agency is crucial in assessing whether or not enforcement action should take place. It is this information which, if it were accessible, could be utilised by those outside the statutory enforcement system to bring an action themselves. Moreover, the public have additional rights of enforcement both through resort to the common law for a private remedy (see Chapter 8) and in the case of the abuse of statutory powers by an enforcement body by an application for judicial review.

Without adequate information, public rights such as these have little value. Although documents containing general information about environmental pollution are freely available, specific information is far more difficult to obtain. For instance, basic information as to who is polluting, where they are polluting, with what they are polluting and how much is being emitted, can be elusive. This chapter examines some of the reasons for this secrecy, in addition to putting forward the possible dangers of keeping environmental information from the general public.

The development of a general environmental secrecy policy

The roots of environmental secrecy can be traced back to the mid-nineteenth century and the age of industrialisation when, in 1864, the Alkali Inspectorate, which was then empowered to regulate atmospheric pollution, commenced its enforcement activities under the Alkali Act 1863 with a policy of keeping any information regarding the alkali industry private unless publication was demanded by a particular statute or was permitted by the owner. Naturally, the alkali industry itself was concerned to keep the information secret in order to ensure that the public did not know of the dangers and consequences of the pollutants emitted into the atmosphere. This, coupled with the beginning of a co-operational approach between enforcers and the polluters, ensured that the Inspectorate was very unlikely to make such information available to members of the public unless specifically required to do so.

Central Government holds important information about the environment. As central policy makers and legislators, its ability to make fundamental changes in the nature of environmental protection heightens the need for proper public accountability. Until recently, the disclosure of information in these areas, when unauthorised, would have resulted in the commission of a criminal offence under the Official Secrets Act 1911, s. 2. Although Central Government has very little detailed information which would be of help to the public, the unamended Official Secrets Act 1911 gave rise to situations which could only be described as bizarre.

The Draconian nature of the restrictions placed upon Central Government organisations led to the reform of the Official Secrets Act in 1989. This Act narrowly protects a certain limited class of information, which does not now include environmental information. However, the time taken to respond to the proposals made by the Franks Committee in 1972 and by a White Paper in 1978 reflects the reluctance of Central Government to take action upon not only general information held by themselves, but also more detailed environmental information held by others.

Mechanisms of secrecy

Historically, secrecy has been endemic in environmental legislation. Many statutes contained specific sections explicitly forbidding the disclosure of information relating to environmental discharges. Even if there were no specific sanctions for disclosure, access to information was prohibited unless another statute specifically required that it be made available to the general public.

Water pollution

The Rivers (Prevention of Pollution) Act 1961 restricted the public right of access to information concerning applications, discharge consents, or effluent samples taken by the enforcing authority, unless the person/company making the discharge permitted its disclosure, or there was a further statutory requirement to disclose. In *The Secrets File*, Maurice Frankel gives an illustration of the type of situation which arose under this old legislation. In a case where a pigment manufacturer was discharging highly polluting substances into the Humber Estuary he says:

> On three occasions the company has been asked for the results of its monitoring — and it has refused on each occasion. Although the water authority has copies of data it is prevented by law from passing it on; an official releasing the information without the company's consent could, under Section 12 of the Rivers (Prevention of Pollution) Act, be jailed for three months. The water authority also carries out its own monitoring of the effluent discharge; again, it is prevented by law from releasing the results without the company's permission.

Such a situation seems inconceivable in a time where access to such information is much more widespread.

Air pollution

The Alkali Inspectorate maintained a policy of secrecy from its inception and, in its very first report in 1864, stressed the importance of keeping information from the public, 'Of course, all information regarding any work must be considered private unless publication is demanded by the Act or permitted by the owner'. This policy was maintained on an informal basis until the introduction of the Health and Safety at Work etc. Act 1974. Under s. 28(7), the Alkali Inspectorate was subject to an unqualified prohibition to ensure that no information was publicised regarding any details of recordings or measurements taken whilst exercising their duties.

Under the Clean Air Acts 1956 and 1968, a local authority's power to publish information could be said to have been somewhat wider than that contained under the Health and Safety at Work etc. Act. Under Part IV of the Control of Pollution Act 1974, local authorities were allowed to publish information on emissions to air from premises other than private dwellings if that information was not information that could be required by the Alkali Inspectorate. Unfortunately, this power was restricted in three ways. First, before publicising information a committee had to be created to involve business/industry and local amenity groups to discuss the proposals to make information public. Secondly, the powers under the Act were directory rather than mandatory, that is to say that the local authorities were not under any legal duty to publish the information. Thirdly, there was an appeal mechanism available to those operators affected by any disclosure if the collection of the information required would have been too expensive, a trade secret or not in the public interest. With these hurdles to overcome and no positive incentive, the expenditure required to set the system in motion would prove to be greater than the benefits received. Additionally, with an enforcement regime based upon the co-operational approach, any attempt to impose discretionary powers upon industry would have fractured the fragile basis of local authority control. As evidence of this, it was reported in 1982 that in the whole country only eight premises had been made the subject of local authority registers and only five local authorities had cut their way through the administrative jungle in order to set up the registers.

Miscellaneous controls

Other examples of the restrictions on the free availability of information can be found in the legislation covering a variety of environmental issues, such as pollution at sea, radioactive substances and hazardous sites. One of the major reasons for such strenuous efforts to keep information away from the public eye stems largely from the views of industry about the free availability of information. This was best characterised in a statement made by the CBI in 1979 entitled 'The Release of Environmental and Technical Information' which stated:

> greater release of data enhances the risk of their misinterpretation and the likelihood of unwarranted alarm or ill-founded 'remedial' actions . . . Data are often highly detailed and technical, requiring interpretation by trained toxicologists; hence the capacity for correct interpretation is limited. This restricts further the amount and type of information which could usefully be released without problems of misinterpretation . . . The threat of legal proceedings would be enhanced by increasing disclosure of data. Applications for injunctions at common law could become more likely, putting industry at greater risk of additional costs and penalties even when it satisfies the requirements of the competent control authorities.

This feeling was amplified when the CBI again attacked existing legislation allowing public access to information on effluent discharges under Part II of the Control of Pollution Act 1974 as 'one of the worst bits of legislation on the statute book'. It was against this background that attempts were made to defend the formal and informal 'cloak of secrecy'.

Commercial confidentiality

Industry's main argument in favour of secrecy was outlined in the evidence submitted by the CBI for the Tenth Report of the Royal Commission on Environmental Pollution. It was suggested that free public access to environmental information could affect the viability of industrial operations:

General disclosure of data about the content of discharges to the environment causes industry concern because it could involve highly sensitive data which may be of commercial advantage to a competitor. Such data are first and foremost the property of the discharger and their disclosure should not be expected or demanded without good reason. In practice, industry often discloses information which relates to the quality of the environment, as a responsible neighbour and part of society; but this disclosure cannot be assumed to be a public right nor can refusal to disclose be taken to mean that there is 'something to hide'. On the contrary, it normally means that the firm believes it right to keep to itself its own property disclosure of which could damage it commercially.

Concern stemmed from the belief that competitors will be able to investigate public registers to gain access to secrets. This could be done in one of two ways. First, by checking the data relating to discharges, it would be open to competitors to calculate the composition of effluents in terms of the types or amounts of raw materials used in a process. This would help in the assessment of the output of a particular factory and thus give competitors a commercial advantage. Secondly, it was often claimed by industrialists that keeping information relating to applications for environmental authorisations on public registers would allow free access to information governing the composition of complex products. These products would often have taken a number of years to research and develop and the costs involved in that process could only be recovered if the information was kept confidential.

In reality, these fears have been overstressed. Any commercial operation intent upon finding out about a rival's business can use far more sophisticated methods of commercial espionage than relying on public information. Even complex compounds can be analysed using fairly simple procedures. Additionally, the constituents of a compound are often widely used within an industry, and the idea that information is commercially confidential only truly applies to those outside the industry.

Moreover the protection of intellectual property is well provided for in the patent and trade mark legislation. The need for additional secrecy is often unwarranted. The situations where this protection is not available seem particularly limited.

Evidence from other countries with free access to environmental information suggested that there were few occasions on which the availability of the information led to the breach of commercial confidentiality. When the CBI were asked to give examples, they were able to point to only three cases which justified these concerns.

The Royal Commission on Environmental Pollution considered the question of trade secrets over a number of reports during the 1970s and 1980s. Their conclusion was always the same, that the reliance upon the concept of confidentiality did not reflect the true nature of the risk involved with greater disclosure. In the Commission's Second Report in 1972 (Cmnd 4894) it was stated that there was:

a need for an increased flow of information to persons of responsibility who can use it for the ultimate benefit of the environment, e.g., MPs, research workers in universities and persons with similar interests in pollution.

In the Commission's Seventh Report in 1979 (Cmnd 7644), this stance was reiterated. Referring to industry's refusal to disclose information on 'trade secret' grounds, it was stated that commercial confidentiality was often a 'reflex action' which did not reflect the commercial risk involved. The Tenth Report of the Commission in 1984 (Cmnd 9149) concluded that the emphasis given to commercial confidentiality was disproportionate and misconceived. Even so, in oral evidence to the House of Lords Select Committee in 1989, the CBI reiterated their view that there was always a risk that technical information taken out of context can be misinterpreted by non-scientists.

Commercial confidentiality continues to be an important issue for many regulated companies. Although there are a significant number of applications to exclude information from registers, the regulatory bodies and the Secretary of State have taken a pragmatic view by only granting exclusions to a small percentage of the applications.

'Green nutters'

The second justification for the maintenance of secrecy often put forward by industry was that open access would lead to mischief-making and an unacceptable level of interference by fanatics. *The Secrets File* gives the example of comments made by an environmental health officer in 1977:

> Action groups, civic societies and pseudo environmental organisations persistently petitioned and pressured local authorities to implement those provisions . . . action groups frequently composed of university research workers, lecturers, people who had failed election through the ballot box and including many cranks, persisted in twisting the truth concerning emissions to atmosphere and their predictions of doom were made to the delight of an ever-waiting national press . . .

This sort of view is not just historical. In 1984 the CBI called Part II of the Control of Pollution Act a 'busybody's charter' and during the passage of the Environmental Protection Bill through the House of Commons, Andrew Hunt, MP for Basingstoke, said that widened rights of prosecution available to the public would 'allow the "green nutters" to get on parade and have a field day of litigation against industry on entirely inconsequential grounds'. Further MPs warned of dire consequences. The chemicals industry would 'disappear from this country', there would be an 'endless stream of prosecutions', and environmental groups would use the information and prosecutions merely as a media tool rather than a means of securing environmental improvements.

The underlying factor in this concern does not stem from misinterpretation of the data. Rather it emphasises the conciliatory strategy employed by the statutory enforcement agencies. If the information supplied on the public register raises issues of non-compliance where industrial operations are breaching their consents, then clearly it serves as evidence that there are difficulties in pursuing a non-confrontational enforcement strategy. In answer to the issues raised in the debate, a junior minister put it thus:

> If an individual has the necessary evidence to mount a case, he should be free to do so . . . we must rely on the courts to deliver justice. The commitment of industry to pollution controls is the surest defence against such litigation.

In other words, if the enforcement agencies are not willing or able to prosecute an offender then an individual should, if there is a proper case to be answered, be allowed to act.

It is not altogether clear who these 'fanatics' would be. It has been alleged that 'they' are amateurs and are unable to analyse properly the data available. In the words of the CBI expressed earlier in the chapter, 'only trained toxicologists' could interpret this information.

The reality is somewhat at odds with this view. Many environmental pressure groups employ specialists as full-time technicians. Others have members who can interpret data perfectly adequately because of many years of experience. The Royal Commission's Tenth Report said that they had seen a growing professionalism in such groups. This had led to high quality reports which compared favourably to those drawn up by trained toxicologists. It is also interesting to note that the Second Report identifies 'research workers' and 'others' as receiving the ultimate benefit of greater disclosure. In the intervening period, the pressure groups have increased in both number and size. Greenpeace and Friends of the Earth often carry out monitoring exercises supplementing statutory enforcement bodies. Clearly, the definition of 'extremists' depends upon which side of the enforcement fence you are. To industrialists, such groups are causing trouble; on the other hand, the pressure groups see themselves as demonstrating the authority that the enforcement agencies lack.

The House of Lords Select Committee did not consider this to be a problem. They said:

> The Committee most emphatically do not subscribe to the public need to be 'protected' on the grounds that raw data may be unintelligible or misleading; many members of non-governmental organisations which may wish to utilise the raw data are familiar with the processes of interpretation. There is inevitably the risk that some raw data may be used mischievously to suit a particular purpose, but that must be accepted as part of the price of openness.

In any event, experience has demonstrated that the fears of industrialists were not justified. Although the numbers of prosecutions brought by enforcement agencies is still relatively small, the proportion of private prosecutions is minute.

Administration costs

In setting up any system of public registration for environmental consents, the CBI pointed out that the administration costs of such an exercise would not be proportionate to the public benefit which would accrue. No doubt this was in the hope of appealing to a political ideology which wanted to cut down on administration and bureaucracy and considered that the creation of a further burden upon an understaffed, over-worked administration would be inadvisable. However, it is clear that records are required to be kept in any event to maintain the proper running of any system and therefore the additional burden would be minimal.

There is, of course, another interpretation to be put upon this argument in favour of non-disclosure. The ability of the public to monitor the success or failure of the enforcement agencies in controlling pollution problems could add to the workload of the agencies in more than a mere administrative fashion. The most likely avenue for complaint once non-compliance is discovered on the register by a member of the public will be to the enforcement agencies. The investigation of these complaints over and above the more general monitoring will amount to an increase in the activity of the agency and therefore increase costs. This underlying argument — that secrecy would be cheaper than openness — cannot be doubted. However, whether 'cheaper' means 'more effective' is perhaps more contentious. The House of Lords Select Committee put it simply, 'The fundamental principle to which the Committee adhere is that information should in no circumstances be protected by price'.

The ability of enforcement agencies to maintain registers in a number of different formats, including the more usual paper records, but also extending to information held on computer, microfiche or photographic record, enables cheaper updating of the information and also cheaper storage and easier access. Whether or not the public interest in the registers is sufficient to justify the expenditure incurred is a different matter.

The Royal Commission's approach

Having had the arguments for restriction of access to environmental information put to them on a number of occasions, the Royal Commission on Environmental Pollution consistently denied their strength. They considered that the public were entitled to know of the risks that they faced from environmental pollution. Furthermore, they took the view that the only way to re-establish public confidence in the enforcement system was to allow the public access to the information which would allow them to take enforcement action themselves, and that the public had a 'beneficial interest' in the environment, and therefore were entitled to know how much it was being polluted. Thus, whilst finding that these concepts held great weight, the Royal Commission rejected the justifications for secrecy and recommended that the public should be:

> . . . entitled to the fullest possible amount of information on all forms of environmental pollution, with the onus placed on the polluter to

substantiate a claim for exceptional treatment. Accordingly, we recommend that a guiding principle behind all legislative and administrative controls relating to environmental pollution should be a presumption in favour of unrestricted access for the public to information which the pollution control authorities obtain or receive by virtue of their statutory powers, with protection for secrecy only in those circumstances where a genuine case can be substantiated.

This was to form the 'guiding principle' for all legislative and administrative control relating to environmental pollution.

The effect of secrecy upon risk perception

Where information is difficult to obtain, the perception of the risk involved in an activity may well be misconceived. The Royal Commission said that 'Secrecy — particularly the half kept secret — fuels fear'. The reality is that there is no widespread conspiracy to keep the public from finding out about environmental pollution. However, when the public is not allowed to judge for itself the incidence of pollution within the environment, the true picture may never be known. It is necessary to disclose such information to enable informed debate not only about the risks to the public and the environment but also as to what steps might be taken to minimise those risks. In their Eleventh Report the Royal Commission commented further on the assessment of risk:

A proper evaluation of the risk requires access to the relevant information and its interpretation, and the public will not be reassured by interpretations provided by the putative polluter who has an interest. In the absence of public confidence in the role of bodies that are both authoritative and independent, interpretations by the press or pressure groups are often accepted even if they go beyond what an informed expert would regard as justified by the evidence.

There are those who believe, however, in a paternalistic form of government. Thus, it could be argued that where there is legislation in place and enforcement agencies are empowered to take action against pollution, there is no need for members of the public to be involved in such activities. However, in Chapter 6 we have seen that, in terms of prosecution rates and compliance with existing standards, the formal enforcement agencies have had limited success. The need to supplement the official enforcement agencies is still required.

The ability to detect environmental pollution is not solely the responsibility of the enforcement agencies. Many incidents are reported first by members of the public, and the availability of information would enable them to assess whether or not criminal activities are taking place. For legislation to be effective, the public will need to have confidence both in the enforcement agencies and their willingness to take action once they have been notified of any pollution.

Environmental rights

The phrase 'environmental rights' is often related to the concept of instilling some form of legal identity in the environment. In the context of access to information, however, we can identify the right that everyone has to information concerning the unowned environment. The general public has an interest in all elements of the environment which competes with other interests, including industrial operations. Where there are such competing interests, access to information on the impacts of those interests allows decisions to be made taking account of all of the relevant factors. In the words of the Royal Commission, 'the public must be considered to have a right, analogous to a beneficial interest, in the condition of the air and water and to be able to obtain information on how far they are being degraded'.

It may be argued by those in industry that these very people who have a beneficial interest in the environment are also the people who are employed in the factories which compete with that right. The right to pollute is essentially a utilitarian right, which has been expressed by those who defend such a right on the basis that the need to maintain a certain standard of living more than outweighs the need to ensure that there is long-term protection of the environment. This view is being increasingly challenged. The need to maintain natural resources and to ensure a proper environmental quality requires that the full extent of any particular problem should be assessed.

The recommendations of the Royal Commission

The history of the Royal Commission, and particularly of the recommendations regarding confidentiality, has been an interesting study of the way in which industry and government have joined together to block at every available opportunity the introduction of a concept which in industry's view could jeopardise the successful and profitable operations of its members. In total, five Royal Commission Reports address the issue of access to environmental information in one way or another, but it was not until the mid 1980s that initial steps were taken to make disclosure more widespread. Furthermore, it was only with the introduction of the EPA 1990 and the Environmental Information Regulations 1992 that disclosure of environmental information in all sectors of control is becoming a reality.

The Royal Commission's tune has hardly changed since 1974 when in its Second Report it stated:

> as a rule . . . the legislation which protects secrecy over industrial effluents and wastes no longer safeguards genuine trade secrets . . . it is in the public interest that information about waste should be available not only to the statutory bodies which have a right to demand it but to research workers and others who make use of it to improve the environment . . .

As a consequence, the Control of Pollution Act 1974 introduced a system of access to public registers of information on water for the first time. The implementation of Part II of the Control of Pollution Act was delayed for more than 10 years until mid 1985, amidst pressure by the CBI to delay disclosure even further. Other areas either remained secret or, in the case of the Health and Safety at Work etc. Act 1974, moved away from informal agreements to more formal statutory non-disclosure powers. In 1986, the Government departed from its previous standpoint when urging the EC to pass a Directive requiring all Member States to allow free access to environmental information. This new-found enthusiasm was short-lived. In 1986, in Pollution Paper No. 23, an inter-departmental Working Party responded to the Royal Commission's criticisms in the Tenth Report by embracing the 'guiding principle' but rejecting the recommendations to move towards a uniform regime of public access to all environmental information. Thus the Working Party charted a difficult course between appeasing the critics and political pragmatism by supporting minimal changes designed to avoid upsetting the system. When in 1989 the first drafts of the Environmental Protection Bill were published, it showed that there were to be no general obligations of disclosure introduced by the new Act. However, when Chris Patten was appointed Secretary of State for the Environment there was a further change in policy and, by January 1990, it was accepted that the public should have free access to information about industry's compliance with environmental authorisations which had been obtained under statutory powers. Clearly there were to be safeguards, but the underlying concept of free access was agreed.

This move towards openness has broadened with the introduction of the Environment Act 1995. Increasingly, access to environmental information is moving into areas such as the provision of general information on the state of the environment (e.g., see the Chemical Release Inventory) and wider consultation on issues of importance (although, for another view, see *R* v *Her Majesty's Inspectorate of Pollution, ex parte Greenpeace* [1994] Env LR 76 and p. 35).

Water pollution

In many ways the provisions on public registers of water pollution have been the model for the introduction of other controls. After much pressure from the Royal Commission, Part II of the Control of Pollution Act 1974 introduced a system of public registration which would contain not only information on the consents granted to a company to allow it to discharge effluent into water, but also the frequency with which the limits of the consent were not complied with. Despite an 11-year gap between the publication of the Act and the implementation of the information requirements, the principles of the register were seen to be a model for other areas of environmental control.

The provisions of Part II of the Control of Pollution Act were re-enacted in the Water Resources Act 1991, s. 190. The public registers contain a wide variety of information. The Act requires that the contents of the register must be available at all reasonable times for inspection by the public free of charge.

Copies of the entries can be taken by anybody on payment of a reasonable charge. The information contained on the register is prescribed in detail by the Control of Pollution (Applications, Appeals and Registers) Regulations 1996 (SI 1996 No. 2971).

Where an application for a discharge consent is made, the EA is obliged to enter the details of the application within 28 days under reg. 15(a). The details contained within the register cover such things as the name of the applicant and any additional information which has been supplied in order to amplify the application. If the application is granted, details of the consent, plus any conditions attached to that consent, also have to be entered within the 28-day limit. These must include the name of the person/company to whom consent is given, where the discharge will take place and when the consent will take effect. If there is any notice served on the holder of the discharge consent, that fact must also be registered on the register (this includes revocation or variation notices). Furthermore, the register must show the time limit within which no variation may be made to the consent.

Normally, the format for recording the information will show the maximum levels of substances to be contained in the effluent as laid down by the original consent alongside a figure showing the content of the effluent as taken on the sample date. The particulars contained in the registers should normally indicate where the sample was taken from, the date and time of day it was taken and whether or not any action was required to be taken on behalf of the EA. Any sample taken, whether it was by or on behalf of the EA or by someone else (e.g., self-monitored samples), must be placed on the register not more than 28 days after the information 'becoming available' to the EA. This provision alters the position under previous legislation, which required the information to be placed on the register within two months of the sampling date.

Some classes of information are exempt and are excluded from the register. In line with other areas of pollution control, all information which is commercially confidential or related to national security issues is excluded (Water Resources Act 1991, ss. 191A and 191B).

Any entry in the register has to be kept there for a period of four years only; thereafter it would be maintained on the register only if it is necessary for the exercise of the EA's pollution control functions.

The register system has been criticised by a number of bodies. It is considered that the 'raw data' showing the results of single samples does not provide lay people with an adequate picture of compliance. There is, as yet, no information relating to environmental quality standards or a summary of any cumulative effects of the discharge. Moreover, some of the samples taken are defined as 'operational' and thus do not fall within the definition of 'samples to be taken as a result of pollution control'.

Other registers in the water industry

There are a range of registers covering different areas in the water industry. Under the Water Industry Act 1991, s. 196, water service companies (in their role as sewerage undertakers) maintain registers containing details of all consents, variations, agreements and directions. Unfortunately, no monitoring data is placed on the register so it is impossible for third parties to check levels of compliance. This has been criticised by a number of environmental groups as there is some conflict between the commercial nature of trade effluent agreements and the discretionary nature of enforcement for breaches. It has been estimated that over £100m is paid by industry to the water services companies and all are negotiated in secret. Where there is no access to levels of compliance it is difficult to see the adequacy (or otherwise) of the system.

Details of private water and sewerage undertakers are maintained on a register by the Director General of Water Services (Water Industry Act 1991, s. 195). This contains details of all directions, consents and enforcement orders.

A register containing details of abstraction and impounding licences is maintained by the EA (s. 189). The register contains details of the holder, the location of the abstraction point, the volume of water abstracted, the provision and location of metering and expiry date. Once again, no metering data are required to be entered on the register and there is no way of checking compliance levels.

Information on drinking water quality is maintained in a register kept under the Water Supply (Water Quality) Regulations 1989 (SI 1989 No. 1147 as amended). Regulation 29 provides for a range of informatiom to be kept on the register including information on any emergency relaxation of standards, sampling results, compliance levels, particulars of action taken to comply with undertakings, and general information on general water quality.

Waste management

Section 64 of the EPA 1990 places a duty upon the EA to maintain a register containing details of information in relation to the waste management licensing system. This duty is subject to ss. 65 — 66 which exclude information on the grounds of confidentiality (see below). There is an additional duty upon all English waste collection authorities to maintain a register of information relating to current or recently current licences and copies of notices affecting the scope or status of the licences (e.g., modification, suspension or revocation notices).

The Waste Management Licensing Regulations 1994 (SI 1994 No. 1056) flesh out the details of the registers. Regulation 10 prescribes the information to be included in the registers which includes:

(a)   full particulars of current or recently current (i.e., in force at any time within the previous 12 months) waste management licences. This should include copies of the licences and working plans;

(b)   full particulars of any application, including a full copy of the application with supporting documentation and copies of consultation responses;

(c)   details of applications for modification and transfer of licences;

(d)   details of suspension, variation or enforcement notices;

(e)   details of convictions for any waste management offence (not necess-arily in connection with any licence in the area) and any details of convictions for 'relevant offences' under the 'fit and proper persons' provision;

(f)   copies of any reports produced by the EA in the exercise of its supervisory duties (whether formal or informal), including information relat-ing to water pollution emanating from waste sites and information obtained on investigations and examinations;

(g)   details of monitoring information from either the applicant or the EA;

(h)   details of directions from the Secretary of State which relate to pollution control and environment rather than administrative matters;

(i)   details of site records in relation to special waste and summary information on arisings of special waste in the area;

(j)   full particulars in relation to the surrender of a waste management licence, including copies of all the documents submitted with the application, any information obtained as a result of any site inspection, a copy of consultation responses and a copy of the determination and certificate of completion in cases where the surrender is accepted;

(k)   details of exempt establishments.

The EA is required to keep the register open to the public at all reasonable times, free of charge and provide copies of all documents on request with the payment of a reasonable charge (s. 64(6)). Although there is no time limit for the provision of information on the register after receipt, Circular 11/94 suggests that it should be entered 'as soon as is reasonably practicable' with a warning that a delay of longer than two months could render the EA liable to be in breach of the Environmental Information Regulations.

Information on licences is to be kept on the register for the lifetime of the licence plus an additional 12 months (i.e., when it is still 'current'). With regard to other information which is not related to the licence, including inspection data or the exercise of emergency powers under s. 70, it is anticipated that it will be kept on the register for a period of four years.

Exclusions

Regulation 11(1) of the Waste Management Licensing Regulations 1994 provides a general exception to the requirements set out above where the information relates to actual or prospective legal proceedings. Thus, where the EA has information which might be used as evidence in a prosecution or even civil proceedings, there is no requirement to disclose the information to the public. Once the case has been heard the requirement to disclose reapplies.

Under EPA 1990, s. 65, information which would, in the Secretary of State's opinion, be contrary to the interests of national security, is to be excluded. This will allow for a fairly limited body of information to be excluded owing to its sensitive nature. There will be no indication on the register that such information has been excluded, as it has been suggested by the Government that even the acknowledgement that there was such infor-mation would be contrary to national security itself.

Under EPA 1990, s. 66, there is the traditional exemption for information which is commercially confidential. However, it is for the Secretary of State to decide whether or not something is commercially confidential, and the Department of the Environment has made it very clear that there will be only a limited number of instances where such an exclusion will apply. There is an additional power under s. 66(7) to allow for an outline description of the process notwithstanding that it is commercially confidential. This aims to provide a general view of a waste disposal site where supplying details would give rise to problems of confidentiality.

Where an application is made for a waste management licence, it is open to the person applying to ask for the information to be excluded from the register because of its commercial confidentiality (s. 66(2)). The EA has 14 days to make a determination, and if it fails to do so then the information is treated as being commercially confidential (s. 66(3)). Where the EA wishes to include the information on the register on the grounds that it is not confidential, it has to allow the applicant an opportunity to make representations on that particular issue and the Agency must take into account the representations made (s. 66(4)). If, after this somewhat complicated procedure, the Agency still decides to publish the information, there is a period of 21 days in which information is not to be published and an appeal is allowed to the Secretary of State (s. 66(5)).

As mentioned earlier, the confidentiality of information depends to a large extent upon whether or not it would prejudice to an unreasonable degree the commercial interests of the person concerned (s. 66(11)). Clearly one of the areas of difficulty will be whether or not this is to be determined by a subjective or an objective test. If it were to be subjective, then clearly any applicant for a waste management licence would be quick to assert that the information would prejudice them to an unreasonable degree and therefore it should be excluded. On the other hand, if objectivity is sought, the waste regulation authority would be able to balance the effect upon an individual with the desirability of making the information public. The Department of the Environment has made it clear that it is for the person opposing the disclosure to substantiate that the disclosure would prejudice to an unreasonable degree some person's commercial interest. There is a need to demonstrate that this disclosure of information would negate or significantly diminish the commercial advantage that one operator has over another. Where information is treated as commercially confidential, under s. 66(8), the information will only be excluded from the register for a period of four years. This allows for the fact that commercial confidentiality endures only for a finite period and after a certain length of time the need to disclose such information to the public will outweigh the harm created to the commercial interests of the individual. There is, however, a right to apply for continuation of the exclusion (s. 66(8)).

Registers in relation to contaminated land

After the withdrawal of the registers of contaminative uses under s. 143 of the EPA 1990, the Environment Act 1995 has introduced a set of registers which reflects those found in other areas of environmental law. Section 78R of the EPA 1990 now provides for each enforcing authority (the EA and local authorities) to maintain a register containing information on the following:

(a)   remediation notices served and remediation statements published by the relevant authority;
(b)   appeals against remediation notices and charging notices;
(c)   notices designating land as a special site and any subsequent notice terminating the designation;
(d)   any notification of remedial steps taken (although the presence of such information on the register is not conclusive proof of either the adequacy of the works nor even that the works have been carried out);
(e)   convictions.

The Secretary of State is expected to make Regulations giving further details of the content of the register. There is the traditional exclusion of information where it would be contrary to national security (s. 78S) or if it is commercially confidential (s. 78T). The provisions in relation to confidentiality reflect those under the IPC register, with the question of determining confidentiality remaining with the enforcing authority and the Secretary of State. They include the right of appeal to the Secretary of State and exclusion of information from the register pending determination.

Integrated pollution control

Under the Health and Safety at Work etc. Act 1974, s. 28(7), all information relating to the works covered by that Act were forbidden to be disclosed by the Industrial Air Pollution Inspectorate. This was criticised on many occasions. The Royal Commission said that these restrictions should be removed as they were an obsolete and unnecessary bar on the disclosure of information. The introduction of the system of integrated pollution control and air pollution control under Part I of the EPA 1990 has now seen the removal of those restrictions and far more open access to information of an environmentally-sensitive type.

The controls are contained in EPA 1990, ss. 20 to 22, and govern both Part A processes controlled by the EA and Part B processes controlled by local authorities. Local authorities will hold information relating to processes they control and processes controlled by the EA which are situated in their area. There are further controls contained within the Environmental Protection (Applications, Appeals and Registers) Regulations 1991 (SI 1991 No. 507) as amended. The format of the registers closely follows those of the waste management licence registers under Part II of the Act.

The register contains details of (reg. 15):

(a)   all particulars of any application of an authorisation made to the authority;

(b)   all particulars of any notice served on the applicant by the authority under paragraph 1(3) of sch. 1 to that Act and of any information furnished in response to such a notice;

(c)   all particulars of any representations made by any person required to be consulted under paragraph 2, 6 or 7 of sch. 1 to the EPA 1990 pursuant to reg. 4(1);

(d)   all particulars of any authorisation granted by the authority;

(e)   all particulars of any variation notice, enforcement notice or prohibition notice issued by the authority;

(f)   all particulars of any notice issued by the authority withdrawing a prohibition notice;

(g)   all particulars of any notification given to the holder of an authorisation by the authority under s. 10(5) of the Act;

(h)   all particulars of any application for the variation of the conditions of an authorisation under s. 11(4)(b) of the Act;

(i)   all particulars of any revocation of an authorisation effected by the authority;

(j)   all particulars of any notice of appeal under s. 15 of the Act against a decision by the authority, the documents relating to the appeal mentioned in reg. 9(2)(a), (d) and (e), any written notification of the Secretary of State's determination of such an appeal and any report accompanying any such written notification;

(k)   details of any conviction of any person for any offence under s. 23(1) of the Act which relates to the carrying on of a prescribed process under an authorisation granted by the authority, including the name of the offender, the date of conviction, the penalty imposed and the name of the court;

(l)   all particulars of any monitoring information relating to the carrying on of a prescribed process under an authorisation granted by the authority obtained by the authority as a result of its own monitoring or furnished to the authority in writing by virtue of a condition of the authorisation or s. 19(2) of the Act;

(m)   in a case where any such monitoring information is omitted from the register by virtue of s. 22 of that Act, a statement by the authority, based on the monitoring information from time to time obtained by or furnished to them, indicating whether or not there has been compliance with any relevant condition of the authorisation;

(n)   all particulars of any report published by an enforcing authority relating to an assessment of the environmental consequences of the carrying on of a prescribed process in the locality of premises where the prescribed process is carried on under an authorisation granted by the authority; and

(o)   all particulars of any direction (other than a direction under s. 21(2) of the Act) given to the authority by the Secretary of State under any provision of Part I of the Act.

Again, these registers have to be freely available at all reasonable times for inspection by the public free of charge and copies are allowed to be taken of the documentation on the payment of a reasonable charge (s. 20(7)).

The EPA 1990 acknowledges the introduction of more sophisticated methods of information retrieval and allows the registers to be kept in any form, which would include computer retrieval, microfiches or photographic storage.

There are two exceptions to the normal rule that information should be freely available. First, there are safeguards against the disclosure of information which is contrary to the interests of national security. Section 21 allows the Secretary of State to direct that information should be excluded if its disclosure would be contrary to national security. This power is also available if a person makes an application to exclude the information on the grounds that it is contrary to national security; they must notify the Secretary of State specifying the information and its apparent nature and then they must notify the enforcing authority of what they have done. There will be no reference to such information on the face of the register because of the chance that any harm might arise out of the disclosure of such sensitive information.

The second exclusion applies to information which is commercially confidential. Section 22 forbids disclosure of information which 'would prejudice to an unreasonable degree the commercial interests' of a person. Unlike s. 21, the determination of what is commercially confidential lies at first with the enforcing authority and then on appeal with the Secretary of State. It is open to a company applying for an authorisation to apply at the same time for information related to that authorisation to be treated as commercially confidential. This also applies when there is an application for a variation of an authorisation, or information is supplied to the authority which concerns compliance with a condition of the authorisation, or which is in response to a formal request by the authority (s. 22(2)). Where a company applies for information to be treated as commercially confidential, the enforcing authority has 14 days to decide whether or not to exclude the information. If the authority fails to make a determination after 14 days it is deemed to have excluded the information (s. 22(3)).

An enforcing authority is permitted to notify an applicant that the information the company has supplied might be commercially confidential. In these particular circumstances, the applicant is then allowed to object to the information being put on the register and to make representations to the authority justifying that objection (s. 22(4)). It is difficult to envisage when this provision will be applied. It seems quite clear that any company wishing to protect its own trade secrets will try to do so from the outset. Moreover, it is not easy to understand quite how an enforcing authority will know that certain information is commercially confidential.

Where the enforcing authority decides that the information supplied is not commercially confidential, it is nevertheless not permitted to enter the information on the register for 21 days, giving time for the company to appeal to the Secretary of State to determine whether or not the information is confidential (s. 22(5)).

The Secretary of State does have an overriding power to direct that information be included on the registers even though it is commercially confidential if it is in the public interest for it to be so included. This may well apply to particularly sensitive operations which cause great public concern and which have been the subject of a large amount of lobbying from members of the public. It is in circumstances where particular concern is expressed to the local authority or to the EA by community groups or local residents that the Secretary of State may find a political bonus in releasing the information required. A good example of when this power could be used would be where there was a large disaster. The then Environment Minister, David Trippier, when explaining this particular section of the EPA 1990 said:

> After the Chernobyl disaster, commercial confidentiality affected the amount of information that we could release. The lack of public information served only to increase public disquiet.

Naturally the right to overrule commercial confidentiality is a draconian one and will only be used in limited circumstances.

The time limit for the exclusion of information from the register is four years from the original exclusion. This obviously takes into account the fact that the confidentiality of information may well have decreased somewhat over that time period and therefore the exclusion of the information from the register is no longer justified. However, it is open to the applicant to apply to the authority for a further exclusion on the grounds that the information is still commercially confidential.

The Environmental Protection (Applications, Appeals and Registers) Regulations 1991 (SI 1991 No. 507) make detailed provision for the maintenance of the registers. There are a number of areas for concern. First, only data obtained by the enforcement agencies as a result of their own monitoring, or as supplied to them in exercise of their powers of information gathering under EPA 1990, s. 19, or under a condition of an authorisation, are to be included.

Secondly, in relation to information concerning 'the assessment of the environmental consequences of a prescribed process', the only requirement is to release 'all particulars of any reports published'. Clearly, the enforcing authority will have a discretion as to whether or not it publishes such 'data'. Once again there is evidence to suggest that informal non-disclosure agreements may preclude the provision of access to environmental information. Lastly, there is no deadline for the entry of information after it has been received.

The Chemical Releases Inventory

The information kept on the IPC registers does not, however, provide enough information to enable a proper assessment to be made of the total effects of releases upon the environment as a whole. Whilst it enables individuals to appraise an individual operator and its performance as set against its authorisation conditions, it does not provide an adequate measure of compliance with general environmental quality objectives.

Therefore, in addition to the registers kept under Part I of the EPA 1990, the EA also publishes a database of aggregated information taken from the registers, which is known as the Chemical Release Inventory (CRI). Information from the database forms the basis of an annual report, which sets out figures for releases from prescribed processes to all environmental media in tabular form.

The main purpose of the CRI was to fulfil part of the Conservative Government's commitment to increase access to environmental information, as set out in *This Common Inheritance*. Secondly, it was intended to clarify the scale and nature of releases from IPC processes and to facilitate an informed analysis of the sources and effects of pollution which should enable priorities for action to be identified. Finally, it was hoped that the CRI will provide a useful resource to enable industry to identify opportunities for waste minimisation. The model for the CRI is taken from the Toxic Release Inventory (TRI) in the US. Since the publication of the TRI in 1987 the so-called 33/50 programme (which was based upon information contained in the TRI) has resulted in over 600 US companies reducing emissions by 33% by the end of 1992 and 50% by the end of 1995.

Although the database was established in 1991, the first printed annual report was published at the end of 1994, with information gathered in the calendar years 1992 and 1993. As IPC was introduced over a number of years for different processes the first report included only a relatively small proportion of information on releases. In later years it has been more comprehensive.

The data which forms the database is gathered from individual operators as a normal part of the requirement to provide monitoring information. It covers over 360 substances (and 125 isotopes). The individual monitoring information is then aggregated by the EA using formulae agreed with the operator so that an overall picture can be gained. This is then incorporated with other information so that regional and sectoral information can be presented. The annual report gives information on the releases of substances released from all processes to all media. It also provides tables that show releases of substances to each media, by country (the database covers England and Wales), by county and by district council, with separate tables covering industry sectors, industry types and process types.

In addition to the annual report, individuals can search the database itself. Searches can be made by reference to EA region, operator details, location, substance, media and authorisation number.

Although the CRI is the first attempt to take environmental information onto a broader scale, it has been the subject of criticism. First, it does not give a completely accurate picture of all releases. For example, it does not include non-point sources such as motor vehicles. This has led to a vast understatement of the quantities of certain chemicals. In the case of methane, where most releases arise from livestock or landfill operations, it is estimated that less than 1% of the total releases are to be found in the database. Secondly, there is no information kept in relation to LAAPC consents and/or discharge consents. The EA has expressed the intention to incorporate such information as soon as practicable and it is expected that the amalgamation of the enforcement agencies under the Environment Act 1995 should help facilitate this.

Air pollution

In the majority of cases, access to information relating to air pollution will be covered under the registers discussed above. However, there are further controls under a number of different statutes. Primarily, smoke pollution is dealt with under the Clean Air Act 1993. There are no specific directions for disclosure, although under s. 34(1) local authorities have vague powers to arrange for research and publicity with regard to air pollution. However, these vague powers are then virtually nullified by s. 34(2), which makes it a criminal offence to disclose any information obtained under the Clean Air Act provisions which relates to a trade secret.

Access to information held by local government

Environmental information held by local authorities is available to the general public under the Local Government (Access to Information) Act 1985 and the Environmental Information Regulations 1992.

Under the 1985 Act all regulatory powers exercised by local authorities can be the subject of public scrutiny where those powers are exercised by way of committee. This would include areas such as planning, waste disposal, environmental health (e.g., statutory nuisances), air pollution and mineral matters. This information is normally available in the form of reports made by officers to committee, which would include any accompanying documentation (for further details, see p. 56).

The Environmental Information Regulations 1992

The pace of moves towards free access to environmental information has quickened with the introduction and adoption of the EC Directive on Freedom of Access to Environmental Information (90/313).

The implementation of the Directive into domestic legislation has seen a move away from the traditional register-based access to environmental information into a broader system. The Environmental Information Regulations (SI 1992 No. 3240), which were brought into force on 31 December 1992, extended the availability of information held by public bodies. The regulations were made under the European Communities Act 1972 and thus follow the terms of the Directive closely. As in the case of the Environmental Assessment Directive 85/337, however, there are some variations, and arguably some exclusions.

Under the regulations, public authorities with responsibilities for the environment must make environmental information available to any person who requests it. 'Environmental information' is defined widely and includes information on the quality and state of air, water, soil, flora, fauna, natural sites and other land. It also covers activities which adversely affect these areas and the measures which are used to protect them.

The regulations apply to all public authorities which have responsibilities for the environment. The Department of the Environment, local authorities, the EA and other public bodies carrying out regulatory functions would come within the definition. There is, however, a whole range of private bodies which carry out public functions in relation to the environment. For instance, the water services companies and the local authority waste disposal companies both carry out roles which are semi-public. It is assumed that such bodies would be subject to the regulations, at least in relation to some of their functions, although the picture is far from clear.

Where a request is made to a public body it has to be responded to as soon as possible, and in any event not more than two months from the date of the request. If the request is refused then any refusal must be in writing and reasons given. The reasons for rejecting the request may vary. The body to whom the request is addressed may consider that it is not subject to the regulations, there may be no information which can usefully be given, or the information requested does not fall within the terms of the regulations. Lastly, the information may be exempt or, where a request is vague, formulated in too general a manner or manifestly unreasonable. In these circumstances the public body is entitled to reject the request.

Exceptions
There is a long list of categories of information which are exempt from the regulations. Certain of these categories are considered to be strictly confidential, whereas others are subject to the discretion of the relevant authority:

(a) *Mandatory confidentiality*.   Certain categories of information are always viewed as being confidential:

(i)   Personal information where an individual has not given consent to its disclosure.
(ii)   Material disclosed voluntarily by a third party.
(iii)   Information which would increase the likelihood of damage to the environment if disclosed.

(b) *Discretionary confidentiality*.   Certain categories of information are considered to be confidential only if the authority determines them to be so:

(i)   Information affecting national security, public defence, or international relations.
(ii)   Information which is or has previously been *sub judice* or the subject of an inquiry.
(iii)   Information from internal communications or unfinished documents.
(iv)   Commercially confidential information.

The availability of information
The information which is available includes anything contained in any records, registers, reports, returns and computer records.

A charge can be made in respect of the costs attributable to the supply of the information, and such a charge can be levied as a condition of the supply of the information. As is usual, the information only has to be available in such a form and at such times and places as is reasonable.

Remedies for failure to supply information

There is no right of appeal against the refusal to supply the information. Central guidance suggests that the only available remedy is that of judicial review. It is, however, difficult to envisage the situation where an individual would be prepared to mount such an action without a firm idea of the type of information which is required.

Access to environmental information in practice

Although the implementation of the Freedom of Access to Environmental Information Directive through the Environmental Information Regulations 1992 has led to wider access to information, there have been criticisms of the Directive and the regulations. In 1996, the House of Lords Select Committee on the European Communities published a report on freedom of access to environmental information. The final report concentrated on the extent to which the Directive is working effectively, rather than considering merely whether the Directive has been properly transposed by the Environmental Information Regulations 1992.

The committee identified a number of areas of weakness including the following:

(a)   The definition of 'information relating to the environment'. There has always been some confusion about whether financial and economic information falls into this category. This would have a direct bearing on the regulated utilities. For example, if such information was excluded from the definition of 'information relating to the environment', water companies could withhold information relating to matters such as leakage and investment programmes, which have a direct environmental impact. In its response to the report the Government accepted that changes which clarify the definition may be required. This should occur as a result of on-going negotiations over a UN/ECE Convention on Access to Environmental Information, expected to necessitate changes to the Directive and regulations.

(b)   The definition of 'relevant persons'. The problems with the scope of this phrase are outlined above. The committee felt that the definition should be fleshed out with a non-exhaustive list of those to whom it applied. Failing that it was felt that the general criteria should be supplemented by greater detail. The Government agreed that clarification of the phrase would be beneficial but felt that a non-exhaustive list would not be helpful. In particular, both bodies thought that legislation which required the water authorities in Scotland and Northern Ireland to supply information but which might not apply to the privatised water utilities in England and Wales was 'unsatisfactory' in terms of environmental protection.

(c)   A more effective means of enforcement. Both the Government and the committee considered that an appeals tribunal should be set up to deal quickly and effectively with aggrieved applicants. The introduction of such a tribunal would probably be integrated into any proposed Environmental Court.

(d)   A revision of the categories of exemption. The report recommended that there be a requirement to demonstrate potential harm where exemption from disclosure is claimed, and an overreaching requirement for disclosure where it was in the public interest. This would obviate the need for the distinction in the regulations (but not the Directive) between mandatory and discretionary exemptions. It was also thought that domestic provisions concerning information relating to legal or other proceedings (reg. 4(2)(b)) should also be tightened to cover only documents specially prepared for the purposes of the legal or other proceedings in question.

The public's utilisation of registers

One of the major difficulties undermining the system of easier access to information within Britain is that research has shown that, even where there is information which can easily be obtained, public participation in the system is said to be low. In their Fourth Report, the Royal Commission stated:

> certainly experience in the local government field has shown that 'public participation' — often consisting of little more than one way provision of information at meagrely attended public meetings — can be an unrewarding ritual for those charged with the task of organising it. However, the essential requirement is that information should be *available,* not that it should be forcefully fed to the public.

It is clear, though, that the basis upon which the system is founded is that the public should have a desire to receive information from the register for themselves. The empirical evidence suggests otherwise. A research project carried out on the utilisation of the registers kept under the Control of Pollution Act 1974 and then the Water Act 1989 has shown that there are relatively few people who are particularly interested in the registers. In the period August 1985 to December 1986, when the registers were first opened, a survey showed that there were 75 enquiries made to Severn Trent Water Authority, 85 to Anglian Water and 70 to Yorkshire Water, making up a total of some 230 requests to look at the register as compared with the millions of people who were resident in each of those areas. Furthermore, when the figures were broken down, by far and away the majority of enquiries were from sellers of septic tank equipment who used the registers as a database from which to sell their wares. Other enquiries came from environmental protection groups who used the registers to check up on information regularly.

The system of registers has received general approval from most parties. The difficulties with the previous systems under COPA 1974 and the Water Act 1989 have, however, underlined some practical problems. In evidence submitted to the House of Lords European Select Committee, Friends of the Earth pointed out that many samples collected were not entered on to the register because they were 'operational' samples rather than samples taken for the purposes of monitoring compliance and legislation. Thus, it was argued that too great a discretion was given to the enforcement agency, which allowed the system to be abused.

Moreover, Friends of the Earth argued that the effectiveness of the register was governed by five factors. They suggested that a system of registers should be:

(a)   conveniently located;
(b)   user friendly;
(c)   not excessively expensive;
(d)   interactive;
(e)   adequately resourced.

The Select Committee regarded it as '. . . of paramount importance that any system of registers should both be accessible geographically and "user friendly". These features should be possible with modern data-processing techniques.'

It was suggested that a two-tier system be utilised. The first tier would contain basic data in a register form with an indication of any further information available at the second tier. The second tier itself might contain the more complicated information which would explain some of the references on the simpler level.

Even so, the registers as they exist have a low level of interest for the members of the general public. Figures available from the NRA's Annual Report in 1989/90 disclosed a marked increase in the utilisation of the registers and this has increased substantially in the 1990s. However, as percentages of the overall population of each individual authority, the use of the registers is still remarkably low. Tim Burton, who has carried out detailed research into access to environmental information in water registers, identified three areas of possible explanation for the low level of utilisation of these registers. These were awareness, accessibility and difficulty with interpreting the data itself. The introduction of the Environment Agency has helped to address some of the issues surrounding accessibility as there are more regional offices and greater efforts made to publicise the EA's activities. There are, however, still real issues relating to the quality and comprehensibility of the data which is available. The challenges in future will centre on the communication of data in a meaningful fashion without imposing controversial value judgments on the raw data which is available.

EIGHT

The common law and the protection of the environment

The development of the law relating to the protection of the environment is not solely governed by the realm of public and administrative law. Although the spread of administrative and bureaucratic controls has accelerated within the last 50 years, traditionally, at first glance anyway, private law has attempted to serve a similar function in controlling damage caused to the environment. This similarity has caused confusion. Private law, essentially the law of tort and contract, serves as a mechanism of environmental protection primarily through the control of competing uses of land rather than the protection of the environment.

The system of common law developed from the time of the Norman conquest in an attempt to cope with new disputes over use and abuse of land. As the system developed, it incidentally became a mechanism for environmental protection. The hybrid nature of the common law's role in environmental protection can be demonstrated by looking at the characteristics which distinguish it from the more usual methods of public law control.

The characteristics of the common law as a mechanism of environmental protection

The common law acts only as a protector of private interest

The primary function of private law actions is to protect interests in land rather than the more nebulous concept of 'environmental rights'. Consequently, the factors governing the decision to take action against polluters are mainly personal. Potential plaintiffs are more concerned about balancing their own interests against the loss suffered, be that financial or the loss of enjoyment of their property. The protection of the environment demands that other factors have to be taken into account. Sometimes it is clear that human interests are contrary to the interests of the environment. For example, it is possible to acquire an easement to pollute a river. It is arguable whether such activity could ever be in the interests of the environment. However, in certain circumstances, the private law seeks to protect the private interests of individuals.

The protection of private rights is based upon imprecise standards

We have already seen in Chapter 5 that the public law controls protecting the environment are based primarily upon standards of environmental quality. Such standards regulate activities specifically by attempting to impose definite limits upon substances which can be emitted into the environment. These levels are often expressed as quantitative limits. These limits allow for relatively simple enforcement as the detection of breaches can be effectively monitored and proper assessments can be made of any discharge.

The monitoring of such discharges involves scientific and technical skills. Without those skills, the accumulation of devastating substances can affect the environment on a long-term basis.

It is this type of pollution which can only be dealt with effectively by quantitative standards and scientific monitoring. Private law mechanisms meet neither criteria. Generally, the common law is based upon imprecise standards unrelated to specified levels. In attempting to balance competing private interests, the common law looks to the reasonableness of actions rather than restricting conduct to specific levels. What is reasonable depends upon the circumstances of each case. Maintaining this balance means that the same result will not be guaranteed from any two cases.

The main mechanism of control, the tort of private nuisance, can broadly be defined as the unreasonable interference with the reasonable use and enjoyment of land. This implies that there are areas which require further analysis. What is a reasonable use? What would be unreasonable? These questions underline the large degree of uncertainty involved in bringing an action in private nuisance. An illustration of the types of uncertainty surrounding private law actions in nuisance and how there can be a detrimental effect to the environment can be found in the so-called locality doctrine in private nuisance.

This doctrine asserts the need to take into account 'the circumstances of the place where the thing complained of actually occurs' (*St Helen's Smelting Co.* v *Tipping* (1865) 11 HL Cas 642). Putting it simply, those who live in towns or close to factories have to expect a dirtier, smellier environment than those who live in the countryside. The flaws in this doctrine are clear. In terms of environmental protection, those areas which require the greatest degree of control are often the same as those to which the most damage has to occur before an action can be founded. The accumulation of polluting substances, be they dust, noise or fumes, actually raises the degree of nuisance required. As one commentator puts it 'Those who suffer most from the ravages of pollution are the least worthy of protection' (McLaren (1972) 10 Osgoode Hall LJ 505).

The right of action is limited

As the common law seeks to balance competing individual rights, the right to take action is normally vested only in those who are directly harmed.

Generally, this means the individual in possession of land which suffers damage. Although there are narrow rights for groups to take action in public nuisance, the basis of an action in common law still remains the protection of land and its ownership rather than the environment. This view has been reaffirmed by the House of Lords in *Hunter* v *Canary Wharf* [1997] 2 WLR 684. The concept of 'environmental rights' is as yet undeveloped in the United Kingdom. The idea that there should be an ability to bring an action on behalf of flora and fauna rather as children bring actions through a guardian *ad litem* seems strange. The private law seeks to compensate one landowner by granting compensation from another. A move away from this system would be difficult. The private law does not properly seek to compensate for environmental damage where there are no rights of ownership to protect or an owner does not wish to pursue an action.

Problems of proof
Whereas, in public law, the proof of the breach of a regulation involves scientific evidence that is more or less irrefutable, there is great difficulty in showing a cause of action for environmental pollution in the common law.

First, there are often problems surrounding the establishment of a causal link between the origins of pollution and the damage. For instance, it is the nature of airborne deposits that they could have originated from a site many miles from the area of damage. Seeking to show that the damage emanates from a particular site in these circumstances is particularly difficult. Moreover, in areas of heavy industrialised activity these difficulties become even more complex. For instance there could be five factories within a two mile radius, all producing and dispersing similar acidic emissions into the atmosphere. Trying to differentiate between each emission requires highly technical evidence. The expense of carrying out investigations such as these will often militate against individuals taking action and it may be that no definite culprit can be identified.

Secondly, there is a large degree of subjectivity involved in assessing the reasonableness of activities. Unfortunately, what would be acceptable to some in terms of environmental damage would not be acceptable to others. Some find the smells of certain fumes offensive whereas others have a high tolerance level. Again, this uncertainty prevents any proper guidelines being laid down as to when activities will incur liability.

Private law as a fault-based system
In certain circumstances, the bringing of an action under common law requires there to be some fault on behalf of the person creating the damage. Very few pollution incidents occur because of deliberate actions by careless and unthinking individuals. Mostly incidents arise because of a number of circumstances which would not normally be foreseeable but which give rise to damage. The common law does not always seek to redress any damage caused by such accidents. It is only in situations where the pollution is foreseeable that an action will normally be founded.

Reactive controls
Private law controls are only reactive and compensatory rather than preventative. It is only very rarely that private law can be used to prevent
environmental damage. Although it is possible in certain circumstances to
seek anticipatory injunctions, on the whole the controls tend to be post-
damage, that is to say, after the harm is discovered. Private law offers no
continuing control, nor does it necessarily seek to remedy harm. When
compensation is paid there are no rules governing the manner in which the
money has to be spent. Damages are often assessed as being the difference in
value between the land as it was before an act of damage and the value
afterwards. This does not necessarily include clean-up costs although those
can form a part of any claim.

Controls are not purely environmental
The wide range of activities covered by civil remedies extends far beyond
those activities covered under the umbrella of the environment. As an
incidental effect, the common law provides for the prevention of pollution or
the protection of the public but the protection spreads much wider to the
coverage of a whole range of civil rights. The effect of this is to ensure that
the system has built up in an unsystematic way and in some ways mirrors the
piecemeal nature of the statutory controls.

Is the common law as a protection mechanism dead?

The criticisms of the private law as being too expensive, too long-winded and
too uncertain have led to its low utilisation as a tool for environmental
protection. The roots of its weaknesses can be traced back to the nineteenth
century when industrial pollution was in its infancy. With no statutory
regulations to control the growth of polluting processes it might be thought
that the common law would serve as the primary mechanism for protection.
However, McLaren presented very cogent arguments that other factors,
including institutional, social and economic matters, outweighed the importance of the environmental benefit to be procured from such control (see
pp. 178 and 185).

The courts have consistently struggled with the use of the common law for
environmental protection. Indeed, the judiciary have often sought to separate
the system of administrative regulatory protection from private law remedies
where, in fact, there is often a significant overlap. In *Wheeler* v *J.J. Saunders
Ltd* [1996] Ch 19 (see below at p. 190) the court took the view that the
planning system (with the emphasis upon the public interest) was entirely
different to the exercise of private rights which protect property interests. In
addition, the House of Lords' judgment in *Cambridge Water Co.* v *Eastern
Counties Leather plc* [1994] 2 AC 264 (see below at p. 193) suggested that the
courts would prefer the relative 'safety' of the growth of administrative
mechanisms to developing the common law. Even more recently, the House
of Lords has reaffirmed the essentially property-based nature of the right to
sue in nuisance. In *Hunter* v *Canary Wharf Ltd* [1997] 2 WLR 684 the Lords

overturned the Court of Appeal's decision to allow those without any legal interest in land to sue in nuisance. The Court of Appeal had held that a plaintiff who could demonstrate a 'substantial link' to the land could bring an action in nuisance. This principle was developed from previous decisions which had seen mere occupiers sue in nuisance in cases of telephone harassment and other threats of violence. The House of Lords, however, reaffirmed the essential nexus between property ownership and the right to sue. In doing so the Law Lords sought to distinguish the right to bring an action in negligence, which was not related to ownership, and nuisance which had historically been intrinsically linked to ownership. Taken together, these strands of judicial thinking would appear to make the development of the common law for environmental protection unlikely. This would be more acceptable if administrative controls were adapted to provide substitutes for private rights, such as compensation.

Civil liability in statutes

In addition to the common law, there is a number of statutes which impose liability by means of private law remedies, rather than the more usual public law methods.

(a) Nuclear Installations Act 1965

The individual problems of nuclear installations are not adequately dealt with by the law of tort. As the incident in Chernobyl demonstrated, the damage caused by nuclear actions can be widespread and not confined to a specific period of time. There are also difficulties of proving a causal link between the injury caused and exposure to radiation. Many diseases that are caused by radiation also occur naturally, and trying to establish whether or not there is an epidemiological link is frequently fraught with difficulties. Therefore, to avoid these difficulties, the Nuclear Installations Act 1965 introduced absolute civil liability for all damage caused from certain occurrences (ss. 7 — 10). Not all loss from nuclear damage is covered under the Act. Economic loss can only be recovered where there is specific physical harm caused to the land. Thus in *Merlin v British Nuclear Fuels plc* [1990] 2 QB 557 a claim for loss in value of a house in the area of the Sellafield nuclear installation resulting from radioactive contamination was refused because the 'contamination' had not given rise to physical harm. The presence of raised radioactivity levels in the house was not sufficient to amount to such harm.

The decision in *Merlin v British Nuclear Fuels plc* was considered in *Blue Circle Industries v Ministry of Defence* [1997] Env LR D7, in which a claim arose out of the contamination of land (owned by Blue Circle) neighbouring the Atomic Weapons Establishment at Aldermaston. Water from ponds on the AWE overflowed on to Blue Circle's land as a result of heavy rain. Blue Circle discovered the radioactive contamination when it attempted to sell the site and failed, even though it transpired the contamination was not at a dangerous level (it did, however, exceed statutory levels laid down under the Radioactive Substances Act 1960). The MOD carried out remediation works on Blue Circle's land which effectively removed the radioactive material.

However, it refused to compensate for the loss in value and saleability of Blue Circle's site, which was due to blight resulting from the contamination. Blue Circle brought an action to recover £5 million in damages arising out of the diminution in value of the estate. The court distinguished the damage in *Merlin* from the contamination at the AWE by linking the economic loss in Blue Circle's case to the actual physical harm caused by the radioactive contamination. In *Merlin* it was thought that there was no physical harm and the nature of the loss was purely economic and non-actionable. In contrast, the Blue Circle site had, in fact, suffered physical harm and therefore the loss was actionable. In finding in favour of Blue Circle the court also found that the 1965 Act imposed liability where there was *any* injury or damage, irrespective of the contamination levels.

(b)   Merchant Shipping (Oil Pollution) Act 1971
In the wake of numerous oil disasters in the mid to late 1960s, international concern led to the introduction of this Act to compensate for damage from oil. It is specific in that liability under the Act only arises from pollution from oil tankers. The implementation of this statute again deals with the inadequacies of tort in trying to cope with transfrontier contamination. The intention of the Act is to impose strict liability on owners of ships in relation to physical damage to property and personal injury from oil pollution (s. 1). The financing of the majority of losses stemming from the Act is covered by a compulsory insurance scheme, although there is a further international fund for compensation which pays out in situations where a shipowner cannot afford to pay the damages. There are a number of statutory defences which cover circumstances such as war, intentional acts of damage by third parties, or poor governmental control of navigation or lighting (s. 2).

(c)   Environmental Protection Act 1990, s. 73
Section 73(6) of EPA 1990 imposes civil liability for the unlawful deposit of waste (see p. 429).

Other private law remedies

The most common application of private law remedies as used for environmental protection is that of the law of tort (see below). However, there are other private law mechanisms which are useful in this context. Restrictive covenants, for instance, govern the activities which can be carried out upon land. A further example can be seen where local planning authorities and/or developers enter into planning obligations under the Town and Country Planning Act 1990, s. 106. Such obligations may be used for a whole variety of purposes, including to restrict the class of occupants of premises or to restrict the type of operation that can be carried out from those premises. These mechanisms have the advantage of maintaining a fairly tight degree of control over the use of land, which can only be varied in a few circumstances.

A mechanism which is being used more frequently is the ability to enter into contractual agreements to restrict the use of land. Management agreements made in nitrate sensitive areas under the Water Resources Act 1991 are essentially contracts between the Minister of Agriculture, Fisheries and Food and an individual to restrict the use of certain agricultural activities so that the nitrates used in farming will not pollute the waters in the area. Under s. 95 of the Act, a voluntary arrangement can be agreed whereby certain agricultural practices will not be carried out on the land and in return compensation will be paid for the restrictions. These types of management agreement are not as wide-ranging as freehold or leasehold covenants as they are not necessarily binding on third parties (unless of course statute makes them so).

The law of tort and environmental protection

This book does not aim to deal specifically with the law of tort as it is more than adequately covered in other textbooks. However, the general principles can, in certain circumstances, be used to protect the environment and these are outlined below.

The law of nuisance

As stated earlier, the law of nuisance is concerned with the unlawful interference with a person's use or enjoyment of land, or of some right over or in connection with it. This definition illustrates one of the primary distinctions between nuisance and other torts in that the protection afforded is directed towards controlling proprietary interests rather than the control of an individual's conduct. As has already been pointed out, the protection of proprietary rights can have the incidental effect of providing a general benefit to the wider community by achieving improvements in environmental quality. There have been occasions where the effect upon the community has been a negative one. In *Bellew* v *Cement Ltd* [1948] IR 61, an interlocutory injunction was granted to restrain the noisy blasting at a quarry This remained effective for several months. The effect of this stoppage upon the supply of cement in Ireland was devastating as 80% of the cement used in Ireland was created by materials from the quarry. Thus the court upheld the protection of the private right involved at the expense of employment and construction.

The basis for a claim in nuisance is founded upon a balancing exercise centred around the question of reasonableness. As was stated in *Sanders Clark* v *Grosvenor Mansions Co. Ltd* [1900] 2 Ch 373:

> . . . the court must consider whether the defendant is using his property reasonably or not. If he is using it reasonably, there is nothing which at law can be considered a nuisance; but if he is not using it reasonably . . . then the plaintiff is entitled to relief.

Thus, in attempting to assess liability in a nuisance action, a balance is made between the reasonableness of the defendant's activity and its impact upon the plaintiff's proprietary rights.

In assessing the balance, a court will take into account a number of specific factors including the locality of the nuisance, the duration of the nuisance, and any hypersensitivity on the part of the plaintiff.

The locality doctrine

The case of *St Helen's Smelting Co.* v *Tipping* (1865) 11 HL Cas 642 illustrates the workings of the doctrine particularly well. In the mid-nineteenth century, St Helens was the centre of the alkali industry. The average life expectancy was well under 25 and it had built up a reputation as one of the dirtiest towns in Britain. The physical impact of the works had left most vegetation in the area dead and adversely affected the health of cattle. Mr Tipping brought an action in private nuisance. The court drew the distinction between actual physical damage to property and a nuisance which would only cause 'personal discomfort'. In the latter situation, the locality of the nuisance would be a material factor in assessing the balancing exercise. In a famous quote in the case of *Sturges* v *Bridgman* (1879) 11 ChD 852, Thesiger LJ stated, 'What would be a nuisance in Belgrave Square would not necessarily be so in Bermondsey'.

The unfortunate consequences of this approach have already been outlined. Although there is a distinction drawn between actual damage done to property and interference with the enjoyment of property, in practice there is often an overlap. It has been alleged that the economic effect of nuisance can be just as detrimental as physical damage to an interest in land. If, for instance, a house is situated by a pig farm, the smells emanating from that may well make the house less attractive to potential buyers, but under the locality doctrine it could be argued that in an agricultural area an owner has to expect such farmyard smells (see, however, *Wheeler* v *J.J. Saunders Ltd* [1996] Ch 19 below at p. 190).

However, even in the most heavily industrialised areas, there is not an absolute freedom to produce polluting materials. An illustration was given in the case of *Rushmer* v *Polsue and Alfieri Ltd* [1906] 1 Ch 234, where Cozens-Hardy LJ said:

> It does not follow that because I live, say, in the manufacturing part of Sheffield I cannot complain if a steam-hammer is introduced next door, and so worked as to render sleep at night almost impossible, although previously to its introduction my house was a reasonably comfortable abode, having regard to the local standard; and it would be no answer to say that the steam-hammer is of the most modern approved pattern and is reasonably worked. In short, if a substantial addition is found as a fact in any particular case, it is no answer to say that the neighbourhood is noisy, and that the defendant's machinery is of first-class character.

In that case, there was an injunction sought against a printing press being operated in Fleet Street, even though there were many other printing presses in the area and others also operated at night. The House of Lords affirmed the decision of the Court of Appeal and granted the injunction.

When viewing the case law on the locality doctrine, two main strands of judicial thinking can be identified. McLaren in his article on the foundation of the law of private nuisance suggests that there are two contradictory judicial views. The first is based upon property rights and is essentially a natural rights theory. Basically, where there is any interference with property rights which is not trivial then there should be a right of action to take steps to prevent such interference (e.g., *Bellew* v *Cement Ltd)*. The second judicial view takes a more rational approach to the problem of environmental pollution and nuisance claims. This could be described as the view of social utility. In this view there tends to be a balance taken between the social utility of the action complained of as weighed against the environmental harm caused (see *St. Helen's Smelting Co.* v *Tipping* and *Sturges* v *Bridgman)*. A third view could be that in the cases involving physical damage it is much easier to be influenced by the natural rights argument as the extent of the damage is easily quantified. With the uncertainty of the assessment of damages for interference with the reasonable enjoyment of land there is a far greater demand for a counterbalance to be taken. In recent cases, the courts have appeared to move away from the social utility view towards the re-emphasis of property rights. In an era when statutory controls have become more sophisticated, the judiciary have refused to develop 'new' concepts of environmental harm. In two significant decisions (*Cambridge Water Co.* v *Eastern Counties Leather plc* [1994] 2 AC 264 and *Hunter* v *Canary Wharf Ltd* [1997] 2 WLR 684) the House of Lords explicitly moved away from expanding liability for harm which was associated with environmental damage. Moreover, in both cases the decisions could actually be viewed as a retrograde step as the judgments specifically restricted ideas which had been developed in the lower courts.

There can, however, be situations where the grant of planning permission has such a significant effect upon the locality that a nuisance will not arise (see *Gillingham Borough Council* v *Medway (Chatham) Dock Co. Ltd* [1993] QB 343 below at p. 190).

Sensibility

One of the balancing factors to be taken into account is the amount to which the nuisance can be 'sensed'. The law does not take into account mere trivial unpleasantness.

Unlike other forms of tort, nuisance is not actionable without proof of damage. The inconvenience has to be able to be 'sensed' by reasonable members of the public. It has to be capable of being seen, smelt or tasted by persons other than the defendant. However, that does not mean to say that where one person senses the nuisance that is sufficient for an action to be founded.

A good example of this rule of *de minimis* can be found in the case of *Attorney-General* v *Gastonia Coaches Ltd* [1977] RTR 219. This case involved a nuisance emanating from a company which was operating a large number of coaches from a residential area. The activities on the site included general maintenance as well as the storage of the vehicles overnight. The judge in the case made a distinction between the two different elements of nuisance. First he said that the nuisance from the smell of the fumes from the engines and the noise from the engines as they were revved could amount to a nuisance. However, he also said that the noise emanating from the vehicles as they were cleaned and repaired did not amount to 'serious interference'.

The duration of nuisance
For a nuisance to be actionable it must be something which is more than temporary. Isolated incidents can give rise to a nuisance only where the use which gives rise to the risk of that isolated nuisance is of itself a continuing use. For example, a factory which produces fumes does not necessarily have to produce those fumes continuously over a period of years for there to be a nuisance. However, where there are isolated incidents occurring regularly then the use of the land for that purpose is of itself a nuisance. The more isolated the occurrence, however, the less the likelihood that the use being carried out is a nuisance. In *Harrison* v *Southwark and Vauxhall Water Co.* [1891] 2 Ch 409, the defendant was a water company which had dug a shaft to pump water from land adjacent to the plaintiffs. As the shaft was being sunk the pumps that were being used created a continuous noise. Mr Harrison brought an action in nuisance to stop the noise. In finding against Mr Harrison the court held that the works were not actionable because they were temporary and that such temporary works would only be actionable if unreasonable methods were used, unless physical damage was caused. Vaughan Williams J said:

> For instance, a man who pulls down his house for the purpose of building a new one no doubt causes considerable inconvenience to his next door neighbours during the process of demolition; but he is not responsible as for a nuisance if he uses all reasonable skill and care to avoid annoyance to his neighbour by the works of demolition. Nor is he liable to an action, even though the noise and dust and the consequent annoyance be such as would constitute a nuisance if the same . . . had been created in sheer wantonness, or in the execution of works for a purpose involving a permanent continuance of the noise and dust.

Again, judicial thinking seems to have been affected by taking a realistic balance of the number and type of occurrences as against the utility involved in the operation itself.

The hypersensitive plaintiff
The test for assessing a nuisance has two elements. Not only must the use of land which is complained of be unreasonable, but also the use of the land to which the nuisance applies must be a reasonable use. If a potential plaintiff is particularly sensitive to one type of nuisance then it will not be actionable unless that nuisance would have affected a 'reasonable' person. In *Robinson* v *Kilvert* (1889) 41 ChD 88, the defendant let out part of his building to the plaintiff to be used as a paper warehouse. The defendant himself kept some

of the space in the building for a particular use which required the air within the building to be kept hot and dry. This use had consequently heated the floor of the paper warehouse and damaged the paper kept there. Unfortunately, the paper stored in the upper rooms was of a particularly sensitive nature. Normal paper would not have been affected to such an extent. The defendant argued that the plaintiff had not told him of the intended use of the premises and in the particular circumstances the Court of Appeal held that there was no nuisance:

> A man who carries on an exceptionally delicate trade cannot complain because it is injured by his neighbour doing something which would not injure anything but an exceptionally delicate trade.

The effect of the rule laid down in that case is perhaps not as wide as first imagined. The principle only applies when the unreasonableness of the conduct is specifically the result of the hypersensitivity of the plaintiff. If there is an independent cause of action brought because of the inherent unreasonableness of the nuisance, then action can still be taken. In the Canadian case of *McKinnon Industries Ltd* v *Walker* [1951] 3 DLR 577, the defendants operated a motor car plant which emitted poisonous gases. The plaintiff grew orchids for sale and the gases unfortunately killed off his stock. He brought an action in nuisance. The defendants argued that the growing of orchids was a hypersensitive activity and therefore any damage suffered was not as a result of the unreasonable use of land. The court disagreed and held that the nuisance was independent of the special sensitivity of the plaintiff.

Thus, in pollution cases, there will be very few occasions where this particular factor will be taken into account. Normally, the type of pollution complained of will be itself a cause of action which can cancel out any arguments put forward about hypersensitivity.

Defences to a claim for nuisance

There are a number of defences which attempt to restrict the ambit of the law of nuisance. However, in practice, they are either so difficult to prove as to be useless, or of dubious merit.

The defence of prescription

Although it is possible in principle to acquire a right to pollute as an easement through 20 years continuous use, there are so many caveats that the practical use of the defence is very restricted. For the defence to apply, the right to pollute must be exercised openly, continuously and not with any specific permission of the person against whom it is so acquired. It must also be the result of a lawful act, so a discharge in breach of a consent would not suffice. For example, in the case of *Sturges* v *Bridgman* (1879) 11 ChD 852, the defendant, a confectioner, had used a noisy pestle and mortar in his premises in Wimpole Street for more than 20 years. There had not been any complaints over that period but a doctor residing at the back of the site built a new consulting room close to the defendant's operational area. Consequently, the noise became a problem. The Court of Appeal held that the defendant in this case had not acquired a right to pollute by prescription. In the court's opinion, the nuisance had commenced only after the consulting room had been constructed, because previously the activities complained of did not give rise to any interference. When the consulting room was occupied, however, such interference began. Thus, the period of 20 years did not start to run until the construction of the consulting rooms.

No defence to say that the plaintiff came to the nuisance
In *Bliss* v *Hall* (1838) 4 Bing NC 183, the defendant operated a business as a tallow chandler. This business had been operated for at least three years when the plaintiff moved in nearby. Unfortunately, the defendant's business created highly toxic fumes which were blown over the plaintiff's land. The defendant argued that, as he had been on the site before the plaintiff, the plaintiff should have realised the state of the premises nearby and should therefore not be able to bring an action in nuisance. Tindal CJ said:

> The Plaintiff came to the house he occupies with all the rights which the common law affords, and one of them is the right to wholesome air. Unless the Defendant shows a prescriptive right to carry on his business in the particular the Plaintiff is entitled to judgement.

When this principle is combined with the principle contained in *Sturges* v *Bridgman,* it is clear that whenever an individual moves into an area there could be the creation of a new 'nuisance history' which negates the prescriptive rights principle because of the need to allow a further 20 years before a prescriptive right attaches.

In practical terms, the principle that it is no defence for a defendant to allege that the plaintiff has come to the nuisance is very important. Many old factories constructed in early Victorian times have now been surrounded by new housing. These potentially antagonistic uses can give rise to conflict. On the one hand, industrialists argue that they have been carrying out polluting activities for a large number of years without complaint and anyone who moved into the area would fully know of any problems. However, in law, the creation of a new right to take action effectively renders the process liable to be brought before the civil courts.

The courts have also held that a planning authority can grant planning permission for a new development even though this is likely to give rise to complaints from the new occupiers as a result of an existing incompatible use (see *R* v *Exeter City Council, ex parte J. L. Thomas and Co. Ltd* [1991] 1 QB 471).

Statutory authority
There may be occasions where nuisances are caused by statutory or non-statutory bodies exercising their statutory authority. Where a body can point to such authority then this will amount to a defence if an action is brought against them for any consequential nuisance.

For example, in *Smeaton* v *Ilford Corporation* [1954] Ch 450, there were particular problems with the Corporation's sewers. The nuisance complained of arose because the sewers in the area were overloaded as a consequence of many new houses in the area utilising their right to be connected to the existing sewer system. Unfortunately, the sewers were not able to cope properly with the amount of sewage. Furthermore, the local authority did not have powers to refuse to connect the houses to the existing sewer system. Upjohn J held that the overloaded sewers were not a nuisance, since the local authority had a statutory duty to take domestic sewage and could not refuse the amount that was causing an overflow. There is, of course, a degree of control over such difficulties by restricting the grant of planning permission for development of housing, or restricting housing development without proper provision being made for discharges to sewers.

Although most statutory obligations are expressly contained within the body of the statute itself, it is also clear that a defendant could claim the defence of statutory authority where there is a clear implication that such activities have been authorised by an Act. In *Allen* v *Gulf Oil Refining Ltd* [1981] AC 1001, the Gulf Oil Refining Act 1965 (a private Act of Parliament) gave the defendants power to acquire land for an oil refinery at Milford Haven. The oil refinery emitted smells, noise and vibration and a local resident brought an action against Gulf Oil in nuisance. The plaintiff argued in that case that although the Act gave the defendant the power to acquire land for the construction of the refinery, it did not give any guidelines as to how the refinery should be operated. Therefore, when the defendant sought to rely upon the defence of statutory authority it was suggested that, as the Act did not specifically allow for the operating of the plant in a manner which gave rise to a nuisance, the defence was unavailable. The House of Lords held that the statute implicitly gave the defendant an immunity to every act inevitably flowing from the construction of the refinery. The only possible exception to this would be where the nuisance complained of was of a greater degree than was necessary or where such activities were carried out in a negligent manner.

It should be pointed out that, where private rights are interfered with, it is often the case that statutes themselves provide for compensation. For example, where a new road is being built, statutory compensation is payable where there is injurious affection to the enjoyment of property which is the direct result of the works carried out. There are, however, situations where the interference with private rights is not compensated.

Private rights under the common law and the grant of planning permission

There is often a conflict between private rights under the common law of nuisance (i.e., the right to have the use of one's property without unreasonable interference) and the public law nature of the grant of planning permission (i.e., development granted in the public interest). Many uses of land which give rise to nuisances have the benefit of planning permission. In determining the grant of permission it must be assumed that the local planning authority has balanced the impact of the development upon private interests (e.g., neighbours) with any competing public interest and has concluded that the public interest in allowing the development to proceed outweighs any detriment (this assumption could be questionable in some cases). There is, however, still some overlap between the two systems as both environmental considerations and private interests are part of the decision-making process and they are, in certain circumstances, concerned with land use (see *Westminster City Council* v *Great Portland Estates plc* [1985] AC 661).

Difficulty arises when considering the nature of the overlap between these two considerations. The question arises, does the grant of planning permission extinguish the private rights of an individual to take action against an inevitable consequence of that which has been allowed to be developed (by virtue of the grant of planning permission)? In *Gillingham Borough Council* v *Medway (Chatham) Dock Co. Ltd* [1993] QB 343, Buckley J decided that the grant of planning permission for a commercial port was analogous to the defence of statutory authority (see above) and that it acted as a defence to a public noise nuisance from lorries travelling to and from the port. This case was criticised by a number of commentators (see Crawford [1992] JEL 262 and Waite [1992] 4 LMELR 119) because a broad interpretation of Buckley J's judgment suggested that the grant of planning permission could negate any action in nuisance. This would, if followed, have serious implications for those seeking to protect their private rights in nuisance. Effectively, it would mean that private rights would be extinguished without any redress or compensation which would be contrary to established principles of English law.

A narrow interpretation of the decision in *Gillingham* suggested that planning permission did not act as a *defence* to an action in nuisance. Instead, Buckley J's decision went to the heart of the *definition* of a nuisance and the locality doctrine in particular. Under this interpretation the case could only be viewed as supporting the proposition that the grant of planning permission may act to change the nature of the area for the purposes of the locality test. Thus, the presence of lorries on the roads leading to and from the port was reasonable in the context of a commercial area.

The Court of Appeal clarified the situation in *Wheeler* v *J.J. Saunders Ltd* [1996] Ch 19 where the narrow interpretation of the *Gillingham* decision was preferred. The case concerned the grant of planning permission for pig-weaning units and allegations of a smell nuisance which occurred after the development was implemented. The court decided that the grant of planning permission could not act as a defence to a nuisance action and did not deprive the plaintiffs of the right to bring an action in nuisance. Moreover, the court sought to distinguish the *Gillingham* decision and redefined the narrow interpretation (to an even narrower definition). First, Gibson LJ sought to apply the *Gillingham* principle only to those developments which demand a consideration of 'strategic' planning issues which necessitated an explicit consideration of the public interest. Thus, in the case of, for example, a commercial port, it was clear that the interference with private rights had been balanced against the public interest and the development was found to be acceptable. This begs the question of what the dividing line is between 'strategic' decisions such as a commercial port, and secondary developments such as pig units; but Gibson LJ left this issue undetermined with the comment that 'it may be — and I express no concluded opinion — that some planning decisions will authorise some nuisances'.

Secondly, the *Gillingham* decision is restricted to those situations where the effects of the development make a specific change to the nature of the locality. In *Wheeler* the pig unit was situated in a rural area and did not bring about such a radical change. Finally, Buckley J in the *Gillingham* case suggested that the mere grant of permission could be sufficient enough to change the nature of the locality and implied that the allocation of land in a development plan could have the same effect. Sir John May made it clear in *Wheeler* that it is the implementation of the development rather than the grant of permission which could change the character of the area. This would appear to be the correct approach as the implementation of a development could have different consequences from that envisaged at the date of grant of planning permission.

The Court of Appeal, therefore, has truly dissected the *Gillingham* principle with the consequence that the decision has little practical effect, although it would still be true to say that major strategic developments can change the character of a locality (which is probably a view which would have been held before the *Gillingham* case). Both decisions demonstrate, however, that the judiciary is uncomfortable with the overlap between the exercise of rights conferred by public law powers and private law remedies. This, perhaps, reflects the essential problem which faces a court when adjudicating between the exercise of a right which has been determined to be acceptable in the public interest, and private rights which have been unreasonably interfered with. Both can be correct (in the court's eyes), yet one must lose. In *Wheeler* Gibson LJ accepted that there can be no assumption that the local planning authority can take away private rights, but suggested that there might be occasions where the regulatory body can legitimately override private rights. There are, of course, situations where the exercise of public powers can override private rights (e.g., the exercise of compulsory purchase powers), but compensation is normally payable to offset the loss. In relation to concepts like environmental harm this type of compensation is difficult to envisage.

An assessment of nuisance as a tool for environmental protection

The common law principles of nuisance were available to counteract the problems of industrial pollution a long time before industrial growth started to bring about an increase in noxious emissions. However, it was still felt necessary to introduce statutory regulations under the Alkali Acts of 1863 to counteract the problems caused. This was not the only example of statutory intervention. There has been much argument amongst academics as to why, given the availability of common law remedies, it was felt necessary to introduce the supplementary administrative/public law controls.

Essentially, the reasons that have been identified for suggesting that the common law was under-utilised echo many of the weaknesses of the other mechanisms in environmental control. Environmental law was not, and is not, in a legal vacuum. The social and political context of pollution and the law neutralised attempts to deal with the environmental issues of increased industrialisation.

Resort to the law in the nineteenth century was always a rich person's prerogative. Taking an action to law was both lengthy and ultimately outside the reach of the vast majority of the population. Until 1854 an action to prevent a nuisance through an injunction required two actions to be taken, one through the common law, and one through the Court of Chancery.

Secondly, as we have seen, to bring an action in nuisance required a proprietary interest. In the mid-nineteenth century it has been estimated that only somewhere in the region of 15% of the population were owner/occupiers. Thus, the vast majority of the population would have great difficulty in even founding an action. When coupled with the level of damages, notoriously low for interference with the enjoyment of land, there was an inevitable reluctance to take action.

Moreover, what has subsequently been identified as a complex system of power relationships ensured that in the social context there was tremendous pressure not to 'cause trouble'. Few workers would wish to proceed against their bosses and it was also clear that there was a certain degree of class solidarity amongst the industrialists themselves. Many factory owners bought up large areas of land surrounding their own sites and constructed low cost, high density housing to house their workers. This, coupled with the fact that it was often the case that the presence of an industry lowered surrounding land prices, meant that a factory owner could purchase the right to pollute the surrounding area very cheaply. Furthermore, although society has become inherently more litigious over the last 50 to 100 years, bringing environmental actions was, and has always been, somewhat different to the norm.

One of the few recorded cases, *St Helen's Smelting Co.* v *Tipping* (1865) 11 HL Cas 642 (referred to above), illustrates these points well. Mr Tipping was a rich cotton magnate who owned 1300 acres of land. He could afford to risk the backlash of industrialists because of the well-documented conflict between the cotton and the chemical industries. The damages received in his case and also in other nuisance cases were appallingly low. In *Halsey* v *Esso Petroleum Co. Ltd* [1961] 1 WLR 683, there had been constant noise, dirt and commotion which had caused great difficulties and misery to the plaintiff for some five years. Finding for the plaintiff, the court awarded the derisory sum of £200 damages.

Although the physical effects of pollution could often be seen, the long-term effects of exposure to noxious fumes and hazardous chemicals were not fully understood. In an era where so many preconditions were placed upon the bringing of an action, the ignorance of many of those subjected to a high level of pollution ensured that no action would ever be taken. Lack of technical knowledge often led to practical difficulties of proving the source of pollution. Without scientific instruments, and without a right to enter onto land and take samples, individuals were restricted in their ability to monitor problems.

The power of industrialists at legislative, local government and magisterial level was too great for the 'person in the street'. Thus, a climate was set in which pollution control received a low priority. Local authorities were most reluctant to use their powers to prosecute for public nuisances, and indeed were often responsible for much pollution themselves. The law of nuisance was just one aspect of a legal regime which included as its other elements political, social, economic and philosophical responses to pollution. The limitations of the civil law in general, which apply more particularly to the law of nuisance, were commented on in the Third Report of the Royal Commission on the Pollution of Rivers in 1867:

> It [bringing a common law action] is an expensive remedy. For the same money which is spent over a hard fought litigation against a single manufacturer, a Conservancy Board armed with proper powers, might for years keep safe from all abuse, a long extensive river with hundreds of manufactories situated on its banks.

The law of nuisance and its relationship with environmental protection was discussed in *Cambridge Water Co.* v *Eastern Counties Leather plc* [1994] 2 AC 264. In that case, the Cambridge Water Company purchased a borehole at Sawston near Cambridge for the purpose of supplying drinking water to the surrounding inhabitants. ECL operated their business in Sawston and used a number of solvents in their processes. They had been established on their site for over 100 years, and until 1976 solvent had been delivered to their premises in 40 gallon drums. During that time fork-lift trucks were used to transport the solvent drums from storage. Over time, there were frequent spillages of solvent which found its way into the underground aquifer.

In 1985, as a result of an earlier EC Directive, regulations were introduced in the UK which restricted the maximum allowable concentration of particular solvents in drinking water. As a matter of chance, the drinking water abstracted from the borehole near Sawston was found to contain high levels of solvent. Further tests identified the tannery as being the main source of the solvent. The water company had to shut down that particular borehole and seek a supply from elsewhere. As a consequence, they brought an action in nuisance (see *Rylands* v *Fletcher* (1868) LR 3 HL 330 below) and negligence against ECL for the monetary losses involved in locating a new supply of ground water.

At first instance, the water company's claims were rejected. The claims in nuisance and negligence were said to depend upon whether or not the consequences of the spillages were reasonably foreseeable. Kennedy J stated that the correct test was: 'What would the reasonable supervisor overseeing the operating of the plant have foreseen to be the possible consequences of repeated spillages over perhaps 10 years?' The judge went on to hold that the supervisors could not have foreseen any environmental hazard from spillages of a mundane and regular nature. For nuisance to be established proof of actual damage was required. The damage suffered arose only upon the introduction of the regulations, and that post-dated the spillage by a number of years. Thus the claims in nuisance and negligence were rejected.

When considering the case under the rule in *Rylands* v *Fletcher,* the main issue was whether the storage of the solvents as an adjunct to a manufacturing process was a non-natural use of land. In determining that point, consideration had to be given to the question of whether the storage created special risks for adjacent occupiers and whether the activity had a general utility for the surrounding community. The court decided that, as the location of the factory was in an industrial village, the storage of solvents did not amount to a non-natural use of land.

The Water Company appealed and the Court of Appeal overturned the decision of the High Court. The court followed the decision in *Ballard* v *Tomlinson* (1885) 29 ChD 115 and decided that the nuisance complained of was an interference with a natural right incidental of the ownership of land (i.e., the right to abstract uncontaminated ground water), liability was therefore strict and the only effective issue was causation which had been adequately demonstrated by the plaintiff.

The defendants appealed to the House of Lords. The Law Lords allowed the appeal on the basis that liability in private nuisance depended upon the foreseeability of the relevant type of damage occurring (i.e., the pollution of ground-water above the levels laid down in the EC Directive). On the facts of the case, it was held to be unforeseeable that repeated spillages of solvent before 1976 would lead to any environmental hazard or damage. *Ballard* v *Tomlinson* could be distinguished as the issue of foreseeability had not arisen in that case.

The court stated that the rule in *Rylands* v *Fletcher* was historically linked to the law of nuisance. Indeed, Lord Goff made it clear that the rule was to be regarded as an extension of the law of nuisance to cases of isolated escapes from land (see the discussion of the rule on p. 199).

Two points arise from this decision. First, the activities which gave rise to the damage took place some time before the introduction of statutory controls over ground-water quality. It is arguable that after the introduction of such controls, the foreseeability of damage would increase. Certainly, in recent times with the introduction of environmental management systems and increased corporate attention to environmental compliance, it would be foreseeable that repeated spillages of toxic material would give rise to environmental damage. Thus, although there is only a small chance of retrospective liability for pollution, damage caused relatively recently or from continuing activities should still be actionable.

Secondly, and perhaps more importantly, the court displayed a marked reluctance to expand or develop the principles of nuisance. Lord Goff made it clear that recent legislation was being put in place to provide for liability in respect of pollution and it was undesirable to develop a common law principle to achieve the same end. If this strand of judicial thinking is followed it would seem as if the future growth of the common law as a mechanism of environmental protection is uncertain.

This judicial antipathy towards the development of the law of nuisance as a tool for environmental protection was further evidenced by the decision of the House of Lords in *Hunter* v *Canary Wharf Ltd* [1997] 2 WLR 684. In two separate actions, over 500 residents in London Docklands brought actions against the developers of Canary Wharf and the London Docklands Development Corporation for nuisance arising out of interference with television signals from Canary Wharf Tower and damage from dust emissions from road construction respectively. In dismissing the appeal the House adopted reasoning which relied heavily upon the established view of nuisance as an interference with property rights. The Law Lords upheld the traditional view that generally, at common law, an owner is entitled to build without restriction. Instead of enlarging the right to bring nuisance actions for the interference with television reception, Lord Hoffmann considered that the planning system was a 'far more appropriate form of control from the point of view of both the developer and the public' — thus reinforcing the decision in *Wheeler* v *J.J. Saunders* [1996] Ch 19 (see above p. 190).

The more important point of principle which was considered by the House was the question of who had the right to bring an action in nuisance. The Court of Appeal had expanded the categories of those with such a right to include those with a 'substantial link' with the enjoyment of the property as a home. This reflected the view that the old ideas of nuisance did not adequately deal with the harm suffered by those parties which had no legal interest in the land (including occupiers and children). By extending the classes of potential plaintiff the Court of Appeal appeared to offer a way in which the tort of nuisance could have been developed and revised to take into account new concepts such as environmental harm.

The House of Lords overturned this part of the decision by reverting to the traditional view that private nuisance actions are essentially concerned with interference with property rights. The House analysed the suffering in nuisance in terms of the diminution of value of the property as opposed to damage suffered by individuals. Thus there was a finite amount of damages which could be claimed as a result of unreasonable interference and it was unconnected with the number of occupiers who had suffered damage.

Lord Cooke of Thorndon, however, delivered a dissenting judgment in which he advocated a more modern approach to liability which took account of the family unit.

Public nuisance

Although seemingly a close relative of private nuisance, the law relating to public nuisances contains both similar elements and distinguishing features. Public nuisance can be defined as a nuisance which affects a wide class of the public in general. It is a criminal offence to cause a public nuisance, though damages can also be claimed as a civil remedy by anyone who suffers special damage over and above that suffered by the rest of the public.

An illustration is the case of *R* v *Lloyd* (1802) 4 Esp 200. A number of people living in Cliffords Inn complained of a noise nuisance which was disturbing their work. Although the court did not rule out the possibility that it might have amounted to a private nuisance it was held that the inhabitants of only three chambers did not constitute a wide class of the public in general. The case of *Attorney-General v PYA Quarries Ltd* [1957] 2 QB 169 demonstrates the width of class required. The defendants operated a quarry. During operations they carried out various blasting activities. These activities caused vibration and noise over a wide area. In attempting to lay down guidelines, Denning LJ declined to specify what numbers would be required to show that a particular nuisance was public rather than private. He did however say:

> I prefer to look to the reason of the thing and to say that a public nuisance is a nuisance which is so widespread in its range or so indiscriminate in its effect that it would not be reasonable to expect one person to take proceedings on his own responsibility to put a stop to it, but that it should be taken on the responsibility of the community at large.

If the need to show an effect over a wide class of the public is set aside, there is a good degree of overlap with the factors that are taken into account when deciding whether or not there is a private nuisance. For an example, in the *PYA Quarries* case above, if there had only been intermittent blasting then it may have arguably fallen foul of the rule in *Harrison v Southwark and Vauxhall Water Co.*, which would have negated any liability not only in private but also in public nuisance.

Trespass

One of the simplest of the torts, trespass, involves direct interference with personal or proprietary rights without lawful excuse. Trespass to the person has never been properly developed in pollution cases, although in theory making someone inhale toxic fumes could give rise to an action in trespass. The main reason for this restriction lies in the requirement of directness. The interference with the personal or proprietary right must be direct rather than consequential. As an example, in *Reynolds v Clarke* (1725) 1 Str 643, Fortescue J said, 'if a man throws a log into the highway and it hits me I may maintain trespass because it is an immediate wrong; but if, as it lies there, I tumble over it and receive an injury, I must bring an action upon the case because it is only prejudicial in consequence'. In relation to trespass onto land a good illustration would be that throwing stones onto someone's property would be a direct trespass, whereas allowing tiles to fall off a badly repaired chimney would not be.

Furthermore, an act of trespass has to be intentional or negligent. *McDonald v Associated Fuels Ltd* [1954] 3 DLR 775 illustrates the distinction well. Although in this Canadian case an action was successfully brought in negligence, the court also decided that a trespass action would have succeeded. The case involved the supply of sawdust fuel to the plaintiff's house. The delivery method was somewhat unusual in that the defendants parked their truck and blew the sawdust into a bin inside the house by means of a blower unit. Unfortunately, the intake mechanism for the sawdust was too close to the exhaust system of the truck. Consequently, as well as sawdust, carbon monoxide was blown into the house, the occupants were overcome and one of the occupants broke a hip when she collapsed. It is clear here that the trespass itself (i.e., the entrance of the carbon monoxide directly into the house) was not intentional. However, the act which caused the trespass was.

A major disadvantage with an action in trespass is that a causal link between the directness of an act and the inevitability of its consequences has to be established. In *Jones* v *Llanrwst Urban District Council* [1911] 1 Ch 393, faecal matter from sewage had collected in the local authority's drains and was passed untreated into the River Conway. As a consequence, it collected on the gravel banks of a river owned by the plaintiff. The question that the court was asked to answer was whether or not this deposit could amount to a trespass as it was not intended to pass onto the plaintiff's land. The court held that it was a trespass as it was intentional in the sense that the sewage was intentionally passed into the river; it was also direct in the sense that it inevitably came onto the plaintiff's land. Thus, even though it may have appeared that the matter was some way away from the plaintiff's land when it first entered the river, it was still both intentional and direct.

Jones v *Llanrwst UDC* was distinguished in the case of *Esso Petroleum Co. Ltd* v *Southport Corporation* [1956] AC 218, which at first glance would seem to fail on similar facts. A 680 tonne tanker was grounded in the Ribble Estuary. In order to lighten the ship, the master discharged much of the cargo of oil. This was then carried by the wind and the tide onto Southport's beach. The beach was under the ownership of the Corporation and they claimed against the company for the clean up costs involved. The case largely concerned the question of negligence as there was more than a suggestion that the cause of the pollution was bad navigation. That case failed, but views were expressed in the House of Lords on the possibility that the output of the oil onto the beach was a trespass. Lords Radcliffe and Tucker expressed the view that this could not be a trespass and sought to distinguish it from the *Llanrwst* case by looking at questions of inevitability. Unlike the river which inevitably flowed downstream, there was no inevitability about the deposit of the oil onto the foreshore, which depended on the action of the wind, waves and tide.

This principle would make it almost impossible to bring an action in trespass for air pollution. In a situation where air currents and wind could throw the pollution in any particular direction, the element of directness required for trespass would be difficult to show.

One of the main advantages of bringing an action in trespass is that there is no need to show damage. Trespass is actionable *per se,* therefore all that needs to be shown is some interference. Whereas most environmental pollution actions will involve some form of damage, the need to show only that trespass has occurred as a matter of fact enables an injunction to be obtained far more easily than with any other common law mechanism (see **Remedies** below).

Negligence

To attempt a full coverage of the law of negligence in a book on environmental protection is unnecessary. There are many other texts which contain a considered study of the principles. Moreover, the utility of the principles of negligence in bringing an action for environmental protection is somewhat limited.

The law of negligence is a fault based system; in order to succeed in negligence there has to be some fault on behalf of the defendant. Thus negligence would only really be utilised where other remedies under the common law (e.g., nuisance and trespass) are not available. Furthermore, proving negligence owes much to the state of technology at the time; where a polluting factory meets the standard expected of other factories of that type at that time, then any action in negligence will fail.

It is also necessary to foresee the type of harm which will result from an activity. In *Cambridge Water Co.* v *Eastern Counties Leather plc* [1994] 2 AC 264 (above), an action in negligence was dismissed at first instance because at the time when the incident giving rise to damage occurred it would not have been reasonably foreseeable that the particular type of damage (i.e., pollution of ground water above levels laid down under an EC Directive) would have been the consequence of routine spillages of solvent. It is not sufficient to show that 'pollution' would have been foreseen as that would be too wide a category of damage.

The three main principles of negligence are that the plaintiff must establish that (a) a duty of care is owed by the defendant to the plaintiff; (b) that the defendant has breached that duty; and (c) that there has been foreseeable damage resulting from the breach. Notably, there is no need to establish a proprietary interest prior to making a claim in negligence. Thus anyone who has suffered damage from the negligence can bring an action. This widens the class of possible claimants.

Considering how often negligence is used to provide a cause of action in other areas of life, it is perhaps surprising to find how little it has been used to control environmental problems. There have historically been fairly few examples, although in recent years there has been an upsurge in the use of the mechanism. Examples include the case of *Tutton* v *A. D. Walter Ltd* [1986] QB 61, which involved the use of insecticide. Farmers had been advised by the manufacturers and central government that using a particular insecticide when oil rape was flowering could lead to the death of insects such as bees. Furthermore, they were told that the insecticide was actually most effective when used after the flowering period. Unfortunately, the defendant sprayed his crop whilst the oil rape was in flower and a number of bees owned by the plaintiff were killed. The court held that the farmer was liable for using the insecticide in a negligent manner.

More importantly perhaps, the case of *Scott-Whitehead* v *National Coal Board* (1987) 53 P & CR 263 showed the court's approach to statutory bodies and the advice they should give concerning environmental matters. The defendants discharged an emission of a chlorinated solution into a river. The river was in drought and therefore there was insufficient water to dilute the strength of the pollutant. The plaintiff was farming down stream and abstracting water to irrigate his crops. The water abstracted from the river contained a high level of pollutant and damage was caused to his crops. The second defendant in this case, the regional water authority, was held to be liable in negligence for not advising the farmer of the potential danger from the condition of the water he was abstracting. Extending the principle in this case, it may well be possible to bring an action against other environmental bodies in negligence if it can be shown that their failure to give adequate warnings of pollution contributed to damage.

The rule in *Rylands* v *Fletcher*

The principle known as 'the rule in *Rylands* v *Fletcher*' was first established in the case of that name ((1886) LR 1 Ex 265 (Exchequer Chamber); LR 3 HL 330 (HL)). It involved the construction of a reservoir on the defendants' land. The contractors failed to block off mine shafts with the result that when the reservoir was filled up, water went into the shafts and flooded a mine belonging to the plaintiff. Although there was no negligence on behalf of the defendants, the House of Lords held that they should be liable. In the lower court, Blackburn J first expounded the principle:

> . . . that the person who for his own purposes brings onto his land and collects and keeps there anything likely to do mischief if it escapes, must keep it in at his peril, and, if he does not do so, is prima facie answerable for all the damage which is the natural consequence of its escape.

Thus, the principle imposes strict liability (but not absolute liability) if something brought onto land or collected there escapes.

The implications as far as environmental protection is concerned are clear. Many acts of pollution are caused by materials and/or substances which are brought onto land escaping from that land. Over the years the rule has been applied in relation to water, fire, gases, electricity, oil, chemicals, colliery spoil, poisonous vegetation and even a chair-o-plane at a fairground! The sheer simplicity of the principle would seem to cover many potentially hazardous situations. However, the limitations of the principle are such that it is rarely successful nowadays.

Non-natural user

By far and away the most important restriction upon the principle is that where a substance is kept on land it must have been kept by means of a 'non-natural user'. Originally, this may have meant only that there is no liability if the water (in the case of *Rylands* v *Fletcher*) had been a natural lake or naturally flooded area rather than a man-made reservoir. In time, it came to mean that the use had to be 'some special use bringing with it increased danger to others and must not merely be the ordinary use of the land or such a use as is proper for the general benefit of the community' (*Rickards* v *Lothian* [1913] AC 263).

Thus a slightly different interpretation to the word natural came about. Instead of meaning 'artificial' the courts began to interpret the phrase as meaning an 'abnormal' use of land. Consequently, some rather strange things have been held to be a natural use of land and a flexible test of what is an *especially* or *unduly* hazardous activity has evolved which has attempted to import some element of public utility.

In *Rainham Chemical Works Ltd* v *Belvedere Fish Guano Company* [1921] 2 AC 465, a factory which manufactured high explosives for the Ministry of Munitions exploded, killing a number of people and damaging the respondent's factory. The House of Lords held it to be a non-natural user and also found that the effects of the explosion amounted to an escape even though it was actually bits of the factory which had escaped rather than the substance stored, i.e., the explosives. However, in a similar case, *Read* v *J. Lyons & Co. Ltd* [1947] AC 156, the defendants managed the Elstow Ordnance Factory where they made high explosive shells for the Government. Ms Read was an inspector in the factory in 1942 when there was an explosion in which she was injured. There was no negligence in their activities, but she argued that the defendants were manufacturing high explosive shells and they knew them to be dangerous, and therefore the rule in *Rylands* v *Fletcher* ought to be applied. In the House of Lords, Lord Macmillan said:

> Every activity in which man engages is fraught with some possible element of danger to others. Experience shows that even from acts apparently innocuous, injury to others may result. The more dangerous the act the greater is the care that must be taken in performing it . . . . one who engages in obviously dangerous operations must be taken to know that if he does not take special precautions, injury to others may very well result. In my opinion it would be impracticable to frame a legal classification of things as things dangerous and things not dangerous, attaching absolute liability in the case of the former but not in the case of the latter . . . . accordingly I am unable to accept the proposition that in law the manufacture of high-explosive shells is a dangerous operation which imposes on the manufacturer an absolute liability . . . .

This decision may well have had something to do with the fact that in war time it would clearly be a natural use of industrial land to make explosives. However, it is now common for a court to find that an ordinary industrial use is a natural use if it is sited with due care and consideration. To that extent, where a factory is given a planning permission, that would, it is suggested, amount to prima facie evidence that consideration had been given as to its suitability as a use. The definition of 'non-natural' user was further discussed in *Cambridge Water Co.* v *Eastern Counties Leather plc* [1994] 2 AC 264 (above), where it appeared, at least in the High Court, as if the extension of the non-natural use exception was so great as to extinguish the rule altogether.

Other restrictions on the use of the rule
Further limitations on the principle do not have the same restrictive nature as the non-natural user principle. However, they are still important in seeking

to restrict the introduction of a strict liability concept into the common law. First, there is a requirement that the substance escapes from the land where it is kept. Therefore, in *Read v J. Lyons & Co. Ltd*, the workers in the ammunition factory could have no action under the rule in *Rylands v Fletcher*. Furthermore, the principle applies specifically to protect landowners and therefore it is generally accepted that no actions for personal injuries received from the escape of substances from a non-natural user of land can lie.

There is also a requirement that the relevant damage be foreseeable. In *Cambridge Water Co. v Eastern Counties Leather plc*, the House of Lords allowed an appeal by Eastern Counties Leather on the ground that foreseeability of damage was a prerequisite of liability under the rule in *Rylands v Fletcher*. In allowing the appeal, the court took the view that the rule should form a natural extension of the law of nuisance to cover isolated escapes from land and should not be developed further.

Although there have been a number of restrictions placed upon the rule in *Rylands v Fletcher*, this does not necessarily condemn an action based on an escape of hazardous substances from land to failure; it merely means that negligence, nuisance or trespass must be shown for liability to accrue. In many circumstances, fault will be able to be shown fairly easily.

Defences

There are a number of defences to an action brought under the rule in *Rylands v Fletcher*. It has been suggested that there is a defence where the plaintiff benefits from the harmful activity. Therefore, where gas, electricity or water supplies have caused damage on the plaintiff's property, no liability should accrue. The concept behind this defence perhaps takes the desire to restrict absolute liability too far (see *Northwestern Utilities Ltd v London Guarantee and Accident Co. Ltd* [1936] AC 108). The thinking behind the development of this principle has been somewhat confused (e.g., the decision in *Anderson v Oppenheimer* (1880) 5 QBD 602). Some have seen the use of this defence as an extension of the defence of consent, which can be simply stated, as in *Attorney-General v Cory Brothers & Co.* [1921] 1 AC 521 — if the plaintiff has allowed the defendant to accumulate the matter or thing which is being complained of, then they are unable to sue if it escapes. Secondly, as in the case of private nuisance, it is a defence that a statute authorises the activity complained of (see *Smeaton v Ilford Corporation* [1954] Ch 454).

Finally, although it is a defence to plead an Act of God (i.e., the nuisance was brought about by a set of extreme circumstances) the relevance of this defence is somewhat restricted. As one commentator has put it (*Street on Torts*, 9th ed.):

> The defence has received in connection with this tort a prominence out of all proportion to its practical importance. If an escape is caused, through natural causes without human intervention, in 'circumstances which no human foresight can provide against, and which human prudence is not

bound to recognise the possibility', there is then said to exist the defence of act of God.

The only things which fall under this defence would be escapes caused by such things as earthquakes, tornadoes or freak acts of nature.

The usefulness of the rule in *Rylands* v *Fletcher*

After the decision of the House of Lords in *Cambridge Water Co.* v *Eastern Counties Leather plc* [1994] 2 AC 264 it could be argued that the effectiveness of the rule in *Rylands* v *Fletcher* has been diluted to such an extent that it is virtually useless. It is perhaps more appropriate to call the rule an extension of the law of private nuisance rather than a specific class on its own. The Court also stated, obiter, that in the light of 'carefully structured legislation' designed for environmental protection there was less need to develop the rule to provide for liability in respect of pollution. Consequently, the future of the rule looks uncertain.

The protection of riparian rights

There is a separate action for interference with the rights of owners of riparian land. Although this action has some similarities with private nuisance, it is in practice used far more frequently owing to the strength of riparian owners' natural rights to water. For further explanation of the law on riparian rights see p. 479.

Civil law remedies

Of course, the use of the common law as a mechanism for environmental protection would be useless unless there were effective remedies once a cause of action had been established. There are three main types of remedies which can be sought: compensatory and preventative remedies, and abatement. Monetary damages act as compensation for any damage suffered but also can pay for any clean up costs involved in rectifying pollution. On the other hand, an injunction allows for actions which are creating an environmental problem to be stopped by order of the court. Lastly, there are certain limited circumstances where plaintiffs can take individual action and abate the activity causing environmental damage.

The utility of the common law in dealing with environmental pollution depends upon the nature of the problem. An isolated occurrence could cause tremendous environmental damage and, where a problem is not likely to recur, it may well be an adequate remedy to pay for the restoration of the environment to its prior state. However, in cases where the pollution is perhaps of a lower level but more persistent, it may be necessary to prevent an accumulation of potentially hazardous substances which cannot be properly compensated through damages alone. Therefore, in certain cases, an injunction may be the only suitable remedy. There are, however, many instances where the remedies available through the common law will give a far wider range of options to potential plaintiffs than are available through seeking to have statutory bodies act on their behalf.

Damages

The aim of awarding damages at common law is to place the plaintiff as far as possible in the position they would have been in had the wrongful act not occurred. This could be calculated in two ways; on the cost of clean-up operations necessary to restore the property to its previous state, or the difference between the value of the property as it was after the pollution had affected it, and before. It is a principle which is not particularly clear. In *Marquis of Granby* v *Bakewell UDC* (1923) 87 JP 105, the defendant operated a gas works which discharged poisonous effluent into a river over which the plaintiff had fishing rights. The effluent killed all the plaintiff's fish and thus he claimed damages against the defendant for the interference with his fishing rights. He received compensation equalling the costs of restocking the river in addition to the loss of a large amount of the food supply for other stocks. The court also took into account the effects of the pollution on higher quality areas of the river and considered that the damages would be higher where environmental pollution was greater.

Damages for all *future* loss are only available in lieu of an injunction. This remedy is used only sparingly because of the ready availability of the more usual injunction procedure.

Lastly, exemplary or punitive damages can be awarded in specific instances. The basis of such an award is to deter the defendant and others from committing torts which may result in financial benefit to the person responsible. The scope for these damages is, however, limited to classes of tort which were the subject of an award of exemplary damages before 1964 (*A.B.* v *South West Water Services Ltd* [1993] QB 507) and cases where there has been oppressive, arbitrary or unconstitutional action by servants of the government, or where the defendant's conduct was calculated to make a profit which would exceed the damages payable (*Rookes* v *Barnard* [1964] AC 1129). Thus a claim for exemplary damages in public nuisance after the public water supply was polluted was rejected on the ground that public nuisance fell outside the above categories (*A.B.* v *South West Water Services Ltd*, above).

Injunctions

The granting of an injunction is a discretionary remedy which can prohibit a defendant from carrying on an activity which is causing pollution. The principles for the granting of an injunction are well established. Normally, either the activity complained of has to be continuing at the date of action, or there has to be a threat that the activity will continue. Even though the activity may have ceased at the time of trial, an injunction can still be sought if it existed when the action was brought.

When exercising its discretion, the court will take a number of factors into consideration. First, it will not grant an injunction if the activity complained of is not of sufficient gravity or duration to justify stopping the defendant's activities. Turner LJ in *Goldsmith* v *Tunbridge Wells Improvement Commissioners* (1866) LR 1 Ch App 349 said:

> it is not in every case of nuisance that this Court should interfere. I think that it ought not to do so in cases in which the injury is merely temporary or trifling; but I think that it ought to do so in cases in which the injury is permanent and serious: and in determining whether the injury is serious or not, regard must be had to all the consequences which may flow from it.

The court attempts to balance the competing interests of the plaintiff and defendant by assessing the balance of convenience between the parties. Where all things are equal, an attempt will be made to assess the social utility of the activity by comparing its public importance with the interference to the private rights of the plaintiff. Basically, the harm suffered to the plaintiff has to be balanced against the effect that granting of an injunction would have upon the defendant.

There are situations where it is possible to obtain an injunction before the occurrence of the event causing injury or damage. A *quia timet* injunction, as it is known, does not require proof of environmental damage at all. However, there must be sufficient proof of imminent damage and it must be demonstrated that if the activity were to continue the damage accruing would be substantial and of such degree that it would be difficult to rectify.

Injunctions are rarely specific in nature; the court merely sets the standard for the defendant to meet and this standard can be achieved in any way possible. For example, it may be met either by closing down a particular plant which is causing environmental difficulties or by fitting new arrestment equipment. Even where an injunction is granted it is often on the basis that a certain amount of time is given for compliance.

Abatement

The remedy of abatement tends to be more of historic interest than it is useful. The remedy involves the removal of a nuisance by the injured party without recourse to legal proceedings. The courts view this remedy unfavourably as it is extra-judicial in nature and therefore open to abuse. An example of the use of abatement can be found in *Lemmon* v *Webb* [1895] AC 1, where action was taken to trim back the branch of a tree which encroached on land from a neighbouring site. Any damages subsequent to an abatement action are restricted to damages in respect of harm prior to the abatement.

Statutory nuisance

The law of statutory nuisance represents a bridge between the common law controls of environmental protection and the more characteristic statutory mechanisms. The law on statutory nuisance was consolidated in the Public Health Act 1936, following previous Acts of 1848, 1855, 1860 and 1875. Originally, the purpose of the Act was to attempt to control matters which, although nuisances in the common law sense, affected sanitation levels and thus public health in Victorian times. The law has been updated yet again and consolidated in Part III of the EPA 1990. The main aim of the statutory nuisance provisions is to provide a quick and easy remedy to abate nuisances with which the common law is too slow or too expensive to deal.

The control of statutory nuisances

District councils and London borough councils are under a duty to inspect their areas for statutory nuisances (EPA 1990, s. 79). The consequence of this is that if an individual within an area complains of a statutory nuisance emanating from within that area then a district council is obliged to investigate. The EPA 1990 implies that the level of such an obligation is only to take such steps as are reasonably practicable. Although the duty imposed is only that inspection be periodic, it is clear that if there is strong evidence to suggest that a statutory nuisance exists within an area, and a local authority refuse to inspect, then it is possible that the remedy of judicial review will lie to any aggrieved applicant. It is important, therefore, for any individual wishing to complain to a local authority to ensure that proper evidence is gathered (e.g., dates, times and length of the nuisance if it has already occurred, or strong evidence to show that the statutory nuisance is about to occur). There are default powers under EPA 1990, sch. 3, para. 4 which allow the Secretary of State to take action if local authorities are not carrying out their duty.

The general control of statutory nuisance is contained in EPA 1990, s. 80. This provides that where a local authority is satisfied that a statutory nuisance exists, or is likely to occur or recur, it is under a mandatory duty to serve an abatement notice on the person responsible for the nuisance or, if that person cannot be found, the owner or occupier of the premises on which the statutory nuisance is present.

The nature of this duty was considered in *R v Carrick District Council, ex parte Shelley* [1996] Env LR 273. The applicants were two residents of a Cornish village. They complained to the council about the discharges of sewage from two outlets on the village beach. Each outfall was subject to a discharge consent under the Water Resources Act 1991. The applicants asked the council to exercise its powers to deal with statutory nuisances. Instead of taking action the council resolved to do nothing (having taken into account the fact that the discharges of sewage were being considered by the Secretary of State in an appeal made by the relevant water company, South West Water). The applicants challenged this refusal by way of judicial review. It was held that the council was under a duty to investigate its area for the existence of statutory nuisances. Once it was found that a statutory nuisance existed, the council was under a duty to serve an abatement notice. Thus the council could not simply resolve to do nothing in the light of a determination that the statutory nuisance existed. A decision has to be made on the state of affairs which are before the council at any given time and it was not possible to wait for any anticipated improvements before coming to a view on the existence of a statutory nuisance.

The categories of statutory nuisance

There are a number of categories of statutory nuisance contained in the EPA 1990, s. 79. These are supplemented by other statutes which declare specific categories to be a statutory nuisance and thus controlled under the provisions of the Act (EPA 1990, s. 79(1)(h)). Much of the language used in s. 79 is somewhat antiquated and difficult to reconcile with modern technology. The categories of statutory nuisance are listed in the headings below. The Act lays down certain activities or states of affairs which will amount to a statutory nuisance if 'prejudicial to health or a nuisance'.

The scope of statutory nuisances has been widened under the Noise and Statutory Nuisance Act 1993, which reinforces local authorities' powers and enables them to take action against noise in the street. This includes noise from vehicles, equipment, machinery or loudspeakers. Another part of the Act deals with powers to take action against faulty burglar alarms.

'Prejudicial to health or a nuisance'

The main criterion for the existence of a statutory nuisance is that anything complained of must be either 'prejudicial to health or a nuisance'. These are not to be read conjunctively.

'Prejudicial to health' is defined under EPA 1990, s. 79(7), as meaning injurious, or likely to cause injury, to health. In *Coventry City Council* v *Cartwright* [1975] 1 WLR 845, the Council owned a vacant site within a residential area on which they allowed people to dump all sorts of materials. These included not only normal household refuse, but also building and construction materials. Occasionally, the Council would move household materials. A nearby resident complained of a statutory nuisance under the Public Health Act 1936. The Divisional Court held that, where the accumulation complained of was inert rather than putrescible, there was no likelihood of disease or that vermin would be attracted which could spread disease. Although there was a chance that physical injury could be caused to people who walked on the site, that did not amount to being prejudicial to health.

In defining the word 'nuisance', it is generally accepted that the word contained within the EPA 1990 has the same definition as that under the common law. In *National Coal Board* v *Thorne* [1976] 1 WLR 543, the nuisance complained of amounted to defective guttering and windows within premises. The complainant argued that the physical condition of the building amounted to a nuisance under the Public Health Act. Watkins J said that a 'nuisance coming within the meaning of the Public Health Act 1936 must be either a public or private nuisance as understood by common law'. Thus, when deciding on the point of whether or not a statutory nuisance could arise when it was the inhabitants of premises who were suffering, such a state of affairs could not amount to nuisance because it was not an interference with the use or enjoyment of neighbouring property. There has to be more than just mere discomfort to the occupier's enjoyment of property unless such a state of affairs would be prejudicial to health.

Any premises in such a state as to be prejudicial to health or a nuisance

Section 79(1)(a) provides that where premises are kept in a state which is prejudicial to health or a nuisance then this will amount to a statutory nuisance. 'Premises' includes land and any vessel not powered by steam-reciprocating machinery. The physical extent of the premises must be viewed in context. In *Stevenage Borough Council* v *Wilson* [1993] Env LR 214, premises extended to the garden of a house where an abatement notice had included only the word 'dwelling'. The provision covers the physical state of premises rather than any use to which those premises are put. Therefore, where noise or dust etc. is emitted from those premises from a use, this is not covered. The aim is to prevent situations where there are physical elements which are either prejudicial to health or a nuisance. Such things would cover the lack of proper insulation of council-owned flats against noise (see *Southwark London Borough Council* v *Ince* (1989) 21 HLR 504) and dwellings which are subject to heavy condensation from poor heating and ventilation (see *Greater London Council* v *Tower Hamlets London Borough Council* (1983) 15 HLR 57).

Smoke emitted from premises so as to be prejudicial to health or a nuisance

Section 79(1)(b) replaced the Clean Air Act 1956, s. 16, which previously made separate provision for the control of smoke from premises. There are exemptions contained within s. 79(3) so that:

(a) smoke emitted from a chimney of a private dwelling within a smoke control area;

(b) dark smoke emitted from a chimney of a building, or a chimney serving the furnace of a boiler or industrial plant attached to a building, or for the time being installed on any land;

(c) smoke emitted from a railway locomotive steam engine;

(d) dark smoke emitted, otherwise than as mentioned above, from industrial or trade premises

will not be statutory nuisances. Section 17 of the Clean Air Act 1993 deals with smoke nuisances in Scotland.

Fumes or gases emitted from premises so as to be prejudicial to health or a nuisance

Section 79(4) controls fumes or gases emitted from private dwellings. Fumes are defined as 'any airborne solid matter smaller than dust, gases including vapour and moisture precipitating from vapour' (EPA 1990, s. 79(7)).

Any dust, steam, smell or other effluvia arising on industrial, trade or business premises and being prejudicial to health or a nuisance

The meanings of dust, steam and smell are fairly well established. However, the term 'effluvia' was defined in *Malton Board of Health* v *Malton Manure Co.*

(1879) 4 ExD 302. This case involved the production of manure by the defendant company which produced vapours. It could not be conclusively demonstrated that these vapours were prejudicial to healthy people in the locality, although the Board of Health did demonstrate that it had the effect of making people who were ill more ill. The court held that this effect could amount to effluvia which were prejudicial to health. It is suggested that the meaning of effluvia covers the outflow of harmful or unpleasant substances.

Any accumulation or deposit which is prejudicial to health or a nuisance

To come within s. 79(1)(e), the accumulation or deposit has to be capable of causing disease rather than injury (see *Coventry City Council* v *Cartwright* [1975] 1 WLR 845, above). The wide range of accumulations or deposits covered by this section have included sheep dung (*Draper* v *Sperring* (1869) 10 CB 113) and cinders which emitted offensive smells (*Bishop Auckland Local Board* v *Bishop Auckland Iron and Steel Co.* (1882) 10 QBD 138). This section can also include discharges of sewage (see *R* v *Carrick District Council, ex parte Shelley* [1996] Env LR 273).

Any animal kept in such a place or manner as to be prejudicial to health or a nuisance

The keeping of a large number of animals on premises can give rise to a number of different enforcement actions. First, the keeping of a large number of animals may amount to sufficient intensification of a use to give rise to a change of use, which could result in enforcement action under the Town and Country Planning Act 1990 (see *Wallington* v *Secretary of State for Wales* (1990) 62 P & CR 150). Secondly, there may be common law actions which could be brought for nuisance. Thirdly, there could be action taken by the local authority under by-laws passed under the Public Health Act 1936, s. 81(2), and finally, there could be action taken under the statutory nuisance provisions of s. 79(1)(f).

Noise emitted from premises so as to be prejudicial to health or a nuisance

This provision replaces Part III of the Control of Pollution Act 1974 dealing with noise from premises. There is an exemption for noise from model aircraft.

Any other matter declared by any enactment to be a statutory nuisance

This provision is to include any statutory nuisance provided for under future statutes. it also includes nuisances from mines, shafts and quarries under the Mines and Quarries Act 1954 (EPA 1990, s. 151).

What is required to satisfy the local authority?

In practice, it is the responsibility of the local environmental health officer to decide upon whether or not a statutory nuisance is occurring or is likely to occur. As has been stated, the test is whether or not a statutory nuisance is prejudicial to health or a nuisance. An environmental health officer will visit the premises and make a subjective decision as to whether or not the state of the premises or anything on those premises amounts to a nuisance. When reverting to the common law for the definition of nuisance, it is up to the environmental health officer to balance the many different factors used when deciding on whether or not a common law nuisance exists. The most important of these factors are:

(a)   the nature and the location of the nuisance;
(b)   the time and duration of the nuisance; and
(c)   the utility of the activity concerned.

Balancing all these factors together is the only way in which an environmental health officer can make an adjudication between respective neighbours' rights, because it is quite clear that a statutory nuisance will only apply to affected neighbours' properties.

Section 80(1) provides that for a local authority to act, the statutory nuisance must exist or be likely to occur or recur. Thus this procedure can be used to prevent a nuisance before it actually occurs, although there has to be evidence that a forthcoming activity is likely to give rise to a statutory nuisance and the standard of evidence required is particularly high. However, where these problems can be overcome, such as in the case of a party where there is more than a suggestion that powerful audio equipment will be used, this may well be the only method of prohibiting certain types of nuisances in advance. Where a local authority has delegated enforcement powers to individual officers then those officers are able to carry out the enforcement procedures on behalf of the local authority.

Who is the 'person responsible'?

The enforcement of a statutory nuisance is normally against the 'person responsible', which is defined in EPA 1990, s. 79(7) as being 'the person to whose act, default or sufferance the nuisance is attributable'. This is a particularly wide definition and can include a local authority (see *Rossall* v *London Borough of Southwark*, unreported), or a landlord who has allowed a tenant to carry on offensive activities. It can also include a tenant who has denied access to a landlord who wished to carry out works to abate a nuisance (see *Carr* v *London Borough of Hackney* [1995] Env LR 372).

If there are any difficulties in locating the 'person responsible' for the existence of a statutory nuisance, EPA 1990, s. 80(2)(c), states that the definition of the person responsible can be extended to include the owner or occupier of the premises in question.

The abatement notice

Once the local authority, through its environmental health officesr, is satisfied that a statutory nuisance exists, it is under a duty to serve an abatement notice which must require any or all of the following:

(a)   the abatement of the nuisance or the prohibiting or restricting of its occurrence or recurrence;
(b)   the execution of works or other steps necessary to comply with the notice.

Where works are specified in the abatement notice the requirement must be clear and precise as the recipient needs to know what must be done to comply because criminal sanctions apply if the notice were to be breached (see *Network Housing Association* v *Westminster City Council* (1994) 93 LGR 280). On the other hand, where the notice simply requires the cessation of the nuisance but does not specify the works there is no need to go into any greater detail (see *R* v *Wheatley* (1885) 16 QBD 34 and *Sterling Homes* v *Birmingham City Council* [1996] Env LR D8). In the case of a noise nuisance, however, it is not necessary to specify maximum noise levels (see *East Northamptonshire District Council* v *Fossett* [1994] Env LR 388). Finally, there is no requirement that the notice be corroborated by evidence of a particular occupier who has suffered unreasonable interference with the enjoyment of property (see *Cooke* v *Adatia* (1988) 153 JP 129). The notice should specify the time within which compliance is required.

Where an individual has been served with an abatement notice, the contravention of that notice, without reasonable excuse renders that person guilty of a criminal offence under the EPA 1990, s. 80(4). Once a notice is served it takes effect in perpetuity even in the case of a notice served under the old Control of Pollution Act powers (see *Aitken* v *South Hams District Council* [1994] 3 All ER 400 overruling *R* v *Folkestone Magistrates' Court, ex parte Kibble* [1993] Env LR 400).

Defences

Where an offence has been committed under s. 80(4) there are a number of defences.

Reasonable excuse
It is a defence to a prosecution for the contravention of an abatement notice to show that there was a reasonable excuse for carrying out the activity which resulted in the contravention. The test laid down for this would seem to be an objective one, i.e., 'would a reasonable person think that the excuse given was consistent with a reasonable standard of conduct?'. The defence is not available where an abatement notice has been contravened deliberately and intentionally in circumstances wholly under the control of the defendant. Thus, a defendant could not argue that because there had been a three year

gap between the service of an abatement notice and its breach and no one had complained about the breach as it was of minimum inconvenience, there was a 'reasonable excuse' (*Wellingborough Borough Council* v *Gordon* [1993] Env LR 218). It is not sufficient to say that there would be a defence to a private law action in nuisance. Indeed, in *A. Lambert Flat Management Ltd* v *Lomas* [1981] 1 WLR 898, it was said that COPA 1974, s. 58(4) was designed to provide a defence to a criminal charge where an individual had some reasonable excuse, such as some special difficulty in relation to compliance with the abatement notice. It was not an opportunity to challenge the notice; that should only properly be done on an appeal (see, in relation to the EPA 1990, *AMEC Building Ltd* v *London Borough of Camden* [1997] Env LR D9).

Best practicable means

Where an abatement notice is served on trade or business premises and the nuisance complained of is caused in the course of the trade or business, it is a defence under certain heads of EPA 1990, s. 70(1), to show that the best practicable means have been used to prevent or counteract the nuisance (s. 80(7)). This does not apply to fumes or gases emitted from premises (s. 79(1)(c)), or the catch-all provision under s. 79(1)(h). Although there is not any complete definition contained within the EPA 1990, certain elements are required to be taken into account under s. 79(9). These include local conditions and circumstances, the current state of technical knowledge, the financial implications, and the design, installation, maintenance, manner and periods of operation of plant and machinery.

The defence has to be established on a balance of probabilities, and the burden of proof lies on the defendant to show that it had taken reasonable steps to prevent or counteract the nuisance. Thus, where a defendant had submitted a planning application for noise reducing bunding to counteract a noise nuisance, but failed to answer the local planning authority's request for further information, it failed to discharge the burden of proof that it was using best practicable means to prevent or counteract the nuisance (*Chapman* v *Gosberton Farm Produce Co. Ltd* [1993] Env LR 191).

Special defences

There are specific defences available in relation to noise and nuisances on construction sites and in areas where there are registered noise levels under the noise abatement zone procedure (see EPA 1990, s. 80(9) and COPA, ss. 60, 61 and 65–67).

The right of appeal against an abatement notice

Where an individual is served with an abatement notice there is a right of appeal against the notice to a magistrates' court. One advantage of the appeal system over a defence to a prosecution under contravention proceedings is that it allows for a far greater range of appeal grounds and therefore provides a greater scope for disputing the nuisance. An appeal normally lies within 21

days of the service of the notice. The grounds of appeal are set down in
regulations made under EPA 1990. The Statutory Nuisance (Appeals)
Regulations 1995 (SI 1995 No. 2644) set out the grounds of appeal against
an abatement notice, which include:

(a)   that the abatement notice is not justified in the terms of s. 80;
(b)   that there has been a substantive or procedural error in the service of
the notice;
(c)   that the authority have unreasonably refused to accept compliance
with alternative requirements, or that their requirements are unreasonable or
unnecessary;
(d)   that the period for compliance is unreasonable;
(e)   that the best practicable means were used to counteract the effect of
a nuisance from trade or business premises.

Furthermore, the regulations allow for the suspension of an abatement notice
pending the court's decision, unless the local authority override the suspension in the abatement notice with a statement to the effect that the notice is
to have effect regardless, and that:

(a)   the nuisance is prejudicial to health;
(b)   suspension would render the notice of no practical effect (e.g., where
nuisances are to cease before the action can be heard in court); or
(c)   any expenditure incurred before an appeal would be disproportionate
to the public benefit.

Individual actions by any person

It is often the case that local authorities' environmental health departments
are overworked and understaffed and have neither the resources nor sometimes the inclination to deal with disputes regarding statutory nuisances.
Section 82 of the Act allows a complaint to be made to a local magistrates'
court by any person who is aggrieved by the existence of a statutory nuisance.
This procedure allows for any person within an area to bring a more
affordable and expeditious proceeding than a private law action. One particular limitation upon this procedure is that the nuisance must be in existence
and therefore cannot be used to anticipate problems. Therefore, a person has
no right of action under this section to stop a nuisance which is likely to occur
in the future (e.g., loud parties). If the person can satisfy the magistrates that
there is an existing nuisance, or that there is likely to be a recurring nuisance,
they are under a duty to issue an abatement notice requiring the defendant
to abate the nuisance within a specified time, and to execute any works
necessary for that purpose and/or prohibiting a recurrence of the nuisance,
and requiring the defendant, within a specified time, to carry out any works
necessary to prevent the recurrence. The magistrates may fine a defendant at
a level not exceeding level 5 on the standard scale (s. 82(2)). There is a notice

procedure, which differs slightly from that which governs local authority actions, in that s. 80(6) provides that where an individual is bringing an action they must give not less than three days' notice in relation to a noise nuisance and, in relation to other statutory nuisances, 21 days' notice, before the bringing of proceedings under s. 80(2).

Sentencing powers for contravention of an abatement notice

Section 80(5) and (6) of the EPA 1990 provide for penalties for a person who is guilty of an offence of contravening an abatement notice. The matter is triable only in the magistrates' court and, if found guilty, a private offender is liable to a fine not exceeding level 5 on the standard scale (£5,000). If the offence continues after the conviction they are liable to a further fine not exceeding one-tenth of that level for each day on which the offence continues. The previous levels of fine included under the Public Health Act and Control of Pollution Act indicated that for major industrial uses there were no real disincentives to carry out works to improve premises. Indeed, it was often cost effective to pay fines at a low level in order to ensure that a particular activity could be carried on rather than abated. Section 80(6) closes this particular loophole by imposing a maximum fine of £20,000 on industrial, trade or business offenders. In addition to these sanctions, the magistrates have a 'discretion to award compensation' up to a maximum of £5,000.

The use of injunctions and proceedings in the High Court

In many cases the provisions of s. 80 would not provide an adequate remedy in terms of either gravity or speed. Under s. 81(5), a local authority may take action in the High Court for the purpose of securing the abatement, prohibition or restriction of any statutory nuisance where it is of the opinion that proceedings for an offence of contravening an abatement notice would not provide a sufficient remedy. The usual method for doing this would be by seeking an injunction in the High Court. In *Hammersmith London Borough Council* v *Magnum Automated Forecourts Ltd* [1978] 1 WLR 50, the Court of Appeal decided that this was an additional power to that contained under the statutory noise nuisance provisions contained within COPA 1974. Thus, the right to take proceedings in the High Court could be used after an abatement notice had been served, but before the prosecution for contravention had been heard, in order to expedite the cessation of the nuisance.

The scope for injunctions has widened considerably with the decision in *Lloyds Bank* v *Guardian Assurance* (1987) 35 BLR 34, which stated that the jurisdiction of the High Court was not affected by any proceedings under the statutory nuisance provisions of COPA 1974. The real effect of this decision has been to suggest that it will not be open to any individual to apply for an injunction under the common law which is in stricter terms than any abatement notice which has already been served under COPA 1974 or the EPA 1990. However, it is open to the local authority to tighten up on a weak abatement notice by applying for an injunction in the High Court under

s. 81(5). In such proceedings it will be a defence to prove that noise was authorised by a construction site consent under COPA 1974, s. 61.

Injunctions are a discretionary remedy and will not be granted lightly. The activity complained of must be of sufficient gravity and/or duration to justify stopping it (*Goldsmith* v *Tunbridge Wells Improvement Commission* (1866) LR 1 Ch App 349).

The powers available to local authorities may flow from primary statute (e.g., EPA 1990) or from s. 222 of the Local Government Act 1972. This general power is available only in circumstances where the local authority has expressly considered that the powers available under the specific provisions would afford an inadequate remedy (see *Vale of White Horse District Council* v *Allen & Partners* [1997] Env LR 212).

PART II   SECTORAL COVERAGE OF ENVIRONMENTAL LAW

NINE
Town and country planning

The British system of town and country planning is undoubtedly one of the most sophisticated systems of land use control in the world. It is virtually unique in incorporating controls over the use of land as well as over the design and form of the built environment. Accordingly, it plays a central role in environmental law because of its enormous importance in relation to locational and siting issues. It is, as stated earlier (see p. 100), perhaps the pre-eminent example in this country of an anticipatory system of control. However, town and country planning is not just about environmental protection. It has a wider role in organising economic development, and in balancing economic, political, social and environmental factors to do with development in a democratic context. This wider role is outside environmental law in the sense in which the term is used in this book, so this chapter is restricted to summarising those parts of planning law which have the greatest importance for environmental protection.

This chapter is written in the firm belief that planning law can be reduced to a number of central principles, and that once the structure of the system is understood, many of the details become self-explanatory. As a result, many matters of detail are omitted, but there are many excellent specialist books and encyclopaedias which readers are urged to consult (see Bibliography).

In particular, it should be noted that, for reasons of space, the specific provisions on listed buildings and conservation areas are not covered in this chapter. Pieces of planning law relevant to other chapters within Part II of the book are summarised at the appropriate places.

The main features of town and country planning

These are as follows:

    (a)   The local planning authority draws up a development plan, which sets out the strategy for development in the area. This involves a measure of public participation. Development plans are permissive (i.e., they do not guarantee what is going to happen, but act as guides to future development) and must be taken into account in any decision.

(b)   All 'development', which is widely construed and includes changes of use as well as physical development, requires planning permission from the local planning authority before it may be carried out.

(c)   Procedures are laid down for applications for planning permission. These involve consultation with other public bodies and some limited public involvement.

(d)   The local planning authority decides on grounds of planning policy whether to grant permission or refuse it, taking into account the development plans, Central Government policies and any other material considerations.

(e)   Unlike most other systems of town planning, which rely heavily on zoning of areas within which certain generalised rules will apply, in this country each case must be considered on its merits.

(f)   If permission is granted, it may be subject to conditions; indeed, this is the normal position. If permission is refused, no compensation is normally payable — the right to develop land was effectively nationalised in the Town and Country Planning Act 1947.

(g)   The applicant has a right of appeal to the Secretary of State against any refusal or conditions. This is a complete rehearing of the whole matter, including the policy issues, and thus enables the Secretary of State to exercise a stranglehold on policy by having the final say on it.

(h)   There is no right of appeal for third parties and no right to appeal against a grant of planning permission.

(i)   There is a further right of appeal from the decision of the Secretary of State to the High Court on what are essentially the same grounds as for judicial review. The courts thus exercise a supervisory jurisdiction over the procedures and the decisions taken. However, the courts will not intervene on grounds of fact or policy.

(j)   Enforcement of the law is through another discretionary procedure in which the local planning authority may serve an enforcement notice requiring specified steps to be taken. It is an offence to fail to comply with an enforcement notice. Once again, a right of appeal to the Secretary of State is provided and, as this may involve consideration of policy issues, it is in most cases deemed a retrospective application for planning permission.

(k)   Planning permission effectively gives a right to develop. Unlike most systems of pollution control, there is no power to vary a planning permission in the future (unless compensation is paid).

Town and country planning as a tool of environmental policy

There are thus three main areas with relevance to environmental law:

(a)   The system of development plans, which ensures that environmental protection is considered at the level of policy-making. These plans often set the basic ground rules for action on the environment in any particular area, although they must be read in conjunction with the policy guidance emanating from Central Government.

(b) The development control process, in which planning permission is required from the local planning authority for acts of development. This is a good example of a 'mixed economy' solution to environmental control (i.e., the initiative for development is normally taken by private developers, but permission to go ahead is required from a public authority). This ensures a strict anticipatory control over many activities before they start and normally involves liaison with the relevant pollution control and environmental agencies.

(c) The power to impose conditions relating to environmental protection on a grant of planning permission. These are capable of creating some form of continuing control over activities.

The traditional conflictual model of a regulatory body regulating the applicant by granting or refusing permission is currently breaking down. Modern town planning may be seen as a negotiative process in which consultation between the prospective developer and the local planning authority in advance of the application is the norm, and in which proposals are both made and considered in the light of local and national policies. The local planning authority and the developer often have a community of interest in carrying out a particular development: the developer gets its proposal granted and the local authority obtains the revitalisation of the economy of an area, or the creation of jobs, or some other economic benefit. (Indeed, developments by local authorities and developers in partnership with each other are now quite common.) In addition, arrangements between developers and local authorities in which 'planning gain' is bargained for are increasingly used to supplement the regulatory controls (see p. 258).

It should also be borne in mind that the impact of planning control is in many ways incomplete or inadequate. Planning permission is not required for all environmentally harmful activities, for example for mobile pollutants such as cars, or in relation to most agricultural activities. There are difficulties where some form of continuing control is required, because of the limitations on planning conditions, or where positive management is required, since it is mainly a preventative system. The system also tends to get circumvented in various ways where nationally important development is desired by Central Government.

A further point is that the planning decision is a political one, and thus environmental issues may be subordinated to other needs. As the Royal Commission on Environmental Pollution commented in its Fifth Report in relation to pollution prevention, 'Our concern is not that pollution is not always given top priority; it is that it is often dealt with inadequately, and sometimes forgotten altogether in the planning process' (Cmnd 6371, 1976).

Nevertheless, the planning system is of central importance in many areas of environmental law, especially when used in conjunction with other regulatory controls. This is seen clearly in relation to waste disposal, where planning permission for a waste disposal site is required before a waste management licence can be granted. In other areas, planning control is arguably of greatest importance where the enforcement of pollution control is inadequate, since non-enforcement at the operational end puts increased pressure on initial siting and design issues.

Town and country planning and some themes of this book

This brief summary of the town and country planning system shows how it illustrates a number of the major themes of this book. For instance, it is a good example of a sophisticated anticipatory regulatory mechanism and it emphasises prevention of harm. That also means that the predominant method of control is through negative, restrictive measures, rather than through positive mechanisms. Local decision-making dominates, although there has been an all too obvious shift of power towards Central Government in recent years (see p. 110). It is a highly discretionary system, in which decisions are made on a case-by-case basis and it is a democratic system in which ultimate political control rests with elected members rather than with officers (on appeal responsibility rests with an elected Secretary of State), although in practice most decisions are actually taken by officers. It is a fairly open and public system. Of course, this last point sets up one of the great conflicts of the system: the more open it is, the slower decisions tend to be.

Enforcement is under-emphasised, being almost exclusively the responsibility of the local planning authority and dependent on political and tactical factors.

But the most important point is that this is a highly political system of decision-making. Local planning authorities and the Secretary of State make discretionary decisions by balancing economic, political, environmental and social factors. It is therefore just as important to understand the prevailing policy in relation to a particular issue as it is to understand the relevant law.

The role of the law and the courts requires some explanation here. The planning system is one where the law exercises a supervisory, or review, function. It is there to define the various concepts used in the planning system (such as what development is, or what types of conditions are legitimate), to ensure that the correct procedures are used and to ensure that discretionary decisions are taken in the proper manner. The law is therefore ultimately about procedures, i.e., about ensuring that decisions are made correctly rather than that the correct decisions are made.

The planning legislation

As Lord Scarman stated in *Pioneer Aggregates (UK) Ltd* v *Secretary of State for the Environment* [1985] AC 132, 'Planning control is the creature of Statute . . . Parliament has provided a comprehensive code of planning control'. This comprehensive code was originally created in the Town and Country Planning Act 1947, when a uniform and mandatory country-wide system of development control was introduced. One of the most remarkable things about planning is that, whilst there have been numerous detailed additions and amendments to the law, the basic structure of much of this system (apart from that relating to development plans) has remained unchanged since then, although the way in which it is operated has in practice changed quite radically.

The legislation is now consolidated in the Town and Country Planning Act 1990. Unless otherwise stated, wherever a section number is given in this chapter without reference to a particular Act, it refers to that Act.

The Planning and Compensation Act 1991 made substantial changes to the 1990 Act, especially in relation to development plans, enforcement and planning obligations. Perhaps the greatest impact of the 1991 Act, however, has been on the relationship between development plans and other material considerations, particularly Central Government policy guidance. This is because of the introduction of a statutory presumption, laid down in s. 54A to the 1990 Act, in favour of following the provisions of the development plan. This presumption obviously reflects a shift in emphasis away from 'developer-led' planning towards 'plan-led' planning (see p. 251). The 1991 Act was brought into force in a piecemeal manner and involved the passage of a large amount of subordinate legislation, but it was effectively fully implemented by the beginning of 1993.

Much of the detail of the law on town and country planning is in subordinate legislation. Of particular importance are the Town and Country Planning (General Permitted Development) Order 1995 (SI 1995 No. 418) as amended and the Town and Country Planning (General Development Procedure) Order 1995 (SI 1995 No. 419) as amended, which have consolidated the old GDO (SI 1988 No. 813). These regulations fulfil different functions: the former grants automatic planning permission for a large number of activities and the latter provides many of the procedures relating to an application for permission.

What is town and country planning?

One respected town planner has described town planning simply as 'How much of what is put where'. This reflects the fact that planning is a *process* through which decisions are made, rather than anything with an absolutely definitive subject matter. As befits a political system, the question of what planning covers has over the years largely been left to those who make planning decisions. The result has been an expansion of the idea, beyond straightforward amenity, public health and land use issues towards taking into account the economic and social impact of decisions.

This widening of the scope of planning has received the support of the courts. In exercising their supervisory jurisdiction they have often had to ask the question 'What is planning?' in order to decide whether a power has been used legitimately. In so doing they have proved willing to decide that most things are within the scope of planning. The most commonly used legal test is given by Lord Scarman in *Westminster City Council v Great Portland Estates plc* [1985] AC 661, who suggested that town planning covers anything that 'relates to the character of the use of land'.

However, this accommodating legal attitude is not shared by all and in recent years there have been fundamental divisions over the legitimate role and scope of planning. Until the 1970s, town and country planning was a relatively uncontroversial topic in party political terms, with the exception of the questions of compensation for refusal of permission and taxation of profits resulting from a grant of permission. There was a degree of consensus over what planning should consist of and over the preferred policies. This has now broken down, with the result that there is open conflict over both the proper role of planning and over the content of the policies that should be adopted.

There is universal agreement that planning includes land use and amenity issues, such as the location and design of new developments. The key question is how far socio-economic issues are a legitimate part of it. Some see planning as one means by which a particular form of social development may be produced. Others wish to see planning restricted as much as possible on the grounds that it interferes unduly with the free market. The second view was effectively the one that was espoused by the previous Conservative Government, with its firm beliefs in deregulation, a minimalist approach to restrictions on commercial activity, the power of the market as a distributor of resources, and the consequent need for speed and certainty in any system of control. It is too early to discern any particular view from the Labour Government of the way in which the planning system might be used. The linking of the Departments of the Environment and Transport and the recognition of the importance of the development of regional policy suggest that planning policy may become much more integrated into other areas (including other environmental policy areas) and there will be a greater reliance upon the contribution of the regions in strategic planning.

Planning policy

Notwithstanding the retention of the basic structure of the system outlined above, town planning has changed radically since the 1970s. Only some of these changes have been to the law. Most have been brought about by administrative means, particularly by the concerted application of strong Central Government policy. This was summarised by Grant in the first updating supplement to *Urban Planning Law* (1986) as follows:

> One of the most distinctive trends of the past five years has been the emergence of Government policy as a dominant force in development control. It has been brought about by a series of hard-hitting Circulars based on the Government's deregulatory and pro-development ideology, coupled to a new willingness to use the appeals process as a means of reinforcing the policies.

The pro-development ideology was arguably the most important aspect of the 1980s, as the then Government sought to increase the role of the free market in generating development. Landmarks in this regard were the publication of

Circular 22/80, with an overt encouragement of small businesses and private housing, and Circular 14/85 with its presumption in favour of development which stated 'There is always a presumption in favour of allowing applications for development, having regard to all material considerations, unless that development would cause demonstrable harm to interests of acknowledged importance'. Circular 1/85 also played an important role, emphasising that conditions should not be attached unless they could be justified on clear grounds. Their role was described as 'anodyne expedients by which objections to offensive developments can be assuaged' (Miller and Wood, *Planning and Pollution*, 1983).

Not only were these Circulars pro-development in terms of policy, they afforded such great weight to this that local planning authorities ignored them at their peril. The result was that in the 1980s these explicitly directory Circulars grew to have far greater importance than local policies such as development plans. As shown below, these were downgraded in importance in the 1980s, though they are enjoying a resurgence at present. The reason for this is straightforward; in a developer-led system, developers value the certainty that is provided by a framework of clear policies, rather than the uncertainty provided by a wholly market-based approach.

The appeals process was used to support this shift in power from local government to Central Government. Pearce ('The changing role of planning appeals', *Development and Planning*, ed. Cross and Whitehead, 1989) showed some dramatic changes here. In the early to mid 1970s the success rate of appeals against refusal of permission was in the region of 20%. This had grown to 32% by 1984 and 40% in 1986/7, at which level it stayed for the rest of the decade. Not surprisingly, the number of appeals also rose sharply, from around 8,000 in the mid 1970s to almost 30,000 each year in the late 1980s. This meant that a quarter of all refusals were appealed. A similar story was apparent in relation to appeals against enforcement notices.

In keeping with the policy of doctrinal neutrality on the content of planning policies, the courts did not interfere with these changes, except to preserve the rationality of the decision-making process by insisting that adequate reasons were given for decisions. In this respect it should be recognised that the planning system has always been pro-development to some extent. This stems from the prominence of property-based ideas within it and is evident in its very structure. For example, third parties and objectors are not given particularly wide rights within the system. Specifically, there is a right to appeal against the refusal of permission, but no right to appeal against a grant of permission (as there is in many other countries, such as the Republic of Ireland). The result is that permission will be granted if *either* the local planning authority or the Secretary of State is in favour of it. The Labour Government has given a previous policy commitment to the idea of giving third parties the right to appeal against the grant of planning permission in cases where the development would be contrary to the development plan — thus taking the concept of 'plan-led' development one stage further. Although the introduction of such third-party rights might appear to be radical, it is perhaps best seen as an extension of the existing power of call-in which is available to the Secretary of State under s. 77 of the 1990 Act. In cases where the Secretary of State refuses to call in an application it would be unlikely for a third party appeal to succeed, as there has already been an implicit acceptance that the departure from the plan is not sufficiently important to warrant calling in.

There has also always been some sort of presumption in favour of granting permission; the difference is that this has changed in substance from the basic public law requirement that reasons be given for a decision affecting some-one's right to develop to a *policy* in favour of development that may have a great weight attached to it by the decision-maker (see p. 249 for a discussion of the court's attitude to the presumption in favour of development). Similarly there have always been restrictions on the scope of conditions, with the courts adopting the attitude that conditions that take away private property rights without compensation are *ultra vires* (see p. 254). Lastly, the statistics on planning permission show that of the large numbers of applica-tions made each year, approximately 90% are granted.

Deregulation

A separate, though related, strand of the changes in the 1980s was the theme of deregulation. This was illustrated by the titles of three White Papers setting out Government policy — *Lifting the Burden* (Cmnd 9571, 1985), *Building Businesses, Not Barriers* (Cmnd 9794, 1986) and *Releasing Enterprise* (Cm 512). A major emphasis was the reduction of red tape and delays. Significant relaxations were made in the General Development Order in 1981, 1985 and 1988 and in the Use Classes Order in 1987 so as to cut out the need for planning permission in many situations, with the objective of encouraging the development of small businesses. Along with the other changes to develop-ment plans referred to at p. 227, the procedures for development plans were streamlined, so that they might be adopted more quickly, leading to a consequent reduction in public opportunities for participation in the process. Regular encouragement was given by Circulars to speed up the process of dealing with planning applications. The politically suspect metropolitan county councils were abolished in the Local Government Act 1985, and this led to the introduction of a new system of unitary development plans in those areas.

The uniformity of the system was also lost. Enterprise zones were introduc-ed in the Local Government, Planning and Land Act 1980 and simplified planning zones in the Housing and Planning Act 1986. Both mechanisms operate so as to remove most or all planning controls in designated areas, though designation and the controls that are retained remain with the local authority. In contrast, urban development areas, also introduced in the Local Government, Planning and Land Act 1980, are designated (or imposed) solely by the Secretary of State and are put under the management of centrally appointed urban development corporations, with local planning authorities losing all their powers (see p. 246). A final point worth mentioning is that an increasing number of environmentally significant developments avoid the planning system entirely by using either the more limited Private Bill procedures or the technical procedures under the Transport and Works Act 1992.

A change of direction?

In summary it can be said that in the 1980s the planning system became far more centralised. This was true in two senses: more decisions were taken at a central level and central policy pervaded every decision even at a local level. One effect was to shift power from local government to Central Government; another to increase the areas of conflict between the two levels. But, interestingly, at the same time the system became in a way less centralised. This was because the changes in policy were designed to increase the role of the market at the expense of the State, and to make the system more developer-led.

However, it is clear that in the 1990s these trends are slowly being reversed as the Conservative Government steered a slightly different course to that charted in the 1980s. There were signs that greater regard was being paid to local decisions (as represented by development plans) and this impression of a shift in the balance between Central Government and local government was reinforced by the presumption in favour of following the development plan mentioned above.

The pace of change in planning policy has slowed significantly from the heady days of the mid to late 1980s. This reflects a number of factors, not the least of which is the deep recession in the development industry in the early to mid 1990s. When this is coupled with the strategic shift from central to local control via the development plan system, it is difficult to identify any significant policy emphasis from Central Government. Perhaps the most notable policy guidance in the mid 1990s has seen the use of the mechanism of planning to contribute to the goal of sustainable development. PPGs on planning and transport and retail development (and more specifically out-of-town retailing) have indicated that the Government is willing to use planning as a means of governing the location of development which would generate significant amounts of traffic. These policy initiatives have been reinforced by a spate of appeal decisions where the Secretary of State has upheld the turned down appeals for a number of out-of-town superstores. Ironically, the use of central policy to *promote* 'environmentally friendly' developments is a cumbersome mechanism, and can be overridden by both local decisions through the development plan process and the courts (see the House of Lords decision in *Bolton MBC* v *Secretary of State for the Environment* [1995] JPL 1043).

Local planning authorities

Initial responsibility for most planning decisions rests with local authorities, which in this context are generically called local planning authorities. As a result of local government reorganisation under the Local Government Act 1992, there are three main types of local planning authority:

(a) Single-tier London boroughs and metropolitan districts.

(b) Non-metropolitan areas in which the planning function is split between county and district authorities by sch. 1 to the 1990 Act (see further below).

(c) Unitary authorities which are responsible for all the development control and related functions that were previously exercised by both county and district authorities, including the preparation of a structure plan and a local plan, unless the Secretary of State provides by order that the authority should prepare a UDP for the area. In certain cases it may be preferable to have a development plan which covers a wider area and the Secretary of State can order authorities to prepare a joint structure plan (see further Circular 4/96).

County councils (called county planning authorities) are responsible for:

(a) structure plans;

(b) local plans relating to certain county subjects, such as minerals planning and waste disposal;

(c) county matters in development control (including minerals developments and any related works or buildings, waste disposal applications, and applications relating to land in national parks);

(d) certain development control decisions where they are able to grant themselves planning permission;

(e) county councils are also consulted by the district planning authority over certain large-scale developments, principally those which affect the structure plan or county matters, and over highway matters in their capacity as highways authorities.

District councils (called district planning authorities) are responsible for all other local plans and for all development control decisions, *except* those relating to county matters.

There are a number of special areas where different rules apply:

(a) In national parks, as from 1 April 1997 all planning decisions are taken by autonomous planning authorities set up under the Environment Act 1995, s. 63. Thus each of the seven national park authorities established under that section are responsible for maintaining the structure and local plans for the area of the National Park. Previously planning matters were administrated by either a joint board established for that purpose or a committee of the County Council (or Councils) responsible for the area.

(b) In the Broads, the similarly constituted Broads Authority takes all decisions (Norfolk and Suffolk Broads Act 1988).

(c) In urban development areas the urban development corporation normally becomes the local planning authority. This was also the case with new town development corporations, but these have now been phased out. (In enterprise zones and simplified planning zones the local planning authority stays the same.)

Forward planning: development plans

Local planning authorities are responsible for producing development plans on a continuing basis, which then guide or influence development in the areas covered. In this country, all development plans are permissive, i.e., they lay down policies, aims, objectives and goals rather than state what is definitely going to happen in an area. They have no immediate effect other than as a statement of what the local planning authority considers is desirable. But they do have a great and growing importance in the decision whether or not to grant planning permission (see p. 232).

There is *no* national plan. The nearest equivalent is the Central Government policy set out in Planning Policy Guidance Notes and Government Circulars. There are also no formal regional plans, although groupings of local planning authorities do produce general regional strategies, and there is formal regional planning guidance issued by Central Government, often based on advice from these regional groupings.

For most areas the existing system is to have two tiers of plan — structure plans and local plans, collectively referred to as the development plan. However, in metropolitan areas, unitary development plans are taking over this function. They were first required by the Local Government Act 1985 (a consequence of the abolition of the metropolitan county councils), and although they are still in the course of being made, will replace structure plans and local plans in those areas in the next few years.

The history and future of development plans

The system of development plans has been one area within planning law where there seems to have been a constant state of change. The original development plans established under the 1947 Act were basically detailed, spatial, land use maps, drawn up by local authorities for all areas, but requiring Central Government approval. Delay was endemic both in making the plans and keeping them up-to-date, and public involvement was not properly catered for, with the result that the two-tier system of structure and local plans was introduced in the Town and Country Planning Act 1968. Increased public participation rights were added by the Town and Country Planning Act 1971.

Before these plans had much of a chance to prove themselves, they became unpopular with a Government unconvinced by the need for strong forward planning and antipathetic to the power of local authorities. Structure plans in particular were downgraded by comparison with local plans by the Local Government, Planning and Land Act 1980 and plans of all types were accorded ever-decreasing weight in decisions compared to Central Government policies. Numerous proposals for reform were produced, the major themes of which were the need for plans to be restricted to land use matters, for less detail to be included in them, and for procedures to be speeded up.

Ultimately, some important changes were enacted by the Planning and Compensation Act 1991, sch. 4, which remodelled the part of the Town and

Country Planning Act 1990 dealing with development plans (Part II). The main changes, which came into force in February 1992, were as follows:

(a) Despite some consideration having been given to their abolition, structure plans were retained. But they should now cover a more restricted range of topics than before.

(b) The requirement that structure plans and modifications to them must be approved by the Secretary of State was removed.

(c) It became mandatory for a local planning authority to make a *district-wide* local plan, something which few had done in the past, preferring to concentrate their plan-making activities on specific parts of their district.

(d) Development plans for the area of a national park became mandatory for the first time, as did a local minerals plan and a waste local plan, the last being intended to complement the waste disposal plan required by the Environmental Protection Act 1990, s. 50, which has limited public involvement. In time any existing waste disposal plans will be replaced by the national waste strategy. Amendments to the Development Plan Regulations require local planning authorities to have regard to any future national waste strategy in formulating development plans (see the Town and Country Planning (Development Plan) (Amendment) Regulations 1997 (SI 1997 No. 531). The national waste strategy has not yet been prepared but the White Paper on a strategy for sustainable waste management in England and Wales, *Making Waste Work*, was published in December 1995 (Cm. 3040 and see p. 365). Any waste disposal plan or modification of such a plan under s. 50 of the EPA 1990, whose content has been finally determined before 1 April 1996, is to continue in force until the content of the national waste strategy is finally determined, notwithstanding the repeal of s. 50.

(e) In relation to all these types of plan (and also to unitary development plans) the procedures were streamlined so as to reduce the delay between initial deposit and final adoption, though the main elements of public participation and consultation were retained.

These changes make it clear that plan-making has assumed a much greater importance — a fact that gains in significance when considered alongside the movement towards a plan-led system of development control and the consequent increase in practical importance of the plans. This increase in importance has, however, led to a marked slowdown in the formal adoption of development plans — leading to problems similar to those experienced with the original development plans under the 1947 Act. The procedure for adopting local plans and UDPs in particular has come under great pressure as developers, local planning authorities and the public have come to recognise the importance of the adopted plan and have therefore subjected the proposals within the plan to great scrutiny. Some public inquiries into development plans have lasted for well over a year. Consequently, the target of achieving complete development plan coverage by the end of 1996 has been missed by some way. Figures show that at that date, only 43% of plans were actually adopted. It is now estimated that full coverage will not take place until after the year 2000. If the plan-led system is to operate effectively, the approval and adoption procedures have to be streamlined.

A consultation paper was issued in January 1997 with some proposals to speed up the process of delivering local plans and UDPs. Some of the proposals would require legislative change and these originally included proposals to replace the right for objections to be heard with a right for them to be considered and the introduction of a presumption that an inspector's recommendations would be binding on the planning authority. Both of these proposals were subsequently rejected by the incoming Labour Government. Proposals still under consideration include:

(a) The use of an inquisitorial mode of hearing for all or part of the inquiry. The inquiry would subsequently take on the character of an examination in public as used in the structure plan process.

(b) The imposition of strict time limits with procedural rules and sanctions.

(c) A streamlined two-stage process for the deposit of the plan. After the initial consultation, there would be a first deposit stage when the full draft would be placed on deposit for a specific period. This would be followed by a period of negotiation (which would be time-limited) which might result in the publication of a revised plan. This revised plan would then be placed on deposit for a further six weeks, allowing time for objections to be raised against that plan alone.

Although the proposals are some way from being adopted, there is consensus over the need to speed up the process of plan approval. At the moment it is estimated that a plan takes five or more years to be adopted. Any changes would be aimed at reducing that time to a more acceptable two or three years.

Structure plans

A structure plan is a statement of general strategic policies set out in the form of a written statement supplemented by representative diagrams and a written memorandum (which is not a formal part of the plan). It will contain major strategic policies for the area of a county. Planning Policy Guidance Note 12 sets out current Government policy, which is to restrict the scope of structure plans to topics undeniably connected with land use. These are listed as housing, green belts, conservation, the rural economy, the urban economy, major employment-generating development, strategic transport and highways issues, minerals matters, waste treatment and disposal, land reclamation, tourism, leisure and recreation, and energy generation, including renewable energy. The impact of the proposals on the environment should also be covered, including the question of the contribution that planning can play in combating global warming. There is a specific duty to include policies for 'the improvement of the physical environment' (s. 31(3)), and many structure plans now include policies on such things as air pollution. These will set out general objectives for the area and act as a framework for land use decisions (see Wood, *Planning Pollution Prevention,* 1989, Ch. 5). On the other hand, the Royal Society for the Protection of Birds has published a report critical of the generally inadequate treatment of nature conservation in structure plans (*RSPB Planscan,* 1990). The structure plan will be relevant to the process of filling out these policies in the local plan and to major development control decisions.

All areas now have a structure plan, but there is a continuing duty for a county planning authority to keep under review matters affecting the development and planning of their area (s. 30), and Planning Policy Guidance Note 12 envisages there should be a formal review every 15 years. In addition, some counties have different structure plans for different parts of the county and are now required to prepare revised plans on a county-wide basis. The procedures for modifying the plan are set out in ss. 31 — 35C and the Town and Country Planning (Development Plan) Regulations 1991 (SI 1991 No. 2794), which allow for limited public involvement. In essence, the county planning authority produces and publicises reasoned proposals. It must consult with a wide range of interested bodies (including the various regulatory agencies with environmental responsibilities), send a copy to the Secretary of State and allow at least six weeks for members of the public to make representations. Unless the Secretary of State directs otherwise, an examination in public (a limited form of public inquiry at which there is no right to present a case unless invited to do so) must be held. This appears to be dispensed with in over half the cases.

In the past, a structure plan required the approval of the Secretary of State. This requirement meant that the Secretary of State had the final say on the scope and content of the plan and its policies, and the power was often used to ensure that policies acceptable to Central Government were adopted rather than those originally proposed by the local planning authority. This requirement has now been dropped, but the Secretary of State has a power to call a plan in (s. 35A), and thus is able to exercise ultimate control over policy. The plan should be in conformity with the Regional Planning Guidance produced by the Secretary of State.

A challenge to a structure plan modification can be made within six weeks of the decision under s. 287 but, given the wide and subjective powers given to the local authority and the Secretary of State, unless the decision is perverse, totally unreasoned or internally contradictory, a successful challenge is most unlikely (see *Edwin H. Bradley & Sons Ltd* v *Secretary of State for the Environment* (1982) 47 P & CR 374).

Local plans

Local plans are more detailed, consisting of written policies and specific land use allocations by reference to a map, so their relevance to individual development control decisions is much greater. Originally there were three types of local plan:

(a)   district plans, including proposals for regulatory controls within a defined area: the district planning authority makes these;

(b)   subject plans, covering proposals for particularly sensitive subjects in an area (e.g., green belt, minerals development, tourism): either county or district planning authorities may make these;

(c)   action area plans, dealing with proposals for the comprehensive redevelopment of small areas.

These last two categories were rendered obsolete with the introduction of district wide local plans. In addition, urban development areas and the few remaining new towns may have their own plans. Automatic planning permission is granted by Special Development Order for the matters in such a plan.

Prior to the passage of the 1991 Act, the local planning authority was given a discretion to include environmental measures in a local plan, but policies varied from the detailed to the non-existent. There is now a duty to include such policies.

Despite their importance for development control, until the passage of the 1991 Act there was no requirement for everywhere to have a local plan. According to the White Paper, *This Common Inheritance* (Cm 1200, 1990), 55 of the 333 district planning authorities at that time had no local plan at all, and most others had only patchy coverage. One reason for this was undoubtedly that the making of local plans was actively discouraged by the Government throughout the 1980s, both in Circular guidance (e.g., Circular 22/84) and through the appeals system. However, there has been a distinct U-turn in policy on this point and the making of local plans became mandatory under the 1991 Act. Each district planning authority is now under a duty to make a single district-wide local plan. Consequently, when the district-wide local plan is introduced other subject plans and action area plans will be phased out.

The procedures for making or modifying a local plan are set out in ss. 36 — 52 and the Town and Country Planning (Development Plan) Regulations 1991 (SI 1991 No. 2794). In the past these procedures allowed for greater individual involvement than structure plans, but the initial procedures are now effectively the same for each type of plan. One important difference is that, if an objection to a draft local plan is made and not withdrawn, the local planning authority *must* hold a public local inquiry before an inspector. Objectors must be given at least six weeks' notice and have a right to appear at the inquiry (s. 42). The procedure is governed by a *Code of Practice on Development Plans,* published as an Annex to Planning Policy Guidance Note 12. The local planning authority must consider the inspector's recommendations and can adopt the local plan formally by resolution, unless the Secretary of State exercises the right to call in the plan for approval — a very rare occurrence (ss. 44 and 45). The local plan should be reviewed every 10 years at least.

The local plan is required to be in 'general conformity' with the structure plan (s. 46). However, if there is a conflict between the two, it is the local plan which prevails, unless the structure plan specifically lists the local plan as not conforming with it (s. 48). Local plans may be challenged within six weeks of their adoption (s. 287). Owing to the procedural duties relating to the public local inquiry, a successful action is more likely than for a challenge to a structure plan.

Unitary development plans

The Local Government Act 1985 introduced unitary development plans to replace structure and local plans in metropolitan areas. This is being done gradually; only one unitary development plan has yet been made, but all metropolitan authorities have been directed to make one. Existing plans remain in force until the Secretary of State brings the new plan into force and existing local plans may be incorporated into it.

The unitary development plan will consist of two parts: Part I will in general correspond to the structure plan and Part II to the local plan. The procedures for them are set out in ss. 12–28. Essentially they allow for a mixture of the current procedures used for structure plans and local plans, combining central supervision over strategic and regional matters with a commitment to some public involvement in more detailed matters. There is a provision for all or part of the plan to be called in for central approval, although it is not expected that this will be usual, even for Part I. The Planning and Compensation Act 1991 imposed a duty to include environmental matters in both Parts I and II.

Development plans and development control

Statutory plans *must* be taken into account in any development control decision. Section 70(2) states that, when making a decision whether to grant planning permission, the local planning authority 'shall have regard to the provisions of the development plan, so far as material to the application, and to any other material considerations'.

This important issue will be covered at p. 251, but it should be noted that, after a period in the 1980s in which plans were downgraded in importance compared to Central Government policy, increased emphasis has been placed on development plans as the framework within which individual planning decisions should be considered. A particular consideration is the need to provide certain guidance for developers on future policy, since, in a developer-led system, developers value clear policies, as opposed to the uncertainty provided by a wholly market-based approach. Section 54A added by the Planning and Compensation Act 1991, s. 26, states:

> where, in making any determination under the planning Acts, regard is to be had to the development plan, the determination shall be made in accordance with the development plan unless material considerations indicate otherwise.

Non-statutory plans and guidance

Local planning authorities frequently have other policies and drafts that have not gone through the statutory procedures. In practice, a large range of such 'non-statutory' material, ranging from draft local plans to design briefs and technical specifications, is used by local planning authorities in making decisions. But there are obvious problems in this practice, because it may be seen as subverting the statutory public participation requirements, and thus the democratic legitimacy of the planning process.

In *Westminster City Council* v *Great Portland Estates plc* [1985] AC 661, a distinction was drawn between different types of non-statutory guidance. The House of Lords required that all matters of *policy* should be included in the statutory plan and that only supplementary matters of detail, or those which relate to the implementation of these policies, should be put in non-statutory guidance. However, as long as this non-statutory material is not illegal (i.e., it must relate to the character of the use of land) it is a material consideration under s. 70(2) and must be considered alongside the statutory development plan, although perhaps not always accorded the same weight. The weight attached to it will depend on the circumstances in which it was produced.

Development control: definition of development

It is in relation to the system of development control that the town and country planning system has its greatest impact on environmental law. Planning permission is required for the carrying out of any development (s. 57(1)). The general approach has been to define development very widely so that virtually everything is included initially, and then to exempt by reference to well-defined categories. This has the effect of shifting the focus in most practical situations from what is included to what is excluded (see the Use Classes Order and the General Permitted Development Order in particular).

Development is defined in s. 55(1), which provides:

Development . . . . means the carrying out of building, engineering, mining or other operations in, on, over or under land, or the making of any material change in the use of any buildings or other land.

This definition has effectively remained unchanged since 1947, so past decisions of the courts, which are the ultimate interpreters of the meaning of the Act, are relevant. Decisions of the Secretary of State on appeal are also of importance in understanding the definition, although these are not binding as legal authority.

The courts have decided that the existence of development is a question of 'fact and degree' in each particular case. It is for the local planning authority (or the Secretary of State on appeal) to apply the relevant law to the facts of each case to decide whether there has been development. The courts limit themselves to supervising and reviewing these decisions, i.e., a decision by a local planning authority that a particular state of affairs amounts to development will only be overturned by the courts if the authority has used an incorrect test, or the correct test incorrectly, or has reached a perverse decision.

There are two limbs to the definition — operational development and change of use development. It is important to make this distinction because:

(a)   enforcement action can only be taken against development that has taken place;

(b)   an enforcement notice should specify which limb of development has taken place;

(c)   the limitation period for serving an enforcement notice is different for the two categories (four years and 10 years respectively).

There are four types of operational development:

(a)   building operations;
(b)   engineering operations;
(c)   mining operations; and
(d)   other operations.

Building operations

These are defined very widely in s. 336. 'Building' 'includes any structure or erection, and any part of a building as so defined, but does not include plant or machinery comprised in a building'. 'Building operations' include rebuilding operations, structural alterations of or additions to buildings, and other operations normally undertaken by a person carrying on business as a builder.

Any significant works are included, such as rebuilding works, works of alteration, the buiding of an extension, and the erection of such things as shop canopies, window grilles, shutters, walls, flagpoles, fences, advertising hoardings, large sculptures, street furniture and many other things. In one celebrated example, the erection of a model shark emerging from the roof of a house was held to amount to a building operation (though it ultimately received planning permission [1993] JPL 194). It is normally considered that very minor alterations such as the installation of ordinary TV aerials, are not significant enough to amount to development.

Exceptions include the following:

(a)   Maintenance, improvement or alterations to a building affecting only its interior, or not materially affecting the external appearance, are not development (s. 55(2)(a)).

(b)   Large numbers of minor and public operations are exempted from the need for planning permission by the General Development Order (see p. 239)

(c)   Movable structures (e.g., caravans) are not normally buildings, unless attached to the land or made permanent in some way (see *Barvis Ltd* v *Secretary of State for the Environment* (1971) 22 P & CR 710).

Demolition raises some interesting points. Until recently the predominant view was that simple demolition of a building was not development, unless it involved such a large amount of removal of materials that it constituted an engineering operation (*Coleshill and District Investment Co. Ltd* v *Minister of Housing and Local Government* [1969] 1 WLR 746). However, in *Cambridge City Council* v *Secretary of State for the Environment* (1991) 62 P & CR 320, David Widdicombe QC decided in the High Court that demolition of part of a building by the removal of roofing materials prior to total demolition was operational development. As a result (and despite the overruling of this decision by the Court of Appeal (1992) 64 P & CR 257), in the Planning and Compensation Act 1991 the Government took the opportunity to amend s. 55 to include demolition within the definition of building operation. But, in order to avoid unnecessary regulatory control, the effect of this step was mitigated by a new s. 55(2)(g), which allows any description of building specified by the Secretary of State to be excluded from the need for planning permission. This power was used to exclude all buildings except dwelling-houses. Even then, the General Development Order (now adopted in the new Order) was amended to grant automatic planning permission in all cases apart from where a building was deliberately allowed to become unsafe or uninhabitable. Before these permitted development rights may be used, however, the developer must notify the local planning authority and the authority may impose restrictions on the method of demolition and the restoration of the site, thus retaining some control over the impact of the demolition on the area. Apart from this limited prior notification require-ment, the position is thus that demolition requires planning permission only where an Article 4 direction has been served withdrawing the permitted development right (see p. 240), or the activity falls within the scope of the *Coleshill* decision, which remains good law.

Whatever the situation for ordinary buildings or structures, demolition of a listed building or of any building in a conservation area is subject to control (see Planning (Listed Buildings and Conservation Areas) Act 1990).

Engineering operations
These include road building, laying out of access to roads, drainage works, land reclamation, and earthmoving works. There are many exceptions for public works in s. 55 and the General Permitted Development Order.

Mining operations
These include all forms of extractive operation, such as mining, quarrying and the removal of materials from mineral deposits and waste tips. There are additional powers over minerals development. County planning authorities are designated mineral planning authorities and given wide powers to review operations and to impose conditions relating to aftercare, restoration of sites and discontinuance of activities.

Other operations
This is a little discussed catch-all category. It appears designed to ensure that matters such as waste disposal and drilling are covered.

An operation has commenced as soon as it has an impact on the land. This includes digging trenches and laying out the lines of roads (s. 56 and *Malvern Hills District Council* v *Secretary of State for the Environment* (1982) 81 LGR 13). The time of commencement is important because every planning permission contains a condition requiring commencement of the work within a stated time, otherwise the permission lapses. If no time is stipulated by the local planning authority, the period is five years from the grant of permission (s. 91). It should also be noted that enforcement action must wait until commencement of the operation, but that the four-year limitation period for serving enforcement notices commences at the substantial completion of the operation.

Material change of use

The power to control changes in the use of land is virtually unique to British town and country planning, and makes it peculiarly able to exercise detailed control over land use. In the debates on the 1947 Act, Lord Reid, then a Conservative MP but later a Law Lord, is reported to have said of material change of use, 'Nobody knows what that means'. Very little guidance is given in the Act on the meaning of this rather vague phrase, but over the years the judges have filled in any gaps by the creation of a number of important explanatory concepts. Nevertheless, this remains a somewhat flexible phrase, and flexibility is aided by the fact that the decision whether development has taken place in any particular case is a matter for the local planning authority, applying the law to the facts.

It is the *change* that is development, not the use itself Accordingly, a use which has been carried on since before 1948 cannot be the subject of control. The change must be *material* in the sense that it has:

(a)   a physical impact on the land;
(b)   a substantial impact; and
(c)   an impact that is relevant to town and country planning.

For example, in *Snook* v *Secretary of State for the Environment* (1975) 33 P & CR 1, a change from builder's storeyard to demolition person's storeyard was held not to be a material change because the change in nature did not have planning effects.

Some uses are *ancillary* or *incidental* to the main use of a property, such as keeping pets in a house. They are ignored for planning puposes. However, if the ancillary use extends beyond a normal degree, as it may do if, for example, extensive breeding of dogs takes place, it cannot be ignored and a change has occurred. There are then two *concurrent* uses (residential and dog breeding). In *Wallington* v *Secretary of State for Wales* (1990) 62 P & CR 150, a material change of use was found where 44 dogs were kept in a dwelling-house and an enforcement notice limiting the number to six on noise grounds was upheld. Similarly, a factory will be treated as one use of a site, even though a number of different activities, such as manufacturing, storage, offices and distribution, are carried on.

The unit of land to be considered when ascertaining whether there has been a change of use is called the *planning unit*. This is normally the unit of occupation prior to the change and it is unusual to aggregate together more than one unit of occupation, or to subdivide one, unless 'two or more physically distinct areas are occupied for substantially different and unrelated purposes' (see *Burdle* v *Secretary of State for the Environment* [1972] 1 WLR 1207). Thus a factory is normally treated as one unit, allowing some internal shifting of activities between manufacturing, storage, office space and car parking. Two factories on separate sites in the same ownership would be treated as two units.

Intensification of an existing use of a site often causes problems. It is not development unless it results in the use becoming different in character or concept. For example, the *Wallington* case illustrates a change in character, whilst a factory which doubles its output, or begins 24-hour working, would not require planning permission.

Certain matters are stated in the Act to be material changes. These are: splitting a single dwellinghouse into separate dwellings (s. 55(3)(a)); the deposit of waste (s. 55(3)(b)); and the display of adverts (s. 55(5)). Conversely, certain matters are stated *not* to be material changes, though in some cases the application of the judicially invented tests would have reached the same conclusions. These include (s. 55(2)(d) and (e)):

(d) the use of any buildings or other land within the curtilage of a dwelling-house for any purpose incidental to the enjoyment of the dwellinghouse as such;

(e) the use of any land for the purpose of agriculture or forestry (including afforestation) and the use for any of those purposes of any building occupied together with land so used.

Use Classes Order

Any change within one of the Use Classes set out in the Schedule to the Town and Country Planning (Use Classes) Order 1987 (SI 1987 No. 764) as amended is not development, thus removing planning barriers that might obstruct a change from one use to another with a similar environmental impact. It is significantly more liberal than previous Orders, part of the deregulatory strategy pursued by the Conservative Government in the 1980s aimed at encouraging changes in business structure. It should also be noted that the General Development Order grants automatic permission for certain innocuous changes from one use class to another.

It is not possible in a book of this kind to explain all of the Classes, but some of them are very wide. For example, Class A1 includes most shops, Class A2 all shop-front financial and professional services where the services are provided principally to visiting members of the public, and Class A3 most food and drink premises. Class B1 — the general business class — is very important, since it includes both use as offices and use for any industrial process which can be carried out in a residential area without significant detriment to its environmental amenity. Class B2 is a general industrial class, including all industrial uses not in other Classes and permits a large range of industrial changes. This Class was extended considerably with an amendment of the 1987 Order which abolished the old Special Industrial Classes B4–7 and brought them under the general B2 Class (see the Town and Country Planning (Use Classes) Amendment Order 1995 (SI 1995 No. 297)). Class B3 was abolished in 1992.

The extension of Class B2 was justified on the basis that there are pollution control powers in place to control the activities of special industrial uses although the extent to which that control is efficient must be questionable. The changes are significant as Classes B4–7 included some of the more polluting developments, and now no permission is required to change between these uses. In addition, the nature of B2 uses has, traditionally, been somewhat more benign than the special uses. The change in the Classes could, for instance, see an engineering use replaced by a blood-boiling factory without any development taking place which would require planning permission. Although both could have an impact upon the amenity of the locality, the nature of the impact could differ widely.

In line with general principle, ancillary and incidental uses are ignored for the purposes of the Order. In addition, a subdivision of a unit (other than a dwelling-house) into two or more units all within the same Class (such as subdivision of a factory unit) is not development. However, it is possible for a planning permission to contain a condition restricting the future operation of the Use Classes Order in relation to that site (*City of London Corporation* v *Secretary of State for the Environment* (1971) 23 P & CR 169), although this type of condition is not favoured by the Government as a matter of policy.

Many unusual uses will not be in any Class, and neither are concurrent uses where the components are in different Classes. The following uses are specifically stated *not* to be in any Class — theatres, amusement arcades, funfairs, launderettes, petrol stations, taxi businesses, car-hire businesses, scrapyards, mineral storeyards and car-breaking yards — so a change to these uses always requires planning permission.

In addition to the exemptions provided by the Use Classes Order, certain changes of use in breach of the law are immune from enforcement action. Prior to the passage of the Planning and Compensation Act 1991 these were changes that took place before 1 January 1964; under the 1991 Act immunity is conferred 10 years after any breach occurred. It should also be noted that s. 57 states that the resumption of a previous, lawful use after a temporary planning permission has expired, or after the service of an enforcement notice, does not require planning permission. The 1991 Act makes it clear, by adding a new s. 191(2), that a use which is immune from enforcement is a lawful use, thus reversing the House of Lords' decision in *Young* v *Secretary of State for the Environment* [1983] 2 AC 662.

Existing uses

Normally there is a right to carry on the existing use of a site, unless it is in breach of planning control. This is roughly equivalent to a property right attaching to the land and has a distinct value. Of course, when the occupier of land voluntarily changes the use, the existing use right switches from the old to the new use.

Existing use rights have been described as 'hardy beasts with a great capacity for survival' (Lord Scarman in *Pioneer Aggregates (UK) Ltd* v *Secretary of State for the Environment* [1985] AC 132), but they may be abandoned by a lengthy period of disuse (*Hartley* v *Minister of Housing and Local Government* [1970] 1 QB 413). It is also possible to lose the benefit of the existing use of a site by carrying out works or changes which effect a *radical change* to the site (*Jennings Motors Ltd* v *Secretary of State for the Environment* [1982] QB 541). This applies whether planning permission is obtained or not. If there is a planning permission, any limitations in it will be operative; if there is no permission, then *any* use of the site will be in breach of planning control. Otherwise, an existing use right can only be removed by a discontinuance order (s. 102), or an order revoking planning permission (ss. 97–100). In both cases compensation is payable.

It is not possible to abandon a planning permission, since it is a public right attaching to the land not the occupier. This is illustrated by *Pioneer Aggregates (UK) Ltd* v *Secretary of State for the Environment* [1984] 3 WLR 32, where a perpetual permission for quarrying was granted in 1950. Quarrying ceased in 1966 and, when it was recommenced in 1980, the local planning authority argued that the use had been abandoned. The House of Lords decided that the planning permission still applied to permit quarrying and any removal of that right would entail payment of compensation.

This position distinguishes planning control from most other areas of environmental control. There is no ability to vary a planning permission once it has been granted, even where circumstances have changed radically in a way that was not foreseen at the time the permission was granted. This emphasises that a grant of planning permission is an irrevocable event, effectively creating rights for the landowner in a way that a consent from a pollution control agency does not.

The General Development Orders

The Town and Country Planning (General Permitted Development) Order 1995 (SI 1995 No. 418) (referred to as the GDO) grants automatic planning permission for 33 classes of development, listed and defined in sch. 1. These are called 'permitted development rights'. There has been some relaxation of the GDO in order to remove what were seen as unnecessary restrictions on development. In addition, the Town and Country Planning (General Development Procedure) Order 1995 (SI 1995 No. 419) (GDPO) sets out various procedural requirements connected with both permitted development and normal planning applications.

Three general types of activity are exempted in this way:

(a) minor developments;
(b) developments carried out by a whole range of public services; and
(c) favoured activities, especially agriculture and forestry.

There are some general restrictions in the Order. An application must always be made for developments involving the formation or widening of an access to a trunk or classified road. Automatic rights may also be restricted by a condition imposed on an earlier grant of planning permission (*City of London Corporation* v *Secretary of State for the Environment* (1971) 23 P & CR 169). In addition, permitted development rights are withdrawn for a number of developments including those which require environmental assessment (see the Town and Country Planning (Environmental Assessment and Permitted Development) Regulations 1995 at p. 285) or which are likely to have a significant impact upon a certain areas of nature conservation value. Certain automatic rights are more restricted in national parks, AONBs and conservation areas.

Under Article 4 of the GDO, a local planning authority may restrict automatic rights by serving a direction withdrawing the automatic planning permission, in which case permission must be sought in the ordinary way. The direction may be general to a type of development or specific to a site. Directions under Article 4 normally require the approval of the Secretary of State, must be made before the development is started and involve the payment of compensation to owners and occupiers, because they amount effectively to the taking away of a right to develop.

Certain automatic rights are more restricted in national parks, areas of outstanding natural beauty and conservation areas (e.g., on extensions to buildings).

It is not possible in a book of this kind to explain all of the Parts to Schedule 1, but the following explanation gives a flavour of the wide range of matters that are covered. For example, Part 1 covers 'the enlargement, improvement or other alteration of a dwellinghouse', subject to very technical limitations on the size, height, forwardmost projection, proximity to a boundary and total coverage of the curtilage. These rights only apply to dwellings, not to offices, and there are further provisions relating to ancillary buildings and developments, such as porches, sheds, garages, animal shelters, stables, swimming pools, oil tanks, hardstanding for cars, and satellite antennae. The limitations have been altered many times, most recently in the 1980s in an attempt to reduce the number of trivial applications. Part 8 covers 'the extension or alteration of an industrial building or a warehouse', again with size, height and other limitations relating to loss of parking and external appearance of the site. Part 4 permits temporary buildings and works, and temporary uses of any type (apart from caravan sites) for up to 28 days in one year (except markets and motor racing, where 14 days only are allowed). Part 6 permits many agricultural operations on agricultural land and Part 7 most forestry operations, both with generous size and height limits, although local planning authorities are given extra powers over the siting and design of otherwise exempted agricultural and forestry buildings. For a more detailed review of agricultural and forestry operations see Chapter 17.

The remaining Parts include a wide range of works carried out by public bodies, many of which will have potentially large environmental effects. They include repairs to services, developments by drainage authorities, many developments on operational land by statutory undertakers (e.g., in connection with railways, waterways, harbours, water, gas, electricity, light-houses and the Post Office), and ancillary mining activities at existing mines.

Is planning permission required?

There is a fairly simple mechanism for ascertaining whether planning per-mission is required. It is now set out in s. 192, which was introduced by the Planning and Compensation Act 1991 and replaced the old mechanism under s. 64, which has been repealed. Section 192 provides that anyone may apply to the district planning authority for a certificate of lawfulness of proposed use or development, specifying the proposed use or operation. A certificate must be granted if the authority is satisfied that the use or operation would be lawful if subsisting or carried out at the time of the application. This is then conclusive of the legality of the development, as long as circumstances do not change before the development takes place. In other words, a certificate is the equivalent of a planning permission for what it covers.

The exact procedures for an application are contained in the GDPO. Since the application has to be specific, it is not possible to make one that relates to a hypothetical situation. Neither is it possible to apply after the develop-ment has taken place. In such a situation, the only way of discovering the position would be to seek a declaration in the High Court (a very expensive step), or to await the service of an enforcement notice and then appeal against it. The applicant may appeal under s. 78 to the Secretary of State against a determination under s. 192, or against a failure to make one within eight weeks.

Applying for planning permission

Anyone can apply for planning permission. It is not necessary to be the owner or occupier of the property, or even a prospective occupier. An application may even be used as a form of publicity stunt. For example, Friends of the Earth once submitted an application for an oversize replica of the Leaning Tower of Pisa in order to draw attention to the inadequacy of the UK Atomic Energy Authority's application for a nuclear reprocessing plant at Dounreay.

There are several types of permission the applicant may seek:

(a) Full permission.
(b) Retrospective permission (allowed under s. 63(2)).
(c) An application for the renewal of a planning permission.
(d) Outline permission (see s. 92 and GDPO, Art. 3). This can be sought for building operations only. Matters of 'siting, design, external appearance, means of access, landscaping of the site' (reserved matters) need not be submitted. Subsequent approval of these is needed within three years of the permission, or any other period stipulated by the local planning authority (s. 92(2)) otherwise the outline permission will lapse. An outline planning permission is legally a full permission in that any conditions, apart from those

relating to reserved matters, must be imposed at this stage, the normal publicity arrangements apply, and revocation entails the payment of compensation.

(e)   Approval of reserved matters (GDPO, Art. 4). Any number of such applications can be made within the three-year period. As this is not a full planning application, no further publicity is required and no new conditions can be added. (It may also be necessary to apply to the local planning authority for other approvals, e.g., where a condition in the planning permission requires future approval of a landscaping plan.)

(f)   Under s. 73, an applicant can ask for a condition to be discharged without putting the rest of the planning permission at risk. The local planning authority (and the Secretary of State on appeal) is limited to considering the condition in question. This procedure is very important in providing a measure of continuing control over planning permissions. It enables a landowner to get an outdated or unwanted condition removed, but in so doing it jeopardises the local planning authority's original discretionary decision. This is because it enables applications for removal of conditions even where the application might never have been granted in the first place had the condition not been attached.

Steps for the applicant to take
The applicant must apply on a form provided by the local planning authority. It must also notify owners and tenants of the land and submit a certificate to the authority stating that it has done so. This enables these people to be aware of the application and to make representations that the authority must take into account. It is an offence knowingly to issue a false certificate.

In *Main* v *Swansea City Council* (1984) 49 P & CR 26, the Court of Appeal decided that failure to carry out such procedures does not necessarily render a subsequent grant of planning permission void: it all depends on whether anyone with *locus standi* has been prejudiced as a result. This applies to most procedures under the Act. In any case, *R* v *Rotherham Metropolitan Borough Council, ex parte Rankin* [1990] 1 PLR 93 shows that an action to quash a permission must be brought without delay.

Fees are payable for all applications for planning permission and deemed applications in connection with an appeal against an enforcement notice. There are fixed charges for different types of application. The categories are set out in the Town and Country Planning (Fees for Applications and Deemed Applications) Regulations 1989 (SI 1989 No. 193). The local planning authority need not consider an application until the requisite fee has been paid.

The current rates (they are periodically increased) are set out in the Town and Country Planning (Fees for Applications and Deemed Applications) (Amendment) Regulations 1997 (SI 1997 No. 37). For example, the rate is £190 for each house and for a material change of use, and £95 for extensions. At present the fees do not cover the full administrative cost to the local planning authoriy of processing applications but, in line with Government policy, the level can be expected to rise so as to do so in the next few years.

Steps for the local planning authority to take

On receipt of an application, the local planning authority will consult with a wide range of public bodies as required for specified situations by the Town and Country Planning (General Development Procedure) Order 1995, Art. 10. These include highways authorities, other local authorities, parish and community councils, the Environment Agency, the Ministry of Agriculture, Fisheries and Food, and the relevant Nature Conservancy Councils. There is a Code of Conduct governing this consultation procedure and those consulted have procedural rights in the event of an appeal. Any representations that are made are material considerations which must be taken into account by the local planning authority before it decides the application. However, it must not slavishly follow the advice of another public body, otherwise the decision will be challengeable for fettering of discretion.

The local planning authority must also publicise *all* applications (GDPO, Arts. 6 — 8). It reflects a major change from the position prior to 1992, when there were no statutory publicity requirements other than for applications which did not conform with the development plan, applications relating to a listed building or in a conservation area (the duties in this respect still exist in addition to those explained below), applications subject to environmental assessment (see Chapter 10), and applications for a number of somewhat randomly selected anti-social activities that were termed 'bad-neighbour' developments.

The rigours of the earlier position were mitigated by the fact that most local planning authorities included provision for publicity in a wider range of cases in their standing orders, and indeed were encouraged to do so by Circular advice. For example, neighbours and others likely to be affected would often be informed of an application. The Local Government Ombudsman formalised some of these practices by deciding that, where a local authority had a policy of publicising applications, it would amount to maladministration not to follow that policy in any given case (see the case at [1983] JPL 613). However, this approach is of limited use since, while it may result in an aggrieved neighbour receiving an apology or some compensation for not being notified, an Ombudsman cannot quash the planning permission. Nevertheless, it remains an alternative course of action should the statutory requirements be ignored.

The new publicity requirements set out in the General Development Procedure Order split applications into three categories:

(a)   major developments, such as developments on sites of more than one hectare, the building of 10 or more houses, developments involving 1,000 square metres or more of floor space, and mineral and waste applications — in these cases an advertisement must be placed in a local newspaper and either a site notice posted or neighbours notified;

(b)   applications covered by the need for an environmental assessment, or which do not accord with the provisions of the development plan, or which affect a public right of way — in these cases a newspaper advertisement and a site notice are required;

(c)   in all other cases either a site notice or neighbour notification can be used.

These requirements involve some discretion being given to the local planning authority. For example, in categories (a) and (c) it has a choice of publicity measures, whilst it has a general power to decide that any development is major enough to fall within category (a).

In addition, the Town and Country Planning (Development Plans and Consultation) Directions 1992 require that certain applications which do not accord with the provisions of the development plan should be referred to the Secretary of State so that a decision can be made whether to call them in.

It must be asked what the legal position is should these procedures not be complied with. On the basis of court decisions such as *Main v Swansea City Council* (1984) 49 P & CR 26 and *R v St Edmundsbury Borough Council, ex parte Investors in Industry Commercial Properties Ltd* [1985] 1 WLR 1168, it must be assumed that a failure may invalidate a decision, but would not necessarily do so because of the hurdles thrown up by judicial review. Reference should also be made to a number of cases in which the courts developed some safeguards for neighbours through the concepts of legitimate expectations and fairness (for a discussion of these cases, see Hinds [1988] JPL 742). However, these cases stopped some way short of recognising any general principle that applications should be publicised and they are rendered of reduced significance by the introduction of statutory publicity in all cases.

Decisions by the local planning authority

The local planning authority may (a) grant planning permission, (b) grant permission subject to conditions, (c) refuse permission, or (d) grant permission for part of the application only, as long as what is granted is not different in substance from the original, or an effective denial of rights to would-be objectors (see *Bernard Wheatcroft Ltd v Secretary of State for the Environment* (1980) 257 EG 934). The decision must be in writing and must include reasons for the decision and for the imposition of any conditions. These are normally brief and it seems that a failure to provide reasons does not make the decision void. In the event of a grievance, the correct (and cheaper) course would be to appeal to the Secretary of State. The decision should be made within eight weeks of receipt by the local planning authority and payment of the fee, otherwise the applicant can appeal to the Secretary of State as if the application had been refused (GDPO, Art. 20). The applicant can agree to a longer time scale.

Section 69 requires the local planning authority to keep public registers of all planning applications and decisions. (There is a further public register of details of enforcement notices and stop notices kept under s. 188.) The GDPO, Arts. 25 and 26 set out the form these registers must take. They are an invaluable source of information on the planning history of a site.

Planning permission attaches to the land, not to the applicant (s. 75(1)). Exceptionally, a condition may limit the persons who can take advantage of the planning permission, though such conditions are discouraged by the Secretary of State (see Circular 11/95). A permission cannot be abandoned, since it is a public document (*Pioneer Aggregates (UK) Ltd* v *Secretary of State for the Environment* [1985] AC 132). However, it is possible for a permission to become spent, either through lapse of time, occurrence of a condition subsequent, or occurrence of a situation which renders carrying it out impossible (*Pilkington* v *Secretary of State for the Environment* [1973] 1 WLR 1527). In any other case where a planning permission is taken away, compensation is payable (ss. 97 — 100).

Alternative and special procedures

The following are ways that ordinary planning procedures may be circumvented, mainly for public developments:

(a) Local authorities are effectively allowed to grant themselves planning permission (s. 316 and the Town and Country Planning General Regulations 1992 (SI 1992 No. 1492)). They can do this for any land within their area which they own or intend to develop, although if they intend to carry out the work themselves the permission is a personal, non-transferable one. The procedures are simple: the local planning authority passes a resolution to seek planning permission, after which it must publicise the application. Having taken any representations into account as material considerations, it may then pass a second resolution granting permission. The resultant planning permission is deemed to have been granted by the Secretary of State, so there is no right of appeal: it can be challenged only by judicial review. In view of the possibility of a conflict of interest, the courts have interpreted the procedural requirements of the General Regulations very strictly (*Steeples* v *Derbyshire County Council* [1985] 1 WLR 256). It is not, however, impermissible for a local planning authority to follow a well-defined policy, provided it considers other possibilities and does not fetter its discretion. Such a course is not contrary to natural justice (*R* v *Amber Valley District Council, ex parte Jackson* [1985] 1 WLR 298).

(b) Developments authorised by a Government Department under other authorisation procedures do not require planning permission (s. 90). This prevents a duplication of effort, but it does result in the decision being taken centrally rather than locally. For example, this option is available in relation to applications for the construction of nuclear power stations, since permission for power stations is also required from the Department of Trade and Industry under the Electricity Act 1989.

(c) Permission may be granted by a Special Development Order made under s. 59. This process has been used for granting blanket permissions in new towns, urban development areas and enterprise zones. The Windscale Thermal Oxide Reprocessing Plant was also permitted by the Town and Country Planning (Windscale and Calder Works) Special Development Order 1978 (see SI 1978 No. 523). In that case the Order followed a public inquiry and a Parliamentary debate, but neither is strictly required.

(d)   Increasing use is being made of Private or Hybrid Acts of Parliament which avoid any of the planning procedures and effectively give the decision to a small Parliamentary joint Committee, with limited public scrutiny. The Channel Tunnel Act 1987 is an example of such an Act with very important environmental effects.

(e)   Under s. 294, Crown land (i.e., all land owned by the Crown, the Duchies of Lancaster and Cornwall, Government Departments, but not nationalised industries) is effectively excluded from the Act by the provision of immunity against service of an enforcement notice. Planning permission can be obtained prior to disposal to private hands and action can be taken against private individuals occupying Crown land. In Circular 18/84, it is stated that the Crown bodies have agreed to abide informally by the same procedures and requirements as apply to private developers, but this system is not legally enforceable. One exception is that Crown immunity has been removed from health authorities and NHS trusts by the National Health Service and Community Care Act 1990. In November 1992, the Government issued a consultation paper proposing the removal of Crown immunity in planning legislation, except for cases involving national security and where there was a need for a particular development to be completed urgently. However, the paper also proposed that the normal enforcement procedures would not apply to Crown land. Instead, a local planning authority would seek a declaration in the High Court and the body in breach would remedy matters of its own accord.

Special areas

One of the features of the 1947 Act was that it applied a uniform system of control nationwide. Exceptions were made for developments in the areas of the new towns, but it was not until the 1980s that further exceptions were made as part of the Government's strategy of deregulation, with the pro-claimed aim of effecting regeneration of the inner cities.

Urban development areas
Urban development areas were introduced in the Local Government, Planning and Land Act 1980. Not only are ordinary planning rules virtually scrapped in these areas, but the local planning authority is replaced by an unelected body. Under s. 134 of the 1980 Act, the Secretary of State may designate an area an urban development area and appoint an urban development corporation, which has general powers to redevelop land, together with wide powers of acquisition, management and resale. It may submit to the Secretary of State proposals for the development of land in its area (s. 148), which establishes a form of master plan. The Secretary of State may then make a Special Development Order, which grants automatic permission for development in accordance with the approved master plan and normally designates the corporation the local planning authority for all planning purposes (1990 Act, s. 7). The local planning authority accordingly loses all planning powers, although there is provision for consultation between it and the corporation. Twelve urban development areas have been designated.

Enterprise zones

Enterprise zones were also introduced by the Local Government, Planning and Land Act 1980. The order establishing an enterprise zone, which is made by the Secretary of State after some limited publicity, grants automatic planning permission for categories of development specified in the enterprise zone scheme (1990 Act, s. 88). However, the local authority draws up the scheme to cover those matters it wishes to permit. Thus, while enterprise zones are formally designated by the Secretary of State, local authorities decide what is to be permitted. They also remain the local planning authority for other development not covered by the scheme.

An enterprise zone normally lasts for 10 years and involves fiscal and administrative advantages for those in it, as well as the planning exemptions. Few new zones are now expected to be made, but development commenced before the expiry of the scheme retains the benefit of the automatic permission.

Simplified planning zones

These were introduced in the Housing and Planning Act 1986. As with an enterprise zone scheme, a simplified planning zone scheme grants automatic planning permission for the matters specified in it, but there are no non-planning effects (1990 Act, s. 82).

Every district planning authority has a duty to consider whether to impose a simplified planning zone in part of its area. It must prepare a scheme if satisfied it is expedient to do so. Anybody may request the making of a scheme and the Secretary of State may direct the making of one. The procedures for making one are set out in the 1990 Act, sch. 7, as amended by the Planning and Compensation Act 1991. There is no requirement that the scheme be approved by the Secretary of State, though it may be called in for approval. A simplified planning zone lasts for 10 years, but development commenced before the expiry of the scheme retains the benefit of the automatic permission. Only a handful have been made.

National parks, areas of outstanding natural beauty, conservation areas, sites of special scientific interest, and designated green belt cannot be the subject of a scheme. County matters are also excluded, as are matters covered by the need for an environmental assessment.

The Secretary of State's powers

Under s. 77, the Secretary of State has an unfettered power to call in any planning application for determination. This immediately transfers jurisdiction from the local planning authority to the Secretary of State. This power is used sparingly, usually only for matters of national or regional importance or of local controversy. There is a right to a public inquiry unless waived by the parties and the Secretary of State and one is normally held. The procedures are virtually the same as for appeals, suitably amended to provide for the fact that this is a first determination. There is no formal power to request the Secretary of State to call in an application: objectors should write to the Secretary of State putting their case for this to happen.

The Secretary of State also has power to make directions relating to an application; this is normally used only for certain classes of case (e.g., applications for large shopping centres must be referred to the Secretary of State), but may also be used to prevent a precipitate decision by a local authority in an individual case.

Summary of rights of third parties

Third parties or objectors have limited specific rights under the legislation, although statutory publicity is now required for all applications and the Local Government (Access to Information) Act 1985 ensures the right to attend council meetings (see p. 56). Any representations made to the local planning authority must be considered as a material consideration.

Since third parties have no right to appeal against a planning decision, they must apply for judicial review of any adverse decision. This entails having *locus standi*, acting without delay, and being able to afford the large costs involved, and has very little chance of success. Only local planning authority decisions can be subject to judicial review: decisions of the Secretary of State are immune from challenge except under s. 288 (see p. 264). If an appeal is brought by the applicant, third parties have wider procedural rights at that stage.

The local planning authority's discretion

Under s. 70(2), in deciding whether or not to grant permission, the local planning authority 'shall have regard to the provisions of the development plan, so far as material to the application, and to any other material considerations'. The Secretary of State is subject to the same requirements in relation to decisions on a s. 78 appeal, or which are called in under s. 77.

It is central to an understanding of planning law to appreciate the scope of s. 70(2):

(a)   It gives the local planning authority a very wide *discretion* whether or not to grant permission.

(b)   This discretion will be exercised on grounds of *policy*.

It should be noted that policy means 'planning policy'. Despite the fact that ultimate responsibility for local authority decisions rests with elected members, decisions may not be 'political' in the sense of being based on party political or personal factors. For example, a decision by elected members that an industrial development should be refused simply because the residents were opposed to it would be *ultra vires*, unless there were valid planning objections.

The discretion is controlled in two ways:

(a)   through judicial review of the legality of decisions; and

(b)   for decisions of the local planning authority, through the appeal system.

There is no doubt that the second way is more important, firstly because of the limited scope of the courts' supervisory jurisdiction, and secondly because of the willingness of the Secretary of State to use the appeals process to impose Central Government policy. In practice, the Secretary of State exercises a stranglehold over the content of the policies that are applied, and has the final say on policy in any case because of the applicant's unlimited right of appeal.

If a local planning authority refuses planning permission, its decision may thus be challenged either on legal grounds (for example, that the objections are not planning objections), or on policy grounds (for example, that too much weight was attached to the objections).

Judicial control of the discretion

The courts control and restrict the discretion through the application of ordinary principles of public law (see in general *E.C. Gransden* v *Secretary of State* [1986] JPL 519 and *Wycombe District Council* v *Secretary of State for the Environment* (1987) 57 P & CR 177). Failure to take something that is relevant into account (or, alternatively, taking into account something that is not relevant) means that the resultant decision is *ultra vires* and may be quashed, although the courts retain a discretion whether to do so. Whether something is relevant is a legal matter for the courts to decide.

As long as the policies that are applied are lawful (i.e., relevant to town planning), the courts do not interfere with their content. This is effectively a principle of non-intervention in policy matters. Accordingly, the *weight* given to any policy is a matter for the decision-maker, unless the decision is perverse. However, it is impermissible to have an absolute policy, or to apply it rigidly, since this would constitute an unlawful fettering of discretion (*Stringer* v *Minister of Housing and Local Government* [1970] 1 WLR 1281). The courts thus see their role as ensuring that decisions are made rationally in the light of all the town planning considerations. This is ensured by the requirement that *reasons* must be given for decisions: something that has attracted a great deal of attention in recent cases.

The application of policy

The decision whether to grant permission will be made by reference to:

(a) the facts of the case;
(b) development plans;
(c) other local policies;
(d) Central Government policies, especially as set out in Circulars and Planning Policy Guidance Notes (policy used to be published in Circulars, but Planning Policy Guidance Notes are now taking over this role, although the process of replacement is not complete, so reference still needs to be made to both types of document);
(e) representations received; and
(f) any other material considerations (see below).

As stated above, the weight given to each of these factors is ultimately a matter for the decision-maker, but, in practice, development plans and Central Government policies are the most important. In the past, this had little to do with the law, because the courts always refused to lay down a rigid hierarchy of the relative importance of the different considerations. Instead it followed from the way that policies were actually applied on appeal. However, things have changed greatly as a result of the enactment of s. 54A (see below).

Nevertheless, the prior legal position must be considered, since it helps to explain how s. 54A is being interpreted. Cases such as *Enfield London Borough Council* v *Secretary of State for the Environment* [1975] JPL 155, established that the policies laid down in a development plan must always be taken into account, but it was made clear that the plan is only one consideration, albeit an important one, in deciding whether to grant planning permission. Thus, unlike the situation in many other countries, a plan did not have to be followed; it was a statement of aims or objectives only. Circulars and Planning Policy Guidance Notes were also material considerations and must therefore be considered where relevant (*J.A. Pye (Oxford) Estates Ltd* v *West Oxfordshire District Council* (1982) 47 P & CR 125). However, it is now normally assumed that a Circular has been considered unless the reasoning is inconsistent with it, or it has obviously been ignored or misunderstood. The correct interpretation of a policy in a development plan or Circular is ultimately a legal matter for the courts to decide. Misunderstanding a policy is accordingly as bad as ignoring it. It is left to the decision-maker in each case to weigh up the competing issues. This shifts the emphasis of legal control on to the reasons given for the decision. As long as adequate reasons are given the courts will not interfere. In practice this means that Central Government policies will normally be applied on appeal.

This judicial reluctance to get involved in policy matters was crucial in the light of the development of Central Government policy in the 1980s. There was a complete overhaul of existing guidance, and the whole political shape of the planning system was altered by the publication of explicitly directory Circulars (such as 22/80 and 14/85) laying down very strong pro-development policies. For example, a policy presumption that development should be permitted 'unless the development would cause demonstrable harm to interests of acknowledged importance' was introduced in Circular 14/85 and repeated in the original Planning Policy Guidance Note 1. This presumption was not restricted in terms of the subject matter of the application, with the result that it applied as much to industrial development as it did to housing development. However, it did not apply where certain restraint policies were applied, such as where inappropriate development was proposed in the Green Belt (see Planning Policy Guidance Note 2), and it would be rebutted by a strong local policy, such as a policy against industrial development in a defined area.

The relevance of the presumption was addressed by the House of Lords in *London Residuary Body* v *Lambeth London Borough Council* [1990] 1 WLR 744, which decided that the policy presumption must be taken into account and had the weight attached to it by the decision-maker. As a matter of interpretation, it was not limited to resolving a deadlock where the factors in favour of permission equalled those against, as suggested by the Court of Appeal. This decision, by confirming the principle of non-intervention in the contents of policies, allowed the Government freedom to accord the presumption a very high value.

The presumption in favour of the development plan

This state of affairs has now changed. The first signs of any change were seen in a number of appeal decisions around the turn of the decade which decided that where there was an up-to-date plan with clear policies that were in conformity with regional and national policies, then it was likely to be followed. Legislative recognition of this point was provided by s. 54A, which was inserted by the Planning and Compensation Act 1991. This states:

> Where, in making any determination under the planning Acts, regard is to be had to the development plan, the determination shall be made in accordance with the development plan unless material considerations indicate otherwise.

This section appears to introduce a presumption in favour of following the provisions of the development plan, because it replaces the existing duty to 'have regard to' the plan with a duty to act 'in accordance with' it. This is certainly the position that has been espoused on a number of occasions by Government Ministers who have suggested that we have left the period of 'market' or 'developer-led' planning far behind.

The courts have considered and interpreted s. 54A on a number of occasions. In one of the first decisions it was suggested that s. 54A did set out a presumption in favour of the development plan but that it could be rebutted fairly easily (at least as a matter of law, if not of policy — see further below) by other considerations, such as central government policy and the presumption in favour of development, as long as the reasoning was clear and rational (see, for example, St Albans District Council v Secretary of State for the Environment (1992) 66 P & CR 432). (This case also shows how the court's general discretion not to quash a decision if the failure identified does not make a difference to the result can be used to water down s. 54A, and that there is no need to mention the section specifically if it is obviously taken into account.) In Loup v Secretary of State for the Environment [1996] JPL 22, however, the Court of Appeal seemingly elevated the strength of the presumption in favour of the development plan by referring to part of PPG1 (subsequently revised — see further below) which referred to the planning system operating 'on the basis that applications for development should be allowed, having regard to the development plan and all material considerations, unless the proposed development would cause demonstrable harm to interests of acknowledged importance'. In doing so, the court acknowledged that the whole purpose of the plan-led system was to give certainty to the development plan, which in turn would lead to greater consistency in decision-making. The relative certainty created by the development plan could itself amount to an interest of acknowledged importance.

More important than the legal position is the policy context, in particular the question of how the legal presumption laid down in s. 54A fits in with the *policy* presumption in favour of granting planning permission. This policy is contained in PPG1, which was revised in 1992 to take into account changes brought about by the introduction of s. 54A. Now that the plan-led system has been in operation for some time, a revised version of the Guidance Note was issued in February 1997. Although the guidance in the 1997 version has a similar tone to that found in the 1992 version there are some significant distinctions. In the latest version the general policy presumption in favour of development continues to be downgraded. Instead there is a greater emphasis on matters such as the promotion of mixed-use development and of improving design to ensure acceptability. On the other hand the guidance appears to reduce the impact of the decision in *Loup* (see above) by reducing the weight which should be attached to the demonstrable harm caused to interests of acknowledged importance. Unlike the previous version of the Guidance Note, which was interpreted by the Court of Appeal on the basis set out above, the revised Guidance now states merely that 'those deciding . . . planning applications or appeals should always *take into account* whether the proposed development would cause demonstrable harm to interests of acknowledged importance' (emphasis added). This could once again lead to a watering down of s. 54A, on the basis that taking the harm into account (when considering the development plan as an interest of acknowledged importance) could mean that there is a return to the position which makes the presumption in favour of the plan rebuttable by fairly weak considerations.

The guidance on the basic approach that decision-makers ought to employ in determining applications or appeals, is virtually unchanged in the 1997 version. The plan is said to be the starting point. If the proposal is in accordance with the plan, it would normally be granted permission. If the proposal is in conflict with it, the developer would normally have to produce 'convincing reasons' to show why the plan should not apply. If the plan is neutral, then the presumption in favour of development has a role to play as one of the material considerations.

It is clear that importance will be attached to such things as the age of the plan, the strength of the relevant policies, how far they are consistent with other national and regional policies, and whether the Secretary of State had intervened during the making of the plan. On this last point, the Guidance Note states that if there was no formal intervention at the plan-making stage it may be assumed that the Secretary of State 'will attach commensurate weight' to the plan on any appeal.

In summary, it appears that the planning system has moved into an age which can be characterised by the description 'plan-led', but that this is no guarantee that the plan will always be followed. One point that has therefore acquired increased significance is the interpretation of development plans. In the past it has often been assumed that this is a matter of law for the courts to decide. This is undoubtedly correct, but it does not solve the question of whether the courts will impose their own interpretation or will be content to adopt the less interventionist method of reviewing whether the decision-maker's interpretation was a reasonable one. This is crucial to the extent to which the courts will interfere with decisions via s. 54A. Past experience suggests that they will continue with their normal non-interventionist approach and adopt the second method, thus reinforcing the view that the real change in planning that is envisaged in the 1990s will result from actual changes in policy rather than from anything the courts require.

Other material considerations

Various matters are always material considerations and thus always have to be taken into account — e.g., plans, Circulars, Planning Policy Guidance Notes, the results of consultations, and any representations made by third parties or objectors. In addition, certain issues are clearly nearly always material on the facts — e.g., the effect on the amenity of an area, safety considerations, potential pollution problems, the effect on the local economy, transport and highways considerations, the balance of land use in an area, and the need for the proposed development. To be material they have to be material to planning and material to the application. 'Planning' has been given a wide meaning here and covers anything that relates to 'the character of the use of the land' (*Westminster City Council* v *Great Portland Estates plc* [1985] AC 661).

This may be illustrated by the range of matters that have been held to be material in certain circumstances: the effect on private rights (*Stringer* v *Minister of Housing and Local Government* [1970] 1 WLR 1281); the existing use of the site (*Clyde & Co.* v *Secretary of State for the Environment* [1977] 1 WLR 926); the personal circumstances of the occupier (*Tameside Metropolitan Borough Council* v *Secretary of State for the Environment* [1984] JPL 180); the precedent effect of a decision (*Collis Radio Ltd* v *Secretary of State for the Environment* (1975) 29 P & CR 390); whether the application is premature in the light of an emerging development plan (*Arlington Securities Ltd* v *Secretary of State for the Environment* (1989) 57 P & CR 407); the achievement of a separate planning objective of the local planning authority — in this case the protection of the Royal Opera House by allowing it to raise funds by carrying out the development permitted (*R* v *Westminster City Council, ex parte Monahan* [1988] JPL 557); the availability of alternative sites, which has great implications for objectors seeking to put forward the argument that another site elsewhere is more suitable for the development (see *Greater London Council* v *Secretary of State for the Environment* (1985) 52 P & CR 158).

In relation to environmental matters, it is clear that planning permission may be refused on a number of grounds. An industrial development may be refused because of possible pollution or safety problems (e.g., it is possible to prevent a plant handling dangerous substances, or a waste disposal site, from being sited near to a sensitive watercourse). A housing estate may be refused because of the inadequacy of the existing sewerage provision. A new work-

place may be refused because of the effect of noise on neighbouring properties. It is not just the potential harm the proposed development may cause
that is relevant. Development may be refused because it would be within a
cordon sanitaire around an existing installation. For example, *Stringer* v
Minister of Housing and Local Government [1970] 1 WLR 1281 concerned an
area around Jodrell Bank that was subject to a policy of restraint on
development to prevent interference with the radio telescope.

However, it must be remembered that these are only some of the matters
that must be taken into account. The final decision involves a balancing of
all the factors. A clear example of the discretion given to the local planning
authority to decide that other factors outweigh environmental ones is *R* v
Exeter City Council, ex parte J. L. Thomas & Co. Ltd [1991] 1 QB 471.
Permission was granted for a housing estate close to an existing animal waste
processing plant, despite arguments put forward by the owners of the plant
that this might mean that it could be closed down by the future occupants of
the houses, exercising their rights in private nuisance. The court held that
such a decision was unchallengeable, as long as the local planning authority
had considered this factor: it had no *duty* to refuse permission on these
grounds.

Conditions

Section 70(1) permits the local planning authority (and the Secretary of State
on appeal) to impose such conditions 'as it thinks fit'. This wide discretionary
power is limited by statutory guidance in ss. 72 and 75, judicial control over
what is permissible, and Central Government policy.

Statutory guidance is limited and relatively unimportant. Section 72 states
that conditions attached to other land under the control of the applicant,
conditions requiring commencement of the development within a specified
time, and temporary permissions are permissible. Section 75(3) enables new
buildings to be used for the purpose for which they were designed, unless the
permission expressly limits the use.

Legal tests for the validity of conditions

Over the years the courts have developed four tests of validity for conditions.
In contrast with the decisions on material considerations, these have produced some rather restrictive results, possibly because the cases were mainly
decided earlier, when a more overt policy of protection of private property
rights was applied. A condition is *ultra vires* if it is:

(a)   not related to planning purposes;
(b)   not related to the development permitted;
(c)   perverse ('so unreasonable that no reasonable authority could impose
it'); or
(d)   hopelessly uncertain.

(a) Conditions not related to planning purposes

In applying this test, the courts have had to define the limits of 'planning'. They have done this by concluding that certain matters of a social planning nature do not relate to town and country planning. For example, in *R v Hillingdon London Borough Council, ex parte Royco Homes Ltd* [1974] 2 QB 720, a condition requiring that houses be occupied by people on the local authority housing list, who should then be granted 10 years security of tenure, was held to be *ultra vires*. However, the dividing line is unclear. An occupancy condition restricting occupation of a rural dwelling to agricultural workers and dependants will be valid (*Fawcett Properties Ltd v Buckingham County Council* [1961] AC 636), as will a personal permission, although in each case the Secretary of State disapproves of the use of such conditions (see Circular 1/85).

(b) Conditions not related to the development permitted

A condition must be geographically and functionally linked to the site to which the application relates. Thus conditions relating to other land controlled by the applicant are valid only if the other land is close by (*Pyx Granite Ltd v Ministry of Housing and Local Government* [1958] 1 QB 554). Equally, a condition requiring works to be carried out on land which is neither included in the application nor under the control of the applicant is *ultra vires* (*Ladbrokes Ltd v Secretary of State* [1981] JPL 427). Thus, a requirement to screen a site by planting trees on neighbouring land would be *ultra vires,* unless that land was under the control of the applicant.

(c) Conditions that are perverse

This test has normally been used as a means of preventing the use of conditions which undermine private property rights by requiring the dedication of land to the public without compensation. In *Hall & Co. Ltd v Shoreham-by-Sea Urban District Council* [1964] 1 WLR 240, a condition was attached to a permission for industrial development which required an access road to be built at the developer's expense and dedicated to the public. This was held to be *ultra vires,* even though the Court of Appeal was clear that the condition was beneficial in planning terms since it created a usable access to otherwise inaccessible land. In *Bradford Metropolitan Council v Secretary of State for the Environment* (1987) 53 P & CR 55 this position was supported. The Court of Appeal stated that a condition requiring donation of land to the public for a road-widening scheme would be *ultra vires* even if the developer suggested it or agreed to it, since *vires* cannot be conferred by consent.

This restriction is bizarre, since it is surely the whole *raison d'être* of development control to take away existing rights without compensation. It ignores the community of interest between the developer and the local planning authority; in the *Bradford* case, the developer included the donation of the land in the application since it was clear that permission would not be granted unless the road was widened. It also prevents any great use of planning conditions to secure 'planning gain' for the local community. In *M. J. Shanley Ltd v Secretary of State for the Environment* [1982] JPL 380, a condition requiring 40 acres of the developer's land to be landscaped and dedicated as public open space, in return for permission to carry out housing development on adjoining land, was stated to be *ultra vires.*

It is interesting, however, that the courts have accepted the validity of conditions restricting existing use rights, or the right to take future advantage of the Use Classes Order or General Permitted Development Order (*City of London Corporation* v *Secretary of State for the Environment* (1971) 23 P & CR 169). They have also accepted negative conditions subjecting development to a condition precedent, even though the condition would be invalid if put in terms of a positive obligation (*Grampian Regional Council* v *Aberdeen District Council* (1983) 47 P & CR 633), and even though the condition precedent may be unlikely to occur (*British Railways Board* v *Secretary of State for the Environment* [1994] 1 EGLR 197).

(d)   Conditions which are hopelessly uncertain
In this category it is clear that a mere ambiguity will not render the condition invalid. In *Alderson* v *Secretary of State for the Environment* (1984) 49 P & CR 307, a condition requiring occupation by people who worked locally was valid because it was sufficiently certain to be understandable to the applicant.

If a condition is *ultra vires,* it may be challenged in the courts. This may result in the whole planning permission being declared void, unless the condition can be severed. Alternatives are to appeal against the condition to the Secretary of State, or to apply for a discharge of the condition under s. 73.

Conditions and policy

On appeal the Secretary of State can add, omit or amend any conditions as part of the total rehearing of the issues. This can be done on legal, factual or policy grounds, so an understanding of the Secretary of State's policy on conditions is essential.

Circular 11/95 requires conditions to be (a) necessary, (b) relevant to planning, (c) relevant to the development permitted, (d) enforceable, (e) precise, and (f) reasonable. In addition, it lays down some very important general policy tests: 'As a matter of policy, a condition ought not to be imposed unless there is a definite need for it'; 'a condition should not be retained unless there are sound and clear cut reasons for doing so'; a condition 'requires special and precise justification' if planning permission would not be refused if the condition were omitted. The local planning authority should also consider whether the imposition of any conditions may render an otherwise objectionable development acceptable, so as to save the application from being refused.

These are not legal requirements, but a local planning authority ignores these tests at its peril because of the applicant's right of appeal. It also appears from *Times Investments Ltd* v *Secretary of State for the Environment* [1990] JPL 433 that a failure to have regard to these policies (e.g., not to demonstrate the harm that would be caused by omitting a particular condition) may render the decision *ultra vires* for failure to have regard to a material consideration. Once again, therefore, the Secretary of State's guidance imposes significant restrictions on the decisions that may be reached. Circular 11/95 notes types of condition that would normally be *ultra vires* and those that require exceptional justification. Appendix A includes a list of model conditions and Appendix B a list of unacceptable ones.

Planning conditions and pollution control

One particular issue relates to the use of planning conditions to achieve continuing pollution control objectives. There is, of course, a slender but marked distinction between the policy tests laid down in PPG 23 and the relevant circulars and the legal tests laid down in *Newbury District Council* v *Secretary of State for the Environment* [1981] AC 578. One of the important differences is that the legal tests do not suggest that a condition will be unlawful if it duplicates other statutory controls. As long as the matter which is sought to be controlled has a planning purpose (a concept which seems to widen with the passing years), it is lawful.

On the other hand, Government policy in Circular 11/95 (echoing the Royal Commission on Pollution in its Fifth Report) makes it clear that planning conditions should not be used to deal with difficulties which are the subject of controls under other legislation. The justification for this approach is that it prevents an unnecessary duplication of control or any argument over the nature of the conditions which are to be imposed. Whether it is desirable in policy terms is another matter and local planning authorities will always be wary of imposing conditions which duplicate other controls as the Secretary of State will, more often than not, amend the condition on appeal.

The problems of overlapping conditions can be significant in pollution control. The Department of the Environment's Report on Planning, Pollution and Waste Management published in 1992 found that there were two main circumstances where planning conditions were used in the control of pollution.

First, there were occasions where the only (or in some cases the most straightforward) means of controlling pollution was by imposing planning conditions (e.g., the control of groundwater pollution from direct or indirect sources, such as storage tanks). Secondly, conditions were used to override existing pollution control systems in circumstances where it was argued that planning authorities had little confidence in the pollution control authorities and wished to maintain a degree of control to protect the amenities of the area. Examples included a condition to impose a release limit which would run with the land, rather than be associated with a licence to operate, and a condition to impose a release limit where the planning authority were concerned that the relevant pollution control authority would not enforce its own controls.

These types of conditions were, and still are, clearly contrary to policy but not unlawful. For example, an Inspector imposed an overlapping condition in the appeal involving Ferro-Alloys and Metals Smelter in Glossop (see

[1990] 2 LMELR 176). In that appeal, the Inspector granted permission for the retention of a chimney at a smelting plant subject to a condition restricting the emission levels of sulphur dioxide. The appellant operators had argued that it was not appropriate for the planning authority to use planning conditions to seek to control matters which were dealt with under other legislation. The Inspector concluded that it was reasonable for the planning authority to take the view that they could not rely upon HMIP taking enforcement action. HMIP had indicated that there were grounds upon which they would review the emission levels or refuse to enforce (e.g., where there were financial difficulties or where there was no danger to health). The powers available to the Environment Agency have improved since that decision but the legality of the determination still appears to be correct. It is, however, unlikely that the Secretary of State would take such a view now. For another example of a condition which was not unlawful by virtue of any potential overlap with environmental legislation see *W. E. Black Ltd* v *Secretary of State for the Environment* [1997] Env LR 1, which involved the imposition of a condition requiring flood drainage works to protect the amenity of the area. Overlapping conditions were used to require the details of pollution control measures which were not available at the time of the planning determination were required to be submitted to and approved by the planning authority prior to development commencing.

PPG 23 suggests that the increasing scope and effectiveness of the regulatory mechanisms of the pollution control authorities should mean that the imposition of conditions which duplicate pollution control measures would not be acceptable. This does not, however, reflect the experience of local authorities, who have to deal with the consequences of unenforced conditions in pollution control consents. For examples of local authorities who have struggled with the inadequacies of Part I of the Environmental Protection Act 1990 when attempting to deal with problems of odour nuisance see *Tameside Metropolitan Borough Council* v *Smith Brothers (Hyde) Ltd* [1996] Env LR D4 and *R* v *Secretary of State for the Environment, ex parte West Wiltshire District Council* [1996] Env LR 312. In such circumstances it would be understandable if local authorities would prefer to deal with such matters by way of a breach of condition notice under the planning system, even where the condition was arguably unlawful.

Planning obligations

The town and country planning legislation has always included powers under which a local planning authority could enter into an agreement relating to the development or use of land. Similar powers are provided in other legislation (e.g., the Local Government (Miscellaneous Provisions) Act 1982 and various Local Acts). Whilst for many years little use was made of these powers, in the 1970s and 1980s they came to be seen as a mechanism for the provision of some form of 'planning gain' (i.e., some gain to the community that would not necessarily have been obtained without the agreement). The increased importance of agreements illustrated the negotiative nature of modern town planning and showed that the concept of planning as a strict system of regulation in which the regulator imposes restrictions on a developer had become rather outdated. But it also gave rise to some concern. There was no need for approval of agreements by the Secretary of State, no provision for publicity or appeal, limited scrutiny of the content of agreements and limited potential for a successful challenge by a third party. As a result, there was a great danger that an agreement could be seen either in terms of the local planning authority 'selling' planning permission or the developer offering a bribe in return for favourable treatment.

When the Town and Country Planning Act was consolidated in 1990, the provisions on agreements were included as s. 106. However, they were soon completely rewritten by the Planning and Compensation Act 1991. The main change was that developers were enabled to give binding unilateral undertakings as well as to enter into agreements. The phrase 'planning obligations' is now used to cover both agreements and undertakings. The idea of unilateral undertakings was attacked by the opposition parties in Parliament as a 'developer's charter', but it appears that they have not been used on any major scale. They are of greatest importance for developers wishing to make proposals in relation to infrastructure costs and requirements and in situations where a local planning authority is unwilling to agree terms. But they can also be used to great effect during an appeal — a developer can lay its proposal on the table and thus enable the Secretary of State to take that into account in deciding whether to allow the appeal. Other changes made by the 1991 Act were that the various powers were set out far more clearly than under the existing legislation and that a new procedure was introduced in which an application can be made for the discharge or modification of an obligation. The Crown was also enabled to create planning obligations.

As a result, the redrafted s. 106 represents the current law, though the old provisions continue to apply to agreements made before 25 October 1991. Planning obligations can only be created by deed and by a person who has an interest in the relevant land. They may include positive as well as negative obligations (s. 106(1)). For example, a developer could offer to build and maintain some facility of benefit to the community on the site, or could agree that traffic flows on to the site would be regulated in a particular way. They are enforceable against successors in title (s. 106(3)) and are local land charges (s. 106(11)). Where there is a breach, they are enforceable by injunction (s. 106(5)), which is often a more attractive method of enforcement for a local planning authority than reliance on the enforcement notice procedures. The local planning authority has an alternative power to enter the land, carry out the appropriate operations and recover its costs, as long as it gives at least 21 days' notice of its intention to do so (s. 106(6)).

It is important to note that the creation of a s. 106 obligation does not replace the need to seek planning permission in the normal way. But the existence of a valid obligation is definitely a material consideration which should be taken into account under s. 70(2). The local planning authority will normally link the permission and the obligation by imposing a condition on the permission that implementation depends on the acceptance of a planning obligation. It thus appears that a planning obligation may enable the local planning authority and the developer to supplement a permission by achieving objectives which could not be achieved by planning conditions.

However, the exact legal extent of this has never been entirely clear, and was not clarified by the 1991 Act. In *R v Gillingham Borough Council, ex parte Parham Ltd* [1988] JPL 336, it was decided that an agreement made under the section as it was then drafted must relate to planning purposes and must not be perverse, although it need not be related to the development permitted. This clearly accepted that the test for agreements was more relaxed than that for conditions, which requires all three tests to be satisfied (see p. 254). The decision, which was supported in *R v Wealden District Council, ex parte Charles Church (South East) Ltd* (1989) 59 P & CR 150, in effect represented a judicial approval of the practice of obtaining planning gain, at least where it was reasonable to do so.

The Court of Appeal took a different view in *R v Plymouth City Council, ex parte Plymouth and South Devon Co-operative Society Ltd* (1993) 67 P & CR 78. In this case, the court had to examine the legality of the offer by two superstore developers of planning gain — including such things as construction of a tourist information centre, provision of a bird-watching hide, a contribution towards a 'Park and Ride' scheme, and up to £1m for infrastructure works at another site. The Court of Appeal decided that community benefits could be material considerations even where they were not necessary to overcome or alleviate planning objections. The court stated that a planning obligation had to satisfy the three tests which applied to conditions, i.e., (a) it must have a planning purpose; (b) it must fairly and reasonably relate to the permitted development; and (c) it must not be perverse or grossly unreasonable. The court decided that the proposed benefits satisfied these tests.

The House of Lords have subsequently refined this decision in *Tesco Stores Ltd v Secretary of State for the Environment* [1995] 1 WLR 759. Once again, the case involved competing superstore developers, one of whom had entered into a planning obligation offering planning gain in the form of private funding for a £6.6m new road, which was intended to relieve traffic congestion in the town of Witney in Oxfordshire, in return for the grant of planning permission for their site. On appeal, the Secretary of State decided that the offer of funding (or the lack of it) was not a good ground for either granting or refusing permission.

In the House of Lords it was argued that the offer of funding was a material consideration and that as the Secretary of State failed to have regard to it his decision was flawed. The House took a different approach to the Court of Appeal in *Plymouth* and distinguished the tests for the legality of conditions and planning obligations. In particular, Lord Hoffmann, in an erudite judgment, held that a planning obligation could be valid even where it would not satisfy the second test set out in *Plymouth* (above) in the sense that the connection to the development had only to be more than *de minimis*. Thus, a planning obligation only has to satisfy tests (a) and (c) above. Whilst accepting that it would be unlawful to take into account an obligation which had no connection *whatsoever* with the development, the weight to be attached to the obligation was entirely a matter for the decision-maker (and different decision-makers could take opposing views on the weight to attach to the same obligation). The court did not, however, give any guidance on the sufficiency of the connection between the development and the obligation. It is difficult to envisage many obligations which could not be linked to the development in some manner (albeit that specific examples could be tortuous). Moreover, Lord Hoffman commented that it was not necessary for the obligation to be proportional to the development, nor did it have to be necessary to allow the development to go ahead.

The decision in the House of Lords in *Tesco* re-emphasises the fact that the earlier reported cases confused the *legal* question of the legitimacy of obligations with the *policy* test laid down in Circular 16/91 and its predecessors. In particular, the requirement that the development relates to a planning purpose merely reflects the legal requirement to take into account material considerations under s. 70(2) of the Town and Country Planning Act 1990.

Moreover, the third test of general reasonableness equates with normal principles of administrative law. On the other hand, the second test set out in *Plymouth* was a test of policy which was specified in Circular 16/91.

The legal tests are amplified by policy guidance on what is permissible by way of planning gain set out in Circular 16/91. Given that policy and practice have arguably been more important than law in this area in the past, the terms of the Circular are of special significance. They suggest that s. 106 should not be used so as to require a developer to provide more than that which is linked to the development in issue in terms of scale and kind. This appears to mean, for example, that a developer may be asked to provide extra sewerage which is needed for the works applied for, but not sewerage for the whole general area. But this limitation seems unenforceable in many cases, since neither the developer nor the local planning authority will wish to challenge an arrangement they have themselves reached (and which may indeed be encouraged by the local plan, which was the situation in the *Plymouth* case), and other objectors may well lack either knowledge of the agreement or *locus standi* to challenge it. It is significant that the reported cases on planning obligations nearly all concern claims by one developer that a rival is being given preferential treatment as a result of an offer of planning gain that is questionable in terms of law or policy. Lord Hoffmann in *Tesco* examined the interface between the law and policy of planning obligations and suggested that there was nothing in the 1990 Act which required the Secretary of State to adopt the second test (i.e., necessity) notwithstanding that it was a policy which was consistent with the policy of a presumption in favour of development. He went on to say, however, that the Secretary of State was entitled to change that policy at any time. Indeed, he went on to suggest that it would be legitimate for the Secretary of State to pursue a policy of granting permissions for 'good reason' and that one of those 'good reasons' could be the willingness of the developer to provide related external benefits.

Section 106A includes provisions on the modification or discharge of obligations. This may be done by agreement, but there is also a right to apply to the local planning authority for modification or discharge after five years, with an appeal against refusal to the Secretary of State provided by s. 106B. The Town and Country Planning (Modification and Discharge of Planning Obligations) Regulations 1992 (SI 1992 No. 2832) provide the procedures for these sections, but it is clear that the right is narrower than that for discharge of conditions set out in s. 73, thus providing another good reason why local authorities may choose an obligation in preference to conditions. Agreements existing on 25 October 1991 are still covered by the old law on variation and extinguishment, which allows restrictive covenants to be looked at under the Law of Property Act 1925, s. 84.

Planning appeals

Section 78 provides a statutory right of appeal to the Secretary of State against refusals of permission or the imposition of any conditions, and where the local planning authority has failed to determine an application within eight weeks. Only the applicant can appeal.

An appeal amounts to a total rehearing of the application. The Secretary of State can make any decision originally open to the local planning authority, i.e., allow or refuse permission or attach any conditions. This is true even where the appeal is against a conditional grant of permission (but not where it is against an application for discharge of conditions under s. 73, since there the local planning authority itself would have been limited to a consideration of the relevant condition). An appeal is thus not primarily a contest, but a forum in which all relevant information may be produced and tested so that the Inspector may make a rational decision. However, it is clear that, over the years, appeals have come to resemble the confrontational model of court proceedings far more than was originally intended although research has indicated that many users of the system are unhappy, and changes to reduce inquiry times have been proposed.

There is also a right to seek judicial review of local planning authority decisions, although an applicant would normally be advised to appeal to the Secretary of State, because the appeal will encompass policy matters and is cheaper. A decision to grant planning permission can only be challenged through judicial review. Such action requires the person initiating the challenge to have *locus standi*, which is fairly easily satisfied for those with some interest in the case (see *R v Sheffield City Council, ex parte Mansfield* (1978) 37 P & CR 1). Alternatively, the Attorney-General can be requested to bring a relator action on behalf of the applicant.

The number of appeals increased rapidly in the 1980s, with a figure of 32,281 being reached in 1989/90. This fell to 22,121 in 1991/92. The success rate currently is around 33%, a significant increase on the 1970s, but not as high as the peak of 40% reached in the late 1980s. There is clear evidence that the appeals process has been politicised, with the opportunity being taken to impose Central Government policy unless there are strong and clear local policies applicable (e.g., in a local plan), or a clear restraint policy, such as the Green Belt, applies.

Procedure on appeals

Either party (or the Secretary of State) has a right to a public hearing. In large cases this will be a public inquiry under ss. 320 and 321. In an attempt to address some of the criticisms of the public inquiry system, there has been a shift towards the use of informal hearings to resolve planning disputes. Circular 15/96 makes it clear that it is central government policy to use hearings in all suitable cases, and to that end the choice of the hearing procedure is made by the Planning Inspectorate in consultation with the parties. Previously, either party to an appeal could request a public inquiry.

In the vast majority of cases, however, an appeal is dealt with by way of written representations. The Town and Country Planning (Written Representations Procedure) Regulations 1987 (SI 1987 No. 701) introduced statutory rules for such procedures for the first time and laid down time limits for the various stages involved. Third parties have some limited rights to make representations on written appeals. However, it is clear that it will be very rare for a decision to be quashed because of inadequacies in the procedures actually adopted.

Apart from a very small number of matters of national importance, the decision is normally taken by an Inspector. In the remaining cases, the Inspector's report goes to the Secretary of State, who then makes the final decision in the light of the recommendations.

If a public inquiry is to be held, there are two similar sets of rules: the Town and Country Planning (Inquiries Procedure) Rules 1992 (SI 1992 No. 2038) and the Town and Country Planning (Determination by Inspectors) (Inquiries Procedure) Rules 1992 (SI 1992 No. 2039). They are an attempt to solve previous criticisms about the delays and costs involved in a public inquiry by setting out formal rules on pre-inquiry exchanges of information and laying down timetables for the various stages. However, there is no remedy to ensure these time scales are kept, except an award of costs.

The inquiry must be public and anyone is entitled to attend. In general, the procedure to be followed is at the discretion of the Inspector, but the rules give the appellant and the local planning authority full participation rights, including access to evidence, calling of witnesses, and the right to cross-examine. A right to appear and present a case is also conferred on other people who have served a statement of case. However, since the rules are supplemented by the rules of natural justice, as indeed are the written representation procedures, an Inspector normally permits anyone with anything new and relevant to say to put their case properly. The Inspector is entitled to make a site inspection at any time, but this is not the place for hearing submissions.

Reasons must be given for the decision. Again, this duty has been supplemented by the courts, which require the reasons to be adequate, intelligible and not self-contradictory. The conclusions should follow from the evidence and all the main points raised at the inquiry should be dealt with (*Givaudan & Co. Ltd* v *Minister of Housing and Local Government* [1967] 1 WLR 250).

Unlike normal civil litigation where the loser will usually pay all the costs of an action, parties to a planning appeal are expected to pay their own costs unless there has been 'unreasonable behaviour' (as defined in Circular 8/93) by one of the parties which justifies an award of costs against them. On the whole, costs can only be awarded where there has been a public inquiry. Costs can also be awarded in the case of a written representations appeal where a public inquiry is cancelled as a result of the withdrawal of one or more grounds of refusal, but the appeal proceeds by way of written representation. In all other cases costs in written representation appeals are irrecoverable. There has been an increase in the number of successful claims in the last few years. The majority of awards are against the local planning authority, rather than the appellant, and very limited use has been made of the power to make awards against third parties. 'Unreasonable behaviour' for the appellant includes making an appeal that has no reasonable chance of success (e.g., an appeal against a refusal prompted by a clear planning policy such as the Green Belt — see the award in the *Bricket Wood* case [1989] JPL 629), and uncooperative behaviour. For the local planning authority, unreasonable refusal of the application is the main ground for an award, which puts great emphasis on the reasons for refusal and the statement of case submitted before the inquiry (see Walker [1988] JPL 598).

An increasing number of cases are now heard by the less formal procedure of a hearing. Hearings are not normally imposed by the Planning Inspectorate on behalf of the Secretary of State where third-party evidence is expected, or there are disputed matters of fact, or complex matters of law or policy. The details are laid out in a Code of Conduct published as part of Circular 15/96, which stresses prehearing exchange of information.

Challenging the decision of the Secretary of State

The Secretary of State's decision can only be challenged under s. 288, owing to s. 284 which ousts all other challenges. Section 288 thus provides a statutory appeal: this must be distinguished from judicial review under RSC Ord. 53 (see Chapter 2). About 150 cases under s. 288 are brought each year. These are the main source of decisions on planning law.

The s. 288 grounds approximate to judicial review grounds. A decision can be challenged either if it is not within the powers of the Act , or if substantial prejudice has been caused by a failure to comply with the relevant procedures (e.g., the Inquiries Rules). These will cover bad faith, perverse decisions, failure to take account of relevant factors, taking into account irrelevant factors, mistakes of law, acting on no evidence, giving inadequate reasons, or a want of natural justice.

Under s. 288, the High Court is limited to quashing the decision of the Secretary of State and remitting the case. It cannot make the decision for the Secretary of State, but can make some fairly explicit directions as to the relevant law. Thus, even if an appeal under s. 288 is successful, there is no guarantee that the redetermination will be any more beneficial. The High Court also has a discretion whether to quash a decision and will refuse to do so if it considers that the defect made no difference to the eventual decision.

Any 'person aggrieved' by the decision can use s. 288. This includes all parties who appeared at the inquiry or made representations, as well as the appellant, the local planning authority, and owners and occupiers of the site (see *Turner* v *Secretary of State for the Environment* (1973) 28 P & CR 123). The time limit for a s. 288 appeal is six weeks from the Secretary of State's decision, after which the decision is unchallengeable, no matter what the grounds of complaint (*Smith* v *East Elloe RDC* [1956] AC 736).

Enforcement of planning law

Planning law has a well-developed system of enforcement, which has just undergone some quite radical changes in the Planning and Compensation Act 1991. Most of these changes stem from the recommendations of the Carnwath Report (*Enforcing Planning Law*, 1989), but it is clear that the system of enforcement has in reality been a weak point of the planning system for many years. It has a number of features which differentiate it from most other enforcement mechanisms in environmental law. In particular, it is a two-stage procedure, in which an enforcement notice is first issued and then may be followed up with a prosecution if it is ignored.

Enforcement notices

The major tool for enforcement against breaches of planning control is the enforcement notice. This is an entirely discretionary procedure under which a local planning authority may serve an enforcement notice in respect of unauthorised development, requiring the owner or occupier to take specified steps to remedy a breach. Unlike most pollution control legislation, a breach of planning law is not in itself a criminal offence; the offence consists of failing to comply with an enforcement notice. There are additional powers relating to stop notices and to injunctions, though these have not been greatly used. There are also new powers on contravention notices and breach of condition notices.

A number of limitations of the enforcement notice procedure should be noted:

(a)   The legislation empowers no one other than the local planning authority to serve an enforcement notice (except the Secretary of State, who has a reserve power in s. 182 that appears never to have been used).

(b)   The local planning authority is given a wide and virtually unchallengeable discretion whether to serve an enforcement notice and over its content. One may be issued where the authority consider it 'expedient' to do so, having regard to the development plan and to any other material considerations (s. 172).

(c)   This makes the exercise of the discretion dependent on policy factors. Government policy advice in Planning Policy Guidance Note 18 is that enforcement action should be taken only where it is essential and commensurate with the breach to which it relates, and that the service of an enforcement notice should be treated as a last resort. The local planning authority will take into account effectively the same things as it would when deciding whether to grant planning permissions (after all, failing to enforce against a breach is almost tantamount to granting unconditional permission).

(d) The whole process of serving an enforcement notice is very lengthy and excessively technical.

(e) There is an appeal to the Secretary of State: not only does this delay matters, since the appeal suspends the operation of the notice, there is a very high success rate on appeal (averaging around 40% in recent years), mainly owing to the deregulatory policies of the Government.

In a survey carried out in 1983, Jowell and Millichap found that enforcement of the law was given a very low profile in many local planning authorities (see [1986] JPL 482), though matters may well have improved since then as a result of the wider range of effective powers now available. A significant number of authorities did not have anyone responsible for enforcement. Monitoring of compliance with conditions and agreements was *ad hoc* and not guaranteed. The most common method of discovery of a breach was from a complaint from a member of the public rather than from investigation. When it came to taking action, informal methods of solving the problem were favoured, such as warning letters and requests for details of ownership of the land (an easily recognised threat of more formal enforcement action). Even if an enforcement notice was served, there was no guarantee that it would itself be enforced if ignored. 40% of metropolitan authorities and 32% of non-metropolitan authorities had not prosecuted once in the two years preceding the survey, low fines being given as a significant reason for failing to do so. Even more starkly, 65% of authorities had not used a stop notice in the previous two years, with fear of compensation being cited as the main reason for reluctance here.

Further surveys have illustrated that enforcement action is more likely to be taken where economic circumstances permit it. For example, enforcement is more common in South East England than in depressed urban areas.

Immunity from enforcement
The following situations provide immunity from the service of an enforcement notice:

(a) Where four years have elapsed from the substantial completion of an operational development (s. 171B(1)).

(b) Where four years have elapsed from a change of use *to* a dwelling-house (s. 171B(2)).

(c) Where 10 years have elapsed from any other breach of planning control (s. 171B(3)). This is a change introduced by the Planning and Compensation Act 1991; prior to that Act there was immunity for changes of use only if the breach took place before 1 January 1964. All cases where there is a breach of a condition attached to a planning permission are now covered by the 10-year period of immunity, thus mitigating the effect of *Harvey* v *Secretary of State for Wales* (1989) 88 LGR 253, which decided, on the original wording of the 1990 Act, that conditions attaching to an operational permission were subject to the four-year rule. This created some potential difficulties for the enforcement of continuing conditions, such as occupancy conditions or those relating to the operation of a site. However, *Harvey* still applies to any breach which took place before the 1991 Act came into force, which was 2 January 1992.

(d) Where there is a certificate of lawfulness of existing use or development, a certificate of lawfulness of proposed use or development, or an established use certificate granted under earlier legislation relating to the alleged breach (see ss. 191 — 194). These certificates are conclusive as to the lawfulness of the matters to which they relate.

(e) Development by, or on behalf of, the Crown on Crown land (s. 294), although it is possible for a special enforcement notice to be served on a private individual who is occupying Crown land (s. 294(3)), a power that is primarily available for the control of trespassers.

Procedure for issuing an enforcement notice
An enforcement notice is first issued by the local planning authority (normally the district planning authority, though the county planning authority has some powers over county matters). It must then be served on all owners and occupiers of the relevant premises, including licensees. The enforcement notice must specify the alleged breach, the steps required to remedy it (these may include any steps to alleviate an injury to amenity), the reasons for issuing the enforcement notice, and the relevant land. It also has to specify the date on which it takes effect, which must be at least 28 days from the date of service, and a further period after that which is for compliance with its requirements.

At the end of the period for compliance, the owner of the land (or in some cases a person with control of or an interest in the land) commits a criminal offence if its requirements have not been met (s. 179). It should be noted that compliance with an enforcement notice does not discharge it: it attaches permanently to the land (s. 181). However, an enforcement notice is a local land charge, so future purchasers of the land should find out about its existence. Each district planning authority must keep a public register of enforcement notices and stop notices (s. 188).

The maximum penalty for these offences is £20,000 on summary conviction, or an unlimited fine for conviction on indictment. In determining the amount of any fine, the court must have regard to any financial benefit accruing to the convicted person. There is no provision for imprisonment. The local planning authority also has a power to enter the land and remedy a breach at the owner's expense (s. 178).

Appeals
Any person with an interest in the relevant land (or an occupier with a written licence) may appeal against the enforcement notice to the Secretary of State. The appeal must be in writing and must be received by the Secretary of State before the enforcement notice takes effect. Thus the period in which an appeal must be lodged could be as short as 28 days.

An appeal will suspend the operation of the enforcement notice until the appeal is finally determined. In *R* v *Kuxhaus* [1988] QB 631, it was held that this could mean until a subsequent court action had been heard; in that case the number of successive appeals meant that the enforcement notice was suspended for over six years. The effect of that decision has now been reversed by the Planning and Compensation Act 1991. Nevertheless, the enforcement notice is still suspended until after the Secretary of State's decision, and it is quite clear that a determined and experienced operator may delay the final operation of an enforcement notice for a considerable period.

There are seven grounds of appeal set out in s. 174(2):

(a)   planning permission ought to be granted for the development, or the relevant condition ought to be discharged;

(b)   the alleged breach has not in fact taken place;

(c)   the matters alleged in the enforcement notice do not in law constitute a breach of planning control;

(d)   the matters alleged in the enforcement notice are immune from enforcement action;

(e)   failures to carry out the correct procedures in serving the enforcement notice;

(f)   the steps required to remedy the breach are excessive;

(g)   the time allowed for compliance with the enforcement notice is unreasonably short.

These grounds are very wide, and cover both policy and legal grounds. Ground (a) is effectively an application for planning permission from the Secretary of State, hence a fee is payable for making an enforcement notice appeal (this is refundable if the appeal is allowed on grounds (b)–(e) or the enforcement notice is withdrawn).

Ground (f) is also important. A local planning authority may not 'over-enforce', i.e., put the recipient of an enforcement notice in a worse position than before the breach took place. This relates mainly to ancillary uses; the local planning authority may not require a developer to cease a use which would always have been ancillary (see *Mansi* v *Elstree Rural District Council* (1964) 16 P & CR 153).

The procedure for enforcement appeals is very similar to that for planning appeals. They are governed by the Town and Country Planning (Enforcement Notices and Appeals) Regulations 1991 (SI 1991 No. 2804) and the Town and Country Planning (Enforcement) (Inquiries Procedure) Rules 1992 (SI 1992 No. 1903). A choice of procedure is provided between a public inquiry, an informal hearing and a written representation procedure, and most cases are decided by Inspectors. Intelligible reasons must be given for the decision.

The Secretary of State may (a) uphold an enforcement notice and refuse the appeal; (b) quash it (often this involves granting retrospective planning permission); (c) vary its terms; or (d) amend it. In the last two cases any error in the enforcement notice may be corrected if it would not cause injustice to the appellant or the local planning authority.

Challenging the validity of an enforcement notice

The service of an enforcement notice is the first step towards the creation of a possible criminal offence, so the procedures set out in the legislation must be strictly observed. However, there is the possibility that the Secretary of State can amend an enforcement notice on appeal. In the past, the courts have tended to adopt very technical reasoning in this area, and have suggested that many procedural shortcomings render an enforcement notice invalid and not capable of correction, but recent decisions suggest that this attitude is changing. In *R v Tower Hamlets London Borough Council, ex parte Ahern (London) Ltd* (1989) 59 P & CR 133, it is made clear that, as long as the enforcement notice tells the recipient what must be done and why, most technicalities may be corrected by the Secretary of State on appeal, if that can be done without prejudice to either party. This point was reinforced by the redrafting of s. 173, on the contents of an enforcement notice, in the Planning and Compensation Act 1991.

Appeal is made the exclusive remedy for the matters laid out in grounds (a) to (g): it is not possible to seek judicial review of an enforcement notice on these grounds (s. 285). However, some may be challenged in the High Court through judicial review as nullities (and therefore void). This may be the case if the notice is hopelessly ambiguous as to what is required, or if essential procedural requirements are not met (see *Miller-Mead v Minister of Housing and Local Government* [1963] 2 QB 196). The validity of an enforcement notice may not be challenged in a prosecution for breach (*R v Smith* (1984) 48 P & CR 392).

There is a further right of appeal on a point of law to the High Court against the decision of the Secretary of State (s. 289). It has no jurisdiction to quash an enforcement notice; if the judge thinks the Secretary of State was wrong in law the matter will be remitted to the Secretary of State.

Stop notices

One of the problems with enforcement notices is that immediate action to remedy the breach cannot be ensured. Accordingly, under s. 183, the local planning authority is given power to serve a stop notice on anyone carrying on an unlawful activity. This makes it an offence to continue any activity which is specified in the notice once it has come into force, which may be between 3 and 28 days from service. The penalties are the same as for breach of an enforcement notice.

There are limits on the application of stop notices. A stop notice is parasitic on an enforcement notice; that is it must be served together with one or after one has been served, and will automatically cease to have effect if the enforcement notice is withdrawn or successfully appealed. It may not be served to stop use as a dwellinghouse, or where an activity has been carried on for more than four years. Most importantly, compensation is payable by the local planning authority if the enforcement notice or the stop notice is withdrawn, or if an enforcement notice appeal is allowed on any other ground than ground (a) – the policy ground. This threat of compensation has meant that service of a stop notice has been quite a rare occurrence, but the availability of compensation was limited by the Planning and Compensation Act 1991 so that it is not payable if the activity stopped is in breach of planning control.

There is no appeal against service of a stop notice. Accordingly, it is permissible to challenge the validity of a stop notice when prosecuted for ignoring it (*R* v *Jenner* [1983] 1 WLR 873).

Injunctions

Under s. 222 of the Local Government Act 1972, a local planning authority has always had a power to seek an injunction against any breach of the law where it is considered 'expedient for the promotion or protection of the interests of the inhabitants of their area'. This power has been interpreted fairly widely in the House of Lords in *Stoke on Trent City Council* v *B & Q (Retail) Ltd* [1984] AC 754, with the result that an injunction may be sought not only where there has been a deliberate and flagrant flouting of the law but where the normal enforcement procedures prove inadequate to deal with the problem. For example, in *Westminster City Council* v *Jones* (1981) 80 LGR 241, a chemist's shop in a residential area was converted to an amusement arcade. The owner ignored an enforcement notice and appealed against it, thus delaying the enforcement process, but the court granted an injunction in the light of the damage to amenity in the area and the deliberate nature of Jones's actions. Section 187B provides a specific power for the local planning authority to seek an injunction if it considers it necessary or expedient to restrain an actual or potential breach of planning control, thus removing the need to rely on the Local Government Act 1972. In *Kirklees Metropolitan Borough Council* v *Wickes Building Supplies Ltd* [1993] AC 227, the House of Lords established that any public authority exercising the functions of law enforcement does not always have to give a cross-undertaking in damages when seeking injunctions, thus removing a serious practical obstacle that had previously restricted their use.

An injunction is a discretionary remedy and will not be granted by a court unless the circumstances warrant such a strong solution. The penalty for breach of an injunction is potentially far higher than for breach of an enforcement notice, since the developer is in contempt of court and imprisonment is a possibility. It seems, however, that there is no requirement that other enforcement methods have been exhausted first.

Other enforcement powers

The Planning and Compensation Act 1991 introduced an additional three enforcement powers as follows:

(a) The local planning authority may serve a planning contravention notice on any owner, occupier, or other person who is using or carrying out operations on land, seeking information from them relating to its use or occupation (s. 171C). It is a summary offence to ignore such a notice, or knowingly to provide incorrect information (s. 171D). The idea behind the procedure is to obtain information relating to suspected breaches and to enable the breach to be remedied without recourse to more formal enforcement procedures. Clearly, the issuing of such a notice will warn the recipient that the local planning authority will take further action if necessary.

(b) A breach of condition notice provides for a simple summary procedure whereby a local planning authority may serve written notice on a person responsible for non-compliance with a condition, or having control over the relevant land, requiring compliance in a period of not less than 28 days (s. 187A). It is an offence not to comply with such a notice, the maximum fine being £1,000. As with enforcement notices, it is made clear that a continuation of the non-compliance constitutes a further offence.

(c) Local planning authorities are provided with wide powers to enter land at any reasonable time to ascertain whether there has been a breach of planning control and what remedial steps may be required (ss. 196A, 196B and 196C).

Enforcement where there is no breach of planning law

There are some courses of action available to the local planning authority where there is no breach of the planning legislation. Normally these require the payment of compensation for the loss of any rights which have been taken away, so they are little used. But they are of importance as reserve powers where there is something creating an environmental problem that may not be removed or controlled in any other way.

Under s. 102 a local planning authority may serve a discontinuance order, which may require that any use be discontinued or that any buildings or works be removed or altered. Under s. 97 a local planning authority may revoke or modify a planning permission that has already been granted. In both these cases there are provisions for a public local inquiry to be held and compensation to be paid. The Secretary of State must also confirm these orders before they have effect and has reserve powers to make either type. Indeed, in March 1991, the Secretary of State took the exceptional step of making an order revoking a planning permission which Poole DC had granted to itself for housing on land designated a site of special scientific interest (SSSI) on Canford Heath in Dorset (thus belatedly rendering unnecessary the litigation in R v Poole Borough Council, ex parte Beebee [1991] JPL 643).

The local planning authority may also conclude a planning agreement under s. 106 in order to remove an existing building or use, although obviously the owner will require something of benefit in return.

Planning and hazardous substances

The storage of hazardous substances was traditionally dealt with under normal planning procedures. There were, however, many occasions when the storage of large amounts of hazardous materials fell outside the scope of existing controls as it was either permitted automatically under the GDO/

UCO or it did not amount to development at all. Thus, it became necessary to control the siting of hazardous materials under a separate but complementary set of controls.

The Planning (Hazardous Substances) Act 1990 was brought into force on 1 June 1992. It requires hazardous substances consent (HSC) to be obtained if hazardous substances are present on, over or under land in an amount at or above a controlled quantity. The Act gives hazardous substances authorities (HSAs) the opportunity to consider whether the proposed storage or use of a hazardous substance is appropriate in a particular location, having regard to the risks arising to persons in the surrounding area, the wider implications for the community and other material considerations.

The controls under the Act are not intended to duplicate the effect of other statutory controls. Thus the Act does not apply to controlled or radioactive wastes. Also, the controls do not apply to explosives, the location of which is controlled by licences specifically issued by the HSE. The Planning (Hazardous Substances) Regulations 1992 (SI 1992 No. 656) outline the categories of substances which are controlled by the Act and the level at which they become subject to the provisions of the Act.

The Act operates by requiring any person wishing to store any listed substances at or above prescribed controlled quantities to obtain prior consent from the relevant HSA.

The role of the hazardous substances authorities
HSAs are defined in ss. 1 and 3 of the 1990 Act. The provisions in the Act are designed to ensure that the HSA will usually be the same council or other body that would act as local planning authority in dealing with an associated application for planning permission.

The relevant responsible bodies are:
—   in non-metropolitan areas, the district council;
—   in metropolitan areas, the metropolitan authority;
—   in Greater London, the borough councils;
—   county councils for county matters;
—   miscellaneous bodies where they are responsible for the planning functions of the area (e.g., UDCs, the Broads Authority, and housing action trusts).

The extent of control
The 1992 Regulations list 71 substances which are subject to control (sch. 1). Section 4(3) and reg. 4 exempt the temporary storage of a controlled amount of a hazardous substance whilst it is being transported or transferred from one mode of transport to another. The exemptions under the Regulations also include aerosol dispensers, substances in pipelines, ammonium nitrates and substances stored on land as a result of a maritime emergency.

Applications for consent
Applications for HSC must be made on a prescribed form and be accompanied by:

(a)   a site plan;

(b)   a plan indicating the intended location of the controlled substances, the plant which the substance will be present in and access points to the site.

Notice of the application must be given in a local newspaper and on a site notice at least 21 days prior to making the application (reg. 6). In addition, an ownership certificate must be submitted with the application on a similar basis to that in a planning application.

The basis for giving consent

Section 9 of the Planning (Hazardous Substances) Act 1990 sets out the powers and duty of HSAs in relation to their decisions on an application for consent. Section 9(1) gives the HSA the power to grant consent either with or without conditions, or to refuse consent. Section 9(5) requires the HSA to have regard to any material considerations and specifies certain considerations to which the HSA shall have regard.

Section 9(2)(d) makes the provisions of a development plan relevant when determining whether to grant consent. It is important to note that the Act is a 'planning Act' within the definition of s. 336 of the Town and Country Planning Act 1990. Thus, s. 54A of the Town and Country Planning Act 1990 applies to the determination of any consent. Consequently, the determination should be in accordance with the development plan unless material considerations indicate otherwise. It is therefore clearly important for a HSA to consider any policies contained in the relevant development plan.

Regulation 10 of the 1992 Regulations sets out a list of bodies that the HSA must consult before granting hazardous substances consent. The list includes, amongst others, the HSE and the NRA.

The role of the Health and Safety Executive

Although the Planning (Hazardous Substances) Act gives the HSE a purely consultative role in the decision-making process that the HSA must undertake, it is clear from Central Government guidance that a great deal of importance is placed upon the expertise that the HSE have in assessing risks to persons from the presence of hazardous substances.

Section 10(2) of the 1990 Act makes particular provision for the conditions that may have been imposed by the HSA. It states that any condition relating to how a hazardous substance is to be kept or used should be imposed only if the HSE have advised the HSA that any consent should be subject to such conditions. Thus, the HSA does not have a free hand when imposing conditions on any consent that it wishes to give. Central guidance in Circular 11/92 states that any advice from the HSE along the lines that hazardous substance consent should be refused should not be overridden without careful consideration. Where an HSA wishes to grant consent against the HSE's advice, it should give advance notice of that intention and allow 21 days for the HSE to give further consideration to the matter. During this period the HSE can request the Secretary of State for the Environment to call in the application for his own determination.

Furthermore, the controls under the Act are designed to complement and not override or duplicate the requirements of the Health and Safety at Work etc. Act 1974 and its relevant statutory provisions. If an HSA, in exercising its powers under the Act, omits or requires something to be done which is (or which becomes) contrary to any of the above statutory provisions, s. 29 of the 1990 Act is designed to ensure that those safety provisions will prevail, as safety must be the overriding concern. Thus, the statutory provisions relating to health and safety clearly take precedence over any consent given by a HSA, and since it is the HSE who enforce safety provisions, it is also clear that they would have the final word if such a conflict arose.

Relationship with other planning controls

The provisions of the 1990 Act and the relevant regulations were designed to fill the gaps in existing planning controls by enabling specific control to be exercised over the presence of hazardous substances, whether or not associated development was involved. Thus, it is now possible for a local body to have control over the siting of hazardous substances even if development has not occurred.

The new requirement for hazardous substances consent, however, does not override the need for planning permission to be obtained where development is involved. This may arise, for example, where it is proposed to erect a building for the storage or processing of hazardous substances. Where both planning permission and hazardous substances consent are required, two separate applications will be necessary and the respective statutory requirements will need to be followed.

Enforcement

Any person in control of land, or any person who knowingly causes or allows:

(a)   more than the controlled quantity of a hazardous substance to be present in, over, or under land without consent or in excess of the quantity allowed by the consent;

(b)   a breach of any condition of a hazardous substances consent;

will be guilty of an offence (s. 23).

The maximum penalty on summary conviction is £20,000 and on indictment an unlimited fine, and regard must be had of any financial benefit which has accrued or is likely to accrue to the defendant as a result of the offence (s. 23(4A)).

It is a defence to prove that the defendant took all reasonable precautions and exercised all diligence to avoid the commission of an offence, or that the defendant did not know and had no reason to believe that an offence had been committed.

Hazardous substances contravention notice

Where it appears to the HSA that there has been a contravention of HSC, s. 24 of the 1990 Act provides for the service of a hazardous substances contravention notice. The notice must be served on the owner and/or person in control of the land and/or anyone with an interest in the land who is materially affected by the notice. The notice must:

(a)   specify the alleged breach;
(b)   outline the steps which are to be taken to remedy the breach;
(c)   identify the land to which notice relates;
(d)   state the date on which the notice takes effect and the time limit for remedying the breach.

There is a right of appeal against the notice prior to the date on which the notice takes effect. Section 26 enables the HSA to apply for an injunction where it considers it necessary or expedient to do so, whether or not it has exercised any other enforcement powers. Under s. 36, a duly authorised person has the power to enter land at any reasonable time for the purpose of surveying in connection with any application for HSC, or for considering the issue of a hazardous substances contravention notice. Furthermore, s. 178 of the Town and Country Planning Act 1990 gives the HSA power to enter land where a notice has not been complied with, to take the steps specified in the notice and to recover the costs of doing so from the landowner.

Modification of consents

There is a variety of mechanisms available to modify existing consents. Under s. 13, applicants can apply to remove or modify conditions on existing consents. In considering the application the HSA must consider only the condition(s) which is (are) to be removed or modified and not the decision about whether or not to grant consent.

The HSA can revoke or modify a consent by order under s. 14 if it considers it expedient to do so having regard to material considerations. Any order made is subject to confirmation by the Secretary of State. Compensation is payable to any person in circumstances where that person has suffered loss as a result of:

(a)   disturbance in the enjoyment of their land;
(b)   depreciation of the value of their land.

Compensation will not be paid where a consent is revoked and:

(a)   planning permission for a change of use is implemented;
(b)   there has been a material change of use to the land in any event;
(c)   controlled substances have not been present on, over or under land for the preceding five years.

Deemed consent

Section 11 of the 1990 Act enabled a deemed consent to be claimed where hazardous substances had been present during the period of 12 months immediately preceding the commencement of the Act (i.e., 1 June 1992).

The purpose of this provision was to avoid undue disruption by enabling the continuation of previous operations involving hazardous substances in a similar way to that which was then in existence, but with some facility for controlled expansion, without a specific grant of consent being required from the HSA.

Provided a valid claim was made prior to 30 November 1992 (i.e., the submitted information was complete and accurate and the statutory requirements of s. 11 and reg. 14 were met), HSC was automatically deemed to be granted, subject to the standard conditions set out in s. 11(7)(a) of the Act and in sch. 3 to the Regulations. The jurisdiction of the HSA to consider the application was limited to the validity of the application submitted and not the criteria in s. 9.

It is clear from s. 11(8) that the quantity of hazardous substances permitted in the case of deemed consent may be up to twice that which was last notified to the HSE under the Notification of Installations Handling Hazardous Substances Regulations 1982 (SI 1982 No. 1357). Therefore, the introduction of the full, established quantity of a hazardous substance as authorised under a deemed consent may well result in the contravention of health and safety provisions.

Hazardous substances register
Section 28 of the 1990 Act requires every HSA to keep a register containing information about a variety of matters. Regulation 23 sets out the detailed requirements for the manner in which the register should be kept. The register contains details of:

(a)   applications for HSC;
(b)   information about deemed consents;
(c)   enforcement action;
(d)   decisions of the HSA and directions of the Secretary of State.

Fees
All applications for full HSC must be accompanied by a fee. Regulations 24 and 25 of the 1992 Regulations set out the detailed provisions relating to fees, the level of which is between £200 and £400, depending on the quantity of substances involved. The aim of the fee is to enable the local authority to cover normal administration costs.

TEN
Environmental assessment

The assessment of the environmental effects of a development has always been an implicit part of the decision-making process in the system of town and country planning operating in Britain. Indeed, there have also been explicit examples where detailed assessments of the environmental effects of developments have been carried out, for instance in relation to power stations and motorways. Environmental harm has always been a material consideration when deciding whether or not to grant planning permission and there are many developments which have had planning permission refused because of their detrimental environmental effects.

This implicit mechanism was raised to a more formal level with the adoption of EC Directive 85/337 on the Assessment of the Effects of Certain Private and Public Projects on the Environment. This Directive established the need for the preparation of a statement outlining the effects of a development on the environment as a mandatory component of the decision-making process in relation to certain specified projects.

The Directive was the subject of fierce debate between the Member States (and has remained controversial ever since). After much discussion, and some alterations, the Directive was implemented in England and Wales by the Town and Country Planning (Assessment of Environmental Effects) Regulations 1988 (SI 1988 No. 1199) (there are similar regulations which apply in Scotland). These regulations were enacted in Britain under the European Communities Act 1972 and are specifically limited, therefore, to the categories of development listed in the Directive. Section 15 of the Planning and Compensation Act 1991 inserted s. 71A of the Town and Country Planning Act 1990, which provides the Secretary of State with the power to make regulations extending the categories of projects which are to be the subject of environmental assessment, and consequently environmental assessment now has a place in primary legislation. This power was used for the first time when the Secretary of State extended the classes of project which are subject to environmental assessment within the Town and Country Planning (Assessment of Environmental Effects) (Amendment) Regulations 1994 (SI 1994 No. 677). This extended the requirement for environmental assessment to wind turbines, motorway service areas, coast protection works and financed toll roads (although it is only in the latter case that a environmental assessment is mandatory).

The Town and Country (Assessment of Environmental Effects) Regulations 1988 ('the Regulations') cover projects which require planning permission and are listed in the Directive. Additionally, certain projects which either do not constitute development, or are permitted under a development order or are dealt with under separate consent procedures, have separate specific regulations. These include such proposals as afforestation, highways, harbour works, salmon farms, power stations and overhead transmission lines. The separate regulations all follow the framework of the general regulations, but specifically apply to projects which do not require planning permission.

What is environmental assessment?

On a simple level, environmental assessment is merely an information-gathering exercise carried out by the developer and other bodies which enables a local planning authority to understand the environmental effects of a development before deciding whether or not to grant planning permission for that proposal. On this level, however, there is little to distinguish this concept from the normal planning process under which environmental effects are a material consideration. The innovation behind the formal environmental assessment process is the systematic use of the best objective sources of information and the emphasis on the use of the best techniques to gather that information. The ideal environmental assessment would involve a totally bias-free collation of information produced in a form which would be coherent, sound and complete. It should then allow the local planning authority and members of the public to scrutinise the proposal, assess the weight of predicted effects and suggest modifications or mitigation where appropriate.

Thus, environmental assessment is a technique and a process. It is inanimate rather than tangible. There are a number of stages to an assessment, but the main part of the process is the collection and presentation of information relating to environmental impacts and any mitigating measures which are proposed to reduce the significance of those impacts. This information is gathered together in a document known as the environmental statement. This 'environmental statement' is the ultimate submission which is made to the determining authority. It forms part of the overall assessment which is brought together from a number of sources. Clearly, most of the information will be supplied by the developer. There are, however, a number of other sources from which information can, and should, be drawn. There are a number of other participants in the process, and these would normally include statutory consultees (EA, MAFF, HSE, etc.), independent third parties (conservation groups and the like), members of the public, and even the local planning authority itself. The large range of bodies involved in the assessment re-emphasises the underlying concept behind environmental assessment as being based on the systematic analysis of all the relevant facts — these relevant facts being drawn from the widest possible sources.

The theory of the stated objectives of environmental assessment is seemingly simple enough. Unfortunately, the difficulties involved in the coordination of a proper assessment have led to a number of criticisms of the process (as to which see p. 295).

Environmental Assessment Directive

Directive 85/337 on the assessment of the effects of certain public and private projects on the environment requires Member States to ensure that projects likely to have significant effects on the environment by virtue of their nature, size or location are assessed with regard to their environmental impact before development consent is given. Projects are categorised into Annex I (where environmental assessment is compulsory) and Annex II (where it is discretionary).

Whereas the term 'project' is defined as the execution of construction works or of other installations or schemes (which would equate roughly with the concept of 'development' in English planning law), 'development consent' is defined as the decision of the competent authority which entitles the developer to proceed with the project. There is some difficulty with the definition of 'proceeding with the project'. This does not necessarily equate with planning permission, as other statutory consents could be required. Whilst certain developments could be built they could not be operated without other licenses.

On one interpretation therefore, it could be argued that, under the terms of the Directive, the Environment Agency (for example) could request an environmental assessment when considering an application for a waste management licence where the local planning authority had failed to require an assessment. Although this is not the case in UK legislation it arguably could be if the Directive was to have direct effect (as to which see below).

The Directive goes on to set out the detailed requirements for an assessment, which should include direct and indirect effects of a project on a variety of factors, including human beings, fauna, flora, the environment and material assets and the cultural heritage.

The developer must then submit certain specified information to the authority dealing with the application (see below for the contents of an environmental statement). There are also provisions for consultation with both the authorities likely to be concerned with the project and members of the general public, although the detailed arrangements for consultation are left to individual Member States.

Amendments to the Directive

The Directive was amended in March 1997 (OJ L73/6). The amendment Directive requires Member States to implement the amendments before 14 March 1999. The main changes which will affect UK law and practice are:

(a) *All* projects which are likely to give rise significant environmental effects will be *required* to obtain a development consent. This clarifies the position for projects which are exempt from the need to obtain planning permission either by virtue of not being 'development' or by having permitted development rights. In most cases this amendment will not require any legislative changes as the introduction of the Town and Country Planning (General Permitted Development) Order 1995 and the Town and Country Planning (Environmental Assessment and Permitted Development) Regulations 1995 ensured that permission was withdrawn in the case of projects which required environmental assessment. The amendment would, however, also include projects which are excluded from the planning system altogether (i.e., those covered under the alternative regulations).

(b) For all Annex II projects, Member States are required to adopt the criteria for assessment on a case-by-case basis or by means of thresholds and criteria for specific classes of project. At the moment, the UK mixes these two approaches by laying down indicative criteria and leaving the decision on whether to require an assessment to the discretion of the competent authority on a case-by-case basis. Whichever approach is adopted, Member States have to take into account criteria for selecting Annex II projects for assessment set out in a new Annex IIa to the Directive. These include the characteristics of the project, sensitivity in terms of location and the nature of the impacts involved. All decisions on whether an assessment is required have to be made public.

(c) Member States are required to introduce measures to ensure that, if a developer makes a request, prior to submitting an application, the competent authority is under an obligation to give an opinion on the information which the developer is obliged to provide. In such a case there is still scope for the competent authority to request further information at a later date.

(d) As far as the environmental information which is supplied as part of the assessment is concerned, developers will be obliged to provide an outline of the main alternatives studied with an indication of the main reasons for choosing the selected option, taking into account the environmental effects.

(e) A competent authority will be under an obligation to make public the result of any consultation. In addition, where the competent authority has decided to grant or refuse the development consent, it is obliged to inform the public of the reasons for the decision and, in a case where consent is granted, give a description of the mitigation measures which are proposed. This duty to give reasons for the grant of a development consent is a significant change to present procedure, which only requires reasons to be given in the case of a refusal. Challenging decisions to grant permission by way of judicial review should be made easier as the decision-making process will be transparent. In addition, such decisions could be used to facilitate the introduction of third-party rights of appeal against the grant of development consent.

(f) The scope of the Directive has been extended with significant amendments to the lists of Annex I and Annex II projects. Whilst some changes are the result of clarification or rationalisation of existing definitions, there are additional projects in both lists.

(g)   Member States may introduce a single procedure to deal with the granting of development consent and pollution control authorisation under the Integrated Pollution Prevention and Control Directive (see p. 336). In the UK there are sophisticated mechanisms which are already in place to deal with these two separate consent/authorisation procedures by virtue of the integrated pollution control system and the separate system giving development consent.

Environmental Assessment Directive and direct effect

Unlike more recent directives (e.g., on Access to information (92/313), Habitats (92/43), and Waste (91/271)), the Environmental Assessment Directive was not translated 'literally' when transposed into UK legislation. Moreover, most Member States (including the UK) failed to implement the Directive within the time frame laid down. This has led to a number of challenges to decisions made on projects which purportedly fall within the terms of the Directive. A central issue in all cases was whether the Directive had direct effect within UK legislation (for a general discussion of the direct effect doctrine in relation to environmental Directives see p. 69).

The answer to the question of whether the Directive has direct effect in the UK is, unfortunately, unclear. Most of the cases involved 'pipe-line projects', i.e., projects which fell within one of the Annexes of the Directive and were applied for or published before the date of the implementation of the directive (3 July 1988) (without the benefit of an environmental assessment) but received consent afterwards or which were applied for after 3 July but before the implementation date for the relevant domestic legislation (15 July 1988).

In *Twyford Parish Council* v *Secretary of State for the Environment* [1993] 3 Env LR 37, McCullough J appeared to accept that the Directive passed the test of being 'unconditional and sufficiently precise' in its terms and was therefore capable of having direct effect in relation to all projects under the Directive (and on the facts to the extension of the M3 motorway across Twyford Down — an Annex I project).

Subsequently, in the Scottish Court of Session in *Kincardine and Deeside District Council* v *Forestry Commissioners* [1993] Env LR 151, Lord Coulsfield (without referring to the *Twyford* decision) held that Art. 4.2 of the Directive (which lays down the framework for Annex II projects) was not 'plain and unconditional' as it allowed the authorities a discretion not as to the means of implementation of the Directive but as to whether an assessment should be required. Therefore, the Directive would not appear to have direct effect in respect of Annex II projects.

The position was further confused by the decision of Tucker J in *Wychavon District Council* v *Secretary of State for the Environment* [1994] Env LR 239. In that case an application for poultry houses and associated dwellings was submitted on 11 July 1988 (i.e., after the implementation date for the Directive but before the implementation date of the domestic regulations). The High Court held that the Directive had no direct effect in relation to any Annex I or Annex II projects. In doing so, Tucker J found that it was unnecessary to analyse each Article of the Directive in order to identify whether every one was sufficiently precise; it was enough to make out one Article which was imprecise and the direct effect of the whole Directive would fall. He proceeded to identify some Articles within the terms of the Directive which were, in his view, insufficiently precise and, therefore, offended the principles which lay behind the direct effect doctrine. Whilst this view could be supported on the ground that the Directive should be interpreted as a unified set of rules (i.e., all the provisions are interdependent), it is clearly wrong when compared to other Directives which have had partial direct effect (i.e., direct effect for some provisions only — see, e.g., *Marshall* v *Southampton and South West Hampshire Area Health Authority (Teaching)* (case 152/84) [1985] QB 401, which gave direct effect to one provision of the Equal Treatment Directive and the decision in *Von Colson* v *Land Nordrhein-Westfalen* (case 14/83) [1984] ECR 1891, where a different provision in the Directive was not given direct effect).

Following the decision in *Wychavon*, there were three separate judicial views on the direct effect of the Directive, none of which referred to the others and one of which was based on an interpretation of European law which appeared to be contrary to the view of the European Court of Justice. In *R* v *North Yorkshire County Council, ex parte Brown* [1997] Env LR 391, in a case concerning a minerals interim development order, Hidden J preferred the *Wychavon* decision over the other two and held that the Directive did not have direct effect. The ECJ has now considered the direct effect of the Directive in a case involving the failure to assess the construction of Dutch dykes. In *Aannemersbedrijf P. K. Kraaijeveld BV* v *Gedeputeerde Staten van Zuid-Holland* (case C-72/95) [1996] ECR I-5403 the court was asked to rule specifically on the question of the direct effect of Article 4.2 of the Directive, which makes provision for the assessment of Annex II projects. The applicants challenged the modification of a zoning plan which dealt with the reinforcement of dykes. They argued that the works were subject to the requirement of environmental assessment under the terms of the Directive. The projects fell within Annex II of the Directive but the modification fell below the threshold set out in the domestic legislation. The UK and Dutch Governments argued that the Annex II procedures were not sufficiently precise to have direct effect. The ECJ did not deal with the issue explicitly, as it phrased its decision in terms of the national court's ability to consider whether a Member State had exceeded the limits of its discretion as to the form and method of implementing the Directive. The ECJ held that anyone concerned with the implementation of the Directive could raise the issue of an improper use of discretion in selecting the method of transposition. Moreover, a national court is obliged to consider whether the Member State has exceeded its discretion, even if the matter is not raised by the parties.

Although this does not necessarily imply that all the Annex II procedures have direct effect, it does undermine the certainty that the whole Directive does not have direct effect as expressed in *Wychavon* and *Brown*. What is disconcerting about all of the UK decisions is the refusal of the UK courts to refer the question to the European Court under the Article 177 procedure.

Whilst there are apparently conflicting decisions it would appear as if the matter could be clarified by a reference. The decision in the *Dutch Dykes* case could, however, give national courts the opportunity to find that the national government had not exceeded its discretion in transposing the Directive. Certainly, the language used by the ECJ would be attractive to English courts, which are used to dealing with discretion in a non-interventionist fashion.

The Dutch dykes decision increases the importance of the amendments to the Directive outlined above. In particular, the introduction of formal detailed 'screening' criteria to determine whether Annex II projects should be subject to an assessment means that the limits on discretion in terms of transposition will be more restricted.

The UK courts' attitude to the direct effect doctrine and the Environmental Assessment directive is also demonstrated by the fact that in both the *Twyford* and *Wychavon* decisions the court went on to discuss its findings on the basis that the Directive had direct effect. In both cases the court expressed the view that the challenges would have been dismissed as the applicant had not suffered substantial prejudice (*Twyford*) and there was a general reluctance to exercise any discretion and grant relief.

The use of the direct effect doctrine in the UK courts has normally been on the basis that the Directive has not been fully or properly implemented in UK legislation. Notwithstanding the courts' views of these challenges, the Government has accepted that the original regulations were ineffective in implementing the Directive (see environmental assessment and permitted development below).

Is the project subject to environmental assessment?

The process of environmental assessment can be broken down into a number of discrete stages. The first stage is to determine whether or not the project falls within the criteria for the requirement of environmental assessment. The projects which should be subject to environmental assessment are listed in a variety of regulations, the main ones being the Town and Country Planning (Assessment of Environmental Effects) Regulations 1988. As mentioned above, there are developments which fall outside the control of the Town and Country Planning Acts which are dealt with in specific regulations. For the purposes of this chapter, reference will be made only to the main regulations.

The Regulations apply to the main groups of projects under what are known as schedule one projects and schedule two projects. Projects falling within schedule one of the Regulations *must* be the subject of environmental assessment, whereas projects falling within schedule two of the Regulations only require environmental assessment where there are *likely to be significant environmental effects*.

Schedule one projects: mandatory environmental assessment
As might be expected, the projects falling within schedule one of the Regulations include major infrastructure projects. For example:

— crude-oil refineries;
— thermal power stations;
— installations for the disposal of radioactive waste;
— chemical installations;
— motorways and major roads;
— trading ports;
— special waste incineration, treatment or landfill.

This list of examples for which environmental assessment is mandatory is not particularly surprising. Indeed, most of these types of projects will have been the subject of some form of environmental assessment before the introduction of the Regulations. Projects of this type have always been subject to thorough scrutiny and are usually considered at major public inquiries which involve many months of preparation and a vast range of documentation. It is fair to say that until recently the public was largely excluded from the technical debate unless they had the financial resources to instruct experts to act on their behalf. If the environmental assessment process operates satisfactorily in disseminating information in intelligible terms, then the public may be able to play a more effective role in these inquiries.

For most projects falling within schedule one, the definition of the project is self-explanatory. There are, however, in certain instances, thresholds which seek to define further the types of project to which mandatory environmental assessment applies. For instance, a thermal power station other than a nuclear power station is subject to mandatory environmental assessment only where it has a heat output of 300 megawatts or more. Where there is any degree of uncertainty over whether or not a project falls within schedule one, a ruling on the need for an assessment can be obtained from either the Secretary of State or the local planning authority (see p. 286).

Schedule two projects: discretionary environmental assessment
The projects within schedule two of the Regulations are, by and large, the types of development which are less sensitive in nature. For example:

— pig/poultry units;
— mineral extraction;
— metal processing;
— glass-making;
— food manufacture;
— holiday villages;
— knackers' yards;
— wool scouring units;
— tanneries;
— paper manufacturers.

The fact that a project falls within schedule two does not mean that environmental assessment is necessarily required. There is a requirement for environmental assessment only where such projects 'are likely to have significant effects on the environment by virtue of factors such as their nature, size or location'.

There is no statutory definition or guidance on what is meant by the phrase 'significant effects on the environment'. There is, however, guidance in the DoE Circular 15/88, which lays down three general criteria as to whether the environmental effects are likely to be 'significant':

(a)   whether the project is of more than local significance in terms of its size and physical scale;

(b)   the sensitivity of the location of the development (where it is proposed to be located in areas such as national parks, areas of outstanding natural beauty or a site of special scientific interest, the effects of the development will undoubtedly increase);

(c)   the polluting effect of the development and whether or not it is likely to give rise to complex or adverse effects.

Aside from these general criteria the Circular sets out specific indicative criteria and thresholds relative to each schedule two project. These thresholds are merely advisory and illustrative and each project is to be taken on a case-by-case basis. Experience has shown that some local planning authorities view the threshold levels as being obligatory, but there is little uniformity in the approach. Most thresholds are size related. For instance, intensive pig-rearing units will normally not require environmental assessment unless they exceed 400 sows or 5,000 fattening pigs. Other thresholds concentrate on the amount of land-take. Manufacturing plants, for example, may require environmental assessments when they exceed 30 hectares in area. There is no apparent allowance made for the cumulative effect of a number of smaller, separate proposals. Thus, the construction of two 15 hectare manufacturing plants would arguably not fall within the criteria for environmental assessment. However, for a judicial view see *R v Swale Borough Council, ex parte Royal Society for the Protection of Birds* [1991] 1 PLR 6 (p. 288).

Environmental assessment and permitted development

Although many developments which do not require planning permission are dealt with under Regulations which are separate from the main Town and Country Planning Regulations (e.g., afforestation and fish farms), there were still, however, some anomalies which enabled developments which gained automatic planning permission by virtue of the General Development Order to escape from the need to have an environmental assessment whereas in other circumstances an assessment, would be required.

Therefore, the Town and Country Planning (General Permitted Development) Order 1995 (SI 1995 No. 418) withdraws permitted development rights from developments which fall within sch. 1 of the 1988 Regulations (mandatory assessment) and for schedule 2 projects where the development is likely to have significant effects. The effect of the Regulations is to require developments with automatic permitted development rights to apply for planning permission where an environmental assessment is required.

In addition, new Regulations set down procedures to be followed where the otherwise permitted development falls within the environmental assessment regime (see the Town and Country Planning (Environmental Assessment and Permitted Development) Regulations 1995 (SI 1995 No. 417)). Where the development is normally permitted and falls within sch. 2 the developer can apply to the local planning authority for a determination as to whether an environmental assessment is required, with a right of appeal to the Secretary of State in cases of dips. Circular 3/95 sets out indicative criteria for nine classes of development which would normally be permitted but which fall within the classes of projects subject to the Regulations. These include field drainage works, reclamation of land from the sea, surface storage of fossil fuels, petroleum, natural gas and chemical products, local authority roads, the construction of harbours and marinas, long-distance aqueducts and water pipelines, waste-water treatment plants and sewage sludge lagoons.

The amendments have been made necessary as a result of pressure from the EC, which has insisted that the Environmental Assessment Directive requires the assessment of all developments listed in the Annexes regardless of the national position in relation to automatic development consent. This view has been formalised with the amendments to the Directive (see above). Although it is not expected to make a dramatic impact upon UK practice there will be a few circumstances where the ability of a planning authority to investigate the impact of a development which would otherwise have automatic permission could prove to be decisive.

In particular, it is interesting to note that the introduction of the new Regulations specifically goes against other deregulatory initiatives brought forward by the Government and, in effect, places hurdles in the way of developers which were absent previously (albeit at the urging of the EC). There is one cautionary note, however; the advice to local authorities contained in the Circular suggests that 'full, clear and precise reasons' are required before the authority can demand an environmental assessment of a development which is viewed in the Government's eyes as being suitable for automatic planning permission. Indeed, it could be argued that there would have to be a particularly serious environmental consequence for the Secretary of State to uphold a planning refusal in circumstances where it would normally receive automatic planning permission.

Pre-application procedures for establishing the need for environmental assessment

With the vagueness of the indicative criteria for schedule two projects and the uncertainty of interpreting the definition for schedule one projects, there is a number of pre-planning application procedures which establish whether or not environmental assessment is required. Many developers of major projects will need to know at an early stage of the development process whether or not an environmental assessment is required, as the potential for delay and expense is great once a planning application has been submitted.

Under reg. 5(1) of the Regulations, it is open to an applicant at any time prior to making a planning application to seek an opinion from the local planning authority as to whether or not a proposed development falls within schedule one or schedule two, and whether it exceeds thresholds or is in any other way suitable for environmental assessment. This request is made to the appropriate planning authority dealing with the application, whether it be the county authority, district authority or metropolitan authority.

When making an application for an adjudication the applicant must provide some basic minimum information about the proposal, including:

(a) a site plan;
(b) a description of the development and its nature and purpose;
(c) its possible effects on the environment.

Local planning authorities can request further information if they consider it to be necessary (reg. 5(3)). They must determine the request within three weeks or any longer period as the developer may agree. If the authority determines that environmental information is required it must give clear and precise reasons for its opinion (reg. 5(4)). All documents relating to the request, including the opinion of the local planning authority and the accompanying statement of reasons, are placed on the public register (reg. 5(5)).

If the local planning authority either fails to give an opinion within the determination period or requires the provision of environmental information before granting planning permission the developer may refer the matter to the Secretary of State for a direction (reg. 5(6)).

Pre-application directions from the Secretary of State

Where developers wish to challenge the local planning authority's determination they are required to send a copy of all the relevant documentation, including any representations made in the light of the local planning authority's opinion and statement of reasons, to the Department of the Environment. The Secretary of State will then give a direction concerning the requirement for environmental assessment within three weeks of the date of the application (reg. 6). Where the direction states that an environmental assessment is required, it must be accompanied by a statement of reasons, giving a full explanation of the Secretary of State's view (reg. 6(5)). The Secretary of State also has a residual power under reg. 3 to direct that a particular form of development is exempt from environmental assessment.

Challenges to the decisions of the Secretary of State or local planning authority

There is clearly a considerable amount of discretion over whether or not an environmental assessment is required. The courts have been given guidance on the exercise of that discretion in two cases, both of which suggest that they will seldom intervene in the decision of a determining authority. In *R* v *Swale Borough Council, ex parte Royal Society for the Protection of Birds* [1991] 1 PLR 6, Swale Borough Council granted planning permission for 'land reclamation' on an area of mud-flats near the mouth of the River Medway. This application for planning permission was to be the first stage in a proposed development of the area for further dock uses and a business park. Notwithstanding these proposals, the application for land reclamation was necessary because of dredging which was taking place in the area. No environmental assessment of the project took place. The RSPB challenged the decision to grant planning permission. One of the grounds of challenge related to the failure to carry out an environmental assessment as required by the Regulations. The RSPB argued that the application could not be viewed in isolation and was part of an integrated development strategy. As such it was either a schedule one project (i.e., a trading port), or a schedule two project with significant environmental effects. The court held that the question of whether or not the project fell within a particular schedule or class was essentially a matter of fact and degree for the determining authority. The issue as to the cumulative effect of other applications was to be dealt with strictly by looking at the nature of the project requiring permission and not any further proposals. However, in assessing the environmental effects of a schedule two project, it was possible, in Simon Brown J's view, to consider the environmental effects of a development in total even though this would mean considering more than what was being applied for. This would seem to go further than the advice laid down in Circular 15/88, which states: 'The individual developer can be asked to provide an environmental statement only in respect of the particular development he proposes'.

The point may well be academic when considering that the main thrust of the decision concerned the discretionary nature of the decision to request an environmental assessment. It does not come as any great surprise that the court was willing to intervene only when the decision was unreasonable in the *Wednesbury* sense. To that extent, it would be open to a local planning authority to request an environmental assessment where the project fell within the class in schedule one or schedule two, but was under the threshold levels, when the environmental effects of the development could not be viewed in isolation. This would not be the case, however, where a number of separate developments which fell outside the Regulations amounted cumulatively to a single development which was above the threshold criteria and would have significant environmental effects.

In *R* v *Poole Borough Council, ex parte Beebee* [1991] JPL 643, Poole Borough Council granted itself planning permission without considering whether or not an environmental assessment was required. Schiemann J took the view that the purpose of an environmental assessment was to draw to the attention of the decision-maker any relevant information which would assist in reaching a decision. On the facts, he thought that the local planning authority had all the relevant information before it and that an environmental statement would have been superfluous. All the information which might have been gleaned from a formal environmental statement had already emerged and ensured that the council had not arrived at an irrational decision.

As the purpose of environmental assessment is to produce a *systematic* approach to the consideration of environmental effects using best practicable techniques and best available sources of information, it is bold to assert that the local planning authority had all the information that would have been contained in an environmental assessment before the assessment itself has been carried out. Indeed, the transcript of the case suggests that the officers' reports to the decision-making committee had a number of omissions, which would imply that there were deficiencies in the local authority's decision.

Other procedures for determining the need for environmental assessment

Although the pre-application procedure will be utilised in most cases, where there is uncertainty over the requirement for an environmental assessment there is a number of alternative methods which can be used.

First, it is open to a developer to volunteer an environmental statement and to state expressly that the document is to be viewed as being an environmental statement for the purposes of the Regulations. This in turn means that the local planning authority has to carry out the other information-gathering exercises for the environmental assessment process. This has led to the growth in the submission of quasi-environmental statements. These documents contain the information which would normally be contained within an environmental statement, but are not submitted as formal statements for the purposes of the Regulations. In such circumstances, if there is any doubt as to the need for environmental assessment the local planning authority can gather the information from one source (i.e., the developer), but is not obliged to go through the whole environmental assessment exercise. One of the consequences of this approach has been that there is a tendency to concentrate on the subjectivity of the developer's assessment of the environmental effects. Thus, the whole purpose and concept of the environmental assessment can be undermined unless this quasi-assessment is carried out thoroughly.

If an environmental statement is submitted and it is not referred to as a statement for the purposes of the Regulations, the local planning authority should consider whether a formal environmental assessment should be undertaken. If it decides that it should be carried out, the statement can be considered as the environmental statement for the purposes of the Regulations. If the authority takes the view that environmental assessment is not required, it is still required to take the information into account when deciding the planning application.

Post-planning application determinations on the need for environmental assessment
Where a planning application has been submitted without an environmental statement the local planning authority should consider whether the application falls within one of the schedules to the Regulations. Additionally, it

should check to see if the Secretary of State has made any directions, or if the authority itself has made any prior determinations on the relevant project.

Where the local planning authority considers that the project falls within one of the schedules, it must inform the applicant within three weeks of the need for an environmental statement to accompany the planning application, giving its full reasons for doing so. Thereafter, the applicant can either ask the Secretary of State for a direction within three weeks, or supply the environmental statement. Failure to do so would mean that the application could not be decided until a statement had been submitted, unless the local planning authority was minded to refuse the application.

Appeals and called-in applications

There is even scope for the Secretary of State to request an environmental statement after he has called in an application or it has gone to appeal. Where there is a direction that an environmental assessment is required, the Secretary of State or an inspector cannot grant planning permission on appeal or after a call-in unless the environmental statement is submitted.

The environmental statement

The main component of any environmental assessment is the environmental statement. The prohibition governing the undertaking of environmental assessment is that planning permission cannot be granted for a project falling within the schedules without the developer submitting an environmental statement. There may, of course, be any number of reasons why a local planning authority might refuse an application on grounds other than the environmental effects of the project, but it would be necessary before granting planning permission to consider information contained within the environmental statement.

There is no statutory provision as to the form of an environmental statement, but it must contain the information contained in schedule three of the Regulations, which reflects Arts. 3 and 5 of Annex III of the Directive. This 'specified information' includes:

(a)   a description of the proposed development, including:

    (i)   the site,
    (ii)   the design,
    (iii) the size and scale of the development;

(b)   the data necessary to identify and assess the main effects which that development is likely to have on the environment;

(c)   a description and assessment of the likely significant effects, direct or indirect, by reference to:

    (i)   human beings, fauna and flora,
    (ii)   soil, water, air, climate and landscape,

(iii) the interaction between these factors,
(iv) material assets and the cultural heritage;

(d) where significant adverse effects are identified, a description of the measures envisaged to avoid, reduce or remedy those effects.

Furthermore, an environmental statement *may* be supported by further information which can amplify or explain any of the specified information. This includes:

(a) the physical characteristics of the proposed development, and the land use requirements;
(b) the main characteristics of the production processes proposed;
(c) the estimated type and quantity of expected emissions resulting from the operation of the proposed development;
(d) the main alternatives studied by the applicant;
(e) the likely significant direct and indirect effects on the environment resulting from:

(i) use of natural resources,
(ii) the emission of pollutants, the creation of nuiances, and the elimination of waste.

The environmental statement should also have a non-technical summary of the information to enable non-experts to understand its findings.

When considering the types of information to be included in the environmental statement it is important that the project is viewed as having two distinct phases — the construction (and commissioning) phase and the operational phase. Clearly the effects of construction may be different from the long-term operational effects.

The Department of the Environment's *Guide to Environmental Assessment* has a checklist of items for inclusion in an environmental statement, which comprises:

(a) information describing the process;
(b) information describing the site and its environment;
(c) assessment of the effects;
(d) mitigating measures and their likely effectiveness;
(e) risk of accidents.

Not all environmental statements should cover every conceivable aspect of a project's potential effects. An environmental statement should deal primarily with the main or significant effects to which a project may give rise. In many cases, the environmental statement should deal only with a few aspects in depth. It is important that there is agreement between the developer and the local planning authority as to the pertinent issues to be dealt with in an environmental statement. This requires a 'screening' and 'scoping' exercise.

Undertaking the process of environmental assessment

Alternative site selection

Although there is no absolute requirement to undertake an alternative site assessment as part of an environmental assessment, it is nevertheless important to consider the rationale behind the choice of the site in question and why alternatives were not thought to be suitable. The decision to carry out a site selection process must be based upon the applicant's assessment of the need to minimise and the possibility of mitigating the environmental impact when selecting the site for the proposed development.

Clearly, the type of development has a marked effect on the depth of search carried out. Where the proposal is for a nuclear power station there would be a significant obligation to undertake a thorough search for the best available site. This may well mean undertaking a national, or at least regional, investigation. Alternatively, if the proposal is to establish an intensive pig-rearing unit there would not be the same degree of obligation. Notwithstanding this, where a farmer managed a 10,000 acre farm there would be an expectation that the site identified for the unit would be the site giving rise to minimal environmental effects.

The site selection process should identify the basis upon which a balance has been struck between the following factors:

(a)   operational requirements;
(b)   economic constraints;
(c)   environmental effects.

Any analysis of these issues, and particularly the weight being attached to the operational economic considerations, is capable of being challenged. It is incumbent upon the developer to establish the criteria and indicate how the particular site chosen strikes an acceptable balance.

The process of identifying the site by reference to other sites is known as the macro-siting process. Once the site has been identified there is then usually a range of alternatives for micro-siting within the site itself. Environmental impacts can be mitigated by adopting the best configuration of the development within the site.

Screening

There are no strict legal rules to govern the substantive nature of the environmental assessment process but it is usual to commence with the screening of the project (i.e., determining whether the project requires an assessment and, if the project is on the margin, whether the impacts can be reduced to an extent where there is no need for a formal assessment). The amendments to the Directive should ensure that the screening process becomes much more formal, with more detailed criteria set down in the Directive, which will govern whether a project should be subject to an assessment, and a requirement that competent authorities publicise the determination on whether an assessment was required.

Scoping

Once it has been determined that a project should be the subject of an assessment it is necessary to undertake a scoping exercise. The developer holds preliminary meetings with the local planning authority and other relevant consultees in order to ascertain the scope of the environmental issues to be examined and the degree of investigation that has to be undertaken. The object of the Directive was to ensure that parties other than the developer and the local planning authority have a role to play in development process. The scoping exercise should enable the environmental assessment to acquire the objectivity which provides an accurate assessment of the environmental effects.

Although the scoping exercise will provide a common ground as to the issues raised by a development, it does not necessarily mean that all parties will agree on the acceptability of those effects. The amendments to the Directive require a formal scoping exercise to be carried out by the competent authority before the assessment can be carried out.

Consultation

In gathering information developers are not only expected to consult local planning authorities; they must also seek views from the statutory consultees and possibly non-statutory consultees.

Ordinarily, the developer will go to the local planning authority first to discuss the project. At that stage the local planning authority may wish to identify the bodies with whom consultations should be undertaken. Such consultees will often extend beyond the range of those specified in the Regulations as statutory consultees. Regulation 8 provides that the statutory consultees should include those bodies which the local planning authority is required by Art. 8 of the Town and Country Planning (General Development Procedure) Order 1995 to consult on the determination of a planning application. These include, where appropriate, the HSE, the highway authority, English Heritage, the Ministry of Agriculture, Food and Fisheries and the Environment Agency. The width of consultation depends precisely upon the type of development proposed. In addition reg. 8 provides that English Nature and the Countryside Commission should be consulted.

It is the developer's responsibility to approach the statutory consultees. Regulation 22 imposes a duty on the statutory consultees to make available, on request, any information in their possession which is relevant to the preparation of the environmental statement. This does not, however, require the public bodies to obtain information they do not have or to disclose confidential information. The consultees can levy a reasonable charge for making such information available (reg. 20).

The information which it is envisaged would be made available would include specialised information, such as the results of ecological monitoring, which would help the identification and assessment of the envoronmental effects.

Furthermore, there may be non-statutory consultees who could assist with this information. Developers can consult with these bodies where they offer some particular expertise or local insight. This type of non-statutory consultee could include such bodies as the RSPB, CPRE, local nature groups and members of the general public.

The consultation exercise (often extensive) forms the backbone of the whole environmental assessment process and produces a number of advantages. First, quite often in development projects some environmental issues are obvious. The benefit of the consultation exercise, however, is that it identifies those issues which are perhaps not so clear. Secondly, a methodical, even approach to the objective analysis of environmental impacts enables alterations to be made to a project at an early stage without great expense or inconvenience. These alterations can mitigate or eliminate adverse effects. Thirdly, where a full and adequate consultation is carried out before a planning application is submitted, the amount of time taken by the local planning authority and other consultees to consider the application when submitted will be greatly reduced. Finally, the consultation process affords the developer the opportunity of communicating with all parties who are likely to have an interest in the project. Misunderstandings can be cleared up on both sides. This then enables the developer and the local planning authority to concentrate on the relevant issues.

Determination of the planning application

The developer is responsible for the content of the environmental statement which is finally submitted. Where the local planning authority considers that the information given is insufficient to allow for proper consideration of the environmental effects of the development, further information can be requested (reg. 21). Where the process of consultation has been carried out properly this should not arise.

Once an environmental statement has been prepared and submitted together with the planning application, there are further procedural steps which closely follow the standard procedure for planning applications. The two main differences are that the determination period for the application is extended to 16 weeks (regs. 14 and 16) and there are increased publicity requirements to ensure that the planning application including the environmental statement is advertised in the local newspaper and in a site notice.

Additionally, each statutory consultee is entitled to a copy of the environmental statement free of charge, and a reasonable number of copies should be made available for sale to the public at a charge which reflects their printing and distribution costs (regs. 18 and 20).

The local planning authority then notifies the statutory consultees of the application (if this is necessary) and they have a minimum of 14 days to comment on the environmental statement.

As a result of the Town and Country Planning (Assessment of Environmental Effects) (Amendment) Regulations 1992 (SI 1992 No. 1494), these procedural requirements now apply in situations where the local planning authority is itself the applicant for planning permission.

It is not open to the local planning authority to invalidate an environmental statement because of its view of the inadequacies of the information supplied.

Should it take the view that the environmental statement is inadequate, it should use its powers to seek further information under reg. 21. Where the developer fails to provide further information and the local planning authority decides to refuse planning permission, or fails to determine the application within the 16-week period, the developer has the usual right of appeal to the Secretary of State.

Environmental assessment in simplified planning zones and enterprise zones

A separate system for environmental assessment is operated in simplified planning zones. Because of their deregulated nature there is a danger that projects which would normally require environmental assessment would not be subject to the Regulations or the Directive. By way of clarification, the DoE Circular 24/88 states that, generally, permission ought not to be given in simplified planning zones created since July 1988 for any project which should be the subject of an environmental assessment.

Schedule one projects are excluded from all simplified planning zone permissions. Where a simplified planning zone scheme purportedly grants permission for a schedule one project, authorities should include a provision expressly excluding development that falls within the definition of a project requiring mandatory environmental assessment.

There are two different approaches for schedule two projects:

(a)   Where a simplified planning zone prescribes the particular types of development permitted, the permission can be divided in such a way that it excludes projects requiring environmental assessment.

(b)   For other simplified planning zones, it will be necessary to include provisions requiring developers to establish with the planning authority that an environmental assessment is not necessary. If an environmental assessment is necessary a separate planning application will be required.

Enterprise zones designated before July 1988 are not affected by the provisions of the Directive. The vast majority of enterprise zones fall into this category. It was recognised, however, that there might be exceptional circumstances for the creation of a new enterprise zone (e.g., in Lanarkshire to compensate for the loss of Ravenscraig). This situation is to be dealt with in a similar way to simplified planning zones.

Environmental assessment in practice

Research by the Institute of Environmental Assessment (IEA) showed that 1,131 projects were the subject of environmental assessment between July 1988 and July 1992. The research suggested that the experience of environmental assessments in general had been mixed. Over 50% of local planning authorities had not received an environmental statement in that time, and over 40% had received only one. Kent County Council, on the other hand, had received 15. In the first few years since the introduction of the system both the environmental assessment process and the environmental statement in particular have been the subject of a number of criticisms.

The low quality of environmental statements
As with any new system, there has been a relatively short period to accumulate the amount of knowledge required to deal with an issue as complex as the environmental effects of a large-scale project. Although many developers have taken a framework for environmental assessment from experience gained in the United States with environmental impact assessment, the IEA found that when they reviewed a sample of environmental statements 30% of their content was graded as unsatisfactory to poor. Most of these deficiencies were to be found in the assessment of the environmental impacts of the project. There are no agreed 'standards' covering the assessment of these impacts and this has led to a wide diversity in the quality of environmental statements.

Lack of objectivity
Many environmental statements have received criticism for being statements of the developer's case in favour of their planning application. Often this is the result of the inadequacy of the scoping exercise. There is no requirement to carry out any form of scoping exercise. One survey showed that as many as 50% of local planning authorities were not consulted at the scoping stage. Thus the assessment may fail to consider material issues which should have been addressed. Where scoping does take place there is a good chance that the environmental assessment will throw up negative effects which can be mitigated. Furthermore, the scoping exercise can sometimes take the form of a general consultation where the developer tells the local planning authority of the issues which need to be addressed. Unfortunately, a combination of factors, including lack of resources, lack of central guidance and a lack of technical support, often dictates that a scoping exercise of such a 'subjective' nature cannot be widened without a contribution from the local authority.

Lack of central guidance
There is an amount of general guidance on the procedural and legal aspects of environmental assessment, but there is very little guidance on the methodology of assessing impact, or on the types of impact which any particular project might produce. The depth to which an assessment is carried out can also be critical, particularly in relation to archaeological or ecological interests. Thus, there is a danger that there will be a period where mistakes will be made and effects unassessed or not dealt with sufficiently. There is now an amount of material available from previous assessments which can demonstrate the 'dos and don'ts' of the process. These environmental statements are not freely available, although the IEA does have a library.

Lack of a consistent approach
A major criticism of the environmental assessment system to date has focused on the failure of the local planning authorities to have a consistent approach

when determining the need for environmental assessment. Research carried out on behalf of the DoE showed that 50% of local planning authorities who had not received any environmental statements had planning applications on their planning registers which were above the relevant thresholds for schedule two projects and which could have been suitable for environmental assessment. A large number of these projects were of the same type or similar in size to projects in other areas which had been the subject of environmental assessment. When questioned further the local planning authorities admitted that a principal cause for these discrepancies was their unfamiliarity with the Regulations.

Complexity of the task

One of the main concerns of the Government when introducing the Regulations was to ensure that environmental assessment did not become another bureaucratic hurdle for developers. Thus the determination period for environmental assessment projects was extended to 16 weeks. In practice, however, only about half of the planning applications were determined within the statutory period. The average period for determination has been around the 36-week mark, with almost a quarter taking over a year to decide. The delay would seem to stem from disagreement between the main parties over the scope of an environmental assessment and the alleged impacts of the development.

The case for reform?

Although the system has been the subject of criticism from both sides of the development industry, very few changes to either the law or practice of environmental assessment have taken place. One suggestion which has been put forward by a number of bodies is that there should be a formal, independent 'Council for Environmental Assessment' who would help with scoping and quality review. This suggestion was formally proposed as an unsuccessful amendment to the Planning and Compensation Bill in 1991 by Lord Nathan.

The amendments to the Environmental Assessment Directive should address some of these criticisms (see above). On a national level, in 1994, after a long wait (it was promised in 1990), the Government finally published some guidance on the quality of environmental statements. The guide sets out a set of procedures which should be followed when preparing an environmental statement. The main emphasis of the guidance is on the need to use approved methodologies for calculating impacts and to differentiate between scientific calculation of impacts and the evaluation of the significance of the impact, which is at best an informed judgment. The statement should, it is suggested, contain a method statement which should set out an explanation of the approach to carrying out the assessment, including an outline of the scoping exercise, the techniques and methods used to assess impacts and the approach taken in appraising the significance and scale of the impacts. Although concrete guidance is to be welcomed, the improvement in the quality of environmental statements is dependent upon local planning authorities and third parties evaluating draft statements and rejecting them if they are below an acceptable standard.

The next phase?: Strategic environmental assessment

At the end of 1996 a draft Directive was proposed dealing with strategic environmental assessment. Although the proposal first surfaced in 1991 it was the subject of strenuous objection from various Member States and it has been significantly altered as a result. The draft Directive applies to new or modified 'land use plans or programmes' and would include all development plans, waste local plans and minerals plans. Arguably it could also cover national strategic documents such as the strategies on waste and air quality under the Environment Act 1995.

Strategic environmental assessment operates in a similar way to project-based assessment but to broader policy-based plans. Thus there would be a requirement to prepare an environmental statement which would set out information on the assessment of the direct and indirect environmental effects of implementing the plan or programme. This would include information on:

(a)   existing environmental problems relevant to the plan including environmentally sensitive areas such as Natura 2000 sites;

(b)   the existing environmental characteristics of the area affected by the plan;

(c)   environmental obligations imposed to meet international, European, and national objectives and how the plan meets those obligations;

(d)   the significant environmental effects which would be brought about through the implementation of the plan;

(e)   alternative ways of achieving the objectives of the plan which were considered, with an explanation of why they were rejected;

(f)   any envisaged mitigating measures which are designed to reduce the significant adverse environmental impacts of implementing the plan.

Once the information was provided in an environmental statement, there would be consultation with statutory consultees and the public.

The overriding intention of the draft Directive is to simplify the procedure for assessing individual projects. Thus, developers of individual projects would be able to incorporate information from the strategic environmental assessment into the environmental statement for the project. In the case of Annex II projects the intention is that a properly conducted strategic assessment would preclude the need for an assessment of many projects as the strategic environmental statement would include sufficient information.

As in the case of the original Directive, the UK Government is likely to object to the draft on the basis that the existing system of development planning provides sufficient strategic assessment of the type of plans and programmes which would be the subject of the draft Directive.

ELEVEN
Integrated pollution control

The development of the regulatory system of pollution control has traditionally been pragmatic, reacting to environmental problems in a piecemeal
fashion. Consequently, the approach has been fragmented; specific media
have been controlled by diverse administrative and enforcement agencies.
Many examples of the reactive nature of environmental law can be seen
throughout this book. The Clean Air Act 1956, the Alkali Act 1863, and the
Deposit of Poisonous Wastes Act 1972 all related to specific problems at a
particular time which had given rise to public concern. The *ad hoc* nature of
these controls resulted in a haphazard approach characterised by legislation
with loopholes enabling offenders to avoid liability.

The end result was that by the 1970s, the British system of pollution
control was characterised by a division in the means of control; there were
separate controls for emissions into the atmosphere, environmental problems
on land, and emissions into the aqueous environment.

Pollution of the atmosphere

Traditionally, the role of environmental law was targeted towards the protection of public health. Although the secondary purpose of such controls was
that the environment was protected from harm, this was not the main
purpose of the legislation. In the 1830s standards of sanitation in the major
cities created a great deal of concern amongst those enlightened individuals
who took an interest in the poorer classes. Consequently, between the years
1840 and 1875, attempts were made to deal with the problem by the setting
up of special local boards of commissioners which were the predecessors of
today's local authorities. These boards were made responsible for the enforcement of minimal sanitation standards.

At approximately the same time, industry started to utilise new materials
and new industrial sectors were formed, such as alkali works, which produced
highly noxious and polluting chemicals as a by-product of their processes.
Even in this respect, the problem was not viewed in purely environmental

terms and the main thrust of the controls was based on technological answers to what were perceived as scientific problems. Thus the Alkali Inspectorate was created in 1863 to fulfil a technical and advisory role in the combating of pollution. However, the legislation was neither properly enforced nor did it address all the difficulties emissions into the atmosphere could cause. Consequently, although noxious fumes were controlled, there was no prohibition on the emission of smoke into the atmosphere, which brought about problems of lower-level pollution with the production of smog. Thus, although the law sought to deal with one problem another problem arose elsewhere.

As new environmental issues emerged, legislation was introduced which often resulted in separate bodies being responsible for enforcement in respect of overlapping emissions. For example, in relation to air pollution the Alkali Inspectorate dealt with noxious fumes under the Alkali etc. Works Regulation Act 1906, but local authorities were responsible for the control of smoke under the Clean Air Acts 1956 and 1968. Other bodies were created to deal with a variety of subject matters such as the control of health and safety within factories, the control of nuclear installations and the control of mines and quarries. The control of emissions to the atmosphere was pieced together by a haphazard jigsaw of administrative controls enforced by a number of different bodies. As will be seen, air pollution was not the only area of confusion. Although the aims of these statutory bodies were different, the reactive approach often meant that the mechanisms used to control individual areas of concern overlapped. This resulted in over-complicated and ineffective enforcement.

The Robens Committee was set up in the early 1970s to report on health and safety at work and to answer specifically some of the criticisms that had been levelled at the many different authorities administering different sectors. In 1972, the Committee recommended that a new unified body should be set up to deal with all aspects of health, safety and welfare at work. Traditionally, there had been some confusion as to the role of the Alkali Inspectorate and whether or not its aim was to protect the environment or to safeguard the health of workers. The Robens Committee recommended that a new Health and Safety Executive (HSE) should be established to include the Alkali Inspectorate. This was duly formed in 1974, in the first real attempt to unify a number of different inspectorates under one organisational umbrella.

Environmentalists viewed this as a retrogressive step. The HSE was a factory-based control agency and sought specifically to protect the interests of workers rather than dealing with environmental protection on a broader basis. Secondly, focusing protection on the factory environment did not necessarily take into account the many environmental difficulties suffered as a result of emissions, although other sectors were subject to statutory control through alternative mechanisms.

Pollution on land

The Control of Pollution Act 1974 created new bodies which were known as waste disposal authorities and had responsibility for the disposal of waste to land. These functions were primarily the responsibility of county authorities. Clearly, this protection was not part of the factory-based approach but, unfortunately, in practice there was little or no coordination between the HSE and those controlling waste disposal, notwithstanding that there is a connection between the production of waste in factories regulated by the HSE and the disposal of waste on sites controlled by waste disposal authorities.

Control of water pollution

Notwithstanding the separation of responsibilities for the control of pollution within factories and on land, there was a further complication with the separation of the control over emissions into water. The River Boards Act 1948 created a number of river boards to control land drainage, fisheries and the prevention of river pollution. Then, under the Water Resources Act 1963, 27 river authorities were created to take over responsibility from the river boards; they themselves were then superseded with the creation of the regional water authorities under the Water Act 1973. (See Chapter 14.)

The regional water authorities were given sole responsibility for regulating all matters concerned with water. Thus, they had control over prevention of river pollution, the supply of water, the control of sewage, water conservation, fisheries and water recreation. The Water Act 1989 attempted to overcome the inherent difficulties by separating the operational side of the authorities from the regulatory side. In dividing the poacher from the gamekeeper, a further two bodies entered the administrative jungle of environmental protection.

The administrative jungle and the mechanisms of protection

Although attempts were made by the Department of the Environment to rationalise environmental control, the plethora of enforcement agencies, including such bodies as the HSE, local authorities, the water authorities, and later the successor to the Alkali Inspectorate (the Industrial Air Pollution Inspectorate) and the waste disposal authorities, created a complicated web of fragmented control. There was no unified concept of environmental protection; a theoretical and unrealistic sectoral approach had fundamental flaws which constantly served to undermine the authority of the law.

In addition to the jungle of administrative bodies, environmental control was also hampered by the vast number of powers and procedures available to each individual enforcement agency. Where powers to control pollution were available to a number of bodies, overlapping controls often meant that a particular incident or process could be regulated by as many as four different authorities. For example, a factory which was subject to control under the Alkali etc. Works Regulation Act 1906, which produced dark smoke and discharged trade effluent into the nearby river could be controlled by the Alkali Inspectorate, the local environmental health department, and the water authority. This often created difficulties, particularly as a particular problem could be approached by each different enforcement body using different enforcement powers. In many cases there were elements of 'too many cooks spoiling the broth'.

The controls available to each enforcement agency also varied tremendously. The traditional basis for environmental pollution control has always been seen as discretionary and technical in a scientific sense. Historically, the main basis of this control has been by the operation of the principle of 'best practicable means' (BPM). This principle was first applied in 1842 in an attempt to control smoke nuisances in Leeds, and was further utilised in the Alkali Acts to control *all* noxious emissions from alkali works by 1874. The concept of BPM has since formed the basis of emission control for all media. Although explicit in the Alkali Acts and other statutes (e.g., the Public Health Act 1936 in relation to statutory nuisances) the *principle* of BPM governed other areas of control implicitly. Even where no statutory reference to the phrase could be found, consideration was given to BPM to guide standard-setting and enforcement.

The phrase 'best practicable means' incorporates both a scientific approach ('means') and a discretionary approach ('best' and 'practicable'). There were three main aims of the BPM legislation. First, there was a prohibition on any emission which could constitute a recognised health hazard. Secondly, emissions had to be reduced to the lowest level, always balancing that requirement with local conditions and circumstances, the current state of pollution control technology, the effects of the substances emitted, the financial effect upon a company using such equipment and the means that were to be used to control the emissions. Thirdly, where there were harmful emissions, the aim was that such emissions should be, so far as possible, diluted and dispersed.

The statutory guidance as to what constituted BPM was sparse so as not to fetter the discretion of the regulatory bodies. Certain guidelines were contained within the various statutory controls (e.g., the Control of Pollution Act 1974, s. 72), but effectively, the concept utilised a presumptive control mechanism. Thus, where the individualised emission levels were complied with, it was presumed that there were no better practicable means in controlling emissions. In practice, the Alkali Inspectorate used the concept of BPM to balance any cost implications with the statutory objective of controlling noxious or offensive gases. The 1981 report of the Alkali Inspectorate put it thus:

The expression 'BPM' takes into account economics and all of its financial implications and we interpret this not just in the narrow sense of a works dipping into its own pocket, but including the wider effect on the community. In the long run it is not the owners of the works who pay for clean air but the public, and it is our duty to see that money is wisely spent on the public's behalf. The country's industries and world's current financial situation have to be weighed against the benefits for which we strive and careful thought has to be given to decisions which could seriously impair competitiveness in the national and international markets. Never do we lose sight of our ultimate goal — that all scheduled works should operate harmlessly and inoffensively and that this state shall be attained at the earliest possible moment.

Notwithstanding this 'ultimate goal' there was no clearly defined environmental quality standard. The use of presumptive standards contained in guidance notes issued on a year to year basis attempted to impose some limits on emissions to the atmosphere. It was clear, however, that these limits were to be applied flexibly and on an individualised basis to ensure that in each particular case the emission controls were 'practicable'.

The flexibility that BPM gave to the Inspectorate meant that there could be a co-operative rather than a confrontational approach to industry. It was only when all the possible avenues of co-operation had been exhausted that breaches of the presumptive standards would result in enforcement action (for some possible explanations of this, see Chapter 6).

Although not explicit within the water industry, similar considerations applied to the control of emissions into water. However, there was one distinguishing feature. EC environmental policy sought to introduce into the legislation of Member States the concept of water quality standards or objectives. These directives covered such areas as the quality of drinking water, bathing waters, and the quality of groundwater. Previously there had been no legally binding limits, although both the National Water Council and the Secretary of State had fulfilled secondary roles in setting administrative standards of quality. In order to implement Directives (e.g., 80/778 and 75/440 on Drinking Water and Surface Water for Drinking), the water authorities utilised their powers in setting limits for emission levels on discharge consents. There was still a certain amount of balancing required between the financial implications of the cost of pollution abatement equipment and the requirement to bring water quality up to certain standards.

Overall, as Britain entered the 1980s, there was a fragmented, individualised, sectoral approach which did not reflect the growing trend within Europe for an integrated approach to the environment with specific quality objectives. As the move to make a fundamental change from the 'British approach' gathered pace, the consequences of the traditional basis of pollution control became clear.

Consequences of the fragmented approach

(a)   Failure to view the environment as a whole
One of the main concerns of those who criticised the sectoral approach to pollution control in Britain was that there was a failure to deal with the environment as a whole. Each individual medium was seen as a separate area of control and no consideration was given to the possible consequences of imposing control on one sector in relation to others. For instance, where strict controls were placed upon the levels of effluent discharge into water, a simple alteration to the production process may shift the effluent to another sector, such as by incineration (air) or landfill.

The environment as a concept is a series of interdependent sectors. When individual bodies controlled separate sectors there was often a reluctance to deal with a problem on a unified basis. Administratively, the idea of two separate bodies with overlapping responsibilities created tremendous logistical difficulties, misunderstandings arose, inter-departmental communication had its own problems, which led to inefficient control.

(b) The discretionary decision-making process
The different regulatory bodies possessed wide discretionary powers with which to enforce their statutory duties. Too much discretion led to uncertainty. Certain bodies took a more rigorous view of enforcement whereas others were content to pursue a conciliatory approach. When a number of statutory bodies controlled the same process, the use of these different criteria led to an imbalance in the protection of the environment as a whole. Where an enforcement body showed a tendency to pursue rigorous levels of enforcement, emissions in that sector were kept at an artificially low level. However, this was often counterbalanced by an increase of emission levels to another medium in relation to which the alternative enforcement bodies exercised their discretion leniently.

(c) The development of a co-operational approach to enforcement
The lack of definitive standards in many areas saw the development of the co-operative approach by many enforcement agencies. It has been argued in favour of such an approach that compliance with standards has resulted rather than producing a wholesale enforcement holiday. However, other consequences have also been identified (see Chapter 6).

(d) Overlapping controls
One of the consequences of failing to deal with the environment as a whole was that each individual enforcement agency had a prescribed area of responsibility. Where, however, there were overlaps in that responsibility, an uncoordinated approach brought about ineffective enforcement of the regulations in question.

For example, where there was a spillage of a hazardous substance within a factory site there could have been as many as five different agencies who could have taken individual action against the company involved. If the substance found its way into a water-course the water authority could take action. Where there was a statutory nuisance arising from smells and fumes, the local environmental health officer could take action. If the substance came within the COSHH Regulations, the Factory Inspectorate could have taken action. The water services company could have also prosecuted for the breach of a discharge consent into sewers, the National Rivers Authority could have prosecuted for pollution of controlled waters and the Fire Service could have taken action for the breach of any storage licence conditions. Where such complex administrative mechanisms are required to cope with a simple single incident there is a chance that the proper mechanism is not utilised. The nature of the bureaucratic system of control was such that where administrative controls overlap, any failure of communication between the enforcement agencies rendered proper enforcement more difficult.

(e) Lack of public accountability

Lastly, where there were so many enforcement agencies, there was often a problem with a lack of public accountability. The trained professional could have difficulty in ascertaining which body is responsible for a particular activity. The person in the street had very little chance of knowing who to turn to. Normally, the local environmental health officer was the first person to receive complaints, not necessarily because the local authority was the proper controlling body for a particular process, but because the public identified the environmental health department of a local authority as being the 'right place' to which to complain. Other more obscure agencies were not fully recognised by members of the public. Where there was such uncertainty then the accountability of these bodies was also obscured. For an administrative and bureaucratic system to work effectively, the public needed to recognise who controls what and how they did so.

Time for a change

The consequences of this fragmented approach were recognised when, in an attempt to address them, the Secretary of State for the Environment asked the Royal Commission on Environmental Pollution in their Fifth Report in 1976 to 'review the efficacy of the methods of the control of air pollution from domestic and industrial sources and to consider the relation between relevant authorities'. After receiving many representations, the Royal Commission identified many of the problems which have already been outlined above. They pointed out specifically that, by treating the disposal of waste to air, land and water as three separate issues, there was a danger that the 'allocation of available resources to each of the media will not reflect an overall view of where the problems are most severe' and also that such an approach would result in the 'haphazard disposal' of emissions to one particular sector without taking into account which of the media a particular pollutant would be best disposed into. As a background to the considerations of the Commission, the proposals of the Robens Committee were being implemented and thus, instead of taking a unified approach to the environment, there was a move away from environmental protection to a more factory-based approach with the creation of the HSE.

Before attempting to deal with the procedural aspects of a unified environmental protection system, there had to be an administrative body in place which could effectively use the powers given to it. Thus, the Commission proposed two changes. First, the Commission recommended that there should be a single unified body to ensure that any regulatory system imposed could be enforced effectively and the full environmental consequences of an operation could be assessed. Secondly, in order to assess the full environmental effect of a process rather than just assessing its impact in terms of different media, it recommended that the new concept of the 'best practicable environmental option' be utilised.

Best practicable environmental option

The concept of 'best practicable environmental option' (BPEO) was intended to adopt some of the more positive benefits of the previous BPM tests whilst maintaining some environmental utility. First, the test allowed the enforcement agency to set emission standards relating to specific prescribed substances and specific prescribed processes. Secondly, they acknowledged that the scientific and technical background that a properly trained Inspectorate could bring to the system of control would provide a technological advantage and would imply that any enforcement agency was seen as more than merely an environmental police force, but also as an adviser/consultant. The concept of BPEO sought to keep the more legalistic standard-setting idea, whilst maintaining the scientific and technological approach to pollution abatement.

The basis of BPEO was in part an extension of the BPM concept but it introduced consideration of the environment as a whole when setting emission standards for industrial processes. In 1988, in their Twelfth Report, the Commission suggested a definition for BPEO as being:

> . . . the outcome of a systematic consultative and decision-making procedure which emphasises the protection of the environment across land, air and water. The BPEO procedure establishes, for a given set of objectives, the option that provides the most benefit or least damage to the environment as a whole, at acceptable cost, in the long as well as the short term.

Thus, although the BPEO concept was considered to be an extension of the BPM test it was much more than that. It was to form the *philosophical basis* for a more practical test.

These recommendations were ignored by Central Government for some time, mainly for political reasons. In 1982, the Department of the Environment's Pollution Paper No. 18 investigated the role of a unified administrative body without taking specific action. However in 1983, William Waldegrave, a new Minister in the Department of the Environment, pressed for a unified agency to implement the Royal Commission's recommendation. Tim O'Riordan and Albert Weale ([1989] PA 277) point out a number of motivating factors for this sudden re-emergence. Amongst the factors identified was the need to implement the idea of BPEO. In the period since their Fifth Report the Royal Commission had not kept quiet about the concept. In particular, the Tenth Report, *Tackling Pollution — Experiences and Prospects,* was particularly scathing in its criticism of Government inaction. However, with the administrative set-up in the 1980s there was no one regulatory body to oversee the new system. The weaknesses of the fragmented, reactive approach finally received official recognition. Mr Waldegrave told the House of Lords Select Committee on the European Communities:

> I have been struck by how often we appear to be dealing with subjects not really on the basis of an objective assessment of environmental priorities but as a result of the changing fashions in pressure from outside.

The difficulties of quasi-governmental organisations being influenced by party political pressures tended to detract from the main priority of environmental protection. Thus, a feeling grew in the Conservative Government and elsewhere that a free-standing body was necessary.

The EC's role in change

At about the same time as the Fifth Report of the Royal Commission on Environmental Pollution, the EC was formally adopting its First Action Programme for the environment. The approach for this Action Programme was fundamentally different to that of Britain as it adopted a continental approach which contained few elements of British tradition. The continental approach was to take a proactive rather than a reactive stance. Thus, its driving principle was one of anticipation of environmental pollution problems rather than trying to deal with problems as they arose on a piecemeal basis.

From the date of implementation of the First Action Programme, a number of Directives were introduced which emphasised these differences in approach. Directive 76/464 on Pollution caused by Dangerous Substances Discharged into the Aquatic Environment was introduced to eliminate or reduce the pollution of water by dangerous substances. This was to be implemented by means of emission standards on authorisations to sewers and controlled waters. Similar Directives were later introduced for Air Pollution (84/360) and Emissions from Large Combustion Plants (86/609).

Increasingly, the flexibility of standard-setting in Britain did not reflect this move towards European-style emission standards defined with reference to 'permissible maximum concentrations of substances' and 'quality objectives'. Other countries within the EC were already developing new and different ideas.

Vorsorgeprinzip: anticipation through foresight

In the 1970s, as environmental issues started to percolate through the political systems of the Member States of the EC, the methodology of pollution control in other Member States was starting to develop significantly. In West Germany, for instance, environmental control evolved around the somewhat different mechanism of the *Vorsorgeprinzip*. This was a stated principle which was to be adhered to when considering the environmental impact of a process and which operated on two bases: first, that the environment should be able to restore itself notwithstanding the effect of industrial activity, and secondly, that environmental controls on emission standards should be set as high as they could, taking into account available technology. These two bases work in tandem to create an overall scheme which takes into account available technology but does not sacrifice environmental quality by putting standards at the margins of environmental deterioration. However, even with the *Vorsorgeprinzip* there was also some need to take into account an economic factor. Thus, the principle of proportionality, which takes into account the balance between the environmental improvement achieved and the cost needed to attain that improvement, was also a factor.

The natural consequence of this three-pronged approach was translated into EC policy in the Directive on Atmospheric Emissions from Industrial Plants (84/360). This required that 'all appropriate preventive measures against air pollution be taken, including the application of best available technology, provided that the application of such measures does not entail excessive cost'. The introduction of this new system — 'the best available technology not entailing excessive cost' or BATNEEC — was to play an important part in the development of an integrated pollution control system in Britain.

Some saw this new principle as being not very far removed from the old principle of BPM, but the method of its utilisation within the British legislation, when coupled with environmental quality objectives, ensured that there was to be a fundamental restructuring of pollution control within Britain.

HMIP: a unified body

Although the Royal Commission on Environmental Pollution made strong recommendations that a unified body be created to deal with environmental problems, this was specifically rejected by the Government of the day and ignored for approximately 10 years until its Tenth Report raised the issue again when considering the concept of BPEO. Whilst considering the *Vorsorgeprinzip* from Germany and the concept of BPEO, the Commission accepted the benefits of such a system, but pointed out that for BPEO to operate effectively it would require a single agency to deal with the day-to-day regulation of environmental matters.

Finally, after an investigation of the efficiency of the Health and Safety Executive, a recommendation was made to create a unified Inspectorate which could not only overcome some of the historical problems surrounding environmental protection but also implement the new system of integrated pollution control.

The Environment Agency and IPC

Although the EPA 1990 attempted to deal with the problems of a diverse range of agencies, some difficulties were still experienced at the boundaries of each agency's controls. In order to deal with some of the obvious areas of overlap a memorandum of understanding was agreed between HMIP and the NRA to cover situations where there were overlapping responsibilities. In the field of waste management, HMIP acted in a technical and advisory capacity, with the regulation of the final disposal of waste on land remaining with local authorities.

The introduction of the Environment Agency is, in one sense therefore, the logical conclusion of the move towards an integrated system of control over pollution. Initially, administrative integration is perhaps the most significant challenge, but there are still a number of legal anomalies which need to be dealt with. For example there is a wider range of enforcement powers available to deal with IPC processes than discharge consents. In time, however, the assimilation of all the powers which were available to the old enforcement agencies should see more consistency in both decision-making and enforcement.

The introduction of integrated pollution control

Any new system of control needed to take into account the requirements of assessing the environment as a whole. With a new administrative agency, Her Majesty's Inspectorate of Pollution, ready to deal with an integrated approach, all that was required was the setting up of the legislation to break down the boundaries between the different sectors. Many of the elements of the new system of integrated pollution control contained some similarity to previous environmental legislation (e.g., the Health and Safety at Work etc. Act 1974 and the Alkali etc. Works Regulation Act 1906). However, there were a number of new concepts which were introduced to enable Britain to fulfil its obligations under the EEC Treaty and also to take a proactive approach to environmental protection.

Thus, the EPA 1990 introduced a system of integrated pollution control (IPC) to improve the regulation of pollution control arising from industrial processes. Part I of the Act establishes two separate systems: first, IPC controlled by the Environment Agency; and secondly, air pollution control (APC) controlled by the local authorities (see Chapter 12). Both systems contain the same principal mechanisms, but differ in two aspects. IPC controls the more polluting processes and is intended to prevent or minimise pollution of any environmental medium, whereas APC solely controls atmospheric releases from the less polluting processes.

The system of integrated pollution control works on the principle that to carry out a scheduled process without an authorisation from the EA is a criminal offence. Secondly, when granting an authorisation, various statutory objectives are required to be met before such an authorisation can be granted. Lastly, the scope of control is wide. When assessing an application for an authorisation in relation to the more polluting (and potentially more damaging) processes, account has to be taken of emissions to all three media when calculating the effect of a process upon the environment as a whole.

Organisation and administration of the system of integrated pollution control

The legislation controlling integrated pollution control is contained in Part I of the EPA 1990. The EPA 1990 is something of a lawyers' paradise in that it is only a framework which requires regulations to be passed to fill out various areas of the primary legislation. The reasons for this have more to do with the need for flexibility in controlling environmental matters than any desire to avoid responsibility within the main Act. It is possible to pass new regulations quickly and this allows for new research into environmental problems to be taken into account when assessing what particular matters ought to fall under the control of the framework legislation. The power to make regulations has been used to amend the scope of control significantly on a number of occasions since the implementation of the EPA 1990.

Thus, the EPA 1990 itself forms only a small part of the controlling legislation. There are further statutory controls under the Environmental Protection (Prescribed Processes and Substances) Regulations 1991 (SI 1991 No. 472 as amended), the Environmental Protection (Applications, Appeals and Registers) Regulations 1991 (SI 1991 No. 507) and the Environmental Protection (Authorisation of Processes) (Determination Periods) Order 1991 (SI 1991 No. 513). Furthermore, there is a system of guidance notes issued by the EA, providing detailed guidance processes which are covered under the regime.

The system of integrated pollution control is administered centrally by the EA (SEPA in Scotland) (EPA 1990, s. 4(2)). It is referred to in the Act as 'the enforcing authority'. A similar system, which relates solely to the control of emissions into the atmosphere from less polluting processes, is controlled by local authorities under the air pollution control regime (SEPA also has control over these processes in Scotland) (see Chapter 12).

The Department of the Environment has stated that the main objectives of integrated pollution control (IPC) are twofold:

(a)   to prevent or minimise the release of prescribed substances and to render harmless any such substances which are released;

(b)   to develop an approach to pollution control that considers discharges from industrial processes to all media in the context of the effect on the environment as a whole.

Additionally, the system aims to improve the administrative structure of pollution control by clarifying the functions and responsibilities of the EA in relation to the most polluting industrial processes and other statutory bodies and by providing 'one-stop shopping' for those processes. It is also hoped that the system will improve public accountability by making the relevant enforcement body easily indentifiable, removing doubts as to who is doing what, and by making it possible to obtain information quickly and simply. Finally, it is hoped that the system will allow a certain degree of flexibility in allowing alterations to be made to the scientific methods of abatement where new information is received, both in respect of abatement technology and in respect of the effect of pollutants. Account can also be taken of new emission standards, whether imposed by the EC or on a more international scale (EPA 1990, s. 7).

Role of the Secretary of State

The Secretary of State has a central role in the IPC system in prescribing the processes and substances which are controlled under the system (see below). In addition the Secretary of State has a range of other functions including:

(a) *Standard setting*. Section 3 of the EPA 1990 gives the Secretary of State power to establish a variety of standards for such things as emission limits, environmental quality objectives for individual media and the measurement or analysis of prescribed substances.

(b) *National plans*. The Secretary of State has the power to make plans to establish overall emission limits for the UK as a whole (or any part of the UK) (s. 3(5)). This power has been exercised in relation to the UK Programme and National Plan for Reducing Emissions of SO_2 and NO_x. This plan was introduced in order to implement the Large Combustion Plants Directive 88/609 (as amended). The plan sets annual targets for SO_2 and NO_x emissions from power stations, refineries and other heavy industry and is implemented through individual authorisations.

(c) *Issuing directions*. There is a range of powers which enable the Secretary of State to issue directions to the EA and local authorities (in the case of LAAPC). These directions could cover the exercise of enforcement powers, the inclusion of specific conditions in any authorisations, the transfer of responsibility for an individual process from a local authority to the EA and the removal of information from a public register. By mid 1996 nearly 50 directions had been given.

(d) *Appeals*. In addition to making regulations governing the appeals system, the Secretary of State has the power to determine appeals or direct that appeals be determined by an inspector.

The requirement for authorisation

The IPC system applies to any process carried out in England and Wales which has been prescribed as being subject to such control by the Secretary of State (EPA 1990, s. 2(1)). The Secretary of State has exercised this power under the Environmental Protection (Prescribed Processes and Substances) Regulations 1991 (SI 1991 No. 472). These Regulations include a list of processes and substances which are controlled either under the IPC system or the air pollution control system. Accordingly the regulations split processes and substances into two parts, Part A and Part B. Part A processes are prescribed for IPC. Part B processes are prescribed for local authority air pollution control (APC) which, although governed by similar principles, has different detailed guidance (see Chapter 12).

Approximately 2,000 installations are regulated in respect of solid, liquid and gaseous wastes under IPC, whereas roughly 12,500 are subject to control purely in respect of the emissions to the atmosphere by local authority environmental health departments. Whether a process is controlled under the system depends on whether it is a process contained in the schedule of prescribed processes in addition to whether or not it is likely to release certain prescribed substances into specified media.

Determination of the need for an authorisation

Unlike the Town and Country Planning Act, there is no formal mechanism for determining whether or not a process falls within the terms of the

Regulations. Furthermore, there is no discretion as to whether or not the EA can extend the categories in the Regulations to include extraordinary processes. Therefore, where there is uncertainty, the only mechanism for clarifying the position is to apply for a declaration in the High Court. In certain instances the Regulations which define prescribed processes and substances have been extended (see the Environmental Protection (Prescribed Processes and Substances) (Amendment) Regulations 1992 (SI 1992 No. 614)). Other difficulties of interpretation are dealt with in specific IPC Notes and General Guidance Notes issued by the DoE and the EA.

Clearly, one of the main difficulties with seeking to avoid making an application for a prescribed process which does not fall within any definition as specified in the Regulations is that there is a risk of prosecution. For most operators that risk will be too great and it will be more appropriate to agree with the EA the scope of the description of the process.

Prescribed processes

Schedule 1 to the Regulations contains a list of the prescribed processes. This list is split into six main chapters outlining various areas of industry. These areas are:

(a) the fuel and power industry;
(b) the chemical industry;
(c) the minerals industry;
(d) the metal industry;
(e) the waste disposal industry; and
(f) miscellaneous industry.

Within these six different headings the processes are further split into those processes likely to cause greater pollution, contained in Part A, and those more suitable for Part B control. Each individual industry grouping also has subsections.

Fuel and power industry
Gasification processes, carbonisation processes, combustion processes and petroleum processes.

Chemical industry
Petrochemical processes, organic processes, chemical pesticide processes, pharmaceutical processes, acid manufacturing processes, halogen processes, chemical fertilizer processes, bulk chemical storage processes and inorganic chemical processes.

Minerals industry
Cement processes, asbestos processes, fibre processes and ceramic processes.

Metal industry
Iron and steel processes, smelting processes and non-ferrous processes.

Waste disposal industry
Incineration processes, chemical recovery processes and waste-derived fuel processes.

Miscellaneous industry
Paper manufacturing processes, di-isocyanate processes, tar and bitumen processes, uranium processes, coating processes, coating manufacturing processes, timber processes, animal and plant treatment processes.

All in all, approximately 105 processes covering some 2,000 different installations are covered under Part A of the Regulations. Essentially, the list of processes extends the previous list regulated under the Health and Safety at Work etc. Act 1974 by including processes which give rise to significant quantities of special waste and processes which give rise to the emission into sewers or controlled waters of Red List substances, which have a particularly damaging effect on the environment.

Meaning of process

Industrial processes are often made up of many individual component parts but, in terms of the integrated pollution control system, a process is defined in relation to the operator and the location. So, where there are a number of processes falling within the same class in sch. 1, only one authorisation will be required if there is only one person operating the process. Where there is an overlap between the control of Part A processes and Part B processes, then the Part A processes will take precedence. Thus, where a small element of the process is subject to APC and one element is subject to IPC, the EA will govern the whole of the process and only one authorisation will be required. Where the processes fall into different categories under sch. 1, different authorisations will be required. Thus, a process involving bulk chemical storage and chemical recovery requires two authorisations. However, it could be possible for one process to fall within Part A whilst another process is within Part B of a different class. In that particular situation, responsibility for each process would fall to different controlling authorities.

The authorisations themselves cover all operations relating to the main process itself. Therefore, where the production of waste from the main operation is incidental to the overall operation of a plant, that would not necessarily fall within the waste disposal class under sch. 1.

The Government has amended the detailed provisions on the scope of Part A and B processes as part of the deregulatory thrust. In the first set of amendments set down in 1994, eight processes were brought within control for the first time, whilst a number were 'demoted' from IPC to LAAPC. Perhaps the most significant change, however, was the alteration of some of the thresholds which took certain processes outside control (see p. 357). Further amendments to the regulations were proposed in June 1995, with deregulation being the aim yet again. In particular the definition of the 'triviality' exemption (see p. 315) in relation to specific levels of releases will exclude many processes in the pulp and paper and leather industries.

Release of prescribed substances

Alongside the regulations controlling individual processes there are also controls over the release of prescribed substances. Often, the release of prescribed substances will be an integral part of the process controlled. However, specific obligations fall upon operators to deal with the listed substances in a particular way. Schedules 4, 5 and 6 to the Regulations lay down those substances which are controlled in this way.

Schedule 4: Releases into the air
The substances listed under sch. 4 are subject to control not only under IPC but also under APC. They are:

Oxides of sulphur and other sulphur compounds.
Oxides of nitrogen and other nitrogen compounds.
Oxides of carbon.
Organic compounds and partial oxidation products.
Metals, metalloids and their compounds.
Asbestos (suspended particulate matter and fibres), glass fibres and mineral fibres.
Halogens and their compounds.
Phosphorus and its compounds.
Particulate matter.

Schedule 5: Releases into water
This list reflects the Red List, which governs the input of substances which are a danger. The following are listed:

Mercury and its compounds.
Cadmium and its compounds.
All isomers of hexachlorocyclohexane.
All isomers of DDT.
Pentachlorophenol and its compounds.
Hexachlorobenzene.
Hexachlorobutadiene.
Aldrin.
Dieldrin.
Endrin.
Polychlorinated biphenyls (PCBs).
Dichlorvos.
1, 2-Dichloroethane.
All isomers of trichlorobenzene.
Atrazine.
Simazine.
Tributyltin.
Triphenyltin.
Trifluralin.

Fenitrothion.
Azinphos-methyl.
Malathion.
Endosulfan.

Schedule 6: Releases to land
The following substances are listed in sch. 6:

Organic solvents.
Azides.
Halogens and their covalent compounds.
Metal carbonyls.
Organo metallic compounds.
Oxidising agents.
Polychlorinated dibenzofuran and any congener thereof.
Polychlorinated dibenzo-p-dioxin and any other congener thereof.
Polyhalogenated biphenyls, terphenyls and naphthalenes.
Phosphorus.
Pesticides.
Alkali metals and their oxides and alkaline earth materials and their oxides.

Exceptions

As in many similar environmental control regulations there are exceptions to the general rule that processes in Part A are to be controlled under the IPC system. Regulation 4 and sch. 2 give a list of criteria for exemptions. A process is exempted if:

(a) it cannot result in emissions to air of a substance contained in sch. 4 or, if there are such emissions, the release of those substances to cause any harm as it is in such trivial amounts;
(b) it cannot result in any discharges to water of any substance listed in sch. 5 beyond background concentration;
(c) it cannot result in any substance listed in sch. 6 being released into land, or if such substances are released they are released in such trivial amounts that the release cannot do any harm.

There is no statutory definition of the term 'trivial', although the thresholds set down in the process regulations can specify concentrations which are to be regarded as 'trivial'. The burden of proving that the release is trivial lies, in effect, with the applicant as the burden of demonstrating that an exception applies in any subsequent prosecution lies with the operator (see *Tandridge District Council* v *P & S Civil Engineering Ltd* [1995] Env LR 67).
Other processes excluded include those carried out in:

(a) working museums demonstrating an industrial process of historic interest, or a school (reg. 4(3));

(b)   certain engines powering aircraft, ships, trains and cars (reg. 4(4));
(c)   those processes carried out as domestic activities in connection with private dwelling.

Notwithstanding these exceptions, if the process gives rise to an offensive smell noticeable outside the premises where the process is carried on then it will be subject to control under Part I.

Overlapping controls

The deposit of controlled waste

Section 28(1) of the EPA 1990 provides that no condition may be attached to an authorisation which regulates the final disposal by deposit in or on land of controlled waste. There is a greater degree of uncertainty, however, over the overlapping responsibilities where waste is treated or kept. The Secretary of State has the power to draw up regulations excluding the deposit, treatment or keeping of waste from the need for a waste management licence under Part II of the Act (s. 33(3)). Under the Waste Management Licensing Regulations 1994 (SI 1994 No. 1056), two main categories of processes are excluded from the waste management regime. Regulation 16(1)(a) excludes any recovery or disposal of waste where it forms part of an IPC process (although s. 28(1) still applies to the final deposit of waste). In addition, reg. 16(1)(b) excludes waste incineration which falls within LAAPC. This exclusion applies only to the parts of the process which are controlled under LAAPC (i.e., the release of prescribed substances to the atmosphere) and does not cover other aspects of the process (including storage and handling of waste).

The pollution of controlled waters

The creation of the Environment Agency has seen the end of an artificial separation of functions between the NRA and HMIP. Under s. 28 of the EPA (1990) (since repealed) there was provision for consultation between the two agencies which is no longer necessary. Section 88 of the Water Resources Act 1991 provides that any discharges made in accordance with an authorisation under Part I of the EPA 1990 would not be an offence under s. 85 (pollution of controlled waters).

Discharge of trade effluent into sewers

The discharge of trade effluent into sewers can be controlled under IPC authorisations. Under the Trade Effluent (Prescribed Processes and Substances) Regulations 1989 (SI 1989 No. 1156) the Secretary of State has prescribed the categories of processes and substances for control as in the case of Part I of the EPA 1990. Any discharge to a sewer is defined as a release to water for the purposes of Part I, although it is not relevant when considering whether there is 'pollution of the environment', presumably because the effluent is likely to be treated before it is actually released into the environment (s. 1(11)(c)).

There is still an overlap of controls, however, as all discharges to sewers require consent from the sewerage undertaker under s. 118 of the Water Industry Act 1991. Such a consent may set limits on the volume, composition and temperature of the discharge in addition to setting out the consent fee (see further p. 487).

Statutory nuisance

Where a local authority wishes to initiate its statutory nuisance powers in relation to a prescribed process it must first obtain the Secretary of State's consent (EPA 1990, s. 79(10)). This power applies only in relation to smoke emitted from premises, dust, steam, smell or other effluvia arising on industrial, trade or business premises, or any accumulation or deposit.

Planning permission

There is no reference to the overlap between the planning system and IPC. There is no obligation on an operator to obtain a planning permission for any development associated with a new or altered process prior to authorisation under Part I of the EPA 1990 (the reverse is also true). PPG 23 on Planning and Pollution Control recommends that both applications are submitted together. There are, of course, inherent dangers of applying for any one before the other as different considerations are taken into account when determining each application. An illustration of the problems was seen in the case of the Point of Ayr gas terminal in North Wales. Planning permission was granted for the project after a public inquiry in 1992. When the IPC application was lodged (on the basis of the location of plant which had received planning permission) in 1994 the application was refused by HMIP as the process did not represent BATNEEC. This led to a fresh application with changes to plant design at a reported cost of several million pounds (see *ENDS Report* 245 at p. 13 and 246 at p. 7).

It is quite normal for a planning application to be submitted along with a staged application for an IPC application (see p. 320). When dealing with the planning application, local authorities are advised to consider only the land-use implications of the development. This leads to the question of the nature of 'land-use' implications. The courts have examined the nature of the overlap between planning and pollution control in *Gateshead Metropolitan Borough Council* v *Secretary of State for the Environment* [1995] Env LR 37. In that case the Secretary of State granted planning permission for a clinical waste incinerator in the north-east. The inspector appointed to hear the appeal recommended that permission be refused. One of the issues which was taken into account by the inspector was the public fear that pollution from the site would be unacceptable. The Secretary of State concluded that the issue could be satisfactorily addressed as part of the IPC application and granted planning permission. That decision was challenged by the local planning authority on the basis that the two systems were so closely inter-linked that it was unreasonable to grant planning permission without knowing if emissions could be adequately controlled under the IPC system. In the

High Court, Sullivan J decided that although the two statutory regimes overlapped, the extent of the overlap would vary on every occasion. It was envisaged that there would be a whole range of cases, from those where environmental considerations could be dealt with adequately under the IPC system to those where environmental considerations could not be overcome by the mere grant of an authorisation. The correct legal test was whether or not it was reasonable in the *Wednesbury* sense to arrive at the decision reached by the decision-maker. On appeal, the Court of Appeal affirmed this decision with only a slight variation of judgment. The issue of whether there was an unacceptable risk was, in the court's view, a matter for HMIP and the fact that the public had expressed concern about the issue was not conclusive. The court went on to say, however, that the fact that planning permission had been granted should not be viewed as a restriction upon HMIP's discretion to refuse the application for IPC authorisation if it thought fit to do so. Thus, the courts have affirmed the Government's implicit view as contained in PPG 23 that there is no definite dividing line between planning and IPC applications, and that each decision-maker is entitled to arrive at different conclusions if it exercises its discretion reasonably.

In order to assist the process of close cooperation between the planning authorities and HMIP (and subsequently the EA), HMIP issued a guidance note on consultation with planning authorities (*Planning Liaison with Local Authorities*). This document recommends simultaneous applications for IPC authorisation and planning permission but in cases where this is not possible it suggests that the role of the enforcing authority is to comment on whether the application would constitute BATNEEC and whether it is likely to be granted an authorisation.

Contaminated land

Where a prescribed process causes land to become contaminated, the powers under Part IIA of the EPA 1990 cannot be exercised in circumstances where powers to remedy harm are available under s. 27 of the Act regardless of whether the powers are in fact exercised (ss. 78YB(1) and 78N(2)).

Applications for authorisation

When IPC governs a prescribed process an authorisation has to be obtained from the EA before that process can be carried out (EPA 1990, s. 6(1)). To carry out a process without authorisation is a criminal offence (s. 23(1)). Thus, the first step in the IPC procedure is to apply for an authorisation.

The Environmental Protection (Applications, Appeals and Registers) Regulations 1991 (SI 1991 No. 507) (as amended) lay down the procedure for an application. Regulation 2 prescribes the information required by the EA. Clearly, certain authorisations can be very complicated and a great deal of information is required. This information includes:

(a)   The name, address and telephone number of the applicant.

(b)   A map of the area within which the process is to be located, with indications of the exact location of the process, the name of the local authority, and the address of the location of the prescribed process.

(c)   A proper description of the process, including such information as relates to the concept of BATNEEC (as to which, see below). This is wider than the information required under the BPM tests and the techniques employed must be described fully.

(d)   Where there is a prescribed substance involved in the process, information regarding the quantity and nature of the releases and also whether or not raw materials are used in the process itself.

(e)   Where techniques are used to prevent or minimise the release of prescribed substances, or such substances are rendered harmless, a full description of the methods used. There should be information as to how waste will be discharged.

(f)   A detailed assessment of the environmental implications of the process. This has to be carried out specifically in relation to the BPEO. It does not have to be a definitive description of the environmental effects but rather an assessment of the environmental impact on a local, regional or global basis and, alongside this, there has to be a justification of the process used in an attempt to balance the harm caused by a process with the techniques used.

(g)   Information regarding the monitoring of the released substances.

Where the EA wishes to impose additional conditions but does not have sufficient information to enable itself to do so, it may ask the applicant to furnish such information as is necessary. If that information is not forthcoming, EPA 1990, sch. 1, para. 1(3), allows the EA to give notice in writing to the operator of the requirement to give any further information within a specified period so that the application can be determined properly.

The application form
The only requirement for a valid application in relation to its form is that it be made in writing. There is, however, an application form available from the EA, which is a short document dealing with the relevant names and addresses of the applicant and the prescribed processes, the application fee, and details of the bodies who may be statutory consultees. Lastly, there is a section which deals with applications for confidentiality.

Additional information
The official application form provided by the EA deals with only a small proportion of the information which is necessary for an application to be determined properly. The vast majority of the information prescribed under the Regulations relates to technical information and is usually provided in separate documentation. Although there is no formal requirement to present the information in a particular way, the EA has suggested that applications can be dealt with swiftly and properly where the technical detail is structured by focusing on the detailed description of the process, the abatement techniques utilised and the environmental effects of the prescribed releases.

Special cases

Although generally the procedure for making an application is the same for every process, there is a number of exceptions to the rule which were either introduced at the outset of the system or have evolved since its inception as a result of unforeseen difficulties.

Staged applications

The development of industrial sites for new and particularly complicated processes inevitably takes many years. Often proposals develop over time and a variety of changes can be made to the plans. In these cases, the EA can agree to a staged application procedure whereby the applicant submits the application for authorisation over an agreed period of time so that there is a degree of flexibility.

Where such a phasing has been agreed it is normal for the applicant to submit an outline of the process design as an initial step. Once this step is complete the application will not be determined within the usual period. Instead, an agreed timetable will be adhered to in which the operator submits details of the process during the design, construction and commissioning stages.

Clearly, the advantage of such an approach from the operator's point of view is that it enables the EA's suggestions for improvements to be made at the design stage so that they can be incorporated in the final proposal.

Aside from the timing of the application all normal procedures will be followed, including publication, consultation and the payment of a fee. There will, however, be a final determination only when it is agreed that such a determination will be appropriate — usually at the commissioning stage.

Envelope applications

The particular operational requirements of the chemicals industry have led to a change in accepted procedures where the process involves either a pilot plant or a facility for manufacturing products under contract. Normally, there is a four-month time limit for issuing an authorisation for a process, although this may be increased by agreement between the parties. This suggests that there would be tremendous difficulties for chemical operators in particular, where they were producing chemicals in response to a particular demand at a particular time. Furthermore, many manufacturers produce small scale runs of products when trying to assess the commercial viability of a particular product. Where operators were obliged to apply for new authorisations every time they received a new contract or carried out a trial, there would not be sufficient time under the normal procedure for the application to be processed. In order to deal with this problem, there is a wider form of application known as envelope authorisation.

For contract operations the envelope application will define the areas of processes which can be carried out before a further authorisation would be required. Essentially, the opportunity is given to applicants to demonstrate that they are competent to deal with a wide range of activities within a single authorisation.

Once the boundary of the envelope has been determined it is still possible to manufacture products outside the envelope by submitting an application for a 'non-substantial variation'. This non-substantial variation is not a full application but would normally be processed relatively quickly so long as it fell within a band of the same or similar processes as those contained within the envelope.

For pilot plants, however, there is a much wider regime. As the processes involved are relatively small-scale the environmental impact is also likely to be small. Therefore, an envelope authorisation for a pilot plant can be much broader. Normally, once an envelope authorisation has been granted it will be necessary only to give the EA seven days' notice of a new project. This procedure will be followed unless the trial is likely to result in the previously agreed envelope limits being exceeded or new processes being utilised.

Complex sites

Although many sites will feature the use of specific waste treatment facilities, there are complex industrial sites where a number of processes may feed into common effluent and/or other abatement facilities. These processes raise difficulties where the processes are of a different nature, some of which may fall within the IPC regime, some of which may not; and even where all the processes are covered by IPC they may come within IPC at different times. the EA has responded to such complicated situations by introducing the concept of 'ring fencing'. The idea of ring fencing is to separate each individual process into artificial 'ring fenced' areas. An application for the processes within each ring fence will be determined separately and on the basis of the release of prescribed processes from the particular process to the common treatment plant. As new processes come within IPC they will all be controlled separately and the limits on the effluent from each process will be dealt with by means of individual authorisations.

When all the processes which feed into the effluent treatment plant have been dealt with by the EA, a unified authorisation can then be considered.

Fees

A valid application has to be accompanied by the appropriate fee (EPA 1990, s. 6(2)). The statutory charging scheme is governed by the general provisions on fees and charges under the Environment Act 1995, ss. 41 and 42 (see p. 52). The charging scheme is made on an annual basis by the EA.

The charges scheme operates on three levels:

(a) An application fee — this is specifically linked to the costs of processing particular applications.

(b) An annual subsistence charge, which covers the annual maintenance of an authorisation, including monitoring, inspection charges and enforcement.

(c) A substantial variation fee — this is levied at a different level to the annual fee and covers the costs of considering an application for a substantial variation of an existing authorisation.

The charges are levied on a component basis. Therefore, there is a flat rate which is multiplied by the number of components in each process. The definition of 'component' is different for each individual process and is contained in an appendix to the charging scheme.

Fee levels are set annually and take effect from 1 April in each year. The aim of the scheme is to recover the administrative costs associated with the system. This was evidenced by a significant rise in fee levels over the first few years of the system. This arose as a direct result of underestimating the costs of administering the system.

Where there has been a mis-calculation as to the amount of fees required, there is provision to enable the EA to send a further invoice to the applicant. If there has been an over-payment this will be refunded.

Where an application is not accompanied by the appropriate fee, or a fee has not been paid within 28 days of being invoiced, the EA has a discretion to decline to consider the application and cannot issue the authorisation. Where the subsistence charge is not paid it is open to the EA to revoke the authorisation or take other enforcement action (s. 8(8)).

Although the charging mechanism has always been seen as a method of raising revenue which contributed to the running costs of the EA (indeed the EA is under a statutory duty to recover costs), it has traditionally been spread equally between all operators. The EA has investigated the use of different charging mechanisms (for the annual subsistence fee) in seeking to make the operators of more polluting processes pay proportionately more by way of charges.

Public participation and other consultation procedures

The right of the public to be notified of environmentally harmful processes has been virtually non-existent in the past. This has been altered under the Environmental Protection (Applications, Appeals and Registers) Regulations 1991 (SI 1991 No. 507), as amended. Regulation 5 obliges the operator of a process to advertise all applications for authorisation and all variations of an authorisation involving a substantial change. This advert has to be published in a local newspaper circulating in the area in which the process is to be operated, and must contain details including:

(a)   the name and address of the applicant and the premises where the process is carried on;
(b)   a description of the process;
(c)   the availability of information on the registers and where those registers can be inspected;
(d)   an invitation for representations to be made within 28 days to the EA.

This advertisement has to appear between 14 and 42 days after the application was made or the day on which the variation notice was served upon the applicant.

Other consultees are given the right to make representations under reg. 4. The list of consultees reflects the many impacts that a process may have upon different areas not only of the environment but also the workplace. The bodies entitled to be consulted include:

(a)   the Health and Safety Executive, specifically in relation to the health and safety at work of people involved in the process;

(b)   water services companies or any other sewerage undertaker, in relation to the release of any substance into a sewer;

(c)   the Minister of Agriculture, Fisheries and Food;

(d)   the relevant Nature Conservancy Council, in relation to the release of a substance which may affect a site of special scientific interest;

(e)   a harbour authority, in relation to the release of any substance into a harbour;

(f)   Local authorities, particlarly in relation to conditions to be imposed which have an impact on air quality management plans under the Environment Act 1995 (see p. 345).

These statutory consultees are entitled to notification within 14 days of receipt of an application for authorisation or variation (EPA 1990, sch. 1). They are then allowed to make representations within 28 days, and any representations made have to be taken into account as a consideration when deciding an application.

Where an application does not contain commercially confidential information, the Environmental Protection (Authorisation of Processes) (Determination Periods) Order 1991 (SI 1991 No. 513) provides that there is a four-month period for determining applications, beginning with the date of receipt (see also EPA 1990, sch. 1, paras. 5(1) and (3)). This time limit can be extended by agreement between the applicant and the enforcing authority.

Call-in procedure

As with an application for planning permission, the Secretary of State has the ability to 'call in' an application for an authorisation, thus ousting the jurisdiction of the enforcing authority (EPA 1990, sch. 3, para. 3(1)). This power can be exercised at the discretion of the Secretary of State. However, it is probable that this power will only be used for particularly sensitive applications, applications of local or national importance, or applications which arouse a great deal of public interest.

When an application is called in, the Secretary of State has no power to grant the authorisation, but instead must direct the enforcing authority as to whether to grant the application and, if so, as to the conditions which are to be attached (sch. 1, para. 3(5)). The manner by which the Secretary of State decides such an issue may be by public local inquiry or by means of informal hearings.

Commercial confidentiality and national security

In normal circumstances, the EPA 1990 seeks to allow free public access to information regarding an application for an authorisation. However, there are exceptions to this on the ground of commercial confidentiality and in relation to issues affecting national security. Where an applicant believes that any information contained within an application should be restricted, then an application may be made under ss. 21 and 22 to exclude such information from the public registers. This application is included along with the information relating to the authorisation, and the EA (in relation to IPC) has to determine whether or not such information is commercially confidential (s. 22(2)(a)).

In the case of information relating to national security, the only criterion is that the Secretary of State has to be of the opinion that the inclusion in the register of that information would be contrary to the interests of national security. On commercial confidentiality grounds, the enforcing authority have 14 days in which to determine whether the information is commercially confidential and, if they fail to make a determination, it is deemed to be treated as such (s. 22(3)). Where the enforcing authority determine that the information is not commercially confidential, they must not enter such information on the register for 21 days so as to allow an applicant to appeal against the decision to the Secretary of State (s. 22(5)). Pending any appeal, the information is also excluded from the register.

The determination of an application

Once the EA has received all representations, it is entitled to grant the authorisation, subject to any conditions required, or to refuse it (s. 6(3)). It is under a duty to refuse an authorisation if it is of the view that an applicant would be unable to carry on the process in compliance with any conditions which would be included in an authorisation (EPA 1990, s. 6(4)). An *inability* to comply with a condition should not be confused with the question of whether it was *likely* that an applicant would comply with conditions. Likelihood of compliance (i.e., the possibility that the applicant could comply with the conditions) is not strictly a relevant consideration. On the other hand, when considering whether an applicant will be able to comply with a condition it is relevant to consider the previous compliance history as that has a direct connection with the ability to comply (see *R v Secretary of State for the Environment, ex parte West Wiltshire District Council* [1996] Env LR 312). Other grounds for refusal are if information required under the Environmental Protection (Applications, Appeals and Registers) Regulations 1991 (SI 1991 No. 507) was not supplied, or the proper fee had not accompanied the application. There is a residual power available to the Secretary of State under s. 6(5) to direct the enforcing authority either to grant or to refuse the authorisation.

In considering whether or not to grant an authorisation, there are a number of statutory objectives which have to be taken into account (s. 7). This section has introduced a new concept into environmental control within Britain of taking a proactive environmental quality approach to emissions to the environment as a whole. The statutory objectives have to be achieved in every authorisation and most of the conditions in an authorisation will relate to them. These objectives are contained in s. 7(2) and are:

(a) ensuring that, in carrying on a prescribed process, the best available techniques not entailing excessive cost (BATNEEC) will be used:

(i) for preventing the release of substances prescribed for any environmental medium into that medium or, where that is not practicable by such means, for reducing the release of such substances to a minimum and for rendering harmless any such substances which are so released; and

(ii) for rendering harmless any other substances which might cause harm if released into any environmental medium;

(b) compliance with any directions by the Secretary of State given for the implementation of any obligations of the United Kingdom under EC Treaties or international law relating to environmental protection;

(c) compliance with any limits or requirements and achievement of any quality standards or quality objectives prescribed by the Secretary of State under any of the relevant enactments;

(d) compliance with any requirements applicable to the grant of authorisations specified by or under a statutory plan made by the Secretary of State under s. 3(5) of the EPA 1990.

Section 7(1) provides for three different types of conditions which may be included in an authorisation:

(a) Conditions to meet the statutory objectives as laid down in s. 7(2).
(b) Conditions imposed by the Secretary of State under s. 7(3).
(c) Any other appropriate conditions.

There is also a general implied condition that a process will be carried on using BATNEEC. Additionally, s. 7(7) specifically provides, in relation to IPC processes involving the release of substances into more than one environmental medium, that BATNEEC will be used for minimising the pollution which may be caused to the environment taken as a whole by the releases, having regard to the best practicable environmental option (BPEO) available in respect of the substances which may be released. Thus, the dual concepts of BATNEEC and BPEO are incorporated into the statutory objectives of Part I as far as IPC is concerned.

BATNEEC

All of the processes controlled by the EA under IPC are subject to the requirement of BATNEEC. BATNEEC is to be applied specifically to each individual process taking into account various individual problems on a case by case basis. The concept of BATNEEC is somewhat wider than the traditional BPM model in that it includes not only the technical means and technology of pollution abatement, but also the number, qualifications, training and supervision of persons employed in the process, in addition to the design, construction, lay-out and maintenance of the buildings in which it is carried on (s. 7(10)). Thus, the umbrella of the control mechanisms covers a whole range of subjects which need to be taken into account on a strategic level.

'Best available techniques'

By way of further guidance as to the meaning of the phrase, the Department of the Environment's guide to IPC states that 'available' should be taken to mean procurable by the operator of the process in question; this does not imply that the technique is in general use, but it does require general accessibility. It includes a technique which has been developed (or proven) at a scale which allows its implementation in the relevant industrial context with the necessary business confidence. It does not imply that sources outside Britain are 'unavailable'. Nor does it imply a competitive supply market; if there is a monopoly supplier, the technique counts as being available provided that the operator can procure it.

This would suggest that the use of easily available abatement equipment would not necessarily satisfy the criteria. Efforts may need to be made to investigate other avenues of technology. 'Best' is defined in relation to the effectiveness of the techniques in minimising, preventing or rendering harmless noxious emissions. 'Best' is not an absolute term and it has been indicated that there may well be a number of different techniques which qualify under this particular word.

The statutory terms are deliberately vague in an attempt to import some flexibility into the decision-making process. There is, however, supplementary guidance contained in the IPC notes. Unfortunately, there has been very little indication of the EA's (or perhaps more importantly, the Secretary of State's views) on the meaning of 'BAT' other than the guidance set out in the IPC notes as there have been very few refusals of authorisations or enforcement notices and therefore few consequent appeals in which policy could be clarified. In one appeal the Secretary of State took the view that an abatement system which was generally available in Germany was not truly available for use in UK processes as there were some differences in the types of plant and machinery used in the UK and the trials of the abatement system with the UK equipment had not been completed.

The DoE is keenly aware that people within industry are particularly concerned that the meaning of BATNEEC should have a clearer definition than that contained in the Act. Overall, the onus is on an applicant to supply a system which properly and effectively deals with emissions so that they minimise the harm caused to the environment as a whole. It need not be the most up-to-date equipment, but it certainly requires an attempt to demonstrate that the particular system used is effective and that there are no more effective methods of dealing with the waste products of an industrial process.

'Not entailing excessive cost'

However, as pointed out earlier, there is always the need to balance one part of the BATNEEC requirement against the other. Thus, if the cost of a particular technique is excessive then, even though it might be the 'best available technique', it need not necessarily become a condition of any authorisation that that technique be used. There are, however, different considerations to take into account, depending on whether a process is an existing process or a new process.

Clearly, where there is an existing process to update, account needs to be taken of the financial consequences of introducing new equipment. Therefore, it is anticipated that the introduction of new plant and equipment will be phased-in over a number of years. Thus, the cost of upgrading environmental plant will be spread over a number of years so that the two balancing factors of 'best available techniques' and 'not entailing excessive cost' can be taken into account.

Although it is clear that some account has to be taken of economic factors, there is some uncertainty over the extent to which the costs will be allowed to tip the balance. There has been comment made that those who cannot afford to equip their factories with up-to-date plant and machinery should not be allowed to carry out operations which could contaminate the environment. Certainly, with new processes, applicants will be required to show that there has been a cost/benefit analysis to show that whatever they are claiming to be excessive in a financial and economic sense is excessive by objective criteria in relation to the pollution caused. Different industry sectors have different levels at which costs become excessive.

HMIP made available its internal guidance notes which formed part of the Inspectorate's Manual on IPC. These made it clear that when issuing authorisations an application would be viewed in terms of a process standard rather than purely looking at the emission levels. Operators had to demonstrate the options that they had considered when selecting the best available techniques. However, in a situation where the best technique is not put forward, the applicant must be able to justify the technique on the grounds that the selection of another option would involve entailing excessive cost. The note stressed the onus was on the operator to:

> describe excessive cost in absolute terms without reference to the cost of the product. The applicant must be able to demonstrate that the increased cost of the product produced by the best available technique is grossly disproportionate to any environmental benefit likely to accrue from that method of production. The extra cost must represent a significant fraction of the cost of the finished product.

Additionally, the EA may be able to relax the BATNEEC requirements where substances are released and are to be rendered harmless. Process standards for new processes will be different to that for existing plant. Geographical effects, such as the volume of water carrying away effluent, could affect whether something is BATNEEC in one place but not in another.

There are, however, to be different considerations when dealing with existing plant. It is stressed that existing processes will have to be upgraded to the BATNEEC standards applicable to new plant within four years of the original date of authorisation. There may be allowable derogations from this period, but the EA has stated that these may not be allowed for more than four years. The tone of the new guidance is that the EA will certainly be looking towards the upgrading of existing plant with as much severity as the implementation of new plant.

Best practicable environmental option

In addition to demonstrating that the process constitutes the BATNEEC, operators must demonstrate that it represents the 'best practicable environmental option' (BPEO). Section 7(7) of the EPA 1990 provides that where the process is subject to control by the EA and results in the release of substances to more than one environmental medium the operator has to demonstrate that the BATNEEC is being used to minimise the release of substances to the environment *having regard* to the BPEO.

Although the Royal Commission on Environmental Pollution (RCEP) put forward a definition in its Report (see p. 306) there is no statutory definition and it has proved to be a particularly difficult concept to pin down in practice. Whilst a BPEO assessment has a number of similarities with a formal environmental assessment, it is the distinguishing features which make the concept of BPEO both wider and narrower than the assessment of a construction project. It is narrower in the sense that with a BPEO assessment there is only a requirement to assess the effects of releases of substances upon air, water and land. It is, however, wider in that there is a requirement to assess the availability and relative cost-benefit ratios of other process options which could be used to deal with the releases.

In a study carried out by the *ENDS Report* the vast majority of operators were found to have ignored other alternative process options and failed to have provided any data on the costs of other options when demonstrating that they were excessive. The EA has issued guidance on carrying out a BPEO which attempts to flesh out the theoretical framework. It includes advice on the selection of options, the assessment of environmental effects and a system for ranking the process options. The underlying concept for the assessment is based upon the assessment of each process option as a proportion of the environmental quality standard for particular substances. In the absence of an environmental quality standard for any particular substance the EA would determine an environmental assessment level (EAL) which would act as the guideline. Many critics complained that the EALs were both arbitrary and imprecise. Although the basis of the methodology has been criticised, it is clear that the introduction of some formal guidance on the issue of carrying out a BPEO assessment is necessary in order for the concept to have any meaning. One of the critics of this approach, the RCEP has promised to look at the issue of environmental standards in its next report. In particular, it will examine the underlying concept behind BPEO and the setting down of environmental quality standards, in an attempt to lay down some ground rules to underpin the comparison of different environmental options.

Integrated pollution control notes

In addition to the limited definition contained within the Act, an inspector determining an application for an authorisation must take into account the particular guidance note applicable to the class of process which is subject to the authorisation. The notes are supposed to provide a coherent context in which decisions can be made in relation to conditions to be imposed upon authorisations. Thus, all parties to an authorisation will know of the ground rules. The introduction of an element of certainty into the system increases both public accountability and also procedural fairness. As general guidance, the guidance note serves as a framework within which the details can be supplemented by scientific and technological advice from the EA. The notes:

(a) give the rationale behind the designation of the process for IPC;
(b) state the environmental quality standards which are relevant to the process;
(c) state the EA's views as to the achievable standards;
(d) describe a number of ways by which those standards can be reached;
(e) give guidance as to what would amount to a substantial change and therefore require authorisation under the variation procedures.

The details contained within the guidance notes act as standards which new processes will have to meet. On the other hand, existing processes are given an appropriate timescale within which to achieve these standards. To ensure that each note represents the 'state of the art' they are to be reviewed at least every four years.

Implementation of the IPC system

IPC was introduced for new processes, substantial variations of existing processes, and large combustion plants on 1 April 1991. Other existing processes were introduced over a five-year period ending on 31 January 1996.

The introduction of a timetable for the implementation of IPC was a direct result of concern expressed over the ineffective implementation of the Control of Pollution Act 1974. Various amendments were proposed to the Environmental Protection Bill requiring implementation within a certain time period. In order to counter such suggestions an official timetable for the implementation of the system was introduced. (See sch. 3 to the Environmental Protection (Prescribed Processes and Substances) Regulations 1991 (SI 1991 No. 472.)

Transfer of authorisations

An authorisation is personal to an applicant/operator. However, it is possible to transfer an authorisation from one operator to another. Therefore, if a business has been sold, it is possible to transfer an existing authorisation to the new owner.

Section 9 of the EPA 1990 provides that the person to whom the authorisation is transferred must notify the EA of the transfer within 21 days. This will allow the EA to take into account any new considerations arising out of the transfer and provides an opportunity for variation notices to be served. Failure to notify the EA of the transfer of an authorisation is an offence (EPA 1990, s. 23).

Enforcement powers

There are a wide range of enforcement options to deal with breaches of authorisations. This includes a series of administrative sanctions such as enforcement, revocation and prohibition notices. This flexibility gives the EA the scope to take action against a variety of breaches of legislation. This is evidenced by the fact that although the rate of prosecutions is low, with approximately 13 — 14 cases a year brought on average, there has been a widespread use of enforcement notices and other administrative mechanisms. The use of enforcement action is publicised heavily by the EA, but the effect of its general enforcement policy is hard to discern, with public complaints about prescribed processes increasing. In particular, there are some doubts about the use of administrative sanctions as there are few indicators to demonstrate whether the enforcement notices served are complied with or to what extent they result in improvements.

Variation notices

The ability to vary an authorisation is not strictly an enforcement power when compared with, for example, enforcement and prohibition notices. However, the effect of a variation may be such that an operator would view it as having no practical distinction from an enforcement notice. The distinctive character of a variation notice relates more to the proactive approach rather than the punitive approach. Where new pollution abatement systems are introduced, or there is an understanding of new environmental dangers, then a variation notice can be served to bring operators 'up to date' (s. 11). Indeed, the EA is under a statutory duty to follow developments in pollution abatement technology and techniques (EPA 1990, s. 4(9)).

Where the EA considers that the conditions to which the authorisation originally applied have changed, it is under a duty under s. 10 of the Act to vary that authorisation. The variation notice specifies what type of variation is required and the date on which the variations have to take effect (s. 10(3)).

It is also open to the applicant to apply for a variation where plant is upgraded or replaced (EPA 1990, s. 11). Thus, s. 11 provides that an operator wishing to make a 'relevant change' can notify the EA and ask for a determination:

(a)   whether the proposed change would involve a breach of any condition of the authorisation;

(b)   if it would not involve such a breach, whether the authority would be likely to vary the conditions of the authorisation as a result of the change;

(c)   if it would involve such a breach, whether the authority would consider varying the conditions of the authorisation so that the change may be made; and

(d)   whether the change would involve a substantial change in the manner in which the process is being carried on.

A relevant change in a prescribed process is defined as a 'change in the manner of carrying on the process which is capable of altering the substances released from the process or of affecting the amount or any other characteristic of any substance so released' (s. 11(11)). Where the change would amount to a substantial change in the manner in which the process is being carried on, this is to be treated as a fresh application and various consultation procedures must be undertaken.

These powers allow a degree of flexibility into the system so that changes which do not affect the authorisation can be made without a great deal of administrative intervention. On the other hand, where there is a change in the circumstances surrounding the authorisation, clearly the EA ought to be able to intervene directly and request certain amendments.

The procedure mentioned above is only a preliminary procedure. Where the EA decides that a formal variation is required, such an application has to be made. The only other alternative for an operator is to request a variation of the conditions of an authorisation.

There are further powers of variation contained in s. 11(5) and (6). The DoE envisages that these particular sections will be used during the construction of a plant where a variation in the authorisation is required but no 'relevant change' as defined in s. 11(11) of the Act is to take place. On the other hand, s. 11(6) allows for a variation of the conditions of an authorisation to take account of a relevant change.

The procedure governing a variation under s. 11 is contained in the Environmental Protection (Applications, Appeals and Registers) Regulations 1991 (SI 1991 No. 507). Regulation 3 states that when an application is made by an operator it must be in writing and include the name, address and telephone number of the operator and the address of the premises where the prescribed process is carried on. The request also has to include a description of the change, any change to the overall techniques used in the process, and any further information which the operator wishes the inspector to take into account.

Revocation notices
Section 12 of the EPA 1990 gives the EA the power to revoke an authorisation at any time by giving notice in writing (s. 12(1)). This power is subject to the right of appeal or subsequently from challenge by way of judicial review. An appeal against a revocation notice suspends the action of the notice. Notwithstanding the nature of this power, the EA is able to revoke an authorisation where it has reason to believe that a prescribed process in respect of which there is an authorisation has not been carried on for a period of 12 months (s. 12(2)). Thus, where authorisations are seen to be redundant, the power to revoke will be exercised to ensure that there is no question of restarting the process. When a revocation notice is served, there is a minimum period of 28 days before it can take effect (s. 12(3)). There is also a residual power open to the Secretary of State to direct the EA as to whether or not it should revoke the authorisation.

The revocation procedure has been used where an operator had consistently failed to comply with a program of improvement for an existing process notwithstanding a number of time extensions and to prevent an operator from reopening in circumstances where the original closure was a result of a failure to achieve upgrading standards.

Enforcement notices
Where the EA is of the opinion that an operator is contravening any condition of an authorisation, or is likely to contravene a condition, it is under a duty to serve an enforcement notice (s. 13). The power to serve such a notice is discretionary as the EA is entitled to arrive at a judgment about the likelihood of contravention. A decision not to take action would be challengeable by way of judicial review.

An enforcement notice must contain the following details:

    (a)   that the enforcing authority is of the opinion that there has been a contravention or that it is likely that there will be;
    (b)   the matters which constitute the contravention or give rise to the likelihood that there will be a contravention;
    (c)   the steps required to remedy the situation;
    (d)   the period within which those steps should be taken (s. 13(2)).

There is a residual power for the Secretary of State to direct the EA to take enforcement action (s. 13(3)).

Prohibition notices
If the EA is of the opinion that the carrying on of an authorised process in a particular manner involves an imminent risk of serious pollution, it is under a mandatory duty to serve a prohibition notice, whether or not the operator is contravening the authorisation (s. 14(1)). The prohibition notice has to include details of the authority's assessment of the risk involved in the process, as well as specifying the steps that must be taken to remove it and the period within which they must be taken. The meaning of imminent risk to the environment is open to all manner of interpretation. Section 1(2) defines the environment as 'all, or any, of the following media, namely, the air, water and land', whereas pollution of the environment means 'pollution of the environment due to the release (into any environmental medium) from any process of substances which are capable of causing harm to man or any other living organisms supported by the environment'. It will be a matter for the subjective judgment of the inspectors as to what amounts to an 'imminent risk' and what amounts to 'serious pollution'.

The prohibition notice empowers the EA to prohibit an authorisation either as a whole or, if it is felt that the risk could be avoided by withdrawing part, then by prohibiting that part only. Additionally, there is power under s. 14 to impose new conditions on the original authorisation and thus avoid imminent risk of serious pollution of the environment.

In attempting to clarify the difference between prohibition notices and enforcement notices, when the Environmental Protection Bill passed through the House of Lords, Lord Reay explained that a prohibition notice would cover:

circumstances in which a process is being operated in a perfectly reasonable manner and within the conditions of the authorisation, but where some event external to the process requires quick and decisive action. For example, an accident at one process could release substances which could react with those normally allowed to be released at a nearby process, so causing serious pollution. In those circumstances, it would be right to close down temporarily the second process even though it was operating within its authorisation.

Therefore, when considering the nature of the prohibition notice, it has to be borne in mind that such a Draconian power cannot be used too widely. The width of this power can be seen in s. 14(3), where it is stated that until the notice is withdrawn, an authorisation will cease to have any effect.

Powers of entry and inspection
The EA has a wide range of powers to carry out inspections, requisition information, take samples and gain entry to premises (s. 108 of the Environment Act 1995; see p. 51).

Offences and remedies

Section 23 of the EPA 1990 gives a long list of offences under Part I. It is a criminal offence to:

(a)   operate a prescribed process without an authorisation;
(b)   contravene the conditions of an authorisation;
(c)   fail to give notice of transfer of an authorisation;
(d)   fail to comply with an enforcement or prohibition notice; or
(e)   intentionally make a false entry in any record required to be kept as a condition of an authorisation.

All offences are triable either way, with the more serious offences having a maximum fine level in the magistrates' court of £20,000. In the Crown Court all offences are subject to a maximum term of imprisonment of two years and/or an unlimited fine (s. 23(2)). The Act also gives rights of audience to inspectors to present prosecutions even though they are not legally qualified (s. 23(5)).

In any trial relating to the breach of the implied condition relating to the use of BATNEEC, the onus of proof falls upon the operator of the process to show that there was no better available technique not entailing excessive cost which could be employed for that particular process (s. 25(1)).

It is open to any court in sentencing an offender for failure to comply with an enforcement or prohibition notice to order that the effects of the offence be remedied (s. 26). This allows for clean-up and compensation costs to come directly out of the offender's pocket. In many instances, these costs will far outstrip any reasonable fine that could be imposed. Perhaps even more importantly, where a process has been operated without any authorisation or has not been in compliance with a condition of an authorisation, the EA can arrange for reasonable steps to be taken towards remedying any harm caused as a consequence and recover the costs of taking such steps from any person committing the offence (s. 27(1)). Before doing so, however, the EA must obtain the Secretary of State's approval in writing. Thus, even where a court is not willing to impose the high financial burden of clean-up costs on an offender, it will be open to the Agency to remedy such harm. There are further remedies available to the EA in the High Court, under s. 24, where there has been a failure to comply with an enforcement or a prohibition notice. This allows the EA to seek injunctions where the enforcement of the criminal law is not securing adequate compliance. It must, however, exhaust other remedies before seeking an injunction (see *Tameside MBC* v *Smith Bros (Hyde) Ltd* [1996] Env LR 312).

Corporate liability

In an age where the concept of individual responsibility for corporate actions is being accepted by both the courts and the general public, s. 157 of the EPA 1990 provides that where an offence is committed by a company and it can be shown that a director, manager, or similar person in the company either consented, connived or was negligent, then criminal liability can attach individually as well as on a corporate basis. Furthermore, where an offence is committed owing to the act of default of an independent third party, proceedings can be brought against either or both under s. 158. These provisions would cover coprorate officers who acknowledged that there was a risk of environmental contanimation from certain activities and took that risk in the full knowledge of the consequences. Furthermore, acitivites where an act of environmental damage is caused by a breach of Part I owing to the activities of an independent contractor and notwithstanding the absence of fault on behalf of the operator of the process, both parties can be prosecuted.

Crown immunity

As in other legislation the Crown will be immune from criminal proceedings by virtue of s. 159. However, where the Crown operates processes subject to IPC it will not be exempt from the general control mechanisms under Part I. Thus there is a need to apply for authorisations and the same statutory objectives will apply as in the case of non-Crown bodies.

There is, under s. 159(2), a subsidiary power which allows for the Crown to be taken to the High Court and any breach of any authorisation to be declared unlawful. It is difficult to envisage a situation where this would be useful except in a case where the proof of civil liability depended to a certain extent upon the ability to show unlawful action on behalf of the Crown.

Appeals

Section 15 of the EPA 1990 governs appeals. It provides that there is a right of appeal against:

(a) revocation, variation, enforcement and prohibition notices;
(b) the refusal to grant or vary an authorisation;
(c) the imposition of unreasonable conditions.

Furthermore, s. 22 gives an applicant a right of appeal where the EA has notified the operator that information contained within an authorisation or an application for an authorisation is not commercially confidential.

The detailed appeals procedure is contained in the Environmental Protection (Applications, Appeals and Registers) Regulations 1991 (SI 1991 No. 507). Generally, the time limit for appeals is similar to that in the planning system, being six months from a refusal or a deemed refusal to grant an authorisation. Where there is an appeal against an enforcement, prohibition or variation notice, the time limit is two months from the date of the notice. Where the EA is seeking notice to revoke an authorisation, the appeal must be submitted before the notice takes effect. Lastly, where there is an appeal concerning commercial confidentiality, it must be submitted within 21 days from the refusal.

Pending the hearing of the appeal, a revocation notice will not have effect. However, in all other cases involving appeals against statutory notices, although there is an appeal made, there is no suspension of the notice. Thus, an operator cannot gain an economic advantage where there is a rush order by appealing against a notice so as to stop the enforcement process, continuing to pollute until the order is completed, and then stopping the process before the appeal is heard.

An appeal must be made in writing to the Secretary of State (reg. 9). The appeal has to be accompanied by any relevant information, including any application, authorisation, correspondence or decision and a statement as to how the appellant wishes the appeal to be determined.

Modes of appeal

An appeal can be heard in one of two ways: either by way of written representations or by a hearing. If either party to the appeal requests that it be heard by way of hearing the Secretary of State has no discretion in the matter, he must hold the hearing (s. 15(5)(a)) although there is a discretion as to whether the hearing is in public. The Secretary of State also has the power to direct that a public inquiry be held (s. 15(5)(b)). There has been an attempt by the DoE to ensure that hearings do not take on a quasi-legal nature, as has happened in the planning system. Thus, the system has very few rules. The DoE Guidance states:

the procedure at a hearing will be left to the Appeals Inspector. He may hear the parties in whatever order he thinks most suitable for the clarification of issues. He may, for instance, review the case based on the papers already provided and then outline what he considers to be the main issues and indicate those matters which require further explanation or clarification. This will not preclude the appellant or the enforcing authority from referring to other aspects which they consider to be relevant. The approach that will be encouraged will be one of informality, for example, hearings may often take the form of a round table discussion, rather than a formal presentation of evidence.

This air of informality is supposedly to alter the hearing system from being adversarial, as is often the case in planning appeals, to inquisitorial. There is to a certain extent a degree of public participation in that reg. 13 states that notice has to be given at least 28 days before the date of the hearing of the date, time and place for the holding of the hearing. The Department does however concede that in more controversial proposals it may be necessary to adopt a formal procedure. Presumably, where issues are likely to be of great consequence to members of the public, there needs to be some element of the adversarial approach to ensure that there is adequate accountability. Otherwise, public confidence in an appeals system, which to the untrained eye and ear would appear to be a meeting of highly trained, highly specialised people discussing hypothetical problems around a table, would be seriously undermined.

The written representations appeal procedure will contain an exchange of views on paper as to the suitability of any proposals. The procedure will vary little from the planning system.

The Secretary of State cannot delegate the above decision-making powers. The inspector who heard the appeal is required to report to the Secretary of State as to any conclusions and recommendations. The Secretary of State in making the decision has to take into account these recommendations but does not have to follow them. The Secretary of State then issues the decision to all interested parties.

Integrated pollution prevention and control

The current IPC system is scheduled to be amended over the next few years as a result of the implementation of the Directive on Integrated Pollution Prevention and Control (96/61), which was adopted in September 1996. It must be brought into force in Member States before 14 October 1999 for new processes (or those which are subject to a 'significant change'). Existing processes must be brought within the regime before October 2007, although the phasing of this implementation is to be left to each Member State. Although the scheme of the Directive bears a great deal of similarity to the IPC regime, it will require a number of changes to the present legislative provisions. These include:

(a) *An extension of the classes of processes which are controlled.* Fewer than 2,500 processes are currently subject to IPC. Implementation of the Directive could bring up to 4,000 new processes under control. Some processes will be covered for the first time whereas others will be transferred from local control under the air pollution control regime. These include large intensive livestock units, food and drink manufacturers, sewage works and some landfill sites.

(b) *An extension of the matters controlled by an authorisation.* The IPPC Directive does not only cover the emissions of a process. It takes a wider approach and considers other matters including energy efficiency, the consumption of raw materials, restoration of a site after closure and noise emissions.

(c) *A wider definition of BPEO.* As the Directive will extend the matters which are to be covered under any authorisation it will also require a much wider consideration of the options which are considered when deciding the BPEO for a process. Thus it will not be sufficient to demonstrate the BPEO in terms of environmental releases — there will need to be consideration of each process option in terms of energy, noise emissions and the consumption of raw materials.

(d) *A reconsideration of the role of the sewerage undertakers.* Under European law, there is some doubt about whether private bodies (such as the sewerage undertakers) can perform the function of permitting authorities. In the case of the new IPPC processes there is some doubt over the role of the sewerage undertakers in relation to any discharges to sewers.

(e) *A redefinition of 'best available techniques'.* The definitions of BAT are broadly similar in tone and intent in the Directive and the current system. There are, however, some significant distinctions between the two. For example, decommissioning of processes is included in the IPPC definition of 'techniques' and does not feature in the domestic scheme.

Perhaps more significantly, the Commission sees this Directive as heralding a new phase in the control of industrial processes and emissions where an integrated approach to authorisations is adopted in preference to emission limits for individual environmental media. The next stage should see the introduction of an integrated approach to the control of releases from smaller industrial installations under a new framework Directive. This Directive would aim to ensure that small installations which released dangerous substances would be required to seek an authorisation with simple controls which are similar in scope to the IPPC Directive. Subsequently, in conjunction with the introduction of the framework Directive on Water Resources this should see the repeal of the controls under the 1976 framework Directive on the discharge of dangerous substances to water.

TWELVE
Atmospheric pollution

The range of problems affecting the atmosphere stretches across the full range of human activities, from highly toxic fumes emitted from a complicated industrial process to such seemingly mundane activities as lighting a fire, driving a car or using spray-on deodorant. The history of atmospheric pollution dates back to early times. The prohibitions on certain activities producing smoke are probably the first instances of environment pollution legislation in Great Britain.

Because such a wide range of activities affects the atmosphere, the range of environmental issues is also wide. On the one hand, there have always been difficulties with polluting activities affecting the locality in which they were situated. International difficulties have arisen with the creation of acid rain. In recent years we have seen a realisation amongst the international community that individual nations' actions can combine to create truly global difficulties. The destruction of the ozone layer and the issue of global warning have brought home the truly awesome consequences of the combined effect of certain industrial activities.

Local atmospheric pollution

The pollution of the local atmosphere from emissions has traditionally been easy to identify. Such problems date back to the early uses of coal in domestic fires. The production of fumes and particulates from fires caused pulmonary infections and related lung diseases. Notwithstanding this effect, coal continued to be used. In 1661, John Evelyn published his famous work on air pollution in city areas, *Fumi Fugium,* which not only outlined the problems that atmospheric pollution from smoke caused, but also, more importantly, tried to suggest methods by which the problems could be resolved.

With the advent of more complicated processes in the late eighteenth century, the problems of atmospheric pollution grew more severe. The industrial revolution increased the use of coal to drive new machinery and, more importantly, produced very acidic emissions as a consequence of the 'alkali works'. These works used the Leblanc process to produce soda, but the by-product of the chemical process used meant that hydrochloric gas was emitted into the atmosphere which, when mixed with water, created a new phenomenon — acid rain.

The consequences of these new processes were that areas of the country were rendered desolate by this very highly acidic moist air, burning trees, shrubs and hedges. One of the centres for the alkali industry, St Helens in Lancashire, was reported as not having a single tree with any foliage on it. Even amongst the people working in such factories, concern was expressed. This concern led to the setting-up of a Royal Commission to look into the problem of alkali pollution, which subsequently made the recommendations which led to the first Alkali Act, passed in 1863. Under this Act, a new Alkali Inspector was appointed who regulated such alkali processes. Although the Act did not attempt to deal with smoke, it did introduce new stricter controls over the production of acidic emissions. It made the first attempts at restricting the composition of emissions with the introduction of primitive emission standard requirements. Under the Act, there was a requirement that 95% of all noxious emissions should be arrested within the plant, so that only 5% of the previously emitted fumes were allowed into the atmosphere.

Even though there were strict emission standards on the volume of noxious gases produced, there were also the first signs of a proactive approach from the newly created Alkali Inspectorate in that they would encourage manufacturers to reduce the emissions to less than 5% in order to protect the environment.

The initial effect of the legislation was a dramatic reduction in the production of acidic emissions from almost 14,000 tonnes to about 45 tonnes. This improvement, however, was only temporary. Within a short time the inadequacy of the legislation was brought home. The imposition of individualised emission standards could not take into account the cumulative effect of a large concentration of such operations. As the Act had only set a reduction for acidic emissions in terms of a percentage for each plant, the overall concentration of such emissions rose as the number of factories increased.

The introduction of the Alkali Act of 1874 attempted to redress the balance by introducing the concept of best practicable means (BPM). The application of BPM was used to widen the scope of the previous emission limits to include all noxious or offensive gases. In essence, the application of BPM relied upon these presumptive limits. The limits saw the introduction of the first proper emission standards in British legislation by specifying actual amounts of certain substances per cubic metre of emitted gas. If these emission limits were being met, then it was presumed that any legislation was being complied with and that the best practicable means were being used. The use of the concept of best practicable means ensured that there was to be a conciliatory and co-operational approach as the Alkali Inspectorate sought a method of enforcement which would not place 'an undue burden on manufacturing industry'.

Neither of these Acts, nor the consolidation Act of 1906, dealt specifically with the control of smoke from either industrial or commercial premises.

Attempts were made to control the emission of smoke through such Acts as the Public Health Act 1875, the Public Health (Smoke Abatement) Act 1926 and the Public Health Act 1936, but these dealt generally with smoke nuisances. These powers could not rid industrial cities of the problems of smoke pollution. The physical evidence of this pollution could be seen on blackened buildings, and by the frequency of smog, which was prevalent from Victorian times. Such smog was caused by fog forming in winter months and combining with smoke particles to produce a compound of gases which could cut visibility to very low levels. Of more concern, however, was the effect that these smogs had upon the dispersion of pollution. With a heavy concentration of smog hanging over a city the air was very still and convection was low. With the onset of these calm conditions, the dispersal of emissions was much more difficult. Such a lethal cocktail was bound to produce tragic effects, but these were fairly minimal until December 1952 when a smog descended upon London which did not clear for five days. Nothing unusual was noticed until prize cattle at the Smithfield Show started to suffer from respiratory problems. The smog got everywhere, even inside the Sadler's Wells Theatre, which resulted in the stoppage of a performance because of the difficulty of seeing the stage. When the smog had lifted it was estimated that nearly 4,000 people had lost their lives as a consequence of the smoke and other emissions.

The Government immediately responded by setting up the Beaver Committee to report on the difficulties surrounding smoke pollution. The recommendation of the Committee was to introduce legislation to eliminate particulate emissions such as smoke, dust and grit so that such conditions would not arise again. With the introduction of the Clean Air Act 1956, later supplemented by the Clean Air Act 1968, controls were introduced for the first time to restrict the production of smoke, grit and dust from all commercial and industrial activities not covered by the Alkali Acts but also, more importantly, domestic fires as well. The Acts introduced such concepts as smoke control areas and the complete prohibition on 'dark smoke' from chimneys.

During the 1970s, the problems of the emission of smoke, dirt, dust and grit lessened and coupled with the new approach to industrial processes a gradual improvement took place in the quality of the atmosphere in the UK. There was a move away from the use of coal as fuel to smokeless substances such as coke and gas. Additionally, the gap left behind with the introduction of clean air zones was met by an increase in the use of electricity for power and heat. The main generator of electricity in Britain, the Central Electricity Generating Board, changed its practices in a direct reaction to the difficulties encountered with local pollution by replacing the short chimneys traditionally used in power stations with larger and taller stacks. The basis of this change was to disperse pollution at a higher level in the hope that any substances would be diluted over greater distances. The consequence would be a reduction in the concentrations of pollutants in the nearby locality. Unfortunately, this reduction in the levels of local pollution only shifted the problems to a different location. Whilst the pollution of the atmosphere declined nationally, the concern internationally rose. The change of policy from short to tall stacks for chimneys saw the creation of the first environmental problem which could properly be identified across national boundaries — the problem of acid rain.

International difficulties: acid rain

The production of electricity from power stations burning fossil fuels produces, amongst other things, sulphur dioxide, nitrous oxide and nitrogen dioxide. The sulphur dioxide created from power stations amounts to some 80% of all such emissions into the atmosphere. In 1953 the Beaver Report had recommended that such plants should be fitted with desulphurisation equipment, but that was rejected specifically at the time as being impracticable for the particular process. Instead, the change from using short chimneys to a dilution and dispersal method from tall chimneys was introduced. It was thought that the dispersal of such emissions into the upper levels of the atmosphere would render such substances harmless before they could contaminate an area. This applied to the areas around the emission plants but, further afield, the evidence suggested that it had little effect.

In smoothly flowing medium speed winds, plumes from power stations travel in a concentrated stream for hundreds of miles. Tall stacks (Drax Power Station is 259 metres tall) can take emissions above a layer of air trapped near the ground into smooth air streams. On a steady south westerly, a plume from Eggborough Power Station, labelled with sodium hexafluoride was tracked all the way across the North Sea to Denmark . . . in clear skies sulphur was being slowly oxidised and deposited. Once it entered low mountain cloud, production of acid increased 14 fold and fall out increased over 200%. The total removal rate shot up to 27% an hour, depositing the sulphur in a concentrated drizzle (Rose, *The Dirty Man of Europe*).

The combination of sulphur dioxide and other acids from power stations and traffic combined with the atmosphere to produce not only acid rain, but also acid deposits in the atmosphere made of ammonium sulphate particles.

The effects of the production of such substances into the atmosphere has increased the acidity of rainfall in some areas to over 40 times the natural level. This has had a terrible effect upon areas of not only England, Scotland and Wales but also other countries within Europe where the prevailing winds have carried such emissions. The Scandinavian countries in particular have received a large percentage of the 'export' of Britain's production of sulphur dioxide and acid rain. Vegetation suffers from the increased acidity, trees and shrubs die and, in Southern Norway, it has been shown that there has been a steady increase in the acidity of lakes so that some lakes and rivers no longer support any life. The specific effects of certain pollutants can range from speckled areas on leaves brought about by acidic deposits through to complete death. These problems require a co-operative approach to be taken between nations. There has been a long running dispute between Britain and the Scandinavian countries as to the cause of the acidic deposits on their countries. The EC has made some steps towards introducing a desulphurisation programme, but it remains to be seen whether or not this is to be successful.

Global issues: ozone depletion and global warming

The Department of the Environment's White Paper *This Common Inheritance*, published in September 1990, brought the international problem of global warming to the top of the environmental agenda.

Global warming is one of the biggest environmental challenges now facing the world. It calls for action by all the world's nations, as no single nation can solve the problem on its own.

The greenhouse effect, as it has come to be known, has arisen because the production of various 'greenhouse' gases have increased in the past century with progressive industrialisation. In the lower atmosphere the production of emissions from power stations, car exhausts and industrial plants have increased by almost 100%. These emissions absorb radiated heat and create a higher ambient temperature level which has led to speculation that there could be shrinking global icecaps and rising water levels.

Additionally, the amount of ozone in the upper atmosphere screens the earth from harmful UV-B radiation. This screen has deteriorated and there have been studies showing a 'hole' above Antarctica. This depletion of ozone has been linked to the use of chlorofluorocarbons (CFCs). The creation of greenhouse gases and the depletion of the ozone layer are worldwide problems which require international co-operation to solve. The use of international law as a mechanism for environmental protection is relatively unusual and there are some limitations to its usefulness. However, the nature of the problems facing the world in terms of these two issues have led to significant steps being taken to prevent any further harm.

Global issues

The Earth Summit in Brazil, attended by over 160 countries, was seen as a watershed in the fight against climate change. At the conference the Climate Treaty was signed in an attempt to reduce the emission of greenhouse gases to 1990 levels by 2000. The Treaty was ratified by 50 countries (including the EU and the UK) and came into force in March 1994. The relative weakness of the use of international obligations to enforce environmental improvements can be seen in the fact that the UK's commitment to the Treaty (as set out in Climate Change — the UK Programme) consists of a set of voluntary measures with the aim of reducing energy consumption, with regulatory or economic instruments only being used where necessary. The New York summit in June 1997 re-emphasised the lack of success for the Rio declaration with the overall trend in air quality in decline and a failure to agree binding commitments to future improvement.

Air pollution policy

The control of air pollution has, as noted above, been the classic example of the use of reactive legal controls to regulate specific problems as they arise. Policy approaches have, until very recently, been sparse and incoherent. Although the legal controls have been modernised and broadened, it is only in the 1990s that a coherent strategy has been developed to deal with the problems of atmospheric pollution. When the Government published its policy on sustainable development in January 1994, urban air quality was identified as a priority area for improvement. In March 1994 the DoE issued a consultation paper on air quality which bluntly described previous policy initiatives on air pollution as 'the fortuitous sum of a large number of unrelated regulatory decisions and individual choices'. It was not until the beginning of 1995 that the first steps were taken towards a coherent air quality management system and the Environment Act 1995 has a variety of framework provisions which are described below.

A variety of factors has led to this acceleration of policy-making. First, there has been increasing evidence linking health problems with poor air quality, with the increase of the incidence of asthma and other diseases connected with a variety of atmospheric pollutants. There has also been a number of occasions (particularly in the summer months) when pollution levels have risen to dangerous levels in cities.

Secondly, the quality of provision of information on air quality has been improved with the number of background monitoring stations increased. Although air quality standards (AQS) have been introduced for a number of pollutants any assessment of measuring improvement depends to a large extent upon the availability of long-term data. Most of England's major cities now have stations to monitor base data in order to assess compliance with standards for the main polluting emissions. It is anticipated that this will increase as the move towards established AQS grows over the next few years (for more on monitoring see p. 346).

Thirdly, the link between air pollution and transport, in particular motor transport, has become much more pronounced. The RCEP's Eighteenth Report concentrated on the environmental effects of vehicle emissions. In addition there has been a range of measures designed to tackle pollution from motor vehicle (see p. 361).

Finally, as in other areas of environmental policy, the EC has made moves towards streamlining policy on atmospheric pollution. This culminated in a new framework Directive on air quality assessment and management with proposals to set AQS for 12 significant pollutants by 1999 (see p. 348).

Air quality strategy

The cornerstone of policy on air pollution is a new national strategy for air quality. The air quality strategy sets out air quality standards, objectives for controlling air pollutants and measures which should be taken by enforcing authorities to meet these objectives. Local authorities are under a duty to review the air quality in their areas from time to time. If the air quality objectives are not being met or are not likely to be met by a target date, the authority is under a duty to designate an air quality management area (AQMA). In an AQMA, a more detailed assessment of air quality must be undertaken within 12 months from the date of designation with an accompanying 'action plan' setting out a timetable for meeting the air quality objectives set for the area. Unlike the Air Quality Standards Regulations 1989, the strategy does not have complete statutory force. This approach may require the Regulations to be amended if the framework Directive prescribes definite limits in the future.

The strategy is relatively uncontroversial, although the target date for meeting AQS (set at 2005) is five years earlier than the date set in the framework Directive (although as a counter to that the AQS in the Directive are more stringent in some cases). There is, however, a great deal of work to be done in fleshing out the bare bones of the strategy. A number of consultation documents have been issued dealing with various aspects of the implementation of the strategy. The most uncertain aspect of the implementation is the extent to which local authorities will be given powers to control activities within AQMAs. These could include changes to:

(a) *Smoke control powers.* The control of smoke from both industrial and domestic premises is an important part of the national air quality strategy. Therefore, a few changes to existing legislation can be envisaged over the next few years. These would include additional measures to control industrial smoke including new provisions on fuel quality, economic instruments to influence fuel use, and a review of the guidance on chimney heights to ensure that emissions from new plant do not lead to high local concentrations.

In relation to domestic smoke control, it is possible that the introduction of new smoke control areas will be reviewed in the light of the drawing up of AQMAs by local authorities. There are likely to be new controls over the sale of unauthorised fuels in smoke control areas and there are proposals to limit the sulphur content of solid fuels to 2%.

(b) *Traffic management.* The ability of local authorities to tackle local hotspots of air quality which result mainly from vehicle transport rests largely in the opportunities for the management of traffic. The Road Traffic Regulation Act 1984 gives local authorities extensive powers to make traffic regulation orders to prohibit, restrict or regulate vehicular traffic or particular types of vehicular traffic. This was not intended, however, to cover situations where traffic fumes were causing harm to the environment or health (see *R v Greenwich London Borough Council, ex parte W* [1997] Env LR 190). Schedule 22 to the Environment Act 1995 extended the purpose for which traffic regulation orders could be made to include explicitly the pursuit of air quality objectives set out in Part IV of the Environment Act 1995. Local authorities could use the new power to manage traffic including, for example, congestion charging and area licensing.

(c) *Land use planning.* The link between land use planning and air pollution has been recognised explicitly in Planning Policy Guidance Notes on Transport (PPG 13) and Retail Development (PPG 6). It is expected that this link will be developed further with stricter limits placed upon the types of development which are allowed in AQMAs.

The potential conflict between national and local measures to meet overall quality objectives and action plans in AQMAs poses some interesting questions about the extent to which local measures can restrict uses to a greater extent than that envisaged in national guidance.

A framework of air quality standards and targets
The implementation of the strategy is largely dependent upon the introduction of AQS for nine pollutants. The standards are generally set in relation to the effect of each pollutant on human health, although the effect upon the environment might also be considered. There are two main levels:

(a) *The alert threshold.* This level is reached when air quality is so poor that an immediate response would be justified to prevent serious damage to health or the environment.

(b) *The guideline level.* This level is to be seen as a long-term goal and represents an equilibrium point at which the pollutant in question is considered to be harmless to health and the environment and which can be achieved through cost effective measures such as the introduction of new plant and technology.

These levels are to be set alongside a timetable for achieving the new objectives, although some doubts have been expressed in relation to the Government's desire to enforce these time limits. The Expert Panel on Air Quality Standards is to have the role of advising in relation to the setting down the numerical standards. As mentioned above, work has already been carried out (and in most cases completed) in respect of the guideline levels, although the more difficult alert threshold is as yet undetermined.

Local air quality management areas
The national framework of new two-level AQS will be implemented on a practical level with the introduction of air quality management areas (AQMAs) laid down and regulated by local authorities (EA 1995, ss. 83 — 4).

Local authorities have a duty to carry out regular assessments of air quality in their areas with a view to the identification of targeted areas for action. It is expected that all major urban areas will be surveyed before the end of 1997.

Where the local authority has identified an area for action it must consider whether to declare an AQMA where it has been shown that the AQS set out in the National Strategy are not likely to be met solely as a result of national policies. The criteria for doing so is to be the subject of Central Government advice. The procedure for declaring an AQMA and the proposed action to comply with the AQS laid down is to be similar to that of the designation of a smoke control area (see p. 356) involving consultation with a variety of bodies (DoE, EA, public and neighbouring councils).

The Environment Act 1995 also contains wide regulation-making powers to enable local authorities to control levels of pollution in AQMAs (s. 84).

Advisory bodies with responsibility for air pollution
There are a number of bodies carrying out an advisory function within the area of air pollution. Three of particular importance are:

(a)   The Expert Panel on Air Quality Standards (EPAQS), set up by the DoE which makes recommendations in respect of AQS. Although the Government seeks advice from a variety of bodies, this group, made up of both medical and air pollution experts, is seen to have the greatest influence when setting new AQS. It has made recommendations for AQS for ozone, benzene, 1,3-butadiene and carbon monoxide with other pollutants to follow over a period of time.
(b)   The Quality of Urban Air Review Group (QUARG) reviews the state on urban air quality and makes recommendations in relation to monitoring stations/networks, types of pollutants monitored, information made available to the public and areas for further research.
(c)   The National Environmental Technology Centre (NETCEN) is responsible for a variety of functions relating to the measurement of air pollution. It coordinates the UK Smoke and Sulphur Dioxide Monitoring Network, prepares an annual National Atmospheric Emissions Inventory giving estimates of atmospheric pollution from all sources and provides training for local authorities in relation to the Enhanced Urban Network (EUN) (see below).

Monitoring of air pollution

The introduction of AQS for a variety of pollutants will rely heavily on the systematic measurement of those pollutants in the atmosphere. Monitoring of smoke, sulphur dioxide, grit and dust has, in fact, taken place since the early part of this century. This is unsurprising given the major impact that these pollutants had upon health and the environment and the relatively unsophisticated methods of measurement. In 1961, the establishment of the National Survey of Air Pollution led to a coordinated network of monitoring sites situated throughout the country. These sites concentrated on the accumulation of data on smoke and sulphur dioxide. The network was, however, unwieldy (nearly 1,200 sites) and unreliable. The National Survey was, in turn, replaced with a more workable Smoke and Sulphur Dioxide Monitoring Network with over 200 sites. Of these, the majority monitor compliance with EU Directives on sulphur dioxide and suspended particulates, with the rest forming the Basic Urban Network, providing basic information for urban areas. There are other monitoring sites which gather information on nitrogen dioxide, lead in the atmosphere and acid deposition.
The most significant recent development in monitoring air pollution has been the introduction of the Enhanced Urban Network (EUN) in 1992 (with an expansion in 1995). A range of pollutants (ozone, nitrogen oxide, sulphur dioxide, carbon monoxide and particulates) are measured continuously at sites throughout the country.
Information on pollutants which are likely to affect health is gathered from the EUN and disseminated to the public via the Met Office weather bulletins, the media, a telephone service and the Internet.

There are specific and separate requirements for the monitoring and dissemination of information on ozone levels. The Ozone Monitoring and Information Regulations 1994 (SI 1994 No. 440) implemented the EC Directive on Air Pollution by Ozone (92/72). The Regulations require the establishment of a monitoring network, the dissemination of information, and a system whereby the public are warned when excessive levels of ozone are in the atmosphere. These warnings should be communicated as soon as possible and on a sufficiently wide scale to enable the public to take precautionary measures. The warnings should contain details of the area affected, the length of time that levels are likely to be excessive and precautionary measures which should be taken. The regulations are implemented by means of the EUN and the public information systems outlined above.

The introduction and expansion of the EUN has been widely welcomed but the quality and accuracy of past monitoring of air pollution has been criticised strongly. The main criticisms have centred around the selection and quantity of sites. The effectiveness of any monitoring network is primarily dependent upon the location of the monitoring equipment. It has been argued that the monitoring sites are not generally located in areas of high exposure and therefore give a false impression of levels of pollution. Secondly, although coverage of monitoring sites is spreading there are still large gaps, particularly in some areas of heavy industry and traffic. More specifically, the EC has criticised the UK for failing to provide an adequate number of sites to monitor nitrogen dioxide levels. The introduction of a National Air Quality Strategy based around specific targets and AQS means that the base data provided by the EUN has to be credible and sufficiently broad to indicate true levels of improvement.

The EC and air pollution

The protection of the atmosphere was not seen as a priority by the EC until the mid 1980s. Indeed, relatively few proposals based purely on environmental protection (as opposed to market harmonisation) were published before 1984. The reasons for this were twofold. First, a lack of political will and, secondly, a genuine desire to move forward in other areas. As a result of the effects of acid rain, however, the German Government pressed for swift action in 1983 and the main framework Directive on emissions from industrial plant (84/360) was introduced nearly 10 years after the framework Directives for waste and water pollution. Since that time, though, the concern about trans-boundary pollution and wider issues such as global warming and ozone depletion has led to a wide range of Directives being introduced.

The Commission's approach to the protection of the atmosphere has been wide-ranging in its scope. Various mechanisms have been used.

Environmental quality standards
Directive 80/779 on Smoke and Sulphur Dioxide sets limit values for the ground level concentration of smoke and sulphur dioxide which must be

adhered to for specified periods. Furthermore, there are more stringent guide
levels which can be set in areas of special need. Other approaches of this sort
are to be found in Directives on Lead (82/884) and Nitrogen Oxide (85/203).
In Britain, these Directives have been implemented by means of the Air
Quality Standards Regulations 1989 (SI 1989 No. 317).

A framework Directive on air quality was formally adopted in September
1996. The Directive is intended to provide a framework for a variety of
pollutants (in the process replacing Directives 80/779, 85/203 and 82/884).

It is intended that the Framework Directive will apply three types of quality
objective — a limit value, a guide value and an alert threshold (which mirrors,
to some extent the new framework found in the draft of the air quality
strategy to be produced under the Environment Act 1995).

Emission limits

Certain Directives impose limits upon the emission levels of pollutants. In the
framework Directive 84/360 this is used in conjunction with the process
standard 'best available technology not entailing excessive cost'.

Directive 88/609 dealing with emissions from large combustion plants
utilises a variation on the normal emission standard. Under that Directive,
each Member State is allocated a total national limit for emissions from power
stations and other large combustion plants. These so-called 'bubble' limits are
then reduced over a period of time. This enables each Member State to have a
degree of flexibility when imposing individual emission limits whilst still
maintaining an overall ceiling. In Britain, these Directives based upon specific
emission levels have been implemented through Part I of the EPA 1990.

The introduction of a national 'plan' for the 'bubble' limits for sulphur
dioxide and nitrogen oxide from combustion plants has been implemented
under s. 3(5) of the EPA 1990. This plan has imposed particular limits upon
individual power stations which cumulatively fall within the overall limits
under the Directive. The national plan is not binding, however, and the limits
which have been placed upon the Part I authorisations for these power
stations are, on the whole, more stringent. This allows an operator with a
number of plants to exceed its allocation under the national plan for one plant
if that can be offset by low levels of emissions at another, provided that it falls
within the limit set by the Part I authorisation.

Product standards

The protection of the atmosphere is one of the few areas where product
standards have been used extensively. One of the main reasons for this is that,
previously, the introduction of such standards was seen to be justifiable in
terms of market harmonisation where environmental justifications were not
accepted by every Member State. Relevant Directives include: lead in petrol
(85/210); emissions from vehicles (88/76, 89/458 and 91/441); and the
sulphur content of gas oil (87/219).

Prohibitions

The phasing out and prohibition of CFCs under Regulations 3322/88 and
594/91 is one of the few examples of that mechanism.

Market mechanisms

Proposals for an EC carbon/energy tax have been progressing through various stages for some time. Compulsory taxation on carbon-based fuel has been accepted by the majority of Member States, with Britain being the main dissenter. The future of the proposal is somewhat uncertain but it is envisaged that some form of taxation will be introduced by the late 1990s.

EC action on a worldwide basis

The EC has encouraged a number of worldwide initiatives by negotiating in its own right on issues which require global action. Thus, the EC is a signatory to the Vienna Convention on Ozone Layer Protection. This in turn led to the implementation of Regulations 3322/88 and 594/91 on CFCs.

Future proposals

A new framework Directive on Air Quality Standards has recently been adopted (see above). This proposal will replace Directives 80/779, 85/203 and 82/884 in respect of air quality and introduce limit values for a range of substances. The objective of the new proposal will be to harmonise the present Directives by putting forward three types of quality objectives which will apply to all substances under the Directive: first, a limit value, secondly, a guide value and, thirdly, an alert threshold. Not all of the substances would be subject to the three parameters immediately and further daughter Directives will be introduced to phase in those substances which are not limited in every category.

The Air Quality Standards Regulations 1989

As Britain was under a duty to implement EC Directives on air quality, steps were taken (prior to the introduction of the provisons under Part I of EPA 1990) to move away from the informal, flexible standards under previous legislation. Therefore, in 1989, mandatory air quality standards were introduced under the Air Quality Standards Regulations 1989 (SI 1989 No. 317). These regulations impose an obligation upon the Secretary of State to ensure that levels of sulphur dioxide, nitrogen dioxide, lead and smoke do not rise above EC limits, and to set up a system of sampling stations to measure air quality.

The control of smoke under the Clean Air Act 1993

As we have seen, the control of smoke, dust and dirt from industrial and domestic fires was largely ineffective in dealing with the problems associated with such emissions in the early part of the twentieth century. Although the Public Health (Smoke Abatement) Act 1926 attempted to control certain categories of industrial smoke, domestic smoke was prohibited only if it amounted to a 'nuisance'. The Clean Air Act 1956, later amended and supplemented by the Clean Air Act 1968, provided a comprehensive control mechanism for the protection of the environment from smoke, dust and fumes. These Acts were consolidated in the Clean Air Act 1993.

This Act constitutes a separate and distinct area of control. Essentially, it controls smoke, dust and grit from all fires and furnaces.

Overlap with Part I of EPA 1990
Section 41 of the 1993 Act specifically excludes prescribed processes from controls regulating the production of smoke and dust. Under that section, Parts I — III of the 1993 Act do not apply to any prescribed process as from the date on which an application for authorisation is granted or refused (whether or not on appeal).

The enforcement agency responsible for the Clean Air Act 1993 is the district authority, metropolitan authority, unitary authority or London borough council (s. 55).

Control of smoke from chimneys
Section 1 of the 1993 Act prohibits the emission of 'dark smoke' from the chimney of any building. Any occupier who breaches s. 1 will be guilty of a criminal offence. The section applies to all types of buildings, from domestic houses to industrial premises and crematoria. The mechanism of control specifically applies to chimneys from buildings. Although the definition of the word 'building' covers such structures as a greenhouse, it would have to be a part of a recognised structure (*Clifford* v *Holt* [1899] 1 Ch 698).

The prohibition applies only to 'dark smoke'; other types of emissions are covered either elsewhere in the Act or under different statutes. In attempting to determine whether smoke is 'dark', enforcement officers are forced to make a visual assessment of the shade of the smoke emission by comparing the darkness of the smoke with a uniform chart known as a Ringelmann chart. The chart contains five shades of grey by cross hatching black lines on a white background from clear (number 0) to black (number 4). The chart is rectangular in shape, measuring some 581 mm × 127 mm. The chart is used in accordance with certain guidelines laid down in British Standard 2742. It is held up by the operator and compared to the smoke from a distance of at least 15 metres and then comparisons are made between the colour of the smoke and the colour on the chart. If the colour of the smoke is as dark as, or darker than, shade 2 on the Ringelmann Scale it then qualifies as dark smoke (s. 3(1)). Where, however, an operator is experienced, s. 3(2) allows for an assessment to be made independent of the Ringelmann chart, often by the use of a smaller, more portable smoke chart (129 mm × 69 mm). Some officers rely purely on their experience to assess whether or not the smoke is darker than shade 2.

The prohibition also only covers smoke emitted from chimneys. The definition of a chimney can be found in s. 64 and is wide enough to cover all structures or openings through which smoke is emitted. Thus, smoke from outdoor fires or, for instance, burning straw or stubble is not covered by s. 1.

Strict liability
As in other environmental legislation, liability is strict, therefore prima facie *any* dark smoke emitted from a chimney would give rise to liability under

s. 1. The Act imposes liabililty on an occupier of a building from which smoke is emitted, irrespective of responsibility.

Exemptions and defences

Section 1(3) provides for certain exemptions to be made by the Secretary of State. These exemptions are restricted by the duration of emissions. The Dark Smoke (Permitted Periods) Regulations 1958 (SI 1958 No. 498) allows three main exemptions for smoke from chimneys. There are time-limits imposed of anything between 10 and 40 minutes during any period of eight hours for emission of dark smoke depending on both the number of furnaces used and whether or not soot is blowing. Secondly, there is a limit of four minutes of continuous emissions of dark smoke where the cause is not owed to burning soot. Lastly, there is a limit of two minutes in each period of 30 minutes where smoke is black (that is, smoke as dark as, or darker than, shade 4 on the Ringelmann chart).

Furthermore, s. 1(4) lays down three statutory defences. These defences are not absolute and require certain qualifying steps to be taken to ensure that the defences apply. The section provides that it is a defence to a charge under s. 1(1) that the emission was:

(a) solely due to the lighting of a furnace, and that all practicable steps were taken to minimise or prevent emissions;

(b) solely due to the failure of a furnace, and that the contravention of s. 1(1) could not reasonably have been foreseen or provided against and prevented by action taken after the failure;

(c) solely due to the unavoidable use of the least unsuitable fuel available when suitable fuel was unavailable, and that practicable steps were taken to minimise or prevent emissions;

(d) any combination of (a), (b) and (c).

Enforcement and offences

Local authorities can take action against dark smoke emitted from outside the area which they control if it affects their area (s. 55(2)). An important prerequisite of bringing a prosecution is that the enforcement authority are under a duty to notify occupiers of the existence of the offence 'as soon as may be'. This notification will normally be given orally by the relevant enforcement officer. If such oral notification is given, it must be confirmed in writing within four days of the date on which the officer became aware of the offence. In any event, written notice of the offence must be given within that time. If notification is not given, it is a defence to charges under ss. 1, 2 or 20 of the Act (s. 51(3)). The offence is only triable in the magistrates' court. There are different maximum levels of fine for emissions from private dwellings (level 3 on the standard scale) and for any other case (level 5 on the standard scale) (s. 1(5)).

Emissions of dark smoke from industrial plants

Section 2 of the Act prohibits the emissions of dark smoke from industrial trade premises other than from a chimney of a building (which is covered under s. 1). 'Premises' include the grounds of factories and open areas such as demolition sites (*Sheffield County Council* v *ADH Demolition Ltd* (1983) 82 LGR 177). Section 2(2)(b) gives the Secretary of State power to pass regulations giving an exemption to the burning of prescribed matter which emits dark smoke in the open. The Clean Air (Emission of Dark Smoke) (Exemption) Regulations 1969 (SI 1969 No. 1263) exempt certain material such as timber, explosives, tar, and waste from animal or poultry carcases. Section 2(6) provides that industrial or trade premises include premises not used for industrial or trade purposes but on which substances or matter are burnt in connection with such processes. Thus, open areas without any connection to industrial activities would fall within control under this section.

Section 2(3) refers to the burden of proof required when attempting to show the causation of dark smoke. On trade or business premises, where circumstances are such that the burning of material would be likely to give rise to an emission of dark smoke, such an emission can be taken as proved unless the occupier or person accused of the offence can show that no dark smoke actually was emitted. When fires have been extinguished but dark smoke has already been emitted there has often been difficulty in proving the source of the dark smoke. This section allows environmental health officers to act against smoke pollution even though there is no smoke emanating from the premises. The prohibition under s. 2 applies not only to occupiers but also to any person who causes or permits the emission of dark smoke from industrial or trade premises.

There is a statutory defence under s. 2(4) that the emission of dark smoke was 'inadvertent'. This would suggest that although the offence has an absolute liability, some degree of blameworthiness is necessary for an action to be successful. If the emission was inadvertent, it is also necessary to show that all practicable steps have been taken to prevent or minimise the emission of dark smoke. Practicability is defined in s. 64 as meaning reasonably practicable having regard to local conditions and circumstances, to the financial implications and to the current state of technical knowledge. An offence under s. 2 is triable only in a magistrates' court, the maximum fine being set at level 5 on the standard scale (s. 2(5)).

The control of grit, dust and fumes

The Act does not only cover smoke. Emissions from furnaces can also contain particulate matter and the Act extends to cover such particulate matter, ranging from the largest (being grit as defined in the Clean Air (Emission of Grit and Dust from Furnaces) Regulations 1971 (SI 1971 No. 162)), through dust and small solid particles between 1 and 75 μm in diameter (as defined in BS3405), to fumes (which are defined as any airborne solid matter smaller than dust) (s. 64). There are proactive measures for preventing smoke, dust, grit and fumes being emitted from furnaces. Section 4 provides that furnaces over a certain energy value (excluding domestic boilers) should, as far as practicable, be smokeless when using a fuel for which it was designed. This control is implemented by s. 4(1), under which anyone wishing to install a furnace has to notify the local authority before doing so. Where the local authority is notified and authorisation has been given, then the furnace is deemed to comply with the provision. This, however, does not exempt the furnace from being subject to the prohibition on dark smoke under s. 1. Where a furnace is operated without such an approval then the person who installed the furnace will be guilty of an offence (s. 4(4)).

This proactive approach is further strengthened by the requirement for grit and dust arrestment plant to be fitted to furnaces. This power is extended by ss. 6 and 7, which control all furnaces partly installed or for which there is an agreement to install after 1 October 1969. Again, details of the type of arrestment plant must be given to the local authority. Prior to 1 October 1969, the only furnaces covered were those in buildings burning pulverised fuel or solid waste or fuel at a rate of 1 tonne or more an hour. After that date, the Clean Air Act 1968 extended the powers to include furnaces in which solid, liquid or gaseous matter is burnt as well as reducing the rate of the use of solid matter to a minimum 100 pounds per hour. The statutory requirements are fleshed out by the Clean Air (Emission of Grit and Dust from Furnaces) Regulations 1971 (SI 1971 No. 162), which contain information as to the quantities of grit and dust which may be emitted by reference to either the heat put out by the furnace or the heat taken in by the furnace.

Exemptions

There are exemptions to the requirement to supply details of plant to the local authority under s. 6; s. 7 gives two main areas of exemption. First, the Secretary of State can exempt certain furnaces by way of the Clean Air (Arrestment Plant) (Exemption) Regulations 1969 (SI 1969 No. 1262), which exclude mobile or transportable furnaces, and certain other furnaces. Secondly, the local authority has a power to exempt a specific furnace if it is satisfied that the emissions from the furnace will not be prejudicial to health or a nuisance. Application for this exemption has to be made by the person installing the furnace. The local authority has eight weeks in which to give a written decision and if no decision is forthcoming in that period then exemption is deemed to have been granted. Where there is a refusal of an application, there is a right of appeal within 28 days from the date of the decision.

Monitoring provisions

To enable the local authority to enforce its responsibilities effectively, s. 10 allows the Secretary of State to make regulations which allow the local authority to monitor the emission of grit and dust from furnaces. This provision does not apply to fumes unless they are controlled specifically under other legislation.

The provisions regulating the measurement of grit and dust are contained in the Clean Air (Measurement of Grit and Dust) Regulations 1971 (SI 1971 No. 616) and the Clean Air (Units of Measurement) Regulations 1992 (SI 1992 No. 35). Under these regulations, the local authority has to give occupiers of premises not less than six weeks' notice in writing requiring them to make adaptations to any chimney serving a furnace to allow for plant and machinery to be installed to monitor the dust and grit from the furnace. Thereafter the local authority must give at least 28 days' notice in writing requiring a test to be carried out in accordance with the procedure specified in an otherwise obscure book, *The Measurement of Solids in Flue Gases* by P. G. W. Hawksley, S. Badzioch and J. H. Blackett. Then, after giving at least 48 hours' notice in writing of the date and time of the tests, the occupier must send to the local authority within 14 days the report of the results of the test, including the date, the number of furnaces and the results in terms of pounds of grit and dust emitted per hour.

These provisions apply only to a number of specific types of furnace including those that burn pulverised fuel or any other solid matter at a rate of 45 kilograms or more per hour.

The control of height of chimneys

As one of the main mechanisms for the control of environmental pollution into the atmosphere was to increase the height of chimneys to disperse the pollutant over a wider area, there is specific legislation to control the height of chimneys. The argument used by many scientists has been that the higher the chimney the higher the emission point, and thus the more diluted any emissions will be when they eventually come back down to the ground.

Under ss. 14 and 15, an application for chimney height approval is required to enable the local authority to assess the height required, taking into account the geographical features and the constitution of the emissions, so as to avoid localised pollution. If approval is not obtained, it will only be an offence if the chimney is used once it has been constructed. The application form is prescribed by the Clean Air (Height of Chimneys) (Prescribed Form) Regulations 1969 (SI 1969 No. 412). An application must be made in the following circumstances:

(a)   where a new chimney is erected;

(b)   where the combustion space of a furnace serving an existing chimney is enlarged by adding a new furnace to an existing number of furnaces all serving the same chimney;

(c)   where a furnace is removed, or replaced, but only where a furnace burns pulverised fuel, or burns solid matter at a rate of 100 pounds or more per hour, or burns more than 1.25 million BTU per hour of any liquid or gas.

In addition to these controls, planning permission must also be applied for.

When deciding whether or not to grant chimney height approval, the local authority must be satisfied that the chimney height will be sufficient to prevent, so far as is practicable, the smoke, grit, dust, gases or fumes emitted from the chimney from being prejudicial to health or a nuisance when taking into account (s. 15(2)):

(a)   the purpose of the chimney;

(b)   the position and descriptions of buildings near it;

(c)   the levels of the neighbouring ground;
(d)   any other matters requiring consideration in the circumstances.

If the local authority decides to grant approval, it can grant it with or without conditions, but these must relate only to the rate and quality of emissions from the chimney (s. 15(3)). If the local authority turns down an application, it has to notify the applicant of its decision in writing with its reasons and an indication as to what it thinks the lowest acceptable height would be. The applicant may appeal to the Secretary of State within 28 days of notification of the decision (s. 15(6)).

As in other areas of control in the Clean Air Act, the Secretary of State has the power to exempt certain boilers or plants from this control for chimney height approval. These exemptions can be found in the Clean Air (Heights of Chimneys) (Exemption) Regulations 1969 (SI 1969 No. 411). The Regulations specifically relate to the need for approval to construct a chimney under s. 10 and include mostly temporary or mobile boilers or plant.

The guidelines on assessing chimney heights are contained in the *Third Memorandum on Chimney Heights,* published by HMSO. This provides specific mathematical calculations which take into account background levels of pollution. Where pollution levels are higher there is a requirement that a chimney should be higher as well. The memorandum indicates that the chimney height required should vary according to the type of area concerned among other factors. It identifies the following types of area:

(a)   an undeveloped area where development is unlikely;
(b)   a partially developed area with scattered houses;
(c)   a built-up residential area;
(d)   an urban area of mixed industrial and residential development;
(e)   a large city or an urban area of mixed heavy industrial and dense residential development.

By assessing the level of pollution in the atmosphere in these generalised ways, it is hoped to achieve an idea of the required height for a particular chimney. In a large city or urban area it will be a requirement that chimneys should be at their highest.

Miscellaneous controls

Aside from chimneys serving a furnace, s. 16 applies similar restrictions on chimneys serving a non-combustion process. There is a much simpler procedure for obtaining approval by submitting building regulation plans. The local authority is entitled to reject the plans if the chimney is not adequate to prevent emissions from becoming prejudicial to health or a nuisance. There is a right of appeal against refusal.

The Building Regulations 1991 (SI 1991 No. 2768) apply not only to non-combustible furnace chimneys but also to those controlled by s. 15. Building regulation approval is therefore required for all chimneys.

Smoke control areas

In order to improve conditions over wide areas and to control non-dark smoke, s. 18 allows local authorities to designate areas which will be smoke control areas. As there are difficulties in defining areas in relation to land, two or more authorities are entitled to join together and declare that a larger area than their own area is to be a smoke control area (s. 61(3)). Most smoke control areas were designated soon after the introduction of the Clean Air Act 1956. Although the process has slowed down since that time, the number of smoke control orders continues to rise. By 1990, nearly 10 million premises were subject to control, and the success of the orders was a major factor in the achievement of compliance with EC Directive 80/779.

The effect of designating a smoke control area is to make it an offence for occupiers of premises to allow any smoke emissions from a chimney.

The Act exempts both authorised fuel and certain fireplaces from control. The Smoke Control Areas (Authorised Fuels) Regulations 1991 (SI 1991 No. 1282), consolidate 17 different regulations made since 1956. These Regulations include all the types of material which can be burnt without emitting smoke. Fireplaces are exempted under various Smoke Control (Exempted Fireplaces) Orders. Therefore, either authorised fuel can be used *per se* or unauthorised fuel can be used on exempted fireplaces, and the use of either could amount to a defence to a prosecution under s. 20. The burden of proof for showing that such exemptions apply falls upon the occupier.

The local authority is entitled under s. 18(2) to exempt specified buildings, classes of building or fireplaces from the smoke control area. It may make different provision for different parts of the area or limit their operation to specified classes of buildings in the area, such as factories rather than houses.

The process for making an order designating a smoke control area is contained in sch. 1. There is a requirement for general publicity, which enables the public to make objections. This publicity is effected by placing advertisements in the *London Gazette* in addition to notices being posted around the area. If there are any objections to the order they must be taken into account as material considerations in deciding whether or not to ratify the order. Where an order is made, its operation is delayed for a minimum of six months whilst the authority brings the effect of the order to the notice of the people within the area.

Department of the Environment Circular 11/81 suggests that there should be sufficient supplies of authorised fuel in the area and the operation of the order should be implemented at some time between 1 July and 1 November to ensure that there are adequate provisions of fuel stocks.

The control of noxious emissions to the atmosphere other than smoke, dust, grit and fumes

Although the control of smoke has remained relatively unaffected by the EPA 1990, the control of more noxious pollutants is controlled under the air pollution control (APC) system contained in Part I of that Act.

The general framework of control under the APC regime is similar to that under IPC. Such things as application procedures, appeals, conditions and enforcement powers broadly reflect the IPC system, as to which see Chapter 11. It is not, therefore, intended to reproduce all the statutory provisions but to concentrate on the distinguishing features of APC where they depart significantly from the IPC system.

Under APC, local authorities regulate atmospheric emissions from a variety of industrial processes and mobile plant. New processes or existing processes which were substantially modified were required to apply for authorisation from 1 April 1991. Unlike IPC all existing processes covered under APC were required to apply for authorisation before the end of 1993.

The scope of air pollution control

The Environmental Protection (Prescribed Processes and Substances) Regulations 1991 (SI 1991 No. 472) (as amended) lists those processes which are to be controlled by the local authority, known as Part B processes. Since the introduction of the Regulations in 1991 there have been two major changes to the content of the Part B list. In a strong deregulatory move in 1994 there was a streamlining of the process list with some Part A processes (under IPC) being transferred to Part B and many threshold levels being raised to take processes outside regulatory control. Further changes have been made and are likely to continue for some time. These amendments should be viewed in the same context as the continuing review of APC guidance notes (see below). As in the planning field, the Government has used both regulatory amendments and policy guidance to refine the scope of the system in an attempt to eliminate what is considered to unnecessary bureaucracy. Critics have, however, argued that the raising of thresholds and other amendments have had a significant impact upon the number of process which are not subject to any regulation. In particular, the choice of defined threshold limits has lead to claims that some limits are almost arbitrary. For example, the threshold for prescribing processes involving the sale of coal and coal products was lifted from a throughput of 3,000 tonnes to 10,000 tonnes. Whilst it might be argued that the impact of operations with a throughput at the former level was insignificant, it is much more difficult to argue that the latter level is a precise indication of a significant impact. If this is the case, is the impact insignificant at a throughput of 9,995 tonnes per year? It is for this reason that some operators have chosen to alter processes to fall beneath the threshold limits and escape direct control.

The substances controlled under APC are set out in sch. 4 to the Regulations and are controlled only in relation to their impact on the atmosphere rather than land or water (see p. 314).

Applications

All Part B process applications must be made to the local authority for the area in which the process will be carried on (in the case of mobile plant it is the local authority in which the applicant's principal place of business is situated). The form and content of the application is set out in the Environmental Protection (Applications, Appeals and Registers) Regulations 1991 (SI 1991 No. 507) (as amended). A application fee is payable under the APC charging scheme. An annual fee is payable thereafter.

An application must contain general information about the location of the process, a description of the process and the name and address of the operator. It should also contain details of any prescribed substances released from the process, with an assessment of the environmental consequences of the emissions and methods of abatement and monitoring all with reference to the BATNEEC for that particular process. It should be borne in mind that this information relates only to atmospheric emissions (s. 7(5)), it is not necessary to include any information on discharges to water and production of solid wastes. It is also not necessary to undertake an exercise to identify the BPEO in relation to the process as this only applies to IPC (s. 7(7)).

The local authority has the power to request further information in writing (sch. 1, para. 1(3)). The procedure in relation to consultation and publicity is similar to that for IPC, with HSE being notified (but unlike IPC not being part of a full consultation exercise) and nature conservation bodies being statutory consultees and publication of details of the application in a newspaper within 42 days of the application being made. Representations can be made within 28 days of the publication of the details of the application. Under the Environmental Protection (Authorisation of Processes) (Determination Periods) Order 1991 (SI 1991 No. 513) the determination period for applications involving new processes is four months whereas this can be extended to nine months for an existing process (see SI 1994 No. 2847). In every case the deadline can be extended with the agreement of the parties.

The determination of the application

The local authority has two choices when determining an application. It can grant the application subject to conditions (including conditions imposed by s. 7) or refuse the application (s. 6(3)). It must refuse an application where it considers that the applicant will not be able to comply with the conditions which would be imposed under the authorisation (s. 6(4)). The High Court has interpreted this provision in a wide manner in *R* v *Secretary of State for the Environment, ex parte West Wiltshire District Council* [1996] Env LR 312. In that case an inspector hearing an appeal against refusal to grant an authorisation concluded that the applicants were unlikely to be able to carry on the process so as to comply with the statutory objectives of the Act as there were no detailed proposals which indicated that the statutory objective of BATNEEC (the best available techniques not entailing excessive costs) could be met in preventing or reducing emissions, nor were there any proposals which demonstrated that management or design shortcomings would be overcome.

The Secretary of State disagreed with the inspector's conclusions. In considering s. 6(4) the Secretary of State considered that there were two issues:

(a) If an authorisation were to be granted, what conditions would be included?

(b) Would it be possible for the applicant to carry on the process in compliance with those conditions?

The Secretary of State stated that the second of these issues was concerned with the question of whether the appellant was *able* to comply with the conditions, not whether he was *likely* to comply. He concluded that he was not persuaded that the appellant was unable to comply with the conditions. He pointed out that there were a large number of enforcement options available under Part I if there was any future breach of any conditions.

The court allowed the appeal and quashed the decision on grounds which were not strictly related to the statutory interpretation of s. 6(4). Part of the judgment did, however, address the meaning of s. 6(4). Although it was only *obiter*, the judge thought that 'will be possible' was not necessarily the same as 'will be able' when considering whether an applicant would comply with conditions. Thus, it was relevant to consider the previous activities of the applicant when determining whether there would be compliance with conditions in any new consent.

Each APC authorisation has an implied condition (where not explicit) that the BATNEEC will be used for preventing the release of prescribed substances into the air or, where that is not practicable, for reducing the release of that substance to a minimum or rendering it harmless. There is a residual duty to render harmless the release of any substance which might cause harm to the air.

Explicit conditions can be imposed to achieve the BATNEEC standards and to ensure compliance with any standards or limits set down by the Secretary of State. It is particularly important to consider the lawfulness of conditions imposed in relation to APC authorisations. GG2 sets out a list of model conditions with tests of clarity, relevance and workability proposed for determining lawfulness. As in a number of other areas where conditions overlap (most notably planning and waste disposal) it is not necessarily easy to identify clear subject boundaries. It should be possible, however, to limit the conditions purely to the operation of the process itself and the consequences for atmospheric emissions. Most guidance notes contain a list of the matters which should be made the subject of conditions.

Air pollution guidance notes

Unlike the IPC guidance note system, central guidance notes for APC are issued centrally by the DoE. There is a large number of guidance notes which cover all Part B processes. Each note contains information relating to recommended emission limits, requirements for monitoring, reporting and record-keeping, as well as miscellaneous matters including the use of equipment to abate pollution, the handling of certain materials and the construction of chimneys and other emission points.

Significantly, the guidance notes cover situations where existing operations must be upgraded to meet new quality objectives. The notes are reviewed on a four-yearly cycle. In a similar fashion to the Prescribed Processes and Substances Regulations, the review has been seen as an attempt to deregulate the system and to simplify, in particular, ongoing requirements for monitoring. It has been suggested that where monitoring information has been initially validated by an external independent party, the gap between a further regular monitoring period may be extended. It is presumed that this is justified by the demonstrated reliability of the information. This move has also been criticised as it increases the chance that breaches of conditions in relation to emissions limits will be much more difficult to detect.

Enforcement provisions

Sections 11 to 14 of the EPA 1990 enable local authorities to enforce the APC system. The provisions are the same as for IPC and include:

(a) variation notices to take into account changes in circumstances (s. 11);

(b) enforcement notices requiring certain steps to be taken (s. 13);

(c) revocation notices to be issued in situations where a process has not been carried out for twelve months (s. 12);

(d) prohibition notices in situations where there is a imminent risk of serious pollution (s. 14).

There is a right of appeal under s. 15. Local Authority officers have the same powers as EA inspectors when dealing with the obtaining of information.

Public registers

Under ss. 20 to 22 of the EPA 1990, there is a duty on local authorities to keep registers and information relating to applications and authorisations, convictions, and monitoring data. They must also hold registers in relation to the IPC system.

Overlap with other controls

Where an authorisation is required under both parts of the regulations, i.e., there are components of a process subject to IPC control and related components subject to Part B of the regulations, the EA will have full control.

The Secretary of State also has power to transfer processes under APC control to the EA (this is intended to smooth the administrative functions of the system in that, where a process is substantially controlled by the EA, but there are a number of processes which are controlled under APC, it would make administrative sense to amalgamate the two controls under the EA). It is also thought that such a power could be used where the Secretary of State is of the opinion that the local authority is not conducting its duties properly.

Where matters which could amount to a statutory nuisance are more properly controlled under APC, the Secretary of State's consent is required before a local authority can institute summary proceedings (s. 79(10)). It is important to note that this is not a complete prohibition on the bringing of an action in statutory nuisance. Indeed, where an operator of a process is guilty of an offence under s. 23, it is undoubtedly for a local authority to fulfil its statutory duty under s. 79 to ensure that statutory nuisances within its area are abated.

The control of emissions from motor vehicles

The effect of transport on the environment is varied. Noise, land-take for roads and other projects and the use of raw materials (petrol, diesel, in addition to manufacturing materials). Emissions from vehicles are, however, probably the most significant issue which needs to be regulated and controlled.

The problems of pollution from motor vehicles was acknowledged as significant in the RCEP's first report where the Royal Commission warned of the dangers of ignoring the environmental implications of traffic growth. With growth forecasts for road traffic of over 140% between 1988 and 2025 the original warnings have taken on a repetitive nature. In particular, the RCEP's Eighteenth Report on Transport and the Environment set out eight key objectives which were intended to make transport policy more sustainable. In relation to atmospheric pollution this included targets for air quality and the reduction of CO_2 emissions.

The law in relation to the control of emissions from motor vehicles is under constant review and too detailed to be covered, other than in principle, in a book of this type. Most controls target product standards in relation to vehicle-type approval, specified emission limits from vehicles, the content of fuel and maintenance tests. Most limits have their origin within EC legislation (see below).

When a new motor vehicle is produced it must comply with all relevant standards, including EC emission limits. The Motor Vehicles (Type Approval) (Great Britain) Regulations (SI 1994 No. 981) sets out type-approval procedures which are applied to specimen examples of vehicles prior to general sale.

The Road Vehicle (Construction and Use) Regulations, are a series of Regulations which set out requirements in reaction to a variety of construction details, including catalytic convertors, the use of unleaded petrol, and emission levels for vehicles in use. In particular, the annual MOT tests (and, more recently, roadside checks) have standards for smoke and carbon monoxide which must not be exceeded.

European policy on motor vehicles

The EC has combined policy with legislative initiatives on transport generally, and motor vehicles specifically, for some time (the earliest Directive on emissions from engines dates back to 1970). European transport policy is to be found in a Green Paper on the Impact of Transport on the Environment, adopted in 1992. UK policy mirrors the approach contained in this document with its integrated approach to transport policy ('sustainable mobility') with an increasing overlap between transport policy and other areas, such as planning and economic policy.

Vehicle emissions have been controlled under a number of increasingly complex amendments to the original controlling Directive 70/220. Generally, Directives have set product standards by fixing emission limits for carbon monoxide, HC and NO_2 and particulates. Various amendments have culminated in Directive 94/12 which sets out limits for cars and light vans which will come into force in 1997 for all new registrations and 1996 for new models. Emissions from larger vans and heavy duty vehicles are controlled under separate Directives (93/59 and 91/542 respectively).

In addition to the fixed emission limits, there have been a number of Directives controlling the roadworthiness of vehicles to ensure that the original product standards are being maintained. Directives 91/238 and 92/55 set out procedures for checking the roadworthiness of private cars and light vehicles and catalytic converters respectively.

These Directives are implemented in UK legislation through the Construction and Use Regulations and the Type Approval Regulations (see above).

THIRTEEN
Waste management

The production of waste is a natural consequence of life in an industrialised society. In the past, both the volume and the types of waste produced were easily dealt with in small, country rubbish dumps. This, of course, was in the days before plastic packaging, aluminium cans and other composite materials which make up a large amount of domestic waste in Britain. Furthermore, the amount of domestic waste disposed of in Britain represents only a small fraction of the total amount of waste produced. In the Second Report of the House of Commons Environment Committee on toxic waste, it was shown that in 1989 Britain produced approximately 2,500m tonnes of waste, of which only 1.5m tonnes was domestic and trade waste. Other types of waste included liquid industrial effluent, agricultural waste, waste from mines and quarries, sewage sludge, waste from power stations, solid industrial waste and hazardous waste.

These vast amounts of waste have increased in recent years. The consumer boom of the post-war Britain has led to the production of more and more products with less and less durability. As consumption increases so does the volume of waste, and a strong impression builds up that we live in a society with a throwaway mentality. The culprits are, however, not just the end users of products, but also the producers and designers of them.

Most of the waste disposed of in Britain is deposited in large holes in the ground, such as old quarries. The difficulties of burying waste are numerous. Substances may break down after a number of years to produce contaminating liquids or hazardous gases, which may then escape from the site. In 1989 and 1990, the House of Commons Environment Committee reported on the issues of toxic waste and contaminated land. The evidence submitted to the Committee painted a horrifying picture of the extent to which there are problems with the state of contaminated land in Britain. Estimates of the area of land contaminated range from a very conservative 10,000 hectares to a possible 100,000 hectares. Britain has already experienced the dangers of waste disposal sites. In 1986, methane produced from a landfill site at Loscoe in Derbyshire exploded, causing injury. Other examples could be given from around the world of housing estates that have been abandoned because of contamination of the land on which they were built, severely polluted water supplies, deaths caused by indiscriminate dumping of waste, and areas that are wholly unusable owing to long-term pollution problems caused by dumping.

Landfill is not the only option for the disposal of waste. Large quantities of waste are discharged to sewers or to natural waters, both matters which are dealt with elsewhere in this book. A small percentage of waste is incinerated or dumped at sea.

Each of these methods of disposal creates its own pollution problems and controversies. As suggested above, landfill sites may give rise to problems of methane emissions and of water pollution as a result of leachate. They also give rise to effects that will be only too obvious to those who live nearby, such as smells, noise, air-borne dust and rubbish, and increased traffic generation. As a result, landfill sites are amongst the uses of land that are most vigorously opposed by local communities. A further factor is that there is a marked tendency for landfill sites to be proposed on 'waste land', which is often precisely that land which is of greatest importance in nature conservation and amenity terms. However, in the 1990s the most important point is simply that many existing sites are reaching their full capacity and that the supply of suitable new locations for landfill sites is very limited indeed. In some areas the problem is acute, leading to the need to transport waste long distances. A particular problem for Britain is that, unlike many other European countries, it has traditionally followed a policy of co-disposal on landfill sites, meaning that different sorts of waste are mixed together.

In relation to incineration, there are obvious problems of air pollution, especially concerning the release of such things as dioxins as a result of incomplete combustion. More recently, the publication of a draft US EPA Report on the effects of dioxins has led some people to take the view that any level of dioxin production, however small, could cause significant harm to both humans and the environment. It is becoming clear that the application of EC standards on air pollution to British incinerators will lead to a reduction in their number and that replacement facilities are being opposed and delayed through the town and country planning system and latterly the authorisation process under EPA 1990, Part I. However, in May 1993, the Royal Commission on Environmental Pollution in its Seventeenth Report, *Incineration of Waste* (Cm 2181), recommended that waste incineration should play a key role in the future development of waste disposal, though critics have pointed to the weakness of the Royal Commission's arguments on waste minimisation.

Dumping at sea is now heavily restricted through international conventions and must be seen as an option which has virtually disappeared. For example, dumping of industrial waste at sea has now effectively ceased and Britain, the only EC country still dumping sewage sludge at sea, has agreed to discontinue this practice by 1998.

These problems illustrate the need to establish a clear framework of policy to provide for the proper disposal of waste, particularly toxic and hazardous waste. However, more importantly, they establish the need to develop policies relating to the reduction of waste and its recycling or re-use.

Waste policy

The response has been to seek to develop policies that tackle the problem of waste at source if possible. The Conservative Government's White Paper, *This Common Inheritance,* states that 'the Government's first priority is to reduce waste at source to a minimum'. It further states that the Government is committed to the promotion of recycling of as much waste as possible and to the tightening of controls over waste disposal standards. This official policy can be summarised as being that waste minimisation is to be preferred to recycling, and recycling preferred to disposal. These policies reflect those of the EC (see below).

Although there has been a tremendous upsurge in policy initiatives in the field of waste management there has been a feeling that the growth has been unstructured and the overall objectives have been difficult to discern. It has also become important to establish central policy themes in order to set down the manner in which the policy objectives can, in practice, be achieved. There has therefore been a need to bring together the various initiatives in a coherent structure and to iron out any minor inconsistencies between individual strategies. The status of official policy on waste management has thus taken a further step forward with the introduction of a formal national waste strategy for England and Wales. Section 44A of the Environmental Protection Act 1990 (inserted by s. 92 of the Environment Act 1995) provides for the Secretary of State to prepare a statement containing policies in relation to the recovery and disposal of waste. It is intended that the strategy will replace waste disposal plans which have been drawn up by waste regulation authorities under s. 50 of EPA 1990 in addition to meeting the requirements of the EC framework Directive's provisions in relation to waste management plans.

A precursor to the adoption of the final version of the national waste strategy is the White Paper, *Making Waste Work* (Cm 3040) published in December 1995. At present, this strategy is non-statutory and advisory but amounts to a material consideration for planning authorities when drawing up development plans. Underpinning the strategy are the three key objectives for waste management: to reduce the amount of waste that society produces; to make best use of the waste that is produced; and to choose waste management practices which minimise the risks of immediate and future environmental pollution and harm to human health. The mechanism for achieving these three objectives is the previously outlined waste hierarchy of waste reduction, reuse, recovery, and disposal.

The White Paper sets two quantifiable targets with a further commitment to set a third target in future. The targets are:

(a)   To reduce the proportion of controlled waste going to landfill to 60% by the year 2005.

(b)   To recover 40% of municipal waste by the year 2005.

(c)   To set a target for overall waste reduction by the end of 1998.

There are a variety of secondary targets set for individual waste streams (for example, the paper adopts the existing target for household waste, namely, to recycle or compost 25% of household wastes by the year 2000).

It is fair to assume that when the statutory national waste strategy is introduced it will bear more than a passing resemblance to the policies set out in the White Paper. The formal strategy does, however, require a full national survey of the production of waste before it can be drawn up. It is unlikely to be finalised for some time.

Although Britain has now firmly established the concept of a hierarchy of waste management it must be recognised that Britain is still some way behind other EC countries in the amount of waste that is recycled and in developing recycling policies. For example, a recent report suggested that less than 6% of British household waste is recycled, against a Government target of 50%, which it believes can mainly be achieved through the use of economic instruments and charging mechanisms. In this respect, the Government's Advisory Committee on Business and the Environment recommended in its first report in November 1991 that the most effective method of encouraging recycling would be to raise landfill prices significantly — they are currently far lower than in many other countries. This is a simple example of the use of an economic instrument.

The introduction of a tax on waste disposed to landfill has been considered for some time. The idea received support from the Royal Commission on Environmental Pollution. The tax was implemented in the fiscal year 1996/97 and it is anticipated that rates will rise in future

The impact of the recent legislation on firms producing waste is clear, particularly when coupled with developments in relation to discharges to sewers and controls over incineration. Waste minimisation is to be encouraged because the costs of disposal, by whatever route, are likely to increase significantly throughout the 1990s.

As has frequently been the case in environmental matters, the British approach to the clean-up of contaminated land has tended to be a fairly pragmatic one. Unlike the position in some other countries, where land is cleaned up to uniformly high standards, the British approach is in general to consider the current use of land and to question whether there is any immediate threat of pollution or harm to human health. The British clean-up powers tend, therefore, not to be activated until there is some problem, and then are used only to the extent that is necessary to remove the problem, rather than to provide an absolutely pristine site (even if that were technically achievable).

This chapter will concentrate on the management of waste throughout the disposal chain and the clean-up of contaminated land. This should not, however, obscure the point that increasingly developments in waste minimisation techniques and recycling technologies are likely to dominate over the coming years.

National plan for exports and imports of waste

The Conservative Government produced a plan which sets out the legal framework controlling the import and export of waste to and from the UK.

The plan came into effect on 1 June 1996. Under the plan, which is legally binding throughout the United Kingdom, all exports of waste for disposal are banned, as are most imports for disposal other than in exceptional cases where wider environmental considerations apply. Exports of waste for recovery to countries within the Organisation for Economic Cooperation and Development (OECD) may continue but, subject to limited exceptions, exports of hazardous waste for recovery to non-OECD countries are banned. Imports of waste for genuine recovery operations may continue. The plan contains some discussion of the phrase 'genuine recovery' and what that means in relation to satisfying the plan. Unlike the national waste strategy described above, which is an advisory and non-binding document, the plan has statutory effect.

The use of economic instruments and waste management

The waste management system has seen the largest number of active initiatives in relation to the use of economic instruments in the field of environmental protection. In particular, provisions to encourage the recycling and the proposed tax on disposal of waste to landfill are intended to reflect the environmental costs of disposing of waste to land.

The landfill tax

In August 1996 the landfill tax was introduced under the Finance Act 1996. The Landfill Tax Regulations 1996, the Landfill Tax (Qualifying Materials) Order 1996 and the Landfill Tax (Contaminated Land) Order 1996 flesh out the statutory framework. The provisions came into force in October 1996 and mean that the vast majority of waste disposed of in landfill sites will be subject to a tax. The rate of tax is currently £7 a tonne, except for specified relatively 'inactive' wastes which will attract a rate of £2 per tonne. The tax is paid by the operators of landfill sites and passed on indirectly to the waste producers. It is intended to offset the money raised by making compensatory reductions in the level of employer National Insurance contributions.

The tax is likely to have a large impact upon those companies which dispose of significant volumes of waste to landfill, although this will be offset by some of the changes in other taxation. Furthermore, it is anticipated that there will be an incentive to produce less waste or recycle where appropriate. Other technologies for waste disposal (e.g., *in-situ* sewage treatment of liquid waste) are also expected to become more prominent as existing price differentials narrow. There have, however, been a number of criticisms of the proposed tax and allegations that it will only lead to more waste being dumped in poorly engineered and unsuitable sites.

The tax is intended to reflect the full environmental costs of disposing of waste to landfill and to apply the 'polluter pays' principle. It is also hoped that the amount of waste going to final disposal will be reduced by 20% over a 20-year period as waste producers seek to reduce costs. It is estimated that approximately 100 million tonnes of waste is dumped in landfill sites every year, with an average cost of £10 per tonne.

Generally, the use of the tax income to reduce National Insurance contributions has been welcomed, but some commentators have criticised the failure to allow the income to be set aside solely for environmental purposes. The Government has attempted to address these criticisms by introducing environmental trusts. These trusts are private sector, non-profit-making bodies, under a duty to distribute funds for approved environmental purposes — reflecting the bodies set up to administrate the proceeds of the National Lottery. In particular, it is intended that most of the funds will be set aside for paying for the clean-up of contaminated sites or closed landfills where primary responsibility cannot be clearly identified. This is one of the few examples of a hypothecated tax and certainly an unusual innovation in the environmental field, which could gain favour with a large number of environmental groups. Landfill tax bills are abated by up to 90% of any payments made by waste producers to the environmental trusts in the previous quarter. They are financed primarily from these rebates but the waste industry still has to contribute 10% of their funds.

Recycling

There is now a number of powers in the legislation which aim to encourage recycling. for example in accordance with Directive 91/156, many types of waste recycling facility are likely to be exempt from the waste management licensings, system and require only to be registered with the EA. However, it is clear that government belief is that recycling ought to be encouraged by voluntary and economic mechanisms rather than be required through compulsory controls. As a result, British legislation does not formally include many specific duties to recycle. This attitude partly explains, for example, the Government's opposition to the introduction of strict recycling targets in the proposed EC Directive on packaging, waste.

The authority with the most important role in relation to recycling is the waste collection authority, since it collects most domestic and commercial waste and is able to separate recyclable wastes at an early stage. The authority may require separate receptacles to be used for household wastes that are to be recycled and those which are not (s. 46(2)). It may buy or acquire waste with a view to recycling it (s. 55) and, if it makes arrangements for recycling waste, it does not have to deliver the waste to the waste disposal authority, as it would otherwise have to do under s. 48. It is also under a duty to draw up a waste recycling plan for its area, which involves publicising the arrangements it intends to make to facilitate recycling (s. 49). By the middle of 1993 all authorities had submitted their draft plan to the Secretary of State.

Perhaps most significant in the light of the Government's policy on economic instruments is that the waste collection authority is entitled to a recycling credit from the waste disposal authority under s. 52 where it recycles waste. The idea behind this provision is that it acts as an incentive to recycle waste by getting the waste disposal authority to pay the waste collection authority the amount of money it saves by not having to dispose of the waste. The amount payable is based on the net saving the waste disposal authority makes as a result of the recycling activities. At present the rate is fixed at half the average cost saving to the waste disposal authority, but the Government has announced that this is to rise to the full amount. The waste disposal authority *may* also make such a payment to anyone else who recycles waste and thus removes it from the waste stream (s. 52(3)).

Producer responsibility

Section 93 of the Environment Act 1995 provides for the introduction of Regulations to impose obligations on the producers of materials or products to recycle, recover or re-use those products or materials. The first set of Regulations imposing such an obligation introduced an obligation to recover and recycle certain percentages of packaging waste. The final version of these Regulations was laid before Parliament at the end of January and came into force at the beginning of March 1997. Under the EU Directive on Packaging and Packaging Waste (94/62 EC), the UK has been set targets for recycling and recovering packaging waste, under which 50% of waste packaging must be re-utilised through recycling and other recovery methods by 2001.

The legislation which translates the EU Directive into UK law is the Producer Responsibility Obligations (Packaging Waste) Regulations 1997 (SI 1997 No. 648). A key feature of the Regulations is the shared approach which spreads the responsibility for meeting the recovery and recycling targets right along the packaging chain from production through to retail.

Not all businesses are forced to comply with the Regulations. The criteria for businesses falling under the Regulations are that they must:

(a)   be involved in the following activities:

    (i)   manufacturing raw material used for packaging,
    (ii)   converting raw materials into packaging,
    (iii)   packing or filling packaging,
    (iv)   selling packaging to the end user (wholesalers will be obligated from January 2000);

(b)   produce, handle or supply more than 50 tonnes of packaging materials or packaging each year, including imported, but not exported, packaging;

(c)   have a turnover of more than £5 million (although from 2000, businesses with a turnover of over £1 million will fall under the Regulations).

The Regulations are being phased in over a period of four years. By the end of August 1997 obligated businesses must either:

(a)   register individually and provide a rough estimate, in tonnes per annum, of packaging handled in 1996, or
(b)   join a 'compliance scheme', which takes on the legal responsibility for meeting its members' targets. These compliance schemes must also be registered with the Environment Agency or SEPA.

Businesses and compliance schemes must re-register on 1 April each year. In 1998 and 1999 businesses must start to reach interim recovery targets of 38% and recycling targets of 7% per material (packaging which is made from metals, plastics, paper and glass). In the year 2000 these interim targets are raised to 43% recovery and 11% recycling per material. Finally, from 2001 onwards businesses must reach full recovery targets of 52% (of which 26% must be through recycling) and recycling targets of 16% per material.

There is an annual registration fee and it is an offence to fail to take 'reasonable steps' to recycle or recover the statutory targets. Obligated businesses have to demonstrate compliance in any year by sending a certificate of compliance to the Environment Agency which states that the company met its obligation in the preceding year. Companies will be monitored by the Agency every three years to ensure that compliance is achieved.

The Regulations have caused fierce debate within UK industry as the impact will be felt amongst a wide range of companies. There has been some disagreement over whether the targets are achievable within the time limits laid down. During the consultation exercise, many within industry complained that the targets were too high and unachievable. Friends of the Earth, however, have pointed out in contrast to the UK recycling targets, Germany is already recycling over three quarters, and the Netherlands half.

The producer responsibility obligation for packaging waste is probably just the first in a series of Regulations which will be introduced under s. 93 of the Environment Act 1995. It is likely that similar Regulations will be introduced to encourage the recycling and recovery of other products and materials including newspapers, electrical goods and batteries. What is most interesting about the scheme of the Regulations is the way that a variety of different mechanisms are used to secure the overall objective. The system operates in practice by compelling obligated businesses to purchase evidence of compliance from reprocessors who recover and recycle packaging materials in the form of packaging recovery notes (PRNs). Thus the Regulations mix the use of the market in these PRNs (which will fluctuate in price under the normal principles of supply and demand) with the prospect of criminal sanctions for non-compliance to encourage businesses to consider the amount of packaging which they use.

Legislative history

The disposal of waste was not seen as an important issue until a public outcry concerning the deposit of hazardous waste in the West Midlands in the early 1970s led to the passage of the Deposit of Poisonous Wastes Act 1972. This Act is a classic example of the reactive nature of environmental legislation in Britain, since it approached the deposit of waste from a narrow viewpoint and sought mainly to combat the type of incident that had occurred. However, it remains the case that the 1972 Act was one of the first ever controls over the deposit of hazardous waste in the world.

The 1972 Act was soon replaced by Part I of the Control of Pollution Act 1974 (COPA 1974). COPA 1974 introduced a more comprehensive system in which a waste disposal licence was required from the waste disposal authority before 'controlled waste' could be disposed of either to landfill or for incineration. This system provided a model for other countries, and in particular for the EC framework Directive on Waste (75/442). At that stage, Britain led the way in legislating against the dumping of waste.

However, over the years COPA 1974 gave rise to a number of problems and itself proved to be too narrow. Accordingly, in Part II of the Environmental Protection Act 1990 (EPA 1990) the framework for a new system of waste management was established. The change in concept from 'waste disposal' (as used in COPA 1974) to that of 'waste management' is significant, since it illustrates that increased control is to be exercised over the whole of the waste cycle 'from cradle to grave'. In particular, the EPA 1990 involves greater controls over waste producers and waste carriers than was the case under COPA 1974. As a result, the full implementation of the EPA 1990 changed the way in which waste is dealt with fundamentally.

After many stops and starts the main provisions of Part II of the EPA 1990 were finally implemented on 1 May 1994. Anyone who would like to think that the statutory regime is now settled and sensibly structured is unfortunately faced with labyrinth of regulations and guidance notes.

The main reason for the delay — and subsequent deluge of statutory and non-statutory material — has been the need to implement the framework Directive on Waste (91/156). In common with many other areas of environmental law the Act itself now provides only a framework which is fleshed out by numerous other documents. In addition to the Waste Management Licensing Regulations (SI 1994 No. 1056) which forms the main body of supplementary legislation, there is the Waste Management Licensing (Fees and Charges) Scheme, Waste Management Papers on the Licensing of Waste Management Facilities (No. 4) and Landfill Completion (No. 26A), and Government guidance in the form of the Department of the Environment Circular 11/94 on Waste Management Licensing and the Framework Directive on Waste. There is further legislation and guidance on the management of special waste in the form of the Special Waste Regulations 1996 (SI 1996 No. 972) as amended and Circulars 6/96 and 14/96. The effect of all this is that the law has now become even more complex and difficult to interpret. In this chapter an attempt will be made to explain some of the principles of the new legislation; unfortunately, the detail of the law falls outside the scope of such a work as this. Although COPA 1974 has now been largely superseded appropriate reference will be made to its provisions where the courts have interpreted concepts which are relevant to Part II of EPA 1990.

Transitional provisions

Most waste disposal licences granted under COPA 1974 and in force on 1 May 1994 are automatically treated as if they were a waste management license under Part II of EPA 1990. There are, however, four situations where the old Act continues to apply (although the significance of each diminishes with passing time):

(a)   old (i.e., made prior to 1 May 1994) applications for a waste disposal licence which are undetermined;

(b)   undetermined appeals against the revocation of a waste disposal licence;

(c)   activities which fall under Part I of the EPA 1990 but which are not yet covered and are exempt from the need for a licence under Part II;

(d)   scrap metal activities which are exempt from the need for a licence under Part II but are controlled under a waste management licence.

All of these transitional arrangements continue to be regulated under COPA 1974. Where applications or appeals are determined there will be an automatic transfer to a waste management licence as if it were 1 May 1994.

Waste disposal and town planning

The disposal of waste on land presents some difficult questions of a land use nature. It has always been necessary to acquire planning permission for landfill operations. Indeed, the Town and Country Planning Acts were the primary control over waste before COPA 1974 was enacted. They still provide an additional, and complementary, layer of controls, one that will remain largely unchanged by the introduction of the EPA 1990.

Waste local plans

On the whole, county authorities have traditionally incorporated policies on waste disposal into county structure plans. Some counties prepared subject local plans, but coverage has been sparse. There is now, however, a duty imposed under s. 38 of the Town and Country Planning Act 1990 (as amended by the Planning and Compensation Act 1991), upon non-metro-politan authorities alone, to prepare a waste local plan.

The plan should cover a variety of issues and should include references to the full range of waste management considerations, including such issues as:

scrap yards, incineration, landfill and landraise, recycling and waste transfer, waste processing, composting, storage and treatment centres.

The plan should be in general conformity with the structure plan and take into account any minerals local plan. It should aim to identify sites already in use, future sites and broad areas of search within which sites may be located. It should also identify policies setting out criteria against which applications for waste management facilities will be determined.

In metropolitan areas, waste policies should be included in unitary development plans in respect of development which involves the depositing of refuse or waste materials other than mineral waste.

When drawing up plans, local planning authorities should take into account factors such as the principle of self-sufficiency, whereby the authority should aim to allocate sufficient land and/or facilities to deal with the waste arising within that area. Other factors which need to be taken into account include targets of waste minimisation and recycling, incineration to reduce land take, the variety of treatment methods which may be required prior to disposal and any extant waste disposal plans made under s. 50 of the EPA 1990.

Waste local plans, waste disposal plans and the national waste strategy
Before the creation of the Environment Agency, the old waste regulation authorities were responsible for producing a waste disposal plan to be used in conjunction with the waste local plan. These plans were primarily concerned with the strategic aspects of treating and disposing of wastes as opposed to the land use issues addressed in the waste local plans. Section 50 of the EPA 1990, which made provision for such plans, was repealed by the Environment Act 1995 on 1 April 1996. From that date, waste disposal plans will be replaced by the national waste strategy. The statutory strategy has not yet been prepared but the White Paper on a strategy for sustainable waste management in England and Wales, *Making Waste Work*, sets out the framework for waste management (see above). Any waste disposal plan or modification of such a plan under s. 50 of the Environmental Protection Act 1990, whose content was finally determined before 1 April 1996, is to continue in force until the content of the national waste strategy is finally determined, notwithstanding the repeal of s. 50.

Development control
Section 55(3)(b) of the Town and Country Planning Act 1990 provides that the deposit of refuse or waste materials on land involves the material change in the use of that land if the area of the deposit is extended or the height of the deposit is extended above the original ground level. In addition, depending upon the facts of the case, tipping can amount to an engineering operation (if it involves technical supervision for instance), or even fall within the catch-all definition of an 'other operation'.

A planning application for the use of land, or the carrying out of operations in or on land, for the deposit of refuse or waste materials and/or the erection of any building, plant or machinery designed to be used wholly or mainly for the purposes of treating, storing, processing or disposing of refuse or waste materials is a county matter (see Town and Country Planning Act 1990, sch. 1). The application is made direct to the county planning authority, which is then under a duty to notify the district authority within 14 days as part of the consultation procedure (art. 12 of the GDPO).

Areas of doubt
Not every application will clearly fall within the above definitions. The ancillary use of waste disposal or management facilities as part of a larger operation would not amount to a county matter.

Planning conditions and obligations
The difficulties with using planning conditions to control environmentally sensitive developments have been covered elsewhere (see p. 257). Planning

permissions for waste disposal operations require special consideration. The main criterion for conditions on a planning permission for waste disposal is that they be for a planning purpose. Examples of matters which would normally be dealt with by way of conditions on the planning permission include:

(a)   phasing of operations;
(b)   the extent of tipping;
(c)   access to and from the site;
(d)   the *general* nature of the waste;
(e)   restoration plans, including site contours, minimum depth of top soil etc.;
(f)   aftercare for a short-term period.

To avoid duplicating environmental controls there are certain areas which should not normally be covered as they are more properly dealt with under the waste management regime. These include:

(a)   the duration of activity;
(b)   supervision of activities (including site offices and other administrative responsibilities);
(c)   the specific types of waste to be covered;
(d)   keeping of records;
(e)   associated works.

As stated above (p. 257), although it is advisable to separate the two areas of control, it is not unlawful to impose conditions which overlap.

EC Directives on waste

In keeping with the general aims of EC environmental policy set out in Art. 130R(2), the EC has adopted as a specific aim the prevention of waste at source through proper design of products and processes. This is linked with such initiatives as the development of clean technology, eco-labelling and the discipline of life cycle analysis. A second aim is to recycle or to re-use waste that is produced, with particular emphasis to be placed on the use of waste as a source of energy, for example through combined heat and power schemes linked to waste incinerators. An obvious example of the EC's role in this area is its development of a Directive on the recycling of packaging waste (although this is in fact based on existing legislation in other EC countries). A third aim is that waste should be disposed of in its country of origin, thus leading to restrictions on the transfrontier shipment of waste.

These aims have been translated into a number of Directives on waste management, each of which has had, and will continue to have, a great impact on the shape of British law in this area. The framework Directive on Waste 75/442 established a general framework of controls for waste management. In accordance with the EC's general policies, it aimed to encourage the recovery of waste and its management at the point of production. It has been significantly amended by Directive 91/156 which should have been complied with by April 1993. The Directive has been fully implemented with the introduction of the Waste Management Licensing Regulations (SI 1994 No. 1056). Together, the two Directives require that a public agency plans waste disposal properly, that waste disposal facilities are licensed by a competent public agency and that any exemptions from the licensing system fall within certain categories and are properly justified. They also lay down a definition of waste. In *Commission* v *Council* (case C-155/91) [1993] ECR I-939, the European Court of Justice decided that the principal objective of the amending Directive 91/156 was the protection of the environment rather than the removal of trade barriers.

There is a separate framework Directive on Hazardous Waste (78/319, as amended by 91/689). These Directives lay down similar requirements to those applicable to all waste. Their main significance is that the amendments set out in 91/689 seek to lay down a common definition of hazardous waste across the EC based on the generic features and constituents of the waste. Implementation of the Directive depended upon the preparation of a list of hazardous wastes by the EC, which were determinative of its scope. The list was finally agreed (after much discussion) in December 1994 and the provisions of the Directive have been implemented in England and Wales, with the introduction of the Special Waste Regulations 1996 (SI 1996 No. 9727).

There is also a Directive on Sewage Sludge (86/278), which lays down restrictions on the content of sewage sludge used on agricultural land. It has a knock-on effect on what sewerage undertakers will allow to be discharged into their sewers.

The EC has proposed a Directive on landfills. The landfill Directive seeks to harmonise landfill standards across the EC by laying down requirements on most matters concerned with the design and operation of a site, including permits, location, operating practices, leachate controls, financial guarantees, site closure, aftercare and liability for harm caused. However, the detail of the proposals has given rise to a great amount of controversy and there is no guarantee of the final form any Directive will take. A Directive on Packaging and Packaging Waste was adopted in December 1994. The objective of the Directive is to harmonise national measures on packaging waste. Member States must take action to achieve certain recycling targets. By June 2001, between 50% and 65% by weight of packaging waste is to be recovered, with 25–45% of this to be recycled. Implementation must take place before the beginning of 1998. This Directive has been implemented in the UK under the Producer Responsibility Regulations made under ss. 93–5 of the Environment Act 1995 (see further p. 369).

As far as transfrontier shipment of waste is concerned, Regulation 259/93 introduces a system of control of shipments of waste within, into and out of the EC. It implements the provisions of the Basle Convention on the Control of Transboundary Movement of Hazardous Wastes and their Disposal 1989 (Cm 984). The central feature of these instruments is a requirement that all shipments of waste must be subject to prior notification to the competent authorities. Transfrontier shipment of wastes, although a topic of great importance, is outside the scope of this book (apart from the national plan, p. 366).

Lastly, there are Directives on the incineration of waste. Directives 89/369 and 89/429 respectively cover new and old municipal incinerators. Both are 'daughter Directives' of the Directive on Air Pollution from Industrial Plants 84/360. They lay down EC standards based on best available technology and are expected to lead to the shutdown of a number of British incinerators that cannot meet those standards. A Directive on hazardous waste incineration was adopted in December 1994: amongst other things, this lays down strict emission limits based on the most up-to-date technology. The provisions of all these Directives are implemented in British law through the integrated pollution control and air pollution control systems in Part I of the EPA 1990. The introduction of the IPPC Directive in 1996 will have an impact on some waste management operations.

Waste disposal under the Control of Pollution Act 1974

Part I of COPA 1974 introduced a fairly comprehensive system of licensing under which a waste disposal licence was required from the waste disposal authority (WDA) for the deposit of household, industrial or commercial waste, referred to generically as 'controlled waste'. Mineral and agricultural wastes were, in general, exempt. So too was a range of activities listed in sch. 6 of the Control of Pollution (Collection and Disposal) Regulations 1988 (SI 1988 No. 819).

In non-metropolitan areas, the WDA was the county council in England and the district council in Wales. In metropolitan areas, it was normally the district council, although in some areas a joint body was established. The WDA had a range of administrative and regulatory functions, including a duty to arrange for the disposal of controlled waste (s. 13), a duty to make a waste disposal plan (s. 2), and responsibility for the operation of the licensing system (s. 5).

An application for a waste disposal licence had to be made in writing to the WDA (s. 51(1)). There were no publicity requirements, although there was a duty for the WDA to consult with the waste collection authority (normally the district council) and the NRA (s. 5(4)). The only mechanism for refusal on environmental grounds was that the disposal would pose a threat of water pollution or to public health (s. 5(3)). The WDA could attach conditions relating to waste disposal (s. 6), but the legislation was narrowly drafted in this respect and a number of desirable conditions were held to be outside its scope. There was a right of appeal to the Secretary of State against refusal or against any conditions (s. 10).

There were, however, parallel controls operated through the town planning system. Before a waste disposal licence could be granted, a valid planning permission (or equivalent exemption under the planning legislation) had to be in existence for the use of the site for waste disposal (s. 5(2)). This requirement placed the emphasis on whether and where to have a waste disposal site at the planning permission stage. Since it was clear that conditions attached to a waste disposal licence should not overlap with the types of condition that could be imposed on a planning permission, it also meant that the conditions attached to the planning permission were crucial to the operation of the site. For example, conditions relating to such important matters as aftercare and traffic movements to and from the site would be included in the planning permission rather than the waste disposal licence, with all the implications for enforcement that were entailed should breach of conditions occur.

Once a licence had been granted, the WDA had a number of supervisory duties (s. 9). However, its powers to take action were limited. Variation or revocation of the licence was possible only in restricted circumstances (s. 7). There were few limitations on the transfer of a licence (s. 8). Most significantly, there were no limitations whatsoever on the surrender of a licence, with the result that a licence holder could abandon its responsibilities under a licence at any time (s. 8(4)). There was a public register of current disposal licences (s. 6(4)).

It was a strict liability offence to deposit, or to cause or knowingly permit the deposit of, controlled waste without a licence (s. 3). Supplementary powers enabled the WDA to carry out a clean-up of illegal deposits of waste (s. 16), and there were provisions establishing strict civil liability for certain illegal deposits (s. 88).

The failings of COPA 1974

Although COPA 1974 provided the first system of comprehensive control over waste disposal in Britain, the practical effect of the Act turned out to be disappointing. Some of the defects were inherent in the system, whilst others became apparent as time passed. In referring to the state of waste management in Britain, the Second Report of the House of Commons Environment Committee on Toxic Waste contained some of the strongest words ever published by a Parliamentary Committee:

> Never, in any of our enquiries into environmental problems, have we experienced such consistent and universal criticism of existing legislation and of central and local government as we have done during the course of this inquiry.

After what appeared to be a bright future in 1974, what went wrong?

(a) Organisational problems

COPA 1974 created a system in which WDAs operated disposal sites themselves at the same time as regulating private sites by means of the licensing system. The inherent conflict between these two activities proved to be the cause of many difficulties. The perception that the WDAs were acting as both 'poacher and gamekeeper' undermined public confidence in the whole waste disposal industry.

(b) A lack of central guidance on acceptable standards
There was a great disparity between standards of control in different parts of
the country. Evidence submitted to the House of Commons Environment
Committee had shown that different WDAs used different standards when
setting and enforcing conditions in disposal licences. As the Committee put
it:

> Against this *laissez faire* background, it is not surprising to find that there
> is no consistency of standards between one waste disposal authority and
> another. In many, the standards are extremely low, encouraging the
> operation of contractors who have no regard for the potential dangers to
> the environment.

A major reason for this *'laissez faire'* approach was the lack of Central
Government guidance. The DoE had the task of supplying WDAs with
scientific guidance as to the manner in which the system ought to be
operated, which could then introduce uniformity into the controls. It committed itself to producing some 13 waste management papers in the 1980s,
but this target was missed and many of the papers were not produced on
time. As Lawrence put it ([1989] 3 Env Law 4):

> These examples of Central Government complacency and neglect send
> clear signals out to the local authorities that waste regulation is not taken
> seriously in this country. This does nothing to engender the professional-
> ism, technical competence and status that is required for efficient waste
> regulation.

(c) A lack of strategic plans
The introduction of waste disposal plans under s. 2 was a mandatory
requirement of EC Directive 75/442. But, for example, by 1 October 1989,
only 23 WDAs out of 79 had completed their plans. Obviously, little
long-term planning could take place where there was no plan, since it should
have provided the strategic background to the disposal of waste in an area.

(d) The need to prove deposit related offences
COPA 1974 emphasised the control of the deposit of waste. But problems
also arise in relation to the storage, treatment and transportation of waste.
These problems could not be tackled effectively by COPA 1974. The need
to prove a deposit in order to activate many of the enforcement provisions
also had the effect of concentrating on the element that was the most difficult
to prove. For example, if waste was fly-tipped, under COPA 1974 only the
person who made the deposit, or who caused or knowingly permitted it, could
be prosecuted, leaving others further up the disposal chain free from control,
even though they may have had a significant degree of responsibility for what
happened. Even when a prosecution was brought, the maximum penalties
were low.

One particular case that illustrated some of the problems in this area was *Leigh Land Reclamation Ltd* v *Walsall Metropolitan Borough Council* (1991) 155 JP 547. Charges were brought against the holder of a waste disposal licence alleging that it was depositing waste at a time when a number of conditions relating to the overall operation of the site were not being complied with. For example, waste was not being compacted and progressively covered during the day as required. The Divisional Court held that, as long as the *deposit* was in accordance with the conditions, it was irrelevant that other conditions relating to the site were not being complied with. Since COPA 1974 included no separate offence of failure to comply with a condition, this rather literal decision meant that there was effectively no way of enforcing many administrative and operational conditions attached to a disposal licence.

(e) Inability to control 'cowboys'
There were some severe defects in the licensing system which meant that proper control over standards was difficult. For example, there were only very limited opportunities to refuse a grant of a waste disposal licence, or to refuse a transfer, or to vary or revoke a licence. In consequence, great weight was placed on the planning permission stage, though in many cases the planning permission had been granted many years previously and did not fully take environmental considerations into account. (Of course, one of the features of the town planning system is that it is not possible to alter or revoke a planning permission once it has been granted, without the payment of compensation.)

A further problem was that, because of the way the legislation was drafted, WDAs were unable to attach some types of condition. For example, aftercare and restoration conditions were not permitted in a waste disposal licence, although they could be attached to a planning permission. A condition that a site should be operated 'so as to avoid creating a nuisance to the inhabitants of the neighbourhood' was held not to be appropriate in a waste disposal licence (*Attorney-General's Reference (No. 2 of 1988)* [1990] 1 QB 77). The reasoning was that it did not fall within the limited purposes of COPA 1974, Part I, which were assumed (by reference to s. 5) to be the prevention of harm to public health, water pollution and serious detriment to the locality. In addition, the court considered that such matters should be controlled through the statutory nuisance procedures.

(f) The ability to surrender a licence
Site operators had a right to surrender a disposal licence at any time, in which case any conditions attached to it would automatically cease to have any effect. In practice, this meant that an operator could abandon a site and relinquish any future responsibility for supervision of it. For example, an operator who was financially or technically incompetent to deal with problems that had arisen on the land could avoid them simply by giving notice to the WDA. Of course, the operator would not thereby avoid any responsibilities imposed by the planning permission, or, if it owned the land, which arose out of ownership, but this right effectively undermined any attempt to impose a proper system of monitoring of waste sites once operations had ceased.

The Environmental Protection Act 1990, Part II

The EPA 1990, Part II enacted a wide range of new powers designed to strengthen control over waste 'from cradle to grave'. It also attempted to grapple with most of the difficulties thrown up by COPA 1974. Unfortunately, implementation of the EPA 1990, Part II has been beset with problems. No timetable for its introduction was originally written into the Act or promised in the debates on the Bill. To some extent this was understandable, since the Act itself largely set out a framework into which details would be inserted by regulations, and it was always accepted that the drafting of the appropriate regulations would involve the solution of some difficult and complex problems. Extensive consultation has taken place on various aspects of the new provisions. Some of these gave rise to great controversy, particularly as far as the waste disposal industry is concerned. As a result, there were persistent delays, a situation that has not been helped by the uncertainty caused by the announcement in 1992 of the Government's intention to create a national Environment Agency, which would take over the waste regulation functions currently exercised by local authorities. In the end, implementation has been piecemeal. The provisions on duty of care were brought into force on 1 April 1992. But, despite several promises of commencement dates, the new waste management licensing system was not brought into operation until 1 May 1994.

The main features of the EPA 1990, Part II are the following:

(a) The operational and regulatory functions of local authorities have been separated, thus avoiding the implication that the regulatory system is biased. The operational body must be at arm's length from the regulatory authority and is subject to competitive tendering from the private sector. These provisions have been in force since 1991. This separation of functions was emphasised when the Environment Agency came into being. The transfer of responsibility from the local-authority-controlled waste regulations authorities to the politically independent Agency should be viewed as the logical conclusion of the separation of operational and regulatory functons started in Part II of the EPA 1990.

(b) A criminal duty of care, which applies to all those who deal with controlled waste, was introduced on 1 April 1992. This important duty is an attempt to ensure that waste is dealt with properly from its production to its ultimate disposal. It imposes greater duties on the producers and intermediate handlers of waste than ever before and effectively necessitates the introduction of effective systems of waste management within firms.

(c) A new, all-embracing criminal offence of treating, keeping or disposing of controlled waste in a manner likely to cause pollution of the environment or harm to human health was introduced on 1 April 1992. It operates independently of the licensing system and effectively imposes minimum standards on the way waste is handled.

(d) A number of sections designed to encourage the recycling of waste have been introduced.

(e) Provisions were enacted establishing a new system of waste management licensing. These seek to remedy many of the defects and close many of the loopholes in the licensing system established under COPA 1974. In particular, there are expanded powers to refuse licences on environmental grounds, new powers to refuse licences on the ground that the applicant is not a 'fit and proper person', more sophisticated powers to modify, suspend and revoke licences, greater powers to impose appropriate conditions, enhanced powers of enforcement, and increased maximum penalties in the event of a breach. A particular feature of the system is that an operator will no longer be able to surrender a licence, but will be subject to the licence conditions until released from these obligations by the Environment Agency issuing a certificate of completion. A complementary change is that the EPA 1990 enables conditions to be attached to site licences which will continue to apply after the site has ceased to be used for depositing waste.

The EPA 1990, Part II is supplemented by the provisions of the Control of Pollution (Amendment) Act 1989, which was brought into force on 1 April 1992. This Act introduced a system of registration of carriers of controlled waste, with strong penalties for operating an unregistered vehicle. Further supplementation is provided by the EPA 1990, Part IV, which creates a fairly comprehensive regime relating to the control of litter.

It is clear that the combined impact of the above changes will be that the whole of the waste cycle is regulated more rigorously than at any stage in the past. Producers of waste will be subject to a number of controls on the production and transfer of waste that did not affect them before. Tighter standards than before will operate in relation to where and how waste can be disposed of. There is little doubt that the cost of disposing of solid waste is set to rise significantly, and that producers should turn their attention to waste minimisation.

Waste authorities

The administration of waste management is divided into three. Under s. 30 of the EPA 1990 as amended by the Environment Act 1995 these are:

(a) *The Environment Agency*, which took over responsibility from the waste regulation authorities in April 1996. Circular 15/95 gives guidance on the transfer of property rights and liabilities from the WRAs to the Agency. The Agency has responsibility for the main regulatory functions in relation to waste management including the administration, supervision and enforcement of licensed activities (ss. 35–42). In addition the Agency is responsible for the system of licensing waste carriers, the special waste provisions, and the operation and enforcement of the duty of care.

(b) *The waste collection authority* (WCA) is the district council or London borough council. It has the responsibility for arranging the collection of household waste (and on request the collection of commercial or industrial waste) (s. 45), drawing up plans for recycling household and commercial waste (s. 49) and making arrangements for the provision of waste bins for household and commercial waste (ss. 46–7).

(c) *The waste disposal authority* (WDA) is the county council in English non-metropolitan areas or the unitary authority in such areas. In some metropolitan areas special arrangements apply (e.g., Greater London and Greater Manchester), but generally the metropolitan district council or London borough council will be the waste disposal authority. The WDA is responsible for the formation of the privatised waste disposal companies (s. 32), arranging for the disposal of waste collected by the WCA (s. 51), arranging for the provision of waste transfer stations and civic amenity sites (s. 51) and waste recycling (s. 55).

What is waste?

The concept of waste has proved to be particularly difficult to define with any certainty. The main reason for this is the subjective nature of the view which one can take when considering whether material is waste. In particular, one person's waste can be another person's raw material, or, as Purdue put it ('Defining waste' [1990] JEL 259):

> the old newspapers blowing down the street may be gathered by boy scouts to be recycled or even used by a vagrant to keep warm. Even at the same moment in time one person may regard an object as waste, while another has a use for it. This makes legal definition difficult.

Of course, the adoption of the waste management hierarchy as outlined above simply adds to the complexity of the tests. Where an emphasis is placed upon the reuse and recycling of material it would not make a great deal of sense to overregulate unnecessarily and thereby discourage those seeking to minimise the final production of waste. On the other hand, many recycling and reclamation processes have the capability of causing harm to the environment if left unregulated. The legislation seeks to balance these two competing considerations.

For many years the definition of waste included substances or articles which were scrap or which required to be disposed of because it was broken, worn out, contaminated or otherwise spoilt (s. 30, COPA 1974 and s. 75, EPA 1990). Under the amendments to the framework Directive, however, a common definition of waste was agreed to apply to all Member States. This differs from the previous definition and thus required amendments to UK legislation. Other amendments have been necessary to ensure full implementation of the Directive. All of the amendments have been incorporated within the Waste Management Licensing Regulations 1994 with subsequent amendments to the EPA 1990.

The Regulations are very complicated and the guidance in Circular 11/94 runs to almost 200 pages. In an attempt to distil the detail into broad principles it is possible to put forward two propositions:

(a) the only waste which is regulated by the WRAs is now known as *Directive waste* to reflect the description of waste as contained in the Directive;

(b)   generally, the activities which are controlled under Part II of the EPA 1990 are now known as *Directive disposal* and *Directive recovery*. These two phrases replace the old single phrase of 'treating keeping or disposing of waste' as contained in s. 33 of EPA 1990.

Directive waste

Article 1 of the framework Directive amends the definition of waste within the UK. Schedule 22 to the Environment Act 1995 formally repeals s. 75(2) of EPA 1990 and the practical effect upon English law is that the previous statutory definition of waste contained in that section has been replaced by the definition of 'Directive waste' which is, itself, contained in regs. 1(3), 24(8) of and para. 9 of sch 4 to the Waste Management Licensing Regulations 1994. These provisions amend the definition of controlled waste in the Controlled Waste Regulations to provide that waste which is not Directive waste shall not be treated as controlled waste (and therefore shall fall outside the scheme of control of Part II of the Act).

The general definition of Directive waste is:

. . . any substance or object which the holder discards or intends or is required to discard . . .

The crucial concept in determining whether material is waste would appear to be 'discarding'. Further guidance on this concept is contained in Circular 11/94 which poses the question:

has the substance or object been discarded so that it is no longer part of the normal commercial cycle or chain of utility?

If the answer to this question is 'no', it should be a reasonable indication that the substance or object is not waste. The Circular goes on to provide the example of glass bottles which are subject to a refundable deposit on safe return. The DoE contends that the bottles are not waste in the hands of the buyer, the shop to which they are returned or the supplier who takes it from the shop. In these circumstances the bottle never leaves the 'chain of utility'. On the other hand bottles, which are placed in a 'bottle bank' for recycling are discarded and should be treated as waste. 'Discard' can also mean 'dispose of' and/or 'get rid of' but attempting to come up with an all-encompassing definition would be impossible.

Further clarification of the concept is given in four broad categories of potential waste:

(1)   worn, but functioning, substances or objects which are still usable (albeit after repair) for the purpose for which they were made — generally not waste;

(2)   substances or objects which can be put to immediate use otherwise than by a specialised waste recovery establishment or undertaking — generally not waste;

(3)   degenerated substances or objects which can be put to use only by establishments or undertakings specialising in waste recovery — generally waste even if transferred for value;

(4)   Substances or objects which the holder does not want and which he has to pay to have taken away — depends upon the facts of the particular disposal. Where there is an intention that the material/substance will be used by the recipient and no special recovery process is required, that material/substance will not be waste, notwithstanding that a price is paid.

Many difficult cases will depend largely upon their facts and the intentions of the parties and it is not possible to give anything other than a general picture.

In addition to the general definition there are more specific categories of Directive waste contained in the Waste Management Licensing Regulations 1994, sch. 4, Part II. The long list of categories includes residual products from industrial processes, products for which the holder has no further use (e.g., household, agricultural, office, commercial and agricultural discards) and production or consumption residues not otherwise mentioned in the Schedule.

There is also a general all inclusive category which includes *any* materials, substances or products which are not contained in any of the other categories. The effect of this category is that there is a two-stage test which applies to the question of whether a substance, material or product is Directive waste:

(a)   is it a substance, material or product and does it therefore come within any of the categories set out in the specific definitions in sch. 4?; *and*

(b)   has the substance, material or product been discarded by its holder or is there an intention or requirement to discard it?.

It is the second of these two questions, however, which gives the key to the definition of Directive waste. For example, material is not waste merely because it falls within sch. 4, nor even because it has been sent to a waste recovery process. The overriding issue is whether it has been discarded.

Waste recovery operations and specialised recovery operations

One of the notable features of the detailed guidance on the definition of Directive waste is the manner in which recycling and recovery operations are dealt with. In an attempt to balance the need for control with the need to encourage reuse the Circular seeks to distinguish waste recovery operations from specialised recovery operations. Waste recovery operations are listed in the Waste Management Licensing Regulations 1994, sch. 4, Part IV. These processes cover the reclamation or recycling of a variety of substances, including solvents, acids and oils. A substance is not considered to be waste solely on the ground that it has been consigned to a recovery process. The main reason for this is that some of the processes listed in the Regulations cannot be distinguished easily from the normal commercial chain of utility (i.e., the recovery process is part and parcel of the overall process). Therefore, the substance might not have been discarded within the meaning of the definition of Directive waste. One example might be the reuse/recovery of waste oil from a process as a source of fuel for another process.

On the other hand, waste consigned to special recovery operations will always be considered to be waste. There is no specific definition of the phrase 'special recovery operations' within the Regulations or the guidance. The phrase is, however, intended to cover operations which either reuse substances or objects which are waste because they have fallen out of the chain of utility or recycles them in a way which eliminates or diminishes sufficiently the threat posed by their original production as waste and produces a raw material which can be used in the same way as raw material of a non-waste compound. Thus, where contaminated waste oil is disposed of to a third party and that third party utilises the waste for its own purposes (after cleaning the oil) the oil will be waste as it will have to the subject of a special recovery operation.

Can the identity of waste change over time?

In the examples above it can be seen that a substance which has been waste can be purified and utilised. Where waste is 'recovered' under the Directive the substance ceases to be waste — this follows the accepted position after the decision in *Kent County Council* v *Queenborough Rolling Mill Co. Ltd* (1990) 89 LGR 306 (see below). The waste is 'recovered' when it is a substance of sufficient beneficial use to eliminate or sufficiently diminish the threat posed by the original production of the waste. In addition, the waste can be altered by a change of intention on behalf of the recipient of the waste. For example, someone who receives a broken, discarded product can mend it so that it ceases to be waste.

Case law

The courts have examined the definition of waste on a number of occasions. Although these decisions are based upon the definition under previous legislation they assist in helping with the interpretation of Directive waste as the principles can, in some cases, be extended to cover the new definition. In *Long* v *Brook* [1980] Crim LR 109 the Crown Court decided that, upon its true construction, COPA 1974 defined 'waste' from the point of view of the person discarding the material. This was followed in *Kent County Council* v *Queenborough Rolling Mill Co. Ltd* (1990) 89 LGR 306, where the defendant company was charged with depositing waste on land without a disposal licence contrary to COPA 1974 (s. 3). The material concerned consisted of ballast, china, china clay and broken pottery from a disused site which was being cleared by a demolition company. It was used to fill an area subject to subsidence. The magistrates decided that such material was not waste as it was inert and was being used for the purposes of infill. On appeal to the Divisional Court the council argued that the material was waste by its very nature. The defendant company argued that the material was not waste because it was put to a useful purpose and therefore was not unwanted. The Divisional Court held that, although the material was put to a useful purpose, that was not a relevant factor in deciding whether the material was waste. The important factor was the nature of the material when it was discarded. If it was waste it would always remain waste until it was adequately reconstituted or recycled. This would still be the case with the redefintion of waste under the Waste Management Licensing Regulations 1994.

In *Cheshire County Council* v *Armstrong's Transport (Wigan) Ltd* [1995] Env LR 62 the defendant company was responsible for processing building site rubble before returning the crushed material to its original site to assist in rebuilding works. The Defendant was prosecuted as it did not seek a waste disposal licence under COPA 1974. The magistrates found that the material was not waste as it was a product. The defendant was able to demonstrate that there was no intention to discard on behalf of the last holder of the material as they were under a contractual obligation to return the material to the site once it had been processed. The Divisional Court held that this obligation meant that the rubble was not waste as the original holder had not wished to dispose of it. Such evidence would, of course, also be required to demonstrate that material had not left the 'chain of utility'.

In *Meston Technical Services Ltd* v *Warwickshire County Council* [1995] Env LR 380 the defendants operated a waste recycling business from a site in an industrial park. They traded in the receipt of liquid controlled waste which was received from various companies and was reprocessed into substances which would either be sold on for industrial or commercial use or otherwise disposed of by way of landfill or incineration. The defendant was prosecuted for breach of licence conditions under COPA 1974. On appeal the defendants argued that the drums of material were not 'waste' within the meaning of COPA 1974 and that the licence did not apply to the storage of the drums. It was argued, that the drums (and the material within it) were not waste because it was wanted by the appellants and was valuable to them. Secondly, it was argued that the defendants could only be guilty of an offence where they themselves regarded the relevant material as waste. If they did not regard it as waste but intended to sell it on if they could, it was not waste and no offence was committed. The Divisional Court held that the value of the material or the views of the defendant were irrelevant when considering the definition of the material as waste, and it was not appropriate to examine the aims and purposes of the holder of the waste when considering what was waste under the Environmental Protection Act 1990. The introduction of the wider definition of Directive Waste does nothing to change the fundamental principles behind these decisions. Indeed, in the case of *Tombesi* (joined cases C-304/94, C-330/94, C-342/94 and C-224/95), [1997] All ER (EC) 639, the ECJ held that Directive Waste extended to all objects and substances discarded by their owners, even if they had a commercial value and were collected on a commercial basis for recycling, reclamation or re-use. Although this decision did not deal with the difficult question of the definition of 'discarding' which is central to Directive Waste, it confirms that the value or probability of reutilisation of a substance is irrelevant when considering whether it is waste.

The national decisions are in line with a decision of the European Court of Justice in *Vessoso* (cases C-206 & 207/88) [1990] ECR I-1461. In these cases, two Italians had been charged with collecting, transporting and storing waste without authorisation, contrary to Italian Presidential Decree. It was argued on their behalf that the material was recyclable raw material and not waste. In its judgment, the Court stated that the definition of waste contained in the original framework Directive on Waste (75/442) was concerned with the potential health and pollution hazard that the materials could bring, and concluded by finding that although recycling was to be encouraged, material could be waste notwithstanding its potential for future use. This has now been clarified with the expansion of the definition of waste in the updated framework Directive (91/156) and the amendments to British legislation.

What is controlled waste?

Most of the provisions of the EPA 1990 apply to controlled waste. The primary definition of controlled waste is defined in EPA 1990, s. 75(4) as meaning household, industrial or commercial waste or any such waste. In *Thanet District Council* v *Kent County Council* [1993] Env LR 391 the Divisional Court held that the phrase 'any such waste' is limited to waste coming within any of the categories and would not cover seaweed deposited on agricultural land. The definition of controlled waste has been amended by the Waste Management Licensing Regulations 1994. Regulation 24(8) amends the Controlled Waste Regulations 1992 (SI 1992 No. 588) by providing that waste which is not Directive waste shall not be treated as household, industrial or commercial waste. Thus, the practical effect is that the previous categories of household, industrial or commercial waste have been amended to the single class of Directive waste.

Exemptions

Regulation 1(3) of the 1994 Regulations excludes anything excluded from the scope of the Directive from the definition of Directive waste (and thus controlled waste). The justification for these exemptions is that they are already covered under existing legislation. There are, however, a few anomalies. Six main categories of waste are exempted.

(a)   Gaseous effluent emitted into the atmosphere: controlled under Part I of the EPA 1990 and the Clean Air Act 1993. Emissions from waste management are, however, covered under the Directive (e.g., from incineration).

(b)   Radioactive waste: controlled under the Radioactive Substances Act 1993.

(c)   Waste resulting from prospecting, extraction, treatment, and storage of mineral resources and the working of quarries: controlled under the Mines and Quarries (Tips) Act 1969. This also accords with s. 75(7) of EPA 1990 which excludes all waste from mines and quarries from the definition of controlled waste. The issue of non-mineral waste from mines and quarries is, however, far from clear-cut. Although the EPA 1990 would exclude this waste from the definition of controlled waste the DoE has said that this would fall within the definition of Directive waste.

(d) Animal carcasses and the following agricultural waste; faecal matter and other natural, non-dangerous substances used in farming: controlled under the Animal By-Products Order 1992 (SI 1992 No. 3303); there is, however, a similar problem to the position in respect of minerals wastes. Agricultural waste is excluded form the definition of controlled waste under s. 75(7) of EPA 1990, yet the DoE takes the view that it should fall within the definition of Directive waste where it falls outside the above exemption.

(e) Waste waters, with the exception of waste in liquid form: broadly controlled under the Water Resources Act 1991 and Water Industry Act 1991. Where, however, waste water or liquid is subjected to Directive recovery or disposal (e.g., effluent treatment plants) the DoE has advised that it is its view that this will amount to the treatment of Directive waste and a licence will be required.

(f) Decommissioned explosives: controlled under the Explosives Act 1875, the Control of Explosives Regulations 1991 (SI 1991 No. 1531), various regulations under the Health and Safety at Work Act 1974 and the Road Traffic (Carriage of Explosives) Regulations 1989 (SI 1989 No. 615).

There is a residual degree of control over non-Directive waste. Any person who deposits or who knowingly causes or knowingly permits the deposit of any non-controlled waste commits an offence if the waste has the characteristics of special waste and is not deposited in accordance with a licence or permission of some description (EPA 1990, s. 63(2)). This rather convoluted subsection appears designed to cover such things as the irresponsible disposal of toxic materials. The maximum penalty is the same as under s. 33. In addition, the Secretary of State may make regulations under s. 63(1) applying specified parts of the EPA 1990 to exempt wastes (specifically agricultural and mine wastes), although no such regulations have ever been made.

The meaning of 'deposit'

The definition of 'deposit' is central to the operation of the EPA 1990 and the courts have adopted a relatively wide definition. Initially in *Leigh Land Reclamation Ltd* v *Walsall Metropolitan Borough Council* (1991) 155 JP 547 it was held that waste was deposited at a landfill site only when there was no realistic prospect of further examination or inspection and it had reached its final resting place. This decision caused enormous practical problems for waste regulation authorities as it became difficult to prove that waste had definitely reached its final resting place when defendants argued it was going to be moved on a future occasion. The decision in *Leigh* was overturned by the Divisional Court in *R* v *Metropolitan Stipendiary Magistrate, ex parte London Waste Regulation Authority* [1993] All ER 113, where it was held that 'deposit' applies to temporary deposits as well as to permanent ones, which seems to reflect both common sense and the wider scope of the EPA 1990 in dealing with waste *management* rather than *disposal*. This definition was widened once again in *Thames Waste Management Ltd* v *Surrey County Council*

[1997] Env LR 148. In that case, the defendant, TWML, was convicted of unlawfully depositing controlled waste on land other than in accordance with the conditions in a waste disposal licence. A condition of the licence required any deposit of waste to be covered over in the prescribed manner on the day that waste was deposited. TWML argued that the failure to cover the waste was not an unlawful deposit because the failure to cover took place after the initial deposit. The court held that 'deposit' could cover continuing activities where the context of the waste management licence would suggest that it was appropriate to do so. On the facts of the case it was reasonable to assume that the deposit continued until such time as it was covered. Thus there has been a significant movement away from a relatively narrow notion where 'deposit' was viewed only in terms of permanence to a view where deposit may take a significant period whilst other activities are carried out.

Waste management licensing

As with the definition of waste, the requirement for a waste management license has been affected by the need to implement the framework Directive. A waste management licence is required for the disposal, keeping or treatment of controlled waste on land or by means of a mobile plant. The effect of the Waste Management Licencing Regulations 1994, however, when taken with the prohibition on the unlawful management of waste in s. 33 is to limit the phrase 'treatment, keeping or disposal of waste' to Directive disposal and recovery operations (sch. 4, para. 9).

Directive disposal operations
The list of Directive disposal operations is found in Part III of sch. 4 to the 1994 Regulations. It includes landfill, incineration on land and at sea, permanent storage of waste, e.g., in a mine, the treatment of waste prior to final disposal and the injection of waste into the earth.

Directive recovery operations
The list of Directive recovery operations is found in Part IV of sch. 4. It includes the reclamation or recycling of a variety of substances (e.g., solvents, organic substances, acids and metals) and the use of wastes obtained from recycling or reclamation.

Exemptions
A lengthy list of exemptions from the need for a waste management licence is set out in reg. 17 and sch. 3. It is not possible in a book of this nature to go through the whole list, or to provide exact details of those things that are mentioned, but the main types of activity that are covered are as follows:

(a) activities that are carried on in accordance with the provisions of consents or authorisations granted under other legislation (e.g., a discharge consent granted under the Water Resources Act 1991, or a licence to dump at sea granted under the Food and Environment Protection Act 1985);

(b)   the storage of Directive waste at the place at which it is produced pending its treatment or disposal elsewhere (this will cover such things as storing waste in a skip — there is no time limit as long as the producer can show that it is genuinely going to be collected);

(c)   the storage of special waste at the place at which it is produced pending its treatment or disposal elsewhere, as long as certain conditions on quantity and security are met;

(d)   various activities relating to the recovery or reuse of waste, such as sorting waste at the place at which it is produced, baling it, shredding it and compacting it;

(e)   storage or deposit of demolition or construction wastes for the purposes of construction work being undertaken on the land;

(f)   deposit of certain organic matter for the purposes of fertilising or conditioning land;

(g)   in order to encourage recycling, a great variety of recycling activities are exempted, although often subject to detailed restrictions on quantity (for example, the collection of paper and cardboard, aluminium and steel cans, plastics, glass and textiles for recycling, or the cleaning and washing of packaging or containers so that they can be reused).

In most of these categories the exemption will not apply if the waste is special waste (see p. 426).

The requirement for a waste management licence (and the exemptions from the need for a licence) must read in conjunction with the offence of unlawful waste management set out in s. 33 (see p. 405). The general offence in s. 33(1)(c) of keeping, treating or disposing of Directive waste in a manner likely to cause pollution of the environment or harm to human health will remain applicable in all the above exemptions apart from those in category (a). By contrast household waste from a private dwelling which is treated, kept or disposed of within the curtilage of the dwelling by, or with the permission of, the occupier, is entirely exempt from s. 33 (s. 33(2)).

Registration

A new requirement of the 1994 Regulations, made necessary by the provisions of Article 11 of the framework Directive, is that certain activities must be registered with the EA even though exempted from the waste management licensing system. The new registration system is based around a new offence in support of the requirement to register. Under reg. 18(1) it is an offence to carry on an exempt activity involving the recovery or disposal of waste without being registered with the appropriate registration authority. The requirement to register covers 'establishments or undertakings' it does not include private individuals. Registration is effected simply by notifying the EA of the relevant activities, where they are carried on, and the exemption which is being relied on (reg. 18(3)). The EA is required to keep a register of exemptions containing the particulars of the registration (reg. 18(4)). The tone of Government advice in Circular 11/94 is that the requirement to register is more administrative in nature than any great step forward in environmental protection. Indeed, the advice in the Circular would suggest that prosecution for the failure to register an exempt activity would only be a last resort. Where serious environmental harm had arisen from exempt activities it would be preferable to rely upon prosecution powers under s. 33(1)(c), if possible (see p. 405).

Applications for a licence

If a waste management licence is required, an application must be made in writing to the EA. There is a standard application form available from the EA. It is an offence to make a statement in an application for a licence (or in an application for modification, transfer or surrender) knowing it to be false in a material particular, or reckless as to such an event (s. 44). The maximum penalty on conviction in the magistrates' court is a £5,000 fine, but in the Crown Court the maximum penalty is an unlimited fine and/or two years in prison.

Where the licence relates to the keeping, treating, or disposal of waste in or on land the licence is called a 'site licence', and the application is made to the EA where the site is situated. An application for a licence for mobile plant is made to the EA where the applicant has its principal place of business, thus allowing for a number of pieces of plant to be covered by one licence. Section 35(2) states that only the occupier of the land or the operator of a mobile plant can apply for a licence. There is no definition of an occupier in the Act, but it must be assumed that it relates to the ability to control the waste operation and the use of the land.

The EA must consult with a number of other public bodies if it proposes to issue a licence, and must consider any representations that those bodies make within 21 days. The Health and Safety Executive is a statutory consultee in all cases. In any case where the site is notified as a site of special scientific interest (SSSI), the relevant NCC is also a statutory consultee, reflecting the fact that a number of SSSIs have been lost to waste disposal over the years — though current planning guidance makes it less likely that planning permission will be granted for waste disposal on a SSSI in the future.

The EA must also take into account any Central Government guidance (s. 35(8)). This will be provided in the form of waste management papers and it is intended that they should produce a situation where a more uniform approach is adopted across the country than has been the case in the past. The most significant paper is Waste Management Paper No. 4, *Licensing of Waste Facilities*, which seeks to provide comprehensive guidance on the criteria for granting a licence, such as the definition of a 'fit and proper person' and on conditions. WMP4 contains a policy that licences should be reviewed annually and fully reconsidered at least every five years. It will also be appropriate to consider the Central Guidance to be found in 11/94.

One feature that is missing is any element of public participation, since the application does not have to be advertised. This situation arises because it is perceived that the grant of a waste management licence is a technical question: the wider question of the appropriateness of the site will have been considered when planning permission was sought.

The powers of the EA

The EA has a discretion to grant or refuse a licence. But this is subject to a number of restrictions. (Similar restrictions apply to the EA's discretion on questions relating to the transfer, modification, suspension or revocation of a licence, though the wording of the relevant sections is usually more restrictive — see below.)

First, an application *must* be refused if planning permission is required for the use of the land and there is no such permission (s. 36(2)). For these purposes, a lawful development certificate granted under the Town and Country Planning Act 1990, s. 191, is treated as a planning permission. An established use certificate granted under earlier legislation will also normally suffice.

Secondly, the EA *may* refuse a licence if it is satisfied that such a step is necessary to prevent pollution of the environment or harm to human health. This gives a fairly wide discretion to the EA, since s. 29 defines pollution of the environment to mean pollution due to the release or escape of substances capable of causing harm to any living organism from the land in or on which waste is kept, treated or deposited. Where there is no planning permission in force (i.e., because it was not required — this would cover a site open since before 1948), the EA may refuse a licence if that is necessary to prevent serious detriment to the amenities of the locality (s. 36(3)).

Further guidance on this point is provided by the Waste Management Licensing Regulations 1994. In order to ensure compliance with Directive 80/68 on Groundwater, the EA is required only to grant applications if technical precautions, enforceable through conditions, can be taken to prevent the discharge of List I substances and to prevent groundwater pollution by List II substances. The EA is also required to review existing licences that may lead to discharges of List I or List II substances and to use its modification and revocation powers accordingly. The risk of groundwater pollution is an important consideration in the grant of any licence. There is a strong set of policies for the protection of groundwater, which were formulated by the NRA (see NRA, *Policy and Practice for the Protection of Groundwater,* 1992). There are some doubts over the ability of measures taken to prevent contamination of groundwater from landfill sites. On most sites the preventative measures will involve some form of impermeable membrane to prevent the egress of leachate. Research has shown that over time even the sturdiest membrane can degrade and the groundwater be threatened. The technical decision on the adequacy of any preventative measures is, however, a question of policy and the decision-maker is entitled to rely upon one technical view even if there are competing views (see *R v Vale of Glamorgan Borough Council, ex parte James* [1996] Env LR 102, where a WRA was held to be entitled to rely on the view of the NRA even though another view was put forward.)

Thirdly, a licence *may* be refused if the applicant is not a fit and proper person. The meaning of this phrase is set out in general terms in s. 74 and in more specific terms in the Waste Management Licensing Regulations. The final form of the Regulations and the guidance on their use was the subject of great controversy and debate between the Government and the waste disposal industry in 1992 and 1993, leading to a position where the standards are not as strict as was once envisaged.

Section 74(3) states that an applicant is not a fit and proper person if:

(a) the applicant or any other relevant person has committed a relevant offence; or

(b) the mangement of the site will not be in the hands of a technically competent person; or

(c) the applicant cannot make financial provision adequate to discharge the obligations arising under the licence.

Section 74(7) explains that a relevant person has committed a relevant offence in this context if:

(i) any employee of the applicant has been convicted of a relevant offence;

(ii) a company of which the applicant was a director, manager, secretary or similar officer has been convicted of a relevant offence; or

(iii) where the applicant is a company, any current director, manager, secretary or similar officer of the company has been convicted of a relevant offence, or was an officer of another company when that company was convicted of a relevant offence. The question of who constitutes a manager will be construed narrowly to mean someone who is part of the 'controlling mind' of the company (see R v Boal [1992] QB 591 and Woodhouse v Walsall Metropolitan Borough Council [1994] Env LR 30).

For the purpose of these provisions, a list of relevant offences is contained in the Waste Management Licensing Regulations 1994, reg. 3). Since the list is wide (but by no means exhaustive of environmental offences), the EA can choose to ignore a conviction if it wishes to do so (s. 74(4)). Waste Management Paper No. 4, Chapter 3 contains guidance on these provisions. It suggests that four factors should be taken into account in exercising the discretion to ignore a conviction. These are: the type of applicant (i.e., individual, partnership or corporate body); whether it is the applicant or another relevant person who has been convicted of the relevant offence; the nature and gravity of the relevant offence(s); and the number of relevant offences which have been committed.

As far as technical competence is concerned reg. 4 applies to the person responsible for the proper management of the site. The regulation provides that a person is technically competent in relation to the prescribed facilities set out in reg. 4 only if they are the holder of the relevant certificate of technical competence awarded by the Waste Management Industry Training Board (WAMITAB).

There are various transitional arrangements for those managers who have experience within the waste industry prior to the implementation of Part II of the EPA 1990 (known as 'existing managers'). A person will qualify as an existing manager if they registered with WAMITAB before 10 August 1994 and in the 12 months prior to that date were a manager of a relevant type of facility. An operator of a site previously controlled under COPA 1974 is also assumed to be a 'fit and proper' person. Both exemptions last until 1999 to enable those who are exempt to gain WAMITAB certification.

The position with regard to financial provision is much less clear cut. WMP 4 suggests that the main ways of providing such financial provision is through insurance via a third party or, if that is not possible, through self-insurance. The paper also identifies four stages in relation to landfill where financial provision may be relevant: site acquisition and preparation; site operation; site restoration and landscaping, or aftercare for a new use; and post-closure control and monitoring. Specific financial provision may be included in a licence in order to meet specified obligations under the licence. The assessment of the financial provision of an applicant is not to be specifically detailed. It is only to be considered in general terms in relation to the obligations under the licence. WMP4 suggests that the main thing that the EA will want to see when assessing financial capability will be a business plan showing the various stages of the life of the landfill. Unfortunately, as history has shown, the provision of a sound business plan does not necessarily guarantee the long-term success of the operation. It is this long-term position which remains to be assessed.

If the EA decides that the applicant is a fit and proper person, it is under a duty to grant a licence (s. 36(3)). This suggests that if the impediment can be avoided by the imposition of appropriate conditions, the licence should be granted with those conditions attached.

Conditions

The EA is given a wide discretion to attach 'appropriate' conditions to a licence (s. 35(3)). Applying ordinary public law principles, conditions must relate to the purposes of Part II of the EPA 1990. In *Attorney-General's Reference (No. 2 of 1988)* [1990] 1 QB 77, the Court of Appeal decided that a condition requiring the site to be operated so as to avoid creating a nuisance was not permissible under COPA 1974, since it did not relate to the purposes of that Act. Even though the purposes of the EPA 1990 are wider than those of COPA 1974 (in that they relate to the protection of the environment as a whole, rather than the protection of water resources), it is still unclear whether such a condition would be acceptable under s. 35(3), since it is still arguable that such matters are more appropriately dealt with under the statutory nuisance provisions in Part III of the EPA 1990.

Unlike many pieces of environmental legislation, the EPA 1990 does not provide a list of the types of conditions that are appropriate. This function however, is carried out by Waste Management Paper 4. This provides a checklist of matters that should be covered, and stresses that they should relate to the operation and management of the site, so as not to duplicate the conditions attached to the planning permission. The Paper also states that conditions should be enforceable, unambiguous, necessary and comprehensive, and that operators should know exactly what they have to do to comply with them. It appears from decisions of the Secretary of State on appeal that conditions should not impose an unreasonable burden on the operator of a site (see Bates, *UK Waste Law* (1992), p. 203). This seems to water down somewhat the environmental protection aim of the legislation, though it is clearly in line with Government policies on restricting unnecessary regulation and on balancing environmental factors with economic ones.

The range of conditions imposed under the EPA 1990 can be wider than under COPA 1974 in a number of ways. Section 35(3) states that conditions may be imposed which must be complied with before activities begin or after they have ceased. For example, conditions requiring insurance cover to be effected before the site is opened, or the monitoring of a site for methane emissions or for leachate after disposal has finished, are legitimate. Under COPA 1974, such aftercare conditions can be imposed only at the planning permission stage. Section 35(4) provides that conditions may require the applicant to carry out works that need the consent of another person. If they do so, the person whose consent is required must grant any rights in relation to the land that will enable the licence holder to comply with the conditions. For example, this subsection could be used to override landlord and tenant law by allowing a tenant to carry out works that would normally require the landlord's consent.

Regulations may be made prescribing conditions which are or are not to be included (s. 35(6)). In addition, the Secretary of State is given wide powers to direct that specified conditions are, or are not, included in a licence (s. 35). For example, the Waste Management Licensing Regulations stipulate that no conditions designed solely to secure health and safety at work can be imposed (reg. 12), and that, in order to comply with Directive 75/439 on Waste Oils, certain conditions relating to waste oils must be included (reg. 14).

Transfer of a licence

A waste management licence may be transferred by the EA under s. 40 if the holder and the proposed transferee make a joint application to the EA. Unless the EA considers that the proposed transferee is not a fit and proper person, it must make the transfer. An application for a transfer has to be made in writing. It must be determined within two months (or any longer period if agreed between the parties). In the absence of any agreement the application is claimed to have been refused.

Surrender of a licence

Under s. 39, a site licence cannot be surrendered at will, though a mobile plant licence can. A surrender of a site licence can take place only if the licence holder applies to the EA and it accepts the surrender. Before that happens, the EA must inspect the land and determine whether it is likely or unlikely that the condition of the land will cause pollution of the environment or harm to human health. In making that determination, it must take into account only matters that relate to the keeping, treatment or disposal of waste on the site, and not extraneous factors.

If the EA considers that the condition of the land is likely to cause such pollution or harm, it *must* refuse the application (s. 39(6)). But if it is satisfied that the condition of the land is unlikely to cause pollution or harm, it *must* accept the surrender. Where a surrender is accepted, the EA will issue a certificate of completion, and any obligations under the licence (such as to monitor for methane emissions) then come to an end. Since s. 39 requires the EA to issue a certificate where pollution or harm is unlikely, it is possible that an operator will be able to surrender a licence even though it has not fully complied with the licence conditions. However, any conditions attached to the planning permission for the site will still apply after surrender: these could cover such things as a requirement to restore the land to its previous use or to landscape it appropriately.

This procedure is of great importance, since until the implementation of the EPA 1990 holders of waste disposal licences can surrender them at will, and thus relinquish any continuing responsibilities for the site. This will no longer be possible under the EPA 1990. One side effect of this change was that, in anticipation of the introduction of stricter standards and more rigorous enforcement powers under the EPA 1990, many holders of waste disposal licences under COPA 1974 surrendered them prior to the implementation of the new system, resulting in a significant shake-out of the waste disposal industry.

Detailed guidance for applying for a surrender have been set out in WMP 4 and WMP 26A which must, as a result of s. 35(8), be taken into account by the EA). Applications for the surrender of a licence must include: information on the licence holder; site location; number of the site licence; and a description of all the different activities (whether licensed or not) which were carried out on the site, the location of those activities, the period over which they were carried out and an estimate of the quantity of waste dealt with at the site. Where the site has involved the disposal of waste to landfill, further detailed information is required relating to such matters as hydrogeology, production of gas and leachate and the quality of groundwater.

Once all the formalities have been complied with, the certificate can be issued and the licence ceases to have effect. There is little previous experience of WRAs accepting the surrender of licences and there has been considerable disagreement between those who consider that, as a matter of commercial fairness, a certificate of completion should be granted as of right where certain specified standards are met, and those who wish to see the EA have greater discretion. It remains to be seen how willing the EA will be to issue a certificate, since not only do they lose any income derived from the annual licence charges, but they may also become liable for future clean-up costs.

The provisions on surrender have given rise to a degree of disagreement between those who consider that, as a matter of commercial fairness, a certificate of completion should be granted virtually as of right where certain specified standards, agreed in advance, are met, and those who wish to see the EA have greater discretion. It remains to be seen how willing the EA will be to issue a certificate, since not only do they lose any income derived from the annual licence charges, but they may also become liable for any future clean-up costs.

Enforcement powers

It is one of the features of most modern systems of pollution control that the regulatory agencies have strong enforcement powers. These are not limited to bringing prosecutions for breaches of the law, but extend to powers to vary and to revoke licences without compensation. These administrative remedies often represent a greater threat to operators than prosecution because of the potential financial consequences. The EA has some of the widest and most varied sets of powers in this respect, including powers to modify a licence, to revoke it in whole or in part, to suspend the operation of licensed activities, and to order the carrying out of specified works. In order to ensure that these powers are used, s. 42 imposes supervisory duties on the EA. In a number of cases the legislation places the EA under a duty to take enforcement action.

The enforcement powers in the EPA 1990 are significantly wider than under COPA 1974. In addition, many of the restrictions that applied to waste disposal licences granted under COPA 1974, for example on the permissible scope of conditions, are removed by the EPA 1990. Many licences granted under COPA 1974 do not protect the environment as much as they might have done. But when (or if) they automatically become waste management licences subject to the EPA 1990 (as a result of s. 77), the modification, suspension and revocation powers can be used to impose new standards more in keeping with modern expectations.

Supervision of a licence
Section 42 puts the EA under a duty to supervise waste management licences. It must take the steps that are needed to ensure that pollution of the environment, harm to human health or serious detriment to the amenities of the locality do not occur. it must also take steps to ensure that licence conditions are complied with.

Where there is an emergency, specific powers are given by s. 42(3). The EA may carry out necessary works on land or in relation to plant or equipment, and may recover any expenditure from the licence holder.

Modification of a licence
Powers to modify a licence are of particular importance where circumstances have changed since the initial grant of the licence. The EA may, at its discretion, modify the conditions of a licence where it considers this is desirable and is unlikely to require unreasonable expense on the part of the licence holder (s. 37(1)(a)). But if it considers that in order to ensure that the authorised activities do not cause pollution of the environment or harm to human health, or become seriously detrimental to the amenities of the locality, it is necessary to modify the conditions, it *must* do so to the extent necessary (s. 37(2)). Alternatively, in such circumstances it may decide to revoke the licence under s. 38(1). The consultation requirements apply to an EA proposal to modify a licence in virtually the same way that they apply to an application under s. 36, except that, in an emergency, a reference to a consultee may be postponed. There is a separate right for the licence holder

to apply for a modification (s. 37(1)(b)). In each situation any modification made under s. 37 must be by notice and must specify when it takes effect (s. 37(4)).

Suspension of a licence

The powers to suspend and to revoke a licence are of great use where licensed activities are giving rise to problems, for example where the site is being inadequately managed or is causing pollution. The grounds for their use are, in general terms, similar to those relating to the refusal of an initial licence application, though they are in fact slightly less wide. They provide an opportunity to police the licence on a continuing basis and may be used in addition to other enforcement mechanisms, such as prosecution or ordering a clean-up.

The EA may suspend a licence by serving a notice on the licence holder. Such a notice must specify when the suspension is to take effect and when it is to cease. This may be on the occurrence either of a specified date or a specified event. A suspension cannot be of the whole of a licence, but can only relate to those parts of the licence that authorise the carrying on of activities. For example, the EA may suspend a licence in so far as it allows certain types of waste to be deposited, whilst retaining in force any conditions that relate to measures the licence holder must take to protect against pollution. Whilst a part of a licence is suspended it does not authorise the licence holder to carry on the activities specified.

The power to suspend is new in the EPA 1990. It is provided for in two separate sections: one where there has been a failure to comply with the licence (s. 42(6)), and another which applies more generally (s. 38(6)).

(a)   Under s. 38(6), if the EA considers that the site is no longer in the hands of a technically competent person, it may suspend those parts of the licence that authorise the carrying on of activities. The same power applies if the EA considers that serious pollution of the environment or serious harm to human health has been caused, or is about to be caused, or that the continuation of the activities will cause serious pollution of the environment or serious harm to human health.

(b)   The alternative power is that if, in exercising its supervisory powers under s. 42, it appears to the EA that a condition is not being complied with, it may by notice require the licence holder to comply within a specified time. If the licence holder does not do so, the EA may suspend the licence (s. 42(6)). In this situation, the availability of the suspension power acts as an incentive to the proper implementation of conditions.

One limitation on these powers is that, if the Secretary of State determines on appeal that the EA acted unreasonably in suspending a licence, the licence holder can claim compensation for consequential loss from the EA (s. 43(7)). This potential financial liability may act as a brake on the use of suspension notices by the EA.

Whilst a licence is suspended, the EA may require the licence holder to take such measures to deal with or avert pollution or harm as it thinks fit

(s. 38(9)). Significantly, this may include matters which fall outside the scope of the original licence conditions. It is an offence to fail to comply with such a requirement (s. 38(10)). The maximum penalty is, on conviction in the magistrates' court, a fine of £5,000 or, on conviction in the Crown Court, two years' imprisonment and/or an unlimited fine. If the waste is special waste, a magistrates' court may imprison for up to six months, and the maximum term of imprisonment on conviction in the Crown Court is five years.

Revocation of a licence

The EA may revoke a licence by serving a notice on the licence holder, specifying when the revocation is to take effect. A revocation may be of the whole of a licence or of part of it — this includes revocation of those parts of the licence that authorise the carrying on of activities, whilst retaining other parts. For example, the EA may revoke a licence in so far as it allows special waste to be deposited, leaving the rest of the licence in force. Revocation of the whole of the licence is likely to be inappropriate in many cases, since it means that any conditions attached to the licence cease to have effect (s. 35(11)). As these may include conditions requiring the licence holder to carry out works of pollution control, or conditions relating to the restoration and aftercare of a site, revocation would effectively remove most of the licence holder's responsibilities. It was once possible that the EA could avoid this difficulty by exercising its powers under s. 61 (a section which has now been repealed), but that section only allowed costs to be recovered from the owner of the site, who may not be the same person as the former licence holder, particularly if the pollution occurs some years later.

(a)   Under s. 38(1), if the EA considers that the holder of a licence has ceased to be a fit and proper person by reason of being convicted of a relevant offence, it may revoke the licence, wholly or in part. The same power applies if the EA considers that the continuation of the activities authorised by the licence would cause pollution of the environment or harm to human health, or would be seriously detrimental to the amenities of the locality, except that, in such a case, it must also consider that the pollution, harm or detriment cannot be avoided by modifying the conditions of the licence.

(b)   Under s. 38(2), if the EA considers that the site is no longer in the hands of a technically competent person, it may revoke those parts of the licence that authorise the carrying out of activities, but not the rest of it.

(c)   The same power of partial revocation applies if the licence holder fails to pay an annual subsistence charge (s. 41(7)).

(d)   As with the power to suspend a licence, if the licence holder fails to comply with a notice served under s. 42 requiring compliance with a condition, the EA may revoke the licence, either wholly or in part (s. 42(6)).

Fees and charges

As part of the Government's objective of transferring funding of the regulation of pollution from the public to polluters, the Environment Act

1995, s. 41, provides for a fees and charges scheme (see the Waste Management Licensing (Fees and Charges) Scheme 1997). The scheme is a cost-recovery scheme, meaning that the levels are supposed to be fixed by the Secretary of State so as to cover, in general terms, the cost to the EA of processing an application and supervising a licence.

In order to achieve this objective and to ensure that different operations pay a reasonably fair charge relative to each other, a fairly complex scheme has been implemented. The types of licensable activity are divided into four main classes, although these are then subdivided to take account of such things as whether the waste is being reused, reclaimed or recycled. These classes are: the treatment of controlled waste; the keeping of controlled waste; the disposal of controlled waste; and situations where a site has closed and a certificate of completion is being sought. Having established these general classes, the type of waste which is concerned (for example, whether it is inert waste, household waste, industrial waste or special waste), and the amount of waste that the site is licensed to receive annually, are taken into account so that the precise category into which the activity falls can be ascertained. The various fees and charges are then worked out by reference to that category.

There are separate fees for initial applications for a licence, and for applications for transfer, modification and surrender respectively. An annual subsistence charge is also payable, which will normally run into thousands of pounds, depending on the type of facility. The EA has a power to revoke a licence in part if the annual charge is not paid (s. 41(6)).

Public registers

The EA is under a duty to maintain a public register of a wide range of information relating to the waste management licensing system (s. 64, supplemented by the Waste Management Licensing Regulations 1994 (SI No. 1056)). Further details of the requirements are given in Chapter 7.

In outline, the registers must contain details of the following: all current or recently current licences and applications, together with any relevant supporting documentation, representations and directions; modification, suspension and revocation notices; matters relating to an application to surrender a licence; reports and monitoring information produced or obtained by the EA in discharging its functions; remedial action taken by the EA; consignment notes and records made for the purposes of the special waste provisions; convictions of licence holders under Part II of the Act; and appeals. A licence is no longer recent 12 months after it ceases to be in force, and an application no longer recent 12 months after its rejection, meaning that the registers are of limited use for historical purposes.

There are powers for the Secretary of State to exclude information from the registers on the ground that its inclusion would be contrary to the interests of national security (s. 65), and for the EA to exclude information on commercial confidentiality grounds (s. 66), though there is an appeal to the Secretary of State if the EA refuses to do so. In relation to exclusions dealt with under s. 66, the register will contain an entry indicating the existence of the information.

These fairly comprehensive registers will provide much useful information to environmental groups. But they will also be of great help to those who need to comply with the duty of care, since a search of the register may answer many relevant questions about waste carriers and waste disposal sites.

The powers of the Secretary of State

Apart from the wide-ranging powers to make regulations under the Act and to issue policy guidance, the Secretary of State is provided with very wide powers to give directions to the EA. For example, where an application is made, the Secretary of State may give a binding direction to the EA in relation to the terms and conditions that must, or must not, be included in the licence (s. 35(7)). This power is the equivalent of the call-in powers that exist in other areas of the law. There are similar powers to give binding directions relating to modification (s. 37(3)) and to suspension and revocation (ss. 38(7) and 42(8)) — in these cases the Secretary of State can effectively force the EA to take action.

Appeals

There are wide-ranging rights of appeal to the Secretary of State contained in s. 43. An appeal can be made where:

(a)   an application for a licence is rejected (or is not determined within four months);

(b)   a licence is subject to conditions;

(c)   the conditions are modified;

(d)   an application for a modification of conditions is rejected (or is not determined within two months);

(e)   a licence is suspended;

(f)   a licence is revoked;

(g)   an application to surrender a licence is rejected (or is not determined within three months);

(h)   an application for a transfer of a licence is rejected (or is not determined within two months).

One exception is where the Secretary of State made the original decision under the various powers of direction. In such a case, an action for judicial review would be the only available option.

There are no specified grounds of appeal. The procedures relating to appeals will be set out in regulations. The Waste Management Licensing Regulations 1994 state that an appeal must be brought within six months of the relevant decision (or deemed decision in cases where the appeal is against a non-determination within the required timescale). As is normal in environmental matters the appellant and the EA have a choice as to whether the appeal is in the form of a hearing or by written representations. Unusually, if a hearing is held, s. 43(2)(c) states that it is open to the person who hears the appeal to hold it in private, in whole or in part. The appeal will commonly be referred to an inspector or other person, who will normally make the decision on behalf of the Secretary of State.

Modifications and revocations normally have no effect while an appeal is pending or being heard (s. 43(4)). However, the EA may reverse this rule by stating in its notice that this is necessary for the purpose of preventing or minimising pollution of the environment or harm to human health (s. 43(6)). Suspension notices are not affected by an appeal (s. 43(5)). One limitation on the exercise of the power under s. 43(6) is that a licence holder may ask the Secretary of State to determine whether the EA acted unreasonably in activating s. 43(6), or in suspending a licence. If the decision goes in favour of the licence holder, it can claim compensation for consequential loss from the EA (s. 43(7)). This may limit the use of suspension notices and of s. 43(6).

Offences

With the introduction of the concepts of Directive waste and Directive disposal and recovery operations the original offences under s. 33 of EPA 1990 have now been reinterpreted. Unless one of the exemptions applies, a combination of s. 33(1) of EPA 1990 and the Waste Management Licensing Regulations 1994, reg. 1(3) and sch. 4, makes it a criminal offence to do the following:

(a)   deposit Directive waste in or on land unless it is in accordance with a waste management licence. This applies to any deposit, whether temporary or permanent, and is not restricted to Directive disposal and recovery operations;

(b)   treat, keep or dispose of Directive waste unless it is under and in accordance with a waste management licence — this offence can be committed either in or on land, or by means of mobile plant. As pointed out above this offence now extends only to Directive disposal and recovery operations;

(c)   knowingly cause or knowingly permit either of the above.

These offences are considerably wider than those under COPA 1974 because they are not limited to deposits but extend to keeping, treating or disposing of controlled waste. However, many acts of storage and treatment will in fact be exempted, as the Waste Management Licensing Regulations 1994 show. It is clear that offences in categories (a) and (b) above are ones of strict liability, but it should be noted that (c) interposes 'knowingly' in front of both 'cause' and 'permit'.

There was some uncertainty over the exact number of offences which could be committed under s. 33. Is the treating, keeping or disposing of Directive waste a single offence committed in the alternative or are there three separate offences? The practical difficulty which arises as a result of this uncertainty is that if the latter position is correct, any indictment alleging all three in one charge would be duplicitous (as the situation is in relation to causing or knowingly permitting pollution of controlled waters, see p. 454). In *R* v *Leighton and Town and Country Refuse Collections Ltd* [1997] Env LR 411 the court considered the specific question of whether there are a number of alternative ways of committing the same offence. The court found that although each relevant paragraph of s. 33(1) created a separate offence, each of those offences could be committed in any of the ways specified within the paragraph. For example, it was possible to bring a charge of disposing or treating or keeping of controlled waste in a manner likely to cause pollution of the environment or harm to human health contrary to s. 33(1)(c) of the EPA 1990. This eases the evidential burden on the prosecution when framing an indictment.

The courts have interpreted the phrase 'knowingly' very strictly. In *Shanks and McEwan (Teesside) Ltd* v *Environment Agency* [1997] Env LR 305 the defendant was charged with knowingly permitting the deposit of controlled waste in contravention of a licence condition. It was argued that although the defendant knew of the deposit of the waste it did not know it was in breach of condition. The court followed the previous decision in *Ashcroft* v *Cambro Waste Products Ltd* [1981] 1 WLR 1349 in taking a very strict view of the phrase. The prosecution need only prove knowledge of the deposit of the waste material. It is not necessary to demonstrate knowledge of the breach of the licence condition which gives rise to the offence. Thus, once the prosecution demonstrate that waste had been knowingly permitted to be deposited, the burden then falls on the defence to establish that the deposit was made in accordance with the conditions of the licence.

It is also possible to infer knowledge. In *Kent County Council* v *Beaney* [1993] Env LR 225 it was held that knowing permission may be inferred from the facts of a case where the deposit of waste was obvious from surrounding events. This concept of constructive knowledge was developed further in the *Shanks and McEwan (Teesside)* decision. In that case, Mance J took the view that it was sufficient that the defendant company (including its senior management) knowingly operated and held out its site for the reception and deposit of controlled waste. Once this was established it was not necessary to demonstrate that there was any knowledge of the specific breach of the licence condition. This approach broadens the offence considerably and in effect places the operators of landfill sites under a strict liability for breaches of waste management licence conditions.

As far as the concept of causation is concerned, this has been discussed on a number of occasions in relation to the similar offences under the Water Resources Act 1991. However, analogies with these cases should be made with care, since they do not consider the situation where 'knowingly' is inserted in front of 'cause'. This appears to suggest that someone who orders another to deposit waste will be guilty under this section only if it is shown that they knew the deposit was to take place unlawfully. One subsection that may help here is s. 33(5), which states that where controlled waste is deposited from a motor vehicle, the person who controls the vehicle, or who is in a position to control its use, will be treated as knowingly causing the deposit. See p. 454 for discussion of the meaning of 'cause or knowingly permit' in the context of the Water Resources Act 1991. There is a separate strict liability offence of contravening any condition of a waste management licence (s. 33(6)). This removes the loophole revealed by *Leigh Land Reclamation Ltd* v *Walsall Metropolitan Borough Council* (1991) 155 JP 547 (see p. 379).

The maximum penalty for these offences is, on conviction in the magistrates' court, six months' imprisonment and/or a fine of £20,000 or, on conviction in the Crown Court, two years' imprisonment and/or an unlimited fine. If the waste is special waste, the maximum term of imprisonment on conviction in the Crown Court is five years. An injunction may also be sought in appropriate cases.

Any director, manager, secretary or other similar officer of a corporate body can be prosecuted personally if the offence is committed with their consent or connivance, or is attributable to their neglect (s. 157). As stated earlier, a 'manager' only covers someone who is part of the 'controlling mind' of the company (see *R v Boal* [1992] QB 591, a case on very similar wording in the Fire Precautions Act 1971). This liability is additional to the individual liability of the person who carried out, or knowingly caused or knowingly permitted the deposit. Waste management is one area of environmental law where sentences of imprisonment have actually been imposed, though they have been reserved for serious offences and where an offender offends repeatedly.

The decision in *Boal* has been applied recently in relation to waste management offences under COPA 1974. In *Woodhouse* v *Walsall Metropolitan Borough Council* [1994] Env LR 30, the general manager of a waste disposal site (along with his employers) was convicted of a waste offence under the Act. Following the decision in *Boal* the crucial issue in determining personal (as opposed to corporate liability) was whether the defendant was 'in a position of real authority' having both 'the power and responsibility to decide corporate policy and strategy'. This is something more than mere authority itself (such as the power to 'hire and fire'). The important test was whether a defendant was in a position to control and guide the corporate body in terms of policy and strategy. This is, of course, a question of fact and degree in every case. For a possible view of the other side of the coin (i.e., corporate vicarious liability for the actions of its employees in relation to the Water Resources Act 1991) see *National Rivers Authority* v *Alfred McAlpine Homes East Ltd* [1994] 4 All ER 286 and p. 457. In *Shanks and McEwan (Teesside) Ltd* v *Environment Agency* [1997] Env LR 305 there was some discussion of the nature of such vicarious liability and although the views expressed were only *obiter* it was thought that where an employee had knowledge of a deposit of waste there would, following the *Alfred McAlpine* case, be a 'powerful' argument in favour of fixing the employer with vicarious knowledge of that deposit.

Defences

There is a defence under s. 33(7)(a) where the defendant took all reasonable precautions and exercised all due diligence to avoid the commission of the offence. This is a familiar defence that is included in many pieces of regulatory legislation. Essentially, it involves the defendant showing either that it took the appropriate steps on the facts of the case, or that it set up an adequate system. In many ways, the requirements are similar to those laid down by the duty of care. For example, the defence is of great use for receivers of waste (i.e., carriers and waste disposal site operators), who may inadvertently deal with it in an illegal fashion if they are misled by the consignor. However, it does impose quite a high standard on them to take steps to ensure that the consignment contains what it is meant to contain. It is arguable that this defence introduces an element of self-policing into the waste disposal chain. For example, in *Durham County Council* v *Peter Connors Industrial Services Ltd* [1993] Env LR 197, a system of operation which relied upon the person disposing of waste regularly collecting a skip which had been filled with waste by another without checking on the contents of the skip every time, was not sufficient to come within an analogous defence under s. 3(4) of COPA 1974. In that case, the court said that the collector of waste had to take care to inform itself on each occasion that it collected the waste as to the nature of the contents of the skip. The defence required a specific enquiry to be made of any person who knew what the waste was and whether or not the future deposit of that waste would involve a breach of the Act.

There are further defences in s. 33(7)(b) and (c) relating respectively to employees who act under instructions from their employer and in ingnorance of the offence, and to acts carried out in an emergency in order to avoid danger to the public (although not danger to the environment) . The onus of proof establishing whether or not an emergency exists rests with the defendant upon the balance of probabilities. In *Waste Incineration Services Ltd* v *Dudley Metropolitan Borough Council* [1993] Env LR 29 the court viewed the phrase 'emergency' (as used in a condition of a waste disposal licence) objectively and without reference to how the licence holder perceived a given set of facts.

Dangerous disposal of waste

There is a very important further offence created by s. 33(1)(c). It is an offence to treat, keep or dispose of controlled waste in a manner likely to cause pollution of the environment or harm to human health. The importance of this paragraph is that it applies irrespective of the need for a waste management licence. In other words, activities which are exempted from the need for a licence are still governed by what is in effect a general requirement to act safely. The paragraph could also be said to supplement the licensing system by acting as a form of residual condition attached to a licence, since in theory it applies even where a licence is being complied with. The offence is drafted remarkably widely, as pollution of the environment is defined in s. 29 by reference to harm to *any* living organism. Harm in this context means any harm to the health of living organisms or interference with the ecological systems of which they form a part.

The paragraph is mainly targeted at providing a straightforward offence that can be used in relation to fly-tipping and other forms of irresponsible waste disposal. However, it also covers such things as storage of wastes on the production site — the harm to human health could be a harm to employees. The maximum penalty for breach of s. 33(1)(c) is the same as for offences relating to a waste management licence. The section does not, however, apply to activities which are under regulations made under s. 33(3). This has only been done in the cases of activities which are adequately controlled under regimes other than waste management.

Overlap with EPA 1990, Part I

Regulation 16 of the Waste Management Licensing Regulations 1994 covers the overlap between control under Parts I and II of the EPA 1990. In relation to integrated pollution control, reg. 16(1)(a) provides that the recovery or disposal of waste under an IPC authorisation, where the activity is or forms part of a process is exempt from the licensing. What is not clear is the extent to which an activity is 'part of the process'. The problem is particularly acute in respect of incineration and other combustion processes which use waste fuels. In particular, where waste is stored or treated on the site of an incinerator it is unclear as to whether a waste management licence is required.

In addition, despite the fact that it is meant to provide an integrated system of control, no condition can be attached to an authorisation which regulates the final disposal of Directive waste in or on land (s. 28(1)).

In relation to other processes, most incinerators (except for very small ones), a number of waste recovery operations, and some other processes in which waste is burned as a fuel are subject to control under the local authority air pollution control provisions of Part I of the EPA 1990 (see Part B of section 5.1 (incineration) of the Prescribed Processes etc Regulations 1991 (SI 1991 No. 472). In these restricted circumstances, where an authorisation is required under Part I of the EPA 1990, this will exempt the premises from the need for a waste management licence. In practice, however, many operators will have operations ancillary to the main process (e.g., waste storage or delivery) and will seek a waste management licence to cover these aspects.

Clean-up powers

Section 59 gives the EA and waste collection authorities powers to require the removal of controlled waste. They apply whenever controlled waste has been deposited on land in contravention of s. 33(1), i.e., the deposit was not in accordance with a waste management licence or it breached s. 33(1)(c).

The initial responsibility falls on the occupier of the land. The EA may serve a notice on the occupier requiring the waste to be removed, or steps to be taken to mitigate the consequences of the deposit. The notice must specify a period within which this action should be taken, though it cannot be less than 21 days. There is a right to appeal to the magistrates' court during the 21-day period. Such an appeal must be allowed if the court is satisfied that the appellant neither deposited nor knowingly caused or knowingly permitted the deposit, or if there is a material defect in the notice (s. 59(3)). An appeal suspends the operation of the notice until it is determined (s. 59(4)). It is a summary offence, with a maximum fine of £5,000 to fail to comply with a notice served under s. 59 (s. 59(5)). This offence is a continuing one and a further fine of up to £1,000 can be imposed for every day on which the failure to comply continues after conviction. Ultimately, the EA has default powers to carry out the steps specified in the notice itself and to recover any expenses reasonably incurred from the person on whom it was served (s. 59(6)).

Where the occupier did not make or knowingly permit the unlawful deposit, or there is no occupier, the EA may remove the waste or take mitigating steps immediately. This course of action is also available if these steps were immediately necessary to remove or prevent pollution or harm to human health (s. 59(7)). The EA may then recover its costs from any person who deposited the waste, or knowingly caused or knowingly permitted its deposit, unless that person can show that the cost was incurred unnecessarily (s. 59(8)). Ultimate responsibility for unlawfully deposited waste therefore falls on the person who deposited it rather than on the occupier. However, it may not be possible to trace the person responsible, or they may have no money to pay the EA's costs, in which case the position is in practice that the EA has a choice whether to leave the waste where it is or pick up the bill itself. Nevertheless, this is an important power which can be used in addition to a prosecution under s. 33, since it tackles directly the problem that faces the EA.

The EA's powers under the Water Resources Act 1991, s. 161, should also be considered in this context, since they may be used to deal with deposits of waste that threaten controlled waters (see p. 472).

Contaminated land

Britain has an industrial legacy which has led to the contamination of some areas of the country. Traditionally, active emissions from industrial processes have been controlled, whereas the long-term harm caused from ground contamination has been ignored. It has been estimated that approximately 27,000 hectares of land in the UK are regarded as potentially contaminated. The law in relation to the harm caused by contaminated land has, however, been pragmatic and piecemeal. Various mechanisms are available to deal with the specific problems associated with contaminated land (see p. 417). Until relatively recently, however, the need to legislate specifically in order to control the problem has not been acknowledged. There is now a recognition of the need to reuse old industrial land and the understanding of the consequences of land contamination has increased. Subsequently, the law and policy in relation to the clean-up of contaminated land is in the process of change.

The Environment Act 1995 has introduced a new system of control specifically targeted at the clean-up of contaminated land. The principles of the system work in a similar way to the statutory nuisance provisions in the

EPA 1990, although there is a hierarchy of sites which involve slightly different actions. Indeed, the new provisions have been inserted into Part II of the EPA 1990 and now sit alongside the nuisance provisions.

Like many other areas of environmental law the framework of the legislation gives only a small part of the legislative picture. Most of the detail is likely to be fleshed out in the guise of Government guidance. At the time of writing only a portion of this guidance has been issued (albeit only in draft and for consultation purposes). It is likely, therefore, that a unified body of law and policy on the clean-up of contaminated land will only be available some (considerable?) time after the Royal Assent of the Environment Act 1995.

The introduction of the Environment Act 1995 was a direct result of the failure of the first initiative intended to deal with the problem, the contaminative uses register. The origin of the register was to be found in the Parliamentary Select Commitee's report on contaminated land in 1989, which recommended the abolition of the *caveat emptor* rule in relation to the sale and purchase of land so that the seller was under an obligation to inform the buyer of any of the defects with the land (including contamination). The Government responded with a consultation paper, *Let the Buyer be Better Informed*. The primary thrust of the proposals was the introduction of a set of registers which would form an objective list of potentially contaminated sites by reference to a selection of potentially contaminative uses. It was intended that regulations prescribing the form of the register were to be introduced in late 1991.

The response to the consultation exercise was overwhelming and generally negative. In the light of many of the observations which were made, the DoE issued a second consultation paper on 31 July 1992. On this occasion, a set of draft regulations was included which were intended to indicate the framework for the registers. It was envisaged that the regulations would be implemented in late 1992 and subsequently local authorities would be given 15 months in which to compile the data which was to form the registers before they would be available for the public.

The second consultation exercise differed from the first in that fewer categories of potentially contaminative uses which would be included on the register were proposed than on the original list. It was intended that the register would cover land on which there had been such uses as oil refineries, chemical works, scrap metal stores, waste tips, lead works and steel works.

Many objections were raised at both stages of the consultation process. It was pointed out that there were no provisions for the removal of the sites from the register even if the land had subsequently been cleaned up. It was suggested therefore that there was little incentive to clean up a site as it would still be included on the register.

The second major area of concern was the problem of blight on land which was included on the register. It was argued that it would be unlikely that developers would wish to buy an identified 'problem' site, as any subsequent resale or leasing would involve an investigation from potential purchasers into the contamination on site.

This in turn, it was argued, would lead to a disincentive to regenerate vacant and derelict land, which would be contrary to existing Government policy. As developers refused to develop on inner-city areas this would subsequently lead to pressures on edge-of-town sites.

Banks and building societies predicted that there would be a large scale reduction in the value of land included on the register. This would lead to lending institutions being reluctant to fund property development on sites included on the register. Thus, it was argued that sites included on the register would be effectively sterilised.

More fundamental criticisms were aimed at the registers and there were many suggestions that the concept behind them was seriously flawed. Most of the criticisms related to the fact that the registers would not record actual contamination but instead would rely upon the previous or existing uses of land. It was suggested that such a blanket approach would not provide sufficient certainty of the presence of contamination. Indeed, there would be a significant number of sites which were heavily contaminated which would not appear on the register at all.

The basic problem, however, was that the registers did not seek to do anything positive to assist remediation where land had been identified as being contaminated. It was argued that it was not the main priority to identify which areas had a chance of being contaminated, as such information was generally acknowledged to be available. Once contamination has been identified, the crucial issue to be addressed is the liability for the costs of remediation and the recovery of those costs. The registers, of course did not attempt to deal with these complicated issues.

In the light of these criticisms it was announced in March 1993 that the Government was withdrawing its proposals to set up the register of contaminative uses. At the same time it was announced that there would be a wide-ranging review of the clean-up of contaminated land including such issues as treatment, allocation of liabilities and cost recovery. The Consultation Paper, *Paying for Our Past* was issued in March 1994. The aim of the paper was to set out a number of 'preliminary conclusions' on a series of seven issues dealing with Government policy objectives, the statutory framework, the relationship with the common law, the extension of strict liability, the identity of the person liable for clean-up, providing the markets with information and the role of public sector bodies.

In November 1994 the Government announced the outcome of the consultation exercise. The result was a policy document, *The Framework for Contaminated Land*. The document sets out the broad future strategy for dealing with contaminated land. The principal elements of this strategy are:

(a)   the adoption of the 'suitable for use' approach when dealing with the issue of clean-up. Thus, remedial action will only be required where the contamination poses unacceptable actual or potential risks to health or the environment. This is to be balanced against the appropriateness and cost effectiveness of the measures, taking into account the actual or intended use of the site. Therefore, the measure required to clean up a site which was to be used for housing would be more stringent than if it were to be used for car-parking;

(b)   to prioritise action to deal with the most urgent and real problems whilst balancing the economic constraints within the economy as a whole and on private businesses and landowners;

(c)   to clarify the law on the clean-up of contaminated sites, thus enabling a proper market to be created for those who own sites which are or have been contaminated;

(d)   to supplement the existing statutory nuisance provisions with a new, modern, specific power to deal with contaminated land.

In addition it was announced that ss. 143 and 61 of the EPA 1990 dealing with the contaminative uses register and closed landfills were to be repealed.

An overview of the new provisions

The legislation and guidance on contaminated land are very complicated. The key points of the system are:

(a)   There is a duty placed on local authorities to inspect their areas for the presence of contaminated land. They are then responsible for carrying out an assessment of the land in order to ascertain whether the contamination is giving rise to significant harm, significant risk of significant harm or pollution of controlled waters. This assessment is governed by statutory guidance. Where the assessment indicates that the land is contaminated, the authority must determine whether the contamination is so serious as to warrant designation of the site as a special site which is regulated by the Environment Agency. In all other cases the local authority is responsible for regulating the clean up of the site. There are registers which hold details of contaminated land in an area.

(b)   Where emergency works are required to deal with any contamination, the enforcing authority can carry out those works and then seek to recover the costs of doing so from the appropriate persons.

(c)   If it is not necessary to carry out emergency works the enforcing authority must identify all persons who might be affected by the service of a remediation notice. This includes owners, occupiers, and those responsible for the contamination.

(d)   The enforcing authority must then formulate a scheme to clean up the land so that it is no longer causing significant harm etc. Any scheme must specify what needs to be done, the cost of doing so and a timescale for carrying out the works. The scheme must be reasonable taking into account the cost of carrying out the works and the seriousness of the harm or pollution caused.

(e)   Once the scheme has been drawn up there is a consultation period with those who are affected. During this time the scheme is finalised or, if possible, agreed. Where the persons affected agree to undertake voluntary measures to clean up, the enforcing authority is precluded from taking any further action.

(f)   Where there is no agreement, the enforcing authority must then identify everyone who could be made responsible for cleaning up the site —

known as the appropriate persons. The primary responsibility for clean up rests with the original polluters, i.e., those who caused or knowingly permitted the substance or any of the substances which have been the cause of the contamination to be in, on or under land. If the original polluter cannot be found, the owner or occupier becomes the appropriate person.

(g)   Once all of the appropriate persons have been identified the enforcing authority excludes less blameworthy persons in accordance with tests set down in statutory guidance. After these tests have been applied the costs of carrying out the clean-up works are apportioned between those remaining. In apportioning costs the enforcing authority must consider whether any person served would suffer hardship if the costs were to be recovered from them. If that is the case, the authority cannot serve a remediation notice on that person.

(i)   Where the enforcing authority can serve a remediation notice it must do so. If it is precluded from serving such a notice, it has a power to carry out the work itself and seek to recover all or part of the costs of doing so.

(j)   Where a notice is served there is a right of appeal within 21 days. In the event of non-compliance with the notice there are criminal sanctions and default powers for the enforcing authority to carry out clean-up works with provision for cost recovery.

Statutory guidance

The new scheme of liability for contaminated land provided by Part II of the Environment Act 1995 is to be supplemented by three levels of guidance to be provided by the Secretary of State and by Rules and Regulations to be introduced by statutory instrument. The guidance is in three 'levels'. In practice this will have very little effect, although the courts may interpret each type in a different manner should it ever be the subject of a challenge. The three levels are:

(a)   Guidance which enforcing authorities must 'act in accordance with'.

(b)   Guidance which enforcing authorities must 'have regard to'.

(c)   Guidance which is merely descriptive and has no status in administrative law.

Why is this hierarchy important in practice? Clearly, the status of the guidance is important when it comes to challenging any decision of the enforcing authority on appeal. Although the guidance is prescriptive in its language in many places it does not have the precision of a statute and we can therefore expect to see many disagreements on the actual meaning of some of the fundamental concepts in the guidance.

The guidance which enforcing authorities are to have regard to is a familiar animal and the extent to which it is binding as a material consideration as well as the approach which the courts will take to its interpretation is fairly well settled. It should be assessed and interpreted under existing principles.

The guidance which enforcing authorities are to act in accordance with is more difficult. This is a new concept in environmental guidance and carries much greater weight than the typical 'material consideration'. In particular it covers mixed questions of law and fact in relation to technical matters.

Some basic concepts

At the time of writing the statutory guidance is still in draft form and so may be subject to change, and in any event the details of the guidance are too complicated to describe in a book of this type. There are, however a few innovative, key concepts within the guidance which are unlikely to change in principle and are fundamental to the understanding of the practical workings of the provisions.

(a)   Class A and class B appropriate persons. The guidance refers to causers and knowing permitters as class A persons and current owners or occupiers as class B persons. The Government's 'view' of 'cause' and 'knowingly permit' is set out in background guidance on the basis of case law in relation to water pollution, with the caveat that these questions are ultimately for the courts.

(b)   Significant pollutant linkage. This concept is used as the foundation for determining the extent of the liability in a particular case and is defined in chapter 2 of the draft guidance. A pollutant linkage will contain a potential pollutant, a receptor and a potential pathway by which the receptor may be exposed to the potential pollutant. A pollutant linkage which forms the basis for determination of land as contaminated land is a significant pollutant linkage ('SPL'). Determination of land as contaminated land is to be made in accordance with s. 78A(2) and the guidance relating to significant harm and significant possibility. Once a SPL has been identified, remediation actions required and liability for the costs of such actions are determined in relation to the particular SPL. Thus a site which is contaminated by a range of different substances will have a number of different SPLs and the clean up will be referable to each of those individually.

(c)   Liability groups. The appropriate persons who may be liable for remediation relating to each SPL form liability groups, with class A persons forming the class A liability group and class B persons forming the class B liability group. Each liability group may consist of one or more persons. It is possible that appropriate persons will, of course, not necessarily be found to form liability groups in relation to each SPL. In such cases the enforcing authority may be responsible for funding remediation actions ('orphan linkages').

(d)   Exclusionary tests. Exclusionary tests are applied to the members of liability groups with different tests applying to class A liability groups and class B liability groups. The purpose of the tests is to exclude from liability those who are thought to be less blameworthy for the contamination. They are not to be applied so as to exclude all members of a liability group and so at least one appropriate person will remain liable. The tests are to be applied in the order in which they are set out in the guidance and so this order may be as significant as the actual content of the tests. A provision is made to prevent exclusion of parent and subsidiary companies where more than one of them is within the liability group at the outset.

What is contaminated land?

For a number of years there has been some discussion about the precise definition of the phrase 'contaminated land'. The main difficulty in seeking to define the phrase is that 'contamination' (with no necessary link to any harm/damage) refers merely to the presence of a foreign substance. This is not the same as 'pollution' which is linked to harm. Thus, arguably, land could be contaminated and pose no threat to either the environment or human health. In such a case it would be unnecessary to carry out any clean-up operations. The DoE, in evidence to the House of Commons Select Committee select, took the view that contaminated land should be defined as land 'which represents an actual hazard to public health or the environment as a result of current or previous use'.

In any event the discussion has now been superseded by the statutory definition contained in s. 78A(2) of the EPA 1990 (as inserted by the Environment Act 1995). In that section 'contaminated land' is defined as being:

land which appears to the local authority in whose area it is situated to be in such a condition, by reason of substances in, on or under land, that

(a)   significant harm is being caused or there is a significant possibility of such harm being caused; or
(b)   pollution of controlled waters is being or is likely to be, caused.

Local authorities are under a duty to have regard to any guidance issued by the Secretary of State when assessing whether land is contaminated (s. 78B(2)). In addition, the assessment of 'significant' harm is also to be the subject of further guidance. There is, however, express provision within the Act for such guidance to make provision for different weight to be attached to different descriptions of harm to health or property and other factors.

Administrative and regulatory responsibilities

The primary responsibility for the role of identifying and cleaning up contaminated land will fall to the district and metropolitan authorities. The local authorities are guided by the Environment Agency (EA), which provides technical expertise and advice. The EA is also responsible for continuing the Government's research programme into contaminated land, with particular reference to publishing guidelines for priority contaminants (s. 78A(6)). Finally, the EA will play an active role in the clean-up of the most contaminated sites (known as 'special sites') after notification from the local authorities (see below). The EA has inspection and entry powers in relation to special sites (s. 78Q). In particular, the EA can terminate the designation of a special site where it appears to the EA that it is no longer suitable for designation (s. 78Q(4)). The EA (and SEPA) is under a duty to prepare a report on the state of contaminated land in England, Wales and Scotland with assistance from local authorities (s. 78U).

The identification of contaminated land

Under s. 78B of the EPA 1990 each local authority is under a duty to inspect its area from time to time for the purposes of identifying:

(a)   contaminated land;
(b)   special sites.

Special sites are designated by the EA after notification by the local authority after carrying out their general inspection duty. Special sites are regulated directly by the EA and will be defined in separate regulations which have yet to be published. The general criteria for special sites are the seriousness of the harm or water pollution which would be (or is being) caused and whether the EA is more likely to have the expertise to act on those particular sites (s. 78C(10)).

When identifying sites, the enforcing authority is entitled to take into account the cumulative impact of two or more sites when assessing the 'significant harm' or 'pollution'. This will be important where the 'cocktail' effect of a number of contaminated sites causes significant harm, whereas any individual site will not give rise to any notable pollution (s. 78X).

Once land has been identified as being contaminated the local authority is under a duty to notify the Agency, the owner/occupier of the land, and anyone who is considered to be the 'appropriate person' (see below).

Remediation notices

Once a site has been identified as contaminated land or a special site the relevant authority is under a duty to prepare, and serve on the 'appropriate person', a remediation notice specifying what must be done by way of remediation (s. 78E). This reflects the existing responsibilities in relation to statutory nuisances. There are, however, a number of circumstances where the duty to serve a remediation notice does not apply. Where the enforcing authority is satisfied that a site is contaminated but remediation works cannot be specified the duty to serve a remediation notice does not apply. Instead, it must publish a remediation document setting out the grounds for taking the view that remediation works cannot be specified (s. 78H(5)–(16)).

If a remediation notice is to be served the relevant authority is then under a duty to carry out a formal consultation exercise before service (s. 78H(1)). This duty does not apply in cases where it appears to the authority that there is an imminent danger of serious harm or pollution of controlled waters (s. 78(H)(4)). The authority is required to notify the appropriate person(s) on whom a notice would be served, the owner of the land, and any person who appears to be in occupation of the whole or part of the land, at least three months before the date of service of the notice (s. 78H(3)).

It is intended that this time would be used by the potential recipient of the notice to come up with alternative proposals for remediation or to locate any alternative person responsible for the contamination.

In an attempt to encourage more voluntary remediation work, the relevant authority is precluded from serving a remediation notice where it is satisfied that appropriate steps are being, or will be taken, without the service of a notice (s. 78H(5)). The appropriate person is required to prepare, within a reasonable period, a remediation statement setting out the works which will be carried out within a specified period.

The remediation notice is to be served on the appropriate persons and is required to set out what must be done and the time period for carrying out the specified steps (s. 78E(1)). In specifying the steps required under a remediation notice the authority is under a duty to take into account guidance produced by the EA and to balance the costs of carrying out the work with the seriousness of the harm/pollution caused (s. 78E(4)). This cost-benefit analysis which is to be carried out by the relevant authority will be crucial in determining the effectiveness of the new provisions. A further restriction is placed upon the authority in that cannot issue a notice where powers are available to the EA under s. 27 of the EPA 1990 in relation to remediation of pollution caused by prescribed processes.

The 'appropriate person'

Although the practicalities of the new system are fairly straightforward, the issue of the identity of the 'appropriate person' on whom the remediation notice is served is perhaps the central element of the new system. In accordance with the 'polluter pays' principle the aprropriate person is defined as the person, or any of the persons, who caused or knowingly permitted the substances, or any of the substances, which have been the cause of the contamination to be in or under the land (s. 78E).

Where there are two or more parties responsible for the presence of contaminative substances in or under land the Act makes provision for joint and several liability in restricted circumstances. Different remediation notices can require different things to be done by way of remediation (s. 78E(2)) although each 'appropriate person' may only be served with a notice in connection with any remediation which is 'to any extent referable' to substances caused or knowingly permitted by that party (s. 78F(9)). On the other hand, it is no defence for the recipient of a remediation notice to argue that any remediation would not be required in consequence only of the presence of the substance introduced by the recipient of the notice. Where the same remediation activity is required from different parties a remediation notice cannot be served requiring remediation measures in respect of other contaminating substances whose presence was not caused or knowingly permitted by them. In such circumstances, where the 'appropriate person' who *is* responsible for the remediation activity cannot be found, after reasonable inquiry, the owner or occupier become 'appropriate persons' (see below). Where there are two or more 'appropriate persons' in relation to any remediation works they will only be responsible for a relative portion of the costs and/or the works and the remediation notice must specify the proportion of the costs which they are liable to bear (s. 78F(7)).

Although primary responsibility for remediation rests with the person who caused or knowingly permitted the substance to be present in land a residual responsibility falls upon owners and occupiers. Where, after reasonable inquiry, the original polluter cannot be 'found' the owner or the occupier for the time being are deemed to be appropriate persons (s. 78F(4)). The liability of owners and occupiers is restricted in relation to remediation works in relation to the pollution of controlled waters (s. 78J). Where a party finds themselves responsible for remediation works solely as a result of their ownership or occupation of land (as opposed to being the original polluter) they will not be liable for any works relating to the pollution of controlled waters (s. 78J(2)). There are other restrictions in relation to liability for contamination which escapes to other land (see below).

'Owner' is defined in s. 78A as being the person entitled to receive the rent for the property. It specifically excludes mortgagees not in possession, which means that lenders can receive remediation notices where they are mortgagees in possession. Insolvency practitioners are also protected from personal liability unless the contamination is attributable to their own negligence (s. 78X). 'Occupier' is not defined.

Escapes of substances to other land

As contamination does not necessarily confine itself to boundaries of ownership or occupation there is provision for the service of remediation notices where substances have escaped from their original resting place onto other land. The basic principle is that the original polluter can be responsible for contamination which has escaped from the original land onto other land (s. 78K(1)). Owners and occupiers are not liable to carry out remediation works in respect of substances which have migrated onto their land other than remediation to land within their ownership or occupation (s. 78K(3)). In addition, owners of land adjoining contaminated land are not liable for remediation in respect of other, further land to which substances have migrated, unless they are the owner of that land (s. 78K(4)).

Although these provisions in respect of responsibility for contamination provide a complicated hierarchy of liability, the practical difficulties of establishing responsibility must not be overlooked. Unfortunately, contamination does not necessarily carry clear identification of responsibility. In particular, in areas where there has been a long history of industrial activity, distinguishing between different polluters will present evidential hurdles which will have to be overcome before a remediation notice can be served. In these circumstances it is clear that the service of a remediation notice will not be a quick-fire remedy.

Non-compliance with a remediation notice

It is an offence to fail to comply with a remediation notice without reasonable excuse (s. 78M). There are, however, relatively minor penalties which undermines the deterrence factor. The offence can only be tried in the magistrates' court. Where the contaminated land is currently industrial, trade or business premises, the maximum penalty is a fine of £20,000, with a further daily fine of up to £2,000 for every day before the enforcing authority has carried out any remediation. In cases of other contaminated land the maximum fine is £5,000, with a maximum daily fine of £500 (10% of Level 5).

The relevant authority has the power to carry out remediation works where the recipient of the remediation has failed to comply either with or without the appropriate person's agreement (s. 78N). The enforcing authority has the power to recover all or part of its reasonable costs. In recovering costs, regard must be had to any hardship which the cost-recovery might impose. In England and Wales the relevant authority also has the power to serve a charging notice on the owner which will constitute a charge on the premises which consist of or include the contaminated land in question. The costs of any charge may be paid by instalments over a maximum 30-year period. A person served with the charging notice has a right of appeal which must be made to the county court within 21 days of the receipt of the notice (s. 78P(8)).

Appeals

Any person who is the recipient of a remediation notice has the right of appeal within 21 days of the service of the notice. Where the notice was served by a local authority the appeal is made to the magistrates' court; in relation to special sites, the right of appeal is to the Secretary of State (s. 78L). The details of the appeals process are to be the subject of regulations which have yet to be published, but it is expected that they will broadly follow the pattern of appeals against statutory nuisances (see s. 78R).

Registers

There is a public register which contains details of remediation statements, notices, appeals and information about remediation work notified to the authority, although there is no official guarantee of compliance with remediation notices.

Other statutory provisions for the clean-up of contaminated land

The new provisions in the Environment Act are designed to replace (and not supplement) the existing statutory nuisance provisions in Part III of the EPA. Once the new provisions in the Environment Act are brought into force, s. 79 of the EPA will be amended to exclude contaminated land from the definition of statutory nuisances (see sch. 22, para. 89, Environment Act 1995).

Although the introduction of the new contaminated land provisions in the Environment Act 1995 is an attempt to update the law there are still a number of other statutory provisions which can be utilised in dealing with land which is causing or likely to cause harm to the environment.

Most statutory powers rely upon the need to prevent actual harm and do not seek to remediate contamination which is in existence but causing no harm. Thus, there is no statutory obligation to clean up contamination unless certain pre-conditions are met. The only occasions where remediation is required as a matter of law is where contamination is likely to lead to:

(a)   pollution of the environment;

(b)   adverse effects on human health or safety;
(c)   an escape of pollutants.

Where remediation is required as a matter of statute the steps which would be taken would only normally be limited to the minimisation of one of these three risks rather than making the site 'clean'. As a matter of practice, however, when sites are remediated it is normally to an accepted standard.

Statutory nuisances

Sections 79 and 80 of the EPA 1990 require local authorities to inspect their areas in order to detect the presence of statutory nuisances. This includes any accumulation or deposit which is prejudicial to health or a nuisance. Once they have detected a statutory nuisance they are under a duty to serve notices requiring abatement of the nuisance. The notice is to be served on the person responsible for the nuisance or, if that person is unable to be found, the owner or occupier of the site. The local authority has a residual right to carry out the works if the owner/occupier does not do so (see s. 81(3)).

There is, however, a loophole which means that contamination which is giving rise to harm (as opposed to significant harm) falls outside the definition of a statutory nuisance. Section 79(1A) of the EPA 1990 will be inserted by the Environment Act 1995 but will probably only be implemented at the same time as the main contaminated land provisions under Part IIA come into force. Under that section land cannot be a statutory nuisance by virtue of it being in a 'contaminated state'. The intention behind this exclusion was to ensure that the main provisions under Part IIA were used in preference to the existing statutory nuisance provisions and thereby avoid difficult overlaps in the legislation. There is, however, a gap between the definition of contaminated land in Part IIA and land in a 'contaminated state' under s. 79. Under s. 79(1B) land is in a 'contaminated state' where harm is being caused. This definition falls short of the Part IIA definition which links contaminated land with *significant* harm. Therefore where harm is being caused by contamination which is not significant (and it is important to bear in mind that the definition of 'harm' adopted in other parts of the EPA 1990 is particularly wide), a local authority is precluded from taking any action to deal with the harm under the statutory nuisance provisions.

Pollution of controlled waters

As in the case of statutory nuisances, there is a significant overlap between the contaminated land provisions and the clean-up powers under the Water Resources Act 1991. Section 161 of the Water Resources Act 1991 enables the EA to take preventative action and/or remedial action to deal with actual or threatened pollution of controlled waters. Again, the notice is to be served on the person responsible for the pollution and the EA can carry out the works and recover the costs from that person (see p. 472).

The overlap arises out of the definition of 'contaminated land', which includes land which appears to be in such condition, by reason of substances in, on or under it, that pollution of controlled waters is being, or is likely to be, caused. Similarly, under s. 161A(1) of the Water Resources Act 1991, where it appears to the EA that any poisonous, noxious or polluting matter or any solid waste matter is likely to enter, or to be, or to have been, present in any controlled waters, the EA shall be entitled to serve a works notice on any person who caused or knowingly permitted the presence of the matter in the place where it was likely to enter any controlled waters, or caused, or knowingly permitted the matter to be present in controlled waters. This power could be used to require the clean up of controlled waters from past contamination.

The overlap between the two powers only arises where there is present or future pollution of controlled waters from contaminated land. Where the polluting matter is no longer entering controlled waters it falls outside the definition in Part IIA and therefore the contaminated land regime does not apply. Where a local authority is determining whether contaminated land exists in relation to the pollution of controlled waters it is intended that a consistent approach is taken. Thus the draft statutory guidance requires local authorities to consult the EA and 'take into account' any comments before determining whether pollution of controlled waters is being or is likely to be caused.

Section 215 of the Town and Country Planning Act 1990

Local planning authorities have the power to require steps to be taken for remedying the condition of land which adversely affects the amenity of their area. They may serve an appropriate notice upon the owner and occupier of that land. This notice can be the subject of an appeal which can effectively negate the power.

Civil liabilities

In addition to the statutory powers which can be used to remediate contaminated land, there are also potential civil liabilities for damage caused from contamination. These liabilities also depend upon actual loss rather than anticipated loss, although it may be possible to bring a mandatory injunction to prevent any damage arising (see Chapter 8).

Section 73 of the Environmental Protection Act

As outlined below (see p. 429) this section applies where any damage is caused by a deposit of controlled waste in contravention of ss. 33(1) or 63(2) (i.e., the deposit was not in accordance with a waste management licence, or it breached s. 33(1)(c), or it breached the provision on disposal of non-controlled waste).

Rylands v *Fletcher*

Strict liability under the rule in *Rylands* v *Fletcher* can be utilised to pay for the clean-up of contaminated sites (see p. 199). There are a number of limitations on this rule in relation to contaminated land:

(a)   it is only the person who brought the substance which escapes on to the land who can be the defendant;

(b)   the thing on the land must truly escape rather than be the consequence of an 'action' (compare spillages of material over a period of time (an action) with the leaking of a faulty underground storage tank (an escape));

(c)   the escape must cause the damage to the plaintiff;

(d)   the use of land must be non-natural.

Many of these issues have been considered in relation to the pollution of ground water in *Cambridge Water Co.* v *Eastern Counties Leather plc* [1994] 2 AC 264 (see p. 182). It is not clear as to the extent to which the principles in that decision will apply to contaminated land, but there would be good grounds to suggest that it would be followed in such cases.

Nuisance

It may be possible to bring an action in private nuisance on the grounds that contamination has caused a substantial and unreasonable interference with the use of adjoining property. Again, the person liable would be the person responsible or, if that person was not found, the owner/occupier of the site.

Other liabilities might arise in negligence and/or breach of statutory duty. Clearly each of these causes of action would depend to a large extent upon the specific circumstances of the contamination.

Duty of care

The most significant new control introduced by the EPA 1990 is the criminal duty of care imposed by s. 34, which came into force on 1 April 1992. All those who deal with controlled waste are required to take reasonable and appropriate steps in relation to it, otherwise they commit a criminal offence. This entails such things as storing and packaging waste properly, describing clearly what it consists of, dealing only with an authorised carrier, providing the carrier with an accurate transfer note relating to the waste, and taking steps to ensure that it is ultimately disposed of correctly. What is reasonable will depend on the exact circumstances and on the identity and resources of the person concerned. Additional, more specific, requirements apply to special waste (see p. 426).

The introduction of the duty of care was prompted primarily by the publication of the Eleventh Report of the Royal Commission on Environmental Pollution, *Managing Waste: The Duty of Care*, in 1985 (Cmnd 9675). This concluded:

The first task is for society to identify where the responsibility lies for ensuring that wastes are properly handled and disposed of. In our judgment, this must rest with the individual or organisation who produces the wastes. The producer incurs a duty of care which is owed to society, and we would like to see this duty reflected in public attitudes and enshrined in legislation and codes of practice.

The Royal Commission went on to stress the need to pass the responsibility for waste from person to person down the disposal chain, thereby suggesting that, rather than the producer retaining total responsibility for the waste, the duty of care would operate by ensuring that everyone in the chain checks the competence of those with whom they deal with regard to handling the waste safely and without harm to the environment. The main purpose behind the duty of care is thus clear. It is to encourage anyone who holds waste to deal with it in a responsible fashion, so that a 'cradle to grave' approach is applied to its management and disposal. It is no longer the case that producers and others necessarily lose responsibility for waste when they cease to have possession of it.

What does the duty entail?

Section 34 provides that the duty of care applies to any person who produces, imports, carries, keeps, treats or disposes of controlled waste, or who, as a broker, has control of it. The only exception is that occupiers of domestic premises are not subject to the duty with regard to household waste produced on the property (s. 34(2)). The duty applies only to controlled waste.

The section itself states that any person to whom the duty applies should take reasonable steps to:

(a) prevent any other person contravening s. 33 (i.e., the law relating to the unauthorised deposit, keeping, treatment or disposal of controlled waste);

(b) prevent the escape of waste;

(c) ensure that the waste is transferred only to an authorised person;

(d) ensure that an adequate written description of the waste is given to anyone to whom the waste is transferred.

Each of these four limbs is discussed below.

The bare duty in s. 34 is supplemented by the Environmental Protection (Duty of Care) Regulations 1991 (SI 1991 No. 2839), which lay down some additional documentation requirements. Contravention of these regulations automatically results in the commission of a criminal offence. There is also a *Code of Practice on the Duty of Care,* made by the Secretary of State. This is a statutory code, made under s. 34(7). Contravention of its provisions is not of itself a criminal offence, but it could be said that contravention gives rise to a presumption that the duty has been breached, since s. 34(10) states that it should be taken into account in deciding whether the duty has been complied with and in fixing any penalty. (The Code may also be used as evidence in civil cases and in prosecutions under s. 33.) The combined effect of s. 34, the regulations and the Code of Practice is to lay down a mixture of general and specific requirements.

It is a criminal offence to breach the duty of care. The maximum penalty is, on conviction in the magistrates' court, a £5,000 fine or, on conviction in the Crown Court, an unlimited fine.

The steps required to be taken under s. 34 (see above) comprise the following:

(a) *The prevention of breaches of s. 33* — This part of the duty of care is concerned with ensuring that a holder of waste (i.e., the person who has control of it at any time) takes responsibility for checking that the waste is dealt with properly by others further down the waste disposal chain. For example, it entails that the transferor of waste should know where the waste is going before parting with it, which in turn involves checking that the site where the waste is to be taken is licensed to take it and that the carrier is actually taking it there. The Code of Practice requires that a transferor of waste must be prepared to stop a transfer of waste if not satisfied that it is being dealt with properly. The standard is objective in the sense that holders of waste ought to act on signs that something is amiss. For example, a transferor of waste who suspects that a carrier is not tipping the waste where it says it is (for instance, because of the short periods of time between journeys), or who is quoted an unrealistically low price for the disposal of waste, ought to check what is actually happening. However, the standard is also related to the resources and knowledge of the individual, with the result that large firms may be expected to carry out more rigorous investigations than small ones.

(b) *Prevention of the escape of waste* — This requirement is mainly related to the correct packaging and labelling of waste. For instance, if waste spills from inadequate drums whilst they are on the back of a lorry, the transferor of the drums may well be in breach as well as the lorry driver. Other examples relate to the nature of the packaging; for example, fire resistant packaging should be used for inflammable wastes. This limb also imposes a duty to ensure that waste is properly stored — using an open skip which allows waste to be blown off by the wind may amount to a breach.

(c) *Transfer to an authorised person* — There are various stages to the disposal of waste and who constitutes an authorised person will vary from stage to stage. If waste is entrusted to a carrier, the duty of care clearly establishes that it should only be given to a carrier who is registered under the Control of Pollution (Amendment) Act 1989 (see below), or who is exempted from registration under that Act. Accordingly, the Code of Practice states that a transferor should check the carrier's certificate of registration, or its grounds for exemption. It even states that a photocopy of the registration certificate is not adequate for this purpose, only an original copy issued by the EA.

If waste is being delivered to a waste disposal site or an incinerator, an authorised person is one who holds a waste management or waste disposal licence or is exempt from the need for one.

(d) *Description of the waste* — The purpose behind this requirement is fairly clear. It is to enable everyone who deals with the waste to know what it consists of. In that way, it should not be treated incorrectly through ignorance. The detail required in a description will depend on the nature of the waste. For example, if it is hazardous the exact nature of the hazard should be identified, whereas in many other cases a general description will suffice. Consideration of the purpose of the requirement should enable decisions to be taken on what is an adequate description. For example, omitting to mention that a skip includes a small amount of dangerous chemicals may lead to the contents being deposited at a site that is not equipped to take it, or to an undesirable mixing of incompatible wastes. Alternatively, a false description could have catastrophic results in the event of a road accident if it meant that the emergency services dealt with it inappropriately.

The requirement of an adequate description is supplemented by the 1991 Regulations (SI 1991 No. 2839). These require that when controlled waste is transferred there must be a transfer note, though this does not actually have to travel with the waste. The transfer note must identify the waste and state its quantity, the kind of container it is in, the time and place of transfer, and the name, address and other relevant details of the transferor and transferee. The Regulations also require that the transferor and transferee sign the transfer note and that the transfer note and the written description are kept for at least two years from the date of transfer. The EA has powers to demand production of the transfer note or written description within this period. The written description and the transfer note may be combined in one document as long as each requirement is fully met. A standard form of transfer note is set out in the Code of Practice. Because of the width of the concept of a transfer, these requirements cover a range of circumstances where the recipient may not at first glance seem like a typical 'waste disposal firm' — for example, a landlord of an industrial estate, office block or large shopping centre could require a transfer note if the waste was collected centrally, unless the transfer was construed as being 'within the same premises'.

It is permissible for multiple consignments of waste up to one year to be covered by one transfer note, as long as the description of the waste, the identity of the parties and all other details remain the same for each consignment.

Enforcement of the duty of care

It should be noted that the duty of care is broken irrespective of whether harm is caused. It is the failure to take reasonable steps that is the criminal offence, not any damage that results from it. This creates a position where offences will be committed frequently. The control mechanism is whether any breach comes to the attention of the EA and whether it considers any enforcement action is justified. In this context, the Government has made it quite clear in its Circular advice that the EA is meant to be reactive in their approach to policing the duty of care and are not expected to go out of their way to look for breaches. Instead, they should treat enforcement work as part of their existing duty to supervise the waste management licensing system. Certainly no extra resources have been given to the EA in order to enable it to monitor the duty of care provisions.

It should also be remembered that everyone in the waste chain is subject to the duty of care. The system should therefore have an element of self-policing. For example, a producer of waste would be well advised not to transfer it to someone they suspect of being a 'cowboy', because if the waste is fly-tipped that could lead the EA to prosecute the producer for breach of the duty of care (and also give rise to possible criminal actions for knowingly permitting the deposit, and to potential liability in civil law, or under the clean-up powers). Equally, a waste carrier should not accept improperly labelled or packaged waste, and should make periodic checks on the waste it receives, since it will have responsibility under the duty of care if there is something wrong.

In summary, the preceding discussion suggests that the main function of the duty of care is to encourage responsible behaviour and the development of appropriate management systems for the storage, transfer and monitoring of waste, rather than to punish wrongdoing. Because of the documentation procedures, it also makes waste consignments easier to trace. The first reported prosecutions illustrate these points. For example, in one case a demolition contractor was fined £800 for failing to ensure that a skip contained only materials described in the transfer note — the infringement came about because employees had not been given sufficient instruction that only certain materials could be put in the skip. However, one of the lessons from the early prosecutions appears to be that the courts are treating many of the breaches, such as failing to make out a transfer note, as technical in nature, and thus are imposing only small fines. This seems to underplay the importance of this type of management-based control.

Carriage of waste

Intimately connected with the duty of care is the requirement that all carriers of waste are registered with the EA. The requirements in this respect arise out of the Control of Pollution (Amendment) Act 1989. This was a private member's bill (although it did ultimately have Government support) which sought to deal with the growing problem of fly-tipping by providing some powers over carriers. The Act is supplemented by the Controlled Waste (Registration of Carriers and Seizure of Vehicles) Regulations 1991 (SI 1991 No. 1624). It came into force on 1 April 1992.

It is an offence under the 1989 Act, s. 1(1), to carry controlled waste without being registered with the EA. The offence is a summary one only, with a maximum fine of £5,000. The defences are very similar to those available for offences under the EPA 1990, s. 33 (see p. 402). It should be remembered that it is normally a separate offence under the duty of care to deal with an unregistered carrier.

Local authorities, British Rail, and charities and voluntary groups are specifically exempt from the requirement to register by virtue of reg. 2, which also states that a producer may carry its own wastes without having to seek registration, as long as the waste is not demolition or construction waste. In addition, s. 1(1) refers only to carrying waste in the course of a business or with a view to profit, meaning that such things as carrying waste to a local authority waste site on behalf of a neighbour are not covered.

An application for registration must be made to the regional office of the EA where the carrier has its principal place of business (reg. 4). There is only one substantive ground for refusal of registration, which is that the applicant is not a desirable carrier. This fulfils a similar function to the 'fit and proper person' requirement in the waste management licensing system. It has two elements: (i) that the carrier, or someone closely connected with the carrier's business, has been convicted of one of the relevant offences listed in sch. 1 to the Regulations; and (ii) that the EA considers it undesirable for the carrier to be authorised to carry controlled waste (reg. 5). There is a power to revoke a registration on these grounds (reg. 10). However, the impact of these provisions is limited somewhat by the Rehabilitation of Offenders Act 1974, which effectively will allow most convictions to become spent after five years. In addition, there is a right to appeal to the Secretary of State against refusal or revocation and, in a recent example, in accordance with the advice in Circular 11/91, a refusal to register was overturned even though the applicant had been convicted of seven waste offences in the past (see (1993) 217 ENDS Report 13). Unless revoked, a registration lasts for three years, when it must be renewed, though the carrier may surrender a registration at any time. A fee is payable for an application or a renewal (reg. 4(9)). The EA must keep a public register, to be open for inspection free of charge, of firms that are registered in their area (reg. 3).

Enforcement of the Act is mainly in the hands of the EA. Appointed officers (and also police officers) are given powers to stop and search vehicles, as long as they have reasonable grounds for believing that controlled waste is being carried by an unregistered carrier (s. 5(1)). They may also require the carrier to produce its certificate of registration. It is a summary offence intentionally to obstruct an officer exercising these powers, with a maximum penalty of £5,000. Environment Agency officers also have the powers provided under the EPA 1990, s. 71, and the Environment Act 1995, ss. 108 and 109 (see below).

In addition, there are separate powers relating to the seizure of vehicles used for unlawful activities (s. 6). If the EA is unable to obtain through its general powers information about the ownership of a vehicle it has reason to believe has been involved in unlawful disposal operations, it may apply for a warrant from a magistrate to seize the vehicle. Once the vehicle has been seized, the EA may take specified publicity measures and, if no one claims it, dispose of it (reg. 23). If the EA does discover who owns the vehicle it can bring a prosecution under the 1989 Act and/or under the EPA 1990, ss. 33 and 34, though in those circumstances it has no power to seize the vehicle.

Waste brokers

There is a growing business in arranging for the disposal or movement of other people's wastes. These people may not require a waste management licence because they never actually handle the waste themselves. The Waste Management Licensing Regulations 1994 now control such brokers/dealers in waste. Regulation 20 makes it an offence for any establishment or undertaking to arrange, as a dealer or broker, for the disposal or recovery of Directive waste on behalf of another person unless they are registered with the EA. Exemptions apply to those with a waste management licence, or other statutory consents (e.g., a discharge consent), charitable or voluntary registered waste carriers, and bodies with statutory responsibilities for waste management (e.g., waste collection and disposal authorities).

Schedule 5 to the Regulations sets out the procedure for registration. Perhaps the most important consideration in determining whether an establishment/undertaking shall be registered is the number of 'relevant offences' committed by the applicant or connected persons. Generally the considerations are the same as the test for 'fit and proper persons' in relation to applications for a waste management licence. A fee is payable on application for registration and the entry in the register is available to the general public. The entry in the register lasts for a maximum of three years unless it is renewed.

General powers of the EA

Section 7 of the EPA supplements the general powers available to the EA under ss. 108 — 9 of the Environment Act 1995. These powers can be exercised in relation to any of their functions, not just in relation to waste management licensing. There are wide powers to require information by notice (s. 71). It is a criminal offence to fail to provide, without reasonable excuse, the information required, or knowingly to provide false information. The maximum penalty is a fine of £5,000 on summary conviction, or an unlimited fine and/or two years in prison on conviction on indictment. When serving such a notice, the EA must have admissible evidence upon which they can base an argument as to their reasons for needing the information in order to fulfil their statutory functions. It is not possible to use these powers as a 'fishing expedition' where no other evidence is available, as there must be cogent evidence available which can form the foundation of any further requests (*JB and M Motor Haulage Ltd* v *London Waste Regulation Authority* [1993] Env LR 243).

Environment Agency officers have wide powers which are set out in s. 108 of the Environment Act 1995. These include rights of entry, rights to carry out investigations on premises, and rights to take and remove samples, including the power to take samples which will be used as evidence and taken into account by the Secretary of State on appeal (*Polymeric Treatments Ltd* v *Walsall Metropolitan Borough Council* [1993] Env LR 427). The inspector may also require any person to answer questions and provide information relevant to the investigation.

A further power in s. 109 allows inspectors who are carrying out investigations to seize and render harmless any article or substance (not just waste) which appears to be a cause of imminent danger of serious pollution or serious harm to human health.

Special waste

As stated earlier, there are additional controls over hazardous waste, which is referred to in the British context as 'special waste'. Such waste is primarily controlled under the Special Waste Regulations 1996 (SI 1996 No. 9727) which came into effect on 1 September 1996. Brought in under s. 62 of the Environmental Protection Act 1990, the new Regulations revoke and replace the Control of Pollution (Special Waste) Regulations 1980. The regulations were primarily introduced in order to transpose the Hazardous Waste Directive (91/689/EEC) into British law. Detailed guidance on the Regulations has been produced by the DoE in the form of a Circular (6/96).

The Regulations are intended to meet a number of objectives including:

(a)   the introduction of new criteria for determining whether or not waste is special;

(b)   a requirement to pre-notification of movements to the Environment Agency by consignment note;

(c)   the provision of better descriptions of waste and their associated hazards by means of a revised design for the consignment note;

(d)   the simplification of arrangements for repetitive movements and collection rounds;

(e)   a ban on mixing by carriers and consignees of categories of special wastes, and of special with non-special wastes, unless for safe disposal;

(f)   a requirement to carry out periodic inspections by regulators of special waste producers; and

(g)   the introduction of fees for many consignments of special wastes.

The new Regulations broaden the scope of waste to be treated as special and effectively broaden the scope of control over sites receiving a variety of wastes. Many sites were restricted to receiving waste which was not considered special under the 1980 Regulations and this required amendments to extant licences.

Regulation 2 defines special waste as any controlled waste which:

(a)   is listed with a six-digit code in part I of sch. 2 to the Regulations (the Hazardous Waste List, taken from the Council Decision mentioned above) and displays any of the properties given in part II of sch. 2 (which reproduces Annex III to the Hazardous Waste Directive); or

(b)   does not appear in the list set out in part I of sch. 2, but displays any of a restricted range of those properties specified in part II of the schedule (namely: highly flammable, irritant, harmful, toxic (including very toxic), carcinogenic or corrosive); or

(c)   is a waste prescription-only medicine.

Fourteen hazard criteria are listed in part II of sch. 2 and, with the exception of 'infectious' and 'formation of hazardous products after disposal', they match the classifications contained in the Chemicals (Hazard Information and Packaging for Supply) Regulations 1994.

The Regulations also apply to radioactive waste, which is not controlled waste by virtue of s. 78 of the Environmental Protection Act 1990, that would come within the definition of special waste but for the fact that it is radioactive. Thus, for example, radioactive waste which is also corrosive will still not be controlled waste, but it will be special waste.

Regulation 2 provides for two exceptions: first, household waste is not special waste unless it consists of clinical waste, asbestos or any mineral or synthetic oil or grease; and secondly, controlled waste that would be special waste because it has any of the restricted range of properties specified in part II of sch. 2 (listed in paragraph (b) above) is not special waste if any of the properties are below the threshold given in part III of sch. 2. For example, a waste in which the total concentration of substances classified as toxic is less than 3% will not be classed as special waste.

Although explosives are specifically named in part I of sch. 2, and 'explosive' is one of the hazardous properties in part II of the schedule, explosives are already controlled under the Explosives Act 1875 and are not subject to the Regulations.

Pre-notification procedure

A key feature of the new system remains the requirement, in most cases, to pre-notify the Environment Agency of any consignments of special waste. (While the Regulations simply state that pre-notification should be made to the Agency, the guidance states that, in practice, this will mean the local or area office for the place to which the waste is being consigned.) The exceptions are lead acid motor vehicle batteries, off-specification products being returned to manufacturers or suppliers, consignments within the same group of companies where the waste is being removed for the purpose of storage, and certain landed ships' waste.

The main points of the new system are:

(a)   Parties will now be referred to as the 'consignor' and 'consignee', rather than 'transferor' and 'transferee'.

(b)   The content of the consignment note is prescribed in sch. 1 to the Regulations and, under reg. 23, this obviates the need for a duty of care transfer note as required by s. 34 of the Environmental Protection Act 1990. The Environment Agency produces consignment notes and supplies them on request. However, users are still able to produce their own or purchase them from commercial suppliers.

(c)   Between three days' and one month's notice is required, although fax and email will be acceptable on condition that paper copies are forwarded before the waste is consigned.

(d)   There is no longer any requirement to send a copy of the consignment note to the consignor's local Agency office. Instead, the consignment note is to be sent to the local Agency office for the area to which the waste is being consigned. This offfice will, within two weeks, send a photocopy of the note to the consignor's local Agency office.

(e)   A single pre-notification is allowed for carriers' rounds and repetitive consignments. The latter will be valid for up to 12 months.

(f)   Each consignment note must contain a unique identifying number issued by the Agency. In the case of repetitive consignments, each consignment must contain its own unique number and also refer to the original number issued by the Agency. Consignment notes produced by the Agency are pre-coded; others have to obtain codes direct from the Agency. Bulk purchases of codes are allowed.

(g) Consignment code numbers should be obtained from the local Agency offfice for the place to which the waste is being taken.

(h) A fee of £15 (£10 for loads consisting entirely of lead acid motor vehicle batteries) is payable for each consignment. This fee also applies to each consignment in a series of repetitive transfers.

Record keeping

In addition to maintaining registers of consignment notes, anyone who deposits special waste in or on any land is also required to record the location of each deposit. Such records are to be cross-referenced to the register of consignment notes except in cases where the waste was disposed of via a pipeline or at the premises where the waste was produced, where no consignment notes will have been produced.

The records may consist of either a site plan marked with a grid or a site plan with overlays showing the deposits in relation to the contours of the site. The records must be maintained and kept for the lifetime of the site and forwarded to the Agency when the site's waste management licence is surrendered or revoked.

The Regulations introduce restrictions on mixing different categories of special waste or mixing special with non-special waste. The restrictions apply to collectors and carriers or to those who recover or dispose of special waste. However, they do not apply if the mixing is authorised by a waste management licence or an IPC authorisation granted under Part I of the Environmental Protection Act 1990. Nor do they apply to an activity exempt from waste management licensing.

The Regulations also place a duty on the Agency to inspect producers of special waste periodically. This is a requirement of the Hazardous Waste Directive and is achieved by amending the Waste Management Licensing Regulations 1994, sch. 4, para. 13(1). This paragraph already requires 'appropriate periodic inspections' by the Agency on other waste operations. The periodicity of inspections is not stipulated, but is left to the discretion of the Agency, giving due consideration to advice contained in DoE Circular 11/94 (waste management licensing guidance).

Offences

The Regulations create the offences of failing to comply with the Regulations, knowingly or recklessly making statements which are false or misleading, or intentionally making a false entry in records. The penalties for each offence are a fine of up to £5,000 on summary conviction (i.e., in a magistrates' court) or an unlimited fine and/or up to two years in prison on conviction on indictment (i.e., in the Crown Court).

Civil liability for unlawful disposal of waste

Civil liability is provided for in s. 73(6), which is significantly wider than the equivalent provision in COPA 1974 (COPA 1974, s. 88). This subsection applies where any damage is caused by a deposit of controlled waste in contravention of ss. 33(1) or 63(2) (i.e., the deposit was not in accordance with a waste management licence, or it breached s. 33(1)(c), or it breached the provision on unlawful disposal of non-controlled waste). Any person who deposited the waste is liable to pay damages for any personal injury or property damage that was caused, except where it was due wholly to the fault of the person who suffered it, or they voluntarily accepted the risk of the damage. Liability also attaches to any person who knowingly caused or knowingly permitted such waste to be deposited, with the result that anyone who orders an unlawful deposit, or who stands by in the knowledge that it is happening, will also be liable. Since liability is linked to the commission of an offence under ss. 33 or 63(2), it is strict and fault need not be shown, though the defences available under those sections will also apply.

Section 73(6) provides an alternative to the common law causes of action which are explained in Chapter 8. The leading case on waste sites is the Canadian case of *Gertsen* v *Municipality of Toronto* (1973) 41 DLR (3d) 646, where an occupier of land successfully claimed damages for personal injury. His injuries were the result of an explosion caused by the spark from his car engine when he started it up in his garage, which had filled with high levels of methane escaping from the disused landfill site on which it was built. The action was successful under *Rylands* v *Fletcher*, nuisance and negligence, although it must be doubted whether, on the current state of the law, all these causes of action would have succeeded in an English court. Section 73(6) will avoid some of the difficulties associated with the common law actions where there has been an unlawful deposit.

Future development of civil law

It is probable that the width of civil liability will be extended in the future, since the EC has a draft Directive on civil liability for damage caused by waste and the Council of Europe has a Convention on Civil Liability for Damage Resulting From Activities Dangerous to the Environment. Both these documents, if adopted, would involve strict liability on a wider scale than in current British law. In March 1993, the EC also issued a green paper on civil liability for environmental damage, which proposed the establishment of a strict liability regime in combination with the provision of central funds to pay for a clean-up where no liable party could be found. These developments are in line with the EC's commitment in its Fifth Action Programme to the development of civil law as an instrument of environmental protection. It is possible that the EC will adopt the Council of Europe Convention, which covers activities such as production and handling of dangerous substances and waste treatment and disposal, though the British Government has refused to ratify it.

The draft Directive has gone through a number of drafts, the most recent of which dates from June 1991 (see [1991] OJ C192). However, it may not survive in its current draft form (it has given rise to a great amount of controversy and debate), so its provisions will not be considered in great detail. It applies to all kinds of waste, with only minor exceptions where there is some other form of liability (e.g., as there is for radioactive waste). It seeks to employ the 'polluter pays' principle to minimise the generation of waste by imposing strict civil liability for damage caused by waste on the producer, who will remain liable until the waste is transferred to a licensed disposal facility. The most significant feature of the draft Directive is that the definition of 'damage' is very wide indeed. It covers not only personal injury and damage to property but also purely environmental harm, referred to as 'impairment of the environment'. Liability is envisaged to include the costs incurred by a public agency or the occupier in restoring the environment to the state it was in before the damage occurred. The potential remedies are also seen as very wide and include: the prohibition of activities; damages to compensate for damage caused; restoration of the environment; reimbursement of expenditure incurred in preventing damage; and reimbursement of expenses incurred in correcting any damage. It appears to be intended that amenity and action groups should have a right to bring an action for the costs they have incurred in preventing or remedying environmental harm. Many of these things would involve some extension of British law, especially in relation to standing to bring an action, the availability of remedies, and the extent of damages that are recoverable. As a result, if the Directive is ever adopted, it would entail a number of far-reaching changes in British laws on tort and procedure. However, despite the fears expressed by some commentators, the current draft still does not approximate to the notorious US 'Superfund' system established in the Comprehensive Environmental Response Compensation and Liability Act 1981, where public bodies may force clean-up irrespective of actual harm and may then recover costs on the basis of strict, joint and several and retroactive liability.

In this respect, the main restriction in the draft Directive is that it is not intended to be retroactive. It is specifically provided that the Directive is only to apply to damage arising from an incident giving rise to injury or damage taking place after the Directive comes into effect. But this does not fully clarify the situation, since it is unclear when an incident takes place. If, for example, cylinders containing hazardous material are dumped and then, after some months of decay, begin to leak into a nearby watercourse and continue to leak for a long period, it is arguable whether the incident causing the damage took place when the cylinders were dumped, or when the leakage occurred, or is a continuing incident as long as the leakage continues. In other words, it is not clear how far the draft Directive will apply to latent damage.

FOURTEEN
Water pollution

This chapter is about the protection of the water environment. It will concentrate on the control of pollution of inland and coastal waters and will not seek to cover in any detail the very wide range of environmental and other issues that arise from the activities of the water industry. Some of these issues, such as the provision of a clean water supply, will be covered briefly, since, although they do not directly concern the protection of inland and coastal waters, they have a significant impact on water pollution policy and controls. Others, such as the effects of land drainage on the landscape and on nature conservation, will be relevant to other chapters. Marine pollution, where different controls apply, will not be covered as it is outside the scope of this book. Discharges to sewers, which have as much in common with waste disposal as with water pollution and which have their own, more basic, regulatory system operated by sewerage undertakers, are dealt with in Chapter 15.

Over the years, the law on water pollution has tended to be the most developed of the systems of pollution control. It has also had the greatest degree of coherence, both in terms of the institutional arrangements and in terms of substantive law. Since 1974, control has been exercised through a relatively sophisticated and public regulatory system, which has thereafter been updated on a number of occasions.

The Environment Agency (EA) has general responsibility for water pollution under the Water Resources Act 1991. Previously, control of water pollution rested with the National Rivers Authority (NRA). The regulatory system involves the setting of water quality objectives for inland, coastal, estuarial and ground waters and a requirement that a discharge consent is obtained from the EA for discharges of trade or sewage effluent to these waters. This system is backed up by criminal offences, including one of discharging trade or sewage effluent without a consent and a general offence which applies when pollution is caused by other matter. It is also supported by further regulatory and administrative controls, notably in relation to the prevention of harm, and by some well-developed and frequently used common law principles. There are separate legislative controls over discharges from certain environmentally hazardous processes under the integrated pollution control provisions of the EPA 1990.

Water pollution

Pollutants of water come in many forms, including:

(a) deoxygenating materials, for example, sewage and other organic wastes, such as silage, farm wastes and wastes from a number of heavily polluting industrial processes (e.g., food processing and the production of smokeless fuel, textiles, paper and dairy products);

(b) nutrient enrichment by such things as fertilisers, which may give rise to eutrophication, causing an accelerated growth of plants and algae and leading to a decline in water quality;

(c) solids, which may impede flows, or block out light for growth;

(d) toxic materials: some materials, such as heavy metals, pesticides or nitrate, are toxic to humans, animals, plants, or all three, often depending on the level of the dose received;

(e) materials which cause an impact on amenity, such as car tyres or shopping trolleys, or old boots in canals;

(f) disease-carrying agents, such as bacteria;

(g) heat, which may affect biological conditions and also deoxygenates water.

The effect of any potential pollutant will vary according to the size, temperature, rate of flow and oxygen content of the receiving waters, as well as the local geology and the presence of other pollutants and any resulting synergistic effects. The use made of a stream is also of enormous importance in deciding whether it can be said to be polluted, and this factor has a large impact on the attitude of the regulatory bodies towards the setting of standards and their enforcement. It is not sufficient to look at pollution of surface waters, since 35% of the public water supply is taken from ground waters. As a result the control of water pollution encompasses the control of liquid discharges to land.

The sources of pollution are also varied. For example:

(a) There are over 100,000 discharges where there is consent for discharge to waters. Many of these will involve toxic materials or organic pollutants.

(b) There are over 4,300 sewage works with discharge consents. The organic content of these discharges makes them highly polluting, and they have had a particularly important role in the history of water pollution.

(c) Agricultural pollution is significant: discharges and escapes of farm wastes are of great importance and accounted for 2,883 pollution incidents in 1993, most incidents being related to slurry stores and escapes of silage (see *Water Pollution Incidents in England and Wales — 1993*, NRA, 1994). A new phenomenon of recent years has been discharges of wastes from fish farms. Run-off from pesticides and fertilisers also create major problems.

(d)   Discharges of waste waters from mines are often highly contaminated (and *abandoned* mines are still largely exempt from the regulatory system, although the exemption will be removed from 31 December 1999 by the Environment Act 1995, s. 60).

(e)   Accidents are frequent causes of pollution, particularly from the storage and transport of hazardous chemicals.

(f)   Leachate from waste sites, including disused ones, is also significant.

The River Quality Survey takes place every five years to give an accurate national picture of water pollution. The 1990 Survey (covering the period 1985–1990) showed a slight deterioration in overall river quality, although this may to some extent have been due to changes in survey methods. However, closer analysis reveals that there was a significant deterioration in some areas, matched by an improvement in others. Given that the period in question coincided with a deep industrial recession and the increased utilisation of alternative disposal routes for wastes, this position reflects a serious problem. The main causes of deterioration were discharges from sewage works and agricultural pollution. The latter is reducing the quality of many once clean rural rivers. Other significant polluters were identified as discharges from mines, run-off from waste tips and fish farms. This illustrates that one issue for the future is how to control non-point discharges and that more inventive legal mechanisms than those used in the past are needed.

The next few years will see the introduction of a new classification system known as the 'general quality assessment' which will replace the existing methods used for the River Quality Survey and will provide a uniform mechanism for measuring water quality. Applying the new system, the NRA found that water quality improved by 10% between 1990 and 1992 (see *The Quality of Rivers and Canals in England and Wales (1990 to 1992)*, NRA, 1994). However, the NRA only looked at the chemical quality of waters, whilst the general quality assessment will ultimately have four separate elements, covering chemical, biological, nutrient and aesthetic matters, and will thus give a more rounded view of overall water quality.

The water industry

The water industry has traditionally been thought of as including a wide range of rather different matters: water collection, treatment and supply; the provision of sewers, sewage works and sewage disposal; water pollution control; the regulation of bodies providing water services; fisheries; navigation; flood defence and land drainage; recreational activities; and conservation responsibilities. From this list it is clear that in reality this is a set of industries, connected in the sense that they all relate to the water cycle, but separate in their objectives. Not all of these matters are relevant to the themes of this book; pollution control is only one function of the water industry, but its place in relation to these other activities needs to be understood.

The industry has historically been dominated by water supply and sewage disposal. Up to the Second World War these tasks largely were carried out by municipal authorities. However, activities such as fishing and pollution control increasingly came to be organised on a river basin basis through a number of specialist, river-related institutions, such as catchment boards (for land drainage), fisheries boards and internal drainage boards, although a significant responsibility for pollution control still rested with the local authorities through their public health functions.

These trends led to an attempt to create a more logical system. The River Boards Act 1948 established 32 river boards, organised on a catchment area basis, which took over a number of regulatory functions. In 1963 the Water Resources Act converted these boards into 27 river authorities, which had a range of regulatory functions, including pollution control and responsibility for the new system of licensing abstractions of water. Water supply and sewage disposal remained in general a local authority function, although the number of water supply undertakings was steadily reduced over the years.

The Water Act 1973 established a fully integrated system of river and water management. Ten regional water authorities became responsible for all water related functions within river basin areas. These included the management of water provision, water treatment and water supply, sewerage, sewage works and sewage disposal, land drainage and flood defence, pollution control, inland fisheries, recreational uses of water and ecological and amenity matters. The idea was to set up a completely planned and integrated service as opposed to the fragmented system then in existence (prior to 1973, there were 27 river authorities, 157 water supply undertakings and no less than 1,393 sewage authorities). The only real exception was the retention of 29 private water companies responsible for water supply in defined areas.

However, this system came to be seen as ineffective. For a start, the industry was clearly massively underfunded, with the result that capital and other works were postponed and the quality of service declined. In consequence, the problem of water quality was never really addressed and this contributed to a general decline in standards. A particular cause of these declining standards was the inadequacy of many sewage works operated by the regional water authorities themselves, which came to be seen as acting the part of both poacher and gamekeeper in relation to water pollution. This conflict of interest led to specific changes in the Water Act 1989.

The Water Act 1989 and the Water Resources Act 1991

The Water Act 1989 carried out a fundamental restructuring of the water industry. The main impetus was undoubtedly the Government's policy of privatisation. One stated aim of this was to increase accountability, though exactly whether this means the industry should be accountable to the public, the Government, or to shareholders is unclear. A further aim was to remove the previous cash limits on public spending that had restricted the regional water authorities, thus opening the way for improvements in the quality of water services, but at a cost to the consumer of those services, who will pay for them.

Originally it was intended to privatise the whole industry en bloc, but the inadequacy of the proposed regulatory mechanisms, particularly those for pollution control, led to the privatisation of the operational end of the industry only (i.e., water supply, sewerage services and certain recreational services) in the form of 10 water services companies. These double as water undertakers and sewerage undertakers in areas corresponding with the old regional water authority ones. The 29 water companies were retained as statutory water companies, having responsibility for water supply only.

The position of Director General of Water Services, who is in charge of the Office of Water Services (OFWAT), was created to exercise regulatory functions in relation to water supply and sewerage provision. The NRA was created as a wide-ranging and independent regulatory agency with responsibility for tackling water pollution amongst other things. Unlike the old regional water authorities, it had no operational responsibilities in relation to sewage works to conflict with its environmental protection role. These arrangements were consolidated in the Water Resources Act 1991 and the Water Industry Act 1991. However, from 1 April 1996 the NRA was subsumed within the Environment Agency (see p. 42).

Water pollution controls

The modern system of control really begins with the Rivers (Prevention of Pollution) Act 1951, a rather rudimentary control system in which consent from the river board was required for industrial or sewage discharges into most inland waters. Prior to that, there had been the Rivers Pollution Prevention Act 1876, which imposed an absolute prohibition on pollution but proved almost totally unworkable. The Clean Rivers (Estuaries and Tidal Waters) Act 1960 extended the controls to tidal and estuarial waters and the Rivers (Prevention of Pollution) Act 1961 ensured that a large number of discharges that had hitherto been exempted were controlled, including those commenced prior to 1951. The Water Resources Act 1963 extended the system to discharges to certain underground waters. However, the system remained essentially secret and with little public accountability. Control over sewage effluents was also compromised because of the local authorities' control of the river authorities.

The next major step forward was in the Control of Pollution Act 1974, which again extended the geographical coverage of the controls so that most discharges to inland, underground, tidal or coastal waters out to the 'three-mile limit' were covered. More importantly, COPA 1974 introduced some advanced provisions on public participation in decisions, established public registers of information and allowed for private prosecutions, which had previously been excluded. In addition a more sophisticated set of preventative and remedial measures was introduced.

However COPA 1974 did not come into force immediately. Like much environmental legislation its implementation relied on commencement orders, and the main measures were not brought into force until the mid-1980s: a delay mainly due to the Government's worries over the economic cost of the new controls, particularly in relation to underperforming sewage works operated by the regional water authorities. Even when COPA 1974 was brought into force, the transitional provisions meant that the full impact was not felt immediately, and indeed certain of the provisions never were implemented.

As explained above, the Water Act 1989 created the NRA. It also continued the process of refining and improving the law. The system of consents set out in COPA 1974 remained roughly the same, though with a few amendments. Important changes included the introduction of sections providing for statutory water quality objectives for the first time, the introduction of a system of charging for trade and sewage discharges, and the improvement of the available preventative and remedial powers. Water pollution law was then consolidated in the Water Resources Act 1991.

The EPA 1990 did not alter the main structure of water pollution law, but, under the Act, Her Majesty's Inspectorate of Pollution took the lead role in relation to processes subject to integrated pollution control, thus robbing the NRA of total control over discharges to inland and coastal waters. The bringing together of the NRA and HMIP in the Environment Agency means that the institutional control of water pollution is once more unified.

Throughout this history the emphasis has been on flexible standards, with most consents being set on an individualised basis by reference to the effect of a discharge on the receiving waters. Particular emphasis has been placed on biochemical oxygen demand (BOD) and the level of suspended solids, rather than on such things as metals and toxic substances, especially in relation to sewage discharges. In a sense, the method of setting consents could almost be described as a 'rule of thumb' method. This approach is, however, changing in response to EC Directives and as a result of the NRA's commitment to creating a more uniform system of control nationwide.

Scotland

It should be noted that in Scotland a slightly different system applies, since the water industry has not been privatised there. Previously, regional councils were responsible for the provision of the water supply and for sewerage and sewage disposal. Apart from the three island councils, which were all-purpose authorities, water pollution was the responsibility of the seven river purification boards. These were independent catchment area bodies with their own budgets financed out of precepts on the regional councils, and with one third of their members appointed by each of the following, namely, regional councils, district councils and the Secretary of State. The Water Act 1989 did not make any institutional changes, but in sch. 23 it did amend the Control of Pollution Act 1974, which still remains in force in Scotland. Unfortunately, this has meant that there are slightly different wordings for some sections on each side of the border. Whilst water pollution law is thus very similar in Scotland, it cannot always be guaranteed that it is exactly the same.

This position has been altered recently. The Local Government etc (Scotland) Act 1994 restructured local government in Scotland by introducing unitary authorities for the mainland, although the three existing island councils are retained. It also established three publicly owned combined water and sewerage authorities, respectively called the East of Scotland, West of Scotland and North of Scotland Water Authorities, to take over from the regional councils. The Environment Act 1995 establishes the Scottish Environment Protection Agency (SEPA), which replaces the river purification boards and Her Majesty's Industrial Pollution Inspectorate (HMIPI) and thus brings together all water pollution functions in one body.

Pollution policy

Until 1989, it was difficult to identify a coherent national water pollution policy. The Department of the Environment had overall responsibility for all water matters, but most policy decisions were left to the regional water authorities, with the DoE appearing more preoccupied with financial matters than with water quality. The one national body in this area, the National Water Council, was abolished in 1983 as superfluous. Of course, there were often unspoken aims, such as that of getting treatable wastes into the sewerage system if possible, and cleaning up waters for economic reasons, since the public water supply was increasingly taken from them. In addition, EC standards effectively laid down a set of priorities, leading to such things as a policy to minimise the discharge of dangerous substances and if possible to cut them out entirely — effectively a 'precautionary' policy.

The establishment of the NRA meant that the opportunity could be taken to establish a truly national policy on water pollution — or at least one applicable to England and Wales. At a general level, this was achieved through the NRA's Corporate Plans, which set out a number of aims on water pollution, such as the assessment of the present quality of waters, the establishment of classification systems so that comparisons can be made, the review of existing policy in relation to the granting of consents and compliance with them, increased attention to prevention of harm in such areas as farm pollution and pollution from abandoned mines, and a more rigorous enforcement policy involving greater use of prosecution. The NRA also had a range of policies and strategy documents on other aspects of the water cycle, including aquifer protection, conservation issues, recreational opportunities and water resources. The general approach adopted by the NRA (and continued by the EA) was that river catchments should be managed on a integrated basis. This process is a good example of aspects of environmental policy being set by a body other than Central Government. However, the Government also has an important role to play here. *River Quality: The Government's Proposals* (DoE, 1992), sets out the general strategy for water quality. This makes it quite clear that the cost-effectiveness of environmental improvements — and the question of who should pay for them — has been a major factor in Government policy, hence the slow progress that is being made on such things as statutory water quality objectives.

More specifically, the NRA has been involved in trying to establish uniformity and consistency on such things as sampling, setting of consents and public participation, where in the past there have tended to be different attitudes in different regions. In the Kinnersley Report (*Discharge Consent and*

Compliance Policy: A Blueprint for the Future, NRA, July 1990), the NRA suggested some mechanisms for unifying the totally different procedures and levels of consents that it inherited from the 10 regional water authorities. It established a national strategy for reviewing all existing consents on a catchment area basis, and this included bringing sewage works consents into line with industrial consents. However, it remains the case that consents are mainly set on an individualised basis, with the main determinant being the effect on the receiving waters.

The EC and water pollution

The EC has had an enormous impact on water pollution law and policy over the years. The First Action Programme on the Environment in 1973 picked out water pollution as a priority matter, and there has been a steady stream of Directives since. These have tackled such diverse topics as the reduction of pollution from dangerous substances, the improvement of the quality of bathing waters, nitrates in water and the progressive introduction of adequate sewage treatment systems. However, it remains the case that EC law only covers water pollution in a selective manner — not all pollutants in all waters are yet covered. The proposed framework Directive on Water Policy may address this deficiency.

EC water Directives tend to follow two basic models (see Somsen, 'EC Water Directives' [1990] Water Law 93):

(a) those which adopt emission standards, which are mainly used for reducing dangerous substances; and

(b) those which impose quality objectives on waters that are mainly set according to the use that is to be made of those waters.

For a full discussion of all the EC Directives relating to water and their implementation, see Haigh, *Manual of Environmental Policy: the EC and Britain,* Longman.

Emission standard approaches

One of the first water Directives, and arguably the most important, is 76/464 on Dangerous Substances in Water. This is a framework Directive passed with the aim of reducing or eliminating certain dangerous substances from water. It covers essentially the same waters as those controlled by the EA and has led to very tight controls over dangerous substances in discharge consents.

The Directive lays down two lists of substances:

(a) List I (the 'black list'); and
(b) List II (the 'grey list').

In relation to black list substances, the Directive seeks the elimination of pollution. Any discharge of a black list substance must be subject to some form of authorisation granted by a competent national authority. Such an authorisation must conform to very strict requirements. It must *either* set an emission standard which does not exceed the appropriate EC limit value, or the emission standard must be set so that the EC environmental quality standard for the receiving waters is kept to at all times. Only Britain has adopted the second approach (see below), the competent authority being the EA, which operates the discharge consent systems so as to ensure that the EC environmental quality standards are met at all times.

However, implementation of this part of the Directive is proceeding slowly. The Directive itself identifies potential black list substances in general terms only — they are those which are highly toxic, persistent, carcinogenic or liable to bio-accumulate. Although in 1982 the EC Commission published a specific list of 129 potential black list substances (made up mainly of pesticides, organic solvents, and a small number of heavy metals), implementation of the Directive ultimately depends on the agreement of subsidiary 'daughter Directives' which set the EC standards for individual substances. Only a few such daughter Directives have been agreed, covering the following substances: cadmium (Directive 83/513); mercury (82/176 and 84/156); hexachlorocyclohexane (84/491); carbon tetrachloride, pentachlorophenol and DDT (86/280); chloroform, hexachlorobenzene, hexachlorobutadiene and the pesticides aldrin, dieldrin, endrin and isodrin (88/347); and 1, 2-dichloroethane, trichloroethylene, tetrachloroethylene and trichlorobenzene (90/415). Where a daughter Directive has not been agreed for a potential black list substance, the substance is treated as on the grey list (see below). The list of 129 (amended slightly in the intervening years) therefore acts as a priority list for future daughter Directives.

For grey list substances, the Directive again lays down a fairly general list. This includes a range of metals (such as zinc, copper, tin, nickel and chromium), biocides, cyanides, fluorides, ammonia and nitrites. The objective is that pollution by these substances should be reduced. Accordingly, if any such substance has a deleterious effect on the aquatic environment, the Directive requires Member States to develop a national environmental quality standard and to ensure that it is met in the receiving waters. These standards are set at a national, rather than at an EC, level. The Member State must also introduce a reduction programme for grey list substances and must control discharges by setting standards in discharge consents which enable the environmental quality standards to be achieved. Britain has either set or has proposed environmental quality standards for all substances on the 'red list' (see p. 487) and for a majority of other substances on the grey list (see *Dangerous Substances in Water: A Practical Guide,* Environmental Data Services Ltd, 1992).

It was Directive 76/464 which first demonstrated the differences between Britain and the rest of the EC over standard setting. Britain's system of a decentralised setting of non-uniform consents by reference to the quality of the receiving waters was seen to be directly contradictory to the EC desire for uniform, centrally set emission standards for dangerous substances. After much argument, this led to the agreement of the alternative approaches for 'black list' substances in the Directive explained above. The same conflict has also led to delays in the process of agreeing daughter Directives, since unanimity is required on the setting of the limit values and environmental quality objectives.

Directive 76/464 has had an enormous impact on British pollution control. Having claimed that it set its consents by reference to quality objectives for the receiving waters, the British Government was forced to introduce such a system on a formal basis, and water quality objectives were introduced for the first time in the late 1970s, at first by administrative action. This was insufficient for compliance with EC law and sections relating to *statutory* water quality objectives were first introduced in the Water Act 1989.

The Directive also led to specific changes in relation to controls over dangerous substances. For example, whilst many existing discharges were given deemed consent when COPA 1974 was finally brought into force, those involving dangerous substances were subject to specified emission standards. In general, significant discharges of 'black list' and 'grey list' substances are subject to integrated pollution control. The rules providing for control by the EA of prescribed substances discharged to sewers are also a result of this Directive.

A similar story attaches to Directive 80/68 on Groundwater, except in this case List I substances are to be prevented from entering ground waters, whilst discharges of List II substances should be limited, in both cases by a consent system. The EC Council has issued a Resolution calling upon the Commission to prepare an action programme for groundwater protection and to draft proposals for a revision of Directive 80/68 (see OJ 1995 C49/1). This will be covered in the proposed new framework Directive (see p. 445).

One problem with the emission standards approach is that it does not work well for pollution from non-point (i.e., diffuse) sources, nor where there are multiple polluters in one catchment area. Directive 86/280 attempts to tackle this issue by requiring all *sources* of 'black list' substances to be monitored.

Quality objective approaches

For the quality approach there are a number of stages:

    (a)   water with particular uses must first be identified (this is usually left to the discretion of the Member States);

    (b)   the EC must establish a number of parameters: these are normally expressed either as Imperative (I) Values, which must be kept to, or Guide (G) Values, which Member States must try to achieve;

    (c)   environmental quality objectives must be set for the waters, having regard to the parameters;

    (d)   a competent national authority must be established for monitoring purposes and uniform sampling techniques are set by EC Directives (e.g., 79/869 on Sampling Surface Water for Drinking);

    (e)   procedures are established for updating the I and G Values in the light of new knowledge.

Directives which have adopted this approach include those on Surface Water for Drinking 75/440, Shellfish Waters 79/923, Water Standards for Freshwater Fish 78/659, Bathing Waters 76/160 and Drinking Water 80/778.

The Directive on Surface Water for Drinking lays down three classes of waters (A1, A2 and A3), and 46 relevant parameters that waters must comply with to fall within any class (see **Water supply** below).

The two Directives on Freshwater Fish and Shellfish lay down standards for waters designated by Member States. The power to designate these waters was delegated to the regional water authorities (now the EA) — another example of a decentralised implementation of policy. But, there is no duty to designate and the main effect of these Directives has been to increase sampling and monitoring of relevant waters.

The Directive on Bathing Waters lays down 19 parameters (mainly bacteriological) with which all 'traditional' bathing waters must comply, within specified percentile compliance rates. It covers fresh and marine waters. The Directive is very vague as to precisely which waters are covered, but unlike the previous two Directives there appears to be no need for any designation for the Directive to apply. The British response was unenthusiastic: identification of the relevant waters was left to the regional water authorities and only 27 were initially identified — fewer than, for example, land-locked Luxembourg (in addition, no inland bathing waters have ever been identified — a bemusing omission). No doubt the reason was the fear of the cost of cleaning up discharges of sewage effluent to the sea. In consequence of a reasoned opinion on non-implementation from the EC Commission, and intense EC and public pressure, the number of designated beaches is now over 400. Nevertheless, Britain was taken to the European Court of Justice over non-implementation of the Directive and in July 1993 was found to be in breach in relation to standards on Blackpool and Southport beaches (see *Commission* v *United Kingdom* (case C-56/90) [1993] ECR I-4109). In 1994 82.5% of designated beaches complied with the standards. The domestic courts have also had occasion to doubt the effectiveness of the implementation of the Directive. In *R* v *National Rivers Authority, ex parte Moreton* [1996] Env LR 234 Harrison J observed that the Government had apparently failed to implement the mandatory standard on entero-viruses from the Directive (although the Government had argued that there was no scientific basis for maintaining the mandatory level).

The Directive on Drinking Water is probably the best known of the water quality Directives. It lays down 62 parameters relating to the quality of all water provided for human consumption or for the purposes of food manufacturing, except for natural mineral waters (as to which, see Directive 80/777). It led directly to the setting in Britain of the first statutory standards of wholesomeness for drinking water, in the Water Supply (Water Quality) Regulations 1989 (SI 1989 No. 1147).

Apart from the delay in complying with the Directive until well after the formal date set for compliance, argument has centred over the provisions for derogating from the Directive, because of problems in some areas in complying with the standards on lead, nitrate and certain pesticides. For example, the Government sought to grant derogations for nitrate levels by reference to Article 9 of the Directive, which refers to geological conditions. This was argued by the Commission to be an inaccurate interpretation of Article 9, since nitrate levels result from self-induced effects on the soil. The British Government has now been held by the European Court of Justice to be in breach of the Directive in relation to nitrate levels in a number of supply areas (see *Commission* v *United Kingdom* (case C-337/89) [1992] ECR I-6103). This case also decided that the duty to comply with the standards laid down in the Directive is absolute, rather than simply to take all practicable steps to comply. However, in *R* v *Secretary of State for the Environment, ex parte Friends of the Earth* [1995] Env LR 11, the question arose whether the Secretary of State was in breach of EC law by accepting undertakings from a number of water companies in relation to admitted breaches of the pesticide standards set out in the Directive. The Court of Appeal decided that there was no breach, because the Secretary of State had taken sufficiently speedy action to remedy the breach.

The Directive on Nitrates 91/676 also adopts a form of quality approach. It requires Member States to designate 'nitrate vulnerable zones' by December 1993. These are defined in the Directive as being where inland waters intended for drinking or groundwaters are likely to contain more than 50mg/1 nitrate if protective action is not taken; or where any inland or coastal waters are liable to suffer from eutrophication if protective action is not taken. Within these designated 'nitrate vulnerable zones', detailed regulatory requirements are laid down in the Directive. For more detail on the Directive and its implementation in Britain, see p. 475.

Other Directives on water pollution

The Directive on Urban Waste Water Treatment 91/271 is potentially the most significant Directive for the future direction of water pollution policy. It lays down minimum standards for the treatment of urban waste waters (i.e., domestic sewage and industrial waste waters). These treatment standards, and the time-scales within which they must be met, vary according to the population of the urban area concerned, but the basic idea is that secondary treatment should be usual for domestic wastes. For example, a secondary or equivalent system of sewage treatment is required by the end of 2000 for a town with a population equivalent of more than 15,000. Stricter standards are required in sensitive areas and lower standards are permitted in certain less-sensitive areas.

Accordingly, the Directive will have an impact on treatment standards (and therefore costs) for most wastes discharged to sewers. It will have a special impact on those areas of Europe where sewage treatment systems are in their infancy and on those countries, such as Britain, which have followed a 'dilute and disperse' policy of discharging virtually untreated sewage into the sea. For example, it has been estimated that only about 2% of British sewage outfalls into the sea receive secondary treatment. The Directive also requires all Member States to cease dumping sewage sludge in the sea by the end of 1998, as agreed at the Conference for the Protection of the North Sea in

March 1990, with an obligation progressively to reduce toxic, persistent or bioaccumulable materials in sludge before then. Britain is the only country currently carrying out this practice.

Directive 91/271 has given rise to the Urban Waste Water Treatment (England and Wales) Regulations 1994 (SI 1994 No. 2841). Although belated in terms of formal implementation of the Directive, these Regulations largely adopt the wording of the Directive, except that instead of 'less-sensitive areas' the Regulations refer to 'high natural dispersion areas'. In addition, there is currently controversy over the classification of a number of estuarial waters as coastal for the purposes of the Regulations, thus allowing lower levels of treatment to be applied. In 1994, the Government announced the identification of 33 sensitive areas and 58 high natural dispersion areas, although more may be classified in the future. In addition there was some controversy over the classification of a number of estuarial waters as coastal for the purposes of the Regulations, thus allowing lower levels of treatment to be applied. In *R* v *Secretary of State for the Environment, ex parte Kingston upon Hull City Council* [1996] Env LR 248 the Secretary of State drew the boundaries of the estuary for the Humber and Severn rivers at the Humber and Severn road bridges thus ensuring lower (and therefore cheaper) levels of treatment for treatment works alongside the rivers. The councils for the areas challenged these decisions on the basis that the Secretary of State had unlawfully taken into account the costs of upgrading the treatment works when drawing the boundaries of the estuary. The court held that the Secretary of State was wrong to take cost into account and that the correct way of drawing the boundary was to carry out a genuine and rational assessment of what actually constituted the estuary. Subsequently, the estuaries were redefined as a line between the two furthest points of land on each side of the river mouth.

Finally, there are two other Directives worth a mention in the light of their different approaches to control. Directive 73/404 on Detergents sets a product standard by prohibiting the marketing of detergents with average biodegradability of less than 90%. Directive 78/176 on Titanium Dioxide sets standards in relation to a specific industry.

Summary of the impact of EC law

The EC has thus had a great impact on British water pollution practice. Whilst there have been many arguments about technical matters, such as the levels laid down for nitrate in drinking water and the need for a Bathing Waters Directive at all, most of the standards required have been introduced in one way or another, although normally belatedly. A formal system of water quality classifications and objectives, statutory regulations on drinking water quality, the introduction of specific standards for dangerous substances, and a dramatic shift in relation to the discharge of sewage effluent to the sea can all be attributed to EC initiatives. The general approach to pollution control has also been altered significantly.

Perhaps the greatest impact, however, has been the great publicity that has been engendered by having specific standards set at EC level against which

Government action can be measured. This has certainly contributed to the intensity of the debate over nitrate. EC requirements also had an impact on the proposals for the privatisation of the water industry. It became clear that the EC would not accept a private pollution regulator as a 'competent authority' for the purposes of Directives, and this was one reason for the creation of the NRA (and also a separate Drinking Water Inspectorate).

The future of EC water pollution policy

EC water pollution policy is on the brink of fundamental change. In February 1997, the European Commission issued its long-awaited proposal for a Water Framework Directive. The Commission's proposal lays the last major building block in a comprehensive overhaul of the EC's water policy. There is a general recognition that the bulk of the Community's water legislation (which dates back to the 1970s and early 1980s) is a little outdated in the approach to pollution control.

The proposal would result in the abandonment of the proposal for a Directive on the Ecological Quality of Water (Com (93) 680 final) and the repeal of the Groundwater Directive (80/68/EEC), the Surface Water Directive (75/440/EEC), the Fish Water Directive (78/659/EEC) and the Shellfish Water Directive (79/923/EEC). These changes must also be seen alongside the prospect of repeal of the Dangerous Substances Directive (76/464/EEC) following the full implementation of the Integrated Pollution Prevention and Control Directive (96/61/EC) and a proposed Directive covering non-IPPC industries.

Unlike previous water legislation, the framework Directive would cover surface water and groundwater together, as well as estuaries and coastal waters. Its purpose is threefold: to prevent further deterioration in, and to protect and enhance, the status of aquatic ecosystems; to promote sustainable water consumption based on the long-term protection of available water resources; and to contribute to the provision of a supply of water in the qualities and quantities needed for its sustainable use.

It is intended to meet these objectives by using the following mechanisms:

(a)   creating an overall framework within which Community, national and regional authorities can develop integrated and coherent water policies;

(b)   providing a 'safety net' for identifying water issues that are not adequately addressed at present, requiring remedial action to be taken at the appropriate level;

(c)   establishing a sound basis for collecting and analysing a large amount of information on the state of the aquatic environment and the pressures upon it; and

(d)   requiring transparency through the publication and dissemination of information and through public consultation.

The Directive's overriding requirement is that Member States ensure that 'good' status is achieved in all waters by the end of 2010. The intention is to achieve this by river basin management, monitoring and planning. For groundwater, good status is measured in terms of both quantity and chemical purity (i.e., abstractions and alterations to the natural rate of recharge are sustainable in the long term without leading to loss of ecological quality); for surface waters ecological quality is an additional criterion (i.e., in addition to ensuring that concentrations of certain, 'black list', substances do not exceed relevant environmental quality standards and other Community legislation setting such standards, 'good ecological status' means that a body of water which is demonstrated to be significantly influenced by human activity, nevertheless has a rich, balanced and sustainable ecosystem). Although the definition of good status is rudimentary, in many cases it will require Member States to improve on the present situation.

One of the framework Directive's innovations is that rivers and lakes will need to be managed by river basin — the natural geographical unit — instead of according to administrative or political boundaries. With each river basin the Directive will make provision for the preparation of a strategic plan, 'a 'river basin management plan', which will need to be updated every six years. This plan will have to include an analysis of the river basin's characteristics, a review of the impact of human activity on the status of waters in the basin, and an economic analysis of water use in the district. The purpose of the plan will be to establish a programme of measures to ensure that all waters in the river basin achieve the objective of good water status.

The Directive avoids some of the problems of adopting a singular approach to environmental standards. Indeed it recognises the strengths of arguments in favour of both approaches which were put forward at the time of the 1976 Directive (see p. 439). It takes a 'combined approach' requiring Member States to set down in their programmes of measures both limit values to control emissions from individual point sources and environmental quality standards to limit the cumulative impact of such emissions.

The emission limit values will be set in line with the IPPC Directive — on the basis of best available techniques — for installations covered by that Directive. The standards laid down by the daughter Directives under the 1976 framework Directive will be incorporated into the new Directive. Member States will be required to set environmental quality standards for each significant body of water that is used for the abstraction of drinking water or that may be in future. The quality standards must be designed to ensure that, under the expected water treatment regime, the abstracted water will meet the requirements of the drinking water Directive.

The framework Directive is the first piece of Community water legislation to address the issue of water quantity. It stipulates that the programme of measures established for each river basin district must aim to ensure a balance between the abstraction and recharge of groundwater. Moreover, the Directive would introduce a requirement to obtain authorisation for all abstraction of surface water, except in areas where it can be demonstrated that this will have no significant impact on the status of the water.

With water resources becoming more scarce the Directive finally attempts to internalise the environmental costs of water use by the introduction of 'full cost recovery' pricing. By 2010 Member States will be required to ensure that the price charged to water users reflects the true cost of supply. Moreover, where methodologies have been established (on the basis of a Commission proposal that will come later), the full cost will also have to include the costs of water use in terms of the damage to the environment it can cause and the depletion of water resources for future generations. The impact of this proposal would be significant, especially for agricultural users and industry which do not presently pay for the environmental costs of water supply.

There is no doubting that the proposals would require a fundamental change in existing law — both European and domestic. There are, however, many potential objections which will be raised prior to the adoption of the proposals. The subsidiarity doctrine will be put forward to weaken any impact of centralised control, as much of the detail of the legislation is to be left to Member States. Secondly there is, at present, little detail on how some of the key concepts behind the proposals will actually work in practice. In particular, the idea of 'full cost recovery pricing' begs a number of questions about the methodology of calculating the cost of 'environmental harm'. The proposals suggest that it will be left to individual Member States to implement the full cost recovery obligation. If some form of pricing can be agreed which is generally applicable, it may provide a firm basis for valuing the environment as a commodity in other areas. The cost of implementing the proposals is likely to give rise to the most fundamental political objections from Member States. The administrative and regulatory changes which would be required by the proposals would be bound to increase costs dramatically. At present, these extra costs have not been estimated.

Water supply

Strictly speaking, the provision of a clean water supply is a consumer protection rather than an environmental protection measure. However, there is an intimate relationship between water supply and pollution control. The public water supply is abstracted from inland and ground waters, so pollution of those waters will lead to a reduction in the available source and to an increase in the cost of treatment of the water that is abstracted. To this end, it is an offence to pollute any 'waterworks' likely to be used for human consumption, which covers pollution of springs, wells, boreholes and service reservoirs (Water Industry Act 1991, s. 72). In addition, Directive 75/440 on Surface Water for Drinking has imposed controls on the quality of inland waters. This Directive seeks to ensure that surface waters which are abstracted for drinking are fit for that purpose and divides waters into three categories — A1, A2 and A3. Classification in these categories depends on the waters meeting the limits set out in the Directive. Any water of below A3 quality should not be abstracted for drinking except in exceptional circumstances. These requirements are implemented in British law by the Surface Waters (Classification) Regulations 1989 (SI 1989 No. 1148), which set out categories DW1, DW2 and DW3 corresponding to those in the Directive, and by the Water Supply (Water Quality) Regulations 1989 (SI 1989 No. 1147).

There is also a more indirect link which is tied up with the highly charged political question of who should pay for the cost of environmental protection, and which requires some understanding of how the water industry as a whole is regulated and paid for. As pointed out earlier in the chapter, the water industry was massively underfunded when it was in public control prior to 1989, with the result that sewage works were major sources of pollution, and the quality of the public water supply was questionable. Since 1989, the public water supply and sewerage services have been provided by the privatised water undertakers under the regulatory oversight of the Director General of Water Services (OFWAT) and the Secretary of State. Water bills have risen considerably above inflation and, compared with the position prior to 1989, the way in which consumers pay for water and sewerage services is more explicit, since the full amount is paid in charges rather than a proportion being hidden in general taxation. However, the water companies' overall charges for water and sewerage services are regulated by the Director General under the Water Industry Act 1991. This is achieved by reference to a formula, known as RPI + K, under which the weighted average charge is allowed to increase by the retail price index plus a company-specific factor set by the Director General (known as the K factor). The Director General has to take water companies' costs, including the cost of 'environmental' improvements such as upgrading of sewage works and improvements in drinking water quality, into account when setting the K factor. Once the K factor is set, the water companies have to operate within it. This means that the trade-offs between environmental improvements by the water companies (for example, improved performance from sewage works, improved water quality from the public water supply and reduced losses from leakage), improvements in levels of service, efficiency savings and increased company profits and directors' pay, are very clear.

The K factors, which were originally set by the Secretary of State in 1989, were redetermined by the Director General in July 1994. In the run-up to that redetermination, there was a very public debate about the cost of environmental improvements. This debate focussed in particular on the cost of complying with EC Directives such as Directive 91/271 on Urban Waste Water Treatment, which requires the upgrading of a large number of sewage works, although the whole issue was complicated by wildly differing views on the actual costs involved. Some, including the Director General to some extent, argued that the economic cost of the environmental standards set out in the Directives was too high a price for consumers to pay, whilst others argued that basic environmental standards must be paid for, and that water companies rather than consumers should pay by making efficiency savings and reducing excessive profits and directors' pay (for a more detailed analysis, see Wilkinson, 'The re-determination of the K factors' [1994] *Water Law* 153). The next round of price determinations is scheduled to take place in 1999 with environmental costs once again playing an important part.

There is a separate issue concerning overall usage of water, which is rising rapidly, and the question whether current patterns of water use are sustainable in the long term. At present, domestic consumers pay mainly for water under a formula that relates to the rateable value of their houses. This method is likely to remain despite the fact that rateable values are redundant for all other purposes, since the Government is opposed to the use of council tax bands for fixing water bills. However, many (including the Director General) argue that such a method provides no incentive to consumers to reduce or control their water usage and that water metering would have the twin benefits of reducing overall usage and of producing a fair system of payment linked to actual usage. Other commentators, however, argue that metering would unfairly penalise those on low incomes in relation to usage of a basic human resource and would lead to social problems. The Environment Act 1995 places a new duty on water companies to promote the efficient use of water by their customers.

As far as the quality of the public water supply is concerned, under the Water Industry Act 1991, s. 67, domestic water must be 'wholesome', a term which was defined in legislation for the first time in the Water Supply (Water Quality) Regulations 1989 (SI 1989 No. 1147). These Regulations lay down a large number of specific criteria with which water must comply if it is supplied for domestic purposes or for the purposes of food production. In each case the limits have been set so as to conform with Directive 80/778 on Drinking Water. The Regulations require that information on water quality must be made available to the public. In addition, it is an offence under the Water Industry Act 1991, s. 70 to supply water that is unfit for human consumption, although prosecutions for this offence may only be brought by the Secretary of State or the Director of Public Prosecutions. A Drinking Water Inspectorate has been established within the Department of the Environment with responsibility for monitoring the provisions relating to water quality. There have now been successful prosecutions of Severn Trent Water (in this case for the s. 70 offence, see (1995) 243 ENDS Report 45) and of Dwr Cymru (Welsh Water) (in this case for contravention of the Regulations, see [1995] Water Law 61). There is also the possibility of an action at common law for breach of statutory duty or negligence (see *Read* v *Croydon Corporation* [1938] 4 All ER 631, where a ratepayer successfully sued in negligence for water supplied to his household which caused his daughter to contract typhoid).

Consents for the discharge of trade or sewage effluents

A consent is required from the EA for:

(a)   any discharge of trade or sewage effluent into 'controlled waters';

(b)   any discharge of trade or sewage effluent through a pipe from land into the sea outside the limits of 'controlled waters';

(c)   any discharge where a prohibition is in force.

It is an offence under the Water Resources Act 1991, s. 85 to 'cause or knowingly permit' such a discharge, although there is a defence if it is carried out in accordance with a consent. This means it is also an offence to breach any conditions attached to a consent, a point made explicit by s. 85(6). There is no need to show that the discharge has polluted the receiving waters because the offence consists of discharging otherwise than in accordance with the consent.

'Trade effluent' is defined in s. 221 and includes any effluent from trade premises (these include agricultural, fish farming and research establishments), other than domestic sewage or surface water. 'Sewage effluent', also defined in s. 221, includes any effluent, other than surface water, from a sewerage works. The discharge must be of effluent, so it seems that if trade materials, such as fuel oil, escape they are covered by the general pollution offence (see below). But there is some doubt here since effluent is defined in s. 221 to mean 'any liquid' and is not specifically limited to wastes.

A further problem relates to the interpretation of the word 'discharge'. This word is not defined in the Act. It is capable of carrying either an active meaning (i.e., that the release of materials has to be part of a deliberate trade or sewage process) or a passive meaning (as in the discharge of blood from a wound). It is suggested that it carries an active meaning, because otherwise potential dischargers would be in the impossible position of having to apply for a consent for something that was not meant to happen. The effect of this reasoning is that accidental and non-routine emissions of trade or sewage effluent do not require a consent and are covered by the general water pollution offence (see below).

The prohibition is a new device first introduced by the Water Act 1989. It is designed to cover those cases where the type of discharge is not necessarily harmful and thus the blanket requirement of a consent is not justified. By prohibiting discharges on a selective basis, control can be exercised over just those situations where it is required.

There are three situations where a prohibition may apply:

(a)   Where the EA by notice prohibits a discharge of trade or sewage effluent from a building or fixed plant to any land or land-locked waters outside the definition of controlled waters. This includes such situations as soakaways from trade premises and some agricultural activities.

(b)   Where it prohibits a discharge of matter other than trade or sewage effluent from a drain or sewer. Trade and sewage effluent are automatically covered by the need for a consent, so the intention here is to restrict such things as discharges of dangerous substances from a storm drain.

(c)   In addition, any such discharges involving substances prescribed by regulations *automatically* invoke the prohibition.

In relation to the first two categories, the prohibition can only come into force three months after notice to the discharger, unless the EA is satisfied that there is an emergency.

Controlled waters

The meaning of 'controlled waters' is given in s. 104. There has been a change in the meaning of this phrase since its usage in COPA 1974 and it now includes virtually all inland and coastal waters. Controlled waters are made up of four sub-categories:

(a)   relevant territorial waters (i.e., the sea within a line three miles out from the baselines from which the territorial sea is measured, despite the extension of the territorial limit to 12 miles in the Territorial Sea Act 1987);

(b)   coastal waters (i.e., the sea within those baselines up to the line of the highest tide, and tidal waters up to the fresh water limit as defined by the Secretary of State on maps produced for that purpose);

(c)   inland waters (i.e., rivers, streams, underground streams, canals, lakes and reservoirs, including those that are temporarily dry); and

(d)   groundwaters (i.e., any waters contained in underground strata or in wells or boreholes).

In addition, the courts have held that a river bed can form part of 'controlled waters' (see *National Rivers Authority* v *Biffa Waste* [1996] Env LR 227).

The only waters that are excluded are land-locked waters that do not drain into other controlled waters. However, the Secretary of State has power to include or exclude specific waters by order. This has been done in the Controlled Waters (Lakes and Ponds) Order 1989 (SI 1989 No. 1149), which includes any reservoirs, apart from those intended for public water supply, which would otherwise be excluded. Water supply mains and pipes, and sewers and drains (where separate controls on discharges apply), are also excluded from the definition of controlled waters.

General pollution offence

There is a general offence under s. 85(1)(a) of causing or knowingly permitting any poisonous, noxious or polluting matter or any solid waste to enter controlled waters. As is common within the flexible definitions of British pollution control, the words 'poisonous, noxious or polluting' are not defined. However, the wording is very wide and in *R* v *Dovermoss Ltd* [1995] Env LR 258, the Court of Appeal decided that 'polluting' requires simply that a likelihood or *capability* of causing harm to animals, plants or those who use the water could be demonstrated. Actual harm is not necessary.

This general offence complements the more specific offence of discharging trade or sewage effluent without consent. Obviously it covers any entry of polluting matter which is not trade or sewage effluent. But, unlike COPA 1974, where the general and the specific offences were made exclusive of each other by s. 31(2)(e), under later Acts this exclusivity has been removed, so an illegal discharge of trade or sewage effluent also amounts to an offence under the general offence if it causes pollution. Indeed, because of the evidential problems of providing a legal sample to prove a breach of a discharge consent, it has been normal for the general offence to be charged even for discharges of trade or sewage effluent.

The general offence also covers accidental and non-routine escapes of trade or sewage effluent because, whilst the specific offence requires a 'discharge', the general offence only requires an entry. In addition, non-point discharges, such as agricultural run-off, are potentially covered by the general offence.

There is a further offence in s. 85(5) of substantially aggravating pollution by impeding the proper flow of inland, non-tidal waters.

Penalties

For all s. 85 offences the potential penalties are the same. On summary conviction there is a maximum fine of £20,000 (this was raised by the EPA 1990, s. 145(1) from the previous maximum of £2,000), and/or three months in prison. On conviction on indictment, there can be an unlimited fine and/ or a two-year jail sentence. The normal six-month period for a summary prosecution to be brought is extended to 12 months by the Water Resources Act 1991, s. 101, as it is for all offences in Part III of the Act.

Defences

A number of defences to these water pollution offences is set out in s. 88. A discharge or entry made in accordance with the following is a defence:

(a) a consent from the EA, or the equivalent consent granted or deemed to have been granted under COPA 1974 or earlier legislation;

(b) an authorisation in relation to integrated pollution control granted under Part I of the EPA 1990;

(c) a waste management licence or a waste disposal licence (except where the offence is of discharging trade or sewage effluent or where a prohibition is in force);

(d) a licence permitting dumping at sea granted by the Ministry of Agriculture, Fisheries and Food under the Food and Environment Protection Act 1985;

(e) an Act of Parliament;

(f) any statutory order (such as a drought order).

Section 89 provides a further defence if the entry or discharge was made in an emergency in order to avoid danger to life or health: in such a case the discharger must inform the EA as soon as reasonably practicable and take reasonable steps to minimise any pollution. It must be assumed that only a danger to human life or health would suffice. In addition, s. 89 excludes from the operation of s. 85 sewage effluent from vessels (which is covered under by-laws) and solid refuse from mines where the EA has given consent for its deposit. There is also a block exemption order relating to certain discharges which had never required a consent until COPA 1974 came into force. This

granted transitional exemption for these discharges, but it is being progressively withdrawn and few discharges are now covered.

There is also a defence in s. 89(3) for water from abandoned mines. However,
the defence applies only to the situation where the defendant 'permits' the entry
of polluted waters. It is strongly arguable that it does not provide a defence to a
charge of 'causing' pollution, which may well be justified where a mine owner
abandons a mine knowing that to cease pumping water from it will inevitably
lead to an overflow and to pollution (see below and *Lockhart* v *National Coal
Board* 1981 SLT 161). In any case, the exemption for abandoned mines is to be
withdrawn from 31 December 1999 (see the Environment Act 1995, s. 60).
The Environment Act 1995 also defines the concept of abandonment for the
first time and imposes a duty on mine operators to give the Environment
Agency at least six months' notice of a proposed abandonment.

There are some complex provisions in s. 87 relating to responsibility for
discharges from sewage works. In addition to the impact of the wide
interpretation given to the concept of 'causing' on sewerage undertakers (see
below), s. 87(1) deems sewerage undertakers to have caused a discharge of
sewage effluent if they were bound to receive into the sewer or works matter
included in the discharge. In other words, they are responsible for all
discharges from sewers or works unless the pollution is caused by an illegal
(i.e., unconsented) discharge into the sewer. However, s. 87(2) provides a
defence where a contravention of s. 85 is attributable to an unconsented
discharge into the sewerage system by a third party which the sewerage
undertaker could not reasonably have been expected to prevent. In *National
Rivers Authority* v *Yorkshire Water Services Ltd* [1995] 1 AC 444, the House of
Lords decided that, notwithstanding the precise wording of s. 87(2), the
defence applies to all the offences in s. 85. It should be noted that the defence
covers the situation where the sewerage undertaker could not reasonably have
prevented the discharge *into* the sewer, rather than *from* the sewer, but that
the original discharger into the sewer can be prosecuted under s. 85 for
causing pollution of controlled waters as well as under the Water Industry Act
1991, s. 118, for the illegal discharge to the sewer (see Chapter 15).

Under COPA 1974, there was a defence to the general offence if it was
committed by a farmer who was acting in accordance with good agricultural
practice. This was defined in a Code of Guidance issued by the Minister of
Agriculture, Fisheries and Food. The defence has been repealed. In its place
is a non-binding *Code of Good Agricultural Practice for the Protection of Water*,
issued jointly in 1991 by MAFF and the Secretary of State after consultation
with the NRA. This code has no legal effect. Contravention does not amount
to a criminal offence and compliance does not afford a legal defence, but
obviously conformity with the Code will affect any decision whether to
prosecute and the level of any fine imposed.

Meaning of 'cause or knowingly permit'

The offences under s. 85 require that the defendant 'cause or knowingly
permit' the relevant discharge or entry. This phrase has been interpreted in

many cases and it is clear that there are two separate offences, 'causing' and 'knowingly permitting', and that the former lays down an offence of strict liability because it is not conditioned by any requirement of knowledge. Indeed, *Alphacell Ltd v Woodward* [1972] AC 824, a case on this wording in the Rivers (Prevention of Pollution) Act 1951, is one of the leading cases in criminal law on the meaning of strict liability.

In *Alphacell v Woodward*, settling tanks at a paper factory overflowed into the River Irwell. The biochemical oxygen demand (BOD) of the discharge was well above the level permitted in the consent. Although the magistrates did not find that the firm had been negligent (a strange decision since pumps which should have stopped the overflow were blocked), the House of Lords held that there was no need to prove negligence or fault. Alphacell were guilty of the general offence of causing pollution simply by carrying on the activity which caused the pollution. As long as their activity was itself intentional all that needed to be shown was a causal link between it and the discharge. The directness of the entry was also irrelevant: in this case the entry was via a channel into the river.

This test has been reiterated in many cases. In *Southern Water Authority v Pegrum* (1989) 153 JP 581 effluent from the defendants' pig farm ran into tanks and from there into specially built lagoons. Owing to a fissure in one of the lagoons, when it reached a certain level it leaked, polluting a nearby stream. The Divisional Court held that, as long as the farmers carried on an active operation such as this and there was no effective intervening cause of the pollution, such as a trespasser or an Act of God, the general offence of causing pollution under COPA 1974, s. 31 (which involved identical wording) had been committed. The defence that the lagoon was filled by heavy rain was rejected on the grounds that it required something quite out of the ordinary to break the causal link. Similarly, in *F.J.H. Wrothwell Ltd v Yorkshire Water Authority* [1984] Crim LR 43, it was held that a director of a company who had poured herbicide into what he thought was a drain leading to the public sewer, but which in fact led to a nearby stream, was guilty of causing pollution of the stream, despite the unintended result of his action.

More recently, in *National Rivers Authority v Yorkshire Water Services Ltd* [1995] 1 AC 444, the House of Lords has reaffirmed the *Alphacell* test, emphasising that the issue of causation is a question of fact in each case. In *Yorkshire Water Services* an industrial solvent had been discharged illegally into the sewers by an unidentified industrial firm. The solvent had travelled through the sewers and, as a result of the design of the sewage works, into controlled waters, in a virtually undiluted condition. The House of Lords stated that there was ample evidence on which a tribunal of fact could find that the sewerage undertaker had caused the discharge from the sewage works (although in fact the conviction was quashed because the sewerage undertaker could take advantage of the special defence in s. 87(2)). In *Attorney-General's Reference (No. 1 of 1994)* [1995] 1 WLR 599, this case was applied by the Court of Appeal, which decided that where a sewerage undertaker had run a sewerage system in an unmaintained state it could be guilty of causing polluting matter to enter controlled waters. It had been argued that this amounted to an omission rather than an active operation, but the court reformulated the issue by pointing out that the active operation was running a sewage disposal system in an unmaintained state. The court also added that it was possible for more than one person to be liable for causing one pollution incident — the offence simply required that the defendant caused the discharge or entry, not that it was the sole, or even the principal, cause. (For example, on the facts of the *Yorkshire Water Services* case, it was entirely possible for both the original discharger into the sewer and the sewerage undertaker to have caused the entry into the river.)

A final case worth mentioning in this context is *CPC (UK) Ltd v National Rivers Authority* [1995] Env LR 131, where the operator of a factory was held to have caused polluting matter to have entered controlled waters when a pipe carrying cleaning fluid had fractured, allowing the fluid to flow into a river via a storm drain. The conviction was upheld even though the cause of the fracture was defective work carried out by subcontractors of the previous owner some time before the current owners had bought the premises. The reasoning was quite straightforward: the current owners had caused the pollution because they were operating the site when the polluting incident took place. Care must be taken, however, in referring to causation as a question of fact in each case. It does not mean that the tribunal of fact has total discretion, since its decision could be overturned if it failed the *Wednesbury* reasonableness requirement.

There have been two lines of cases which have suggested some limits to this wide interpretation of the concept of causing pollution. One line concerns the situation where a third party has acted in such a way as to interrupt the chain of causation. In *Impress (Worcester) Ltd v Rees* [1971] 2 All ER 357, fuel oil from a tank was released into the River Severn. The defendant successfully pleaded that this was the act of a trespasser. Similarly, in *Welsh Water Authority v Williams Motors (Cwmdu) Ltd* (1988) *The Times*, 5 December 1988, the owner of a petrol station was held not guilty of causing oil pollution where an independent lorry driver had spilt a delivery of diesel oil. In *National Rivers Authority v Wright Engineering Co. Ltd* [1994] 4 All ER 281, vandals had interfered with an oil storage tank, which had then leaked into controlled waters. Once again, the company was held not to have caused the polluting entry, although it was accepted that the foreseeability of vandalism would be one relevant factor in deciding who caused the pollution incident. It should also be recognised that the decision in *Attorney-General's Reference (No. 1 of 1994)* that more than one person can cause one pollution incident (see above) must mean that the availability of a defence cannot be taken for granted whenever a third party is involved.

The second line of cases relates to situations where the defendant can be said to be passive rather than active. It is illustrated most clearly by *Price v Cromack* [1975] 1 WLR 988, where a farmer had a contract permitting an animal products firm to discharge waste into lagoons on his land. One lagoon wall failed and the resulting escape severely polluted a river. The farmer was charged with causing pollution, but was acquitted on the ground that he had only permitted the accumulation and had not caused the pollution. *Price v*

Cromack was followed in *Wychavon District Council* v *National Rivers Authority* [1993] 1 WLR 125 and *National Rivers Authority* v *Welsh Development Agency* [1993] Env LR 407. In the *Wychavon* case, raw sewage escaped from a sewer that was under the control of Wychavon DC, which was at the time acting as agent of the water company in maintaining and repairing the sewerage system. The immediate cause was a blockage in the sewer. The Divisional Court decided that the Council was not guilty of the causing offence since it had not done anything positive but had merely remained inactive. In the *Welsh Development Agency* case, the court decided that the landlord of an industrial estate did not cause a discharge of trade effluent from the estate's surface water drains when the effluent originated from one of the units on the estate. These two cases both purport to follow Lord Wilberforce's statement in *Alphacell* v *Woodward* that causing 'must involve some active operation or chain of operations involving as the result the pollution of the stream'. But both appear to ignore the fact that in *Alphacell* it is made clear that it is not the immediate cause of the pollution that must be active, but the operation that underlies it. (For example, the active operation in *Alphacell* was identified as a complex one that involved the carrying on of a paper factory with an effluent treatment plant situated next to a river and which had an overflow channel that led directly to a river: it was inevitable that if something went wrong, polluting matter would enter the river.) None of these cases has been overruled, but they must be treated as limited to their own facts as a result of the reaffirmation of *Alphacell* in *National Rivers Authority* v *Yorkshire Water Services Ltd* and *Attorney-General's Reference (No. 1 of 1994)*.

The offence of 'knowingly permitting' has given rise to fewer cases and is clearly more limited than the 'causing' offence because of the knowledge requirement. However, it may be of use in situations where a person is passive even after knowing of the polluting incident. For example, in *Price* v *Cromack* the judge suggested the farmer could well have been charged with knowingly permitting the pollution; and in the *Wychavon* case it is fairly clear that the local authority could have been charged with knowingly permitting the pollution once it had been drawn to its attention (on the facts it had delayed for some time before taking steps to remedy the situation). One issue of great importance to the 'knowingly permitting' offence is the level of knowledge required. In *Schulmans Incorporated Ltd* v *National Rivers Authority* [1993] Env LR D1 the judge held that constructive knowledge was sufficient, although he did not go on to elaborate the point (see Wilkinson, 'Causing and knowingly permitting pollution offences: a review' [1993] Water Law 25, for a discussion of the possible implications of this case).

Two final cases are of importance for the s. 85 offences. In *Taylor Woodrow Property Management Ltd* v *National Rivers Authority* (1994) 158 JP 1101, a property company held a discharge consent relating to an outfall from an industrial estate. Even though it did not itself actually make any discharge, it was held liable under s. 85(6) for contravening the conditions of the consent. It thus appears that the holder of a consent is always capable of being prosecuted for breach of positive conditions attached to the consent. It can also be noted that this is a very neat way of avoiding any argument concerning whether the defendant has carried out an active operation, but only where there is a consent.

In *National Rivers Authority* v *Alfred McAlpine Homes East Ltd* [1994] 4 All ER 286, the company was held to be vicariously liable for acts of its employees, irrespective of whether those employees exercised 'the controlling mind' of the company. This appears to be a straightforward application of the principle of vicarious liability, but it does illustrate the need for companies to establish proper environmental management systems. The *McAlpine* case is also noteworthy for the approach of Morland J, who commented that any other answer 'would render important environmental legislation almost entirely nugatory', before stating:

> In my judgment to make the offence an effective weapon in the defence of environmental protection, a company must by necessary implication be criminally liable for the acts or omissions of its servants or agents during activities being done for the company. I do not find that this offends our concept of a just and fair criminal legal system, having regard to the magnitude of environmental pollution, even though no due diligence defence was provided for.

It is quite clear from this quotation, and from other comments in the cases referred to above, that the judges have been prepared to adopt a fairly purposive view of the legislation in order to further the aim of environmental protection. One result has been that the s. 85 offences have been given a very wide interpretation. This has had a number of implications. First, a wide range of accidental occurrences are offences. Secondly, any excess over the requirements of a numerical consent amounts to a criminal offence, no matter how small it is. Thirdly, firms are given a clear incentive to adopt an appropriate environmental management system so that accidents and breaches of consent do not occur. (This is, of course, accentuated by the possible personal liability of directors and senior managers under s. 217.) Fourthly, when a prosecution is brought there is a very high success rate (it is currently over 95%). However, the EA has a discretion whether to prosecute and has adopted a policy which means that a prosecution will not be brought in every possible case (see Chapter 6).

The consent system

The system for acquiring a consent is set out in the Water Resources Act 1991, sch. 10, and the Control of Pollution (Applications, Appeals and Registers) Regulations 1996 (SI 1996 No. 2971), and it involves a higher degree of public involvement than many other licensing-type systems.

Consents which have already been granted under COPA 1974 or earlier legislation are simply translated into valid consents for the purposes of the Act. However, they may be varied or revoked in the future under the terms of sch. 10 (see below).

A consent is required for each discharge, so if a factory has three discharge pipes it needs a consent for each one. The applicant applies to the EA, which has a discretion as to the details required. Normally the applicant will have to state the place, nature, quantity, rate of flow, composition and temperature of the proposed discharge. It is an offence under s. 206 to give incorrect information.

The applicant must publicise the application in a local newspaper and in the *London Gazette* and notify any relevant local authorities and water undertakers. However, this publicity may be dispensed with if the EA considers that the discharge will have 'no appreciable effect' on the receiving waters. Great use was made of this dispensation by the regional water authorities in the past, so that an estimated 90% of all applications were exempted from publicity in this way. Guidance on this vague and subjective discretion is given in DoE Circular 17/84, which suggests a complex set of tests to be considered, the main one being that a change is not to be considered appreciable if there is less than a 10% increase on all relevant parameters, unless some significant environmental amenity is affected. This is a good example of the use of administrative methods to define a legal requirement. It is objectionable that the operation of such an important publicity procedure rests on a rather restrictive interpretation given in a Departmental Circular.

Where the application contains information which would affect matters of national security the agency can exempt the application from the requirement to advertise (s. 191A and reg. 4).

The EA must take into account written representations made within six weeks of the notice appearing in the *London Gazette*. It has the power to grant consent, either unconditionally or subject to conditions, or to refuse consent.

A fee for making an application for a new or revised consent was introduced from 1 October 1990. The intention is that the EA should recover the overall costs incurred in processing applications. A standard charge is payable for each new or revised consent. There is a reduced charge for certain minor discharges of sewage effluent or cooling waters and for those surface water discharges which require consent (see *Scheme of Charges in Respect of Applications and Consents for Discharges to Controlled Waters*).

Conditions

The EA may attach 'such conditions as it may think fit' and sch. 10, para. 2(5) includes a non-exhaustive list. This includes such things as the quality, quantity, nature, composition and temperature of the discharge, the siting and design of the outlet, the provision of meters for measuring these matters, the taking and recording of samples by the discharger, and the provision of information to the EA. Frequently the most significant conditions will relate to biochemical oxygen demand, levels of toxic or dangerous materials, and suspended solids, although it has been suggested, amongst other recommendations relating to consents, the introduction of a more sophisticated test based on the toxicity of the discharge (*Discharge Consent and Compliance Policy: A Blueprint for the Future*, NRA, 1990). For industrial discharges it is normal to attach absolute numerical limits for the various parameters covered in the consent, with the result that any excess amounts to a breach of the consent. For sewage discharges a test based on 95% compliance has in the past been more normal, though sewage works consents are now being brought into line with industrial consents (see p. 467).

Conditions requiring a specified treatment process are legal, but it remains to be seen whether such conditions will be imposed, since in the past it has been Government policy to require compliance with environmental standards whilst giving a discharger a choice of methods to achieve the standard. It is permissible for conditions to be staggered so that they get progressively stricter. This was accepted in *Trent River Authority* v *F. H. Drabble & Sons Ltd* [1970] 1 WLR 98 and is now specifically covered in sch. 10.

A consent is personal to the operator but can be transferred under provisions contained in sch. 10, para. 11.

There is a procedure for granting a retrospective consent in para. 5. This involves the payment of the relevant fee and the same publicity requirements as for any other application. However, the paragraph is not fully retrospective since it affords no immunity for offences committed before the consent was granted. It enables the EA to formalise the legal position in relation to a discharge and also to attach conditions to an existing discharge.

A significant problem under COPA 1974 was the position of new pollutants. This phrase covers substances which the discharger introduces into the discharge after the consent has been obtained, or new substances unknown at the time the consent was set, or substances which were only later traceable or later considered to be polluting. Such substances would not be mentioned in the consent, and it appeared that discharging them may not have been in breach of the consent, since there was a breach only if the conditions were not met. It seems that this possible loophole has been avoided by the Water Resources Act 1991, which requires that the discharge must be 'under and in accordance with' the consent in order for the defence in s. 88 to apply. However, to make matters clear, the EA has recommended that all consents should include a general condition excluding the discharge of any substance not specified in the consent.

Revocation and variation

Under sch. 10, para. 7, the EA has a discretion to review consents from time to time. A variation or a revocation can be made simply by notifying the discharger. Alternatively the Secretary of State may direct that a variation take place (sch. 10, para. 9). No compensation is payable except in one case considered below. There is no provision for public participation in relation to a variation or revocation. This power to make variations or revocations is a wide one which reflects the need to cater for new circumstances, such as a new polluter in the catchment area, or a newly perceived pollution threat, or a change in EC or international obligations. It also reasserts the position that no one has a right to pollute.

However, there are limits on when a variation or revocation can be made. A period will be stipulated in the original consent. This cannot be less than four years and a variation or revocation cannot take place within that period (measured from the setting of the original consent or the last variation), except with the permission of the discharger. Exceptionally, the Secretary of State may direct a modification within the period in order to give effect to an EC or international obligation, or to protect public health, or flora and fauna dependent on an aquatic environment. There is no right to vary early solely because the discharger has been in breach of the consent, or in order to cater for a new pollutant: both are situations where such a right would be desirable. The EA will have to pay compensation to the discharger if a direction is made on the public health or protection of flora and fauna ground within the period.

Transitional provisions

In any regulatory system, when a new Act comes into force the transitional provisions are of importance. For the Water Act 1989, because most discharges were already covered by the provisions of COPA 1974, the transition was fairly straightforward. Existing consents were simply translated into Water Act consents and later into consents under the Water Resources Act 1991. This hides a continuation of a transitional provision from COPA 1974. Some discharges which did not require a consent before that Act were deemed to have been granted consent for the current level of discharge under COPA 1974, s. 40(4), as long as an application was made. These applications are slowly being decided by the EA but the process is not yet complete. Such discharges include many pre-1974 discharges to estuaries, which are effectively permitted to continue with their previous discharge uncontrolled.

Annual charges for discharge consents

The EA is empowered to make annual charges for discharge consents under the general charging provisions of ss. 41–42 of the Environment Act 1995, although any scheme requires the approval of the Secretary of State and the consent of the Treasury. The current scheme, the National Rivers Authority Applications and Discharges Scheme (which was made under the previous powers under s. 131 of the Water Resources Act 1991), applies from 1 April 1994 until 31 March 1999 with the fees and charges revised every year on 1 April.

The basic philosophy underpinning the charging scheme is that of cost-recovery charging, i.e., that the EA should recover from dischargers the actual cost of its activities connected with discharges. This includes the sampling of discharges, inspection of discharges, discharge-related impact monitoring, work on the review of consents, laboratory services and direct administration connected to these matters. Expenditure on general water quality monitoring, general administration and pollution incidents is not recovered by these charges, but will come from the general budget of the EA.

Further principles are that the charges are uniform throughout the country and are not to vary locally; that they relate to what is consented to rather than to the actual discharge; and that they are set according to a formula which has three separate elements — the volume of the discharge, its content, and the nature of the receiving waters. For each of these three elements broad bands have been devised, each being accorded a weighted value (i.e., a number of units). For volume, there are eight broad bands, with larger volume discharges having a higher value than lower ones. There are exceptions for emergency discharges, intermittent discharges and rainwater drains. For content, there are seven bands, reflecting the relative complexity and cost of monitoring the discharge. For receiving waters, there are four bands, with estuarine waters having a higher weighting than inland watercourses, which in turn are weighted more highly than discharges to coastal waters or to groundwaters.

Each discharge thus has three separate values, which are multiplied together to give a final figure in terms of a number of units. This final figure is then multiplied by a national financial factor, so that all dischargers know in advance what their charge is going to be. This financial factor will be varied annually. It can be expected that most dischargers will face a significant annual bill for their discharges.

At present there is no proposal for additional charges for 'Red List' or other hazardous substances on the grounds that the presence of these in a discharge will tend to take it into the more highly weighted categories as far as content is concerned. In a way, therefore, the polluter pays principle is being partially operated in relation to these charges. However, the White Paper (*This Common Inheritance,* 1990, Cm 1200, para. 12.25 and Annex A) suggests that the Conservative Government was looking at charging methods related to the pollution load, or environmental effect, of a discharge, and commissioned studies to look at such a system. This would be far more in keeping with the true meaning of the polluter pays principle. The Chancellor of the Exchequer raised the issue of water pollution levies in the 1997 summer budget. It is likely that any system will be introduced before the end of the life of this Parliament.

The role of the Secretary of State

The Secretary of State has a general, and very wide, power under the Environment Act 1995 to issue directions of a general or specific nature to the EA in relation to pollution control, amongst other matters. The supplementary powers of the Secretary of State to require information from the EA in s. 202 should also be noted. The reason for the width of the s. 40 power is the fact that large policy-making powers have effectively been delegated to the EA, making some mechanism for central control desirable. The use of directions to achieve this should be compared with the use of Circular guidance in other areas of environmental law, since they fulfil similar purposes.

The previous power to issue directions to the NRA under the Water Resources Act 1991, s. 5 was used in relation to a range of issues, including nitrate pollution, the Groundwater Directive and the Titanium Dioxide Directive.

At any stage the Secretary of State may call in an application for decision (sch. 10, para. 5). This is an unfettered discretion and ousts the jurisdiction of the EA to consider the consent. It is rarely exercised.

Appeals

The applicant or discharger has a right to appeal to the Secretary of State against a refusal of consent, the attachment of unreasonable conditions, any adverse variation or revocation of a consent, or the setting of the period in which a consent cannot be varied (s. 91). An application is deemed to have been refused if no decision is given within four months.

An appeal is a general rehearing of the matter in issue and the Secretary of State has the same powers as the EA originally had. Compared to the system of planning appeals, which accords enormous opportunities for argument on policy, it seems that this appeal right will be less commonly used, since there is little perceived difference in policy between the Secretary of State and the EA. However, one criticism that has been made of the appeals system is the length of time it takes for appeals to be decided, with the result that an understanding of the principles to be applied on appeal is only building up slowly.

The procedures for called in applications and for appeals are set out in the Control of Pollution (Applications, Appeals and Registers) Regulations 1996 (SI 1996 No. 2971). These regulations retain the procedures for other applications with modified wording, and also provide for the rights of objectors. One significant change is that the discretion not to publicise where there is no appreciable effect on the receiving waters does not apply.

A final power of the Secretary of State is that the EA must apply to the Secretary of State if it wishes to make any discharges. Similar procedures apply as for ordinary consent applications (SI 1996 No. 2971, sch. 2). Given the limited operational activities of the EA, few such applications will be necessary.

How are consents set?

The EA, or the Secretary of State on appeal, has a wide discretion in setting the consent and it will be set by reference to a variety of factors. Although sch. 10 is silent as to the factors which must be taken into account, applying ordinary public law principles the EA must have regard to all material considerations. In addition, certain requirements appear from other sections of the Act, especially s. 84, and from EC law.

As stated before, it is important to grasp the individualised and flexible nature of these consents, although uniformity and consistency is now being sought by the EA. Relevant matters include:

(a)   The water quality objectives and standards set for the receiving waters under s. 83 (see below). This emphasises that one of the crucial elements in fixing a consent is the effect on the receiving waters. This in turn depends on the use that is intended for those receiving waters.

(b)   Any other effects on the receiving waters, such as on a fishery or downstream user. In particular, regard will be had to whether the waters are used for abstraction for water supply or irrigation.

(c)   Any relevant EC standards for the discharge concerned or for the quality of the receiving waters.

(d)   Any 'cocktail' effect of the discharge. The EA will consider not only the immediate effect of the discharge but also any impact the discharge will have in combination with the current contents of the waters and any potential future discharges.

(e)   The desirability of minimising discharges of hazardous substances as far as possible in accordance with Directive 76/464.

(f)   The EA's environmental duties laid out in the Environment Act 1995, s. 6 (see p. 48).

(g)   The specific duty in relation to sites of special scientific interest set out in s. 8 (see p. 439).

(h)   Any relevant objections and representations made and the results of any consultation carried out.

(i)   Certain informal standard tests for particular types of discharge. For example, 'normal' standards for sewage works were suggested by the Eighth Report of the Royal Commission on Sewage Disposal in 1912 and these were applied for many years. The EA is now seeking to establish some uniformity of standards across the country for all types of discharge.

(j)   Any other material considerations.

Water quality objectives

Although the British approach to the control of water pollution has tended over the years to concentrate on the environmental impact of pollutants, the development of *statutory* water quality objectives owes a great deal to the EC. In the 1970s, in debates on EC Directives such as 76/464 on Dangerous Substances in Water, the British Government argued that its system of water pollution control was different to the systems operated by other EC Member States in that it was based on individualised consent standards set by reference to local environmental quality objectives, rather than on uniform emission standards or limit values which did not take the environmental effects fully into account. At the time, however, there were no formally set quality objectives, so in order to show that this was indeed how the system worked, the Government was forced to introduce more explicit objectives.

In 1978, the National Water Council developed a water quality classification (see *River Water Quality: The Next Stage*, National Water Council, 1978). This had five basic classes of river waters (there was a similar but separate classification for estuaries):

1A   High quality waters suitable for all abstraction purposes with only modest treatment. Capable of supporting game or other high class fisheries. High amenity value.

1B   Good quality waters usable for substantially the same purposes as 1A though not as high quality.

2   Fair quality waters viable as coarse fisheries and capable of use for drinking water provided advanced treatment is given. Moderate amenity value.

3 Poor waters polluted to the extent that fish are absent or only sporadically present. Suitable only for low grade industrial abstractions.

4 Bad quality waters which are grossly polluted and likely to cause a nuisance.

This classification was adopted by the regional water authorities in setting informal river quality objectives over the next few years. It was also used for the five-yearly national survey of water quality. However, as an administrative method of implementing EC Directives, it was clearly insufficient to satisfy EC law (see *Commission* v *Belgium* (case 102/79) [1980] ECR 1473, which requires implementation of EC Directives to be done by legislative means), so it became inevitable that a statutory system would be adopted.

The Water Act 1989 introduced statutory water quality classifications and objectives for the first time. The provisions are now reproduced in the Water Resources Act 1991, ss. 82–84. When fully operational (which will not be for many years), statutory water quality objectives will make the system more open and will be an important element in the general process of establishing a rationally planned, transparent and properly accountable system of water resources management.

The essential features are that, over the next few years, classification regulations will be made which set the standards that waters must reach in order to come within a certain classification. This will be done under s. 82. The Secretary of State will then establish (under s. 83) a water quality *objective* for each stretch of controlled waters. This will set specified classifications as an objective, and will accordingly incorporate the relevant water quality *standards*. These will then act as explicit policy goals for the EA, which will be under a legal duty under s. 84 to exercise its functions, including the granting of discharge consents, so as to achieve and maintain the statutory water quality objective at all times, at least as far as it is practicable to do so. There are thus three different processes involved, although these are intertwined.

The first process is the setting of classification systems for waters under s. 82. In order to comply with certain EC Directives, this process was started with the publication of three sets of regulations:

(a) The Surface Waters (Classification) Regulations 1989 (SI 1989 No. 1148), which classify inland waters (i.e., fresh waters) into three categories according to their suitability as drinking waters. The classification is based on the mandatory values in Directive 75/440 on Surface Water for Drinking. To qualify as within any category, the specified limits must not be exceeded.

(b) The Bathing Waters (Classification) Regulations 1991 (SI 1991 No. 1597), which establish a classification that reflects the mandatory standards laid down in Directive 76/160 on Bathing Waters.

(c) The Surface Waters (Dangerous Substances) (Classification) Regulations 1989 and 1992 (SIs 1989 No. 2286 and 1992 No. 337), which set classifications in accordance with Directive 76/464 on Dangerous Substances in Water and its daughter Directives. These Regulations specify annual mean concentrations of a limited range of substances (mainly 'Red List' substances) which should not be exceeded. In order to comply with EC law, these classifications have also been issued as initial water quality objectives under s. 83, this action having been taken by the Secretary of State under the power to make directions then contained in s. 5 of the Water Resources Act 1991. In so doing the publicity requirements set out in s. 83(4) were dispensed with.

The process has now been taken further with the Surface Waters (River Ecosystem) (Classification) Regulations 1994 (SI 1994 No. 1057), which were introduced following extensive consultation. These Regulations lay down five classifications, RE1–RE5, which are defined according to conformity with seven parameters: dissolved oxygen, biochemical oxygen demand (BOD), total ammonia, un-ionised ammonia, pH, dissolved copper and total zinc. Standard sampling and analysis methods are laid down, as are methods for determining compliance with the classifications. The absence of biological parameters, which were originally proposed by the NRA, has been criticised, but the view has been taken that they would be inappropriate for the statutory classification scheme. They will, however, be used in future as part of a uniform system of analysis for the five-yearly national survey of water quality (see p. 434). Classification systems are still awaited for controlled waters apart from rivers.

The second process is that water quality objectives for individual stretches of controlled waters may be set by the Secretary of State (s. 83). The choice of an objective by the Secretary of State would mean that the appropriate standards laid down for that objective in the classification regulations would apply to the stretch of water. In addition, appropriate EC standards laid down in Directives would be incorporated where relevant (for example, if the waters were bathing waters designated under Directive 76/160).

The procedures for setting a statutory water quality objective involve at least three months' publicity of the proposed objective 'in such manner as the Secretary of State considers appropriate for bringing it to the attention of persons likely to be affected by it' (i.e., these provisions are less specific than many other publicity provisions in relation to pollution control). The EA must also be notified. All representations and objections must be considered, and the Secretary of State may modify the proposals in the light of these representations. A public local inquiry may be held under s. 213. Obviously it is in the interests of anyone discharging into a catchment to get involved in the setting of these objectives. Similar advice applies to those who discharge into sewers, because discharges from sewage works will also be affected by the statutory water quality objective. The Secretary of State may review and, in the light of the review, vary water quality objectives by going through the same procedures, but this may only take place five years after the objective was last set or varied, or alternatively if the EA requests a review, which it may do only after consulting relevant water undertakers.

The third process is that, as stated above, under s. 84 the EA and Secretary of State are placed under a duty to exercise their powers under the Act so as to achieve statutory water quality objectives at all times, so far as it is practicable to do so. This duty already applies to the objectives set in the Surface Waters (Dangerous Substances) (Classification) Regulations, but will only apply to other objectives when they are formally established. It does not follow that the EA is in breach of s. 84 simply by failing to achieve the appropriate standards. But it does mean that its powers in relation to the setting and variation of consents, remedial and enforcement action, and preventative controls should be exercised to achieve the standards if practicable, since a judicial review action could conceivably be brought to ensure the enforcement of the duty. Under the EPA 1990, s. 7(2)(c), a similar duty is placed on the EA to try to achieve statutory water quality objectives when considering authorisations for integrated pollution control.

One of the criticisms of the sections on statutory water quality objectives when they were first passed was that no timetable was set for the introduction of the system. It is now clear that full implementation will take many years. There is still some work to be done on the development of precise classification criteria. After that, the process of setting individual objectives will, in the Conservative Government's words, extend 'over a number of years', starting with a very limited number of selected river catchments. Even then, the current proposals relate only to rivers — statutory water quality objectives for estuaries, coastal waters, groundwaters, canals and lakes are clearly many years off. The existing informal river quality objectives will remain in force until superseded by the statutory objectives. There is little doubt that there is little enthusiasm for the costs involved in setting statutory water quality objectives, despite the great benefits they would produce in terms of a rational and transparent system of pollution control.

Public registers

For the first time, the Control of Pollution Act 1974 provided for public registers of a range of environmental information relating to water pollution, although these provisions were not implemented until 1985. Prior to that the system tended to be operated with a fair degree of secrecy about consents and samples taken. The relevant provisions are repeated in the Water Resources Act 1991 with some amendments.

Under s. 190, a public register must be kept by the EA of all applications for consent, consents actually granted, any conditions attached to a consent, notices of water quality objectives made under s. 83. Prescribed details of authorisations granted for the purposes of integrated pollution control must also be recorded on the water registers. In addition, the results of any samples of the receiving waters or of effluent, and any information produced by analysis of them, must be registered. This requirement is worded more widely than under COPA 1974, and samples taken by *any* person must be registered; this includes samples taken by a discharger as a condition of consent.

Section 190 requires that the register is open for inspection by any member of the public free of charge at all reasonable times and that reasonable facilities for taking copies are afforded on payment of a reasonable fee. The

Control of Pollution (Applications, Appeals and Legislation) Regulations 1996 (SI 1996 No. 2971) specify the detailed shape of the registers, including a requirement that details of any sample must be entered on the register within two months of the date of the sample.

The public register provides an invaluable database for groups and individuals wishing to monitor water quality. It can be used to mount a private prosecution (as in *Wales* v *Thames Water Authority* (1987) 1(3) *Environmental Law* 3, where the Water Authority was successfully prosecuted for pollution from a sewage works in reliance on the information which it had itself recorded on the register), or to provide evidence for a civil claim, or to provide general information on the state of the water environment. The admissibility of the registers as evidence seems quite clear now that they are kept by the EA (see p. 162).

In addition, s. 204 prohibits the EA or any officer from disclosing information obtained under the Act. Any person who does disclose such information without the permission of the person or company which provided it is guilty of an offence and liable, on summary conviction, to a fine not exceeding £5,000, and on conviction on indictment, to imprisonment for up to two years or an unlimited fine, or both. Of course, this restriction does not apply to matters required to be entered on the register. Nor does it apply to such things as the disclosure of information for criminal proceedings, or in pursuance of an EC obligation, and a range of other matters listed in s. 204. It also does not apply where a company has ceased trading.

Integrated pollution control

There are separate controls for those processes prescribed for Part I of the EPA 1990 (i.e., those processes subject to integrated pollution control). Acting in accordance with an integrated pollution control authorisation will be a defence to the water pollution offences under s. 85 of the Water Resources Act 1991.

Sewage discharges

Sewage discharges have always caused problems, firstly because of their potent polluting power and secondly because of the conflict of interest between regulator and regulated. These points were seen at their clearest in the 1970s and 1980s when capital expenditure cuts led to a number of badly underperforming sewage works at a time when the regulator and regulated was the same body, the regional water authority. However, the same conflict also existed prior to that: the local authorities which ran the sewage works also provided members for the rivers authorities, for example, and thus exercised an influence on their decisions.

Under the Water Resources Act 1991, there is no conflict of interest. Sewerage undertakers are treated similarly to other dischargers in requiring a consent from the EA. One slight difference relates to the offences under s. 85. Because sewerage undertakers treat wastes discharged by other people, and thus have limited control over what is actually put into the sewers, they have a special defence under s. 87(2). This operates if the contravention of their discharge consent was due to an unconsented discharge made into the sewer by another person which they could not reasonably have prevented (see *National Rivers Authority* v *Yorkshire Water Services Ltd* [1995] 1 AC 444, which is discussed at p. 454).

A more significant difference is that sewage works have traditionally had their consents set on different terms from other dischargers. The standard practice for other dischargers has been to set absolute numerical limits, with the result that any breach of the limit amounts to a criminal offence. For sewage discharges, in the past the conditions of consents have normally been set by reference to 'look-up tables' intended to ensure a 95% compliance rate over a rolling 12-month period. This leeway was allowed for in recognition of the variable quality of sewage effluents and the comparative lack of control that sewage works operators could exercise over them. The result is that it has been difficult to prove the offence under s. 85, since a single sample which exceeds the consent will not amount to a breach, and a number of legal samples over a 12-month period are needed.

The treatment of sewage works is currently under review. This includes the introduction of consents that set absolute limits, although some percentile compliance tests have been retained in order to provide control over discharge (see *Discharge Consent and Compliance Policy: A Blueprint for the Future,* NRA, 1990). The EA is also reviewing and tightening the levels of many consents. These steps have led to a steady rise in the number of prosecutions for illegal sewage discharges and have also had a marked knock-on effect on trade effluent consents granted by the sewerage undertakers under the Water Industry Act 1991.

An understanding of the present position requires some explanation of the position prior to 1989. Between 1951 and 1985 (when the relevant provisions of the Control of Pollution Act 1974 came into force), consents had been set and monitored in virtual secrecy, though they tended to follow the biochemical oxygen demand (BOD) and suspended solids standards recommended by the Eighth Report of the Royal Commission on Sewage Disposal in 1912. Under the 1974 Act, because of the conflict of interest within regional water authorities, a special procedure was established whereby consents were formally set by the Secretary of State (through HMIP after 1987). Similar procedures for applying for consent to those set up for industrial discharges were provided for in regulations. However, most sewage works consents were already in existence, which meant that under COPA 1974, s. 40 there was no need for a new application and hence the publicity requirements were rarely used.

In the 1970s and 1980s many consents were relaxed. For example, the National Water Council had commenced a review of consents in the late-1970s which led to the relaxation of some sewage works consents. This review was never completed and the results never published. Consents were also relaxed in the 1980s in anticipation of the implementation of COPA and the consequent availability of a right to bring private prosecutions, and again in the run-up to water privatisation in order to protect the sewerage undertakers. Notwithstanding these events, there was evidence that up to a quarter of sewage works were still regularly exceeding their consents in 1989. The NRA's actions (which have been continued by the EA) are clearly an attempt to control sewage discharges more rigorously and it is also significant that the privatised water companies figure prominently in lists of those who have been prosecuted most frequently.

Radioactive discharges

Under the Control of Pollution (Radioactive Waste) Regulations, 1989 (SI 1989 No. 1158), the radioactivity of a discharge is to be ignored for the purposes of the Water Resources Act 1991. In other words, the non-radioactive elements of a discharge or entry are dealt with under the Water Resources Act 1991 and the radioactive elements under the Radioactive Substances Act 1993 by the EA or the Minister of Agriculture, Fisheries and Food.

Sampling and enforcement powers

Environment Agency officers have wide rights of entry to property under s. 108 of the Environment Act 1995. In relation to non-pollution control water-related enforcement the EA has powers under ss. 169–174, WRA, to ascertain if any powers or duties require implementation, or to inspect for breaches of controls. Reserve powers of entry under a warrant from a magistrate are granted in sch. 20 for cases of difficulty.

The powers include a right to take samples of water or effluent or to install monitoring equipment. However, until its repeal by the Environment Act 1995, s. 111, s. 209 posed some problems in this respect. Under s. 209, the result of the analysis of a sample taken on behalf of the NRA was not admissible in legal proceedings unless it was a 'legal', or tripartite, sample (i.e., one that was taken in accordance with s. 209(1), which required that the occupier of the land concerned was notified of the intention to have the sample analysed and it was divided into three parts, one of which was sent for analysis, one given to the occupier and one retained for future comparison). Despite the fact that there is no requirement that a sample be produced in evidence at all (some cases, for example, can easily be proved by visual evidence or the presence of dead fish), this section provided some practical difficulties for the NRA, especially since it costs approximately five times as much to take a tripartite sample as it does to take a routine one.

The section was discussed in a number of cases. In *National Rivers Authority* v *Harcros Timber and Building Supplies Ltd* [1993] Env LR 172, the Divisional Court decided that the requirement of a legal sample applied to both samples of effluent and samples of the receiving waters. In *CPC (UK) Ltd* v *National Rivers Authority* [1995] Env LR 131, a more restrictive interpretation was adopted by the Court of Appeal and it was decided that, where readings were obtained by the NRA from a continuous water monitor, this was not a 'sample' for the purposes of s. 209. In *Attorney-General's*

Reference (No. 2 of 1994) [1995] Env LR 143, the Court of Appeal adopted a purposive view of the section and decided that the notification to the occupier did not necessarily have to precede the taking of the sample or its division, and that the requirement that the sample be divided 'there and then' simply meant at *or proximate to* the site and on the occasion of taking the sample, which is effectively a continuous event rather than a single moment in time. It would also appear from the wording of the section that it applied only to samples taken by or on behalf of the NRA; therefore, a privately taken sample would be admissible, although its scientific accuracy might be challenged. It is worth noting that a private sample taken by trespassing on the discharger's land, although admissible, may be excluded as improperly obtained evidence at the discretion of the court, although such a course of action is unlikely (see the Police and Criminal Evidence Act 1984, s. 78).

The Environment Act 1995 circumvents this rather confusing position by repealing s. 209, although not without significant opposition in Parliament from industrial interests. Section 111 states simply that information provided or obtained as a result of a licence condition is admissible, including where it is provided by means of an apparatus (i.e., some form of measuring device). There is a rebuttable presumption that such an apparatus is accurate. This should reduce the number of offenders who escape prosecution on evidential technicalities.

There is also a potential problem relating to the admissibility of the public registers, since it is fairly clearly hearsay evidence. It appears that samples taken by the EA are admissible under the Criminal Justice Act 1988, s. 24. This section also seems to avoid any problem relating to self-incrimination where the discharger's own data are used, as that data will count as a confession (see the Police and Criminal Evidence Act 1984, ss. 76 and 82).

Enforcement policy

A central issue relating to water pollution, and indeed of this whole book, is whether the rules are actually enforced by the regulators (see Chapter 6 for a general survey of attitudes towards enforcement by regulatory bodies). The NRA established a national prosecution policy and it is clear that the traditional recipe of a conciliatory approach to enforcement with low prosecution rates has been rapidly reformulated.

For example, from 1980 to 1987 the regional water authorities collectively prosecuted between 91 and 254 cases of water pollution each year (Birch, *Poison in the System,* Greenpeace, 1988). By comparison, in its first year of operation (1989/90), the NRA successfully prosecuted 370 cases. Fuller details of more recent prosecutions are given in *Water Pollution Incidents in England and Wales — 1993*, NRA, 1994. This report records 25,299 substantiated pollution incidents in 1993 and states that by 31 March 1994, 286 prosecutions had been brought, with a further 133 cases still to come to court. (This actually compares with a figure of 592 prosecutions for incidents occurring in 1990, which can be explained by the higher number of major incidents that year, which was a time of drought in many areas.) In addition, in a further 206 cases a formal caution was issued, this course of action being used where the polluter admits the offence yet a prosecution is considered unnecessary.

This increase in prosecution activity was linked to the NRA's internal practices. It divided pollution incidents into three categories according to their severity — major, significant and minor. For example, a major incident involved one or more of the following:

(a) a potential or actual persistent effect on water quality or aquatic life;
(b) the closure of a potable water, industrial or agricultural abstraction point;
(c) an extensive fish kill;
(d) excessive breaches of consent conditions;
(e) a major effect on amenity values; or
(f) extensive remedial measures are necessary.

It then applied its internal prosecution policy. Although this remains unpublished, essentially it involved prosecuting for major incidents where there was sufficient evidence to do so, and leaving it to the discretion of individual officers where a significant incident occurred (see Jewell, 'Agricultural water pollution issues and NRA enforcement policy' [1991] LMELR 110). The proportion of major incidents for which a prosecution was brought is over 30%. It is too early to analyse any trend in prosecution rates after the demise of the NRA and the birth of the EA, although there is now a formal enforcement policy which sets out the manner in which the EA is to act and when it will take prosecution action (see p. 147). It is likely that the NRA's policy will continue to be relied upon by EA officers for some time, at least informally.

However, it remains the case that most prosecutions are for accidental or other unusual incidents, rather than for consistent breaches of consent, a characteristic that was noted by Greenpeace in *Poison in the System,* and which has given rise to continued complaints from environmental groups that the NRA (and subsequently the EA) was not taking action against persistent polluters with sufficient rigour. In this regard, it is appropriate to note that private prosecution remains a possibility under the Water Resources Act 1991. Whilst little used, its availability remains a threat to dischargers, particularly in the light of the information on the public registers, and it may also be used by environmental groups as a means of registering their disquiet over the EA's perceived failure to take action over certain discharges. This was the case, for example, when Greenpeace successfully prosecuted Albright & Wilson in 1991.

Owing to the strict liability nature of the offences most prosecutions are successful. Of the 286 prosecutions referred to above, 277 resulted in conviction, a success rate of 97%. The level of fines imposed by magistrates is also rising. Before the EPA 1990 raised the maximum fine on summary conviction to £20,000, it was £2,000. However, even this was rarely imposed and the average fine in the late — 1980s was estimated to be around £250.

This has clearly increased since then, most probably as a result of greater publicity of the costs of environmental pollution, so that the maximum fine has been imposed on a number of occasions and a fine of over £1,000 would now be expected in most cases. Another emerging trend is an increased willingness by the EA to bring a prosecution in the Crown Court, where fines may be higher. This has resulted in several very large fines, most notably the £1m fine imposed on Shell (*National Rivers Authority* v *Shell (UK)* [1990] Water Law 40). There has, as yet, been no reported case of a sentence of imprisonment being imposed for a water pollution offence.

Preventative and remedial powers

In common with other areas of pollution control, the regulatory system which controls water pollution has a range of powers in relation to the prevention of harm. The exercise of these powers is undoubtedly aided by the presence of water quality objectives against which action may be justified.

Under s. 161, the EA has widely drafted powers to prevent pollution incidents where there is a threat of water pollution, to clean up after them and to carry out remedial or restorative works. For example, s. 161 covers such things as diverting a potential pollutant spilt in an accident in order to prevent it from entering a watercourse, cleaning up the effects of a spillage, and restocking a river with fish, and following an amendment made by the Environment Act 1995, s. 60, it also covers investigations into pollution incidents. The main problem with these provisions is that they require the EA to undertake works or operations before recovering the costs, thus adding to uncertainty over the prospect of cost recovery which can, in turn, mean that the power to carry out works is often not exercised. The Environment Act 1995 introduced new provisions which have addressed this problem by ensuring that the EA can only carry out works and operations where a works notice is served on the appropriate responsible person, unless it is necessary to carry out works 'forthwith'. There is a right of appeal against such a notice. Failure to comply with a works notice is an offence (s. 161A–C).

The EA can recover the costs incurred in these works, operations or investigations from anyone who has caused or knowingly permitted the pollutant to be present in controlled waters, or who has caused or knowingly permitted the pollutant to be a threat to controlled waters. There is a degree of overlap between these powers and the power to clean up contaminated sites. The Government has promised to issue guidance on the manner in which each of these powers should be exercised (see further p. 418). There are two exceptions: expenses cannot normally be recovered in relation to waters from an abandoned mine (these are also exempted from some of the criminal provisions in the Act), although this exemption will lapse after 31 December 1999 as a result of an amendment made by the Environment Act 1995, s. 60; and these powers cannot be exercised so as to impede or prevent the making of a discharge in pursuance of a consent. In this second case the EA is limited to a consideration of whether the consent should be varied, though it should be noted that there is no power to override the period of immunity against variation merely on the grounds that a discharger has committed a breach or an act of pollution.

Section 161 is mainly used for accidental acts of pollution, although it can be used where there has been a breach of the conditions of a consent (although it is much more likely that the EA would choose to issue an enforcement notice: see below). It is particularly useful because the potential cost may act as a greater deterrent than the threat of prosecution. The costs of a clean-up operation are likely in many cases to be higher than the potential fine. For example, in *National Rivers Authority v Shell (UK)* [1990] Water Law 40, Shell was fined £1m for a major leak of oil into the River Mersey, but it has been reported as having paid over £6m in clean-up costs. In *Bruton v Clarke* [1994] Water Law 145, a county court case concerning damage to a fishery, the approach to valuing a claim under s. 161 is shown, with the judge limiting the NRA to costs necessarily incurred as a result of the pollution incident and not allowing costs incurred in *improving* the fishery. The case also illustrated that there does not have to be a successful prosecution for s. 161 to be successful. However, in *National Rivers Authority: River Pollution from Farms in England* (National Audit Office, 1995), the National Audit Office reports that the NRA only obtains recovery of costs in a minority of cases (42% of the sample taken), which is a low figure considering the NRA's stated policy that polluters should pay for the consequences of their actions.

In cases where there has been or is likely to be a breach of a discharge consent condition, the EA has the power to serve an enforcement notice under powers inserted by the Environment Act 1995 (s. 90B, Water Resources Act 1991). An enforcement notice must identify the breach (or likely breach), the steps which are required to remedy the breach and the time within which those steps must be carried out. Failure to comply with an enforcement notice is an offence and there are the normal rights of appeal (see above). This addition to the range of enforcement mechanisms is significant in that it gives the EA another option other than prosecution when faced with a pollution incident. It is also useful in preventing pollution from non-accidental sources and requiring improvements in situations where there is an 'accident waiting to happen'.

Precautions against pollution

Under s. 92, the Secretary of State is empowered to make regulations concerning precautions to be taken in relation to any poisonous, noxious or polluting matter to prevent it from entering controlled waters. Such regulations may prevent anyone having custody or control of poisonous, noxious or polluting matter unless the steps required in the regulations or specified by the EA are carried out. These regulations may create additional criminal offences and administrative remedies in relation to breaches, although these may not have penalties higher than for the pollution offences under s. 85.

The Control of Pollution (Silage, Slurry and Agricultural Fuel Oil) Regulations 1991 (SI 1991 No. 324) are, as yet, the only regulations made under s. 92. They introduce precautionary controls over the design and operation of some potentially very polluting activities by imposing specific controls over silage making operations, slurry stores and agricultural fuel oil stores. All new or substantially altered facilities are covered by the new standards (many of which are performance standards rather than strict design requirements), though it is possible for the EA to bring existing activities under control if it is satisfied there is a significant risk of pollution to controlled waters. These Regulations have the potential to complement the planning system in preventing pollution problems arising. However, control is exercisable over operational details in a more specific way than is possible through the planning system, oversight and monitoring will be carried out by a more specialist body, and the controls relate to agricultural matters not normally covered by planning powers. It is likely that a second set of regulations relating to industrial fuel oil stores will be introduced before the end of 1997, with a possibility of new rules on chemical storage sometime in the future.

Water protection zones

Under s. 93, the Secretary of State may designate water protection zones by order. Such an order may effectively establish a system of local law within the zone with regard to water pollution. It is envisaged that an order under this section may either prohibit or restrict specified activities within the designated zone with a view to preventing or controlling the entry of poisonous, noxious or polluting matter into controlled waters, or provide for a system whereby the EA determine prohibited or restricted activities. It is not possible to require the carrying out of positive works. An order may also include provisions relating to procedures for obtaining consent for such restricted activities from the EA, with criminal sanctions being available for breaches.

The procedure for the making of an order is set out in sch. 11. This requires that the EA must apply for an order by submitting a draft to the Secretary of State. Fairly precise publicity requirements are laid down, including a duty to notify any local authority and water undertaker within the designated area. The Secretary of State may modify the order and has a power (not a duty) to hold a public inquiry before making it. In England, the Secretary of State must consult with the Minister of Agriculture, Fisheries and Food.

Similar provisions were included in COPA 1974 but were never used, and no water protection zones have yet been designated under the Water Resources Act either, though one has been proposed for the River Dee catchment. They would be excellent tools for protecting certain sensitive areas and for combating non-point discharges, such as pesticide or fertiliser run-off, and would enable steps to be taken to protect against groundwater pollution. However, the use of these powers has always been strongly opposed by agricultural interests. Significantly, there is no specific provision in the Act for an order to include compensation payments, but it may include such supplemental and consequential provision as the Secretary of State 'considers appropriate'.

One limitation, in s. 93(3), is that a water protection zone should not concern itself with nitrate from agricultural sources. This is because protection against nitrate is provided for in s. 94: a section which was hurriedly written into the legislation during its passage in response to public worries about nitrate in groundwaters used for water supply and the action against the British Government in the European Court of Justice for non-compliance with EC Directive 80/778 on Drinking Water. From a legal point of view it is difficult to see why the nitrate problem could not have been tackled through the designation of water protection zones, and it is hard to avoid the conclusion that specific nitrate sensitive area provisions are something of a political gesture.

Nitrate sensitive areas

The powers in relation to nitrate are set out in s. 94, which provides that an area may be designated a nitrate sensitive area by order with a view to preventing or controlling the entry of nitrate into controlled waters as a result of agriculture. In this case the designation is made by the Secretary of State and the Minister of Agriculture, Fisheries and Food acting jointly if the area is in England, and by the Secretary of State for Wales alone if it is in Wales. An order can only be made if requested by the EA, which must identify controlled waters likely to be affected and the agricultural land likely to result in the entry of nitrate into waters. It must also appear to the EA that its other powers are inadequate to control nitrate pollution before applying for an order. The consent of the Treasury is required before an order is made.

There are two types of order that may be made, respectively imposing voluntary and mandatory controls. Voluntary controls are available where *any* nitrate sensitive area has been designated: the Minister of Agriculture, Fisheries and Food may enter into a management agreement with any owner of an interest in agricultural land, with compensation payable. Such an agreement will bind those deriving title from the original party.

A mandatory order is similar to an order designating a water protection zone. However, there are significant differences. In nitrate sensitive areas the order may require positive obligations, such as the construction of containment walls around agricultural stores, as well as prohibitions and restrictions on activities. If consent is required, it is obtained from the Minister responsible for the designation, not the EA. In addition, the order may provide for compensation to be paid to anyone affected by the obligations. No guidelines on the criteria for awarding compensation are set out in the Act.

The procedure for making a mandatory order is set out in sch. 12. This requires that the EA must apply for an order by submitting a draft to the relevant Minister. Once again, precise publicity requirements are laid down, including a duty to notify any local authority and water undertaker within the designated area, and to notify any owner or occupier appearing to the relevant Minister to be likely to be affected by the compensation provisions. The relevant Minister may modify an order and has a power (not a duty) to hold a public inquiry before making an order.

The Government has made public its intention to use only the voluntary methods initially, in keeping with its stated preference for such methods. It designated 10 pilot areas in the Nitrate Sensitive Areas (Designation) Order 1990 (SI 1990 No. 1013), which provided for two types of scheme, a 'basic scheme' and a 'premium scheme', with more significant restrictions on agricultural operations (and higher payments) available in the latter than in the former. The take-up rate was, in general, good (about 87% of the agricultural land in the 10 areas), but the premium scheme was little used, so the payment rates were increased in an amendment order (SI 1993 No. 3198).

Since then, the perceived success of the pilot scheme has led the Government to expand the number of nitrate sensitive areas to 22 and to introduce a new scheme in the Nitrate Sensitive Areas Regulations 1994 (SI 1994 No. 1729). These Regulations are formally made under the European Communities Act 1972, s. 2(2), in order to comply with the EC Agri-Environment Regulation 2078/92, and thus technically concern the de-intensification of agriculture rather than pollution control. They provide for three separate schemes: a 'premium arable scheme', a 'premium grass scheme' and a 'basic scheme', with farmers being required to give undertakings as to their farming operations for a period of five years in return for payments of specified amounts per hectare per year. It is significant that the payment rates may be revised during the five years.

There are further regulations which implement Directive 91/676 on nitrates but the position is still not entirely clear. The Conservative Government failed to meet the December 1993 deadline for designating nitrate vulnerable zones and only set out the proposed zones in a consultation paper in May 1994, although admittedly it did propose that an area of about 650,000 hectares be designated. Whilst there is no doubt that the 1994 Regulations represent a fairly sophisticated response to nitrate pollution in designated nitrate sensitive areas, it is clear that the Regulations and accompanying voluntary mechanisms such as the *Code of Good Agricultural Practice for the Protection of Water*, issued by the Ministry of Agriculture, Food and Fisheries, are insufficient to comply with the Directive.

The Protection of Water against Agricultural and Nitrate Pollution (England and Wales) Regulations 1996 (SI 1996 No. 888) were introduced to address the incomplete implementation of the 1991 Directive. The Regulations designate Nitrate Vulnerable Zones (NVZs) in specific areas where there are excessive levels of nitrate pollution from agricultural sources. As a result of the consultation process referred to above, 68 NVZs were designated on the basis that nitrate levels were either above Drinking Water Directive levels (for surface water) or in the case of groundwater in excess of 50mg/l. The EA is under a duty to monitor nitrate levels so that designations can be continuously assessed and revised. The Secretary of State must then draw up action plans for each NVZ which are designed to reduce and prevent water pollution from nitrates and agricultural sources.

The future of these Regulations is uncertain as they have been the subject of challenge in the High Court. In *R v Secretary of State for the Environment and Minister of Agriculture, Fisheries and Food, ex parte Standley* 268 ENDS Report 47, several farmers challenged the designation of some of the NVZs.

The main ground of challenge was that the Government, when drawing up the NVZs, had failed to consider whether the excessive nitrate levels were caused by non-agricultural sources. It was argued, on behalf of the farmers, that this failure discriminated against agricultural users in the NVZ as the cost of reducing the nitrate concentrations to an acceptable level was to be borne wholly by the farmers when there were other users which may have been responsible for the nitrate pollution. The High Court referred the matter to the European Court of Justice as the arguments involve difficult issues of interpretation of the 1991 Directive (notably, the first occasion that the High Court has done so). The outcome of the case is unlikely to be heard for some time and the already delayed implementation of the Directive is once again clouded with uncertainty.

Planning controls

Local planning authorities have the ability to make important decisions relating to water pollution through the town and country planning system. However. it is clearly recommended in Central Government guidance, such as Circular 11/95 on planning conditions and Planning Policy Guidance Note 23, *Planning and Pollution Control* (PPG 23), that planning powers should be used mainly for locational and siting decisions and that matters about the regulation of pollution should be left to the specialist regulators to control through the specialist consent systems.

It is clear that potential water pollution arising from a proposed develop-ment is a material consideration in any planning decision, and the EA is a statutory consultee under the General Development Procedure Order in relation to many applications for planning permission. This is of great importance in relation to groundwaters, since the NRA published a set of very strong policy statements on the protection of groundwater (*Policy and Practice for the Protection of Groundwater*, NRA, 1992). In addition, planning per-mission may be refused because of inadequate sewerage in the area. Of course, the EA will also have an important role to play in the making of development plans. The generous exemptions for agricultural activities and buildings may be of significance in the context of increasing evidence of water pollution by agriculture.

Other water pollution offences

There are a number of other offences which may be committed in relation to water pollution. A few of the main ones are considered here: to these should be added offences concerning the dumping of waste, which often involve the pollution of water, and many by-laws of a local or specific nature.

Under the Water Resources Act 1991, s. 90(1), it is an offence to remove any part of the bed of inland waters so as to cause it to be carried away in suspension. Section 90(2) provides for an offence of causing or permitting vegetation to be cut or uprooted so as to fall into inland waters, and then failing to take reasonable steps to remove it. In both cases the EA may grant its consent subject to any conditions it considers appropriate. The offences are summary only, with a maximum fine of £2,500.

Under the Water Resources Act 1991, sch. 25, the EA has powers to make by-laws in relation to the washing or cleaning of anything in controlled waters, or in relation to sanitary appliances on vessels. The maximum fine for an offence under these by-laws is £2,500.

Under the Salmon and Freshwater Fisheries Act 1975, s. 4(1), it is an offence to cause or knowingly permit any liquid or solid matter to flow or be put into waters containing fish so as to cause those waters to be poisonous or injurious to fish, their food or their spawning grounds. This offence is more limited than the Water Resoures Act 1991, s. 85; it requires proof of the presence of fish and injury to them. A prosecution cannot be brought except by the EA or anyone who has obtained a certificate from the Minister of Agriculture, Fisheries and Food (or, in Wales, the Secretary of State) that they have a material interest in the waters affected. The maximum fine on summary conviction is also less than for s. 85 (£5,000 rather than £20,000) although the penalties for conviction on indictment are the same. The Water Consolidation (Consequential Provisions) Act 1991, sch. 1 provides that a consent under the 1991 Act is a defence to the offence under the 1975 Act.

Under EPA 1990, s. 140, the Secretary of State is given powers to make regulations to prohibit the importation, use, supply or storage of any substance or article for the purpose of preventing it causing pollution of the environment, or harm to the health of humans, animals or plants. This very wide power includes the power to order the disposal or treatment of restricted articles. It replaces the similar power under COPA 1974, s. 100. That section was used to make regulations banning the supply of lead weights for use by anglers (see Control of Pollution (Anglers' Lead Weights) Regulations 1986 (SI 1986 No. 1992)), prohibiting the supply and use of PCBs (see Control of Pollution (Supply and Use of Injurious Substances) Regulations 1986 (SI 1986 No. 902)), and prohibiting the supply of tri-organotin compound paints (see Control of Pollution (Anti-Fouling Paints and Treatments) Regulations 1987 (SI 1987 No. 783)). Interestingly, the regulations on anglers' lead weights have been amended as a result of the EC single internal market. The original regulations had banned the import of lead weights as well as their supply. The Control of Pollution (Anglers' Lead Weights) (Amendment) Regulations 1993 (SI 1993 No. 49) amended this so that only their supply is banned, since the Government considered, despite the clear implications of the *Danish Bottles* case (see p. 81), that the import ban could no longer be justified.

Statutory nuisances

In addition to the statutory nuisances listed in Part III of the EPA 1990 (see p. 205), two further statutory nuisances are provided for in the Public Health Act 1936, s. 259. Section 259(1)(a) provides that any pool, pond, ditch, gutter or watercourse which is in a state that is prejudicial to health or a nuisance is a statutory nuisance. This will cover small ponds and ditches which are not within the consent system, as well as controlled waters. Section 259(1)(b) covers any watercourse which is silted up or choked so as to obstruct the proper flow of water and thus causing a nuisance or which is prejudicial to health. This is limited to watercourses which are not normally navigated. The normal procedures for statutory nuisance apply to these situations, thus creating an alternative course of action for a local authority or individual wishing to clean up a grossly polluted watercourse.

Water pollution and the common law

The common law still plays a significant role in the control of water pollution. Indeed, for various technical reasons it is probably of greater use for water pollution than for other forms of pollution and may be used to produce, directly or indirectly, environmental improvements.

One right which has already been mentioned is the right of private prosecution for breaches of the criminal law. This has been available for many water pollution offences since 1985 as a result of the removal by COPA 1974 of the restrictions on it. More significant, however, are the various civil law claims that may be brought. For example, the Anglers' Cooperative Association is estimated to have been involved in over 1,000 cases involving water pollution since the Second World War. The two main remedies available are damages to compensate an owner of the river bed, the river banks, or a fishery for any losses caused, and an injunction to restrain future breaches of the law.

There are a number of reasons why water pollution cases have proved easier to bring than air pollution cases:

(a)   Causation is easier to show because of the defined channels in which water normally flows.

(b)   Many rural landowners have the money to bring an action: indeed, pollution to fisheries will often justify an action in commercial terms, as the claim by pop star Roger Daltrey for the loss of an estimated 500,000 fish from his fish farm, caused by the bursting of an upstream fertiliser storage tank, illustrates (*Beju Bop Ltd* v *Home Farm (Iwerne Minister) Ltd* [1990] Water Law 90). Damages of £500,000 were claimed, although the case was settled out of court for £150,000.

(c)   There are a number of campaigning and amenity bodies concerned with water problems, far more than are concerned with air or noise pollution.

(d)   The acquisition of evidence is more straightforward, particularly since the advent of the public registers, which may provide evidence relating to the quality of the receiving waters before and after an incident and also relating to discharges. Nevertheless, there will still be problems with an individual acquiring scientifically valid evidence (see Macrory, *Water Law*, Ch. 5:2).

Riparian rights

The usefulness of the civil law in this area stems mainly from the nature of riparian rights. Owners of land adjoining a watercourse (including estuaries), termed riparian owners, normally own the river bed, but not the water itself.

However, as a natural incident of the soil itself, they have the right to receive the water in its natural state, subject only to reasonable usage by an upstream owner for ordinary purposes (*Chasemore* v *Richards* (1859) 7 HL Cas 349). Owners of other property rights such as fisheries have the same right.

The most authoritative statement of this principle was given by Lord Macnaghten in *John Young & Co.* v *Bankier Distillery Co.* [1893] AC 691. He stated, at p. 698:

> A riparian proprietor is entitled to have the water of the stream, on the bank of which his property lies, flow down as it has been accustomed to flow down to his property, subject to the ordinary use of the flowing water by upper proprietors, and to such further use, if any, on their part in connection with their property as may be reasonable in the circumstances. Every riparian owner is thus entitled to the water of his stream, in its natural flow, without sensible diminution or increase, and without sensible alteration in its character or quality.

This means that any interference with the natural quantity or quality of the water is an actionable nuisance. The strictness of this test was shown in *John Young & Co.* v *Bankier Distillery Co.* An upstream mineowner discharged water into a stream from a mine. This altered the chemistry of the water from soft to hard and thus altered the quality of the downstream distillery's whisky. The water had not been made impure, but the distillery obtained an injunction because the nature of the water had been changed. The case illustrates the relative nature of the definition of water pollution and indeed emphasises that the common law does not lay down any absolute standards in relation to water quality. It is worth noting, however, that this test only applies where the upstream usage is not ordinary; a good example of the balancing process the law of nuisance tries to carry out.

Some of the technical difficulties relating to the law of nuisance, such as the causation question and the locality doctrine, have been neatly answered in the water pollution cases. It appears from the reasoning in *Young & Co.* v *Bankier Distillery Co.* (above) that an invasion of the natural right to water is treated as equivalent to damage to land, thus circumventing the locality doctrine. It is also clear that actual harm need not be shown, merely a 'sensible alteration', a position that is supported by *Nicholls* v *Ely Beet Sugar Factory Ltd* [1936] Ch 343, where the claim of interference with riparian rights was held to be analogous to trespass. It follows that an action can be brought against any upstream polluter, even if only one of many and responsible for only a part of the whole pollution. All that needs to be shown is that the polluter is contributing to the pollution (*Crossley and Sons Ltd* v *Lightowler* (1867) LR 2 Ch App 478).

Pollution of groundwater
Liability will also arise in nuisance for polluting percolating groundwaters, as long as causation can be shown. This was first established in *Ballard* v *Tomlinson* (1885) 29 ChD 115, where a brewery sued successfully for the

contamination of its well caused by a neighbour who used his own well for the disposal of sewage. However, the exact extent of this liability has recently been clarified by the House of Lords in *Cambridge Water Co.* v *Eastern Counties Leather plc* [1994] 2 AC 264. In this case, a water company claimed £1m damages for the pollution of one of its boreholes by spillages of organic solvents from a nearby leather tannery. These solvents had seeped into the aquifer over a number of years, resulting in water abstracted from the borehole failing the standards laid down in EC Directive 80/778 on Drinking Water by large margins. The Court of Appeal had followed *Ballard* v *Tomlinson* and decided that the tannery had interfered with a natural right incidental to the water company's ownership, that liability was strict, and that all the water company needed to do was to show causation, which it had done. This was hailed by some commentators as an acceptance of the central role of strict liability in water pollution law and a reflection of the 'polluter pays' principle. However, other observers, including those representing most potential polluters, argued that the Court of Appeal's decision raised the question of retrospective strict liability, since the spillages in issue had taken place many years previously. In this regard, the judge at first instance had decided that it was not foreseeable at the time the spillages took place that they might lead to the contamination of the public water supply.

The House of Lords allowed the appeal on the ground that, following Lord Reid's comments in *The Wagon Mound (No. 2)* [1967] 1 AC 617, the recovery of damages in private nuisance depends on foreseeability by the defendant of the type of damage that occurred. It also considered that the same foreseeability requirement applied to liability under the rule in *Rylands* v *Fletcher*. *Ballard* v *Tomlinson*, where this point did not arise, was distinguished.

This decision places significant restrictions on liability for *past* activities. However, it does not necessarily restrict the recovery of damages, or the imposition of an injunction, in cases where polluting activities *currently* cause damage to groundwaters or, indeed, where the cause of the pollution was recent. It must also be pointed out that liability in nuisance is personal in the sense that, even if the original polluter is liable for pollution damage, it does not follow that a subsequent purchaser of the site would also be liable. But, purchasers of potentially contaminated land must bear in mind the possible implications of cases such as *Goldman* v *Hargrave* [1967] 1 AC 645, which establish that there is liability for 'adopting' a nuisance in certain circumstances.

Other claims

Other common law claims may also be available. In *Jones* v *Llanrwst Urban District Council* [1911] 1 Ch 393, the owner of a river bed claimed successfully in trespass for deposits of solid wastes. In *Scott-Whitehead* v *National Coal Board* (1985) 53 P & CR 263, Southern Water Authority was held liable in negligence for the loss of a farmer's potato crop. The loss was caused by saline water abstracted in accordance with an abstraction licence granted by the Authority: the salinity in turn was caused by an upstream colliery discharge permitted by the Authority, which was not being diluted properly in the circumstances of the 1976 drought. The judge held the Authority liable for not warning the farmer of the potential damage to his crop if he used excessively saline water, although the exact reasoning behind this decision must now be reassessed in the light of the restriction on the liability of public authorities for negligence in the exercise of their duties in *Murphy* v *Brentwood District Council* [1991] 1 AC 398.

Lastly, it is often stated that a prescriptive right to acquire an easement to pollute can be acquired. Whilst this remains true as a matter of principle, such an occurrence will be rare owing to the fact that it is not possible to acquire a prescriptive right where the act relied upon to gain the right is illegal. In most water pollution cases the polluting activity will be illegal.

Remedies

Damages will be recoverable for any loss to the person whose rights have been infringed. This will include such things as any clean-up costs, the cost of restocking the water with fish, any loss of profits from subscriptions for such things as fishing rights and, in some circumstances, loss of amenity (see *Bruton* v *Clarke* [1994] Water Law 145).

Injunctions are also available for water pollution, though they will normally be suspended to allow the defendants time to correct matters. For example, in *Pride of Derby and Derbyshire Angling Association Ltd* v *British Celanese Ltd* [1953] Ch 149, injunctions and damages were obtained against British Celanese Ltd (for industrial effluent), Derby Corporation (for untreated sewage), and the British Electricity Authority (for thermal pollution from a power station).

It is important to note that acting within the terms of a discharge consent does not act as a defence to a civil action, since the private law system operates separately from the public regulatory mechanisms. This is made explicit in the Water Resources Act 1991, s. 100(b), but it can also be implied from the important decision in *Wheeler* v *J.J. Saunders Ltd* [1996] Ch 19, which decided that a planning permission cannot license what is otherwise a nuisance.

FIFTEEN
Disposal of waste to sewers

In this book disposals of waste to the sewerage system are dealt with in a self-contained chapter because they are a separate form of waste disposal with their own particular and unique regulatory regime. The treatment of wastes at sewage works is an integral part of general policies on waste disposal and protection of the natural environment. The alternative to such disposal (waste minimisation apart) is often some form of direct discharge to the environment, so sewage treatment offers an important weapon in the search for the best practicable environmental option (BPEO).

There are other links with environmental protection that justify detailed consideration of sewage disposal. Sewage treatment is only an intermediate step in the ultimate disposal of waste and the operators of sewers and sewage works must dispose of their own wastes. This will often (though not always) be after a treatment process and will involve a combination of liquid discharges into watercourses or the sea, the dumping of sludge on land or at sea, and incineration. Indeed, sewage works have been responsible for the low quality of many of our inland and coastal waters (see *The Quality of Rivers, Canals and Estuaries in England and Wales*, NRA, 1991). The Government announced a commitment to phase out the dumping of sewage sludge at sea by 1998 at the Third International Conference for the Protection of the North Sea in March 1990.

Sewerage and sewage treatment have always been closely related with the water industry and most books have tended to treat discharges to sewers as a part of the law on water pollution. This can be explained on the grounds that discharges to sewers are liquid and that most sewage works themselves discharge into watercourses, but it also relates to the historical institutional connections. Sewerage, public water supply and the prevention of water pollution have often been carried out by the same bodies, most notably between 1974 and 1989 when the 10 regional water authorities in England and Wales carried out all functions in relation to water and sewage on an integrated basis. This included regulating discharges both to the sewers and to surface waters.

Since 1 September 1989 there has been a reversion to a system of split responsibilities. Private water and sewerage undertakers provide the public water supply and own and operate the sewerage network and the sewage works, as well as regulating discharges to sewers, whilst the EA (originally the NRA) regulates abstractions from and discharges to the natural environment and has responsibility for combating surface water pollution.

Trade effluent discharges

The sewerage undertaker plays its most important environmental protection role in the regulation of trade effluent discharges, although since 1989 certain dangerous discharges have been regulated by HMIP and now the EA (see below). Measured in terms of pollutant load, a far greater quantity of industrial effluent is discharged into the sewers than directly into surface waters or by any other disposal route.

The regulatory regime relating to discharges to sewers is an old and somewhat rudimentary one, though there have been periodic developments designed to bring it more up-to-date. It involves a rather basic system of individualised consents set by the operators of the sewers, involving little input from other bodies or from the public at any of the various stages of policy-making, standard-setting, consent-setting or enforcement. The legislation is contained in the Water Industry Act 1991, to which all section numbers refer.

It is a criminal offence to discharge any trade effluent from trade premises into sewers unless a trade effluent consent is obtained from the sewerage undertaker (s. 118). 'Trade effluent' and 'trade premises' are defined widely in s. 141 to include all liquid discharges from industry, shops, research establishments, launderettes and agriculture, except for domestic sewage. It is also an offence to breach the terms of a consent. This is a unique system of control in that it is the only example in this country of a private body exercising regulatory functions with regard to environmental protection.

Applying for a trade effluent consent

The discharger applies for a trade effluent consent by serving a trade effluent notice on the sewerage undertaker at least two months prior to the commencement of the discharge. This notice is effectively an application and must state the nature and composition of the proposed effluent, the maximum daily volume and the maximum rate of discharge in order to enable the sewerage undertaker to establish its likely effect.

The sewerage undertaker then has a discretion whether to grant or refuse consent, though if the sewerage system can cope with the discharge, it is normal for consent to be granted subject to conditions. The scope of these conditions is laid down in s. 121. They may include such matters as the place of discharge, the nature, temperature and composition of the discharge (including requirements as to the elimination or maximum concentration of any specified constituent), the rate and timing of discharges, and ancillary matters such as the fixing of meters to register the volume of the discharge, the monitoring of the nature and volume of the discharge and the keeping of records. Most importantly, conditions on the payment of effluent charges will also be included.

It is not permissible to attach conditions which require the fitting of specified treatment plant. The normal practice is to specify the effluent standards that must be met and to leave it to the discharger to determine how to meet those standards, albeit often with advice from the sewerage under-taker. One reason for this is the widespread belief that most effluent is better and more efficiently treated at the sewage works than at each factory, but it also reflects the policy of preserving some element of choice for producers.

How are consents set?

Since discharges to sewers are distinct from other discharges in being to an artificial environment, the matters that are taken into account in setting a consent differ from other consents and licences. In particular, environmental protection is only one factor.

The objectives of trade effluent control are set out clearly in a booklet produced by the Water Authorities Association in September 1986 entitled *Trade Effluent Discharged to the Sewer*. They are that the system of control seeks:

(a)   to protect the sewerage system and the personnel who work in it;

(b)   to protect the sewage works and their efficient operation (for example, most sewage works operate by a biological process and care has to be taken not to neutralise that process);

(c)   to protect the environment generally from the residues of the sewage treatment process or from direct discharges from parts of the system such as storm drains; and

(d)   to ensure that dischargers pay a reasonable charge for the cost of the treatment.

In addition, the booklet stresses that it is important for correct information on discharges to be kept, so that dischargers can know how to improve their trade effluent control and sewerage undertakers can plan for future sewerage provision and operate the treatment process efficiently.

With these factors in mind, the consent will in general be set by reference to the receiving capabilities of the sewer and sewage works. If the works are already overburdened, the consent may be refused or subject to tight limits, whereas if there is spare capacity at the works, the limits will be much more generous. Certain pollutants, such as heavy metals or persistent chemicals, may be unsuitable for sewage treatment and may be banned from the discharge. The discharger may then have to pre-treat the effluent to remove these constituents, or find an alternative method of disposal. Other relevant matters are taken into account, such as the sewerage undertaker's own potential liability for discharges from the works under the Water Resources Act 1991 and the requirements of EC law.

The sewerage undertaker has a power to vary a consent unilaterally by giving two months' notice to the discharger (s. 124). This enables it to take steps to meet the terms of the consent for the sewage works set by the EA. Since 1989, variation has been a common occurrence, as sewerage undertakers have renegotiated consents inherited from the regional water authorities and established a more uniform system for their areas and also as the NRA and now the EA have tightened consents relating to discharges from sewage works. It should be noted, however, that there is no power for the sewerage undertaker to revoke a consent.

Variation of a consent is, however, possible only after two years have elapsed from the grant of the consent or the last variation. Exceptionally, a variation may be made within this period if it is necessary to provide proper protection for people likely to be affected by the discharge. In this situation, compensation will be payable to the discharger unless the variation was necessary as a result of a change of circumstances unforeseeable at the time of the grant of the consent or its last variation (s. 125).

The discharger has a right of appeal to the Director General of Water Services (i.e., to OFWAT) against a refusal or variation of consent or the imposition of conditions, except that there is no appeal against trade effluent charges (ss. 122, 126). An appeal against a deemed refusal may also be brought if no decision is given on the trade effluent notice within two months. (It used to be the case that such a failure to determine an application led to an automatic consent, but that rule was removed by the Water Act 1989.) As with planning appeals, an appeal is effectively a rehearing and the Director General may make any decision that the sewerage undertaker could have made. There is a further right of appeal to the High Court on a matter of law.

An alternative to seeking a consent is for the discharger and the sewerage undertaker to reach an agreement for the reception or disposal of trade effluent under s. 129. Such an agreement may provide for the discharger to pay for works necessary to treat the wastes, such as an extension to a sewage works.

Trade effluent charges

Trade effluent charges are levied for discharges to sewers and a charges scheme may be made under the Water Industry Act 1991, s. 143. All the sewerage undertakers currently use a similar formula based on the so-called 'Mogden Formula', in which charges are calculated according to the volume and strength of the effluent, as measured by the chemical oxygen demand (COD) and the solids content. Dischargers are therefore advised to consider whether their processes can be changed so as to minimise wastes, and thus costs. No extra charges are currently levied by the sewerage undertakers in relation to metals or other hazardous items: undesirable levels of these are controlled by the consent limits rather than by charging mechanisms. However, levels of charges are rising as a consequence of the fact that sewerage undertakers are themselves liable for charges for their own discharges from sewage works. The charging system thus operates in tandem with the consent system to reduce discharges. To a limited extent it encourages the reduction of pollution, although it does not make dischargers fully responsible for the environmental costs of their discharges. It remains to be seen whether a system of incentive charging will be introduced in this area: that would require legislation.

Public participation

Public rights in relation to the trade effluent system are very limited. There is no right for a member of the public to be informed of an application for a trade effluent consent and no right to participate in the decision whether to grant one, or in any appeal. Under the Water Industry Act 1991, s. 196, all consents, variations, agreements and directions by the sewerage undertaker or the Director General, and all decisions by the Secretary of State (effectively the EA in this context) must be placed on a public register.

However, this is a limited right, since there is no public right to information on any samples taken. Indeed, it is a criminal offence under s. 206 for an employee of the sewerage undertaker to disclose information furnished under the Act. There is also no right of private prosecution for breach of a consent, except by a 'person aggrieved' or with the consent of the Attorney-General. It remains to be seen whether the Environmental Information Regulations 1992 (SI 1992 No. 3240) will confer wider rights (see p. 172).

'Red List' substances

In order to ensure compliance with EC Directives, such as 76/464 on Dangerous Substances in Water, an additional control has been introduced for specified dangerous substances. The Secretary of State is empowered to prescribe certain substances or processes for which the EA is effectively made the consenting body. Currently 24 such substances are listed in sch. 1 to the Trade Effluents (Prescribed Processes and Substances) Regulations 1989 (SI 1989 No. 1156, as amended by SI 1990 No. 1629), and five processes involving asbestos or chloroform are listed in sch. 2. The 24 prescribed substances consist of the 'Red List', plus carbon tetrachloride.

All discharges where any of these substances is present in more than background concentration, or where a prescribed process is carried on, must be referred to the EA, which may then issue a direction (against which there is no appeal) to the sewerage undertaker on whether to grant a consent and on any conditions it might impose. Before deciding an application, the EA must provide the sewerage undertaker and the applicant with an opportunity to make representations. The same procedures apply where more than 30 kg per year of trichloroethylene or perchloroethylene is discharged (Trade Effluent (Prescribed Processes and Substances) Regulations (SI 1992 No. 339)).

Existing discharges covered by the regulations are also reviewable by the EA. As with ordinary trade effluent discharges, a review may not normally be made within two years of the previous review. However, review is possible within two years if there has been a contravention of a consent or agreement, to give effect to an international or EC obligation, or to protect public health or aquatic flora and fauna. Compensation is payable in some of these circumstances, unless the review resulted from a change of circumstances unforeseeable at the time of the setting of the consent or the previous review.

This system is affected by the introduction of integrated pollution control in the EPA 1990. Any process discharging significant amounts of 'Red List' substances will normally be a prescribed process for the purposes of integrated pollution control and therefore will require an authorisation from the EA. In these circumstances a trade effluent consent will be required as well as an authorisation.

Enforcement

The penalty for the offence of discharging without consent, or in breach of a condition, is, on summary conviction, a fine not exceeding £5,000, and on conviction on indictment, an unlimited fine (ss. 118, 121).

Enforcement of the legislation is by the sewerage undertaker. In the past this has led to a conciliatory approach to enforcement, since officials have seen themselves as problem-solvers rather than as police officers. Indeed, one of the main surveys of enforcement attitudes (Richardson, Ogus and Burrows, *Policing Pollution,* 1983) was a survey of trade effluent control officers.

Discharges from sewage works

Under the Water Resources Act 1991, sewerage undertakers have consents set for their own discharges into controlled waters and may be prosecuted by the EA or any individual if they breach them. They are responsible for all discharges from their sewers or works, subject only to a defence that the breach was caused by an illegal discharge to the sewer that they could not reasonably have been expected to prevent (Water Resources Act 1991, s. 87(2) and *National Rivers Authority* v *Yorkshire Water Services Ltd* [1995] 1 AC 444). This means that sewerage undertakers are ultimately responsible if they are unable to treat adequately discharges they have permitted. They thus have an incentive to restrict discharges to those which are treatable.

Domestic sewage discharges

Some discharges are prohibited entirely by the Water Industry Act 1991, s. 111 (although a trade effluent consent is a defence). These are discharges of anything liable to damage the sewer, or to stop its flow, or to prejudice the sewage works treatment; any chemicals, or any liquids over 110°F, which will be dangerous or a nuisance; and any petroleum spirit, including motor oils. For example, drainage of used car oils is an offence under this section. The maximum penalties are, on summary conviction, a fine of up to £5,000, and, on conviction on indictment, an unlimited fine and/or up to two years' imprisonment.

Otherwise, there is no restriction on discharges of domestic sewage. There is a right of connection to the public sewer conferred on owners and occupiers by the Water Industry Act 1991, s. 106, with very limited powers of refusal. These do not include the potential overloading of the system: as Upjohn J stated in *Smeaton* v *Ilford Corporation* [1954] Ch 450, 'they [i.e., the sewerage undertakers] are bound to permit occupiers of premises to make connections to the sewer and to discharge their sewage therein'. Powers to requisition new sewers for domestic purposes are set out in the Water Industry Act 1991, s. 98.

However, it is permissible for the local planning authority to refuse planning permission on the ground that the local sewage works are overburdened or inadequate, since that is a material consideration. Alternatively, it could seek some planning gain in relation to the provision of sewers by the use of conditions or planning obligations under the Town and Country Planning Act 1990 (see Chapter 9 for the limitations on this course of action).

SIXTEEN

The conservation of nature

This chapter looks at the laws which set out specifically to protect plants, animals and habitat. This has become a popular subject in recent years, partly as a result of the dramatic growth of interest in all things connected with nature and conservation, but also as a consequence of the appalling rate of decline in and loss of the natural environment. The Wildlife and Countryside Act 1981, the major piece of legislation in this area, reflects this popularity: it still holds the record for the number of amendments tabled to a Parliamentary Bill and its controversial passage brought nature conservation firmly into the arena of political debate, where it has stayed.

At the outset, a distinction must be made between nature conservation and matters of amenity and landscape, which are dealt with in Chapter 17. Even though these topics are often closely related, it is possible to distinguish between those laws which are justified as a matter of straight wildlife protection and those which relate more to human uses of the environment. It must also be borne in mind that the preservation of a balanced ecosystem and the survival of many species depends as much on the responses to the other environmental threats covered in this book, such as pollution and development, as on the specific methods of protection mentioned in this chapter, which would probably be useless if applied in isolation.

History

A brief history of nature conservation will help to explain the current structure of the law. Up to less than 200 years ago, the need to protect wildlife was normally perceived solely in human terms, such as the desirability of preserving game and quarry species and protected areas in which to hunt them. There is little doubt that an incidental benefit of this human-centred approach was the protection of other animals and plants and the preservation of whole areas (for example the New Forest) in a fairly natural state, but there were few laws designed specifically to protect wildlife.

From Victorian times, the tendency was to enact legislation outlawing unwelcome activities in response to particular problems as they were identified. The rationale for this intervention was as much based on concern about cruelty as on any positive desire to conserve nature for its own sake. Some good examples are the Sea Birds Protection Acts of 1869, 1872 and 1880, passed to combat the slaughter of birds at places such as Flamborough Head, and various pieces of legislation intended to restrict the international trade in feathers for clothing and hats. However, there was no grand design underlying these restrictions. The weight of conservation fell on voluntary organisations — indeed Britain had the world's first developed conservation movement — and no official bodies were established to monitor or enforce the legislation that did exist. This unplanned approach persisted; the Protection of Birds Act 1954, which established protection for birds that was far stronger than that for other animals and plants, was a Private Member's Bill brought forward on behalf of the Royal Society for the Protection of Birds.

These voluntary organisations gradually developed a strategy which became, and remains, the typical approach to nature conservation. This is the designation of selected areas or sites that are specially protected. The first modern uses of this technique related to the protection of common lands for recreational purposes, but it was soon used for the development of nature reserves, even though at this time they were seen as a somewhat peripheral interest of the nature conservation movement. For example, the National Trust acquired parts of Wicken Fen in 1899, the Norfolk Naturalists Trust was founded to buy Cley Marshes in 1926 and the Royal Society for the Protection of Birds bought its first nature reserve (on Romney Marsh) in 1929. However, in the absence of any legislative protection for such sites, their safety lay in the exercise of ordinary property rights. After all, the property owner's freedom to exclude others and to use the land for any purposes is one mechanism for controlling land use in limited areas. The limitations of this approach are well illustrated by the RSPB's first reserve, which had to be abandoned when drainage activities on neighbouring land destroyed its natural interest.

The post-war period

In the immediate post-war period, the site designation approach was adopted as a matter of national policy. The beginning of the modern age of nature conservation can be traced to that time in the publication of two influential reports, *Conservation of Nature in England and Wales* from the Wildlife Conservation Special Committee (the Huxley Committee, Cmd 7122) and *Nature Reserves in Scotland* from the Scottish Wild Life Conservation Committee (the Ritchie Committee, Cmd 7184), many (though not all) of whose recommendations were accepted and acted upon.

A specialist national nature conservation body — the Nature Conservancy — was established and one of its main roles was to create a series of protected sites across the nation, rather than the somewhat random series produced by private acquisition. The two main habitat protection measures, the national nature reserve (NNR) and the site of special scientific interest (SSSI), both date from this period. The scientific basis of nature conservation was emphasised and it was linked firmly to education and research on the natural environment. Nature conservation was also split from amenity, recreation and landscape matters, which were given their own separate institutions and laws, and it is worth reflecting that the powers for nature conservation at that time were both stronger and met with far less opposition than those for recreation in the countryside.

Current policy

Many of the features of this post-war structure remain, but the climate in which they operate has changed radically, with the result that many of the similarities the current system has with that structure are illusory. There have been devastating changes in both the urban and rural environments and these have altered the role of site designation dramatically from an educational to a safeguarding one. One result has been the expansion of the NNR and SSSI system way beyond that envisaged, or indeed considered necessary, by the Huxley and Ritchie Committees, in order to ensure that at least a basic pool of key sites is protected.

Another result is that general environmental awareness has now shifted the focus of policy away from the designation and protection of certain key sites towards the protection of the wider countryside. It is now accepted that there is little future in having isolated and ever-decreasing areas of protected wildlife in an otherwise barren countryside, and so nature conservation is increasingly seen as a factor to weigh in the balance when considering all rural policies. This adds to the political dimension which nature conservation has rapidly acquired. It also leads nature conservation law into a potential head-on collision with traditional views of property and personal rights.

In addition, the enjoyment of nature has emerged as a major leisure pursuit, blurring the distinction in the public mind and in policy between nature conservation as a scientifically justified discipline and as a recreation. There has been an undreamt-of increase in voluntary activity in relation to the countryside, resulting in large numbers of reserves and sites protected by voluntary bodies and non-statutory designations. There has also been an increase in international activity on the natural environment, mainly through conventions such as the Washington Convention on International Trade in Endangered Species (usually known as CITES), and the pressure on the Government to carry out internationally agreed policies is immense. Nowhere is it greater than in relation to the EC, which has important Directives on Wild Birds and on Habitats. The Wild Birds Directive (79/409) required changes in British law and led to the Wildlife and Countryside Act 1981, effectively the first major Government sponsored measure on nature conservation and one that revealed some severe differences in philosophy between the political parties, whilst the Habitats Directive (92/43) has led to a significant increase in protection for certain internationally important sites.

Types of legal protection

From this brief historical survey it can be seen that the protections offered by the law can be divided into four rough categories:

(a)   protecting individual animals and plants;
(b)   habitat protection through the designation of key sites;
(c)   the use of grants and incentives; and
(d)   incidental protection.

(a)   Protecting individual animals and plants

This is still done on a somewhat ad hoc basis, though a degree of coherence is provided by the Wildlife and Countryside Act 1981. Nature conservation is not the only aim being pursued: there is still a large element of protection against cruelty, and there are important exceptions relating to game and quarry species.

(b)   Habitat protection through the designation of key sites

This has been a favoured technique, and a bewildering array of legislative designations has built up, the special rules and protections differing for each one. There is quite a degree of overlap here and many designations are cumulative. In *Nature Conservation in Great Britain* (1984), the Nature Conservancy Council set out its policy that 10% of the country be covered by one designation or another, so that a bedrock of essential sites may be protected.

(c)   The use of grants and incentives in the wider countryside

The realisation that the protection of isolated sites is insufficient, both in scientific terms and in terms of the expectations of people who are interested in nature, has led to the search for general policies conducive to nature conservation, especially as part of agriculture and forestry policy. This is all part of the general trend towards integrating environmental considerations into all aspects of policy.

(d)   Incidental protection

It remains clear that nature conservation interests are often served by taking advantage of legal powers which were not designed with nature conservation in mind. The best example is the purchase of private nature reserves by voluntary bodies, thus taking advantage of ordinary property rights, but another good example is the nature conservation value of the large tracts of land used for Ministry of Defence training grounds.

The nature conservation agencies

In 1949, on the basis of recommendations contained in the Huxley and Ritchie Reports, the Nature Conservancy was established by Royal Charter. This was a scientifically-orientated national body with responsibility throughout Great Britain for nature conservation matters ranging from education and research to the designation and management of national nature reserves. Under the Nature Conservancy Council Act 1973, this body became the Nature Conservancy Council (NCC), an autonomous body independent of government departments, but whose Council members were appointed by the Secretaries of State. However, the new NCC was split from its active research ecology arm (this is now the Institute of Terrestrial Ecology), a separation which resulted in a greater concentration on its remaining roles of advice and site protection. When coupled with the increasingly political flavour of nature conservation in the 1970s and 1980s, this turned the NCC into what could almost be described as a pressure group within Government.

Under the EPA 1990, from 1 April 1991 the NCC (and hence responsibilty for nature conservation) was split into three national bodies; an NCC for England (called English Nature); a Countryside Council for Wales, combining the functions of the NCC and the Countryside Commission in the principality (i.e., combining nature conservation with amenity and recreational matters); and an NCC for Scotland. In the case of Scotland, the position was further changed by the Natural Heritage (Scotland) Act 1991. This Act established a new body called Scottish Natural Heritage, effectively through a merger of the NCC for Scotland with the Countryside Commission for Scotland. In the EPA, the three national bodies — English Nature, the Countryside Council for Wales and Scottish Natural Heritage — inherited most of the responsibilities of the NCC within the appropriate geographical area and thus have very similar powers and duties relating to nature conservation to each other. For ease of explanation, the name 'NCC' is retained throughout this book to refer to the relevant national body in its own area.

Each of the three national bodies is established on a similar basis to the old NCC (see EPA 1990, sch. 6). They receive annual grant in aid from the Treasury and have to submit annual reports and accounts to Parliament. Council members are appointed by the appropriate Secretary of State. They are the Government's statutory advisers on nature conservation issues, with specific responsibilities for advising on species and habitat protection, the dissemination of knowledge about nature conservation, the support and conduct of research into nature conservation, and the safeguarding of protected sites (see EPA 1990, s. 132). In particular, they are responsible for the selection and management of NNRs and for the designation and oversight of SSSIs. They are also statutory consultees in relation to a large number of decisions made by other public bodies, including decisions on applications for planning permission and for pollution consents. In one sense, therefore, the three bodies are classic quangos and could be said to be largely unaccountable for many of their decisions: but they could also be said to be accountable to the interests of wildlife and ecology.

The dismantling of the NCC was undoubtedly the most controversial part of the EPA 1990. The Conservative Government sought to justify it on the ground of administrative efficiency, but the result has been to add to the adminstrative complexity (and thus to the administrative cost) of nature conservation activities. A further justification was that power was devolved to Scotland and Wales and away from a GB body based in Peterborough. Whilst there was a significant degree of support for such devolution, particularly in Scotland, this explanation scarcely fits in with the Conservative Government's general record on devolution of powers. The clear impression that is left is that the main motivation behind the splitting up of the NCC was the political desirability of reducing the NCC's power in Scotland, where it had been active in opposing such things as afforestation of the unique flow country of Caithness and Sutherland.

Critics of the dismantling of the NCC point to the irrationality of dividing responsibility for nature conservation along national borders, when ecological criteria demand that a wider approach is adopted. They also stress the fact that three smaller bodies are inevitably weaker than one large one. In addition, there is a significant possibility that uniformity in the implementation of the law will be lost. This follows inexorably from the wide discretions in the legislation and the fact that in Scotland and Wales in particular there is a greater willingness to accept that economic factors outweigh nature conservation considerations. As the last Chairman of the NCC, Sir William Wilkinson, put it when presenting the NCC's 16th Annual Report, 'As a result of the Government's attitude, nature conservation has been set back three, or possibly up to five, years'.

The controversy over the splitting up of the NCC led to the establishment in the EPA 1990 of a further GB-wide body. There was initial opposition to such an idea from the Government, but during the debates on the Bill a separate Joint Nature Conservation Committee emerged. The final form of this body is provided for in sch. 7. It has few executive functions, but carries out important roles in relation to the international responsibilities of the old NCC (e.g., under the Ramsar Convention and other international agreements), matters affecting Great Britain as a whole, and the retention of common standards throughout Great Britain (for example, common criteria for the designation of SSSIs). Since it is really a committee of the three national bodies, the Joint Nature Conservation Committee relies on them for its funding, staffing and other resources. It consists of an independent chair and three other independent people appointed by the Secretary of State, together with two representatives from each of the three national bodies and the chair of the English Countryside Commission. Two non-voting members are appointed by the Department of the Environment for Northern Ireland.

The protection of individual animals and plants

The common law is generally unsympathetic to wild creatures, according them no rights of their own. However, property rights may usefully be exercised in order to protect them. Wild animals are subject to the qualified ownership of the landowner whose land they are on, whilst wild plants are part of the land itself. As a result, wild animals and plants have no common law protection against the landowner. But anyone else who kills or injures a wild animal or picks a wild plant commits the torts of trespass and interference with property. Whilst the normal remedy would be damages for the value of the item taken (and thus is of little practical use), it would be possible to seek an injunction to restrain continued breaches. An owner of a nature reserve could in theory use these property rights to protect against threats to the wildlife on it. In addition, a person who uproots plants may commit the crimes of theft and criminal damage, though there is an exception in the Theft Act 1968, s. 4(3) for picking flowers, fruit, foliage and fungi.

As a consequence of the limitations of the common law, the main protection for wild creatures is statutory. The Wildlife and Countryside Act 1981, Part I, contains the bulk of the law in this area, although the Conservation (Natural Habitats etc.) Regulations 1994 (SI 1994 No. 2716) have made some changes to ensure compliance with the Habitats Directive 92/43. Three more specific conservation Acts are the Conservation of Seals Act 1970, the Protection of Badgers Act 1992 and the Wild Mammals (Protection) Act 1996. There are numerous pieces of legislation relating to hunted species, such as deer, game birds, wildfowl, rabbits and of course fish, though in all these Acts protection of individual animals is incidental. Reference to specialist books is recommended.

The chosen method of control is to establish blanket criminal offences of interfering with specified wildlife, together with a long list of exceptions and defences for acceptable activities, many of which require permission or a licence from an official body. The strongest provisions relate to wild birds (a legacy of the historical influence of the voluntary bodies here, but also a result of the EC Directive on Wild Birds 79/409, which requires certain legislative protections) in the sense that they are reverse listed — i.e., the Act applies unless they are exempted in the Schedules covering pest and quarry species. Animals and plants are covered only if specifically listed in other Schedules. As with all Schedules under the Act, the Secretary of State has powers to vary them by order to include or exclude species (s. 22), and this power has been exercised fairly frequently to take account of changes in the conservation status of the species concerned. The Joint Nature Conservation Committee has a specific duty to carry out a quinquennial review of schs. 5 and 8, which deal with protected animals and plants respectively, although its advice is not binding on the Secretary of State.

Wild birds

It is an offence intentionally to kill, injure or take any wild bird and this is backed up by offences of intentionally taking, damaging or destroying a nest whilst it is in use or being built and intentionally taking or destroying eggs (s. 1(1)). It is also an offence to be in possession of a wild bird or egg, live or dead (s. 1(2)). There are further offences relating to illegal methods of killing or taking wild birds (s. 5) and the sale or advertising for sale of wild birds (s. 6). For these purposes a bird is presumed to be wild unless proved otherwise.

Birds are divided into two categories. Rarer birds are listed in sch. 1 and are specially protected. This means that the maximum penalty for committing any of these offences is increased from the normal £1,000 to £5,000 (s. 1(4)). In addition, intentionally disturbing a Schedule 1 bird on or near its nest, or disturbing its dependent young, is an offence (s. 1(5)).

Areas may be designated as bird sanctuaries by the Secretary of State, but only with the consent or acquiescence of the owners and occupiers. By-laws may be made for bird sanctuaries which create extra offences, including unauthorised access to the site (s. 3).

There are a number of exceptions and defences to these various offences. Game birds (i.e., pheasant, partridge, grouse and ptarmigan) are excluded from the protection provided by the Act, apart from that relating to illegal methods of killing or taking them (s. 27). Wildfowl listed in sch. 2, Part I may be killed or taken outside the close season (s. 2(1)). (The close season can be varied by the Secretary of State and there is also a power to provide for special protection periods in the event of bad weather in the open season.) Pest species listed in sch. 2, Part II may be killed or taken and their nests or eggs destroyed, but only by the owner or occupier of the land or any other authorised person (s. 2(2)).

Under s. 4, there are defences relating to the killing of injured birds and where the action is an 'incidental result of a lawful operation and could not reasonably have been avoided', or where it is necessary for crop protection, disease prevention or the protection of public health and safety. None of these defences requires permission, though the last three are only available to owners and occupiers and other authorised persons.

Section 16 also includes a long list of further exceptions which apply if a licence has been obtained from the appropriate official authority. It includes such things as the carrying out of research, educational activities, ringing of birds, falconry and keeping bird or egg collections.

Animals

Only the animals listed in sch. 5 are protected by the legislation. This includes all bats, reptiles and amphibians, but only the rarest mammals, fish, butterflies and other forms of life.

For those animals which are protected, there is a range of offences similar to those for wild birds. It is an offence intentionally to kill, injure or take any scheduled wild animal (s. 9(1)), or to have in one's possession any such animal, live or dead, or any part of one (s. 9(2)). Additional offences relate to the sale or advertisement for sale of wild animals (s. 9(5)), illegal methods of killing or taking any wild animal (s. 11(1)), and illegal methods of killing or taking those animals listed in sch. 6 (s. 11(2)). There is also an offence of intentionally damaging, destroying or obstructing any structure or place used for shelter or protection by a sch. 5 animal, or disturbing such an animal whilst it is occupying such a structure (s. 9(4)). This provision is of greatest significance for the protection of bats roosting in such typical places as attics, outbuildings, caves and belfries, since they cannot be disturbed by, for example, rebuilding or timber treatment unless the NCC is notified in advance. For all these offences the maximum penalty is £5,000. In ss. 10 and 16 there are similar provisions relating to defences and licences to those available for wild birds.

In addition, the Conservation (Natural Habitats etc.) Regulations 1994 (SI 1994 No. 2716) create some further offences in relation to the animals defined as 'European protected species', which are listed in sch. 2 to the Regulations (this is a short list which includes all native bats, the dormouse, the great crested newt, the otter, the large blue butterfly and a few other species). In order to ensure compliance with the Habitats Directive 92/43, the

Government has chosen to set out the requirements of the Directive in full, rather than seek to amend the existing legislation. The result is that the Regulations cover similar ground to the 1981 Act, but with some occasional subtle changes in wording to make the offences wider: for example, it is an offence under reg. 39 deliberately to disturb an animal of a European protected species or deliberately to take or destroy the eggs of such an animal.

There is more general protection for wild mammals which are not covered under the Wildlife and Countryside Act 1981. Under the Wild Mammals (Protection) Act 1996 it is an offence to commit a wide range of cruel acts to any wild mammal with intent to inflict unnecessary suffering. There are defences if the acts constituted a mercy killing or were otherwise lawful (e.g., trapping or the use of poisons). The maximum fine is £5,000 per animal affected. The operation of the Act is somewhat restricted by the range of defences and the need to prove the mental element of the offence but it does at least bring a degree of parity in the law relating to domestic animals and that relating to wild mammals.

Badgers

Badgers are given special protection under their own legislation. This has been developed over many years and is now consolidated in the Protection of Badgers Act 1992. The general scheme is similar to that for animals protected under the Wildlife and Countryside Act 1981, sch. 5, but there are some unique features to the provisions. It is an offence to do any of the following: wilfully kill, injure or take a badger, or attempt any of those things (s. 1(1)); possess a dead badger (s. 1(3)); cruelly ill-treat a badger, use badger tongs, or dig for a badger (s. 2); sell or have possession of a live badger (s. 4); mark or attach a marking device to a badger, except under licence (s. 5). In recognition of the evidential problems thrown up in prosecutions for the barbaric activity of badger baiting, in relation to the attempt offences under s. 1(1) and the offence of digging for a badger, the burden of proof is effectively reversed. Once there is reasonable evidence of the offence it is up to the defendant to prove that no offence has been committed. For all these offences there is a defence if a licence is obtained from the appropriate authority (s. 10).

There is a further, very important, offence of interference with a badger sett that shows signs of current use (s. 3). This covers such things as damaging the sett, destroying it, obstructing access to it, causing a dog to enter it, or disturbing a badger that is in occupation. The provisions are unusually strong in that, even where there is a valid planning permission, a separate licence will be required under s. 10 if the carrying out of the permission would involve damage or disturbance to a sett. This has led to a situation where the existence of a badger sett is a very significant factor if development is envisaged. There is a general defence if the action was the incidental result of a lawful operation and could not reasonably have been avoided, and a more specific defence in relation to temporary interference in the course of fox-hunting (s. 8).

The maximum fine for all the offences under the 1992 Act is £5,000 per badger affected, and in relation to most of the offences a prison term of up to six months may also be imposed. If a dog is used in connection with the offence, the court may order its destruction or disposal.

Plants

Section 13 makes it an offence for anyone other than the owner, occupier or other authorised person intentionally to uproot any wild plant. In addition, it is an offence for anyone intentionally to pick, uproot or destroy any of the numerous species of rare wild plants listed in sch. 8. The sale or advertisement for sale of sch. 8 plants is also an offence. Once again, there are similar provisions relating to defences and licences to those available for wild birds.

In addition, the Conservation (Natural Habitats etc.) Regulations 1994 (SI 1994 No. 2716) create some further offences in relation to the small number of European protected species of plants which are listed in sch. 4. As with the offences concerning European protected species of animals, in order to ensure compliance with the Habitats Directive 92/43, the offences are similar to, but slightly wider than, those in the 1981 Act: for example, it is an offence deliberately to collect or cut a wild plant of a European protected species.

Introducing foreign animals or plants to Great Britain

A final section of the 1981 Act worth mentioning is s. 14, which makes it an offence to introduce into the wild any animal not normally resident in Great Britain or any wild animal or plant listed in sch. 9. This section aims to protect against further repetitions of the ecological havoc wrought by alien introductions such as grey squirrel, coypu and giant hogweed.

Habitat protection

Although there is a rapidly growing number of protective designations for areas of habitat, the main domestic ones remain the interrelated categories of NNR and SSSI. The increasingly important international designations are discussed later in this chapter. Both NNRs and SSSIs were originally introduced in the National Parks and Access to the Countryside Act 1949 on the recommendation of the Huxley and Ritchie Committees. The NNR powers remain essentially those enacted in 1949, but the SSSI provisions have been significantly altered and strengthened by the Wildlife and Countryside Act 1981, Part II. This reflects the changing role of SSSIs in the light of the enormous environmental changes since 1949.

Two preliminary points need to be made about the 1981 Act, the passage of which would justify a book by itself. First, the whole structure of Part II rests on the policy of voluntariness favoured by the Conservative Government. This is the view that compulsory controls should only be used as a last resort, because they will only serve to antagonise landowners, who are seen as having the main responsibility for site protection. Pursuant to this policy, the favoured mechanism of control is the management agreement: the NCC is to seek to enter into agreements with landowners to protect the site, with compensation being paid for losses incurred by owners (see p. 509). In order to achieve this, many of the legal requirements focus on a duty to notify the NCC of threats to sites.

Secondly, Part II was significantly altered during its passage through Parliament. Originally the Government intended to confer statutory protection only on the limited number of sites to be accorded nature conservation order status, leaving the majority of SSSIs protected by the narrow existing limitations on development in the planning system. Many saw this as wholly inadequate, particularly when the NCC released statistics showing that between 10 and 15% of SSSIs had suffered significant damage or loss in 1980 alone, the majority of the damage being caused by agriculture rather than urban-type developments. Statutory powers relating to *all* SSSIs were hurriedly introduced. One effect is that the provisions on SSSIs (and the confusingly similar nature conservation orders) are not well drafted and many detailed matters remain particularly unclear, although there have subsequently been drafting amendments in the Wildlife and Countryside (Amendment) Act 1985, the Wildlife and Countryside (Service of Notices) Act 1985 and the EPA 1990.

The difference between NNRs and SSSIs can best be explained by saying that NNRs are actively controlled and managed by the NCC, whereas in SSSIs the occupier of the land retains control subject to a number of restrictions on use decided by the NCC. In one sense, therefore, the NNRs are the top tier of sites which merit extra controls and the expenditure of money on positive management. However, since they are all notified as SSSIs and benefit from the restrictions on them, it is clearer if the protections available to SSSIs are explained first.

Sites of special scientific interest (SSSIs)

It is important to understand the function of SSSIs. In an explanatory paper, *The Selection of Sites of Special Scientific Interest,* it is explained that they are a representative sample of British habitats, with each site seen as 'an integral part of a national series' established with the aim of 'maintaining the present diversity of wild animals and plants in Great Britain'. It is emphasised that selection is on scientific grounds rather than to enhance amenity or provide recreation. For biological sites, the best examples of various habitat types (including natural, semi-natural and man-made landscapes) are chosen, determined on the basis of 'naturalness, diversity, typicalness and size', along with sites catering for rare habitats and species. A geographical spread is ensured by selecting typical sites within sub-regional areas (see, in general, *Guidelines for Selection of Biological SSSIs,* NCC, 1989). Geological SSSIs are treated differently, the intention being to 'conserve those localities essential to the continued conduct of research and education in the earth sciences'. again in the context of a national representative series (see *Geological Conservation Review,* NCC).

By the end of March 1992, throughout Great Britain there were 5,801 SSSIs notified under the 1981 Act (3,621 in England, 841 in Wales, and 1,339 in Scotland). Together they covered 1,777,619 hectares, which is over

7% of the land area, though the proportion is far higher in some regions. The size of individual SSSIs ranges from over 10,000 hectares for some upland moorland sites, to less than one hectare. Also included are a number of linear sites, such as rivers.

The NCC is given a wide discretion both to formulate reasonable criteria for notification and to carry out the task of individual selection. The 1981 Act, s. 28(1), states:

> Where the Nature Conservancy Council are of the opinion that any area of land is of special interest by reason of any of its flora, fauna, or geological or physiographical features, it shall be the duty of the Council to notify that fact —
>
> (a)   to the local planning authority in whose area the land is situated;
> (b)   to every owner and occupier of any of that land; and
> (c)   to the Secretary of State.

One effect of this definition is that the list is not unchanging. New SSSIs will be notified as new information about sites is acquired, and as the importance of safeguarding certain habitats increases. It must also be understood that, in an age when sites are being damaged and destroyed, one site may become of greater importance simply because of the loss of another site. The NCC will, in practice, denotify a site which loses its scientific interest, although it is unclear whether there is any legislative sanction for such a step.

Section 28(1) states that it is the 'duty' of the NCC to notify the people and bodies listed. This is a very rare example, as far as environmental legislation is concerned, of a duty rather than a discretionary power being referred to. It is especially remarkable given the largely unaccountable nature of the notifying agencies. It has now been discussed in *R* v *Nature Conservancy Council, ex parte London Brick Co. Ltd* [1996] Env LR 1, which concerned a challenge to the notification of a SSSI on a brickworks in Peterborough. May J discussed the procedures for establishing a SSSI and decided that there are, in fact, two steps involved.

> (a)   Under s. 28(1), a *duty* is imposed on the NCC to notify a site which fulfils the appropriate scientific criteria. This notification has provisional effect, but a period of three months is provided during which representations or objections can be made (s. 28(2), as inserted by the Wildlife and Countryside (Amendment) Act 1985).
>
> (b)   The NCC must consider these representations or objections and then has a *discretion* under s. 28(4A) whether to confirm the notification (with or without modifications). If confirmation is not made within nine months of the date when the notification was served, the notification lapses.

May J then went on to accept that English Nature's policy normally to confirm a notification unless the site is unavoidably going to be destroyed is a reasonable policy, and he upheld the confirmation.

The implications of this decision are significant, since it suggests that it would be illegal for the NCC to refuse to notify on political or tactical grounds (although it could arguably refuse to confirm a notification), and that it may well be possible for an environmental group to succeed in an action to compel the NCC to notify a site. Conversely, it appears that it will be difficult to mount a successful challenge against an unwelcome notification where the requisite special interest can be shown.

It is up to the NCC to define the boundaries of the SSSI and it appears from *Sweet* v *Secretary of State and Nature Conservancy Council* [1989] JEL 245 (actually a case about s. 29, as to which, see below) that it is permissible for land of lesser intrinsic scientific interest to be notified if it is part of the same environmental unit as land which is of interest. However the position of surrounding buffer lands is less clear and it must be doubted whether they could be notified. One geographical limitation is that SSSIs cannot be notified for waters below the low water mark (thus excluding many estuaries), although inland waters are included within the definition of land in the Act.

In carrying out the notification to owners and occupiers, the NCC must specify the features of the land which are of special interest and must also specify any operations which are likely to damage those features. These have traditionally been called 'potentially damaging operations' and it is clear from the decision in *Sweet* that a very wide interpretation will be given to this phrase. It can include virtually anything that has an impact on the site and 'operations' is not limited to its meaning under the Town and Country Planning Act 1990. In *Sweet,* it was held to include:

> cultivation, including ploughing, rotavation, harrowing and reseeding; grazing; mowing or other methods of cutting vegetation; application of manure, fertilisers and lime; burning; the release into the site of any wild feral or domestic animal, reptile, amphibian, bird, fish or invertebrate, or any plant or seed; the storage of materials; the use of materials; the use of vehicles or craft likely to damage or disturb features of interest.

Such things as drainage, building operations and the application of pesticides are clearly covered. One thing which is not covered, however, is doing nothing, and on many sites this is potentially bad for the nature conservation interest.

In the Scottish case of *North Uist Fisheries Ltd* v *Secretary of State for Scotland* 1992 SLT 333 (again a case on similar wording in s. 29), the judge suggested that the use of the word 'likely' required any potential damage to be probable rather than a bare possibility. If this interpretation (which was strictly *obiter*) is correct, it would undermine the whole of the legislation on SSSIs. It is submitted that the judge's reasoning should not be followed, since it seems to be based on an entirely incorrect understanding of the context of the legislation.

Duties on owners and occupiers

The process of notification is a lengthy one, since every owner and occupier, which includes approximately 30,000 people, must be notified in relation to the whole of each site. The NCC has only recently finished the process, started in 1981, of renotifying all the sites which existed at that time. This was important because, until it did so, the protection of the 1981 Act did not apply to those sites.

Once they have been notified, owners and occupiers are placed under a reciprocal duty. They must notify the NCC in writing before carrying out any potentially damaging operation. However, four months after this notification, or earlier if the written consent of the NCC is obtained, the operation can go ahead unimpeded — unless of course it requires and fails to get planning permission, which must still be sought for operations and material changes of use as defined in the Town and Country Planning Act 1990. It is an offence 'without reasonable excuse' to carry out a potentially damaging operation either without notifying the NCC, or within the four-month period, but the maximum penalty is only a £2,500 fine. The restrictive effect of designation as an SSSI is therefore to impose a four-month ban on potentially damaging operations.

Liability for the commission of the offence is strict, but it can only be committed by owners and occupiers of the SSSI. They should know about the designation, either because they have been notified, or because it is a local land charge (s. 28(11)). There are two specific defences available: that the operation was carried out in an emergency, and that planning permission had been granted by the local planning authority. This does not include an automatic permission granted by the General Permitted Development Order (s. 28(8)), but it does mean that a planning permission overrides a SSSI designation.

These provisions illustrate the 'voluntary' mechanism which was favoured by the Conservative Government. The whole purpose of the reciprocal notification requirement and the four-month ban is to give the NCC an opportunity to arrange a management agreement with the owner or occupier.

One question which has often arisen relates to the meaning of the word 'occupier' in this context. This is important because there is no need for the NCC to notify anyone who is less than an occupier. It is also true that such a person cannot commit an offence under s. 28 and cannot be offered a management agreement. In *Southern Water Authority* v *Nature Conservancy Council* [1992] 1 WLR 775, the House of Lords decided that for the purposes of s. 28 someone is an occupier if they have some form of stable relationship with the land. As a result, a water authority which carried out drainage works whilst temporarily on an SSSI did not commit an offence under s. 28, even though it knew that these were potentially damaging operations and that they would cause significant harm (the House of Lords referred to its actions as 'ecological vandalism'). This decision did not specifically answer the important question whether commoners are covered by the definition of an occupier, but it is the practice of the NCC to treat them as such, relying on a clear statement to that effect given by a Government Minister during the debates on the Environmental Protection Bill (see Withrington & Jones, 'The Enforcement of Conservation Legislation' in *Agriculture, Conservation and Land Use*, ed. Howarth and Rodgers, University of Wales Press, 1992). Support for

this stance can now be gained from the House of Lords decision in *Pepper* v
Hart [1993] AC 593 that it is permissible to refer to Parliamentary debates
in certain limited circumstances to establish the meaning of a statute, since
the statement was given in the context of a refusal to bring forward an
amendment to clarify the situation on the grounds that the position was
already clear.

As pointed out earlier in this chapter, the drafting of the provisions of the
1981 Act leave a lot to be desired. But maybe the final words on the
effectiveness of the provisions on SSSIs should be left to Lord Mustill in
Southern Water Authority v *Nature Conservancy Council*, who stated (at p. 778):

> It needs only a moment to see that this regime is toothless, for it demands
> no more from the owner or occupier of an SSSI than a little patience. . . .
> In truth the Act does no more in the great majority of cases than give the
> council a breathing space within which to apply moral pressure, with a view
> to persuading the owner or occupier to make a voluntary agreement.

Specific nature conservation duties

Specific duties in relation to SSSIs are imposed upon the Environment
Agency and the NCCs in the Environment Act 1995, s. 8. Similar duties
apply to the water and sewerage undertakers under the Water Industry Act
1991, s. 4. The NCC must notify the EA of SSSIs that may be affected by
its activities (including operational and regulatory functions). If the agency is
notified, it must consult the NCC over any operation or activity it intends to
carry out which it thinks is likely to damage or destroy the SSSI. In addition
the agency is obliged to consult the NCC before authorising anything it
thinks is likely to damage the SSSI. This covers all the range of the agency's
functions, including IPC authorisations, waste management licensing, abstraction licences, discharge consents and land drainage consents. There is a
code of practice, which was published under previous powers (applicable to
the NRA under the Water Resources Act 1991, s. 17) which suggests that *all*
operations should be notified to the NCC, rather than just those that the
agency *thinks* will damage the SSSI, otherwise detrimental ones may be
inadvertently missed (*Code of Practice on Conservation, Access and Recreation*,
1989).

These duties are wider than the normal ones imposed on owners and
occupiers. They apply to all operations, not just to potentially damaging
operations notified by the NCC, and they cover activities in the vicinity of an
SSSI which may affect it, such as drainage works, an upstream discharge or
even an industrial process with potentially detrimental atmospheric emissions
some distance away. However, there is no remedy if the relevant body fails
to consult the NCC, and these duties are unenforceable unless the NCC
brings a successful action for judicial review. This reflects that the real
purpose of these duties is to bring the matter to the attention of the NCC so
that it may give advice (it does not normally offer a management agreement
to public bodies, considering that their general environmental duties should

suffice to make them act in a responsible fashion). Note should therefore be made of the general environmental duties in the Environment Act 1995, ss. 6, 7 and 9.

Nature conservation orders

Section 29 provides stronger powers for areas subject to a nature conservation order. Even so, they have been sparingly used. About 40 have been made over the years, mainly to protect sites imminently threatened with destruction.

The powers in relation to nature conservation orders are superficially similar to those on SSSIs, but there are significant differences. The order will list potentially damaging operations which must be notified to the NCC before being carried out, and a three month ban is imposed. The NCC can extend this ban to 12 months by offering a management agreement, or by offering to purchase the interest of the person seeking to carry out the operation. At the end of the 12 months, the operation can go ahead. Once again, the purpose of this ban is to enable the NCC to conclude a management agreement, or terms for the purchase of the site.

It is an offence to carry out a potentially damaging operation without notifying the NCC, or within the period of the ban. The offence carries a maximum fine of £5,000 on summary conviction, or an unlimited fine for a conviction on indictment, and it can be committed by anyone, not just owners and occupiers. Thus, contractors, trespassers or visiting members of the public could be prosecuted under this section, a position justified by the publicity given to a nature conservation order (see below).

Certain ancillary arrangements differ from s. 28. The NCC is authorised to enter land to see if an order ought to be made, or to see if an offence against one has been committed (s. 51), powers which are not available for SSSIs (a significant gap in the legislation). Anyone can prosecute for a s. 29 offence (under s. 28 it is only the NCC and anyone who has the permission of the Director of Public Prosecutions). A convicting court has powers to make a restoration order (s. 31), ordering that the offender carry out specified works for the purpose of restoring the land to its former condition, although in many cases this power will be next to useless because the damage will be irreversible. Compensation is also payable to the owner or occupier for any reduction in the value of an agricultural holding as a result of an order, and for any loss directly attributable to the ban on operations (s. 30).

These wider powers are complemented by a much more complex system for making nature conservation orders. After consulting the NCC, the Secretary of State is empowered to designate areas by order. They must be of special interest and national importance, or required to ensure the survival in Great Britain of a plant or animal, or to comply with an international obligation. Although it is arguable that all SSSIs are of national importance, it is apparent that the Secretary of State has in practice refused to designate some SSSIs under s. 29 on the grounds that the land was not of national importance, even when the NCC has requested it. It is clear from *Sweet* v *Secretary of State and Nature Conservancy Council* [1989] JEL 245 that it is permissible to designate the whole of an environmental unit even though only part of it is of national importance.

Schedule 11 provides for the making of an order. It comes into effect immediately it is made. It must then be notified to owners, occupiers and the local planning authority and must be publicised generally for any objections to be made. Twenty-eight days are allowed for representations to the Secretary of State, who must appoint an inspector or hold a public inquiry if any objections are not withdrawn. The Secretary of State has a discretion to confirm the order, or to amend or revoke it.

Despite their complexity, nature conservation orders provide the NCC with few extra powers not available for all SSSIs. They are basically used to provide more time for the NCC to negotiate a management agreement where the owner or occupier is being awkward. They also serve notice of intent to use whatever powers are available to protect the site. This may include compulsory purchase (see below). For example, in *Sweet* the land was eventually obtained in 1989 as part of a new national nature reserve.

National nature reserves (NNRs)

NNRs owe their existence to the National Parks and Access to the Countryside Act 1949, s. 15, which defines them as areas managed for study or research into flora, fauna or geological or physiographical interest, or for preserving such features which are of special interest. Before declaring an area an NNR, the NCC must consider that it is expedient in the national interest to manage the area as an NNR.

Designation as an NNR is a simple process: the NCC merely declares that an area is one. In order to do this it has to have control of the site so that it can manage it. Control may be achieved either by buying the land, leasing it, or entering into a nature reserve agreement with the owner under the National Parks and Access to the Countryside Act, s. 16. Such an agreement is enforceable against successors in title. In addition, the Wildlife and Countryside Act 1981, s. 35 permits the NCC to declare an NNR on land which is of national importance and which is being managed by an approved body (meaning a voluntary conservation organisation).

The NCC also has powers to seek a compulsory purchase order if it is unable to conclude a satisfactory management agreement with the owner (1949 Act, s. 17), or if an unremedied breach of an agreement occurs. An order will require the approval of the Secretary of State. These compulsory powers are intended as reserve powers only and are very rarely used. However, they remain the only compulsory powers available to the NCC: if a maverick landowner were to refuse to enter into a management agreement on an SSSI and refused to sell the property, a compulsory purchase order would be the only remaining weapon.

There are no additional statutory restrictions on the use of a NNR other than those imposed on all SSSIs (as a matter of practice all NNRs are designated as SSSIs), since the nature reserve agreement will cover anything extra. However, the NCC is empowered to make by-laws for the protection of the reserve (1949 Act, s. 20). They require confirmation by the Secretary of State and the procedures for making them are set out in the 1949 Act, s. 106. These by-laws may include wide restrictions on such things as entry to the reserve, taking, killing or interference with animals, plants or the soil, dropping of litter and lighting fires. Shooting of birds can also be restricted in areas surrounding the reserve. By-laws may not restrict the rights of the owner or occupier, public rights of way (though this does not include rights of navigation — *Evans* v *Godber* [1974] 1 WLR 1317), or statutory undertakers and some other public bodies carrying out their statutory functions.

There are over 250 NNRs in Great Britain, but it cannot be assumed that they are necessarily the very best sites. Designation of a site as an NNR imposes heavy costs on the NCC, which has accordingly to be selective, and it has tended to follow a policy of opportunism. Given a chronic shortage of money, it will buy or take control of sites that are threatened or available, rather than those which are in safe hands, such as those owned by a voluntary conservation body. Notwithstanding this, the NCC does have a list of proposed nature reserves, and has published *A Nature Conservation Review* (Ratcliffe, 1977 and updated), a description of around 900 key sites representing the range of British flora and fauna, which provides a list of possible future NNRs.

Local nature reserves

Under the National Parks and Access to the Countryside Act 1949, s. 21, local authorities are given the same powers to designate and manage local nature reserves as the NCC has in relation to NNRs. A local nature reserve must have local, as opposed to national, importance and the local authority must consult with the NCC before designation.

Marine nature reserves (MNRs)

MNRs are the counterparts to NNRs in tidal and coastal waters and may be designated for any area of land or water from the high tide mark to a line three miles from the baselines established for measuring the territorial sea (see the Territorial Sea Act 1987). They are provided for in the Wildlife and Countryside Act 1981, s. 36, and may be designated on the same grounds of conservation and study as NNRs. They are actively managed by the NCC.

There are a number of differences from NNRs. Some stem from the absence of property rights over most of the potential area of MNRS, others are a consequence of the limited vision of MNRs in the 1981 Act. Designation of an MNR is by the Secretary of State on the application of the NCC. There is a lengthy procedure, similar to that for nature conservation orders, in which the proposed designation and any by-laws are publicised, followed by a period for representations from interested parties, with the possibility of a public inquiry and of a judicial review both being catered for (see Wildlife and Countryside Act 1981, sch. 12). Only two MNRs have ever been designated (around the islands of Lundy and Skomer), although this may reflect the fact that the NCC's priorities lay elsewhere in the 1980s. It is also true that there are a few voluntary marine reserves.

In common with NNRs, the main additional control conferred by MNR status is the power of the NCC to make by-laws. These may be made as part of the original designation, or may be issued separately, but in either case require confirmation by the Secretary of State. The 1981 Act, s. 37, sets out the range of possible by-laws, which is much more limited than the range for NNRs. Restrictions may be introduced on the killing, taking and disturbance of plants and animals and on the deposit of litter. The by-laws may also prohibit or restrict access by people or vessels to the MNR, but this is limited by the provision in s. 37(3) that by-laws may not restrict any lawful right of passage by vessels, except for pleasure boats. This is an important limitation, since most boats will be able to take advantage of the right of passage in tidal waters, and there are no proprietary limitations on access in such waters. In addition, it must be noted that MNRs cannot take any real advantage from the protection relating to SSSIs, since SSSIs cannot be designated below the low water mark.

Limestone pavements

Limestone pavements are rare landscape features limited to a small number of areas in North-West Europe. In the light of the devastating damage that has been done to them, particularly in gathering stone for garden rockeries, specific powers to protect them were introduced in the Wildlife and Countryside Act 1981, s. 34.

There are two distinct controls. Under s. 34(1), the NCC or the Countryside Commission must notify limestone pavements of special interest to the local planning authority. Amongst other things this will then be taken into account in any planning application. Under s. 34(2), the Secretary of State, a county planning authority or a national park authority may by order prohibit the removal from, or disturbance of, any limestone on a site notified under s. 34(1), if they consider it is likely to be affected adversely by such acts. The making of a limestone pavement order is subject to the same procedures as a nature conservation order (1981 Act, sch. 11). It is an offence without reasonable excuse to remove or disturb any limestone on or in an area subject to an order, although it is a defence to have planning permission to do so. The penalty is a maximum fine of £5,000 on summary conviction and an unlimited fine on conviction on indictment. It was originally intended to protect most areas of substantial pavement, but the cumbersome nature of designation has meant that only a handful of orders have ever been made, mainly (as with nature conservation orders) to deal with threats of imminent damage.

This dual form of protection differs from all other conservation designations. But it must be noted that this is the form that the Government originally proposed in 1981 should apply to SSSIs, with only a few specially protected areas having extra restrictions and the ordinary SSSIs being protected only by notification to the local planning authority.

Management agreements

The NCC has a power to enter into management agreements with owners and occupiers of SSSIs (Countryside Act 1968, s. 15). This was extended by the EPA 1990, sch. 9 to enable agreements to be made with owners or occupiers of land adjoining an SSSI, which will be of use, for example, in wetland areas to control drainage. There is a similar power to make nature reserve agreements for NNRs (National Parks and Access to the Countryside Act 1949, s. 16), although these normally provide for the NCC to manage the land itself.

Management agreements underpin the voluntary approach to nature conservation favoured by the current Government. They are effectively contracts in which owners or occupiers of land agree to manage it in the interests of nature conservation in return for payment from the NCC. They normally provide for positive management of the site as well as for restrictions, but it appears that only restrictive arrangements in the agreement will be binding on successors in title (s. 15(4)).

Prior to the Wildlife and Countryside Act 1981, little use was made of management agreements — only 70 were in force in 1980/81. But since the 1981 Act, numbers have grown, so that in 1990/91 the NCC paid out over £6.85m on 2,032 management agreements on SSSIs (see NCC 16th Annual Report).

Standard rates of compensation have been established in financial guidelines made by Ministers under the 1981 Act, s. 50 (these are set out in the Appendix to Circular 4/83). These are generous to landowners, because they are based on the principle of compensation for profits forgone, which will include such things as lost agricultural grants or lost revenues had the land been converted to a more profitable use. The owner or occupier also has a choice between a lump sum payment or an index-linked annual payment. However, one of the drawbacks of the legislation is that, unlike the position for agreements in environmentally sensitive areas (see p. 530) and under many other schemes, the terms of each SSSI management agreement have to be negotiated individually. This uses up valuable time and resources and has led to a much slower rate of agreement than under these other schemes. Land of outstanding scientific interest may also qualify for tax relief (see *Capital Taxation and Nature Conservation*, English Nature, 1992). Another drawback is that the legislation revolves around compensating people for *not* doing something, rather than paying them to do something, which is inappropriate in nature conservation terms.

There is little doubt that the cost of management agreements has proved more expensive than the Government originally anticipated. Only £600,000 was originally provided for them in 1981, although this figure has risen considerably since. It is also clear that lack of money has caused the NCC to be inhibited in negotiations. For example, in 1982 in Romney Marsh the NCC pulled out of negotiations when no extra Government money was provided for a potentially expensive agreement (see *Cash or Crisis*, Rose and Secrett, 1982). However, when the current figures for damage to SSSIs are considered (see below), it appears that the strategy of relying on management agreements has had some success in reducing damage caused by agricultural activities (although wider issues connected with the profitability of agriculture are also probably of great significance).

Planning permission

In addition to any controls specific to SSSIs and NNRs, planning permission will be required for operations and material changes of use which fall within the definition of development in the Town and Country Planning Act 1990, s. 55 (see p. 233). Where the application relates to an SSSI or is likely to affect an SSSI, the Town and Country Planning (General Development Procedure) Order 1995, Art. 10, requires the local planning authority to consult with the NCC before making a decision. The objective is the familiar one of informing the NCC in advance of a potential threat to the site, so it may give advice or offer a management agreement. Prior to the 1981 Act, this was the *only* legal protection for SSSIs.

These requirements are very limited in practice. Many activities likely to damage SSSIs, such as those relating to agriculture, forestry and works carried out by statutory undertakers, are not covered by the need for planning permission, either because they are not development or because they are granted exemption. In any case, the local planning authority is not bound by the NCC's advice — it is just one material consideration to be taken into account. The economic and other arguments in favour of the development may well outweigh the need to protect the SSSI. For example, in 1990 Havering DC granted outline planning permission for a large theme park on Rainham Marshes, the largest SSSI in Greater London. The Secretary of State refused to call the application in, even though this would have been the largest ever loss of SSSI land to a development with planning permission (it has not gone ahead). In another example, Poole BC granted itself planning permission for housing on Canford Heath, an SSSI within the town's boundaries. After an unsuccessful High Court challenge (see *R v Poole Borough Council, ex parte Beebee* [1991] JPL 643), the Secretary of State took the almost unprecedented step of revoking the planning permission under the Town and Country Planning Act 1990, s. 100.

Government policy on planning and nature conservation is now set out in Planning Policy Guidance Note 9, *Nature Conservation* (PPG 9, October 1994). As well as explaining the various statutory and international protections, PPG 9 emphasises that the nature conservation interest of a site, and the importance of the site in national and international terms, is clearly a material consideration when it comes to a decision whether to grant planning permission, although it does refer to the potential use of conditions or planning obligations to avoid damaging impacts. In particular, PPG 9 includes some especially strong policies in relation to international sites, including that environmental assessment will normally be required where such a site (including a proposed site) could be affected (see below for a discussion of internationally important sites).

However, there is a difficulty here concerning the relationship between safeguarding sites through the planning machinery and the formal designation of SSSIs. If a formal policy against granting planning permission on internationally important sites is adopted, which is likely, many people would then argue that the procedures for designation of those sites need to be upgraded so as to include rights of objection, the possibility of a public inquiry and so on, since such a restraint policy would effectively take away any real chance of realising the development value of the land.

If planning permission is granted for development, it acts as a defence to a prosecution for damaging an SSSI (1981 Act, s. 28(8)). This does not just apply to new permissions. It also exempts existing mineral and peat extraction permissions over SSSIs from the 1981 Act. These are on sites which tend not to have been identified as of importance when the permission was originally granted. The NCC's options are limited and all involve the payment of potentially large sums of money: revocation of the planning permission entails a liability to pay compensation, a management agreement would have to compensate for lost profits, and purchase would normally be at the market price.

Loss and damage to SSSIs

Despite the strengthening of the law relating to SSSIs in the 1981 Act, it remains clear that damage and loss to sites is still continuing, though probably at lower rates than before the passage of the Act. The three national conservation agencies currently divide incidents into four categories: complete loss, partial loss, long-term damage and short-term damage (although it must be recognised that the three agencies adopt slightly different criteria and that short-term damage can easily turn into long-term damage if appropriate management of a site is not undertaken). In 1991/92 they reported a total of one complete loss, six cases of partial loss, 46 cases of long-term damage and 196 cases of short-term damage. In 1994, the National Audit Office reported that 869 SSSIs in England suffered loss and damage between 1987 and 1993, which amounts to over one-fifth of the total number of SSSIs notified, although there was some element of double counting in these figures. These continuing losses illustrate that the traditional British approach to environmental issues identified in Chapter 5, of balancing the various factors and reaching a compromise, simply does not work when it comes to safeguarding key nature conservation sites.

The statistics on loss and damage show that the causes of damage have changed somewhat over the last 14 years, a point reinforced by a number of independent analyses (see Rowell, *SSSIs: A Health Check*, Wildlife Link, 1991). It is true that agricultural activities still account for the majority of incidents, but nowadays only a small proportion of these give rise to the loss of a site. The major problems in relation to agriculture appear to be those with which the Act is ill-equipped to deal, such as overgrazing (especially by commoners) and neglect, both of which create difficult issues of management and control. This point, that the main causes of damage are from those things that the Act cannot deal with properly, is reinforced when non-agricultural causes are looked at. Many cases of loss or long-term damage are caused by activities that are effectively exempt from the Act, such as: activities granted planning permission (for example, the perpetual permissions for peat extraction on lowland moors); major developments promoted by government departments (such as the Channel Tunnel, or the road-building programme); activities by statutory undertakers (the prosecution of Southern Water Authority mentioned earlier is a good example); recreational activities, which are often not controlled because those who are neither owners nor occupiers cannot commit an offence under s. 28; and activities taking place below the low water mark. These cases all point towards the existence of a number of defects in the scheme of the Act which urgently require to be addressed.

The international perspective

There are some international conventions relating to nature conservation whose significance in the context of domestic law should not be underestimated. The Bern Convention on the Conservation of European Wildlife and Natural Habitats (Cmnd 8738, 1979), could, arguably, be seen as the driving force behind the two EC Directives discussed in detail below, whilst the Ramsar Convention on Wetlands of International Importance (Cmnd 6465, 1971, which is discussed below) has played a key role in relation to the protection of one particular habitat which the UK has in relative abundance. There is also the Bonn Convention on the Conservation of Migratory Species of Wild Animals, 1979 and the Washington Convention on International Trade in Endangered Species of Wild Fauna and Flora (Cmnd 6647, 1973).

However, in terms of the impact on British law, two EC Directives, the Wild Birds Directive 79/409 and the Habitats Directive 92/43, have undoubtedly had the greatest influence and will continue to be of importance in the future. The main reason relates to the very specific requirements that these Directives lay down concerning the designation of protected sites, but they also include some significant measures on the protection of individual animals and plants (which have been discussed above).

EC Wild Birds Directive 79/409

Under the Wild Birds Directive, Member States are required in general terms to take measures, including the creation of protected areas, to maintain a sufficient diversity of habitats for *all* European bird species (Arts. 1, 2 and 3). They are also required to take special conservation measures to conserve the habitats of the rare or vulnerable species listed in Annex I and of all regularly occurring migratory species (Art. 4). These special measures should include the designation of special protection areas for such birds. Once a special protection area has been designated, Member States must take appropriate steps to avoid significant pollution or deterioration of the habitat or disturbance of the birds within it (Art. 4(4)).

In *Commission* v *Spain* (case C-355/90) [1993] ECR I-4221, the European Court of Justice held that the Spanish Government was in breach of Art. 4

by failing to designate an important wetland area, the Marismas de Santoña, as a special protection area. The case established that a Member State is effectively under a duty to designate an area as a special protection area (and thus to protect it) if it fulfils the objective ornithological criteria laid down in the Directive.

In an earlier, though no less important, case, *Commission* v *Germany* (case C-57/89) [1991] ECR I-883, the European Court of Justice addressed the meaning of Art. 4(4) in relation to an area known as the Leybucht Dykes. It established that reduction in the area of a special protection area was only justified on very limited grounds, such as where the works were necessary for reasons of public health or public safety (which was actually the situation in the case itself), and that works could not be permitted for economic or recreational reasons, thus creating a strong presumption against development in such an area. This point was reinforced by *Commission* v *Spain*, which applied the same test to the deterioration of a site as a result of pollution or other works and also suggested that Art. 4(4) is sufficiently clear to be directly effective. The effect of these rulings was very quickly mitigated by an amendment that was made to Art. 4 by the Habitats Directive, which brought the Wild Birds Directive into line with the less restrictive exceptions laid down in Art. 6(4) of that Directive (see below), but a more limited presumption against development in special protection areas remains. The nature of the requirement to designate SPAs was re-examined by the ECJ in *R* v *Secretary of State for the Environment, ex parte Royal Society for the Protection of Birds* (case C-44/55) [1997] QB 206. In this case the RSPB challenged the failure of the Government to designate an area known as Lappel Bank within the Medway Estuary and Marshes as a SPA. The main point of contention was the extent to which it was permissible to take into account economic factors in the decision whether, and over what area, to designate a SPA. The UK Government argued that economic considerations were relevant whilst the RSPB relied on the ECJ decision in *Commission* v *Spain* (case C-355/90) to argue that at the designation stage ornithological criteria were the only relevant consideration. In the Court of Appeal, the judges were split, with the majority deciding in the Government's favour. However, the RSPB appealed to the House of Lords, which refused interim relief (with the consequent destruction of much of the habitat) but referred the matter to the European Court of Justice under Article 177 of the EC Treaty (see [1995] JEL 245). Given the nature of previous decisions on the point, it came as no surprise when the ECJ ruled in favour of the RSPB (see [1997] JEL 139). The ECJ followed the decisions in *Commission* v *Spain* (case C-355/90) and *Commission* v *Germany* (case C-57/89) and ruled that economic considerations were not relevant considerations when designating or drawing up the boundaries of a SPA.

Apart from the requirement to designate special protection areas, the Directive does not specify how its objectives are to be achieved, giving a degree of flexibility to Member States. In Britain, the approach that was adopted was initially to provide protection through the town planning and SSSI systems. All special protection areas are, in practice, notified as SSSIs before being designated, but it should be noted that, prior to the passage of the Conservation (Natural Habitats etc.) Regulations 1994 (which are discussed in detail below), designation as a special protection area (or as a Ramsar site, where a similar policy was adopted) did not impose any additional domestic requirements on owners or occupiers to those applicable to all SSSIs. There is also a crucial gap in the legislation on SSSIs in that there is no SSSI protection for parts of many special protection areas (and also many Ramsar sites) because they are below low-water mark. Estuarine sites in particular are under great pressure; an NCC report has shown that 56 out of 136 estuarine SSSIs suffered damage between 1986 and 1989, many through permanent developments (see *Nature Conservation and Estuaries in Great Britain* (NCC, 1991)). The two European Court of Justice cases suggested that the British approach was no longer adequate and the position has now been radically altered by the 1994 Regulations.

The NCC has produced some extensive criteria for qualification as a special protection area (see *Protecting Internationally Important Bird Sites* (NCC, 1990), in which it identified a total of 218 candidate sites and stated that it was considering the merits of a further 43). At present there are over 100 areas waiting to be designated as SPAs. It is also important to note that the Government has accepted, as a matter of planning policy, that all sites that meet the criteria for designation as a special protection area should be treated as if they had been formally designated. For example, in July 1992 the Secretary of State refused planning permission for a number of major developments in North Kent, giving the need to protect a candidate special protection area as one of the main reasons (see [1993] Water Law 89). This policy is now enshrined in Planning Policy Guidance Note 9, *Nature Conservation* (PPG 9, October 1994).

EC Habitats Directive 92/43

The full title of this Directive refers to the Conservation of Natural Habitats and of Wild Fauna and Flora. However, whilst it does require some measures of importance to the protection of individual animals and plants to be taken, its main importance relates to habitat protection. Accordingly, it is commonly referred to as the Habitats Directive. It was adopted in May 1992 after many years of argument within the EC and has led to some important changes to British law and policy on habitat protection, which are discussed below.

The central feature of the Directive is that it provides for the creation of a coherent ecological network of special areas of conservation, which will make up a system of European sites known as Natura 2000. The network will consist of sites containing the natural habitat types listed in Annex I of the Directive and sites containing the habitats of the species listed in Annex II. It will incorporate the special protection areas classified under the Wild Birds Directive. However, the Directive also includes some more general duties, including a requirement that Member States monitor the conservation status of *all* habitats and species (Art. 11) and a general duty relating to the management of certain important landscape features (Art. 10).

The procedures for producing the list of special areas of conservation are complex. By June 1995, Member States were required to send to the Commission a list of proposed sites, drawn up by reference to the criteria laid down in Annex III (Stage 1). At present, 255 sites in the UK are under consideration at the Commission, although the list is not yet complete. The Commission is then under a duty to draw up, by June 1998, a draft list of 'sites of Community importance', taking account of the criteria set out in Annex III (Stage 2). The Commission adopts a final list thereafter in the light of scientific advice from a committee of independent experts. The Commission will produce a separate list of those sites which host one or more of the *priority* habitat types or species which are identified in Annexes I and II (these can be termed 'priority sites'). There are provisions for a bilateral consultation process between the Commission and a Member State where the Commission considers that a priority site has been left off a Member State's list, with ultimate recourse to the EC Council (Art. 5). In addition, the Commission is under a duty to review the list in the future, whilst Member States and the Commission are required to submit detailed implementation reports. Once the Commission has adopted the list of sites of Community importance, Member States are under a duty to designate any site on the list as a special area of conservation as soon as possible and within six years at the latest (Art. 4(4)).

The protection provided by the Habitats Directive is as follows:

(a) for special areas of conservation (once designated), Member States must adopt 'necessary conservation measures' and 'appropriate statutory, administrative or contractual measures' (Art 6(1));

(b) for sites adopted by the Commission as sites of Community importance, special protection areas designated under the Wild Birds Directive and sites subject to the Art. 5 consultation procedure, Member States are required to take appropriate steps to avoid the deterioration of the sites and significant disturbance of the species for which the areas have been designated (Art. 6(2)); and

(c) for sites adopted by the Commission as sites of Community importance and special protection areas designated under the Wild Birds Directive, any plan or project not directly connected with the management of the site which is likely to have a significant effect on it must be subject to an appropriate assessment of the implications; the competent national authorities can then agree to the plan or project only if it will not 'adversely affect the integrity of the site concerned' (Art. 6(3)).

However, if there is no alternative solution, a plan or project may be carried out if there are 'imperative reasons of overriding public interest, including those of a social or economic nature'. In such a case, the Member State has to take compensatory measures in order to ensure the overall coherence of Natura 2000 and must inform the Commission of those measures. When compared with the position set out in *Commission v Germany* (case C–57/89) [1991] ECR I–883 (the *Leybucht Dykes* case), this exception lessens the protection that is offered. However, for priority sites the exception is limited to considerations relating to human health or public safety, situations where the impact is beneficial to the environment, and cases where the Commission has accepted that there are reasons of overriding public interest (art 6(4)), in effect retaining the *Leybucht Dykes* position for priority sites. It is of relevance, therefore, that there are no priority bird species, and thus the stronger controls applicable to priority sites cannot apply to special protection areas designated under the Wild Birds Directive.

In *Commission* v *Spain* (case C-355/90) [1993] ECR I-4221 the ECJ suggested that Art. 4(4) of the Wild Birds Directive had direct effect. Since paras (2)–(4) of Art. 6 of the Habitats Directive are in very similar terms, in that they lay down clear requirements, it is arguable that they are also directly effective, with all the implications for enforcement of the law in Member States that this entails.

The 1994 Regulations

Initially, the British Government envisaged that the Habitats Directive could be implemented without new legislation. It intended to adopt the approach that had hitherto been used in relation to the Wild Birds Directive, i.e., judicious use of the SSSI and town planning systems. However, in the light of the two European Court of Justice cases it became clear that this would be inadequate in legal terms. As a result, in order to implement the provisions of the Directive, the European Communities Act 1972, s. 2(2) was used to pass the Conservation (Natural Habitats etc.) Regulations 1994 (SI 1994 No. 2716).

However, rather than remodel the law on nature conservation entirely, the Government adopted a minimalist approach. It simply engrafted onto the existing SSSI and town planning mechanisms the additional protections required by the Directive, and then only where absolutely necessary. In essence, the Regulations apply additional protections to 'European sites', which are defined as follows:

(a)   a special area of conservation (once designated — the Regulations reproduce the procedures and timetable in the Directive relating to designation, the Secretary of State being placed under a duty to propose a list of sites on or before 5 June 1995 (reg. 7) and required to designate sites adopted by the Commission as special areas of conservation 'as soon as possible and within six years at most' (reg. 8));

(b)   a site adopted by the Commission as a site of Community importance;

(c)   a special protection area designated under the Wild Birds Directive; and

(d)   a site subject to consultation under Art. 5 of the Directive (although in this case the protection is limited in the same way as under the Directive to the obligations under Art. 6(2)).

The Secretary of State will draw up a public register of European sites (Art. 11) and notify them to English Nature (Art. 12), which will then notify local planning authorities, owners and occupiers and anyone else the Secretary of State may direct (Art.13).

Under the Regulations, the basic protection given to terrestrial European sites is the same as under the Wildlife and Countryside Act 1981, s. 28 for all SSSIs, with the following exceptions:

(a)   English Nature may amend the original notification made under s. 28 of the special interest of the site and of the potentially damaging operations (reg. 18);

(b)   the process through which English Nature grants consent for potentially damaging operations is altered in the light of Art. 6 of the Directive so that:

(i)   if it appears to English Nature that a plan or project is likely to have a significant effect on the site, it must carry out an appropriate assessment and may only give consent if the plan or project will not affect the integrity of the site; and

(ii)   if it considers that there is a risk that the operation will be carried out without consent, it must notify the Secretary of State, who has the powers described below to make a special nature conservation order (reg. 20);

(c)   existing consents must be reviewed by English Nature and may be withdrawn or modified without compensation (reg. 21); and

(d)   by-laws may be made for terrestrial European sites (and over surrounding or adjoining sites) as if they were nature reserves (reg. 28).

In addition, the Secretary of State has a power to make a special nature conservation order over a European site (reg. 22). This is a new type of protection, which, although based on the Wildlife and Countryside Act 1981, s. 29, is potentially far stronger because it produces a situation where the ban on potentially damaging operations is permanent.

Where a special nature conservation order has been made, reg. 24 sets out the procedure to be followed where an owner or occupier applies for consent to carry out a plan or project. If it appears to English Nature that the plan or project is likely to have a significant effect on the site, it must carry out an appropriate assessment and *must* refuse consent, unless it is satisfied that the plan or project will not affect the integrity of the site. The owner or occupier may refer the refusal to the Secretary of State, who is given a power to direct English Nature to grant consent. But this power of direction can be used only if: (i) there is no alternative solution; and (ii) the plan or project must be carried out 'for imperative reasons of overriding public interest' (which is defined as in Art. 6(4) of the Directive and includes the more restrictive test for priority sites). If consent is granted, appropriate compensatory measures must be carried out.

This is the central feature of the whole Regulations, since it provides a form of absolute protection by introducing a mechanism through which a damaging activity may be prevented permanently. However, the success of the whole Regulations (at least in terms of whether the Directive is properly implemented in practice) depends on the willingness of the Secretary of State to make a special nature conservation order and then to refuse consent where appropriate. These are matters that may not become clear for some time since, until the Commission adopts the list of sites of Community importance, the only sites that are covered by the Habitats Directive are the special protection areas designated under the Wild Birds Directive. Nevertheless, it is clear from the whole scheme of protection that the Government envisages special nature conservation orders as instruments of last resort to be used only when absolutely necessary. Set against that, reg. 3(2) requires the Secretary of State and the nature conservation bodies to exercise their nature conservation functions 'so as to secure compliance' with the Directive. It must also be noted that the Regulations repeat many of the opaque words and phrases used in the Directive; in line with standard principles of EC law, these should be interpreted in accordance with the Directive.

European marine sites

As far as European sites which are marine or tidal are concerned, the Regulations are far more loosely worded. Every public body having functions relevant to marine conservation is required to exercise its functions so as to secure compliance with the requirements of the Directive (reg. 3(3)). In addition, more specific powers and duties are laid down in regs. 33 — 36. English Nature must advise other relevant authorities (a term which includes local authorities, the Environment Agency, water and sewerage undertakers, internal drainage boards, navigation authorities, harbour authorities, lighthouse authorities and fisheries committees) as to the conservation objectives for the site and any potentially damaging operations. Any relevant authority *may* then establish a management scheme for the site and English Nature *may* make by-laws under the Wildlife and Countryside Act 1981, s. 37 as if the site were a marine nature reserve. The relevant Minister is given a wide power to make directions to the relevant authorities concerning management schemes. It must be doubted whether these vague arrangements, which in the absence of town planning and SSSI controls are the only real powers available below the low-water mark, are adequate to ensure the proper implementation of the Directive.

European sites and other regulatory systems

The Regulations also make important amendments to a number of regulatory systems. Where a plan or project is likely to have a significant effect on a European site, before granting such things as planning permission or a pollution authorisation, the relevant regulatory agency must consult with English Nature and carry out an appropriate assessment of the implications of the plan or project for the site (reg. 48). The agency must agree to the plan or project only if it will not adversely affect the integrity of the site, unless the provisions of regs. 49 and 53 are satisfied (these repeat the exceptions laid down in Art. 6(4) of the Directive). The Secretary of State is also given powers to prohibit the plan or project, either temporarily or permanently. In addition, existing permissions, consents and authorisations must be reviewed as soon as reasonably practicable. If the integrity of the site is adversely affected, the agency should use its normal powers of revocation or modification, paying compensation if that would be the usual position. There are also restrictions on a developer taking advantage of a development order in order to carry out development on a European site (regs. 60 — 64).

In relation to applications for planning permission, PPG 9, *Nature Conservation* (October 1994), creates some additional protections as a matter of policy, including that for development control purposes potential special protection areas and candidate special areas of conservation included in the list sent to the EC Commission should be treated in the same way as designated sites, and that environmental assessment will normally be required where a Ramsar site or a candidate or designated European site could be affected.

The Ramsar Convention

The Ramsar Convention on Wetlands of International Importance Especially as Waterfowl Habitat, 1971, was the first international convention dealing solely with habitat. It came into force in 1975 and currently there are over 50 Contracting Parties, of which the UK is one.

The Convention establishes a number of protections, though it can be criticised for being too general and unenforceable. First it imposes on the Contracting Parties a general duty to promote the conservation of wetlands and waterfowl, especially by establishing nature reserves. Secondly it adopts a site designation approach and provides for the compilation of a list of wetlands of international importance. Contracting Parties are under a duty to formulate their planning so as to promote the conservation of wetlands included in the list. Each Contracting Party must designate at least one site within its territory and deletion or reduction in size of a site is allowed only on the grounds of 'urgent national interests'. Guidelines on the definition of international importance have been drawn up, although ultimately it is up to each Contracting Party to decide whether and where it will designate. In addition to these powers, there are provisions under the Convention for the monitoring of wetlands, the establishment of a database, the funding of projects, educational work and publications. It also provides for a Ramsar Bureau, which is based in Switzerland.

'Wetland' is interpreted very widely to include 'areas of marsh, fen, peatland or water, whether natural or artificial, permanent or temporary, with water that is static or flowing, fresh, brackish or salt, including areas of marine water the depth of which does not exceed six metres'. Designation may also include adjacent areas of land, such as coasts, riverbanks and islands.

As with the Wild Birds Directive, the Ramsar Convention was initially implemented through the planning and SSSI systems. In practice, this still remains the case, since the sites are not European sites for the purposes of the 1994 Regulations. However, it must be pointed out that Ramsar sites are now given significant protection in practice through PPG 9 and that many of the 90 sites designated (which cover 385,000 hectares) are also special protection areas under the Wild Birds Directive or candidate special areas of conservation.

Summary of protection of internationally important sites

There is little doubt that the 1994 Regulations have increased the protection available to European sites and that PPG 9 reinforces that protection within the planning system. However, it is difficult to say whether they implement the Habitats Directive fully, since the crucial issues relate to whether the powers will be used in practice. As pointed out above, the willingness of the Secretary of State to designate European sites and then to protect them by making special nature conservation orders is central. In this respect it is relevant that the Government has sent to the EC Commission a total of 255 candidate special areas of conservation, although it is accepted that this is not a final list. The Government's approach to the selection of appropriate sites was set out in *A List of Possible Special Areas of Conservation in the UK*, issued in March 1995, which confirmed that there will be few priority sites in the UK.

There are other potential defects with the Regulations. They impose a very heavy administrative burden on English Nature and the various regulatory agencies which are required to review consents. This burden may well prove to be too great. It must also be asked whether the extra attention paid to European sites means that, in practice, the resources and goodwill available to protect other sites has been significantly eroded. Many commentators have already queried why, in the light of the defects identified in the legislation relating to SSSIs, the opportunity was not taken to improve the protection given to *all* SSSIs.

SEVENTEEN
The protection of the countryside

This chapter looks at the protection of the features which make the British countryside distinctive. There are a number of different things involved here: the restriction of urban expansion and urban developments in the countryside; the preservation of the particularly rural character of an area; and the protection of distinctive landscapes or landscape types. Since the shape of most of what is to be protected is the result of hundreds of years of human intervention, its protection poses some difficult problems, involving positive action as well as restrictive controls.

Three main methods of control may be discerned:

(a) One is to rely on the town and country planning legislation to control developments in the countryside in the same way that they are controlled in towns.

(b) A second is to impose special protections in designated areas, or in relation to designated features. In practice, these added protections often tend to stem from the town and country planning system as well, though there are some that do not.

(c) A third mechanism is to utilise grants and other incentives to ensure the proper care of the countryside, again with special schemes available in selected areas.

A particular feature of both the second and third mechanisms is the reliance on voluntary controls, rather than on compulsion.

Town and country planning

The starting point for the protection of the countryside has always been the development control system. But it has never proved particularly successful, because despite its name, it has always had an urban bias. There have been very few adaptations of the basic structure to cope with countryside matters. Indeed, it is commonly referred to as the 'town planning' system, the countryside aspect being forgotten.

There are a number of reasons for this. A major one is the history of the system, which had a consequent effect on the nature of the legal mechanisms that were adopted. The town and country planning system developed in 1947 was specifically designed to meet predominantly urban problems, such as community layout and design, industrial location, post-war reconstruction, public health and overcrowding, and transportation changes. As far as the rural environment was concerned, the main policy was the protection of the countryside against urban creep and expansion. The legal mechanisms that were adopted were thus mainly negative, such as the need for planning permission, and did not reflect the need for positive management in the countryside.

In addition, there was in 1947 perceived to be little need to control developments in the countryside, since it was generally considered that landowners and farmers had done a good job in shaping the landscape, and in any case agriculture itself required protection after the rural depression of the 1930s and the Atlantic Blockade of the Second World War. Agriculture and forestry, the two main activities likely to have an impact on the landscape, were granted generous exemptions in the legislation which, despite some minor changes, still remain today.

As a result there are distinct limitations on the use of development control in the countryside, and its most important role is in controlling new buildings and structures:

(a) Many rural activities which have a significant impact on the landscape do not constitute development. For example, afforestation or deforestation, hedgerow or stone wall removal, ploughing, and the cultivation of new crops (such as oil seed rape) are all entirely excluded from the development control system.

(b) The Town and Country Planning Act 1990, s. 55(2)(e), provides that a change of use to agriculture or forestry is not development. Whilst it is obvious that this covers a change from an urban to a rural use, in landscape terms it is more significant that this paragraph excludes from development control a change from unused land (often of high nature conservation or landscape value) to agriculture or forestry, or from agriculture to forestry, or from forestry to agriculture, or from one type of agriculture or forestry to another. 'Agriculture' is defined very widely in the Town and Country Planning Act 1990, s. 336, to include such diverse things as intensive livestock production, fish farming, horticulture and extensive grazing.

(c) Further exemptions are set out in the Town and Country Planning (General Permitted Development) Order 1995 (SI 1995 No. 418) (the GDO) sch. 2, under which blanket automatic planning permissions (permitted development rights) are granted. For example, the GDO exempts the construction of fences and walls up to 2 metres in height, and temporary uses up to 28 days per year (although not war games, motor sports and clay pigeon shooting within SSSIs).

(d) The GDO, sch. 2, parts 6 and 7 provide permitted development rights for a wide range of agricultural and forestry operations, such as new roads,

buildings, drainage works and excavations, subject to some generous limitations on size and height (for example, each building may be up to 465 square
metres in area and 12 metres in height). There are other, more technical
limitations, such as that the erection or alteration of structures for the
accommodation of livestock, or for storing slurry or sewage sludge, within
400 metres of non-agricultural dwellings or other buildings is not permitted
under the GDO.

Prior to 1992, the exemption in part 6 applied to all farms over 0.4
hectares. An amendment that came into force in January 1992 raised that
limit for most operations (termed 'Class A operations') to 5 hectares (even
then, development is not permitted on a seperate parcel of land which is less
than 1 hectare in area). A far more limited list of 'Class B operations' is
granted permitted development rights on units between 0.4 and 5 hectares.
There are thus different permitted development rights depending on the size
of the farm concerned. In relation to both Class A and Class B operations,
the development has to be reasonably necessary for the purposes of agriculture within the agricultural unit.

(e) A final limitation on the usefulness of the development control system
in the countryside is that this is a political system. Decisions are made by local
planning authorities and are likely to reflect the economic needs and policy
preferences of local residents, although reference must always be made to
Planning Policy Guidance Note 7, *The Countryside and the Rural Economy*,
which sets out general Government planning policies towards the countryside. Local authorities may also underestimate the importance of a local area
in national terms. (In passing it should be noted that these same limitations
explain why the network of SSSIs is not protected properly by controls
dependent on the town and country planning system (see p. 510).

Extra protections

In some circumstances, there are extra protections provided by the town and
country planning system in the countryside:

(a) The extent of development permitted under the GDO is limited in
national parks, the Norfolk and Suffolk Broads, areas of outstanding natural
beauty, conservation areas and any area specified by the Secretary of State
and Minister of Agriculture under the Wildlife and Countryside Act 1981,
s. 41(3) (collectively these areas are known as Article 1(5) land). Whilst the
limitations are not great, this does mean that stricter controls apply to such
things as extensions to houses and other buildings.

(b) A system of prior notification applies to farm or forestry developments
otherwise permitted by the GDO, sch. 2, parts 6 and 7. This means that 28
days' prior notification of the proposed development must be submitted to
the local planning authority, which may then impose conditions relating to
the siting, design and external appearance of the development in the light of
the likely effects on the surroundings. In making this decision, the local
planning authority is required to take into account not only the visual aspects

of the development, but also the desirability of preserving ancient monuments and their settings, archaeological sites, the setting of listed buildings and sites of recognised nature conservation value. A fee is payable with the initial notification. Between 1950 and 1992 this requirement applied only in national parks and certain adjoining areas, but from the beginning of 1992 it was extended to all parts of England and Wales.

(c)   As a matter of policy, the local planning authority may impose restrictive conditions on activities requiring permission. For example, specific design criteria are commonly imposed where there is a local style. It may also make non-statutory designations of such things as sites of high landscape value in its development plan.

(d)   An Article 4 direction may be imposed under the GDO, requiring planning permission to be sought for something that would otherwise be granted automatic permission (see p. 240). For example, this mechanism was used on Halvergate Marsh in the Norfolk grazing marshes in 1984 to prevent agricultural drainage and ploughing damaging the landscape importance of the area, though in confirming the direction, the DoE stressed that the main purpose was to compel the farmer involved to accept a management agreement on the land. Since Article 4 directions entail the payment of compensation by the local planning authority if planning permission is then refused, their use is rare (even though the cost is sometimes grant-aided by central government agencies).

The Countryside Commission

The Countryside Commission was originally created in 1949 as the National Parks Commission. It is now established as an independent body, with its members appointed by the Secretary of State and with its finance provided by grant aid from central government (Wildlife and Countryside Act 1981, sch. 13). It has responsibilities in relation to the preservation and enhancement of natural beauty in England and the provision of recreational activities, including rights of way. These amenity functions distinguish its role from that of English Nature. It has few operational powers, apart from the designation of national parks and areas of outstanding natural beauty, but it has an important role in providing advice and finance in relation to its objectives. The equivalent responsibilities are carried out in Scotland by Scottish Natural Heritage and in Wales by the Countryside Council for Wales.

Landscape protection and management agreements

Apart from the limited protection accorded to landscapes by planning law, there are a number of designations of land that may be made. However, these depend ultimately either on the town planning system, or on voluntary powers. There are few, if any, compulsory powers to support landscape protection.

In line with this voluntary philosophy, there is a power for any local planning authority to enter into a management agreement with any owner of land for conserving or enhancing its natural beauty or amenity, or for promoting its enjoyment by the public (Wildlife and Countryside Act 1981, s. 39). Such an agreement is grant aided by the Countryside Commission. Unlike the position for agreements made in relation to SSSIs, the financial guidelines laid down in the Wildlife and Countryside Act 1981, s. 50 do not apply to agreements made under s. 39 (see p. 509 for those guidelines).

National parks

National parks in Britain do not equate to the concept of a national park used in most other countries. instead of being wilderness areas with few, if any, inhabitants, they contain land on which large numbers of people live. They are effectively working environments. The aim of national park designation is to plan and manage the area so as to create a balance between recreation, amenity, wildlife and economic development. Land ownership is unaffected by designation, although various public bodies are given powers to purchase land, and in practice much of some parks is in the ownership of a public body, or of the National Trust.

National parks were first provided for in the National Parks and Access to the Countryside Act 1949. This Act still provides the basic structure of the legislation on national parks, although it has been much amended, especially by the Countryside Act 1968 and the Environment Act 1995, Part III, which came into force in September 1995. The purposes of national parks were originally stated in the Hobhouse Report (*National Parks in England and Wales*, 1947), and set out in the National Parks and Access to the Countryside Act 1949, s. 5, in terms of two general objectives: the preservation and enhancement of the natural beauty of the areas; and the promotion of their enjoyment by the public. In recognition of the way that attitudes towards the national parks have changed since 1949, the Environment Act 1995, s. 61 substitutes a new s. 5 which sets out somewhat wider purposes:

(a) conserving and enhancing the natural beauty, wildlife and cultural heritage of the areas . . .; and

(b) . . . promoting opportunities for the understanding and enjoyment of the special qualities of those areas by the public.

The impact of the changed purposes is reinforced by a new s. 11A(2) to the 1949 Act, which requires all public bodies and statutory undertakers to have regard to the new purposes when exercising or performing any functions affecting land in a national park. The new s. 11A(2) also gives statutory effect to the so-called 'Sandford principle', which is that where there is a conflict between purposes (a) and (b), then greater weight should be attached to purpose (a). The balance between environmental, amenity and economic factors is also made explicit in a new s. 11A(1), which requires national park authorities to seek to foster the economic and social well-being of local communities within the national park, albeit in the context of pursuing the purposes set out in s. 5.

Responsibility for proposing and designating a national park originally lay with the National Parks Commission, which designated the 10 existing parks in the 1950s. This responsibility has now devolved to the Countryside Commission and the Countryside Council for Wales, which are currently reviewing the boundaries of existing parks and the question of new designations. If a new park is proposed (and it has been suggested that the New Forest, which is currently managed by the Forestry Commission, with environmental purposes very much to the fore, should be formally recognised as a national park), it would require extensive publicity and consultation and would normally also require a public inquiry, after which the designation requires confirmation by the Secretary of State.

Currently there are 10 national parks, covering 9% of the area of England and Wales and with almost 250,000 permanent residents. There is no national park in Scotland, although there are designations with a roughly similar impact. The parks are the Peak District, the Lake District, the Yorkshire Dales, the North York Moors, Northumberland, Snowdonia, the Brecon Beacons, the Pembrokeshire Coast, Exmoor and Dartmoor. In addition, the Broads Authority was established by the Norfolk and Suffolk Broads Act 1988. This has a similar constitution and powers to the national parks, with the inclusion of powers over navigation and water space. For the purposes of most legal protections it is treated as a national park.

The national parks are the only areas where a new institutional structure has been created in an attempt to protect the countryside. However, control remains essentially local, since the Countryside Commission and the Countryside Council for Wales have no executive functions. Under s. 63 of the Environment Act 1995, the Secretary of the State has power to establish by order a national park authority in the form set out in sch. 7. This has altered the previous arrangements whereby each national park was administered by an authority run by a committee of the relevant county council or a separate, autonomous board. This has the effect of creating autonomous local authorities for national parks with primary responsibility for planning functions.

The Environment Act 1995, Part III, alters this position. Section 63 enables the Secretary of State to establish by order a national park authority in the form set out in sch. 7. It is clear that this section has been used to convert the existing authorities into what will effectively be autonomous local authorities (and also to establish national park authorities on this model for any new national parks that are designated). The national park authorities were formally established on 1 April 1997. Schedule 7 provides that a national park authority is a body corporate and is subject to most legislative provisions affecting local authorities, including those on access to meetings, audit, competitive tendering and the jurisdiction of the Commissioner for Local Administration (the Ombudsman). Following a late amendment to the Act, for national parks in England the balance between the various appointees to the authorities was altered, a change that led to accusations from some quarters that national park authorities will be turned into centralised quangos. (In Wales, one-third of the members are still to be appointed by the Secretary of State, after consultation with the Countryside Council for Wales, and two-thirds appointed by the constituent local authorities.) One half plus two of the members will be appointed by the constituent county and district councils, with the remainder appointed by the Secretary of State, after consultation with the Countryside Commission. Of those Secretary of State appointees, one half minus one must be members of parish councils in the national park. The total number on the authority and the exact number of appointees each local authority will have will be set out in the specific order establishing each national park authority. The authority will then elect its own chair and deputy chair.

Under the previous legislation each national park had a national park officer and a national park management plan. This position remains the same for the new authorities, which are empowered to adopt the existing management plan, subject to provisions concerning regular review (Environment Act 1995, s. 66). There are new powers to provide funding for the national park authorities. Under the Environment Act 1995, s. 72, the relevant Secretary of State has a wide discretion to make grants to a national park authority, whilst s. 71 empowers the authorities to issue levies to the constituent local authorities, and it has been announced that the principle of 75% central funding will remain. In addition, it should be noted that grants from the Countryside Commission and the Countryside Council for Wales for works and schemes are normally payable at a higher rate in a national park than they are outside.

Protection of the parks has always been strongly tied to the town and country planning system. The national park authority is designated the sole local planning authority for its area, taking over all of the planning functions from the national park committee or board. One exception concerns tree preservation orders, where the district council retains concurrent jurisdiction with the national park authority. Strategic planning in national parks centres around the national park development plan that was first required by the Planning and Compensation Act 1991 (as with all plan-making in national parks, this requires consultation with the Countryside Commission or the Countryside Council for Wales). In addition under s. 68 of the Environment Act 1995 the national park authorities are under a duty to prepare a national park management plan before April 1999. This will replace the national park plans made under the Local Government Act 1972 (though existing plans can be adopted as the management plan). The management plan performs a different strategic function from the purely planning-based development plan, covering wider management policy issues.

As far as the substantive details of planning law is concerned, apart from the limited restrictions referred to above, the main protection lies in the formulation and application of sensitive policies for the protection of the park through the planning process. But national parks are certainly not inviolable, as the siting of Fylingdales Early Warning Station, Milford Haven Oil Terminal, and numerous quarries in the Peak District illustrate. National park authorities also have positive powers in relation to such things as the purchase of land, the arrangement of public access, the provision of facilities and the appointment of rangers.

Every national park authority is under a duty to prepare a map of 'any area of mountain, moor, heath, woodland, down, cliff or foreshore' within the national park, whose natural beauty it is important to conserve (Wildlife and Countryside Act 1981, s. 43, as amended by the Wildlife and Countryside (Amendment) Act 1985). These maps will provide a reliable picture of the landscape of the parks and how it is changing. They will be used as the basis for policies relating to landscape protection within the parks, in line with guidance issued by the Countryside Commission.

Areas of outstanding natural beauty

Areas of outstanding natural beauty (AONBs) are designated under the National Parks and Access to the Countryside Act 1949, s. 87, for their natural beauty, with the objective of protecting and enhancing these features. Even though in landscape terms they are meant to be the equivalent of national parks, by comparison with the parks they are little known and understood, and many of the powers available within them are optional for the local planning authority. Indeed, Marion Shoard in *The Theft of the Countryside* (1981) described them as the 'Cinderellas of the planning system'.

AONBs have a number of similarities with national parks. They tend to be extensive areas: 41 have been designated, covering over 14% of England and Wales. They are designated in the same way as national parks, i.e., the Countryside Commission makes a proposal for designation which requires confirmation by the Secretary of State, normally after extensive consultation and a public inquiry. They rely on town planning procedures for their legal protection and the town planning powers are essentially the same as in national parks, including the duty to consult with the Countryside Commission over the making of development plans.

However, there are significant differences too. AONBs do not have a statutory role as far as recreation is concerned. No specific extra finance is provided for AONBs. But perhaps the major difference from national parks is that the local planning authority remains unchanged. In order to combat some of the weaknesses inherent in the powers relating to AONBs, the Countryside Commission issued a policy statement in which it suggested the preparation of a management plan for each one and the appointment of AONB officers, similar to national park officers. Current policy is also to encourage the coordinated planning of AONBs by the creation of joint advisory committees in those areas where more than one local planning authority has responsibility for the area.

Other landscape protections

A further type of designation is heritage coast. Areas are selected by the Countryside Commission and the local planning authority acting together and are subject to protective policies within the planning process. Forty-four areas covering 1,493 km of coast were designated by 1991. It should also be noted that there is a fairly strong Planning Policy Guidance Note No. 20, entitled *Coastal Planning,* which establishes a number of restraint policies on coastal development.

There is a power for the Secretary of State and the Minister of Agriculture to make moorland conservation orders by statutory instrument (Wildlife and

Countryside Act 1981, s. 42). These orders impose a notification requirement similar to that applied to SSSIs, with the intention that the national
park authority may offer a management agreement. It is accordingly a
criminal offence to plough or convert any moor or heath subject to an order
which has not been agricultural land within the preceding 20 years, unless the
national park authority has been notified in advance. This section is distinctly
limited. Orders can only be made in a national park and only provide for a
temporary ban on operations, and works can go ahead after 12 months even
if the national park authority refuses consent for them. It does not appear that
any such orders have ever been made.

Landscape protection orders were recommended by the House of Commons Select Committee on the Environment in 1985. Despite support from
the Countryside Commission, this proposal produced a very limited response
from the Government, which envisaged their use only as a stopgap power
pending the making of a management agreement, and the proposals have
never been acted upon.

Agriculture and landscape

There is insufficient space in this book to trace the history of agricultural
grants and their relationship with damage to the countryside, but in the past
their availability has often been held responsible for a great number of
damaging changes (see, for example, Shoard, *The Theft of The Countryside*,
1981). The nature of agricultural grants and, indeed, of the whole shape of
agriculture has changed dramatically in the last few years, and this is reflected
in such things as the so-called EC Agri-Environment Regulation 2078/92, the
EC scheme on agricultural set-aside, and the domestic Farm and Conservation Grant Scheme. There is also a number of schemes seeking to protect
landscapes, such as the Countryside Stewardship Scheme, introduced in
1991 by the Countryside Commission with the aim of encouraging farmers
to recreate traditional landscapes in return for incentive payments, although
the Ministry of Agriculture, Fisheries and Food took over this in 1996.

There are three protective procedures which have an important impact on
the protection of the landscape and deserve greater attention:

(a)   Prior notification
Since 1980 there has been a scheme in which farmers in national parks and
the Broads should give advance notification to the national park authority of
their intention to seek agricultural grants. (A similar scheme applies in
relation to SSSIs, requiring prior notification of the relevant NCC.) The
scheme is non-statutory and therefore is not backed up by any legal sanctions,
but it has had a high success rate in preventing objectionable proposals from
being carried out (see *Farm Grant Notifications in National Parks*, Countryside
Commission, 1987). The Countryside Commission has recommended that
the scheme be extended to cover AONBs.

The scheme works as follows. The farmer should notify the national park
authority of an intention to seek agricultural grant. If no objection is received,

the work may go ahead. If there is an objection, discussions follow between the two parties, and the Agricultural Development and Advisory Service of the Ministry of Agriculture, Fisheries and Food (ADAS) are able to mediate at this stage. If a satisfactory arrangement cannot be reached informally, one solution is for a management agreement to be concluded under the Wildlife and Countryside Act, s. 39.

If no agreement can be reached, the farmer may seek a decision on the grant from the Minister of Agriculture, who may approve or refuse it. The possibilities for damaging development are thus either:

(a)   that the Minister approves the grant against the opposition of the national park authority; or

(b)   that the farmer goes ahead with the works without grant.

It should be noted that, in making the decision, the Minister is under a duty to seek to achieve a reasonable balance between the interests of agriculture and of conservation of the natural beauty of the countryside (Agriculture Act 1986, s. 17), and this may be given as the reason for a refusal. However, the Minister may give as the reason for the refusal of grant the objection by the national park authority, in which case the authority is under a duty to offer a management agreement, to which the financial guidelines made under the Wildlife and Countryside Act 1981, s. 50 will apply (see the 1981 Act, s. 41(4)), although it does not appear that this procedure has ever been used.

(b)   Environmentally sensitive areas (ESAs)

These designations formally date from EC Regulation 797/85 on Improving the Efficiency of Agricultural Structures, which permitted Member States to give special aid to farmers in environmentally sensitive areas. However, the current powers are modelled on an experimental scheme established earlier in the Broads to solve the problems experienced in Halvergate Marsh as a result of proposals to plough part of the Marsh (see the Broads Grazing Marshes Conservation Scheme 1985 — 88). Effect was given to the EC Regulation in Britain by the Agriculture Act 1986, s. 18, which allows MAFF to designate an ESA after consultation with the Countryside Commission and the relevant NCC, with the aim of conserving landscape and wildlife. Over 20 ESAs have been designated in England and Wales.

Within these ESAs standard rates of annual payment are made by MAFF to farmers in return for their agreeing to farm in accordance with specified practices. The order establishing each ESA includes a list of practices (and of grant rates) specially tailored for that ESA, but the exact terms of each agreement are a matter for the management agreement between the farmer and MAFF. One important point about these protections, apart from the fact that they rely wholly on the voluntary agreement of the farmer, is that payment is made by MAFF rather than by the conservation bodies. Another is that, by providing for standard rates of payment for standard practices, the system is administratively far simpler than the one established for SSSIs, where each management agreement has to be negotiated individually. As a result, the take-up rate for the ESA scheme is far higher. The Countryside Commission has proposed that ESA-type arrangements should be available throughout the whole country (see *Protected Landscapes in the UK,* 1987).

(c) Grant schemes under the Agri-Environment Regulation 2078/92
Four sets of regulations were made in 1994 in order to assist in the implementation of Regulation 2078/92. Each of them enables the Minister of Agriculture, Fisheries and Food to make payments for certain types of countryside management and each specifies rates of payment and precise management requirements. In keeping with the usual Government policy in this area, occupiers are given a choice whether to join the schemes or not. The Habitat (Water Fringe) Regulations 1994 (SI 1994 No. 1291) apply where an occupier within 20 metres of a designated watercourse or lake agrees not to use arable land or permanent grassland for agricultural purposes for 20 years and undertakes to manage the land to protect or improve a wildlife habitat. The Habitat (Salt-Marsh) Regulations 1994 (SI 1994 No. 1293) apply where the occupier undertakes to manage land with the objective of establishing an area of salt-marsh. The Habitat (Former Set-Aside Land) Regulations 1994 (SI 1994 No. 1292) apply a similar system in relation to land which has previously been the subject of agricultural set-aside. The fourth set of regulations, the Nitrate Sensitive Areas Regulations 1994 (SI 1994 No. 1729), are discussed in Chapter 14 in the context of nitrate sensitive areas, although their impact is somewhat wider than pollution control. Finally, under the Environment Act 1995, s. 98, the Minister of Agriculture, Fisheries and Food and the Secretary of State for Wales are empowered to make grants for any purposes which are conducive to the conservation or enhancement of the natural beauty or amenity of the countryside (including its flora and fauna) or any features of archaeological interest, or the promotion of the enjoyment of the countryside by the public.

EIGHTEEN
The protection of trees and woodlands

In seeking to protect trees and woodlands, the law has to grapple with two familiar and related difficulties — controlling destructive, rather than constructive, acts and establishing adequate control over natural things. There have been protections for selected trees in the town and country planning legislation since 1932, and the powers have been strengthened regularly since then. But planning law tends to concentrate on negative, restrictive controls while the proper management of natural resources such as trees requires positive measures. Ordinary town planning rules have a limited impact, but further protection for trees comes from specific legislation. This is now mainly provided by ss. 197 — 214 of the Town and Country Planning Act 1990, which deal with tree preservation orders (TPOs), and all references to section numbers in this chapter refer to this Act.

TPO protection is based on considerations of amenity rather than the nature conservation value of the trees. There are no nature conservation protections specific to trees, but most of the nature conservation and landscape designations may be used to protect trees. There are also protections which arise out of the forestry legislation, though this primarily tends to concern trees as commercial items, and will therefore be covered only briefly.

Trees and planning permission

Planning permission is not required for the planting or cutting down of trees or woodland, because trees, being natural, are not structures or buildings for the purposes of the development control system. Section 55(2)(e) also excludes from the definition of development any change of use of land to forestry or woodland.

However, s. 197 imposes a general duty on local planning authorities to make adequate provision for trees when planning permission is granted. This may involve attaching conditions relating to trees to the permission (e.g., that certain trees should be retained or replaced by others, or that new trees should be planted as part of the landscaping of the site). It also involves considering whether to impose a TPO on any existing trees. A further possibility is to refuse permission on the grounds that existing trees or woodland should be retained. Full advice on trees and the planning system is given in DoE Circular 36/78, which is how supplemented by *Tree Preservation Orders: A Guide to the Law and Good Practice* (DoE, 1994).

Tree preservation orders (TPOs)

A TPO is a means by which individual trees, groups of trees or woodlands may be protected against damage. A TPO may be imposed on specified trees 'if it appears to a local planning authority that it is expedient in the interests of amenity' (s. 198). Since the section refers explictly to amenity, it does not seem that a tree could be protected for nature conservation purposes. Most TPOs are made in urban areas, though rural woodland may also be protected.

TPO offences

Any person who, in contravention of a TPO, '(a) cuts down, uproots or wilfully destroys a tree, or (b) wilfully damages, tops or lops a tree in such a manner as to be likely to destroy it', commits an offence, unless consent has been obtained from the local planning authority (s. 210(1)). The maximum penalties for this offence were increased by the Planning and Compensation Act 1991. On summary conviction the maximum fine is £20,000. On conviction on indictment the level of the fine is unlimited. In determining the amount of any fine, the court must have regard to the financial benefit accruing, or likely to accrue, to the convicted person in consequence of the offence. This is a significant provision, since many offences against TPOs are committed by developers who stand to make a substantial gain on the development value of their land (see, for example, the £50,000 fine imposed on a property company for deliberately felling 25 trees after designation, which is reported at [1991] JPL 101). There is a further offence of contravening the provisions of a TPO (s. 210(4)), for which the maximum fine is £2,500. This will cover such things as ignoring conditions imposed on works permitted by a TPO. If no other enforcement action works, an injunction to stop contravention of a TPO is available (s. 214A), though courts will be reluctant to exercise their discretion to issue an injunction except in clear cases. One notorious persistent offender (a Kent farmer) has, however, been imprisoned for failing to comply with the terms of an injunction.

These offences may be committed by any person, not just the owner or occupier of the property. They are offences of strict liability. Thus, in *Maidstone Borough Council* v *Mortimer* [1980] 3 All ER 552, a contractor was held to have committed an offence even though the owner of the site had assured him that consent for the works had been given. (It seems that the owner would also commit an offence in such a situation, because the contractor is acting as an agent.) This strict position is justified by the fact that a TPO is a public document (it is a local land charge), so anyone can check the position before carrying out works.

Part of the offence requires that it be committed 'wilfully'. This has been interpreted to mean that it is the act of damaging or destroying the tree that must be wilful (i.e., deliberate), not the contravention of the TPO. *Barnet London Borough Council v Eastern Electricity Board* [1973] 1 WLR 430, illustrates that this may include a negligent act. In that case, contractors negligently damaged the roots of six trees subject to a TPO, shortening their life expectancy. The Divisional Court held that this amounted to a wilful destruction. The case also illustrates that the concept of destruction includes something less than immediate death to the tree.

Making a TPO

The local planning authority has responsibility for making TPOs. This normally means the district planning authority, or the national park authority in a national park, though a county planning authority does have jurisdiction over its own land and where it grants planning permission (e.g., on waste disposal or minerals applications). The authority which imposes the TPO is then the relevant local authority for all procedures for consent and for enforcement purposes. The Secretary of State has a reserve power to make a TPO under s. 202, although this is unlikely to be used much.

The procedures for making a TPO are set out in the Town and Country Planning (Tree Preservation Order) Regulations 1969 (SI 1969 No. 17, as amended by SI 1981 No. 14 and SI 1988 No. 963), which are made under the authority of s. 199. The local planning authority produces a draft TPO, which is placed on public deposit, and all owners, occupiers and those with felling rights are notified. At least 28 days are then allowed for objections, which must be considered before the local planning authority itself confirms the TPO (prior to 1980 a TPO required confirmation by the Secretary of State). There is no appeal against the making of a TPO, though there is right to challenge its validity in the High Court under s. 288. In practice, arguments about the desirability of protecting the tree are considered at the stage of seeking consent to fell.

Normally a TPO does not have effect until it is confirmed. But under s. 201 a provisional (or interim) TPO may be made by the local planning authority. This is done simply by stating that s. 201 applies and the TPO will then have immediate effect, though it will lapse if not confirmed within six months. Such a provisional TPO is of obvious use where there is an imminent threat of felling.

Each TPO is separately drafted and accompanied by a map. This position allows for flexibility (for example, conditions specific to that TPO may be attached, or permitted woodland management operations may be established for a coppiced woodland), but it does make the making of a TPO quite a cumbersome process — certainly more cumberstone than those protective designations where all that is required is that standard rules or restrictions apply to the designated land. However, there is a standard form, which is set out in the schedule to the 1969 Regulations, and accordingly most TPOs will be substantially in the form set out in the schedule. The normal position is therefore that TPOs include a list of permitted operations and of prohibited operations, some of which are especially tailored for that site.

One particular difficulty relates to the definition of a tree. In *Kent County Council v Batchelor* (1976) 33 P & CR 185, Lord Denning MR somewhat arbitrarily suggested that a diameter of 7 — 8 inches at least was needed before something could be said to be a tree. However, this was expressly not accepted by Phillips J in *Bullock* v *Secretary of State for the Environment* (1980) 40 P & CR 246, who thought that anything ordinarily called a tree could be covered by a TPO. In that case he accepted expressly that a coppiced woodland could be covered, a position which seems sensible, since from an ecological point of view a coppice is effectively a single entity and not a collection of unconnected trees. Phillips J's view is to be preferred and is supported by s. 206(4), which states that a TPO will attach to any tree planted as a replacement for one subject to a TPO — such a replacement will often be a sapling or smaller tree. However, although the dividing line is imprecise, it remains clear that some things cannot be the subject of a TPO, such as hedges, bushes and shrubs. It appears to be accepted that a stump of a tree is capable of remaining a tree if it is still alive — a proposition that enables a TPO to continue to apply to trees which have been felled, but not to those which have been uprooted.

A further issue relates to whether local authorities actually have the resources to make TPOs. It appears that a number of local authorities have adopted a policy of not making any further TPOs because of the time and expense involved. The legality of such a policy must be questioned, as it appears to amount to an effective fettering of discretion.

Defences to TPO offences
There is a number of exceptions to these offences:

(a) Some works are permitted in the TPO itself. For example, the standard form of TPO exempts many works by statutory undertakers on operational land, and also works on cultivated fruit trees. More importantly, it exempts from control 'cutting down, topping or lopping a tree . . . where immediately required for the purpose of carrying out development authorised by a planning permission' (this includes a permission granted by the GDO — as to which, see p. 239).

(b) It is possible to seek consent from the local planning authority (see below).

(c) It is an exception to cut down, uproot, to or lop trees which are dead, dying or dangerous, or 'so far as may be necessary for the prevention or abatement of a nuisance' (s. 198(6)). The nuisance exception relates to the position where a tree is a civil nuisance. It is potentially a very wide exception, because it is a civil nuisance for a tree to affect a neighbour's foundations or access. *Elliott* v *Islington London Borough Council* [1991] 1 EGLR 167 illustrates the potential for conflict between public and private rights when dealing with private nuisance. Mr Elliott obtained a mandatory injunction against Islington LBC requiring that a horse chestnut tree, which was in an adjoining park and was damaging his garden wall, be removed. (The tree was not actually subject to a TPO because it was the council's practice not to designate trees on their own land, but this does not affect the point being made.) It is believed that the injunction was in fact never enforced following a later compromise agreed between the parties, but in the Court of Appeal Lord Donaldson MR showed the primacy accorded to private rights over the public interest when he stated, 'It is not generally appropriate to refuse to enforce specific private rights on the basis that that would cause hardship to the public: the court would be legislating to deprive people of their rights'.

(d) There are further exceptions where the Forestry Commission is already effectively controlling forestry activities on the land through a forestry dedication covenant, or a grant or loan made under the Forestry Acts (s. 200).

Consent

It is possible to apply to the local planning authority for consent to carry out any works which are prohibited by a TPO. Any consent which is granted may be subject to conditions, such as the planting of replacement trees. There are no publicity requirements for an application for consent, though Circular 36/78 encourages it and notification of neighbours and the placing of site notices are common. There is an appeal to the Secretary of State against a refusal of consent, and the procedures and powers on an appeal are exactly the same as for an appeal against refusal of planning permission. Technically, the Secretary of State cannot remove a TPO, but granting consent to fell with no obligation to replant achieves the same result.

Replacement trees

The replacement of trees covered by a TPO may be required by the terms of the TPO itself (e.g., in return for permitted works), by a condition attached to a planning permission, by the terms of a consent, or by s. 206.

Section 206 provides that, if a tree is removed or destroyed in contravention of a TPO, or because it was dead, dying or dangerous, a replacement tree of appropriate size and species must be planted at the same place as soon as reasonably possible. The owner may ask the local planning authority for this requirement to be lifted. The TPO attaches to the replacement tree.

Special provisions apply to woodlands. There is no need to replace a dead, dying or dangerous tree, and the obligation is to replace the same number of trees on or near those removed, or as agreed by the local planning authority. Flexibility has been provided in such a case because it will often be impossible to determine exactly how many trees were removed and from where.

Enforcement notices

Since contravening a TPO is itself a criminal offence, there is less need for an enforcement notice requirement than for ordinary breaches of development control. But there is a power for the local planning authority to serve an enforcement notice where a replanting obligation is not complied with. Such a notice must be served within four years of the failure and may require such replanting as is specified by the authority (s. 207). There is a right of appeal against an enforcement notice to the Secretary of State, who may uphold, modify, or quash it (s. 208).

Failure to comply with an enforcement notice is not a criminal offence but the local planning authority may enter the relevant land, carry out the replanting as required, and recover the cost from the owner (s. 209).

Conservation areas

All trees in a designated conservation area are subject to a statutory restriction (effectively a statutory TPO) which prohibits the cutting down, lopping, topping, uprooting, wilful damage or wilful destruction of the tree (s. 211). This is more limited than most individual TPOs. In addition, regulations may be made by the Secretary of State that exempt specified works (s. 212).

There is one crucial difference between these statutory TPOs and ordinary ones: prohibited acts may go ahead six weeks after notification of an intention to do them has been given to the local planning authority. The purpose of this section is to enable the local planning authority to have prior notification of potentially damaging works to trees in conservation areas. (A similar form of control is applied for the protection of SSSIs — see p. 500.) It then has six weeks in which to decide whether to impose a TPO: if it does not the works may go ahead. It is an offence to do any of the prohibited acts without notifying the local planning authority and waiting six weeks, unless consent is given earlier. The penalties for this offence, and the replanting and enforcement provisions, are the same as for ordinary TPOs.

Compensation

No compensation is payable for the imposition of a TPO, but it is payable where loss or damage is caused by a refusal of consent or by a conditional consent (s. 203).

Originally it was thought that this compensation was payable to compensate for the value of cut timber forgone, but this assumption was shown to be unwarranted by *Bell* v *Canterbury City Council* [1989] 1 JEL 90. In this case the Court of Appeal confirmed that the level of compensation payable was for the loss in value of the land. Accordingly, it awarded compensation at £1,000 per acre to a farmer who was prevented from converting a coppiced woodland to beef or sheep farming. Such large amounts of compensation would obviously limit the use of TPOs by local authorities, especially on woodlands which may have potential for agricultural or urban development.

An immediate response was to alter the TPO Regulations. It had always been possible for the local planning authority to certify that refusal was in the interests of good forestry or that the trees were of outstanding or special amenity value: in such a case no compensation would be payable. This certificate was originally available for individual trees, but the Regulations were amended (in SI 1988 No. 963) to apply the procedure to woodlands. However, a more significant response was to alter the practice of the Forestry Commission in relation to woodland TPOs. In woodland, the volume of timber being cut will normally require a felling licence from the Forestry Commission (see below). Normally, the Commission would refer any application relating to trees subject to a TPO to the local planning authority. However, a change of practice consequent to *Bell* v *Canterbury CC* was that the Commission agreed to refuse a felling licence if TPO consent would be refused. The effect is that the Commission pays compensation, but at the level set out in the Forestry Act 1967, which relates to the value of the timber.

Felling licences

Under s. 9(2) of the Forestry Act 1967, a felling licence is required from the Forestry Commission for the felling of trees over 8 cm in diameter (15 cm in coppices) measured 1.3 m from the ground. It is an offence to fell without a licence, which again may be committed by anyone (see *Forestry Commission* v *Frost* (1989) 154 JP 14). This control is based on commercial factors, rather than on amenity factors. However, the Forestry Commission is under a duty to endeavour to achieve a balance between the management of forests and the conservation of landscape and nature (Forestry Act 1967 s. 1(3A), inserted by the Wildlife and Countryside (Amendment) Act 1985 s. 4). A felling licence is not required for fruit trees, trees in gardens, orchards, churchyards or public open space, topping or lopping of trees, operations under a forestry dedication scheme, or where less than 30 cm^3 of timber per quarter is harvested.

To avoid duplication of effort, if a felling licence is required and there is a TPO in force, the following procedure applies. The application goes to the Forestry Commission, which has three choices: it may refer the matter to the local planning authority, in which case the TPO legislation applies; it may refuse the licence, in which case it will pay compensation under the Forestry Act 1967; or it may grant a licence. A felling licence is the equivalent of a TPO consent, but before the Commission grants a licence it must consult with the local planning authority. If the authority objects to a proposed grant of a licence, the matter is referred to the Secretary of State for decision. If a licence is granted there is an obligation to restock the land, unless the Commission waives it (see the Forestry Act 1986).

Proposals for change

In December 1990, the Conservative Government issued a consultation paper entitled *Review of Tree Preservation Policies and Legislation,* which stated its intention to strengthen the TPO legislation. These proposals included the establishment of a standard form of TPO in legislation, that all TPOs should have immediate effect, more flexible arrangements on the siting of replacement trees, and legislation to limit compensation for refusal of consent in woodlands to the value of the lost timber. There are also proposals to give local authorities positive powers to demand works on protected trees.

In 1994 the Government announced its intention to implement many of these proposals and thus to make the TPO legislation more coherent. However, no Parliamentary time was found during the passage of the Environment Act 1995, which perhaps suggests that the Government's commitment to amendment of the law is somewhat qualified. In addition, it is extremely disappointing that neither Circular 36/78 nor the 1969 Regulations, both of which still refer to legislation which is now completely out-of-date, has ever been updated to reflect the significant changes in society and the law since then.

Hedgerows

There has been an enormous loss of hedgerows since 1945, mainly as a result of agricultural intensification. However, hedges have never had the same protection as trees, because the definition of a tree means that the TPO legislation does not apply to hedges, though it is capable of applying to trees in hedgerows. Numerous promises have been made in relation to hedgerow protection and finally the Environment Act 1995, s. 97, makes provision for the protection of special categories of hedgerows. Under this section, the Secretary of State has the power to make regulations prohibiting the removal, damage or destruction of 'important hedgerows'.

The Hedgerows Regulations 1997 (SI 1997 No. 1160) make provision for the protection of important hedgerows in England and Wales. The Regulations generally apply to a wide class of hedgerows (in particular to hedgerows which are 20 metres or more long or which meet another hedgerow at each end and which, in each case, are on or adjacent to land used for certain specified purposes). Domestic hedgerows are excluded.

The protection is basic, to say the least. An owner (or in certain cases a relevant utility operator) must notify the local planning authority before removing any hedgerow, or stretch of hedgerow. The local planning authority has 28 days in which to give or refuse consent, failing which consent is deemed to have been given. Consent can only be refused if the hedgerow is important. The 'unimportant' hedgerows can be removed after that period. It is presumed that the intention would be for the planning authority to negotiate over the continued protection of this class of hedgerow, thus continuing the tradition of voluntariness found in other areas.

To qualify as an important hedgerow the hedge must be not less than 30 years old and must comply with certain detailed criteria laid down within the regulations relating to such matters as the number and type of species contained in the hedgerow. Thus, the range of hedgerows which can actually be protected is relatively narrow.

Fines can be imposed on defaulters (the courts being directed to take account of any financial benefit accruing from the removal) and the courts can also order replanting.

The Regulations have been the subject of criticism from many parties for the primary reason that the protection is restricted to a small category of hedgerows (mainly of historic importance) and there are no further provisions dealing with the protection of hedgerows of nature conservation interest. The Government has announced that it is planning to review the operation of the Regulations with the intention that new provisions will be introduced.

Bibliography

This bibliography is intended as slightly more than just a list of books mentioned in the text. Because of our sparing use of references (which we think often serve to distract the reader), we have sought to identify, with brief comments, some of the more important pieces of writing on each area.

As the book tries to illustrate, there is a need to be familiar with the policy of environmental protection as well as with the law: indeed, the two are often indistinguishable. One way to achieve this is to read official publications and a clear picture of the whole range of policies and issues can be obtained from the Conservative Government's White Paper on the Environment, *This Common Inheritance: Britain's Environmental Strategy* (Cm 1200, 1990). This has been supplemented by annual reports on the progress that is being made on the policies set out in it. More recently, the Conservative Government issued four, more reflective, documents in January 1994, *Sustainable Development: The UK Strategy* (Cm 2426), *Climate Change: The UK Programme* (Cm 2427), *Biodiversity: The UK Action Plan* (Cm 2428); and *Sustainable Forestry: The UK Programme* (Cm 2429). These policy documents are now dated by the change in Government. Indeed, when the Department sends out copies of extant policy documents it is accompanied by a slip which states that the information contained in the document does not represent the thinking of the current government. Unfortunately, there are no ready replacements available. *In trust for tomorrow* and the Labour Manifesto are the nearest things we have to a coherent policy statement on the environment from the Labour party (and the former document looks like it will be progressively disowned).

Any Report by the Royal Commission on Environmental Pollution, the House of Commons Select Committee on the Environment, or the House of Lords Select Committee on the European Communities is worth reading. Each of these bodies has a firm grasp of the policy issues and is not afraid to challenge the adequacy of the existing situation.

However, often the best way to get an insight into what is happening is to read literature produced by environmentalists and environmental organisations. We recommend Rose, *The Dirty Man of Europe: The Great British Pollution Scandal* (Simon & Schuster, 1990) and Secrett & Porritt, *The*

Environment: The Government's Record (Friends of the Earth, 1989), which is a good antidote to the claims in *This Common Inheritance*. In recent years, there have also been some interesting books attempting to counter what are seen by some as an excessive 'green pessimism': a good example of the genre is North, *Life on a Modern Planet: A Manifesto for Progress* (Manchester University Press, 1995). There is a need for books which attempt to cross the multi-disciplinary divide between law, politics, science and economics. A good reader (for those with an understanding of the legal aspects) on the complexities of this interrelationship can be found in Elworthy and Holder, *Environmental Protection: Text and Materials* (Butterworths, 1997). Although the materials are selective it does seek to place the law into some sort of context even if the breadth of the coverage is relatively narrow.

For those seeking an overview of environmental law, the books can be divided into two main categories: those for environmental practitioners and those that are written for a more general audience.

In the first category, there is a range of texts covering the practice of environmental law. In particular, *The Encyclopaedia of Environmental Law* (Sweet & Maxwell), *Commercial Environmental Law and Liability* (FT Law & Tax), and *Garner's Environmental Law* (Butterworths) are all looseleaf works which provide comprehensive and regularly updated coverage of the law and some important policy documents. Burnett-Hall's *Environmental Law* (Sweet & Maxwell, 1995) is a comprehensive textbook aimed at the practitioner which deals with most of the mainstream areas of environmental protection law. It suffers from two main defects, the first of which is characteristic of all non-looseleaf works, namely it became out of date almost on the day it was published. The second problem is that it is extremely expensive and falls well outside the range of most pockets. The first problem will no doubt be addressed with the publication of a supplement, the second is more fundamental. Nevertheless it is an extremely impressive work. Other titles of interest include *Tolley's Environmental Handbook* (Tolley, 1993), which has a very wide coverage of subject matter in the form of chapters written by different authors, and Salter, *Corporate Environmental Responsibility - Law and Practice* (Butterworths, 1992), though neither has much analysis at times.

As far as general textbooks are concerned, Hughes, *Environmental Law*, 3rd ed. (Butterworths, 1996) contains more detail and width of coverage than we provide in this book, whilst clear and accessible accounts of the law are given in Leeson, *Environmental Law* (Pitman, 1995), Mumma, *Environmental Law: Meeting UK and EC Requirements* (McGraw-Hill, 1995) and *NSCA Pollution Handbook* (National Society for Clean Air), which is updated annually. It should also be noted that, since environmental law is heavily based on statutes, some good (if disjointed) discussions can be found in the various commentaries on the relevant Acts. There is also Duxbury and Morton, *Blackstone's Statutes on Environmental Law*, 2nd ed., (Blackstone Press, 1995), which includes the text of the most useful Acts and pieces of delegated legislation.

Frontiers of Environmental Law, ed. Lomas (Chancery Law Publishing, 1991) is a stimulating set of essays on the subject: Chapter 2 by Macrory on the 'new formalism' is particularly valuable. A further set of essays entitled *Law, Policy and the Environment*, a special issue of the *Journal of Law and Society*, edited by Churchill, Gibson and Warren, 1991, includes background material on a number of areas. In particular, the article by Churchill, 'International Environmental Law and the UK', is an excellent survey of the role of international law. *Public Interest Perspectives in Environmental Law*, ed. Robinson & Dunkley (Wiley Chancery, 1995) is an excellent and valuable set of essays: it includes good chapters on public interest environmental litigation in the US and access to justice in the EC, as well as on the Australian experience of environmental courts, legal standing in the UK and the whole concept of public interest environmental law. Essays explaining the position in Scotland are collected in *Green's Guide to Environmental Law in Scotland*, ed. Reid (W.Green & Son, 1992).

Birnie and Boyle, *International Law and the Environment* (Oxford, 1993) is an excellent and comprehensive book that more than fills the gap on international law left in the text of this book. Sands, *Principles of International Environmental Law* (Manchester University Press, 1995) is also highly recommended.

Journals

Of course one of the most important things in environmental law is keeping up to date. There are a number of journals which attempt to do this, though one thing that any environmental law researcher quickly discovers is just how difficult it is to establish what has happened recently and what is going to happen next. This is perhaps a good illustration of the secrecy traditionally surrounding policy-making in this country (though the difficulties pale into insignificance when compared with those involved in finding material on EC proposals). There are many Consultation Papers currently being produced by Government on proposed changes in the law. These often summarise the current position and the reasons for change. The problem is finding out about their existence.

Since environmental law includes news and policy from a wide range of sources, the best way to keep up is to read *ENDS Report* (Environmental Data Services Ltd), a topical monthly digest of a wide range of news on environmental matters, with good coverage of legal and policy developments.

Environmental Law and Management (Wiley Chancery), formerly *Land Management and Environmental Law Report*, appears bi-monthly and attempts to cover all areas of environmental law through articles and current survey. *Water Law* (Wiley Chancery) is also bi-monthly, and as its name suggests, covers those things connected to the water industry, also through articles and current survey.

The Journal of Environmental Law (Oxford University Press), is published twice a year and includes more lengthy and reflective articles. It can be said to fill the need for a more academic journal, though a disadvantage is the slowness with which it is published. There is also *Environmental Law*, the journal of the UK Environmental Law Association (UKELA), published four times a year and including short articles and items of news.

All these journals — and the *Journal of Planning and Environment Law* (Sweet & Maxwell) — include summaries and reports of cases, usually with illuminating comments. The *Environmental Law Reports* (quarterly, Sweet & Maxwell) are the only source in which to find the full transcripts of some environmental cases.

Chapters 1, 2, 3 and 5

These chapters attempt to tackle in introductory form a number of more general issues. An excellent starting point for any deeper reading is Rehbinder and Stewart, *Environmental Protection Policy* (De Gruyter, 1985), though McLoughlin & Bellinger, *Environmental Pollution Control: An Introduction to Principles and Practice of Administration* (Graham & Trotman, 1993) is a very readable account which combines legal and administrative insights. On the specific issue of the various types of standard that are available, see Haigh, *EEC Environmental Policy and Britain*, 2nd ed. (Longmans, 1989), Chapter 3. There is also some useful material in the Department of the Environment Pollution Paper No. 11, *Environmental Standards — The UK Practice* (1975) and Wood, *Planning Pollution Prevention* (Heinemann Newnes, 1989).

On the 'British approach' to pollution control, see Vogel, *National Styles of Regulation* (Cornell University Press, 1986), a comparison of British and American approaches, though it is somewhat out-of-date in the 1990s. Ridley, *Policies Against Pollution: The Conservative Record and Principles* (Centre for Policy Studies, 1989) includes an explanation of Government policy in the late 1980s, though it is easier to look at the policy documents mentioned earlier for an explanation of what has happened in the 1990s. Also recommended are a PhD thesis from the University of Sheffield, Hilson, *Pollution Control and the Rule of Law* (1995), which addresses whether current regulatory and market mechanisms fulfil the requirements of equity, efficiency, effectiveness and accountability, and Ogus, *Regulation: Legal Form and Economic Theory* (Oxford, 1994).

For a sound explanation of general legal principles in the UK, see Waite, 'Criminal and Administrative Sanctions in English Environmental Law' [1989 — 90] LMELR 38 and 74. For some thoughts on the civil liability system, see Ball, 'Liability for Environmental Harm' [1995] *Contemporary Issues in Law*, vol. 2. Some useful reflections on *locus standi* are Purdue, 'A Harpoon for Greenpeace?: Judicial Review of the Regulation of Radioactive Substances' [1994] JEL 297; Geddes, '*Locus Standi* and EEC Environmental Measures' [1992] JEL 29; and Macrory, 'Environmental Assessment and EC Law' [1992] JEL 273. For a comprehensive analysis of the law on standing pre *ex parte Garnett* and *ex parte Dixon*, there is an excellent, if difficult, article by Hilson and Cram, 'Judicial review and environmental law — is there a coherent view of standing?' (1996) 16 LS 1.

The relationship between economics and environmental law is covered in many books, but the starting point should be Pearce, Markandya and Barbier, *Blueprint for a Green Economy* (Earthscan, 1989), which now has a sequel, Pearce *et al, Blueprint 3: Measuring Sustainable Development* (Earthscan,

1993). Alternative views can be read in Bowers, *Economics of the Environment: The Conservationists' Response to the Pearce Report* (British Association of Nature Conservationists, 1990) and Jacobs, *The Green Economy* (Pluto Press, 1991). As environmental issues become more complex there is an increasing need for lawyers to understand the theories which contribute to the spectrum of views which comprise environmentalism. An excellent introduction to this area can be found in Pepper, *Modern Environmentalism: An Introduction* (Routledge, 1996). Other more advanced texts are Eckersley, *Environmentalism and Political Theory: Towards an Ecocentric Approach* (UCL Press, 1992), Dobson, *Green Political Thought*, 2nd ed. (Unwin Hyman, 1995) and O'Riordan, *Environmentalism*, 2nd ed. (Pion, 1981).

Some other useful articles on issues that are relevant to the future of environmental law are Walton, Ross-Robertson and Rowan-Robinson, 'The Precautionary Principle and the UK Planning System' [1995] ELM 35; Winter, 'Planning and Sustainability: An Examination of the Role of the Planning System as an Instrument for the Delivery of Sustainable Development' [1994] JPL 883; and Fairley, 'Environmental Policy and Audit — What's In It For Us?' [1995] ELM 31. As suggested in the text, the creation of an environmental court has been discussed on a number of occasions. See, especially, Woolf, 'Are the Judiciary Environmentally Myopic?' [1992] JEL 1; Carnwath, 'Environmental Enforcement: the Need for a Specialist Court' [1992] JPL 799; and McAuslan, 'The Role of Courts and Other Judicial Type Bodies in Environmental Management' [1991] JEL 195.

Chapter 4

The basic materials on EC environmental law are to be found in Haigh, *Manual of Environmental Policy: The EC and Britain* (Longmans, 1992), an expensive looseleaf work that replaced the excellent Haigh, *EEC Environmental Policy and Britain* 2nd ed. (Longmans, 1989). A major part of these works consists of an analysis of the history and scope of each Directive which could be said to be within the sphere of environmental policy.

For a more legalistic look at the legal basis of EC policy, a good book is Krämer, *EC Treaty and Environmental Law* (Sweet & Maxwell, 1995), written by the former Head of Application of Community Law in Directorate-General XI in the EC Commission. Also see Krämer, *Focus on European Environmental Law*, 2nd ed. (Sweet & Maxwell, 1997), which is a stimulating collection of essays on relevant topics and Krämer, *European Environmental Law Casebook* (Sweet & Maxwell, 1993).

There are a number of books on the general constitutional law of the EC. The easiest to read is Steiner and Woods, *Textbook on EC Law*, 5th ed. (Blackstone Press, 1996), which is now supplemented by Steiner, *Enforcing EC Law* (Blackstone Press, 1995). These should be used to supplement any shortcomings in the explanations in this book on the general law of the EC.

Keeping up with changes in EC law is almost impossible. Very few people have the time to look through the pages of the *Official Journal or Europe*, though this is really the only way to do it. It is often a better bet to scan the reports of current events in the general environmental journals. There cannot really be any greater indictment of the secrecy that surrounds the decision-making processes in the EC! The only thing that makes this less disturbing is the fact that most pieces of environmental legislation take such a long time to get agreed that their import is known long before they are adopted.

Other recommended publications: Haigh and Baldock, *Environmental Policy and 1992* (European Cultural Foundation, 1989); Somsen, EC Water Directives [1990] 1 *Water Law* 93; the *European Environmental Law Review* (Graham & Trotman), a monthly journal combining news with articles; a set of essays, Somsen, *Protecting the European Environment: The Enforcement of EC Environmental Law* (Blackstone Press, 1997); and Stuart, 'Combating Non-Compliance with EC Environmental Directives' [1994] ELM 160.

Chapter 6

Anyone looking for some wider reading material on the enforcement of environmental law will find a number of extremely useful works. Most of these studies have tended to concentrate on the socio-legal aspects of empirical studies. Two seminal articles by Carson investigated the use of enforcement mechanisms in the Factory Inspectorate and described how the Factory Inspectorate first incorporated the idea of 'moral blame' in making any decision to prosecute for the breach of strict liability offences (see 'White Collar Crime and The Enforcement of Factory Legislation' (1970) 10 *British Journal of Criminology* 383 and 'Some Sociological Aspects of Strict Liability' and 'The Enforcement of Factory Legislation' (1970) 33 MLR 39).

Following on from these and other works, a number of in-depth studies were carried out by the SSRC Centre for Socio-Legal Studies, Wolfson College, Oxford. Two further works were produced as a result, Richardson, Ogus and Burrows, *Policing Pollution — A Study of Regulation and Enforcement,* (Clarendon Press, 1982) and Hawkins *Environment and Enforcement: Regulation and the Social Definition of Pollution* (Clarendon Press, 1984). Both these studies examine the work of the water industry, the former looking specifically at the discharge of trade effluents into public sewers whereas the latter deals with the discharge of the trade effluents directly into watercourses. The final work in the series, Hutter, *The Reasonable Arm of the Law* (Clarendon Press, 1988) examines the enforcement processes of environmental health officers. All three works support the view that the enforcement of strict liability offences relies heavily upon the individual officers view of the offender and the offence.

Alternative (and more up to date) views on the enforcement of environmental law can be found in Rowan-Robinson and Ross, 'The enforcement of environmental regulation in Britain' [1994] JPL 200. The effects of deregulation on enforcement are considered in Burton, 'Environmental aspects of the proposed legislation on "Cutting Red Tape"' [1994] WLAW 93. The most contemporary figures on enforcement can be found in the most recent edition of the Environment Agency's Annual Report. For an analysis of these figures have a look at a recent Friends of the Earth Study 'Slippery Customers' (September 1997) on the statistics on water pollution.

Chapter 7

The Royal Commission on Environmental Pollution has long campaigned for free access to environmental information. See generally: *Three Issues in Industrial Pollution* (The Second Report, Cmnd 4894, 1972); *Pollution in Some British Estuaries and Coastal Waters* (The Third Report, Cmnd 5054, 1972); *Air Pollution Control: An Integrated Approach* (The Fifth Report, Cmnd 6371, 1976); *Agriculture and Pollution* (The Seventh Report, Cmnd 7644, 1979). More specifically, however, *Tackling Pollution — Experience and Prospects* (The Tenth Report, Cmnd 9149, 1984) gives a good introductory account of the arguments for and against disclosure. For a more informal essay *The Secrets File* ed. Wilson (Heinemann Educational Books, 1984) provides good anecdotal evidence of the use and abuse of secrecy. More particularly, Frankel, *How Secrecy Protects the Polluter,* Chapter 3, suggests that there are real benefits to be gained from a greater degree of openness. These works are largely made up of contributions from members of the Campaign for Freedom of Information in Britain whose periodical *Secrets* gives up-to-date briefings on access to official information of all types. Indeed, the success of the organisation is demonstrated by the two Acts of Parliament introduced by their lobbying — the Local Government (Access to Information) Act 1985 and the Environment and Safety Information Act 1988.

The Conservative Government replied to the criticisms contained in the Royal Commission's Tenth Report in Pollution Paper No. 23, which gives an overview of Government policy on access to environmental information. Other recommended reading: Birkenshaw, *Government and Information* (Butterworths, 1990); Birtles, 'A Right to Know; The Environmental Information Regulations 1992' [1993] JPL 615; Fairley, 'Integrated Pollution Control — Public Registers and Commercial Confidentiality' [1993] ELM 111; Jenn, 'Public Interest Litigation and Access to Environmental Information' [1993] *Water Law* 163; and *Environmental Information: Law, Policy and Experience* (Cameron May, 1993).

Chapter 8

This chapter looks at the law of tort from a single perspective and therefore does not attempt to cover all aspects of that particular field. More specialised works include Rogers, *Winfield and Jolowicz on Tort,* 14th ed. (Sweet & Maxwell, 1994), Dias, *Clerk and Lindsell on Tort,* 17th ed. (Sweet & Maxwell, 1995 and first supplement 1997). For a more general survey of about the protection of private rights see Pugh-Smith, *Neighbours and the Law* (Sweet & Maxwell).

There are a number of articles dealing with the narrower area of the overlapping nature of the common law and the protection of the environment: McLaren, 'Nuisance-Law and the Industrial Revolution — Some Lessons from Social History' (1983) 3 OJLS 155; Ogus and Richardson, 'Economics and the Environment: A Study of Private Nuisance' [1977] CLJ 284. Both these deal with the socio-legal aspects of common law control. A thorough examination of the overlap can be found in Steele 'Private Law and the Environment: Nuisance in context' (1995) 15 LS 236.

Other recommended reading for those interested in the practical aspects of the common law include Croft, 'The Environmental Protection Act 1990 — Part III, Statutory Nuisance — Consolidation or Change?' [1991] LMELR 2, and Waite, 'Private Civil Litigation and the Environment', [1989] LMELR 113. The problem of historic liability for contamination in the wake of the *Cambridge Water* case (but pre-Environment Act) is discussed in Shelbourn, 'Historic Pollution — does the Polluter Pay?' [1994] JPL 703.

Chapter 9

There are many excellent books on the law relating to town and country planning which cover it in far greater detail than could be attempted in the confines of one chapter. They tend to vary between those which see the subject as a set of rules and those which put it in its policy context. Quite simply, the best book is Grant, *Urban Planning Law* (Sweet & Maxwell, 1982, supplement 1990), though it is now somewhat out of date. This large book combines clear explanations of the law with analysis of its difficulties, as well as providing coverage of the practical context and policy factors that are so important in planning law.

Those who wish to get an immediate impression of what planning law is all about would be best advised to supplement Grant by familiarising themselves with the Planning Policy Guidance Notes and Circulars and to ensure that they look at a few copies of development plans. In addition, some useful pieces on the direction of planning law are: Grant and McAuslan, 'The Scope of Planning: Back to the Future?', *Development & Planning* (editors Cross and Whitehead, Policy Journals, 1989); Garner, 'The Decline of Planning Control' [1985] JPL 756; McAuslan, 'Planning Law's Contribution to the Problems of an Urban Society' [1974] 37 MLR 134 and McAuslan, *Ideologies of Planning Law* (Pergamon Press, 1980) especially Chapters 1 and 6.

Other good textbooks on planning law are: Moore, *A Practical Approach to Planning Law*, 6th ed. (Blackstone Press, 1997). This is the clearest of the standard textbooks, but is rather too much orientated towards the exposition of principles through cases and hence fails fully to convey the central role that policy plays in the subject; Heap, *An Outline of Planning Law*, 11th ed. (Sweet & Maxwell, 1997) — a solid but a rather uncritical explanation of the law, though it is very full in its coverage; Telling and Duxbury, *Planning Law and Procedure*, 10th ed. (Butterworths, 1996), is more readable, but less complete than Heap. Purdue, Young and Rowan-Robinson, *Planning Law and Procedure* (Butterworths, 1990) is a very full practical guide to the area but is again somewhat out of date.

All of these books use the space available to explain the law on matters not covered in this book, such as advertisements, compensation, listed buildings and conservation areas, although a good introductory book on this last area is Ross, *Planning and the Heritage* (E & FN Spon, 1991).

An excellent and stimulating book which analyses the public law issues underlying the development control system is Alder, *Development Control*, 2nd ed. (Sweet & Maxwell, 1989).

Two good books on the relationship between planning and pollution control are: Miller and Wood, *Planning and Pollution* (Oxford University Press, 1983) and; Wood, *Planning Pollution Prevention* (Heinemann Newnes, 1989). Both include some interesting case studies of the application of the law in practice, and the second book also carries material on the USA by way of comparison.

The *Journal of Planning and Environment Law* (JPL), includes most important cases in the area. It has the advantage of having comments on the cases by Professor Purdue. It is, however, somewhat misnamed since in the past its contents almost exclusively related to the planning side of the title.

Keeping up-to-date is crucial in the planning area. *The Encyclopaedia of Planning Law* (Sweet & Maxwell), includes all the relevant statutory and non-statutory material and is updated each month. It also has the distinct advantage of Professor Grant's annotations and analysis.

Chapter 10

Basic material on environmental assessment can be found in a set of essays, *Planning and Environmental Impact Assessment in Practice*, ed. Weston, (Longman, 1997) which covers the operation of the system of environment assessment during the first 11 years from a variety of perspectives including some interesting case studies. There is a large number of 'how to' books including Fortlage, *Environmental Assessment: A Practical Guide* (Gower Technical, 1990), Glasson et al, *Introduction to Environmental Impact Assessment* (UCL, 1994) and *Environmental Impact Assessment: Theory and Practice*, ed. Walthern (Routledge, 1992).

On the legal issues of implementation of the Environmental Assessment Directive and the applicability of the direct effect doctrine see Salter, 'Environmental assessment — the question of implementation' [1992] JPL 313, Alder, 'Environmental impact assessment — the inadequacies of English law' [1993] JEL 203 and Boch, 'The Enforcement of the Environmental Assessment Directive in the National Courts: A Breach in the "Dyke"' [1997] JEL 129. Finally, there is an entertaining, illuminating and ultimately depressing account of the full saga of the campaign to save Twyford Down written by those directly involved. *Twyford Down: Roads, Campaigning and Environmental Law*, ed. Bryant (E & F Spon, 1996) illustrates very clearly the gap between the aspirations for environmental assessment and actual events.

Chapter 11

For a critical evaluation of the historical development of environmental law the Royal Commission on Environment Pollution Reports provide a good background to the introduction of integrated pollution control. The Fifth Report, *Air Pollution Control: An Integrated Approach* (HMSO, Cmnd 6371,

1976), the Tenth Report, *Tackling Pollution — Experience and Prospects* (HMSO, Cmnd 9149, 1984) and the Twelfth Report, *Best Practicable Environmental Option* (HMSO, Cmnd 310, 1988) all trace the development of the principles of integrated pollution control. Other works of interest include UKELA's 'Best Practicable Environmental Option — A New Jerusalem?' (1987). Also see 'Best Practicable Environmental Option and its Antecedents' [1986] JPL 643.

There is an excellent book which uncovers many of the problems which were encountered when the system of IPC was introduced. Allot, *Integrated Pollution Control — The first three years* (ENDS, 1994) helps to flesh out some of the rather tedious legislative material with a mixture of facts, figures and case studies which puts the system into a practical context and clarifies many of the aspects of an otherwise difficult area. For other guides to the legal intricacies of the IPC system under the EPA see Waite, 'Integrated Pollution Control and Local Authority Air Pollution Control — The New Regime' [1991] LMELR 11. Also HMIP's *Integrated Pollution Control — A Practical Guide* (HMSO, 1993) is helpful in giving a view of the enforcement bodies thinking. For further information see Purdue, 'Integrated Pollution Control and the Environmental Protection Act 1990: The Coming of Age of Environmental Law?' [1991] 54 MLR 534 and Layfield, 'The Environmental Protection Act 1990 — The System of Integrated Pollution Control' [1992] JPL 3.

For a view of how integrated pollution control systems have developed elsewhere in the world see *Integrated Pollution Control in Europe and North America* (edited by Haigh and Irwin, Institute for Environmental Policy, 1990).

Chapter 12

Good introductory background works on air pollution include Ashby and Anderson, *The Politics of Clean Air* (Clarendon Press, 1981) and Elson, *Atmospheric Pollution* (Basil Blackwell, 1987). The Royal Commission on Environmental Pollution's Reports in 1976 and 1984 also provide a good overview of the legislation historically.

Other areas which may be of interest include the overlap between planning and environmental regulations (see Wood, *Planning Pollution Prevention* (Heinemann Newnes, 1989) and Forster, 'Plugging the Gaps — The Revision of the Ozone Layer Protocol' [1990] 2 LMELR 74). Finally, for an overview of the workings of the local authority air pollution control system see Waite, 'Integrated Pollution Control and Local Authority Air Pollution Control — The New Regime'[1991] LMELR 11.

Chapter 13

The starting point for any research on waste should be the Royal Commission on Environmental Pollution's Eleventh *Report — Managing Waste: The Duty of Care* (HMSO, Cmnd 9675, 1985). This Report not only deals with waste management law and practice but also some of the wider issues surrounding the disposal of waste in Britain. Other helpful official publications include, House of Lords Select Committee on Science and Technology, Fourth Report, Session 1988 — 90, *Hazardous Waste Disposal* (HMSO, 1989); House of Lords Environment Committee Second Reports Session 1988/9, *Toxic Waste* (February 1989); House of Commons Environment Committee First Report Session 1988 — 90, *Contaminated Land* (January 1990).

For an excellent article dealing with the problems of defining waste see Purdue, 'Defining Waste', JEL (1990) 250. For a short discussion of the problems in the enforcement of the Control of Pollution Act 1974, see Hawke, *Waste Management Law and Enforcement* (Leicester Polytechnic Law Monographs, 1989). This contains a good overview of the old system and provides a quick guide to its defects. See also Ball, 'The Waste Management Licensing Regulations' [1994] Water Law 124.

There is now an excellent book on the law relating to waste in both the old and the new systems — Bates, *UK Waste Law* (Sweet & Maxwell, 1992), though it does not contain much by way of critical evaluation.

The clean-up of contaminated land has given rise to a host of articles and publications. The most comprehensive coverage of the law prior to the implementation of the Environment Act is to be found in Tromans and Turrell-Clarke, *Contaminated Land* (Sweet & Maxwell, 1994).

For a stimulating examination of the problems of trying to regulate the clean-up of contaminated land whilst taking note of market effects (the stumbling block for the Contaminative Uses Register) see Steele, 'Remedies and Remediation: Issues in Environmental Liability' (1995) 58 MLR 615.

Chapters 14 and 15

There are good existing books on water pollution law. The best detailed coverage is Howarth, *Water Pollution Law* (Shaw and Sons, 1988, supplement 1990), though as the publication dates suggest, this is now somewhat out-of-date. Howarth, *The Law of Aquaculture* (Fishing News Books, 1991), though on a restricted subject matter, is also a most impressive book. Elworthy, *Farming for Drinking Water* (Avebury, 1994) is also worth reading on agricultural issues. Bates, *Water and Drainage Law* (looseleaf, Sweet & Maxwell) provides a comprehensive survey of the law relating to the water industry for practitioners.

On the policy side, the National Rivers Authority has published strategy documents on each issue for which it has responsibility. It also produces an Annual Report and regular reports in its Water Quality Series, all of which are worth looking at. For a non-official view, see Birch, *Poison in the System* (Greenpeace, 1988). Up-to-date information is provided by *Water Law* (bi-monthly, Wiley Chancery) and, in news form, the NRA's monthly publication, *The Water Guardians*.

The history of the water industry from its early days to privatisation in 1989 is well covered in Kinnersley, *Troubled Water* (Hilary Shipman, 1988). Recommended writings on the current law are Wilkinson, 'The

Re-determination of the K Factors', [1994] *Water Law* 153 (which covers the relationship between water prices and environmental protection); Waite, 'Water Pollution Law After the Water Act 1989' [1989] LMELR 146; Macrory, 'The Privatisation and Regulation of the Water Industry' [1990] 53 MLR 78; Wilkinson, 'Causing and Knowingly Permitting Pollution Offences: A Review' [1993] *Water Law* 25; Ball, 'Causing Water Pollution' [1993] JEL 128; Howarth, 'Poisonous, Noxious or Polluting' [1993] MLR 171; Ball, 'Cambridge Water; What Does it Decide?' [1994] *Water Law* 61; and McGillivray, 'Discharge Consents and the Unforeseen' [1995] *Water Law* 72 and 101, the titles of which are all fairly self-explanatory.

Chapters 16, 17 and 18

Reid, *Nature Conservation Law* (W. Green, 1994) provides a clear and full summary of nature conservation law (both north and south of the border). However, it is out-of-date in the sense that the Conservation (Natural Habitats &c) Regulations 1994 are not covered. Some thoughts on these and on nature conservation generally can be found in Ball, 'Reforming the Law of Habitat Protection' in a very useful set of essays, *Nature Conservation and Countryside Law*, ed. Rodgers (University of Wales Press, 1996). Another general book worth reading is Gregory, *Conservation Law in the Countryside* (Tolley, 1994). A stimulating analysis of the issues surrounding the Wild Birds Directive and the *Lappel Bank* saga can be found in Harte, 'Nature Conservation: The Framework for Designating Special Protection Areas for Birds' [1995] JEL 267, and the follow-up article, Harte, 'Nature Conservation: The Rule of Law in European Community Environmental Protection' [1997] JEL 168.

However, there is a wealth of information on the state of our natural heritage and on nature conservation policy. As far as the former is concerned, the Annual Reports of the NCC (now English Nature) are of enormous interest. The NCC also publishes a wide range of literature on specific issues, and a general strategy is set out in *Nature Conservation in Great Britain* (NCC, 1984). The starting point for any reading on the shape of modern nature conservation must be the Huxley Report, *Conservation of Nature in England and Wales* (Cmd. 7122, 1947), which sets out all the arguments as to why nature conservation is important. There are many good books on the history of nature conservation (and also landscape protection). A stimulating introduction to the science of nature conservation is Moore, *Bird of Time: The Science and Politics of Nature Conservation* (Cambridge University Press, 1987), written by a former Chief Scientist at the NCC who had a special involvement in the drawing up of the current SSSI criteria. Adams, *Nature's Place: Conservation Sites and Countryside Change* (Allen and Unwin, 1986), provides another readable summary of conservation history.

Shoard, *The Theft of the Countryside* (Temple Smith, 1980), is a book which caused enormous controversy when it first appeared in the run-up to the Wildlife and Countryside Act 1981, and it provides a polemical view of what was (and arguably still is) happening in the countryside. The story is taken on further by Pye-Smith and Rose, *Crisis and Conservation Conflict in the British Countryside* (Penguin, 1984), and Lowe, Cox, MacEwen, O'Riordan and Winter, *Countryside Conflicts: The Politics of Farming, Forestry and Conservation* (Temple Smith Gower, 1986), which includes a number of case studies in the light of the Act. Most recently, there is Harvey, *The Killing of the Countryside* (Jonathan Cape, 1997) which examines wider issues of countryside destruction and attacks the Common Agricultural Policy as one of the primary causes of excessive farming and loss of biodiversity. International instruments on wildlife protection are well explained in Lyster, *International Wildlife Law* (Grotius Publications Ltd, 1985). The law on species protection is well covered in a practical manner in Parkes and Thornley, *Fair Grant: The Law of Country Sports and the Protection of Wildlife* (Pelham Books, 1994).

A wide-ranging set of essays on the law and the countryside is *Agriculture, Conservation and Land Use* (ed. Howarth and Rodgers, University of Wales Press, 1992). More detailed information on landscape protection can be found in *Protected Landscapes in the UK* (Countryside Commission, 1987). As far as tree protection is concerned, many books on planning law include a brief chapter on this topic, though the best place for a review of the difficulties in the current law is the Department of the Environment consultation paper, *Review of Tree Preservation Policies and Legislation*, 1990.

Index